The Encyclopedia of LONDON Crime & Vice

The Encyclopedia of LONDON Crime & Vice

FERGUS LINNANE

SUTTON PUBLISHING

First published in 2003 by
Sutton Publishing Limited · Phoenix Mill · Thrupp · Stroud · Gloucestershire · GL5 2BU

This paperback edition first published in 2005

British Library Cataloguing in Publication Data
A catalogue record for this book is available from the British Library.

ISBN 0 7509 3303 8

Typeset in 9/11pt Times.
Typesetting and origination by
Sutton Publishing Limited.
Printed and bound in England by
J.H. Haynes & Co. Ltd, Sparkford.

ACKNOWLEDGEMENTS

I am indebted to innumerable authors for the information herein. My apologies to any whom I may have forgotten to credit. I am also grateful to Herbert Pearson, who read much of the text and saved me from myself in many instances. To my editor, Christopher Feeney, for his long and eloquent silences and brief but vital interventions, picture editor Jane Entrican for her tireless research and the many friends who looked up long-forgotten crimes on the Internet and elsewhere. I am again grateful to the Edinburgh University Press for its permission to publish extracts from its edition of Boswell's *London Journal*, edited by Frederick Pottle (1991). This material is quoted by permission of Yale University.

The author and publishers are grateful to the following for permission to reproduce illustrations:

The Bridgeman Art Library: pp. 79, 158, 205
The British Museum: p. 171
Guildhall Library, Corporation of London: pp. 14, 48, 50, 169, 210, 211, 217, 228, 266, 276, 280, 291
Hulton Archive: pp. 36, 189, 261
Hulton Deutsch Collection: pp. 148
Hulton Deutsch Collection/CORBIS: p. 132
Hulton Getty: p. 152
Mary Evans Picture Library: pp. 32, 67, 190
Mirrorpix: p. 146
Thurston Hopkins/Hulton Archive: p. 209

The tempestuous Sally Salisbury stabs her lover in a jealous quarrel. He lived, but she died in jail. This exquisite beauty was as wild as the eighteenth century, witty, foul-mouthed, dangerous and irresistible.

INTRODUCTION

This book arose out of frustration with standard works of reference. Biographical dictionaries are full of here-today-and-gone-tomorrow politicians, sportsmen and practitioners of popular music, but you look in vain for information about the twin underworlds of vice and crime. These important strands in London's history are virtually ignored. So the *Cambridge Biographical Encyclopedia* gives us James Hill (1838–1916), Canadian railways magnate, but not BILLY HILL (1911–84), overlord of crime in the capital in the middle of the twentieth century. We get Joseph Needham (1900–95), a British historian of science, but not MOTHER NEEDHAM (*c.* 1660–1732), vicious bawd and innovative businesswoman. We get John Solomon (1931–), croquet player, but not ISAAC (IKEY) SOLOMONS (?–1850), prince of fences, model for Fagin in Dickens's *Oliver Twist*. We find Sir Edward Salisbury (1886–1978), botanist, but not Sally Salisbury (1690–1724), the greatest courtesan of her time, the first proletarian Toast of the Town, a wild and lawless creature of great beauty and wit.

Crime and vice in London have been economically important since the first red-light district was officially established by royal decree on Bankside in 1161. More importantly for the purposes of this book, they have fascinated writers and readers of the many histories and novels devoted to London's underworlds (*The Newgate Calendar*, HARRIS's *List of the Covent Garden Ladies*, DICKENS's *Oliver Twist*, BILLY HILL's *Boss of Britain's Underworld*, John Pearson's *The Profession of Violence*, Fergus Linnane's *London's Underworld*). Dickens was fascinated by London's wicked underbelly. For him areas such as the criminal ghetto of ST GILES, around what is now New Oxford Street, had 'a profound attraction of repulsion'. He would persuade people to accompany him as he prowled its wretched alleys and courts.'Good Heaven!', he exclaimed, 'what wild visions of prodigies of wickedness, want and beggary arose in my mind out of that place!'

The documentation of London's underworld is voluminous, and its story could be told by quoting its literature. The earliest document referred to here is the Act of Henry II which established the red-light district on Bankside (BANKSIDE BROTHELS). We can follow the spread of whoredom in the long series of Acts and other measures which vainly sought to curb it. In the seventeenth and eighteenth centuries, as fear of growing gangland violence grew in a city without a real police force, writers voiced public concerns. The novelist and reforming magistrate HENRY FIELDING, founder with his brother JOHN of the proto-police the BOW STREET RUNNERS, wrote in 1751 in his *Inquiry into the Causes of the late Increase of Robbers*: 'It is a melancholy Truth that, at this very Day, a Rogue no sooner gives the Alarm, within certain Purlieus, than twenty or thirty armed Villains are found ready to come to his Assistance.' Here is HORACE WALPOLE, the aesthete and writer, describing how he was held up by highwaymen in Hyde Park:

> As I was returning from Holland House by moonlight, about ten at night, I was attacked by two highwaymen in Hyde Park, and the pistol of one of them going off accidentally, grazed the skin under my eye, left some marks of shot on my face, and stunned me . . . I was sitting in my own dining room on Sunday night, the clock had not struck eleven, when I heard a loud cry of 'Stop thief!': a highwayman had attacked a post-chaise in Piccadilly, within fifty yards of this house: the fellow was pursued, rode over the watchman, almost killed him, and escaped.

Law and order of a sort was brought to early Georgian London by JONATHAN WILD, who contrived to be both London's police chief and its most powerful gangster ever. In his role of bounty hunter or, as he preferred, Thief-Taker General of Great Britain and Ireland, he broke up the major gangs and consigned their members to the gallows. Before he too was hanged he had a memorable rivalry with the burglar and jailbreaker JACK SHEPPARD, a rivalry immortalised in JOHN GAY's *Beggar's Opera*.

In the following century, as the city exploded in size and population, lawlessness increased. The criminal ghettos or rookeries, 'ancient citadels of vice and crime', existed cheek by jowl with fashionable residential and shopping districts, and their squalor and mystery made them no-go areas to all but a few like Dickens. Every morning desperate young thieves poured out of the rookeries to prey on the wealth of the growing middle class: RAMPSMEN, magsmen and coiners all tried to live on their wits. Swarms of young prostitutes pestered men in the streets and theatres.

The Victorian underworld was much less violent than its Georgian equivalent. Reckless violence was out, thieves were now respected among their peers for ingenuity and thoughtfulness. However, towards the end of the nineteenth century the first signs of the violent gang culture that has made today's underworld so dangerous began to appear. The first gangs were street fighters who used fists and leather belts with heavy buckles. It was legal to carry firearms, and with the arrival of anarchist revolutionaries and Jewish refugees from persecution in the Russian empire their use became more common. The East End gangster ARTHUR HARDING, who was born in 1886 in the notorious NICHOL ghetto and lived into the KRAY era, dying in 1962, led a criminal gang which carried and used guns. Raphael Samuel's *East End Underworld: Chapters in the Life of Arthur Harding* (1981) takes the story up to the rise of the Anglo-Italian DARBY SABINI gang from Clerkenwell, which exercised an even greater control over the underworld than the Krays. Harding clashed with the long-lived TITANICS from Hoxton. The Sabinis and the Titanics were racecourse gangs, criminals who forced bookmakers to pay protection money and fought pitched battles for supremacy. Gradually the Sabinis widened their interests until they dominated the clubs and pubs of the West End. The takeover led to shootings and knifings in streets and pubs all over London. When they were interned as enemy aliens at the beginning of the Second World War their empire passed to their former allies the WHITES, who quickly lost control to an alliance of the racecourse thug and gang leader JACK SPOT, and BILLY HILL, who eventually fell out with Spot and claimed the title of underworld czar. Hill's autobiography *Boss of Britain's Underworld* tells the story of the battle for control of the West End. Although they modelled themselves on American gangsters Spot and Hill were more Ealing comedy than Hollywood, more *The Ladykillers* than *The Godfather*. Their rivalry had an *opera buffa* character. They were succeeded by the ultra-violent KRAYS and RICHARDSONS, gangsters with an even greater love of the literary limelight. Today their violence is being surpassed by new gangs fighting to control drugs.

In past centuries Londoners were more frankly carnal and took their pleasures with unsurpassed gusto. Enterprising women escaped the poverty trap by creating a vibrant sex industry. There was a wide price-range for the sexually adventurous. The biographer JAMES BOSWELL wrote of 'the splendid Madam at fifty guineas a night down to the civil nymph [who] will resign her engaging person . . . for a pint of wine and a shilling'. The perils of unprotected sex were great, as Boswell knew to his cost. He caught gonorrhoea seventeen times. CONDOMS or cundums as they were called, were available but uncomfortable to use. Both Boswell and 'WALTER', the Victorian lecher whose *My Secret Life* chronicled his encounters with 1,200 women, disliked using them.

At first the girls who disseminated venereal diseases were largely unorganised, but Arthur Harding describes how Jews began to prey on prostitutes in the East End, and from the 1930s on gangsters such as the MESSINAS and The Syndicate of BERNIE SILVER and FRANK MIFSUD controlled vice in the West End. The vice of the East End was controlled by Maltese. The major gang leaders despised the vice czars, but vice was where the major fortunes were made.

This A–Z of London's underworld over the ages consists of short portraits of remarkable characters (CHICAGO MAY, LORD BALTIMORE), descriptions of significant events (the BATTLE OF CABLE STREET, the downfall of the PORN SQUAD), criminal customs and practices (RECEIVING, the KINCHIN LAY) and longer sections on generic subjects (POLICE, DRUGS, EXECUTIONS). Apart from the gamut of human aberration and folly I have included some events and people not directly involved in the underworld, but which give an indication of the moral tenor of an age (HICKORY PUCKERY, FAYED, SLEAZE). In the end the choice of some topics is purely personal.

The intention of this book is to be informative, amusing and browsable. It would be a pity if it increased popular fears about crime in London, which afflicted even the Kray twins. They worried that the capital was becoming unsafe for old ladies. Such fears have been common since records of the city began. Another writer, Richard of Devizes, warned in the twelfth century: 'Do not associate with the crowd of pimps . . . avoid dice and gambling, the theatre and the tavern . . . Actors, jesters, smooth-skinned lads, moors, flatterers, pretty-boys, effeminates, paederasts, singing and dancing girls, quacks, belly-dancers, sorceresses, extortioners, night-wanderers, magicians, mimes . . . if you do not want to dwell with evil-livers, do not live in London.' But by all means enjoy reading about them.

Words in CAPITALS cross-refer to other entries.

ABBOTT, GEORGE (1562–1633) Archbishop of Canterbury who shot a gamekeeper dead in 1621. Abbott was a mediocrity distinguished only by his cruelty. He had 140 Oxford undergraduates sent to prison for failing to remove their hats in his presence, and he prosecuted dissent with implacable zeal. One preacher, Alexander Leighton, was 'tied to a stake and received thirty-six stripes with a heavy cord upon his naked back; he was placed in the pillory for two hours in November's frost and snow; he was branded in the face, had his nose split and his ears cut off, and was condemned to life imprisonment' (Durant, *Age of Reason Begins*). However, Abbott's killing of the gamekeeper on 24 July 1621 was accidental. Abbott was with a hunting party on the estate of Lord Zouch at Bramshill Park, Hampshire, and his misguided arrow hit the gamekeeper, Peter Hawkins. A coroner decided it was Hawkins's own fault, and King James I agreed, saying 'an angel might have miscarried in that sort'.

Three newly elected bishops, including William Laud, refused to be consecrated by Abbott and in an effort to unseat him forced an inquiry into the killing. It failed to reach a verdict and said the King should decide: he did, exonerating Abbott.

ACCOMMODATION HOUSES Premises which hired rooms to prostitutes by the hour or the night. A room in a slum might cost a shilling, a more discreet and luxurious house in the centre of the city a guinea or two. The average was about five shillings. The owner of a successful establishment in the Haymarket retired to a villa in Camberwell and called it Dollar House after all the 'dollars' (the Victorian equivalent of 25p) she earned by letting her rooms again and again throughout each day.

Accommodation houses abounded in many parts of London. The important vice area around the Haymarket and Leicester Square had its share, and Kellow Chesney (*The Victorian Underworld*) has described 'an accommodation-house belt' stretching from Bond Street to beyond Covent Garden, 'through the heart of fashionable and raffish west London'. The poorer areas and the slums also had a variety of accommodation houses. There were large houses in the slums of ST GILES and Seven Dials, one of which had thirty-two bedrooms. SOHO and the slums north of Leicester Square offered cheap rooms for assignations. WALTER, the Victorian diarist who left a record of his encounters with 1,200 women, described how a prostitute called Brighton Bessie took him to an accommodation house in Bow Street. It was dearer than the usual house of its type but had the advantage that couples were not interrupted by the landlord asking them to hurry up. Walter described it as a large building nearly opposite the Opera House. It had large and small rooms, well or poorly furnished according to price. 'In it there must have been twenty rooms, and there were more sighs of pleasure in that house nightly than in any other house in London, I should think.' In winter there were large fires in the rooms, and wine and liquor 'of fair quality' was available. The beds, 'large enough for three', always had clean linen. 'It was one of the most quiet, comfortable accommodation-shops I ever was in, and with Brighton Bessie I passed there many voluptuous evenings.'

ACID BATH MURDERS John George Haigh (1909–49) killed at least at least six people for their money before immersing their bodies to dissolve in steel drums full of sulphuric acid. His last victim was Olivia Durand-Deacon. In February 1949 a woman went to Chelsea police station to report Mrs Durand-Deacon missing. With her was Haigh, who claimed Mrs Durand-Deacon had failed to turn up for a business appointment with him. A woman sergeant became suspicious of Haigh, and when police checked with Scotland Yard they discovered that he had a long criminal record.

Far from denying the crime, Haigh, who believed wrongly that he had destroyed all traces of his victims and so could not be prosecuted, boasted to police that he had killed Mrs Durand-Deacon and several others who were known to have disappeared. He had dissolved their bodies at a storehouse in Crawley. Haigh said he had an ungovernable compulsion to drink human blood, and after killing his victims had done so. He claimed to have killed nine people.

Haigh did not realise that the acid had failed to destroy vital evidence, including Mrs Durand-

John George Haigh, the Acid Bath Murderer. Haigh killed at least six people for their money, then immersed their bodies in drums of sulphuric acid. He was executed in 1949.

Deacon's dentures. He had carefully tried to establish his insanity, but a succession of doctors who examined him both before and after his trial concluded that he was sane. The jury at his trial in Lewes, Sussex, in July 1949, took only fifteen minutes to find him guilty. He was executed in August 1949 at Wandsworth Prison. He left his clothes to Madame Tussaud's Chamber of Horrors, where a wax dummy of him was exhibited. Haigh made the bequest on condition that the figure must always be kept in perfect condition, the trousers creased, the hair parted, his shirt cuffs showing.

In March 1949 the *Daily Mirror* and its editor, Sylvester Bolam, were convicted of contempt of court over their reporting of the arrest of Haigh. This included a lurid account of his claim that he drank his victims' blood. Bolam was sent to Brixton Prison for three months and the paper was fined £10,000. It proved to be an exemplary punishment. For years newspapers took great care not to prejudice trials in their pre-trial reports. The situation is sadly different today.

ADAMS, AGNES Woman sentenced to six months in prison for passing risible counterfeit notes. Between 1808 and 1811 a wave of forgeries troubled tradesmen in the capital. The notes originated in the Fleet Prison, and typically bore face values of a few pence. Instead of being issued by the 'Governor and Company of the Bank of England' they bore the words 'Governor and Company of the Bank of Fleet'. But they were on good paper, and, when passed to a busy tradesman with only the figure one, two, etc. showing, they were readily accepted as being for a sum in pounds. Adams was caught by a Mr Spratz, a publican of St John Street, Clerkenwell. After she had been jailed in 1811, the forgeries stopped. The notes were known in the underworld cant vocabulary as 'flash screens'.

ADAMS FAMILY The most powerful criminal organisation in London, based in Islington. They have widespread interests in clubs and, according to Geoffrey Levy in the *Daily Mail* (7 December 1998), control a drugs empire with international ramifications. They hold the whole underworld in a thrall of terror, and are credited with ordering up to thirty murders (William Donaldson, *Brewer's Rogues, Villains and Eccentrics*). These, so the story goes, were subcontracted to Afro-Caribbean gangsters. The family is immensely wealthy, one of them, Tommy, alone being worth £50 million, according to Philip Beresford, compiler of the *Sunday Times*'s annual 'Rich List' (Donaldson). The oldest of the three brothers involved, Terry, 49, is said to operate like the managing director of a public company. According to Levy, he used to hold meetings four times a week with the gang's financial adviser Solly Nahome, before the latter was shot dead at his front door in December 1998. Nahome was a Hatton Garden diamond merchant, and newspapers said he was the man who laundered the Adams' illegal drugs millions. Nahome, 41, funnelled the cash into diamonds and off-shore accounts, or used it to finance property deals. The gang's plans are said to have included the takeover of the Tottenham Hotspur football club before entrepreneur Alan Sugar bought it. The other family members are Patsy, 48, said to be the gang's enforcer, and Tommy, 45, who was jailed for seven and a half years for drugs offences in 1998. Because of their criminal activities both at home and abroad – they are believed by police to distribute drugs including cocaine and Ecstasy to clubs throughout Europe – they have been subjected to the most intensive police surveillance in British criminal history. Scotland Yard, Interpol, the Customs and

MI5 have all at one time or another tried to find a weak spot in a criminal empire that now encompasses money laundering, drugs, loan sharking and counterfeiting. In March 2000 Crown Prosecution Service clerk Mark Herbert was found guilty at the Old Bailey of passing the names of thirty-three police informers to an Adams family intermediary. He got £1,000 for his treachery. Police intercepted the list before it reached the Adamses.

In 1998 Tommy was trapped by electronic listening devices hidden in a black taxi he used to do his drugs deals. Sentencing him to seven and a half years in prison, the judge at his trial ordered that he hand over £1 million or serve another five years in prison. In May 2002 he was released on parole after his wife Androulla had delivered the money into court. She carried the huge sum in used notes in two briefcases. Police had hoped the judge would make an order for £6 million.

There are many stories of the family's brutality. Geoffrey Levy wrote in the *Daily Mail*: 'The Adams family are known to be "worse than the Krays" when there is "work" to be done. And no one likes doing his work more than Patsy. "When he is after someone his eyes light up," says one underworld figure. "He's a very frightening man."'

Levy then recounts a tale of the murder of an accountant. This man is said to have stolen £40,000 from the family while working for them. He was found cowering in a car with his girlfriend. He pleaded to be allowed to live because he was with her. According to the story, one man shot her through the head, said, 'You're not with her now', and shot the accountant dead. Levy says a criminal known as 'Manchester John' borrowed £100,000 for a drugs deal but could not pay the money back on time. He was beaten up and made to sign over the deeds to his flat instead. When it was found that the flat was worth £20,000 less than the debt, he was 'believed to have [been] taken . . . "up north", killed . . . and buried . . .'.

Gilbert Wynter, an associate of the Adams family, stabbed the former British high-jump champion Claude Moseley through the back with a Japanese samurai sword. The brothers had found that the athlete, who was working for them, was ripping them off in drugs deals. Wynter was charged with murder, but the Old Bailey trial collapsed when the prosecution's key witness was said to be too terrified to give evidence. Wynter disappeared in 1998. Levy said there were rumours that he had been strangled and his body dumped in the foundations of the Millennium Dome.

The Adams family have clashed with members of the underworld aristocracy, the DIAMOND GEEZERS or old-timers who have survived from the SPOT-HILL and KRAY eras. MAD FRANKIE FRASER, a harmless relic of the south London RICHARDSON gang, was gunned down outside a Clerkenwell night-club, and it is widely believed that the shooting was ordered by the Adamses. Fraser survived and made a joke about it, but younger south London gangsters are said to harbour resentments. There was the potential for widespread mayhem after a member of the Adams family was said to have cut off the ear of FREDDIE FOREMAN's son on Spain's COSTA DEL CRIME. Foreman reportedly threatened revenge and there were peace talks. Gangs in south and east London have not forgiven the Adams family for these slights, but whether they have the firepower to take on the north Londoners is debatable (Wensley Clarkson, *Gangsters*).

AGAR, EDWARD (1816–81) Businessman and master criminal who led the team which carried out the GREAT TRAIN ROBBERY of 1855.

AGE OF CONSENT The youngest age at which the law recognises a girl can agree to sexual intercourse. It was set at 10 in 1576 and later rose to 13. The journalist W.T. STEAD fought a successful campaign to get it raised to 16, at the cost of a prison sentence.

AITKEN, JONATHAN (1940–) Tory Cabinet Minister jailed for perjury in 1999. Once regarded by some as a future Prime Minister, he made the mistake of suing the *Guardian* and Granada Television over allegations of impropriety when he was Minister of Defence Procurement. He had lied about who paid the bill of almost £1,000 for his stay at the Paris Ritz Hotel in September 1993 and when challenged made a ringing declaration of his determination to fight: 'If it falls to me to start a fight to cut out the cancer of bent and twisted journalism in our country with the simple sword of truth and the trusty shield of British fair play, so be it.' The *Guardian* claimed that Aitken had been staying at the Ritz to meet Saudi Arabian contacts to discuss commissions from the vast Al Yamamah arms deals – the Saudis were spending many billions on British arms, and there were stupendous rake-offs involved. In the course of his libel action it was dramatically revealed that he was lying about the bill. He claimed it was paid by his wife Lolicia, but the *Guardian* proved that she had not been to Paris that weekend. Aitken had persuaded his wife and daughter to back up his story. After his libel action collapsed Aitken resigned from the Privy Council. In June 1999 he pleaded guilty to two charges of perjury and perverting the course of justice. He was sentenced to eighteen months' imprisonment. Later he was declared bankrupt. He began a course in theology at Oxford University and appeared frequently on television to comment on other fallen politicians, including JEFFREY ARCHER.

ALSATIA Sanctuary which was the largest of London's 'ancient citadels of vice and crime'. It was situated between Fleet Street and the Thames, its other boundaries being the Temple and Whitefriars Street. Because of the area's ancient monastic associations, the inhabitants claimed exemption from City jurisdiction, and the area became notorious for lawlessness. When William Hogarth showed his Idle Apprentice being arrested, having been betrayed by his whore, he located the event in a cellar in Alsatia. The historian Macauley wrote that 'at any attempt to extradite a criminal, bullies with swords and cudgels, termagent hags with spits and broomsticks poured forth by the hundred and the intruder was lucky if he escaped back to Fleet Street, hustled, stripped and jumped upon'. The Chief Justice needed the backing of a company of musketeers to serve a warrant there. Troops were used to suppress it in 1697, but it continued to cause problems for many years. *See* ROOKERIES

AMERY, JOHN British Nazi sympathiser hanged in London in 1945. The son of the Conservative politician Leo Amery, he made Nazi broadcasts from Berlin in 1942 and later tried to raise an anti-Bolshevik force in a British prisoner-of-war camp in France.

ANDREASSON, MICHAEL Fraudster who ordered lavish meals in restaurants, then said he had lost his credit card. Andreasson, 39, a former financial adviser, was jailed for twenty-seven months in August 2002. Southwark Crown Court heard that seven days after he had been given an eighteen-month rehabilitation order for failing to pay a £430 bill at Planet Hollywood, Andreasson sat down to another expensive meal at the Ristorante

A murderous riot in Alsatia, the criminal ghetto south of Fleet Street. The Chief Justice needed the backing of a company of musketeers to serve a warrant there. Troops were used to suppress it in 1697, but it continued to cause problems for many years. The word 'Alsatia' came to be used for any criminal district.

Italiano in west London. He drank nine Bacardis, a bottle of Montepulciano and a bottle of champagne. When he was presented with a bill for £146, he made the excuse about his credit card. It was the sixth time in two years he had swindled a restaurant.

ANDREWS, JANE Former dresser of the Duchess of York who was jailed for life for murdering her boyfriend with a cricket bat. Andrews, 34, battered and stabbed wealthy Tom Cressman after he told her their affair was over. She fled to the West Country, where the duchess sent her voicemail messages telling her to give herself up to the police. At her Old Bailey trial in 2001 she claimed she had merely sought to defend herself because 39-year-old Cressman had punched, beaten and raped her. The court was not told that she was known as 'bunny boiler' after the character played by Glenn Close in the film *Fatal Attraction*. She had a history of obsessive behaviour after being rejected by other men. In one brief phone call to Cressman she had sworn eighteen times. In September 2003 she was refused leave to appeal.

ANGRY BRIGADE A small group of anarchists and libertarians who carried out a bombing campaign in London in the early 1970s. Their targets were Tory Ministers and symbols of what they regarded as an uncaring Establishment. Nobody was killed. The trial of eight members of the group at the Old Bailey in 1972 lasted six months – one of the longest trials in British criminal history – and resulted in ten-year jail sentences for four of those in the dock. The other four were acquitted.

On 20 August 1971 officers of the Bomb Squad, which had been set up specifically to catch the bombers, raided a house in Amherst Road, Stoke Newington. The jury were told that they found firearms, explosives and other incriminating evidence. The police arrested Cambridge university drop-outs James Greenfield and John Barker. Also arrested were Anna Mendleson and Hilary Creek, who had studied at Essex University but dropped out to become part of the political underworld in London communes and squats. The following day the police arrested two more callers to the house in Amherst Road: Stuart Christie, already wanted for a series of anti-Franco attacks on Spanish targets in London, and Chris Bott, who had been an activist at Essex University.

Barker, Greenfield, Creek and Mendleson were sentenced to fifteen years in jail, reduced to ten after pleas for clemency by the jury. They were convicted of conspiracy to cause explosions. No one was ever found guilty of planting the bombs. The trial was remarkable for the way in which the defendants politicised it. Issues that are still contentious – terrorism, asylum, police power, homelessness – were central.

The Angry Brigade were regarded with suspicion and even hostility by other left-wing groups whose main focus at the time was the campaign against the Vietnam War. The militant Tariq Ali recalls being approached by someone claiming to represent the brigade. This person suggested bombing the American Embassy. 'I told them it was a terrible idea. They were a distraction. It was difficult enough building an anti-war movement without the press linking this kind of action to the wider Left.'

ANNET, PETER Victim of religious bigotry. In 1762 Annet, a deist, was convicted in the Court of the King's Bench of writing blasphemous remarks. Although he was over 70 years of age, he was sentenced to a month in NEWGATE PRISON, during which he was to stand in the pillory at Charing Cross and at the Royal Exchange, followed by a year's hard labour in the BRIDEWELL. He was also fined six shillings and eight pence and ordered to find securities for his future good behaviour.

ARCHER, JEFFREY (1941–) Politician, writer and perjurer who served a prison sentence after lying to a jury. Archer was a rising young Conservative MP when, in 1974, he lost almost £500,000 he had invested in a fraudulent company. He resigned from Parliament and began writing thrillers. His first, *Not a Penny More, Not a Penny Less*, produced in ten weeks, was a best-seller. Other successful books followed. In 1985 the Prime Minister, Mrs Thatcher, made him deputy chairman of the Conservative Party. A year later he resigned after a newspaper revealed that he tried to pay prostitute Monica Coghlan £2,000. When the *Daily Star* newspaper followed this up with the allegation that he had sex with Coghlan, Archer sued. He claimed he had never met Coghlan, but arranged for a friend to pay her off to stop her making allegations about him. He told the jury: 'I made a fool of myself, but I am not a liar.' He was awarded libel damages of £500,000. It was during this trial that the judge said of Archer's wife Mary: 'Is she not fragrant?' In 1994, after questions were raised about his dealings in the shares of a television company, Archer denied insider dealing, but accepted that he had made serious errors of judgement. In 1999 he was forced to drop out of the race to be Mayor of London after a former friend revealed that Archer had asked him to lie during the Coghlan libel case. Archer was later found guilty of perjury and perverting the course of justice, and jailed for four years. In October 2002 it was reported that Archer had repaid the *Daily Star* £2.7 million libel damages and legal costs. He also agreed to repay damages awarded against the *News of the World*. Friends said the settlement would be 'painful' for the disgraced peer, but would not affect his lifestyle. Archer continued to misbehave. He was transferred from an open prison to Lincoln jail for breaching the terms of his weekend home leave by attending a lunch party given by former Tory Cabinet Minister Gillian Shephard. He had also broken the rules by naming some of his fellow prisoners in his prison memoirs, which were serialised in the *Daily Mail*. Around the same time, Lady Archer's former personal assistant was telling an employment tribunal that she had told the peer's wife about Archer's various extramarital affairs. Jane Williams said Lady Archer replied: 'Well, you know, I've never been bothered about all that'. Monica Coghlan, who said her life was ruined by her encounter with Archer, was killed in a car crash just before his disgrace. Archer was made a life peer in 1992, taking the title Baron Archer of Weston-super-Mare. In 2003 it was announced that legislation was proposed under which he could be stripped of the title. *See* WILLIAM ARCHER

ARCHER, WILLIAM Conman and father of JEFFREY ARCHER. William, who died in 1957, had a long series of convictions and prison sentences, mainly for petty crimes. One of his swindles will be particularly interesting to those who follow his son's career. In America in 1916 he posed as an army surgeon recovering from war wounds. He had even faked an album of photographs showing himself in uniform. He also had a bogus degree from Oxford University. Thus furnished with a completely false identity, he set up a bogus charity for wounded soldiers.

AREA DIVING A form of opportunistic thieving, also called area sneaking, mentioned by HENRY MAYHEW's colleague John Binney. Thieves would sneak down into basement areas or up to back doors in the suburbs, try the door handles and snatch anything of value before fleeing.

ARGYLL, DUCHESS OF (1912–93) Defendant in a memorable divorce case featuring the HEADLESS MAN. Margaret Wigham, daughter of a Glasgow businessman and Deb of the Year in 1930, married the Duke of Argyll after a failed marriage and many affairs. In 1963 the Duke sued for divorce and in a 40,000-word summing-up the judge found she had committed adultery with at least four men – a German ambassador, the public relations officer at the Savoy Hotel, an American businessman and the Headless Man. The jury were shown Polaroid photographs of the Duchess fellating this unnamed man, of whom little could be seen except his penis. The Duke got his divorce, and the antics of the Duchess, sexual and otherwise, continued to amuse the readers of newspapers.

ARIF GANG South London criminals of Turkish-Cypriot origin, successors to the RICHARDSONS. The family have been involved in a murderous feud with another south London gang, the BRINDLES, which has claimed nine lives. Because of their links to the ADAMS FAMILY, some observers expect them to come out on top, if they can stay out of prison long enough. They have been described as the Kings of the Old Kent Road. Pubs, restaurants and clubs are said to have been bought with the proceeds of a series of major armed robberies. In a shoot-out at Reigate in November 1990 one of the gang, Kenny Baker, was shot dead by police after he and three members of the family ambushed a Securicor van. Dennis Arif was jailed for twenty-two years: his brother-in-law, Anthony Downer, got eighteen years, as did Dennis's brother Mehmet, who was wounded. Dogan Arif, who is regarded as the head of the family, got fourteen years for an £8.5 million cannabis smuggling plot. Police believe the Arifs had been successful armed robbers for more than twenty years. 'We reckon they have made millions,' a detective told the *Sun* newspaper. In 1990 there was a £30,000 family wedding party at the Savoy in London. The Securicor robbery trial was told that many other families had attended the party including 'the Colemans, FRASERS, Whites, ADAMS and Hiscocks'. *See* HITMEN

ARMISTEAD, ELIZABETH Courtesan who married well. Originally Elizabeth Bridget Cane, she became the wife of the Whig leader Charles James Fox in 1795 when she was about 45, and lived to be 91. She had graduated from MRS GOADBY's luxury brothel and passed through the arms and beds of the Duke of Dorset, the earls of Loudoun and Cholmondeley and the Prince of Wales, later GEORGE IV.

ASHBEE, HENRY (1834–1900) Pornographer believed by some to be 'WALTER', author of *My Secret Life*. He almost certainly wasn't, but his life is nevertheless interesting. Ashbee was a wealthy businessman and book collector. He amassed a splendid collection of pornographic books and in 1877 published *Index Librorum Prohibitorum*, the first major English work of its kind. He had also formed the finest collections of books about Cervantes outside Spain, and when he left his collections to the British Museum they overcame their distaste for the erotica to get their hands on the latter. The erotica was locked away, to be seen only in special circumstances.

The Walter of the *Secret Life* describes his encounters with 1,200 prostitutes and servants over forty years. There are good reasons for believing that Ashbee merely arranged the publication of the diaries rather than wrote them: for one thing, his dates don't match those of the diarist. There are, however, those who feel there is internal evidence to support Ashbee's authorship, including Ian Gibson, author of *The Erotomaniac: The Secret Life of Henry Spencer Ashbee*.

In the *Index Librorum Prohibitorum* Ashbee provides a list of brothels which indulged flagellants. *See* FLAGELLATION

ASKE, ROBERT (d. 1537) Leader of the Pilgrimage of Grace against Henry VIII. Aske was a successful London lawyer when the rising broke out in Yorkshire in October 1536. It had various causes, including the suppression of the religious houses and taxation. The King promised to pardon those who had taken part, and to order an inquiry into their grievances. He invited Aske to London, and sent him back with promises to placate the rebels. Later Aske helped settle another rising, and was thanked personally by the King. But Henry had been waiting for an opportunity to strike back, and by May 1537 Aske was in prison in London. He was sentenced to be hanged, drawn and quartered. He begged to be hanged until dead before being disembowelled, and the King granted his request.

ATKINSON, ISAAC (1614–40) Highwayman who specialised in robbing lawyers and at his execution at Tyburn shouted 'Gentlemen, there's nothing like a merry life and a short one.' Atkinson was a clever boy but when sent to Brasenose College Oxford at the age of 16 'soon learned to rail at the statutes of the university and lampoon the rulers, to wear his clothes after the mode, to curse his tutor, and sell his books' (*Newgate Calendar*). His father took him back to his country estate in Berkshire, where he gave him the job of steward. Soon the boy was begetting bastards. 'Not a maidservant could live with the old gentleman for the son's importunities, unless she gave up her honour to his desires. Not a handsome wife or daughter in the neighbourhood but either submitted to his pleasure or complained of him to his father.' The old man turned him out and Isaac went to London, where he lived the life of a character in a picaresque novel. He burgled his father's house, stole a large sum, and left the following verses with five pieces of gold in his father's Bible:

> Sir, you your son did often bully,
> Because he never read in Tully;
> What parents teach they ought to practise,
> And I confess your test exact is
> 'Tis just to turn it on yourself
> Your Bible stands upon the shelf;
> The gold is yours, if you unclose it;
> Else I shall find the dear deposit
> Safe in a place by all forgotten,
> When you, good man, are dead and rotten.

Shortly afterwards his father died of grief. On his way back to London, Isaac robbed a parson. 'Another time he met with the famous Noy, Attorney-General to King Charles I, on horseback. As he knew him very well, he was resolved to accost him in his own language: "Sir," says he, "I have a writ of Capias ad Computandum against you, which requires an account of all the money in your pocket." Noy was a merry man naturally, and he was sure it would do him little service to be sour upon this occasion, so he pleasantly asked our desperado by what authority he acted. Isaac, upon this, pulled out a brace of pistols, and told him that those weapons had as much authority in them as any tipstaff in England, which he should be convinced of, if he made any delays. The Attorney-General had no more to say, but very contentedly gave him a purse well lined, and then they parted with mutual compliments.'

After this Atkinson took to following the lawyers as they went on circuit around the courts of England. 'In less than eight months he stopped above one hundred and sixty attorneys only in the county of Norfolk, and took from them upwards of three thousand pounds.'

He was caught after robbing a market-woman of her bag of halfpence at Turnham Green. She raised a hue and cry and Atkinson was taken, after killing four men with his pistols and another with his sword. After his trial and condemnation at the Old Bailey 'he desperately stabbed himself with a pen-knife; but the wound not proving mortal he was afterwards carried to Tyburn, and hanged, in the year 1640, being twenty-six years of age'.

AUDLEY, BARON (1573–1631) Mervyn Castleford, the second baron, was executed at the Tower in 1631 for what *The Oxford History of Britain* describes as 'every known sexual felony'. His second wife, Lady Ann, a famous beauty, was surprised on their wedding night when they were joined in bed by Lord Audley's servant, Anthill. She told Audley's trial at Westminster Hall: 'Anthill came to our bed, and the Lord Audley talked lasciviously to me and told me that my body was his and that if I lay with any man with his consent 'twas not my fault but his.' Other servants, including Skipwith the groom, also joined in. Lord Audley was something of a sexual exhibitionist. 'He took delight in calling up his servants to show their nudities and forced me to look upon them and commend those that had the longest.' When the butler, Broadway, was invited to join them, Lady Ann objected. Lord Audley pinned her down by the hands and feet. 'He delighted to see the act done, and made Broadway lie with me in such a way that he might see it, and though I cried out he never regarded the complaint I made but encouraged the ravisher.' His lordship then buggered the butler and the cook.

Lady Ann had a daughter, Elizabeth, by her first husband. Elizabeth told the court that when she was 12 Lord Audley had her raped by Skipwith. 'He used oyl to enter my body first for I was then but twelve years old, and he usually lay with me by the Baron's privity and command.'

Audley's son James, whom he had forced to marry Elizabeth, informed on his father, who was arrested. He was charged with 'abetting a Rape upon his Countess, Committing Sodomy with his servants, and Commanding and Countenancing the Debauching of his daughter'.

B

BABY FARMING Prostitutes and servants could seldom afford to keep their illegitimate children, and usually either killed them or handed them over to professional nurses. This was often tantamount to a slow death sentence. Dr Cadogan argued in *Essay on the Nursing and Management of Children* in 1750 that 'the ancient custom of exposing them to wild beasts or drowning them would be a much quicker way of dispatching them' than the slow death through neglect they would otherwise suffer. Being brought up by the parish was little better. The philanthropist Jonas Hanway thought 80 to 90 per cent of parish and workhouse children died, and Thomas Coram, founder of the Foundling Hospital in 1742, wrote of 'wicked and barbarous nurses'.

Handing over illegitimate children to professional child-minders was common in the nineteenth century – one Victorian expert reckoned that there were more than 30,000 children in the hands of baby farmers. Some looked after their charges well. Others were simply homicidal. The most sensational case of murderous child-minders was that of two sisters, Sarah Ellis and and Margaret Waters, the 'Brixton Baby Farmers'. In 1870 the bodies of several babies were found on the streets of Lambeth, and police visited Ellis's lodgings, where they found five babies dying from malnutrition and opium poisoning. Waters was later hanged, but Ellis escaped with only eighteen months' hard labour.

BACCHUS, REGINALD (1858–1921) Theologian and pornographer. Bacchus was a contributor of learned articles to the religious press and translator of French novels, and at the same time a member of the louche circle around Oscar Wilde, including the poet Ernest Dowson. His wife, the young actress Isa Bowman, was one of the children the Revd Charles Dodgson (Lewis Carroll) invited to holidays at Eastbourne, and she was the first to play Alice (in Wonderland) on stage. Bacchus's erotic novels included *Maudie*, *Pleasure Bound Afloat* and *Pleasure Bound Ashore*.

BACON, FRANCIS (1561–1626) Eminent philosopher and scientist who pleaded guilty to corruption. After he had been made Lord Chancellor

Francis Bacon, the eminent scientist and philosopher who was a corrupt Lord Chancellor. He was fined a vast sum in 1621 for taking bribes, and held in the Tower. After he was released he never again held public office.

in 1618, he took bribes, and in 1621 confessed that he was 'guilty of corruption and do renounce all defence'. He had charged one man 400 guineas for a favourable verdict, but the man complained that the verdict went against him. The historian A.L. Rowse said he confessed to corruption in order to avoid a charge of sodomy. One of his servants, Godrick, was his 'catamite and bedfellow'.

Bacon was fined a colossal £40,000, held in the TOWER, and banished from the court and public office. He was soon released, but never returned to public office. He died in poverty of pneumonia after observing the effects of refrigeration on a winter's day. His procedure of verifying hypotheses through experiment and empirical observation was highly influential on the development of science.

BADDELEY, SOPHIA (1745–86) Actress-courtesan who failed to cash in on her renowned beauty. One night in June 1771 the audience at the Little Theatre in the Haymarket applauded her for fifteen minutes. She was not on the stage – she was watching the play from a box. It was her sheer beauty that brought them to their feet. The Duke of Ancaster told her that she was 'absolutely one of the wonders of the age . . . no man can gaze on you unwounded. You are in this respect like the Basilisk, whose eyes kill those whom they fix on.' Lord Falmouth told her 'Half the world is in love with you', and noblewomen, who usually snubbed actresses, never mind courtesans, were said to speak of her 'with rapture'. Fifteen years later she was dead, a pauper and a laudanum addict. She lacked the financial acuity of her kind. Several noblemen offered great sums in return for the exclusive right to her charms, but she preferred her freedom. Their gifts made her wealthy, but she spent at a prodigious rate. When her companion Elizabeth Steele suggested she could dress on £100 per annum, Sophia replied: 'Christ, that is not enough for millinery! . . . one may as well be dead as not in the fashion.' Mrs Steele wrote a six-volume biography of her.

BADGER GAME, THE Confidence trick with many variations in which a man is lured into a compromising situation in a hotel room, or in an alley, with a woman and then threatened with exposure. JENNY DIVER and CHICAGO MAY were exponents, SIR HARI SINGH a notable victim.

BAGNIOS Bath houses that were really brothels, many of them in the Covent Garden area. They were very expensive but popular. Men could send out for the prostitute of their choice, or relax after the rigours of an encounter. Casanova, who visited a London bagnio, wrote: 'I also visited the bagnios, where a rich man can sup, bathe and sleep with a fashionable courtesan, of which species there are many in London. It makes a magnificent debauch, and only costs six guineas.' The Swiss traveller J.W. von Archenholz wrote in *A Picture of England*:

> In London there is a certain kind of house, called bagnios, which are supposed to be baths; their real purpose, however, is to provide persons of both sexes with pleasure. These houses are well, and often richly furnished, and every device for exciting the senses is either at hand or can be provided. Girls do not live here, but they are fetched in [sedan] chairs when required. None but those who are specially attractive in all ways are so honoured, and for this reason they often send their address to a hundred of these bagnios in order to make themselves known. A girl who is sent for and does not please receives no gratuity, the chair alone being paid for. The English retain their solemnity even as regards their pleasures, and consequently the business of such a house is conducted with a seriousness and propriety which is hard to credit. All noise and uproar is banned here; no loud footsteps are heard, every corner is carpeted and the numerous attendants speak quietly among themselves. Old people and degenerates can here receive flagellation, for which all establishments are prepared. In every bagnio there is found a formula regarding baths, but they are seldom needed . . . Most of them are quite close to the theatres, and many taverns are in the same neighbourhood.

BAKER, COLONEL VALENTINE (1825–87) Soldier whose trial for attempted rape was a Victorian sensation. Baker, a friend of the Prince of Wales, later EDWARD VII, met 22-year-old Rebecca Dickenson on the Portsmouth-to-London train in June 1875. Baker at first made polite conversation, but when the train left Woking he slipped his arm round Miss Dickenson's waist and kissed her. She opened the outside door and scrambled out on to the running board, clinging precariously to the door handle. The train was stopped at Esher station, Miss Dickenson was helped inside and a clergyman got into her compartment and accompanied her to London. She made a statement to police, and three days later Baker was arrested.

His trial at Croydon in August 1875 drew enormous crowds. Apart from his royal connections Baker, 49, who was married and had two daughters, had recently been commanding officer of the 10th Hussars and moved in the highest social circles. Among his friends in court were Lord Lucan and the Marquess of Tavistock. He had served with distinction in the Crimean War and elsewhere. The judge said Baker had tried to 'win the girl's consent to intercourse by exciting her passions'. Miss Dickenson was pretty and winsome, captivating the jury and the judge, who seems not to have realised how trivial the whole thing was: 'Prisoner at the bar, when this appalling story was first published, a thrill of horror rang through the country at learning that a young and innocent girl, travelling by a public conveyance, was compelled to risk her life in order to protect herself from gross outrage . . .'.

Baker was found guilty of indecent assault, jailed for a year and fined £500. He was also cashiered, a move believed to have been instigated by Queen Victoria. She deeply disapproved of her son Edward's disreputable friends and way of life. After his release Baker became a general in the Ottoman army, taking part in the Russo-Turkish war. Later he became a commander of police in Egypt. He was shot in the leg during the war in the Sudan, and when he returned to London to recuperate he was greeted by a cheering crowd at Victoria Station. After he died of typhoid in Egypt in 1887 the Queen consented to him being buried in Cairo with full military honours.

BALCOMBE STREET SIEGE In 1976 a group of IRA men on the run from police took over a flat at 22b, and held a man and his wife hostage. Police surrounded the building and after six days the terrorists surrendered. *See* TERRORISM

BALL, JOHN Cleric who was the ideological leader of the Peasants' Revolt of 1381. He had been an egalitarian trouble-maker for some time, and was rescued by the rebels from 'perpetual imprisonment' at Maidstone. He preached an extreme form of communism:

> When Adam delved and Eve span
> Who was then the gentleman?

The aristocracy and the senior officers of church and state were to be killed and their property shared among the common people. Ball himself was to be an archbishop. After the leader of the rebels, WAT TYLER, had been killed at Smithfield, Ball was unable to keep the men together. He was caught and executed at St Albans.

BALTIC EXCHANGE Important maritime freight chartering centre wrecked by an IRA bomb in April 1992. *See* TERRORISM

BALTIMORE, LORD (1706–78) Wealthy eccentric who kept a harem in his London house. Frederick Lord Baltimore travelled in the East in the 1730s, and when he returned to London used his immense fortune to build a fine house and install a harem, on the lines of those he had seen at Constantinople. His seraglio consisted of 'five white and one black woman'. They were not permitted to go out unchaperoned, but otherwise could have anything they wanted. When he tired of them, he loaded them with presents, even dowries, and sent them on their way. They were presided over by his wife, Lady Diane Egerton, who 'acted as the Mistress of her husband's harem . . . chaperoning the girls in their outdoor excursions . . .'.

Songs and satires were written about him. What seemed at worst genial eccentricity became something much more sinister in 1764 when he was accused of rape by 16-year-old Sarah Woodcock, whom he had kidnapped from her father's shop on Tower Hill. She was a strict Dissenter. To help him slake his lust on the young girl he enlisted the help of a corrupt German physician, his wife and a bawd. Sarah was taken to Baltimore's house and held captive while her four kidnappers tried to break her will. She did not eat or sleep for three days. On the fourth, when she was too weak to resist, Baltimore raped her twice. Then they induced her to sign a letter saying she had gone to the house of her own free will. It was this letter that formed the basis of Baltimore's successful defence when he was tried for rape.

'A criminal process was instituted in consequence of this accusation; but his lordship vindicated his innocence, and triumphed over the malice of his enemies. This affair, however, made a lively impression on his mind; he dismissed his mistresses, sold his house . . . gave away the magnificent furniture, and in a short time left his native country' (von Archenholz, *A Picture of England*). Baltimore died shortly afterwards in Naples.

BANK OF ENGLAND SWINDLERS *see* p. 15

BANK NUN, THE In 1811 Bank of England clerk Philip Whitehead forged a bill of exchange after losing money gambling on stocks and shares. He was caught, tried and executed. Friends told his 19-year-old sister Sarah that he had gone on a long journey, but one day she called at the bank and was told the truth. She went mad, and for the next twenty-five years went to the bank every day, dressed all in black and looking like a nun, and asked whether her brother had yet returned from his journey.

BANKS, W.J. Member of Parliament found not guilty of attempting to commit 'an unnatural crime' (buggery) in the grounds of Westminster Abbey in 1833. Charles Greville, clerk to the Privy Council, wrote in his diary: 'Nobody can read the trial without being satisfied of his guilt . . . The foreman said he left the court without a stain.' To which a wit added: 'On his shirt.'

BANKSIDE The first official red-light district in London. In 1161 King Henry II guaranteed the Bishop of Winchester's right to exploit the eighteen brothels on Bankside in Southwark for the next 400 years. It was said that the area had been associated with brothels or stews 'since time out of mind'. The women who worked in Southwark's Bankside

Continued on p. 17

Miss Whitehead. insane. she daily attended the Bank of England.

Sarah Whitehead was the sister of a Bank of England clerk who was executed for forgery. When she learned of his death she went mad, and called at the bank every day for twenty years to enquire about him.

BANK OF ENGLAND SWINDLERS

A gang of audacious forgers swindled the Bank of England out of £100,000 in 1873. They were all Americans: the brothers George and Austin Bidwell, George Macdonnell and Edwin Noyes. George Bidwell, who was in his thirties, had arrived in Britain in 1872 via France, where he had swindled various banks out of £6,000. He was joined by the others, who were all in their late twenties. Austin Bidwell, posing as a businessman who had exclusive rights to build Pullman railway cars in England, opened an account at the Bank of England. This account was soon busy as he deposited genuine bills of exchange. These bills, which were issued by banks to their customers, were more secure than banknotes. When they were presented at a bank for payment, they would be scrutinised carefully, and, unlike banknotes, they could not be readily transferred from one person to another.

In December 1872 George Bidwell sent ten genuine bills of exchange with a face value of £4,307 into the account. They were posted from Birmingham, where his brother was supposedly building the Pullman railway cars. His brother Austin travelled to Paris and bought another bill of exchange with a face value of £4,500 from Rothschilds Bank. The accomplices had already bought blank forms for bills of exchange in various languages, and while in Paris Austin Bidwell also bought forms identical to

The four men accused of swindling the Bank of England out of £100,000 in 1873. They were the brothers George and Austin Bidwell, George Macdonnell and Edwin Noyes.

those used by the Rothschilds. First the Bidwell gang passed the genuine Rothschilds bill, on 17 January 1873. They then changed three forgeries, for £4,250. On 25 January eight bills with a face value of £9,350 were passed. They were followed by bills for £11,072.

The only limit on the gang's greed was time. The bills were due to be redeemed by the issuing banks after three months – at the end of March. The forgeries would then be discovered. So the forgers stepped up the pace. On 21 January the gang swindled the bank of £4,250. After that the amounts usually increased sharply, and on 27 February they got away with £26,265. Their haul amounted to £100,405 7*s* 3*d*.

George Bidwell said later: 'It appears as if the bank managers had heaped a mountain of gold out in the street, and put up a notice, "Please do not touch this" and then left it unguarded with the guileless confidingness of an Arcadian.'

The gang were using their haul to buy gold coins and negotiable bonds, both untraceable. These were then moved into accounts abroad. They were preparing to depart. But on 28 February, when the last of their forged bills of exchange were presented to the Bank of England, a clerk noticed that two £1,000 bills lacked an essential date. The bills had been forged in the name of a London bank, B.W. Blydenstein and Co. Thinking it a mere oversight, an official of the Bank of England sent the bills back to have the date written in. Blydensteins replied: 'We have no record of these bills and can only assume they are forgeries.'

Noyes was arrested as he called at a bank to collect foreign currency. George Bidwell, who had been waiting for him, saw Noyes taken into custody and managed to get away. Austin Bidwell was arrested in Cuba on 20 March. Macdonnell managed to board a ship for America but was arrested as he arrived in New York. George Bidwell was arrested in Edinburgh on 2 April.

The scene in court during the trial of the Bank of England swindlers. The judge carried a gun under his robes because of rumours of attempts to spring the prisoners. The state took revenge with harsh sentences.

George Bidwell, who left prison a broken man. He wrote about his release: 'Though I began those years a black-haired, robust young man, at the end I found myself a grey-haired cripple; yet, on this first opening of the world anew before my ravished eyes, how beautiful everything appeared!'

The trial was sensational in several ways. Rumours that guns had been smuggled to the prisoners led to the courtroom being searched, and the judge, Mr Justice Archibald, carried a gun under his robes. Three Newgate warders accepted bribes to help the gang escape.

The four were sentenced to penal servitude for life. George Bidwell was released in 1887 because of ill-health, his brother in 1890, and the others in 1891. George Bidwell, who left prison a broken man, wrote about his release: 'Though I began those years a black-haired, robust young man, at the end I found myself a grey-haired cripple; yet, on this first opening of the world anew before my ravished eyes, how beautiful everything appeared! Even dull-looking old London appeared glorious. And the throngs of people in the streets! I could not tire of looking at them.'

brothels were known as 'Winchester Geese', and the brothels had to be painted white and carry a distinctive mark: one of the best known was the Cardinal's Hat. The historian John Stow's *Survey of London* says that originally there were about eighteen of these brothels. Others were called The Boar's Head, The Cross Keys, The Castle, The Half Moon, The Elephant, very much as though they were inns or pubs. Ferrymen ran a shuttle-service of customers from the northern bank of the Thames, but were ordered to keep their craft tied up at night. *See* PROSTITUTION

BAREBONE (OR BARBON), PRAISE-GOD Preacher nominated by Cromwell to the Short Parliament of 1653, also called Barebone's Parliament. He was an inflammatory preacher, who attracted huge and sometimes riotous crowds. Vehement opponent of the restoration of Charles II. Although not an advocate of violence, he was arrested after VENNER'S RISING of 1661 and held in the TOWER for two years.

BARETTI, GIUSEPPE (1719–89) Italian scholar who killed a man in an affray and whose trial became

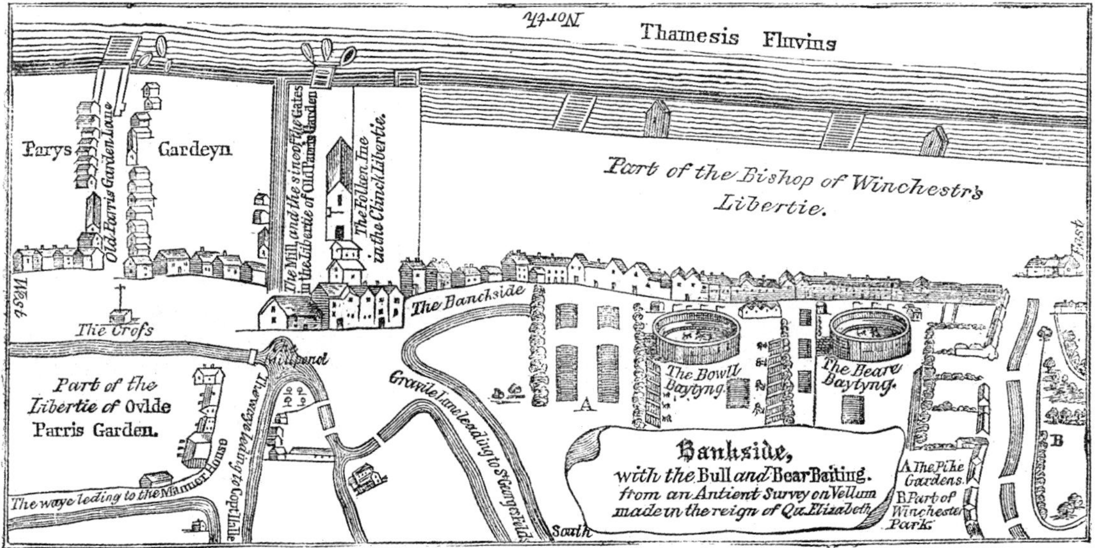

The red-light district of Bankside in Southwark early in the seventeenth century. The area had long been the heart of the sex industry. In 1161 King Henry II guaranteed the Bishop of Winchester's right to exploit the eighteen brothels on Bankside for the next 400 years. By the eighteenth century Covent Garden had superseded it.

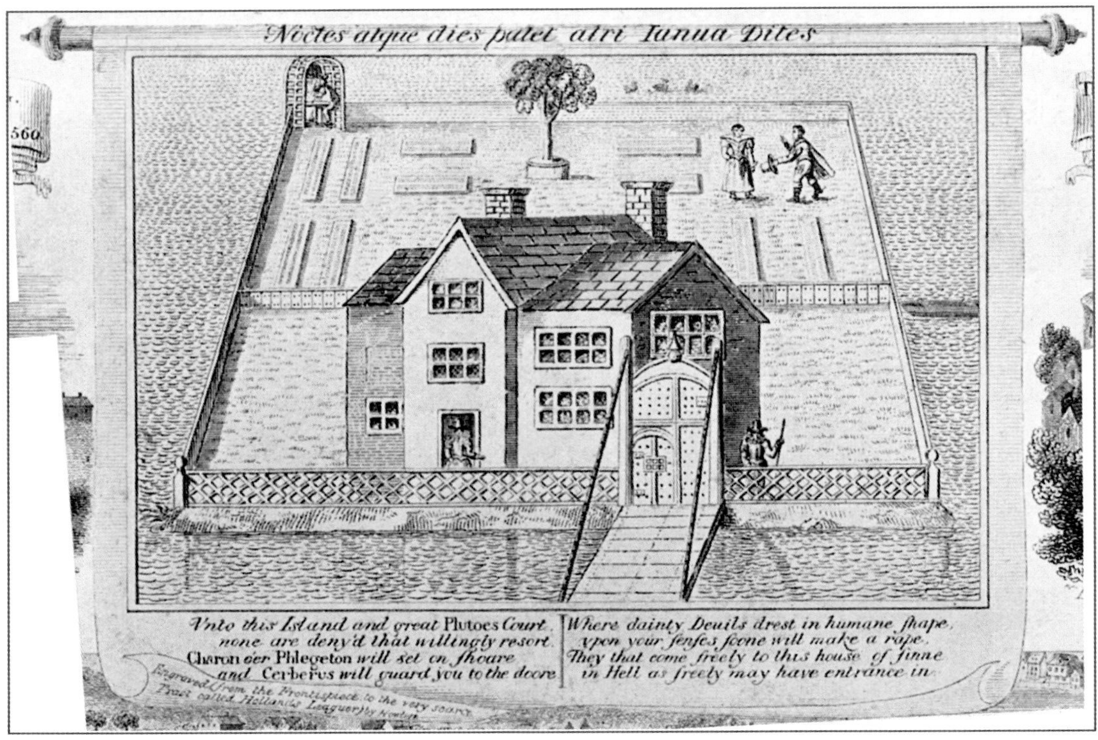

The first luxury brothel, Holland's Leaguer on Bankside, about 1630. The bawd, Elizabeth Holland, charged the highest prices for the greatest pleasure. Her motto was 'this chastitie is clean out of date'.

one of the most famous of the eighteenth century. As he walked home from a coffee house in the Haymarket in 1796, a woman who had been sitting on a doorstep jumped up and kneed him in the genitals. It was a typical criminal 'lay': she hoped to create a scene so that her criminal friends could intervene and rob Baretti. The Italian, who was of a choleric disposition, struck her back. Three ruffians used this as an excuse to set about him, and he stabbed one with a small fruit knife. Unfortunately the wound was fatal. At his trial at the Old Bailey an extraordinary array of London's intellectual elite gave evidence as to his character: Johnson, Burke, Reynolds, Garrick, Goldsmith and others went into the witness box. Johnson described Baretti as 'a man of literature, a very studious man . . . I have no reason to believe that he was ever disordered with liquor in his life'. The defence also established that in continental countries it was the custom to carry a knife, because inns there provided only forks for eating. Baretti was acquitted of murder and freed.

BARINGS BANK Eminent and venerable merchant bank brought down by an obscure currency dealer. Nick Leeson from Watford, the son of a plasterer, was given a free hand to gamble on currencies on the Singapore International Monetary Exchange. In 1993, a year after he had been posted to Asia, the 26-year-old trader personally made more than £10 million for the bank – about a tenth of their profit for that year. The following year he made £25 million in just seven months. 'We were all driven to make profits, profits and more profits . . . I was the rising star,' he wrote in his autobiography, *Rogue Trader*. In his case the profits turned to losses, which he concealed. By the time senior officials discovered what was happening Leeson had gambled away £850 million and the bank was broke. Leeson went on the run to Borneo with his wife Lisa. He was arrested and sentenced to six and a half years in prison.

Barings was founded by Francis Baring in a house in Queen Street, Cheapside, in 1763. Forty years later the diarist Joseph Farrington noted: 'Sir Francis Baring's House is now unquestionably the first Mercantile House in the City . . . Other houses, comparatively, only come in for gleanings.'

BARKER, COLONEL LESLIE IVOR GAUNTLETT (1889–1960) Much self-decorated impostor. Barker was a boxer, cricketer, farmer, teashop manager, butler, Fascist and soldier in the Home Guard. The colonel was arrested for bankruptcy at the Regent Palace Hotel in 1925 and found to be a woman. She had started out life as Lillias Valerie Barker and educated at a convent. In 1918 she married an Australian and later had two children by another Australian. Within a few years she was Captain Barker and dressing as a man. Promotion quickly followed, to Colonel with a DSO. She married the daughter of a Brighton chemist, to whom she blamed her impotence on war wounds.

After her arrest she was sentenced to nine months for making a false entry in a marriage register. She consoled herself with a bar to her DSO, and became a member of the National Fascist Party. When the party's headquarters were raided in 1927 she was charged with having a firearm without a licence. She appeared in court with her eyes bandaged, explaining that she had been blinded in the war. Ten years later she was living with an actress as man and wife, and working as a butler. When she was arrested for stealing £5 from her employer, he described her as 'the perfect manservant'. She moved with her wife to a Suffolk village and during the Second World War served in the Home Guard, using the name Geoffrey Norton. When she died in 1960 the newspapers revealed her true identity, to the surprise of the villagers.

BARRINGTON, GEORGE (*c.* 1755–after 1790) Pickpocket of skill and ambition, caught trying to steal a jewelled snuffbox from Count Gregory Orloff, the discarded lover of Catherine the Great of Russia, at a Covent Garden first night. He was held on a Thames HULK from which he was released as an act of mercy because of his bad health, but several times returned because of further crimes. Transported to Australia in 1790, he became high constable of Parramatta, New South Wales, where his estate was tended by convicts. Such was his fame that books were published under his name, but according to Robert Hughes in *The Fatal Shore* he was not the author.

BARRY, ELIZABETH (1658–1713) Rapacious whore turned into a great actress by LORD ROCHESTER. She made a disastrous stage debut in 1674, at the age of 16. Lord Rochester laid a wager with a friend that he could make a real actress of her, despite her lack of looks or talent. It took him six months, and then the actor-manager Thomas Betterton said Rochester had trained her 'to enter into the meaning of every sentiment; he taught her not only the proper cadence or sounding of the voice, but to seize also the passions, and adopt her whole behaviour to the situations of the characters'. The public agreed. Betterton described her triumphant return to the stage as 'incomparable'.

Her hardheartedness was notorious. Tom Browne said 'should you lie with her all night, she would not know you the next morning, unless you had another five pounds at your service'. She was dissolute, bad-tempered and violent. She and her fellow cast member Betty Boutel quarrelled over a scarf just as Lee's play *The Rival Queens* was about to begin. As she uttered the line: 'Die, sorceress, die and all my wrongs die with thee!' Mrs Barry stabbed Mrs Boutel with such force that her blunted stage dagger penetrated Mrs Boutel's stays and pierced the flesh beneath. After a long and successful career she retired to the country at Acton when she was in her fifties. She died in 1713, possibly from the bite of a rabid pet dog.

BARTLETT, ADELAIDE (1856–after 1886) Woman acquitted of an ingenious murder. Adelaide's 40-year-old husband Edwin was found dead at their Pimlico lodgings on New Year's Day 1886, with a large amount of chloroform in his stomach. She had married him when she was 19 and he 30. He had odd ideas about marriage, believing that a man should have two 'wives', one for intellectual companionship and the other for 'use': the unfortunate Adelaide was for the former. Bartlett had even agreed not to consummate the marriage until she was 21. The couple had a curious relationship with a young Wesleyan minister, George Dyson. The clergyman claimed Edwin had told him that in the event of his death he wished to 'give' Adelaide to him. Edwin even enjoyed watching George and Adelaide kissing in his presence. As Dyson's visits became more frequent, Edwin became ill, and a doctor diagnosed acute gastritis. After his death Adelaide was charged with murder, and her trial began at the Old Bailey in April 1886. The jury heard that Dyson had bought chloroform from chemists three days before Edwin's death. Adelaide explained this away by saying that she used it in tiny amounts to calm her husband, who had begun to show an unwonted sexual interest in her. What she could not explain was how her husband had managed to swallow a bottle of the burning liquid, or why there was no sign of blisters around his mouth or in the windpipe. The jury decided there was insufficient evidence to show how the chloroform got there, and Adelaide was acquitted. After the trial the surgeon Sir James Paget is said to have remarked: 'Now she's acquitted she should tell us, in the interests of science, how she did it.'

BARTON, ELIZABETH The Holy Maid of Kent, executed in 1534 for preaching against HENRY VIII. In 1525 Barton, a domestic servant, fell ill, perhaps with epilepsy. She fell into trances and made prophesies. After she performed miracles her gift was recognised by, among others, the King, SIR THOMAS MORE, Wolsey and the Archbishop of Canterbury. The King planned to divorce his wife and marry ANNE BOLEYN. Barton prophesied that, if he married Anne, Henry would die 'a villain's death' within a month, and should no longer be king. Henry himself heard her prophecies on three occasions. After he had married Anne, the Holy Maid announced that he was no longer king. She was arrested, and in November 1533 Henry called an assembly of high officers of church and state to debate the affair. It lasted three days. Barton was forced to admit she was a fraud, and on 20 April 1534 she was hanged at Tyburn.

BATE, REVD HENRY (1745–1824) Pugilistic priest, editor and playwright. Although he was rector of an Essex village, Bate fought five duels, was co-respondent in an adultery trial and spent a year in prison for criminal libel. Bate was walking in VAUXHALL GARDENS one evening with the actress Mrs Hartley. He challenged a Captain Croft to a duel because he didn't like the way he looked at Mrs Hartley. The captain recruited his friend, the notoriously hot-headed Irish peer George Fitzgerald, who fought more than thirty duels, and the latter's footman, a former professional boxer, to help him. The encounter took place at the Turk's Head Coffee House, Croft and his allies having to be helped away afterwards in a coach. The *Morning Chronicle* referred to the 'bullying, boxing Vauxhall parson' and the *Morning Post*, of which Bate was editor, gave a full account of the fight. It boosted circulation and Bate began to look for opportunities to repeat his success by insulting public figures. On one occasion he accused the Duke of Richmond of treachery in opposing an increase in the armed forces. Instead of seeking satisfaction in a duel, as Bate had hoped, the Duke sued for libel, and Bate was imprisoned. When his proprietor told him to be more careful in future, there was a row and Bates wounded the proprietor in a duel. In 1788 Bate, now the editor of the respectable *Morning Herald*, was accused of adultery with a Mrs Dodwell. He argued that it was not surprising that Mrs Dodwell had strayed, as her husband, an amateur anatomist, liked to dissect bodies in the bedroom. Bate was acquitted and was made a baronet for his work as a magistrate. He died in 1824.

BATTLE OF THE FRATELLANZA CLUB Defining moment in the internecine warfare between DARBY SABINI gang and their former allies, the CORTESIS and the Yiddishers. Darby and his brother Harryboy were set upon by the Cortesis in the club in Great Bath Street, Clerkenwell, on 19 November 1922. They had let their guard down and been ambushed on enemy territory – the Cortesis lived only a few doors away from the club. Harryboy was shot and wounded, and Darby was punched and beaten with bottles. He later told a court that his false teeth were broken in the affray. He added: 'I am a quiet peaceable man. I never begin a fight. I do a little bit of work as a commission agent, sometimes for myself and sometimes for someone else. I live by my brains.' During the trial the Cortesis' lawyer, who had been told that Darby always carried a big revolver, asked him if he was armed. When Darby replied that he wasn't, the lawyer insisted on his being searched. Nothing was found. As Darby left the court at the end of the day one of his team handed him back his gun.

The Old Bailey judge, Mr Justice Darling, who prided himself on his skill as a linguist, addressed Darby in Italian. Darby, who had never spoken anything but English, was baffled. Later the judge told the jury that the name Sabini meant the family were descended from the Sabines, an ancient Italian tribe whose women were raped by the Romans. Despite this rough treatment, he said, the women seemed to have fared rather well in the years that followed. Two of the Cortesis were each sentenced to three years' penal servitude. Judge Darling turned down the jury's suggestion that the brothers should be deported and commented:

> I look upon this as part of a faction fight which has raged between you and other Italians in consequence of some difference which the police do not entirely understand. You appear to be two lawless bands – the Sabinis and the Cortesis. Sometimes you are employed against the Birmingham people, and sometimes you are employed against each other. I have the power to recommend an order for your deportation. I am not going to do it. I can see no reason to suppose that you two men are worse than others who have been convicted in these feuds and have not been recommended for deportation. But the whole

of the Italian colony should know of the Grand Jury's recommendation, and I wish to say to you all, if this kind of lawless conduct goes on, those who get convicted in future will be turned out of this country with their wives and children.

That was the end of the Cortesi challenge. The Sabinis were free to extend their empire into the West End, taking shares in gambling and drinking clubs and installing one-armed bandits.

BATTLE OF LEWES, 1936 Last of the big set pieces of the racecourse wars. In June 1936 rival London gangsters clashed at a race meeting at Lewes in Sussex. About thirty men from the Hackney and Hoxton areas attacked the SABINI associate and bookie ALF SOLOMON and his clerk, Mark Frater. One of the attackers, James Spinks, shouted: 'There they are, boys, get your tools ready.' The tools included an axe with which Spinks struck Frater on the head. The blow was partly deflected by Frater's bowler hat. Sixteen of the attackers, who also carried knives, truncheons, chisels and knuckledusters, were jailed for a total of fifty-three years.

BATTLE OF NILE STREET Encounter between the SABINIS and the TITANICS now encrusted with myth and speculation. It apparently began with a fight in a West End gambling club in the early 1920s. The Sabinis got the worst of it, and Darby Sabini decided to take the battle to the Titanics' heartland. According to gangland legend, a convoy of cars drove from one of the pubs the Sabinis used as their headquarters, the Griffin in Clerkenwell, and travelled eastwards towards Hoxton. Their destination was a pub called the Albion, known as the 'Blood Tub', one of the Titanics' haunts. In the cars were about twenty men with at least ten guns. The Titanics had been warned, and when the convoy drove into Nile Street on its way to the Albion they were armed and waiting. One of their leaders, Jimmy Bond, a war hero, had positioned ten gunmen behind upturned market barrows along a fifty-yard length of Nile Street. Other gunmen were placed in the Albion, which commanded a view west along Nile Street. They opened a lively fire on Darby's men, who took cover behind fruit barrows on the other side of the street and returned fire. Two of the Titanics were wounded, and Sabini soldier Paul Boffa was knocked unconscious with a length of lead pipe. He was stripped by the Titanics' women, who gave him a vicious beating. Bond intervened to save him. They were the only casualties, surprisingly in view of the firepower deployed. The death penalty was in force at the time, and neither side wanted a murder on their hands.

BAWDY BASKETS Itinerant whores who went from house to house in the seventeenth century selling pins and other trifles, and sometimes themselves. 'And as they walk by the way, they often gain some money with their instrument by such as they suddenly meet withal.' Their main purpose, however, was to spy out opportunities for burglary and pass the information on to their male accomplices. They were often allied with the 'upright men', bullies who were the elite of the travelling criminal class.

BAWDY HOUSE RIOTS Attacks by apprentices on brothels, which began on Shrove Tuesday, 1668. Apprentices had traditionally attacked bawdy houses in an excess of moral zeal on Shrove Tuesday, their holiday. The riots of 1668, which lasted five days, were probably caused by a royal proclamation requiring enforcement of the laws against Dissenters. The rioters saw the bawdy houses as symbolic of Charles II's 'flagrantly debauched' court. Pepys wrote that 'these idle fellows' regretted only that they had destroyed small bawdy houses and not 'the great bawdy house at Whitehall'. His diary entry for 24 March tells of a tumult about Moorfields where the apprentices pulled down the local brothels.

This caused consternation at court, where all the available troops, both cavalry and infantry, were called to arms, and alarms were sounded with drums and trumpets. It was, he wrote, 'as if the French were coming into the town'.

Some of the rioters broke open the prisons where their fellow rioters were held. 'With veterans of Cromwell's army rumoured to be involved, the government behaved as though the destruction of the brothels was the prelude to civil war' (Gilmour, *Riot, Risings and Revolution*). Retribution was savage: the offences were treated as if they were high treason, and four apprentices were found guilty of high treason and were hanged, drawn and quartered.

BCCI Crooked bank whose collapse still reverberates. On 5 July 1991 regulators swooped on the Bank of Credit and Commerce International. The Bank of England had obtained a provisional winding-up order, and in coordinated international action BCCI's worldwide assets were frozen. As depositors desperate to withdraw their savings queued outside BCCI branches, police and accountants began one of the biggest financial investigations ever. At their headquarters in Finsbury Square in the City of London the investigators collected such a mountain of paperwork the foundations had to be strengthened to take the weight.

BCCI was created in 1972 by Agha Hasan Abedi, a Pakistani 'banker and mystic'. He had links with Arab sheiks, and Bank of America bought into BCCI to get access to Middle Eastern clients. At one stage Bank of America owned 30 per cent, but sold out long before the crash. By 1988 the bank had 400 branches in seventy-three countries and claimed to have assets of $20 billion. The UK was central to its operations: it was run from offices in Leadenhall Street in the City, and there were branches in Bradford, Birmingham and Southall. It was popular with Pakistani small investors, but its customers may also have included the Abu Nidal terrorist group and Colombian drug barons. General Manuel Noreiga of Panama held accounts in London.

There were guilty verdicts in all six BCCI trials at the Old Bailey. In 1997 shipping tycoon Abbas Gokal, 61, was jailed for fourteen years for his part in the fraud. This was increased to seventeen years after he had failed to pay £2.9 million under a confiscation order. The only UK subject among the BCCI defendants was Nazmu Virani. He was jailed for two and a half years in 1994 on charges of false accounting and misleading BCCI's auditors. Other BCCI suspects remain in Pakistan, which has refused to extradite them. Agha Hasan Abedi died in 1995. Investigators have recovered $7 billion of the $12 billion involved in the fraud (Jon Ashworth, *The Times*, 30 June 2001).

BEDLAM For many years one of the entertainments of London was going to see the poor distracted inmates of the lunatic asylum known as Bedlam. Its real name was Bethlehem Royal Hospital, and it had originally been the Priory of St Mary Bethlehem, founded near Bishopsgate in 1247. It became an asylum for the mentally ill in the fourteenth century. Patients were kept in chains, and whipped or ducked in water if violent. When the priory was dissolved in 1547 the Corporation of London bought the site and used it again for a lunatic asylum. In 1675 the hospital moved to a building in Moorfields designed by Robert Hooke. Evelyn said the building was very beautiful, but the treatment continued to be cruel. Plate 8 of Hogarth's *A Rake's Progress*, while not a literal depiction of Bedlam, gives a fair idea of how it looked, with the demented, the melancholy and people suffering from various manias objects of amused interest to well-dressed visitors. These visits ended in 1770: patients had been upset by people 'making sport and diversion' of them. Reforms were gradually introduced, partly under the influence of the prison reformer JOHN HOWARD, and in 1815 the hospital moved to Lambeth, on a site now occupied by the War Museum. It moved again in 1930 to Addington in Surrey. Today the Bethlehem Royal Hospital is at Beckenham in Kent. Among the patients in Bedlam over the years were Daniel McNaghton, after whom the MCNAGHTON RULES on criminal responsibility were named, and the architect Augustus Pugin.

BELASCO, DAVID Jewish brothel-owner in Victorian London. HENRY MAYHEW's associate Bracebridge Hemyng believed that KATE HAMILTON's Café Royal was owned by a Jewish family, who also owned several other night houses. This may have been Belasco and his associates, who were known to have wide interests in brothels. Belasco went bankrupt, and was later reported to be working as a waiter (Chesney, *The Victorian Underworld*). This is one of the few glimpses we get of the shadowy figures behind the chains of Victorian brothels.

BELCHER, JOHN (1904–64) Labour minister who was forced to resign for accepting gifts. Belcher became an MP in the 1945 election and was promoted to junior minister at the important Board of Trade in 1946. He was clever, honest, hard-working and successful. Unfortunately his duties brought him into contact with Sidney Stanley, 'the Spider of Park Lane', a confidence trickster and a supreme example of the lobbyist. At a time of stringent controls on trade, Stanley, a Polish Jew, obtained staggering amounts of money from businessmen by falsely claiming he had great influence in Whitehall. He courted Belcher, becoming a personal friend. Belcher had been quite legitimately accepting small gifts from businessmen, mainly samples of products, although this was against the spirit of the Labour administration. He usually gave them to people in his office. Barbara Castle, then a Parliamentary Private Secretary, was given a hairbrush by a manufacturer. 'I took it as gingerly as if it had been a time bomb, and brought it back to the Department where I asked one of the top civil servants what I should do with it. They had a solemn conclave and decided I could keep the hairbrush.' Stanley took Belcher to restaurants, boxing matches and greyhound races. He paid for a holiday for the Belcher family in Margate. There

Two elegant society women view the lunatics in Bedlam, the asylum for the insane, in Hogarth's A Rake's Progress*, Plate 8. This was considered an entertainment in the eighteenth century, much like going to the theatre or the pleasure gardens.*

was also a gold cigarette case and a new suit. Rumours began to circulate and in October 1948 the Prime Minister, Clement Attlee, set up a Tribunal of Inquiry, under Mr Justice Lynskey. It reported in January 1949 and found that Belcher had used his ministerial office improperly in return for gifts. Belcher resigned immediately, and Stanley was deported. Belcher went back to his old job on the railways, and rose to the position of assistant goods master at King's Cross.

BELL, LAURA (1829–94) Courtesan who became an evangelical preacher and whose husband died in very mysterious circumstances. Laura was born in County Antrim, worked as a street prostitute in Belfast, became a high-priced Dublin whore with her own carriage and made her London debut in 1850. She lived in Wilton Crescent and cut a swathe through the swells. When she attended the opera, the entire house would stand to watch her leave. Prince Jung Bahadoor, brother of the Maharaja of Nepal, was said to have given her £250,000 (the equivalent of more than £10 million today) to enjoy her for a single night. Katie Hickman (*Courtesans*) speculates that this may have been the total sum he spent on Laura while he knew her. In any case, she had no trouble spending the money. Two years after her arrival in London she married Captain Augustus Thistlethwaythe. When she became a preacher, her extravagant ways did not end, and her husband was forced to disclaim her debts. In August 1887 he was found shot dead in his bedroom. Most improbably it was supposed that he had had a fit, knocking over a table with a revolver on it. According to this theory, the revolver went off, shooting him dead. Laura's preaching was described as 'impassioned . . . not eloquent nor convincing, but certainly effective'. The society hostess Lady St Helier heard her conducting a revivalist service in Scotland when her stunning blonde beauty was fading:

> She was a very striking-looking woman, and the great black mantilla which covered her masses of golden hair, the magnificent jewels she wore around her neck, and the flashing rings on the hands with which she gesticulated, added to the soft tones of her very beautiful voice, made a great impression on those who listened to her.

BELLAMY, GEORGE ANN (*c.* 1727–88) Actress whose brilliant theatrical career was overshadowed by lust and profligacy. 'She was a most beautiful woman, an accomplished actress, and extraordinarily lascivious. Her whoring was as much from inclination as necessity.'

George – the name seems to have been a mistake at the christening – was the illegitimate daughter of Lord Tyrawley. There was clearly more to her than fleshly charms. Her intimate friends included Garrick, Fox, Lord Chesterfield and many other figures from the diplomatic and literary worlds of London. Women too were charmed, and even virtuous society women courted her and allowed their daughters to do so too. She was an early advocate of women's liberation, which may have helped. Baron d'Archenholz wrote in 1773 that 'her beauty, her wit, her intelligence, her talents, and her generosity and refined manners irresistibly attracted everyone to her'. Her friend Barney Thornton, proprietor of the mischievous *Drury Lane Journal*, wrote of her: 'Oh! the Mrs Bellamy! the fine, the charming, the Every Thing Mrs Bellamy – the best actress and the handsomest woman in the world!'

Her great success on the stage and her rich lovers could not always keep her out of the debtors' prison. The diplomat Count Haszlang tried to save her by giving her diplomatic immunity as his 'housekeeper'. She died in poverty in 1788. She told her story in the autobiographical *Apology*.

BENEFIT OF CLERGY A medieval privilege that allowed those in holy orders to be tried by the lenient ecclesiastical courts rather than the lay courts. At the time most of those who could read were clerics and the privilege was gradually extended to all who were literate and to the criminal courts. To prove their status, all they had to do was read or recite a passage from the Bible. For obvious reasons the passage was known as the 'neck verse'. It came from Psalm 51: 'Have mercy upon me, O God, after thy great goodness: according unto the multitude of thy tender mercies blot out my transgressions.' Many common criminals took advantage of this privilege. If they were illiterate, they were rehearsed in reciting it by fellow criminals or sympathetic jailers until they were word-perfect. This ploy was so successful that by the end of the sixteenth century as many as half the men convicted of felony were successfully using it to escape execution. Those who pleaded it were branded on the hand so the ploy could be used only once. Benefit of clergy gave a way out to courts reluctant to sentence men to death for minor offences. But transportation and imprisonment became acceptable alternatives to hanging, and gradually benefit of clergy was removed from most crimes. It was abolished for murder in 1532 and altogether in 1827. The playwright Ben Jonson pleaded benefit of clergy after he had killed a fellow actor in a duel. Benefit of clergy was illogically extended to women in the seventeenth century.

Ben Jonson, who pleaded benefit of clergy.

BENSON, HARRY Conman who was the chief prosecution witness in the TRIAL OF THE DETECTIVES in 1877. Benson lived in style in a large house on the Isle of Wight, with maids and other servants. He owned three local papers and was a talented musician. At one stage he was making £4,000 a week from crime, and he paid lavish bribes to Scotland Yard detectives for tip-offs about inquiries into racing scams, which were among his rackets. After serving a fifteen-year sentence, he went to the United States, where he continued to profit from various swindles. In 1911 he committed suicide in the Tombs prison in New York rather than face extradition to Mexico, where he had sold fake tickets for a tour by the singer Adelina Patti.

BENTHAM, JEREMY (1748–1832) Philosopher who devised a new kind of prison. Bentham came from a line of London lawyers, but his legal studies disgusted him with the current state of the law and, rather than practise it, he became a reformer. His design for a circular prison, called the Panopticon, where warders could sit in the centre and observe all the prisoners like spiders at the centre of a web, influenced the construction of Millbank Prison (1816), which stood on the Thames site now occupied by the old Tate Gallery. He called his ideal prison 'a mill for grinding rogues honest' and hoped to be appointed its manager. It was never built, owing to the opposition of landowners, but after twenty years he was compensated by Parliament.

Bentham argued against capital punishment, but prosecuted the family's elderly servant, who was hanged. The man, John Franks, stole two silver spoons. Mr and Mrs Bentham gave evidence against him at the Old Bailey in January 1780.

BENTLEY, DEREK (*c*. 1933–53) Thief whose execution in January 1953 when he was 19 for being 'concerned' in the murder of a policeman hastened the abolition of the death penalty. Bentley and 16-year-old Christopher Craig were seen breaking into a warehouse in Croydon. When Bentley was arrested, Craig opened fire with a revolver, wounding the detective who was holding his accomplice and killing PC Sidney Miles. Bentley was found guilty of murder in a trial remarkable for the prejudicial remarks of the judge, LORD CHIEF JUSTICE GODDARD. He was executed at Wandsworth prison. Craig was also found guilty of murder but was too young to be executed. He was released in 1963. The execution of Bentley, who was mentally subnormal, the judge's behaviour and the refusal of the Home Secretary to accept the jury's recommendation for mercy caused widespread misgivings and helped the abolitionist cause.

BERKLEY, THERESA Successful Victorian flagellant who made a fortune and owned the ingenious Berkley Horse. So popular were flagellation houses in the early nineteenth century that Mrs Berkley was reputed to have made £10,000 in eight years. The book *Venus School Mistress*, published in 1830 with a preface by another madam, MARY WILSON, and devoted wholly to flagellation, gives an account of Mrs Berkley's establishment at 28 Charlotte Street. Mary Wilson says: 'She is a clever, pleasing, and trustworthy woman, in the prime of life, and perfectly mistress of her business. She is an excellent *ontologist*, and therefore quite *au fait* in treating the *aberrations* of the human mind. Her museum of natural and artificial curiosities and her collection of "*Illustrations de arcanis Veneris et amoris*" are by far the most extensive to be found in any similar institution.' *Venus School Mistress* lists Mrs Berkley's extraordinary equipment:

> Her instruments of torture were more numerous than those of any other governess. Her supply of birch was extensive, and kept in water so that it was always green and pliant; she had shafts with a dozen whip thongs on each of them; a dozen different sizes of thin bending canes; leather straps like coach trades; battledoors, made of thick sole-leather, with inch-nails run through to docket and curry-comb tough hides rendered callous by many years' flagellation. Holly brushes, furze brushes, a prickly evergreen called butcher's brush; and during the summer, glass and china vases, filled with a constant supply of green nettles, with which she often restored the dead to life. Thus, at her shop, whoever went with plenty of money could be birched, whipped, fustigated, scourged, needle-pricked, half-hung, holly-brushed, furze-brushed, butcher-brushed, stinging-nettled, curry-combed, phlebotomised and tortured . . .

For those who preferred to scourge rather than be scourged, Mrs Berkley was prepared to act the role of victim in return for a large fee, as long as the beating was not too violent. For sadists who wanted to inflict serious pain, she kept a number of strong women to play victim, among them One-Eyed Peg, Bald-Cunted Poll and Ebony Bet. Mrs Berkley's greatest claim to the considerable fame she acquired in these circles was the Berkley Horse. This was invented in 1828 for her to flog her clients on. *Venus School Mistress* says:

> It is capable of being opened to a considerable extent, so as to bring the body to any angle that might be desirable. There is a print in Mrs Berkley's memoirs, representing a man upon it quite naked. A woman is sitting in a chair exactly under it, with her bosom, belly and bush exposed she is manualizing his embolon, while Mrs Berkley is birching his posteriors . . . When the new flogging machine was invented the designer told her that it would bring her into notice, and go by her name after her death; and it did cause her to be talked about, and brought her a great deal of business . . . Mrs Berkley also had in her second floor, a hook and pulley attached to the ceiling by which she could draw a man up by the hands . . .

Mrs Berkley died in 1836 and her brother, who had been a missionary in Australia for thirty years, returned to claim her fortune as his inheritance. When he learned how she had earned it, he renounced his claim and returned to Australia. Mrs Berkley's executor, a Dr Vance, refused to administer the estate, and the wages of sin became the property of the Crown. As the executor the Crown suppressed Mrs Berkley's autobiography because she had named her royal and aristocratic clients. The Berkley Horse was given to the Royal Society of Arts. *See* FLAGELLATION

BERNHARDT, SARAH (1844–1923) French actress and mistress of EDWARD VII. Lady Frederick Cavendish referred to her in a letter as 'a woman of notorious, shameless character . . . not content with being run after on stage, this woman is asked to respectable people's houses to act, and even to luncheon and dinner; and all the world goes. It is an outrageous scandal.' Not everyone ran after or even accepted her. In July 1881, at a party in the Rothschild mansion in Piccadilly given at the request of the Prince of Wales, 'the fashionable ladies present refused to speak to the actress, and the whole affair was a dismal frost . . .' (Pearsall, *The Worm in the Bud*). She was one of the king's women in the 'loose box' in Westminster Abbey at the Coronation.

BESSARABIANS, THE A gang of largely Russian-Jewish protection racketeers from the Whitechapel area at the end of the nineteenth century. They extorted money from fellow immigrants, brothel-keepers, men who ran illegal gaming clubs known as spielers, shopkeepers and the proprietors of coffee stalls. Detective Sergeant B. Leeson, who joined the police in 1895, called the Bessarabians the 'Stop at Nothing' gang. 'They were the greatest menace ever known in London,' he wrote, and claimed that in the early years of the century they made the capital 'almost as dangerous a place to live in as Chicago is today . . . In fact there is every good reason to believe that a good many members of the Bessarabian gang which we broke up in the East End thirty years ago are still to be found in the ranks of the gunmen plying their gentle trade in that American city.' Leeson says one of their scams was to approach wealthy families whose daughters were about to be married and threaten to spread defamatory rumours about the brides. If their methods now seem clumsy and naive, they could bring terror to the streets, hunting in packs of up to forty and meeting any resistance with guns, bottles, knives and fists. FREDERICK WENSLEY, one of Scotland Yard's most famous commanders, wrote in his autobiography *Detective Days* in 1931: 'In the main . . . the victims were persons who for some reason or another were a little shy of bringing their troubles to the notice of the police. Keepers of shady restaurants, runners of gambling dens, landlords of houses of resort, street bookmakers and other people on the fringes of the underworld were among those peculiarly open to trouble.'

Their main rivals were the Odessians. The Bessarabians had met their match when they tried to collect protection money from a giant Jew named Weinstein, who ran a restaurant called the Odessa. Weinstein fought back with an iron bar and put five of the Bessarabians in hospital. Admirers of this exploit founded the Odessians. The gang warfare between the two groups came to a head at a pub and music hall called the York Minster in Philpot Street, off the Commercial Road. The proprietor heard the Bessarabians planned to show up during a display of Russian dancing, and he turned to the Odessians for help. When the Bessarabians arrived, a fight broke out in the hall. A man named Kaufman was surrounded by Odessians and stabbed to death. A successful Jewish boxer, Kid McCoy, was arrested. He told the police: 'If they are going to top me [hang me] I will give you the name of the actual murderer. Otherwise I will keep my mouth shut.'

He got ten years' penal servitude and kept his promise of silence. But others in the East End, shocked by the scale of the violence, talked, and the gangs were finally broken up by the police.

BIGGS, RONALD (1928–) Incompetent criminal who found fame as a member of the gang that carried out the Great Train Robbery of 1963. He escaped from Wandsworth Prison and made his way to Brazil. Instead of paying the Brazilians to keep him there, the British authorities tried to bring him back. In 2000, old and ill, he returned voluntarily and was arrested.

BLACK ACT A rare example of state terrorism in Britain. The Act was rushed through Parliament by SIR ROBERT WALPOLE in 1723, ostensibly to deal with an increase in poaching, but it reinforced the BLOODY CODE, under which innumerable more or less petty crimes mainly against property were made punishable by death. By 1820 the number of capital offences had risen to more than 200. Hanging crimes included cutting down trees in an avenue, destroying turnpikes, sending threatening letters, being disguised within the Mint, maliciously cutting hop-binds growing on poles, being a soldier or seaman and wandering about without a pass, consorting with gipsies, stealing a fish out of a river or pond, stealing turnips, and impersonating the out-pensioners at Greenwich Hospital. This savagery was reflected in the figures for hangings. The total for London (not including Southwark) between 1701 and 1750 was 281. After that the total rose sharply: 246 hangings in the 1760s and 501 in the 1780s. *See* EXECUTIONS

BLACK ASSIZE In April 1750 two prisoners with typhus were taken from NEWGATE PRISON to the OLD BAILEY. They infected everyone in the courtroom, and among those who died were the judge, all the trial lawyers, all twelve jurymen and many spectators.

BLACK BOY ALLEY GANG Murderous confederation that controlled a vast network of criminals from their headquarters near Smithfield Market. At their strongest in the 1740s, they were said to claim hegemony over about 7,000 criminals in Southwark, the Mint, St Giles and the City. Whores would try to lure clients to these strongholds and into the clutches of the gang. The gang was broken up after 'several assassination attempts against the constabulary and magistracy'. Among the members were Barefoot, Gentleman Harry, Captain Poney, Nobby, Scampey, Jack the Sailor and Country Dick (Linebaugh, *The London Hanged*).

BLACK HARRIOTT A brothel in the elite vice enclave of King's Place, St James, was operated by a Miss Harriott, known as Black Harriott, a Negress from Guinea who had been captured in a slave raid as a child and shipped to Jamaica. Her beauty and intelligence attracted William Lewis, a plantation-owner and captain in the merchant navy. He bought her and treated her as his wife, teaching her to read and write and grooming her to appear in English high society. In London they lived just off Piccadilly and mixed in the highest circles. Lewis died of smallpox in 1772, leaving her penniless, and she was committed to the King's Bench debtors' prison. She was freed with the help of some admirers, and was soon running a flourishing brothel, with seventy regular customers, of whom at least twenty were members of the House of Lords. In 1774 she took over No. 3 King's Place, where her clients included the Earl of Sandwich, one of the leaders of the MEDMENHAM ABBEY set and famous to posterity for inventing the snack that bears his name. Harriott's downfall was said to be a passion she developed for a Guards officer. She neglected her business and the whores sold the contents of her brothel. She was imprisoned for debt, and, although she later ran another brothel in King's Place, she was now seriously ill, and died of tuberculosis. Harriott was the only black woman to run a brothel in what was the heart of the upper-class enclave of Royal St James's, although BOSWELL was told of a brothel staffed entirely by black women.

BLACK LUCY Whore saved from the gallows by the GORDON RIOTERS when they sacked Newgate Prison in 1780. Lucy Johnson lured a schoolteacher to a lodging house on the pretext of selling him old clothes. Once inside she threw him to the ground, and several other women helped her rob him. They ripped open his trousers and stole a guinea and eight half-crowns. She was sentenced to hang, but was one of the many prisoners freed by the rioters.

BLACK MARKET During the Second World War the boundary between honesty and criminality was blurred by the growth of the black market in scarce goods. Citizens irritated by shortages and exhortations to scrimp and save were eager buyers of what criminals such as BILLY HILL had to offer. People who would otherwise have led blameless lives joined in: businessmen who diverted part of their production to take advantage of the higher prices on the black market, farmers who did the same with their produce, and of course the resentful citizens who bought the goods. Market towns around London – Romford was the centre of the black market – saw a huge rise in business, as traders from London arrived to exchange their goods for agricultural produce. There was also a brisk trade in stolen clothing coupons and ration books. Another source of supply for the black market was bomb-damaged shops and businesses. Criminals raided warehouses and hijacked lorries. Deserters and spivs swelled the ranks of those involved in this commodity crime. Spivs were an important link, essentially contact men, fixers who acted as an interface between the public and the real criminals.

BLACKBURNE, ARCHBISHOP LANCELOT Scandalous cleric who became a pirate and then Archbishop of York. Blackburne was ordained in 1681. He served on board a privateer in the Caribbean, accepting his share of the spoils when Spanish ships were captured. In 1694 he was appointed sub-dean at Exeter, where he had an affair with the wife of a Mr Martyr. He ingratiated himself at court, became Bishop of Exeter and then Archbishop of York. An old pirate friend who returned to London and asked 'How's old Blackburne?' was astonished to hear that his former colleague was now an archbishop. His womanising left him little time for ecclesiastical duties. In 1743, the year of his death, a satirist described him enjoying two women at once:

> One had her charms below, and one above.
> So I together blended either bliss
> Lydia lay on, Dolly had my kiss.

BLACKSTONE, SIR WILLIAM (1723–80) Jurist, born in London, who published the celebrated *Commentaries on the Laws of England* between 1765 and 1769. He was an MP, Solicitor General and a judge in the Court of Common Pleas.

BLAKE, GEORGE British agent who defected to the Russians and betrayed hundreds of his colleagues. Blake was sentenced to forty-two years' imprisonment for passing secrets to the Soviets after being tried *in camera* at the Old Bailey in 1961. In 1966 he escaped from Wormwood Scrubs prison and fled to Moscow. Intelligence sources say up to forty agents he named were executed by the KGB.

BLAKE, JOSEPH, known as 'Blueskin' (1688–1724) Burglar who stabbed the gangster JONATHAN WILD. Blueskin had been a member of Wild's Corporation of Thieves but later teamed up with the burglar and jailbreaker Jack Sheppard. This was enough to turn Wild against him, and he tracked him to his lodgings. His henchman Quilt Arnold broke down the door, and Blueskin drew a knife and threatened to kill the first man who entered the room. Arnold replied: 'Then I am the first man, and Mr Wild is not far behind, and if you do not deliver your knife immediately, I will chop your arm off.' Blueskin surrendered, and was condemned to death on Wild's evidence. When Wild went to his cell to gloat Blueskin stabbed him in the throat. Blueskin was asked whether the attack was premeditated. He replied: 'Had it been, I would have provided a knife sharp enough to cut his head off.' Wild survived, Blueskin was executed in 1724 at the age of about 26. He had a ready tongue. One night he held up a coach in which the notorious bawd Mother Wisebourne was travelling back from Hampstead after selling the virginity of one of her young girls for twenty guineas. When Blake demanded her purse, she said she recognised him, and would see him hanged. Blueskin replied: 'You double-poxed salivating bitch, you deserve hanging more than I, for ruining both body and soul of many a poor man and woman, whom you procure to work iniquity for your own profit; there is nobody your friends, but the beadle and justice clerks who for a bribe may work your peace with [their] masters. Come, no dallying, deliver your money, or else your life must be a sacrifice to my fury.'

Mother Wisebourne paid up with such bad grace, swearing at Blueskin 'a thousand names' that he stripped her naked and left her (Anon, *The History of the Remarkable Lives and Action of Jonathan Wild, Thief-Taker, Joseph Blake alia Blueskin, Footpad, and John Sheppard, Housebreaker*). 'Salivating' in this context was the result of the mercury cure for syphilis.

BLOOD, COLONEL THOMAS (*c*. 1618–80) Irish adventurer who stole the Crown Jewels in 1671. Blood already had a series of wild escapades behind him, including an attempt to capture Dublin Castle and a plot to assassinate the King. He befriended the Jewel-House Keeper, Talbot Edwards, who invited him to supper. The following morning Blood and his accomplices arrived to view the jewels. They gagged and bound the Keeper, but were disturbed as they stole the regalia. One of them stuffed the orb down his trousers but was caught on Tower Wharf. Another who fled with the sceptre was knocked from his horse by a barber's pole. Blood was caught by the garrison as he fled with the crown in a bag. He refused to speak to anyone but Charles II. His effrontery amused the King, who gave him back his sequestered Irish estate and a pension of £500 a year. He became a familiar figure at court. His three accomplices were also released. The generosity of their treatment led to rumours that the King himself was behind the plot to steal the Crown Jewels. Charles was hard up, and there was speculation that he intended to sell the jewels. Blood said enigmatically when he was caught, 'It was a bold attempt, but it was for a Crown.'

BLOODY CODE Name given to the English criminal law system between 1688 and 1815, under which the number of offences punishable by death increased greatly. In 1688 there were about fifty capital felonies: by 1815 the figure had risen to about 225. Most of these penalties were for property crime. However, the death penalty could in theory be imposed for a much greater range of crimes. Sir Erskine May said of the Code: 'The lives of men were sacrificed with a reckless barbarity, worthier of an eastern despot or African chief than of a Christian state' (May, *The Constitutional History of England*). Judges and juries often did what they could to mitigate the severity of the Code. The juries would undervalue stolen goods so that a lesser penalty could be imposed. McLynn (*Crime and Punishment in Eighteenth-Century England*) points out that by 1800 only about a third of those condemned were executed. And execution rates in London were likely to be higher than elsewhere. Two-thirds of the 527 people sentenced to death in London and Middlesex between 1749 and 1758 were executed. The figure for the Norfolk and West Midlands circuits in 1750–72 was under a quarter. *See* the BLACK ACT and EXECUTIONS

BLOODY SUNDAY RIOTS Protest on 13 November 1887, which led to two deaths. Unrest during a period of economic depression brought a ban on demonstrations in Trafalgar Square. A mass meeting to challenge this was called, and troops and police were used to break it up. Apart from the two dead many were injured. Karl Marx's daughter was present and complained of police brutality. William Morris and Bernard Shaw joined a march from Clerkenwell. In St Martin's Lane the marchers were routed by a force of 4,000 police and soldiers. The socialist Helen Taylor had her red flag ripped from her grasp by a policeman. *See* RIOTS

BLOOM, JOHN (1934–) Washing-machine salesman and bankrupt. Bloom had the idea in 1958 of buying washing machines in Holland for £29 and selling them direct to British housewives for £50. The business was wildly successful and he merged with a company called Rolls Razor. He made a fortune, but at the height of his success a partner left and set up a rival business. He persuaded Bloom's Dutch suppliers to sell to him instead, and Bloom was forced to make his own machines. They were a disaster, and in 1964 Rolls Razor went into liquidation owing £4 million. Two years later Bloom was charged with intent to deceive shareholders and fined £30,000. Among his many subsequent unsuccessful ventures was the Crazy Horse Saloon in Marylebone, taken over from him at gunpoint by gangsters. Bloom later ran a restaurant bar in Majorca.

BLUNT, ANTHONY (1907–83) Member of the Establishment and spy. Blunt was an art historian and a don at Trinity College, Cambridge, where he recruited a group of Communist sympathisers to spy for the Soviet Union. He himself had been recruited by his fellow homosexual, GUY BURGESS. In 1940 he joined the security service MI5. The flat he and Burgess shared in Bentinck Street in the West End was the scene of homosexual orgies. Blunt left MI5 in 1945. After the defection of Burgess and fellow spy Donald Maclean, Blunt came under suspicion and bluffed his way through many security interrogations. In 1964 he confessed after being promised immunity from prosecution. The Queen knew of his treachery but he was allowed to keep his post as Surveyor of the Queen's Pictures, although he was later stripped of his knighthood. He was finally exposed to the public by the Prime Minister, Margaret Thatcher, in 1979. Despite the honours and the immunity, he did not tell the whole truth.

BODY SNATCHING The highly profitable practice of digging up bodies and selling them to surgeons. The supply of executed criminals, the only legal source of human bodies, was inadequate to the needs of the surgeons and the anatomy schools in the early nineteenth century. *See* BOROUGH BOYS and JOSEPH NAPLES

BOGARD, ISAAC, known as Darky the Coon, Jewish gangster involved in a violent feud with ARTHUR HARDING in the early years of the twentieth century. Bogard was typical of ethnic gangsters in the East End before and since, preying on his own people and organising prostitutes. He was decorated for bravery during the First World War.

BOILED ALIVE In 1532 Richard Rose was boiled alive at Smithfield. Rose, a cook, had poisoned gruel made for the household of the Bishop of Rochester. Two people died and fifteen more were made ill. Like missionaries supposedly boiled by cannibals, Rose was forced into an iron cauldron and a fire was lit underneath it. It took him two hours to die. Ten years later Margaret Davy was also boiled alive at the same spot for poisoning. *See* SMITHFIELD

BOLEYN, ANNE (*c.* 1504–36) Second wife of HENRY VIII, executed for treason in 1536. She was no beauty, but was witty and vivacious. Her sister Mary had already been a mistress of the King, and in January 1533 he married Anne, who was already some months pregnant. The birth of a daughter – later Elizabeth I – instead of a male heir was a great disappointment to Henry, whose ardour was anyhow rapidly cooling. In January 1536 Anne gave birth to a son, but it was still-born. A combination of politics and Henry's disappointment doomed her. In May 1536 Henry abruptly rode away from a tournament at Greenwich, leaving Anne behind. The next day she was arrested and taken to the TOWER. She was accused of adultery with five men, one of them her own brother. Anne was tried by twenty-six peers and sentenced to death by her uncle, the Duke of Norfolk. The Duke wept as he pronounced the sentence. Anne spent the last night before execution in the same room in the Tower she had occupied before her coronation exactly three years earlier. She chose to be beheaded with a sword rather than the axe, and an executioner was brought over from France. On the scaffold on Tower Green she said: 'I am not here to preach to you but to die. Pray for the King, for he is a good man and has treated me as good could be. I do not accuse anyone for causing my death, neither the judges nor anyone else for I am condemned by the law of the land and die willingly.'

BOLLAND, JAMES Extortionist and fraudster executed in 1772. Bolland was a sheriff's officer who arrested people for debt and held them, quite legally, at his large SPUNGING HOUSE near Temple Bar. There he ruthlessly stripped them of their assets by fraud and cheating at cards. When he had bled them dry he consigned them to Newgate Prison. He became notorious for a wide range of frauds. He had an accomplice whom he installed in a large house with a footman and carriage. This man practised an early form of the LONG FRAUD. He would order goods on credit and then, when he was about to be arrested, Bolland would have him thrown into Newgate for debt, putting him beyond the reach of his creditors. Reports of Bolland's villainy appeared in the newspapers, and the sheriffs suspended him. Short of cash, Bolland asked an acquaintance to cash a 'note of hand', a sort of IOU, for £100. The note was legal tender once Bolland had endorsed it. The acquaintance objected that Bolland's signature on the note would make it hard to cash, and so Bolland crossed out his own name and substituted 'Banks'. Technically this was forgery, the authorities enforced the law and Bolland was executed in March 1772.

BONNER, BISHOP (*c.* 1500–69) Sadistic cleric and zealous persecutor of Protestants. Edward Bonner became Bishop of London in 1539. He refused to accept Edward VI's religious reforms and was imprisoned for six years. He was freed when the Catholic Queen Mary came to the throne in 1553, and quickly got a reputation as a cruel inquisitor of Protestants. He examined Thomas Tomkins, a Protestant weaver from Shoreditch, in his palace at Fulham. He held Tomkins's hand directly over a flame before the man was taken to be burned alive at Smithfield. He particularly enjoyed flogging: he beat a man named John Miles so furiously that he wore a willow rod down to its stump, and had to call for another rod to continue the torture. On another occasion he thrashed an apprentice named Thomas Hinshaw almost to death. It is not hard to see a sexual motive in this. Bonner was arrested when Elizabeth I came to the throne, and died in the MARSHALSEA PRISON.

BOOTHBY, SIR ROBERT (1900–86) Tory politician at the centre of a scandal involving the KRAYS. Boothby was bisexual and shared Ronnie Kray's appetite for good-looking young men. He was having an affair with a young criminal friend of the Krays, a burglar named Lesley Holt, in 1964 when the *Sunday Mirror* claimed that the Metropolitan Police Commissioner had ordered an investigation into the homosexual relationship between a peer who was a 'household name' and a leading gangster involved in West End protection rackets. Among the things the police were said to be looking into were Mayfair parties the thug and the peer had been to, the peer's visits to Brighton along with a number of 'prominent public men', his relationships with East End gangsters and a number of clergymen. There were also allegations of blackmail. The following day the *Daily Mirror* ran an editorial saying: 'This gang is so rich, powerful and ruthless that the police are unable to crack down on it . . . The police, who know what is happening but cannot pin any evidence on the villains, are powerless.'

Boothby issued a statement denying everything. He was saved by the timidity of Cecil King, boss of the Mirror Group. King was a member of the Establishment, and in the climate of deference that then pervaded journalism he was not going to implicate the top echelons of the Tory party in a major scandal. The *Daily Mirror* printed 'an unqualified apology' and Boothby was paid damages of £40,000 – around £500,000 in today's money. Ronnie Kray also got an unqualified apology, but no money. Boothby's earlier political career had been controversial. *See* TOM DRIBERG

BOROUGH BOYS Gang of body-snatchers who operated from the area south of the Thames. They were the main suppliers of bodies to Guy's and St Thomas's hospitals. Low (*The Regency Underworld*) describes them as the most successful of London's grave robbers. *See* BODY-SNATCHERS and JOSEPH NAPLES

BORSTAL Training centre for young offenders, named after a village in Kent. Since 1982 such centres have been replaced by young offender institutions.

BOSWELL, JAMES (1740–95) The great biographer of Dr Johnson was also a very frank diarist. Boswell's descriptions of his many encounters with streetwalkers enrich our knowledge of Georgian street prostitution. Unhappily for him, he was reluctant to use condoms, or 'armour' as he called them. The results were sometimes painful. Between the ages of 20 and 29 he slept with three married gentlewomen, four actresses and Rousseau's mistress Thérèse Le Vasseur, kept three lower-class women as regular mistresses, and had sex with about sixty streetwalkers. He caught gonorrhoea seventeen times. He complained that the first time he wore a condom it gave him little satisfaction. This is how he described the encounter in his 1763 diary:

> As I was coming home this night, I felt carnal inclinations raging through my frame . . . went to St James's Park and . . . picked up a whore. For the first time did I engage in armour which I found but a dull satisfaction. She who submitted to my lusty embraces was a young Shropshire girl, only seventeen, very well-looked, her name Elizabeth Parker.

Another brief and sordid episode took place the same year in the same park.

> I strolled into the park and took the first whore I met, whom I without many words copulated with free from danger, being safely sheathed. She was ugly and lean and her breath smelled of spirits . . . When it was done, she slunk off. I had a low opinion of this gross practice and resolved to do it no more.

Boswell used condoms again from time to time, but greatly preferred not to. His diary for 1763 also tells of an encounter with a prostitute in the Strand.

> I picked up a girl in the Strand; went into a court with intention to enjoy her in armour. But she had none. I toyed with her. She wondered at my size, and said if I ever took a girl's maidenhead, I would make her squeak. I gave her a shilling, and had command enough of myself to go without touching her.

After this Boswell resolved to abstain until he found a girl he could be sure was disease-free, or was 'liked by some woman of fashion'. However, he was unable to keep his resolution. Later that same year he picked up a 'strong, jolly young damsel',

> and taking her under the arm I conducted her to Westminster Bridge, and then in armour complete did I engage her upon this noble edifice. The whim of doing it there with the noble Thames rolling below us amused me much. Yet after the brutish appetite was sated, I could not but despise myself for being so closely united with such a low wretch.

Yet another encounter shows him again taking risks, and suffering the pangs of remorse for his recklessness.

> . . . so I sallied to the streets, and just at the bottom of my own, I picked up a fresh, agreeable young girl called Alice Gibbs. We went down a lane to a snug place, and I took out my armour, but she begged that I might not put it on, as the sport was much pleasanter without it, and as she was quite safe. I was so rash as to trust her, and had a very agreeable congress . . .

BOTTOMLEY, HORATIO (1860–1933) Journalist, publisher and swindler. He ran away from an orphanage and became an errand boy. By the age of 37 he was worth £3 million and had collected sixty-seven bankruptcy writs in five years. Bottomley used the weekly *John Bull*, which he founded in 1906, to promote competitions and pocketed the proceeds, naming non-existent prizewinners in the paper. He was charged with fraud in 1891 and 1909 and was acquitted both times. In 1906 he was elected to Parliament for South Hackney as an Independent, but had to resign in 1909 because of bankruptcy. During the First World War he was a popular speaker on patriotic themes, and was later re-elected as an MP. In 1922 he was again prosecuted for fraud: he had been spending much of the £900,000 subscriptions to his Victory Bond Club, heavily touted in *John Bull*, on lavish living, including betting on horses and

Horatio Bottomley, newspaper proprietor and one of the greatest of all fraudsters. He siphoned off vast sums from competitions he ran in his popular paper John Bull *and spent it on high living.*

keeping mistresses. At his trial Bottomley told the jury that if they found him guilty the sword of justice that was hanging on the wall behind the judge would fall from its scabbard. Nevertheless they found him guilty, and he was sentenced to seven years' penal servitude. Released in 1927, Bottomley tried to make a new start in journalism and failed. One of his mistresses got him a stage appearance at the Windmill Theatre, where he rambled on incoherently about a past and forgotten era. The audience was not amused and he collapsed. He was bankrupted for the third time in 1930, and died penniless in 1933, aged about 73.

BOULTON AND PARK Transvestites whose trial in 1871 was a cause célèbre. Ernest Boulton was the son of a respectable Peckham gent, and worked at a stockbroker's. When he was 6 his mother began to dress him as a girl. His friend Frederick Park was articled to a solicitor. They were charged with 'conspiring and inciting persons to commit an unnatural offence'. Four other men were also charged. Three failed to appear and the fourth, Lord Arthur Clinton, third son of the Duke of Newcastle, committed suicide before the trial began.

The gravity with which officialdom viewed the affair was evident from the big guns ranged against the two harmless men: the Attorney General and the Solicitor General led the prosecution. The Attorney General pointed out that Boulton and Park had been seen dressed as women in the Alhambra in Leicester Square, in the Surrey Theatre and the Burlington Arcade. The latter could have caused confusion, as high-priced prostitutes were known to ply their trade there, and some even had access to rooms behind the shops. A man named Cox, who flirted with Boulton in a public house, believing him to be a woman, told in a deposition how he had kissed 'him, she or it'. Later, after he had learned the truth, he confronted Boulton and Lord Arthur Clinton in Evans's in Covent Garden, saying: 'You damned set of infernal scoundrels, you ought to be kicked out of this place.' There were letters between Lord Arthur and Boulton ('I am consoling myself in your absence by getting screwed') and Park and Lord Arthur ('the weather has turned so showery that I can't go out without a dread of my back hair coming out of curl'). When the two men were arrested, they were examined by a police surgeon, who paid particular attention to their anuses. The judge asked him whether he thought he should have got an order from a magistrate before doing this, and the surgeon replied: 'No, my lord, I never wait for a magistrate's order in any case.' Summing up, the judge said that if he had behaved like that with two strong instead of two effeminate men, he 'might have met with summary punishment for such unwarrantable conduct'. The police had also behaved crassly in going to Edinburgh to collect evidence without the permission of the Scottish authorities. But the judge made it clear that he thought the behaviour of Boulton and Park was outrageous: 'When it is done even as a frolic, it ought to be the subject of severe and summary punishment . . . If the law cannot reach it as it is, it ought to be made the subject of . . . legislation, and a punishment of two or three months' imprisonment, with the treadmill attached to it, with, in case of repetition of the offence, a little wholesome corporal discipline, would, I think, be effective, not only in such cases, but in all cases of outrage against public decency.' Despite this huffing and puffing, the jury took less than an hour to find the two men not guilty. A limerick was soon doing the rounds:

> There was an old person of Sark
> Who buggered a pig in the dark;

The swine in surprise
Murmured: 'God blast your eyes
Do you take me for Boulton or Park?'

BOW STREET RUNNERS The FIELDING brothers, Henry and John, created a team of constables, known as the Bow Street Runners because of their supposed fleetness of foot, paid a guinea a week and a share in the rewards from successful prosecutions. This system of payment was later to lead to accusations of corruption: some officers were said to encourage young criminals in lawbreaking until they had built up a record and had a price on their heads. Then they were arrested for the reward. After the Fieldings had died the Bow Street Runners were reputed to have become very corrupt. One officer, TOWNSEND, was believed to have left a fortune of £20,000, and another, Sayer, £30,000. Sayer must have been among the most corrupt policemen London has known. He was in league with a notorious thief named Mackoull, who was arrested after a bank robbery. Mackoull's offer to return the loot in return for immunity from prosecution was accepted by Sayer, but the bank got little of its money back. The assumption is that Sayer managed to hang on to most of it.

Sir John Moylan, in his book *Scotland Yard and the Metropolitan Police*, wrote that 'the Runners were hand in glove with the thieves'. But for years there was no proof. Finally a House of Commons committee seems to have got at the truth in 1828. The Runners were acting as go-betweens for thieves and banks. Banknotes and bonds stolen from the banks would be restored for a price, and no questions asked, with the Runners getting a cut.

The Runners could not live on their pay of a guinea a week, later raised to twenty-five shillings, or on their share of rewards, which brought in only a further twenty to thirty pounds a year, as a House of Commons committee was told in 1816. But they could make a good living from private detective work, which they seem to have been remarkably free to undertake.

The confused hubbub at Bow Street Magistrates Office off Drury Lane as prisoners and witnesses are questioned. Here the Fielding brothers, founders of the Bow Street Runners, established some control over the underworld. The Runners were later notorious for corruption.

Two cases show that the Runners could be effective. In 1762 LORD HARRINGTON employed John Wesket as a porter. Wesket was a criminal, and in 1763 with his accomplices John Bradley and James Cooper he robbed Lord Harrington. He let Bradley into the house, and together they stole £3,000 in cash and other valuables. After Bradley had gone, Wesket daubed a windowsill with dirty shoes to make it look as if an intruder had got in that way. However, he did not continue the footprints on the ground outside the window. When the theft was discovered he was suspected but nothing could be proved. Lord Harrington dismissed him.

Wesket quarrelled with his girlfriend and kicked her out. She became a prostitute and told a client of the theft. He went to the Runners, and Sir John Fielding questioned Wesket. Again nothing could be proved. Then Bradley tried to cash a £30 banknote, which was part of the haul. Harrington had circulated details of his banknotes, and payment was stopped. Cooper was arrested and talked. Wesket and Bradley were executed.

A Runner named Henry Goddard, who was born in 1800 and enlisted in the Foot Patrol in 1824, left an invaluable record, *Memoirs of a Bow Street Runner*. One case he was involved in will give a flavour of the times and police methods. On the evening of 30 October 1836 the Defiance mail coach left Dover for London, carrying among other things bags of gold. When the coach arrived in London, the gold was checked and one bag was missing.

Goddard questioned the guard and coachman, and the porter who had loaded the gold into the coach, a man called Matthews. He also visited all the stations between Dover and London where the coach had changed horses, questioning all the ostlers, stable-keepers and passengers involved and searching stables and lofts. He finally came to the conclusion that the porter Matthews was the thief, although the owners of the hotel where the man was employed told him he was mistaken, as Matthews had worked for them for many years and was thoroughly honest.

Goddard had Matthews's garden dug over, without finding any gold. A month later he searched Matthews's house again, finding that he had bought new furniture, and then discovered twenty gold sovereigns hidden in one of the rooms. Matthews was arrested but acquitted at his trial.

Three months later, as Goddard was standing on the steps of Bow Street police station, Matthews approached him and asked him if he would meet him that afternoon. Goddard agreed, but at the last moment was sent off on Home Office business. When he failed to turn up Matthews went to Dover and 'told the inspector of police there that he was a wretched man and had never been happy since his trial. He admitted to the inspector that he stole the bag of gold, and had buried it in his next-door neighbour's garden.'

BRADDOCK, LADY ALMERIA Woman who fought a duel with another woman. In 1792 Lady Almeria quarrelled with Mrs Elphinstone about her age. They met in Hyde Park, and began with pistols, Mrs Elphinstone hitting Lady Almeria's hat. They continued with swords, Lady Almeria slightly wounding Mrs Elphinstone. Honour was then thought to have been satisfied and hostilities ceased.

BRADLAUGH, CHARLES (1833–91) Social reformer convicted for advocating birth control. In 1880 he was elected to Parliament but as an atheist refused to take the oath. He was expelled and re-elected regularly until he relented and took the oath in 1886. That same year he was prosecuted with Annie Besant for publishing the birth-control pamphlet *The Fruits of Philosophy*. His conviction was reversed on appeal.

BRAMAH, JOSEPH Inventor who revolutionised lock design in the 1780s. He said he had got the idea for a thief-proof lock 'by the alarming increase of house robberies'.

BRANDING This medieval torture was continued until the late eighteenth century because it provided visible evidence of a conviction. People who successfully pleaded BENEFIT OF CLERGY were branded on the thumb to stop them using this ploy again. Other offenders were burned in the cheek or hand with a letter denoting their offence – T for thief, V for vagrant and so on. The Puritan WILLIAM PRYNNE was branded twice, the second time on each cheek with the letters S L for seditious libeller. The branding was done in court immediately after sentence. The brander, sometimes the common hangman, would apply the hot iron to the flesh, then turn to the judge and announce: 'A fair mark, my lord!' But, if the prisoner had bribed him first, the branding iron might not be red hot.

BRAVO, FLORENCE (*c.* 1846–78) Wife at the centre of a sensational Victorian murder case. On 21 April 1876 Charles Bravo, a prosperous barrister, died at his home in Balham after suffering several days of agony. His attractive young wife Florence, to whom he had been married only five months, had called in seven doctors but they could not help the dying man. An autopsy showed that he had been killed by the poison antimony, and Florence's companion, Jane Cox, said Mr Bravo had told her while in his death agony that he had taken poison.

An inquest jury returned a verdict of death from the effects of poison, adding that they had no way of knowing how it got into his body. There seemed to be no reason why Mr Bravo should kill himself, and his body was exhumed and a second inquest held. This concluded that Charles Bravo was wilfully murdered, but there was not enough evidence to bring anyone to trial. The chief suspect was, and remains, Florence Bravo. She was a wealthy young widow when Charles Bravo married her, having been left £40,000 by her first husband, Captain Alexander Ricardo of the Grenadier Guards. She was the mistress of a doctor named James Gully, an affair Charles was aware of. She promised to end the affair, but there were suggestions that she did not keep this promise. She was drinking heavily, and indeed died of alcoholism two years later.

The other main suspect was Dr Gully. He was a distinguished medical practitioner whose patients included Dickens, Disraeli, George Eliot and Tennyson. He was 67 at the time of Bravo's death. It was suggested that he had supplied the poison, which was administered by either Florence or Mrs Cox. The crime novelist Agatha Christie believed Dr Gully either killed Bravo himself or helped Florence kill him. Other writers have suggested that Mrs Cox had a motive: Bravo disliked her and wanted his wife to dismiss her.

BRENNAN, JAMES Agent of the Royal Mint who was an tireless pursuer of COINERS in the 1850s. He and his men sometimes had to fight battles with criminals. Newspaper reports described how they arrested five out of a gang of seven in a fight which raged over three floors of a building in Southwark.

Brennan was confronted on the top landing by three toughs, one of whom was a professional wrestler named Brown. Brennan tackled two of them: the third jumped over his head and ran down the stairs. At this point a fourth man came from a room at the top of the stairs, hit Brennan over the head with an iron saucepan and forced him against a window. He was saved by two other officers, one of them his son, and the fight went on.

Brennan's son struck his father's attacker with a crowbar, and the man fell through the window into the courtyard below. Another of the gang jumped from a window and tried to escape across the roof of a shed, which gave way under him. The leader of the gang, a man named Green, was trapped with another man and two women in the third-floor room. He tried to destroy the plaster moulds used to make the coins, but enough were saved to secure convictions at the Old Bailey trial that followed in 1855. The judge awarded Brennan £10 for his 'manly and efficient part' in the affair.

In the dense and hostile slums of the period arresting coiners was dangerous. In a raid on a master coiner named Morris, Brennan rushed up a dark stairs and crashed into a spiked flap that had been lowered to block off the stairwell. The three-inch iron prongs pierced his hat.

Morris escaped by jumping down 25 feet to an outbuilding. He was badly hurt but friends got him away to Birmingham, where he went into hospital until he had recovered. He returned to the capital two years later and started coining again in Southwark. Brennan tracked him down but Morris flung himself from a first-floor window on to an officer standing below. He ran off with Brennan in pursuit, plunged through a doorway into a room where a man and woman were sitting by the fire with their children in bed nearby. Brennan fell across the bed but managed to trip Morris. Other officers arrived and they handcuffed him. As they left with the prisoner a crowd gathered and stoned the officers. Morris was sentenced to thirty years' transportation. Little wonder that he had tried to kill himself under the wheels of a passing wagon while Brennan was taking him in.

Another of Brennan's targets was the master criminal BOB CUMMINGS. Brennan and his men raided Cummings's forgers' den in Westminster and arrested several men. On their way out they found the flooring at the bottom of the stairs had been removed to leave a gaping pit to trap them.

BRIAN, JOHN HERMAN Respectable manservant whose execution was probably a miscarriage of justice. In 1707 Brian, who had been dismissed by a man named Persuade, was accused of breaking into his house and, after robbing it, burning it to the ground. The court was told that Mrs Persuade had locked up her valuables, including a needle case called an etui, before going to bed. Later she smelt fire and she and Mr Persuade escaped as the house went up in flames. A woman who was passing said she had seen a man clambering over the Persuades' garden wall. 'Damn you!' he cried out to her, 'calling on people at this time of night. Are you drunk?'

Before working for Mr Persuade Brian had served several respectable masters, and had given no trouble. He had an alibi for the night of the fire – a witness confirmed his story that he was in his lodgings in Soho. But Mr Persuade's fowling piece was found in his trunk, and the jury did not believe him when he said he had bought it from a stranger. Six weeks after he was hanged the old woman who claimed she had seen him climbing over the garden wall tried to sell Mrs Persuade's etui case to a jeweller in Covent Garden.

BRIDES IN THE BATH George Joseph Smith, who was hanged in 1915, perfected an ingenious method of murdering his women victims. As they lay in the bath he would crook his arm under their legs and lift, at the same time holding their heads under the water with his other hand. As he had previously carefully laid the groundwork by telling a local doctor that the victim suffered from fits, the deaths were treated as natural. He was undone by carelessness and greed, otherwise he might have murdered more than his known tally of three victims.

Smith, who was born in the East End, preyed on women for their savings. To begin with he usually simply abandoned them once he had got their money. He would take them to an art gallery and leave them there while he went back to their homes and stripped them of anything saleable. Then he would move on. In August 1910 he met Beatrice Mundy in Clifton, near Bristol. She was attractive, middle class, well educated. Smith quickly found out that she had independent means. Like the many other women he duped, Beatrice fell for Smith. Some thought his power over women was due to hypnotic power. (The great barrister EDWARD MARSHALL HALL, who defended him, once had to end a consultation because he thought Smith was trying to hypnotise him.) Apart from his piercing eyes Smith was tall, with a military bearing.

Brides in the Bath murderer George Smith with one of his victims, Beatrice Mundy. Smith perfected a technique of killing his brides in the bath by pulling up their legs and holding their heads under the water.

Three days after they had met Beatrice married Smith. He hoped to get his hands on the large inheritance of £2,500 from her father, but settled for her savings of £138. He then left, leaving her a letter accusing her of giving him a venereal disease. Some time later she was in Weston-super-Mare when she saw Smith gazing out of a window. She was overjoyed. Smith claimed he had been looking for her for the past year. They were reunited. Smith offered to repay her the £138 and made out a will in her favour. Beatrice also made a will, leaving Smith her £2,500. She was with him when he bought a metal portable bath – the house they were staying in had no bath. He haggled over the price, beating the ironmonger down from £2 to £1 17*s* 6*d*.

Smith consulted a local doctor about his wife's health, saying she suffered from fits. Beatrice wrote a letter, obviously dictated by Smith, to her uncle, saying she had had two fits. The following day she took an early morning bath. There was a hurried call to the doctor, who arrived to find her dead in the bath and Smith apparently grieving. Beatrice's family tried in vain to stop Smith getting his hands on her £2,500. He returned the bath to the ironmonger, reclaiming his money.

In October 1913 at Southsea in Hampshire he found his next victim, Alice Burnham. She was worth only £130 in cash, but Smith insured her life for £500 and persuaded her to make a will in his favour. He took her to Blackpool, made sure their hotel had a bath, consulted a local doctor about his wife's health. Then the landlady noticed water seeping through the kitchen ceiling from the bathroom above.

The landlady was shocked by Smith's indifference to the death of his new bride. He refused to buy her an expensive coffin, saying 'when they're dead, they're done for'. As he left she called out 'Crippen'.

Smith's ninth marriage was to his third known victim, Margaret Lofty. She had little money but he insured her life for £700. He took her to a boarding house in Highgate, London. After she had made a will and visited a doctor where she complained of headaches she took a bath . . . While his latest wife lay dead in the bath upstairs, Smith sat at the piano downstairs playing *Nearer My God to Thee*.

The story of a bride found naked and dead in her bath while on her honeymoon was news. Alice Burnham's father and the husband of the Blackpool landlady both saw reports of Margaret Lofty's unusual death. Soon Detective Inspector Arthur Neil was unravelling a tangled tale of baths, boarding houses, wills and bank accounts.

In court the pathologist Bernard Spilsbury got a woman volunteer to lie in a bathful of water. When a policeman pulled her feet upwards her head was submerged. It took the jury less than half an hour to find Smith guilty. After his execution both Marshall Hall and his assistant stated that they thought Smith had not used force to murder his victims, but had somehow induced them to kill themselves by 'hypnotic suggestion'.

BRIDEWELL Prison on the north bank of the Thames, at the entrance to the Fleet River. It had been a royal palace. In 1553 Edward VI gave it to the City to house vagrants and homeless children. It was also used as a place of punishment for petty offenders and disorderly women. Flogging was almost invariably part of the punishment. The author NED WARD visited the Bridewell and described a flogging:

> A grave gentleman whose awful looks bespoke him some honourable citizen, was mounted in the judgment seat, armed with a hammer . . . and a woman under the lash was in the next room, where folding doors were opened so that the whole court might see the punishment inflicted. At last went down the hammer and the scourging ceased . . . Another accusation being then delivered by a flat-cap [citizen] against a poor wretch, who had no friend to speak on her behalf, proclamation was made, viz.: 'All you who are willing E——th T——ll should have present punishment, pray hold up your hands.'

The audience having voted for instant punishment, the woman was stripped to the waist 'as if it were designed rather to feast the eyes of the spectators than to correct vice or correct manners' and lashed.

In 1791 the flogging of women was abolished. The prison introduced reforms, including straw beds and medical staff, before other London prisons. The buildings were demolished in 1863–4 and today the Unilever Building occupies the site. The name Bridewell was given to other prisons throughout the country.

BRIDGEWATER, DOCTOR TALBOT Successful Edwardian medical practitioner and master criminal. His surgery in Oxford Street was a front for forgery, burglaries and post robberies. Behind the façade of this 'tremendous medical practice', as it was described when he was arrested in 1905, the doctor's expert assistants were altering stolen cheques and certificates greatly to increase their face value. They got the cheques and other forms of securities by burgling houses and breaking into post boxes. Even when police caught up with some of his accomplices they did not give evidence against Doctor Bridgewater. Bill the Barman, as one was called, was sent to prison and hanged himself there. Dicer Cobb shot himself as the police closed in. But Robert Fisher, known as the Key King, finally gave the police the evidence they needed. Caught and jailed for ten years, he had a grudge against Bridgewater, whom he suspected of cheating him. On his evidence Bridgewater was arrested and jailed for seven years.

BRIEF ENCOUNTERS Some whores did brisk business among the lawyers of the inns of court. NED WARD wrote in the *London Spy*:

> They have now extraordinary business upon their hands, with many of the young lawyers . . . They are such considerable dealers, that they can afford to give credit for a whole vacation, and now in term-time they are industrious in picking up their debts. You are now, I assure you, in one of the greatest places in town for dealing in that sort of commodity; for most ladies who, for want of fortunes, despair of husbands, and are willing to give themselves up to love, without waiting for matrimony, come hither to be truly qualified for their mercenary undertaking. By the time any condescending nymph has a month's conversation with the airy blades of this honourable society, she will doubtless find herself as well fitted for the employment, as if she had a twelvemonth's education under the most experienced bawd in Christendom; and if you ever chance to meet with any of the trading madams, and ask her who was her first lover, it's ten to one her answer will be A Gentleman of the Temple.

The seventeenth-century guide to London whoredom JOHN GARFIELD mentions the veteran whore Fair Rosamund Sugarcunt, and Burford (*London: The Synfulle Citie*) says she operated around the Law Courts.

BRIGHTON DIVORCES In 1923 the Divorce Reform Act made it possible for women to obtain a divorce on the ground of a single act of adultery by their husbands. This led to a golden age for resort towns, particularly, for some reason, Brighton, that 'heaving Sodom of the South Coast'. Young showgirls and night-club hostesses would be hired by men to spend a weekend with them in a Brighton hotel. Chambermaids and waiters who served the couples breakfast in bed would confirm the fact of adultery. Since journalists and their photographers were sometimes on hand to record the fact, it was also a golden age for the *News of the World*.

BRILLIANT CHANG Chinese drug-dealer, supplier to the Bright Young Things of London in the 1920s. He was linked to the death of the popular actress Billie Carleton in November 1918. Carleton had attended the Victory Ball at the Albert Hall, and the following morning her maid found her dead in bed, with a gold box containing cocaine on the dressing table. The drug had been supplied by her boyfriend, a costume designer named Reggie de Veuille, whose suppliers were a Chinese named Lau Ping You and his Scottish wife Ada. She was sentenced to five months' hard labour: the Marlborough Street magistrate Frederick Mead called her the 'high priestess of unholy rites'. Her husband was fined £10. Reggie de Veuille admitted conspiracy to supply cocaine and was given eight months' hard labour.

There were calls in Parliament for the deportation of all Chinese and attention soon focused on Chang. He was a close friend of Billie Carleton. The *World Pictorial News* said he 'dispensed Chinese delicacies and the drugs and vices of the Orient' at his restaurant in Regent Street.

In March 1922 Freda Kempton, a young dancing teacher, was found dead from a cocaine overdose. Chang had been with her the night before. He told the coroner at her inquest: 'She was a friend of mine but I know nothing about the cocaine. It is all a mystery to me.' The coroner ruled that the evidence was not strong enough to link Chang with the death, but commented that it was 'disgraceful that such a dangerous drug as cocaine should be handed about London to ruin the bodies and souls of inexperienced girls'. Good-looking young women were waiting outside the court to congratulate Chang.

Chang moved from Regent Street and opened the Shanghai restaurant in Limehouse, which was then London's Chinatown. In 1924 the premises were raided by the police, who found a large quantity of cocaine. Chang was jailed for eighteen months and then deported. After his deportation there were rumours that Chang was living in Europe and directing the London drug scene from afar. There were also rumours – perhaps put about by his own men – that he was a penniless derelict. The *Daily Telegraph*'s crime reporter, Stanley Firmin, wrote: 'A strange Nemesis overtook him. He went blind and ended his days not in luxury and rich silks but as a sightless worker in a little kitchen garden.' Since it was estimated that he made more than a million pounds from drug trafficking, this seems unlikely. In 1927 he was arrested for drug dealing in Paris, and absconded with a young woman while on bail. *See* DRUGS

BRINDLES, THE South London gang involved in a long-running and murderous vendetta with the ARIF family. By April 2001 police estimated that the feud had cost nine lives. The cause is believed to be attempts by the Brindles to spread their drugs empire into south London territory over which the Arifs claim hegemony. Unravelling the feud is complicated by the fact that the Brindles and the Arifs, like other south London crime families, are related by marriage. After a series of reciprocal shootings the first killing took place in a betting shop in Walworth in March 1991. Ahmet 'Abby' Abdullah, a cousin of the Arifs, was shot dead. Five months later two strangers wearing ski masks entered the Bell pub in East Street, Walworth, where Dave Brindle was drinking. They opened fire with handguns, and within seconds Brindle and a man named Anthony Silk, who was not involved, were dead. The barman, John Plows, who had thrown a stool at one of the killers to protect his 15-year-old daughter, was shot four times, but survived. In May 1991 Tony Brindle and his brother Patrick were acquitted of the murder of Abdullah. The *Sun* newspaper had printed a picture of them before they were picked out at an identification parade, and it was argued that this made evidence of identity unsafe.

On 1 June 1993 JIMMY MOODY was drinking a pint of bitter in the Royal Hotel in Hackney, east London. Moody, a veteran gangster, former member of the RICHARDSON gang and survivor of the MR SMITH's club shoot-out in 1966, had been on the run for thirteen years since escaping from Brixton Prison with IRA man Gerard Tuite. Another man entered the pub and ordered a drink. When it arrived, he pulled out a revolver and shot Moody dead, cursing as he did so. He escaped in a stolen Ford Fiesta, which had been parked outside. There was speculation that Moody was himself a hit man, and that he had been involved in the killing of David Brindle. Just over a year later two innocent men, Peter McCormack and John Ogden, were shot dead in Cavendish Road, Balham. Police believe it was a case of mistaken identity – one of the men looked like a criminal who was an enemy of the Brindles. The stakes were raised in September 1995 when an Irish terrorist gunman shot Tony Brindle three times outside his flat in Docklands. Police had been tipped off by Irish police about Michael Boyle, an INLA hitman. They saw him leave a 'safe house' wearing a wig and drive to Brindle's luxury home in Rotherhithe. Tony Brindle was walking to his car when Boyle, who was armed with a Magnum revolver and a Browning pistol, opened fire from inside his van. Horrified police who were videoing the scene then saw Boyle leap from the van and run towards Brindle. The officers cut him down with rifle fire, hitting him in the arm, elbow, chest, heel and between the shoulder blades. Boyle was later given three life sentences at the Old Bailey after the court had been told that the shooting was the latest incident in an eleven-year feud. Boyle, 50, had also planned to kill Brindle's brothers Patrick and George. After the trial Tony Brindle launched a lawsuit against the police, claiming they failed to ensure his safety. Brindle got legal aid to pursue his claim. In April 2001 David Roads, who had been convicted at the Old Bailey in 1997 of being the armourer in the Boyle shooting, was shot dead in an alley in Kingston upon Thames. The Brindles' mother Grace said: 'My lovely boys wouldn't hurt a fly.'

BRINKLEY, RICHARD Murderer executed in 1907 for killing two people by accident. Brinkley, a carpenter, planned to kill a widow, Johanna Blume, for her fortune of £800. He got Mrs Blume, who lived with her daughter in Fulham, to sign a will by folding it so she could not see the contents. She thought she was signing up for a seaside holiday. He tricked the witnesses to the will in the same way. Mrs Blume died two days later and a coroner recorded a verdict of death by natural causes.

Mrs Blume's daughter consulted a solicitor about the will and Brinkley, fearing that the witnesses would be traced and would realise that they had been tricked, decided to kill them too. He called on one of them, a Mr Parker, at Croydon and gave him a bottle of stout that he had laced with poison. While Parker was out his landlord, Richard Beck, saw the bottle and he and his wife and daughter tasted it. Beck and his wife died, their daughter recovered. Brinkley said when he was arrested, 'Well, I'm sugared. That's very awkward, isn't it?' He was hanged on 13 August 1907. Mrs Blume's body was exhumed and there was no trace of poison.

BRINK'S-MAT ROBBERY The biggest bullion raid in British history took place on a trading estate at Heathrow Airport on 26 November 1983. Early that morning a gang of six armed men got into the Brink's-Mat depository where valuable cargoes were stored. The alarm had been switched off so that a guard who was late for work could get in. Once inside, the gang handcuffed the guards and poured petrol over one of them, threatening to set him alight if he did not give them the combination to the vault. They loaded three tons of gold and other precious metals, worth £26 million, into a van and left. Instead of the gold, they had been expecting to get between £1 million and £2 million in cash.

Police questioned the guard who was late for work, Anthony Black, who confessed that he had tipped off robber BRIAN 'THE COLONEL' ROBINSON, who was living with his sister, about large cash deposits regularly made on Friday nights. Black also gave police the names of Micky McAvoy and Tony White, who were arrested. Black pleaded guilty and got six years. Robinson and McAvoy were each given twenty-five years and White was acquitted.

Meanwhile the search for the gold went on. Police began watching the Kent home of a criminal named KENNETH NOYE. In January 1985 undercover policeman John Fordham was stabbed to death by Noye, who found him hiding in the grounds of the house. Noye was acquitted of murder after claiming that he had feared that Fordham, who was wearing a balaclava helmet, was an intruder who was going to kill him. But police established that he was part of the criminal chain set up to dispose of the gold. Noye passed it to Brian Reader, and it then went to Garth Chappell, managing director of a Bristol bullion company, where it was smelted. Chappell and six others were charged with, among other things, disposing of the stolen gold. Chappell got ten years, Reader got nine. Noye got the maximum sentence of fourteen years. JOHN 'GOLDFINGER' PALMER was cleared of melting down the gold.

The investigation touched many of London's criminal elite, including the ADAMS FAMILY. In various trials associated with it over the years crooks large and small were given sentences of more than 200 years. Noye later got life for another killing.

BRITISH UNION OF FASCISTS The gangster JACK SPOT was just one of the London Jews who made a stand against OSWALD MOSLEY's British Union of Fascists. By 1934 the BUF had become openly anti-Semitic, and was getting support in parts of London that had large or growing Jewish populations, among them Hackney and Stoke Newington. As support elsewhere waned, Mosley organised a series of rallies in Jewish areas in East London in 1936. There was fighting at Victoria Park in 1936 between the BUF and anti-Fascists, and a proposed march through the East End on 4 October united a coalition of left-wing organisations, including the Communist Party, with the Jews. The BUF mustered 3,000 Blackshirts, but the route they planned through Stepney was lined by up to 100,000 anti-Fascists and the BUF took police advice and marched away to the west. The Battle of Cable Street was largely between the police and the anti-Fascists.

As marches and demonstrations continued, the authorities acted. The Public Order Act of December 1936 outlawed the wearing of uniforms for political ends and banned paramilitary organisations. The BUF nevertheless held its biggest indoor meeting just two months before the outbreak of the Second World War, when an estimated 20,000 people gathered at Earl's Court. In 1940 the leaders of the BUF were arrested and interned. *See* OSWALD MOSLEY

BRIXTON RIOTS The most serious racial unrest in Britain in the twentieth century broke out in this south London area in April 1981. It followed a five-day police operation against crime. Officers had saturated the streets, stopping and searching 943 people, mostly young blacks. This was the ostensible cause of the riots, but the official report by Lord Scarman concluded that economic deprivation was an important factor. Another was black distrust of the police. Large numbers of white youths joined blacks in attacking the officers. On Saturday, 11 April alone more than 300 police and civilians were injured and twenty-eight buildings set alight.

Trouble broke out in Brixton again in September 1985, after police had shot a woman in an armed raid. The local police station was attacked and a man later died. A week later rioting broke out on the Broadwater Farm Estate in Tottenham after Mrs Cynthia Jarrett died of a heart attack after being searched by police. A local community policeman, Keith Blakelock, was surrounded by a mob and hacked to death.

BROTHERS, RICHARD Prophet prosecuted for treason. Early in 1795 Brothers wrote *A Revealed Knowledge of the Prophecies and Times*, forecasting that on 19 May of that year he would be revealed as the Ruler of the World. He suggested that George III should abdicate in his favour. The pamphlet, which also forecast that the rebuilding of Jerusalem would begin in 1798, attracted followers, particularly among millenarians. One such, the MP Nathaniel Brassey Halhed, gave a three-hour speech in the House of Commons supporting Brothers. When support grew, the authorities, already nervous about republican unrest, arrested Brothers and charged him with treason. He was sentenced to eleven years in prison, but was transferred to an insane asylum. Halhed resigned his seat.

BROWN, WILLIAM War veteran hanged for stealing a shilling during the GORDON RIOTS in 1780. Brown, a sailor, approached a Bishopsgate cheesemonger, Carter Daking, who was looking out of his window. Brown held out his hat and said: 'Damn your eyes and limbs, put a shilling into my hat, or by God I have a party that can destroy your house presently.' Daking gave him the shilling. At Brown's trial a witness said he was 'so much in liquor that he did not know what he was about'. The witness added that he had known Brown 'since he went out in the *Serapis*'. This recalled a famous battle during the American War of Independence. In 1779 the American sea captain John Paul Jones's ship the *Bonhomme Richard* won a hard-fought engagement with the *Serapis* off Flamborough Head, Yorkshire. The battle lasted most of a day and night, and although the *Bonhomme Richard* suffered 150 casualties to 100 British, the captain of the *Serapis* surrendered and the Americans took 500 prisoners, including Brown. He told the court: 'I was wounded in the engagement with Paul Jones, and I lose my senses when I have drank a little. I have done a great deal of good to the nation, my lord, and I hope you will save my life and let me serve his majesty again.'

BROWNRIGG, ELIZABETH Midwife and sadistic murderer, executed at Tyburn in September 1767. She took in young girls from the Foundling Hospital to her home in Fetter Lane to help with her work, and treated them with almost maniacal cruelty. Mary Clifford, 16, was tied up and beaten with a cane, a whip and a broom handle. She had to sleep in a coal-hole and was fed on bread and water. When she broke into a cupboard looking for food, she was stripped naked and chained to a door. She was then beaten with the whip handle for a whole day before being thrust back into the coal-hole with her hands tied behind her back. After she complained to a

The fiendishly cruel Elizabeth Brownrigg, who tortured young girls from the Foundling Hospital at her home in Fetter Lane. She is depicted whipping Mary Clifford, who died in hospital. When Brownrigg was executed, the spectators called down eternal damnation on her.

woman lodger about her treatment Brownrigg tried to cut out her tongue. The screams of Mary and another girl alerted the neighbours, and eventually law officers visited the house. Mary was so ill, her body covered in ulcers and bruises, that she died in St Bartholomew's Hospital. When Brownrigg was executed, a large mob called down eternal damnation on her.

BRUMMELL, GEORGE 'BEAU' (1778–1840) Dandy and wit, arbiter of taste and style in Regency London. Close friend of the Prince of Wales, later Prince Regent and King George IV. After coming into a fortune, Brummell devoted himself to perfecting a personal style in dress and behaviour. He went to ridiculous lengths over minor details of dress, but nevertheless was a restraining influence over the exuberance of dandy taste. He would hold court sitting in the bow window at White's Club in St James's. In 1813 he quarrelled with the Prince of Wales – 'who's your fat friend?' – and, overwhelmed by debts, fled to France. He died in a lunatic asylum at Caen in 1840.

BUCKINGHAM, DUKE OF (1637–87) Debauched courtier and playwright who popularised duelling in England. George Villiers, the second Duke, was the son of James I's favourite of the same name and title. He went into exile with the defeat of the Royalists in the Civil War, and his estates were forfeited. At the Restoration his estates were restored and he became a Privy Councillor. He was an intriguer, and Bishop Burnett said he was a man with 'no principles of religion, virtue or friendship'. Buckingham was also a bully: he became the lover of the Countess of Shrewsbury, and when her husband objected he killed him in a duel, with the countess looking on disguised as a page.

BURDETT, SIR FRANCIS (1770–1844) Radical politician jailed for his views. In 1810 he published a letter declaring the conduct of the House of Commons illegal in imprisoning another radical. A warrant was issued for his arrest and he barricaded himself in his house. Sympathetic members of the public surrounded it in an attempt to stop the military seizing him, and one person was killed. After two days the authorities forced an entry and he was taken to the Tower. In 1820 he was jailed for three months and heavily fined after a letter he had written condemning the Peterloo Massacre was discovered.

BURGESS, GUY (1910–63) Diplomat and spy. Burgess joined the intelligence services during the war and later became personal assistant to a Minister of State, despite having been sacked by another Minister for being 'dirty, drunk and idle'. His private life was scandalous, even for a diplomat. Neighbours complained of noisy and rowdy all-male parties at his flat. On one occasion he was thrown down the stairs by another diplomat, and ended up in hospital on the danger list. In spite of these shenanigans he found time to pass on secrets to the Russians. In 1950 he was sent to the British embassy in Washington where his Cambridge friend and fellow traitor Kim Philby was already working. They were told by Russian intelligence that a third member of the group, Donald Maclean, who was stationed in London, was about to be unmasked. Burgess got himself sent back to London in disgrace so he could warn Maclean. He was met off the boat at Southampton by ANTHONY BLUNT, yet another traitor, who helped plan Maclean's escape. Burgess drove Maclean to Southampton to catch a boat to Russia, and at the last moment decided to join him.

He died in Russia in 1963, aged 52. His years in the Soviet Union were captured memorably in Alan Bennett's television play *An Englishman Abroad*.

BURNING AT THE STAKE The last woman sentenced to be burned alive at the stake was Prudence Lee, who was executed in 1652 for murdering her husband. After that the practice was to strangle the condemned woman on a low gibbet before covering her with faggots and setting them alight. But in 1726 the executioner, Richard Arnet, bungled the killing of CATHERINE HAYES at Tyburn. Instead of first garrotting Hayes, who had incited two men to murder and dismember her husband, Arnet, who may have been drunk, lit the faggots and was driven off by the flames before he could put her out of her agony. Spectators horrified by her screams threw logs of wood at her in a vain attempt to knock her unconscious. In 1789 Christiane Murphy was strangled and burnt at Newgate for coining. The following year the practice ended. Many people were burned alive at the stake during the reign of the Catholic Queen Mary. Most of these executions took place at SMITHFIELD.

BURRELL, PAUL Royal butler whose prosecution for theft collapsed after a dramatic intervention by the Queen. In October 2002 Burrell went on trial at the Old Bailey accused of stealing hundreds of items from the estate of his late employer, Diana Princess of Wales. Just as he was about to go into the witness box the Queen suddenly remembered a private audience with Mr Burrell in which he said he was going to retain certain items for safe keeping. The trial, which had already cost £1.5 million, was therefore terminated, to the consternation of the prosecution, the police and the Palace. Republicans and royalists squared up in an amusing reprise of old arguments. Dennis Skinner, a veteran left-wing Labour MP, wrote to the Lord Chancellor, saying: 'This seems to me to be a clear-cut case of withholding vital information before and during the trial . . . and of obstructing the course of justice . . . At the risk of finishing up in the TOWER, I cannot see why people, however high and mighty, should be allowed to escape the full rigour of the law.' Others suggested the Queen should pay part of the costs, and that prosecutions should no longer be carried out in her name – the trial had of course been *Regina* v. *Burrell*. The former butler sold his story to a newspaper for a sum variously reported as £300,000 and £500,000 and, despite having vowed never to disclose royal secrets – 'my middle name is discretion' – described his audience with the Queen. He said she warned him that dark forces were at work. The story became daily more bizarre, with allegations about a missing tape recording made by Diana. It was said to be of a conversation with the victim of an alleged homosexual rape by a member of Prince Charles's staff. The police said they had investigated and found there was nothing in the allegation, but the self-proclaimed victim renewed his claims in a Sunday newspaper. The Prime Minister, Tony Blair, rose in the Commons to defend the Queen, in the course of his statement disclosing the contents of a private conversation with the Monarch, the first time it had been done. There were further allegations of misconduct at St James's Palace, one said to involve a member of the royal family. Prince Charles appointed his private secretary to carry out an inquiry into the affair. It transpired that when Prince Charles heard of the rape allegations he ordered that the servant who made them should be sacked. The inquiry report suggested that standards in the prince's household were low. The prince himself said it made uncomfortable reading.

In October 2003 Burrell was accused by Diana's children, Prince William and Prince Harry, of 'cold and overt betrayal', after he did precisely what he had promised not to do – he published a book, *A Royal Duty*, about his years as her butler. It included confidential letters, in one of which Diana said there was a plot to kill her. Letters from Prince Philip took Diana's side in her marital troubles with Prince Charles. Philip is said to have written: 'I cannot imagine anyone in their right mind leaving you for Camilla' – Prince Charles's mistress, Camilla Parker Bowles. Princes William and Harry said the book would have 'mortified' their mother if she was alive, but Burrell refused to apologise. He said of the book: 'I am extremely proud of it, and I am convinced the princess would be proud of it too.' He claimed that the princess had entrusted the letters to him.

BUTLER, JOSEPHINE (1828–1906) Social reformer who campaigned against the licensing of brothels and the white slave trade. She also campaigned, sometimes at personal risk, against the CONTAGIOUS DISEASES ACTS, which empowered the police to detain women and examine them for venereal disease, often in the most humiliating circumstances. Butler was an ardent Christian who wanted to abolish prostitution, but she was also a feminist. *The Women's Manifesto* published in the *Daily News* on 1 January 1870, stated:

> We . . . enter our solemn protest against these Acts . . . Because it is unjust to punish the sex

> who are the victims of vice, and leave unpunished the sex who are the main cause, both of the vice and its dreaded consequence: and we consider the liability to arrest, forced medical treatment, and (where this is resisted) imprisonment with hard labour, to which these Acts subject women, are punishments of the most degrading kind . . .

Butler wrote in her autobiography (*Personal Reminiscences of a Great Crusade*) that 'among the two thousand signatures which [the manifesto] obtained in a short time were those of Florence Nightingale, Harriet Martineau, Mary Carpenter, the sisters and other relatives of the late John Bright, all the leading ladies of the Society of Friends, and many well known in the literary and philanthropic world'.

Women from Butler's Ladies National Association went into working-class areas of towns where the CD Acts were in operation and incited whores to rebel against forced registration and examination. Mrs Butler led from the front, as the following extracts from a history of the movement for repeal by one of the campaigners, Benjamin Scott, makes clear:

> Mrs Butler and Professor Stuart, with others, went down to Colchester to join the fray . . . They distributed thousands of handbills . . . on prostitution . . . The blood of the Liberal partisans was up. They attacked the hotel in which Mrs Butler and her friends were staying, and when Dr Baxter Langley began to hold a meeting they went mad and created a riot . . . Dr Langley tried to hold a meeting in the theatre, but he and Professor Stuart were . . . driven from the platform and chased to their hotel, which they reached, Langley covered with flour and dirt from head to foot, his clothes torn, his face bleeding, and Stuart wounded in the arm by a heavy blow . . . the followers of Storks may have justified this playfulness as one of the amenities of political warfare, but there was no sort of justification for the next thing they did. They posted on the wall an exact description of Mrs Butler's dress in order that she might be recognised and mobbed . . . Her friends never addressed her by name in the streets lest some listener should rally the ever-present mob to attack her . . . On one occasion, after repeated flights from different houses, a room was taken for her in a Tory hotel, under the name of Grey. There she had gone to bed, and was falling asleep when she heard a knock on the door of her room, followed by the shout of the proprietor, 'Madam, I am sorry to find you are Mrs Butler; please get up and dress at once and leave the house. The mob are round the house, breaking the windows. They threaten to set fire to it if you don't leave at once . . .' Then he harangued the mob while Mrs Butler was dressing, and, led by one of the servant girls, ran along a little back street as fast as she could go, until she found shelter . . .'

Faced with this strange new power, a women's movement, the government eventually caved in. An MP told Butler: 'We know how to manage any other opposition in the House or in the country, but this is very awkward for us – this revolt of women. It is quite a new thing: what are we to do with such an opposition as this?' After years of agitation the repealers won in the House of Commons. On 20 April 1883 the Acts were suspended. They were later repealed.

BYRON, LORD Peer tried in Westminster Hall in 1765 after killing a man in a duel. Byron and his friend and neighbour, a Mr Chaworth, had been drinking for hours in the Star and Garter club in St James's Street, reputed to serve the best claret in London, when they disagreed about the relative merits of the game on their estates. They withdrew to a back room and, a tallow candle being lit, drew their swords and fought a duel. Mr Chaworth was killed.

At 7 a.m. on 16 April the trial began in a packed Westminster Hall. Apart from royalty and peers, four thousand tickets had been issued to the general public. These were later changing hands at six guineas each. Ladies paraded in the latest finery, the children of the nobility threw bits of apple into the Lord High Steward's periwig, the choristers of St Paul's misbehaved. After eleven hours Byron was found not guilty of murder but guilty of manslaughter, paid his fees and went home. Five days later he was back at Westminster Hall, mixing with his fellow peers on an equal footing. However, he was stigmatised for fighting without seconds, though not for taking advantage of the fact that Chaworth believed him to be fatally wounded to run him through. There were consequences: his wife left him and he lost the mastership of the royal staghounds. He consoled himself with his housekeeper and sold off the valuable contents of his residence, Newstead Abbey, leaving an impoverished inheritance to his great-nephew, the poet Byron.

CADE, JACK Rebel leader. In the summer of 1450 Cade, the so-called Captain of Kent, an obscure but talented leader, led a popular revolt, marching on London with a large group of followers. They seized and executed Lord Saye and looted and burned. Cade held the city for a number of days, but an offer of pardon split his followers, who dispersed. He fled with a price on his head, and was killed resisting arrest near Heathfield, East Sussex. After further risings 'a harvest of heads' put an end to the troubles. The risings were essentially conservative, seeking an end to corrupt government.

CALVEY, LINDA Killer known as the Black Widow. In 1990 she was jailed for life for murdering her lover Ron Cook. While Cook, an armed robber, was in prison she had taken another lover, Daniel Reece. She persuaded Reece to kill Cook while he was on day release from prison. He could not go through with it and Calvey made Cook kneel before shooting him herself. It was suggested that she had spent all Cook's money while he was serving his sentence. She was the widow of bank robber Micky Calvey, shot dead by police in 1978 during a robbery.

CALVI, ROBERTO Italian banker, found hanging from Blackfriars Bridge in June 1982. His wallet held a large sum of money, and the body was weighted down with bricks. An inquest decided he had committed suicide. Further investigation however showed that Calvi was involved with crooked financial figures close to the Vatican Bank in massive frauds, and a new inquest returned an open verdict. A new investigation is ongoing.

CAMBRIDGE SPIES A group of Communist sympathisers at Cambridge University in the 1930s went on to become collectively the most notorious spies the country has known. In 1951 Donald Maclean, head of the American Department at the Foreign Office, fled to Moscow. With him went GUY BURGESS, an important Foreign Office employee. They had been tipped off by Kim Philby, First Secretary at the British Embassy in Moscow, that Maclean was being investigated. Philby defected to Moscow in 1963.

For years there were rumours that others were involved in the Cambridge ring. In 1979 Prime Minister Margaret Thatcher revealed that the fourth man was the art historian SIR ANTHONY BLUNT, Surveyor of the Queen's Pictures. The authorities had known about his role since 1964, when he had been granted immunity from prosecution in return for a confession. After he was unmasked in 1979 he was stripped of his knighthood and other honours. He died in 1983. A KGB defector later named Sir James Cairncross, a senior Civil Servant, as the fifth member of the Cambridge ring.

CAMDEN TOWN MURDER OF 1907 A triumph for the great advocate EDWARD MARSHALL HALL. The victim, Emily May Dimmock, a young prostitute, was found murdered in the Camden Town lodgings she shared with her common-law husband. She was lying naked on a bed, and her head had been all but severed. After a long and painstaking investigation the police arrested Robert Wood, a young artist and designer in a glass factory. Wood had been with Dimmock on the night of the murder, a fact he had gone to great lengths to conceal. At the trial at the Old Bailey in 1907 Marshall Hall demolished the prosecution's case and their witnesses, and fearlessly stood up to the judge, Mr Justice Grantham. When the judge said to a witness that Wood had been leading an 'immoral life' – by which he meant that he had been Dimmock's lover – Marshall Hall objected. The judge said to him: 'I am addressing the witness, and I must ask you not to argue with me.' Marshall Hall refused to be silenced. 'I want to point out,' he said, 'in the interests of justice, that there is not a particle of evidence that the prisoner ever had any improper intercourse with Emily Dimmock.'

Perhaps his master-stroke was to call Wood to give evidence. The Criminal Evidence Act of 1898 allowed the defendant to give evidence in his own defence, but none had thus far done so successfully. Wood was a charming, good-looking, mild-mannered young man, and this came over to the jury. The newspapers had been exciting public sympathy for Wood, and when the Not Guilty verdict was announced there was applause in the courtroom, echoed in the crowd waiting outside.

The Camden Town Murder was one of those cases which, from time to time, seizes the public's attention for no clear reason. It also exercised the imagination of the painter Walter Sickert, who painted several pictures relating to it.

CAMELFORD, LORD Aristocratic bruiser who met an untimely end. Thomas Pitt, the second Lord

Lord Camelford, an aristocratic bruiser who toured the streets of the West End picking fights. A cousin of Pitt the Younger, he was killed in a duel after provoking a friend whom he knew to be a better shot.

Camelford, cousin of Pitt the Younger, had a history of troublemaking before he inherited the title, vast estates and an income of £20,000 a year. As a young naval officer he had challenged a fellow officer to a duel, shot another in a quarrel over seniority and was court-martialled for mutiny. He would prowl the streets of the West End, accompanied by his footman, a black prizefighter, trying to stir up trouble and get into fights. When the Treaty of Amiens of 1802 led to a respite in the wars against Napoleon Londoners decided to celebrate with illuminations. Camelford refused to join in the celebrations which were general throughout the West End, and his house was in darkness when a mob arrived outside and in protest at his curmudgeonliness began to stone his windows. Camelford armed himself with a blunderbuss and opened his front door. The gun was taken from him and he drew his sword. He was knocked to the ground, and his servants rushed out and rescued him. He was next seen at an upstairs window with a pistol. At this the mob dispersed.

Two and a half years later he was killed in a duel. He had deliberately provoked a friend whom he knew to be a much better shot. He was 29.

CAMPBELL ROAD A notorious criminal slum, known as 'the Bunk'. Campbell Road near Finsbury Park, a terraced street of 100 houses built in the 1860s, was described by the local sanitary inspector in 1909 as 'the king of all roads'. Here crime was petty but the poverty was of the type MAYHEW would have recognised. The residents included costermongers, street-sellers, dealers, entertainers, charwomen and casual labourers in the building and haulage industries. Others earned a living from begging, crime or prostitution. The sanitary inspector's report said:

> I have been in practically all the slums in London: Notting Hill, Chelsea, Battersea, Fulham, Nine Elms, and also the East End, but there is nothing so lively as this road. Thieves, Prostitutes, cripples, Blind People, Hawkers of all sorts of wares from boot laces to watches and chains are to be found in this road, Pugilists, Card Sharpers, Counter Jumpers, Purse Snatchers, street singers and Gamblers of all kinds, and things they call men who live on the earnings of women . . . Of course, there are a few who perhaps get an honest living, but they want a lot of picking out.

In the 1920s the road was still conspicuous for poverty and crime. The police still entered the street with caution, and the traditional crime of rescuing arrested men still prevailed in Campbell Road.

CAMPION, EDMUND Jesuit and martyr executed in 1581. Campion had been an Anglican deacon but fled to the Continent and was reconciled with the Catholic Church. He was sent to England on a mission to preach, was betrayed and captured. He was examined before Queen Elizabeth, who offered him a pardon and advancement if he would attend Anglican services. He refused, and a plot to murder the queen was then invented, and Campion was tortured. He had been racked so severely that he could not raise his hand to plead not guilty. He was hanged at Tyburn.

CANNING, ELIZABETH Perjurer who almost sent an innocent woman to the gallows. Canning was 18

ELIZABETH CANNING Aged 19.
the remarkable Quaker
Convicted of Perjury May 8th 1754.

Elizabeth Canning, perjurer who almost sent an innocent woman to the gallows. She claimed she was kidnapped in 1753, and identified an old gypsy as one of her captors. After the woman had been sentenced to death, it was proved that Canning was lying.

when she disappeared in the Houndsditch area on New Year's Day 1753. Her family organised a widespread search, without result. A month later she turned up again at her home, confused, hysterical, dirty, hungry and exhausted. Instead of the clothes she had on at the time of her disappearance she was wearing an old petticoat and a bathrobe. She said she had been kidnapped in a dark street by two men who ripped off most of her clothes and forced her to walk a long distance to a brothel. There the brothel-keeper attempted to make her become a prostitute: when she refused she was locked in a hayloft where she lived on bread and water for a month before escaping.

She could not remember where the house was, but from her description a neighbour suggested that it was the home of a bawd named Susannah Wells, known as Mother Wells. That name seemed familiar to Elizabeth. A warrant was issued, and law officers went with her to the house, where they found several men and women. Elizabeth was asked to point out the people who stole her clothes. Instead of pointing out Mrs Wells she singled out an old gypsy, Mary Squires, whose face was hideously disfigured by illness. Elizabeth had never mentioned these truly memorable features. Mary Squires, moreover, claimed she had been in Dorset on the day Elizabeth vanished. All the people in the house were taken to prison where one of the prostitutes, Virtue Hall, changed her story when she was questioned by the Bow Street magistrate HENRY FIELDING. In return for immunity she testified that Elizabeth Canning was telling the truth. At the Old Bailey Mary Squires was sentenced to death, and Susannah Wells was branded on the hand for harbouring a thief and sent to Newgate for six months.

The Lord Mayor of London, Sir Crisp Gascoyne, who was one of the judges, felt uneasy about the evidence and intervened to get a postponement of the execution while the background to the case was investigated. Over the next fifteen months it gradually became clear that Elizabeth Canning was lying. She had never been to the house before the day she accused Mary Squires. Virtue Hall withdrew her testimony and claimed she had been bullied into giving it by Fielding, who had questioned her for six hours. Canning was tried for perjury and sentenced to seven years' transportation. She never told where she had been during the month after she disappeared. There was speculation that she had been pregnant and had gone away to have the baby. She married in America and died there in 1773.

The action of Gascoyne showed considerable public-spiritedness. At the time there was violent prejudice against gypsies, and there had been attempts to banish them by statute from the kingdom. 'It was a felony even to be in their company' (McLynn, *Crime and Punishment in Eighteenth-Century England*), and a girl of 14 was executed for this crime. The affair cost Gascoyne a subsequent election. Even though he had opposed the unpopular JEW BILL, he was abused as the 'King of the Gypsies', pelted and threatened with murder.

CANT Underworld slang. The canting vocabulary has ancient origins. In the eighteenth century London was 'Romeville' and thieves might 'bite the bill from the cull' – steal a sword from a man's side. They would take 'lobs' from behind 'rattlers' – remove luggage from a moving coach. Some would 'nim the nab' – steal a man's hat from his head and make off with it. 'Clouters' took handkerchiefs from pockets, 'files' took watches or cash. Burglars would 'mill a ken' – rob a house. 'Milling the gig with a betty' was breaking down the door with an iron crowbar, 'milling the glaze' was smashing the window. 'Faggot and stall' was gagging all the people in a house before the thieves escaped with the loot. Horse thieves were, most poetically, 'priggers of prancers'.

Many of the criminal customers at MOLL KING's coffee house in Covent Garden in the eighteenth century used cant to frustrate police spies. A little pamphlet entitled *The Humours of the Flashy Boys at Moll King's*, in the form of a conversation between Moll and a customer named Harry Moythen, who was later murdered, gives us an idea of how it sounded.

> Harry: To pay, Moll, for I must hike.
> Moll: Let me see! There's a Grunter's Gig, is a Si-Buxom; Five Cats' Heads, a Whyn; a double Gage of Rum Slobber, is Thrums; and a quartern of Max is three Megs. That makes a Traveller, all but a Meg.
> Harry: Here, take your Traveller, and tip the Meg to the Kinchin . . . But Moll, don't Puff, you must tip me your Clout before I Derrick, for my Bloss has Milled me of mine. But I shall catch her at Maddox's gin-ken, Sluicing her Gob by the Tinney. And if she has Morric'd it, Knocks and Socks, Thumps and Plumps shall attend the Froe-File-Buttocking bitch

And so on. To Hike meant to go home, a Grunter's Gig was a hog's cheek, Si-Buxom was sixpence, a Cat's Head a ha'penny roll, a Whyn a penny, a Gage of Rum-Slobber a pot of porter, Thrums was threepence, Max was gin, Kinchin a little child. To Puff, to impeach, Clout, a handkerchief, Derrick, to go away, Froe-file-buttock, a woman pickpocket-prostitute. *See* KINCHIN LAY

CANTILLON, RICHARD Wealthy London banker murdered by his cook. In 1734 the cook, who had been sacked, used a ladder to climb into Cantillon's house in Albemarle Street. He stole cash and valuables, murdered the banker and then burned the house to the ground. He went to Holland but the authorities offered a large reward and the master of the ship which had carried him recognised him from a 'wanted' poster. He was arrested in Holland, brought back to London and executed.

CARDIGAN, EARL OF (1797–1868) Aristocrat tried for attempted murder, and acquitted for the silliest possible reason. James Thomas Brudenell, 7th Earl of Cardigan, who went on to lead the Charge of the Light Brigade at Balaclava, fought a duel in September 1840 on Wimbledon Common with a man named Harvey Garnett Phipps Tuckett, whom he accused of insulting him. Tuckett was wounded, and all concerned were arrested. Cardigan was tried at the Bar of the House. Tuckett's full name was set out in the indictment, but there was no proof in court that he bore all those names, and so on this technicality Cardigan was acquitted. Cardigan was challenged to another duel in 1843. He was having an affair with the wife of Lord William Paget, who demanded satisfaction. Cardigan refused, reasoning that he was unlikely to get away with it a second time. Lord Paget brought an action for CRIMINAL CONVERSATION. His butler, who had once hidden under a sofa to spy on Cardigan and Lady Paget, failed to appear and the case failed. Cardigan indignantly denied that he had paid the butler to disappear. He returned a hero after leading the light cavalry brigade to destruction in the Crimea (1854). He gave his name to a knitted woollen jacket, which he used as protection against the Russian winter. *See* TRIALS

CARLESS, BETSY Beautiful Covent Garden bawd and whore known as Careless. After the death of SALLY SALISBURY she was briefly the chief Toast of the Town before drink and an unquenchable appetite for dissipation caused her early death in October 1739. The *Gentlemen's Magazine* recalled that she had 'helped the gay gentlemen of this country to squander £50,000'. Henry Fielding had once seen her on the balcony of a theatre and recalled her sweet and innocent appearance. He thought it a 'pity she was on the way to ruin in such company' until he recalled that a few days earlier he had seen her 'in bed in a bagnio, smoking tobacco, drinking punch, talking and swearing obscenely and cursing with all the impudence and impiety of the lowest most abandoned trull of a soldier'.

CARMAN, GEORGE (1930–2001) Wily lawyer who made his name as defence counsel for Jeremy Thorpe. His clients over the years included Ken Dodd, Elton John and Richard Branson. His theatrical style and one-liners made him feared, his cross-examinations were regarded as ordeals. On receiving a libel writ from Jonathan Aitken the *Guardian* editor Alan Rusbridger is reputed to have said: 'We'd better get Carman before Aitken gets him.' Defending the comedian Ken Dodd on a charge of tax fraud Carman remarked: 'Some accountants are comedians, but comedians are never accountants.' The Liberal politician Jeremy Thorpe was acquitted of conspiracy to murder in a trial which made Carman as famous as his client. One of

The Toast of the Town Betsy Carless, known as Careless, is carried home dead drunk through Covent Garden. She was briefly the chief Toast before drink and an unquenchable appetite for dissipation caused her early death in October 1739. The man on top of the sedan chair is her lover, Mad Jack Montague.

his last cases was representing MOHAMED FAYED in a case involving the HAMILTONS.

CARPENTER, GEORGE (?–*c.* 1785) Covent Garden porter who took over MOLL KING's Coffee House. It was named after him. WILLIAM HICKEY wrote of the unappetising beverage sold there, 'they still continued to dole out a Spartan mixture, difficult to ascertain the ingredients of, but which was served as coffee'. Carpenter's was also known as The Finish. It is interesting that in Victorian times disreputable late-night boozing dens were also known as 'FINISHES'.

CARR, THOMAS Lawyer hanged with his lover for murder. Carr was an attorney in the Temple. In October 1737 he and Elizabeth Adams were tried for robbing a man of 93 guineas and a gold ring at the Angel & Crown Tavern near Temple Bar. Carr petitioned for mercy but the Privy Council ruled that his offence was aggravated by his being a lawyer. Before the cart drew away to leave them dangling from the gallows at Tyburn the couple kissed and held hands.

CARRINGTON, CHARLES Victorian pornographer, publisher of such classics as *Raped on the Railway: A True Story of a Lady Who Was First Ravished and then Flagellated on the Scotch Express* and *Flossie: A Venus of Fifteen*. He had the good sense to base himself in Paris, away from the prying Vice Society and Scotland Yard. He was the publisher of the first part of WALTER's memoirs of sexual encounters *My Secret Life* in 1901. *See* HENRY SPENCER ASHBEE

CASANOVA, GIACOMO (1725–98) Noted seducer, but also clergyman, secretary, soldier, musician, spy, alchemist, librarian and cabalist. In 1755 he was imprisoned for being a magician but escaped. His autobiography gives interesting accounts of London whores and bawds including KITTY FISHER and MADAME CORNELYS.

CASELEY, THOMAS Successful burglar of the mid-Victorian period. In a spell of a few months he and his accomplices stole £10,000 from safes in Lombard Street, £4,000 from Threadneedle Street and £1,000 from the Strand. A greater challenge was John Walker's jewellers at 63 Cornhill. It had a 'Quadruple Patent' Milner safe, advertised as 'thief-proof', and when the shop was closed it contained large amounts of jewellery and gold. The safe stood in a room with walls reinforced by iron plates. The plates had a slit through which passing policemen could inspect the room. The gas lights were left on, and mirrors enabled the observer to see every part of the room.

Caseley and his team 'cased' the shop. It was obvious that opening the safe would take many hours. Caseley bought a second-hand Milner safe and practised breaking into it. He realised that they would need a whole weekend for the task. The gang chose the weekend of 4–6 February 1865. On the Saturday they entered the building while it was still open and went to some offices on the floor above the shop. There they hid until the building was locked up. Then they made a hole in the ceiling of a tailor's shop adjoining the jeweller's and climbed down a rope ladder. When they tried to break through the wall into the jeweller's they found the iron plates were too strong. They descended to the cellar and found a spot where they could break through the floor into the jeweller's. A lookout in the street outside signalled every time a policeman or curious passer-by approached the shop. The cracksmen would gather up their tools and hide behind a partition until the coast was clear again.

The method of opening the safe was crude. They hammered iron wedges into the narrow gap between the door and wall of the safe. After hours of toil the gap was wide enough to insert an iron bar and the lock was prised open. When Mr Walker opened up his shop on Monday morning he found that the safe had been emptied of £6,000-worth of gold and jewels.

As in the case of the first GREAT TRAIN ROBBERY, it was a woman who spoiled what otherwise seemed to be a perfect crime. She felt she had been betrayed by a member of the gang, and talked. Caseley was sentenced to fourteen years' penal servitude.

CASEMENT, SIR ROGER (1864–1916) Irish nationalist executed for treason. Casement, who was born in Dublin, had a distinguished career as a British diplomat in various parts of Africa and Brazil. He denounced colonialist atrocities against natives. He was knighted in 1911, and retired because of ill health, going back to live in Ireland. He was an ardent nationalist, and in 1916 was arrested as he landed in Ireland from a German submarine. He had hoped to lead the Sinn Fein rebellion in Dublin. To discredit him extracts from his controversial 'Black Diaries' were discreetly leaked, although the diaries themselves were not published until 1959. They revealed that Casement was a homosexual. He was tried in London for high treason and executed at Pentonville Prison in 1916.

CASTANAR, JUAN ANTONIO Soho vice racketeer who murdered his rival Casimir Micheletti. The two men dominated the vice trade in the 1920s. Castanar, a Spaniard who drove a Rolls-Royce, was a famous tango dancer and had a dancing school in Archer Street, Soho. Underworld legend had it that he used this to lure pretty young women into white slavery abroad. The war between the two factions led to stabbings and shootings, and questions in the House of Commons. Finally the two gang leaders were arrested and deported. Castanar tracked Micheletti to Montmartre and shot him dead. *See* WHITE SLAVERY

CASTLEMAINE, LADY (1640–1709) Mistress of King Charles II, notorious for greed, profligacy, rages and sexual incontinence. She was Barbara Villiers, her accommodating husband being made Earl of Castlemaine. Pepys paid tribute to Villiers's beauty in August 1662, 'I glutted myself with looking on her'. She was widely disliked and feared, the diarist John Evelyn calling her 'the curse of our nation'. When Charles's wife Catherine of Braganza heard that Lady Castlemaine was to be one of her ladies of the bedchamber she fainted.

For a while her sexual stamina, enthusiasm and expertise completely infatuated the King and made him oblivious to the harm she was doing to his reputation. But she became a termagant, once forcing him to beg forgiveness on his knees. Finally he was willing to pay almost any price to get rid of her, lavishing sums from the privy purse, houses and a pension of £4,700 a year from the Post Office revenues on her.

Castlemaine had many lovers besides Charles. They included John Churchill, later to become the nation's greatest soldier and Duke of Marlborough, the playwright William Wycherley, the Earl of Chesterfield and the rope-dancer Jacob Hall. She had herself painted with Hall. She was said to have seduced the running footman who accompanied her coach:

> She through her lackey's drawers, as he ran,
> Discern's love's cause, and a new flame began . . .
> Full forty men a day have swiv'd this whore,
> Yet like a bitch she wags her tail for more.

After she went to live in Paris in 1676 she had affairs with the English ambassador Ralph Montague and, it was rumoured, the Archbishop of Paris. Another lover was an actor and highwayman named Cardonell Goodman, nicknamed Scum, who was found guilty of trying to poison two of her children. This 'lewd imperial whore' had acquired riches and titles, one estimate being that she consumed half a million pounds of public money. Much of it went in gambling, or was wasted on favourites. She was described by Bishop Burnet as 'enormously vicious and ravenous'. In spite of all Charles made her Baroness Nonsuch, Countess of Southampton and Duchess of Cleveland. She had five children by him. As she grew older her life became if anything more scandalous. When the body of Bishop Robert Braybrook, who died in 1440, was exhumed, it was found to be remarkably well preserved. The Duchess is said to have gone to see it and asked to be left alone. Afterwards it was noticed that the penis was missing. A document in the British Museum quotes a witness: 'and though some ladys of late have got Bishopricks for others, yet I have not heard of any but this that got one for herself . . .' (Masters, *The Mistresses of Charles II*). Her descendants include Diana Princess of Wales and Sarah Ferguson, Duchess of York.

CATO STREET CONSPIRACY Plot to murder the government. Arthur Thistlewood, a former soldier who developed radical ideas while serving in America and France and joined London's revolutionary underworld, planned to murder Castlereagh and other ministers as they dined with Lord Harrowby at a house in Grosvenor Square in February 1820. The government knew all about the plan. A government agent named George Edwards had infiltrated the group and as they met to plan the crime in the stable loft of No 6 Cato Street WI troops and Bow Street Runners burst in. Thistlewood, an expert swordsman, ran one of the police officers through. Some of the conspirators,

The moment the police burst in on the Cato Street plotters. Arthur Thistlewood runs one of the officers through, his fellow conspirators seize weapons to resist arrest. Five conspirators were hanged.

including Thistlewood, escaped. He was caught next day. On 1 May 1820 he and four other ringleaders were hanged at Newgate. On the scaffold he declared: 'I desire all here to remember that I die in the cause of liberty.' Because the government feared public sympathy for the conspirators they were spared being drawn and quartered.

After their bodies had been hanging for an hour they were taken down and their heads cut off by a masked man. The mob, seeing how expertly the heads were removed, suspected a medical man, and a rumour went round that the executioner was the surgeon Thomas Wakeley. That night his house was set ablaze, and Wakeley was badly injured. He lived, and went on to found the medical journal *The Lancet* and to lead campaigns for improved medical standards. The beheadings of the Cato Street conspirators were the last in London. The plotters had played into the hands of the government, which was looking for excuses to attack and discredit the whole radical reform movement. Cobbett said: 'They sigh for a PLOT . . . they are absolutely pining and dying for a plot!'

CHALLENOR, DETECTIVE SERGEANT HAROLD Corrupt police officer who planted evidence. Challenor arrested a number of protesters at a demonstration against a state visit by the unpopular Queen Frederika of Greece outside Claridge's Hotel in July 1963. He roughed them up, then planted half-bricks on them and told them: 'There you are, me old darling. Carrying an offensive weapon can get you two years.' When he was brought to trial he was found unfit to plead because of mental problems.

Challenor was at least eccentric and probably a little crazy. He had been decorated while serving in the Special Air Service during the Second World War, then joined the police. At West End Central, the division covering Soho, he soon had a reputation as a relentless pursuer of criminals. At the same time he was said to be corrupt, taking money from, among others, JIMMY HUMPHREYS. He told his wife he was being prepared for a secret mission by being brainwashed and hypnotised. He later worked as a solicitor's clerk and wrote his memoirs.

CHAPMAN, EDDIE Safe breaker and war hero. His extraordinary story was made into a film, *Triple X*, starring Christopher Plummer. Chapman was a successful London burglar in the 1930s. When the Second World War broke out he was in jail in Jersey. He offered his services to the Germans when they invaded the island, and after training he was sent back to Britain with instructions to destroy an aircraft factory at Hatfield, Herts. Instead he went to the intelligence service MI5 and became a double agent. MI5 staged a fake explosion at the aircraft factory and Chapman returned to Germany a hero. MI5 files opened in July 2001 said 'the Germans came to love Chapman. But although he went cynically through all the forms he did not reciprocate. Chapman loved himself, loved adventure and loved his country, probably in that order.'

The Germans sent Chapman to Norway, to teach at a spy school in Oslo. After the invasion of Europe by the Allies he was parachuted back into Britain to check on the damage being done by the German rocket-propelled V bombs. There he confessed to his MI5 handlers that he had fallen in love with a Norwegian girl and had told her that he was working for the British secret service. His chiefs decided it was too dangerous for him to return to Germany and he was retired with a £6,000 payoff and a pardon for all his crimes. He was also allowed to keep £1,000 which the Germans had given him. With his intelligence role as cover he had gone on blowing safes. 'The deal was that any money I made with the Germans I kept,' he said later. 'I was working under British Intelligence and they behaved like a lot of Boy Scouts.' Chapman used the proceeds of *Triple X* to open a successful health farm with his wife. He died in 1997.

CHAPMAN, GEORGE Poisoner thought by some to have been JACK THE RIPPER. Chapman was a Pole, real name Severin Klosovski. He was apprenticed to a surgeon, although he failed to get a degree. He arrived in England in 1888, and took a job as a barber in Whitechapel. He lived with a long succession of women, and poisoned three of them. The first to die was Mary Spinks, on Christmas Day, 1897. By now Chapman was keeping a pub, and advertised for a barmaid. Bessie Taylor, a domestic servant, answered and although Chapman had a wife they 'married'. She died in February 1901, the death being attributed to 'exhaustion from vomiting and diarrhoea'. The final victim, Maud Marsh, also became a barmaid at Chapman's Monument Tavern in Union Street, Borough. She soon began to show the same symptoms as Bessie Taylor, and her suspicious mother tasted a drink Chapman had prepared for her daughter. She became ill, as did a nurse who had also tried the drink. Mrs Marsh called in a doctor and Chapman, alarmed, decided to kill Maud with a large dose of the poison antimony. She died in October 1902. Chapman was arrested, and the detective in charge of the Jack the Ripper investigations is said to have remarked: 'You've caught the Ripper, then?' Chapman had been under suspicion in 1888, the year of the Ripper murders. He was executed in April 1903 for the murder of Maud Marsh.

CHARLES I (1600–49) King of Britain and Ireland, beheaded in Whitehall on 30 January 1649. His duplicity while in negotiations with Parliament and his secret agreement with the Scots to start the second Civil War in 1646 exasperated the army. After CROMWELL's defeat of the Scots at Preston in 1648, the king was brought to trial. His refusal to plead was interpreted as a confession of guilt. The 'man of blood' went to the scaffold along a walkway erected through a window of the Banqueting House in Whitehall. For years there was speculation about the identity of the masked executioner. There were rumours that Richard Brandon, the hangman, had refused the job, and the French claimed Cromwell and Fairfax were the executioners.

After the restoration of the monarchy in 1660 retribution followed for the signatories of Charles's death warrant. Forty-one of the fifty-nine regicides were still alive. Fifteen of them fled abroad, nine were tried and hanged, drawn and quartered. Others said they had been brow-beaten into signing, one even claiming his hand had been held forcing him to write his signature. Of these some were sentenced to life imprisonment and others were freed.

The three most important signatories, Cromwell, his son-in-law Henry Ireton and John Bradshaw, president of the regicide court, had died and been buried in Westminster Abbey. Their bodies were dug up and exposed on gibbets at Tyburn. Afterwards they were flung into the ditch used for the bodies of common criminals.

CHARLES II King who was more famous for his mistresses than for any act of statemanship. 'Pretty, witty' NELL GWYN is the best known, but the vicious and greedy nymphomaniac Barbara Villiers, COUNTESS OF CASTLEMAINE, Louise de Kéroualle, Duchess of Portsmouth, Hortense Mancini, Duchesse de Mazarin and others were among the great European beauties of their time.

CHARTERIS, COLONEL FRANCIS (1675–1731) Rake, rapist, card-sharp and fraudster. Charteris, who made a fortune from South Sea stock and from cheating at cards and had great estates in Lancashire, was known as the Rape-Master of Great Britain: he boasted of seducing more than a hundred women, and sent out servants to find 'none but such as were strong, lusty and fresh Country Wenches, of the first size, their B–tt–cks as hard as Cheshire Cheeses, that could make a Dint in a Wooden Chair, and work like a parish Engine at a Conflagration'. He turned his house into a brothel, and his escapades made entertaining reading in a flood of pamphlets. He was accused of rape, using loaded dice, fraud, bearing false witness, denying his bastard children and, not least, being an associate of the corrupt Prime Minister Robert Walpole. He used his army rank, although he had been cashiered for embezzlement. His aristocratic connections got him out of several scrapes, as when he drew his sword on a constable in St James's Park, and when he raped a young virgin in the Scotch Ale-House in Pall Mall. He had to pay maintenance for the bastard child born to the girl. A Scots woman giving evidence against him said: 'This is the huge raw beast that . . . got me with Bairn . . . I know him by his nastie Legg for he has wrapt it round my Arse mony a guid time!' (Burford and Wotton, *Private Vices, Public Virtues*). He owned brothels, financed by cheating at cards. He won £3,000 from the Duchess of Queensberry by placing her in front of a mirror in which he could see her cards. This got him banned from several clubs. He was reputed to be the first lover of the noted courtesan Sally Salisbury, when she was little more than a child.

Charteris is shown in Plate 1 of Hogarth's print series *A Harlot's Progress*. A sweet young country girl newly arrived in town is propositioned by a bawd, easily recognised by contemporaries as the notorious MOTHER NEEDHAM. The colonel lurks nearby in a doorway with his cringing servant Jack Gourlay, who acted as his pander.

Shortly before Hogarth began his series early in 1730 Charteris was tried for the rape of his servant Anne Bond. The court was told that as soon as she took up her post he offered her money for sex. She refused, but at seven one morning 'the Colonel rang a Bell and bid the Clerk of the Kitchen call the Lancashire Bitch into the Dining Room'. Charteris locked the door, threw her onto the couch, gagged her with his nightcap and raped her. When she threatened to tell her friends he horse-whipped her and took away her clothes and money. Charteris's rich and aristocratic friends and relatives packed into the court to hear him sentenced to death for rape. He was in Newgate less than a month, and received a royal pardon, negotiated by his son-in-law Lord Wemyss, who bribed Lord President Forbes of Culloden. It also helped that Charteris was the cousin the Duke of Wharton, friend and protector of some of the great bawds of the age. In return for his pardon Charteris had to settle a large annuity on Anne Bond.

There are many stories told against Charteris. One night at an inn he fancied a beautiful young servant girl. At first she indignantly refused his gold, but was eventually worn down by his experienced persistence and left his room a guinea richer. In the morning Charteris told the landlord that he had given the girl a guinea to change into silver for him, and that she had not yet returned it. The girl was called, and had to produce the guinea. Charteris pocketed it, then told the landlord what had really happened. The girl was dismissed. After another girl had been rescued from him by her sister, neighbours stormed Charteris's house with 'Stones, Brickbats, and other such vulgar Ammunition'. When he was released from Newgate following the Anne Bond case, he was set upon by a London crowd. He died in 1731, probably from venereal disease, and the mob threw 'dead dogs &c. into the grave' with him. Pope lampooned him in his Moral Essays.

CHATHAM, GEORGE Successful burglar of the mid-twentieth century known as 'Taters' Chatham. His victims included the hairdresser 'Teasy Weasy' Raymond, the restaurateur Madame Prunier and Lady 'Bubbles' Rothermere, wife of the owner of Associated Newspapers. He fell four floors while attempting to break into the house of Princess Diana's stepmother, Raine Spencer. After being patched up with plaster and bandages he broke in again and was caught. During his long career he served thirty-five years in prison.

He justified his crimes thus: 'They were usually very rich people, millionaires. Some of them regarded it as a nice thing to talk about at dinner parties.' Another time he said: 'I was a rebel against authority and I had no respect for the police. If I could outwit them in any way, I would.' His raid on the Victoria and Albert Museum, when he stole the Wellington swords, was perhaps the high point of his anti-Establishment campaign. He removed jewels from the swords, sold some of them and gave others away to his girlfriend. He chose his victims from *Debrett's* and *Burke's Peerage* and *Landed Gentry*. Although he estimated that he stole millions, he gambled it all away. There were stories that after a particularly heavy night's gambling he would drop out of a game for a few hours for a profitable foray into Mayfair – only to lose everything on his return. When Chatham was 76 he was arrested for shoplifting. 'What have I got,' he asked. 'A lot of sad memories and thirty years inside.'

CHATTERTON, THOMAS (1752–70) Literary forger and suicide. Chatterton was 11 when he produced his first forgery, *Elinore and Juga*, imitating the style of the fifteenth century. He sent his more ambitious *The Legend of Thomas Rowley* to Horace Walpole, the author of the medievalising *Castle of Otranto*. Walpole showed it to the poet Thomas Grey, who denounced it as a forgery. Walpole advised Chatterton to give up forgeries, but instead the young man went to London, where he mixed with politicians and writers. Samuel Johnson described him as 'the most extraordinary young man that has encountered my knowledge'. Others who praised him included Wordsworth – 'the marvellous boy' – Shelley and Byron, and Keats dedicated *Endymion* to him. But his work didn't sell, and in August 1770 he tore up his poems and killed himself with arsenic in his Holborn garret. Walpole thereafter had to live with the accusation that he was responsible for the death of a genius. Chatterton enjoyed posthumously the fame and critical respect he craved. He became a romantic hero to later poets, and his Rowley verses are now seen as highly talented. The artist Henry Wallis's high Victorian *The Death of Chatterton* in the old Tate Gallery renewed interest in him when he was largely forgotten.

CHICAGO MAY (*c*. 1876–1935) Exponent of the BADGER GAME, real name Beatrice Desmond. In 1889 at the age of 13 she stole her family's entire savings and ran off to America, where she married a member of the Dalton Gang of outlaws. He was caught during a train robbery in Arizona and strung up by vigilantes. May, a 15-year-old widow, went to Chicago and made £300,000 over the next four years playing the Badger Game. She lured her victims to hotel rooms where with the help an accomplice she would steal their personal papers. Later she would write to them, reminding them of what a good time they had and threatening to tell their wives unless they paid up. She moved to New York and met Mark Twain, whom she invited to join her in Connecticut for a week. 'I cannot thank you enough for an amusing time,' said Twain as he politely declined, 'but I haven't believed a word of your story that you are an English noblewoman.' May returned to Europe and became the lover of EDDIE GUERIN, with whom she had been involved in a £250,000 robbery in Paris. They fell out and May and her latest lover shot Guerin outside Russell Street underground station. She got fifteen years, and after her release was deported to America. Her luck had run out, and in the 1930s she had become a street prostitute charging $2 a time.

CHILDREN'S BROTHELS In 1816 a Parliamentary inquiry was told of brothels especially for children.

The prostitutes were mainly under 14, and some only 11 or 12. The customers were also youngsters. A witness named a girl then aged 16 who had been working as a prostitute in her father's brothel for the past five or six years. In 1852 a London judge told a Select Committee about girls aged 14 or 15 who could not remember when they first had intercourse. A 9-year-old boy named Burnet, who had a long criminal record and had been sentenced to hang but reprieved, had a mistress aged 13. Some low lodging house known as FLASH HOUSES were exclusively for the young. In one of them, in ST GILES, according to the reformer William Crawford '. . . four hundred beds are made up every night; a boy who was in the habit of visiting this house confessed that he had slept there upwards of 30 times with girls of his own age, and he particularly named five: this boy was 14 years of age, the girls were to be met with at the flash houses to which he resorted'. The promiscuity of flash houses was shocking to the Victorians, with their pronounced attitudes to female modesty. The beds were verminous and inmates of both sexes often lay on them entirely naked. A girl recalled: 'There were very wicked carryings on. The boys, if any difference, was the worst. We lay packed on a full night, a dozen boys and girls squeedged into one bed . . . I can't go into all the particulars, but whatever could take place in words or acts between boys and girls did take place, and in the midst of the others . . . Some boys and girls slept without any clothes, and would dance about the room in that way. I have seen them and, wicked as I was, I felt ashamed . . .'.

CHRISTIE, JOHN (1898–1953) Sex killer who let another man hang for two of his murders. Christie lived with his wife at 10 Rillington Place in Notting Hill. In March 1953, after he had moved out, the new tenant found a cupboard in the kitchen which had been covered over with wallpaper. Inside were the bodies of three women. Under the floorboards in another room police found the body of another woman, wrapped in a blanket. Buried in the garden were the skeletons of two more bodies – a human femur was used to prop up the fence.

The case revived interest in a previous double murder at the same house. In 1949 two bodies had been found in Christie's garden shed. They were those of Mrs Evans and her baby daughter Geraldine, who also lived in the house with Mrs Evans's husband Timothy, and they had been strangled. Evans, an illiterate man of low intelligence, was executed for murder. Was Christie really their killer?

Serial sex killer John Christie in his uniform as a wartime policeman. He let another man die for two of his murders.

A week after the discovery of the bodies in the cupboard Christie was arrested. He admitted murdering the six women. He claimed he had strangled his wife because she was having a fit, and he 'could not bear to see her'. The other three women in the house were all prostitutes, aged twenty-five and twenty-six. One of the women in the garden was an Austrian, whom Christie claimed he had murdered during intercourse, the other was Muriel Eady, a fellow employee at the Ultra Radio factory where Christie had worked in late 1944.

Christie went on trial at the Old Bailey in June 1953 charged only with murdering his wife. He admitted that he invited the other women to his house and got them partly drunk. He then placed a gas pipe near them and turned it on. When they lost consciousness he strangled and then raped them.

He later confessed to killing Mrs Evans. He said he found her lying on the floor by the gas fire, having attempted suicide. She asked him to help her die, he claimed, and he strangled her with a stocking. When Evans returned he told him that his wife had committed suicide, and Evans left the house, going to Wales where he gave himself up to

Timothy Evans with his wife and daughter. He was hanged for murder, but given a posthumous pardon. The killer was John Christie.

police and said he had killed his wife and hidden her body in a drain. Exactly how the child died is unknown. At one stage Evans said Christie was the murderer. The jury rejected Christie's defence of insanity, and Christie was executed in July 1953. In 1966, after a special inquiry, Evans was granted a free pardon (Wilson and Pitman, *Encyclopedia of Murder*). Christie was hanged for the murder of his own wife.

CHRISTOFI, STYLLOU Jealous mother who murdered two women. On 29 July 1954 she murdered her son's wife Hella at their Hampstead home by hitting her on the head and strangling her. She tried to burn the body. She was hanged in December 1954. In 1925 Mrs Christofi had been charged with murdering her mother-in-law in Cyprus

Police search the garden at 10 Rillington Place after the bodies of some of Christie's victims had been found there. Others were in a concealed cupboard inside the house.

by thrusting a burning torch down her throat. It was part of a village vendetta – the woman was being held down by neighbours at the time – and she was acquitted.

CHURCH, REVD JOHN Priest and sodomite. Church had a history of homosexual affairs before he became a notorious preacher in London in the early 1800s. In 1808, after the 25-year-old clergyman had been appointed rector at Banbury in Oxfordshire, he was accused of seducing a string of men. He replied: 'If there was anything of which you speak, it must have been when I was asleep and supposing that I was in bed with my wife.' In London he became preacher at the Obelisk Chapel, a homosexual brothel in Vere Street, running north from Oxford Street. In July 1810 the premises were raided by Bow Street Runners, backed by a unit of troops. Twenty-three people were arrested. Seven of them were sentenced to prison terms ranging from one to three years' imprisonment. They also had to endure a battering in the pillory, described below under VERE STREET COTERIE. The journalist Robert Holloway wrote up the scandal in a book. Although it didn't name Church he was pictured on the front cover and the picture was recognised by a man named Clarke, whose son had been seduced by Church the year before. Clarke armed himself with a brace of pistols and confronted Church. The excitement was too much for Clarke and he fainted before he could fire a shot.

Church officiated at transvestite weddings and at funerals of men executed for sodomy. His sermons were so popular that in 1813 he opened a larger Obelisk Chapel. In 1817 he was jailed for two years for attempting to sodomise an apprentice potter named Adam Foreman. The lad told the Old Bailey that he woke one night after someone took hold of him 'very tight'. When he asked who it was the man replied 'Don't you know me, Adam? It is your mistress.' When Church emerged from prison he was more popular than ever.

CLAP, MOTHER In 1726 the SOCIETIES FOR THE REFORMATION OF MANNERS succeeded in closing down more than twenty homosexual brothels or 'mollies' houses', including Mother Clap's in Holborn. She was found guilty of keeping a 'sodomitical house' and put in the pillory at Smithfield. Three of her male prostitutes were hanged. The trial record shows that Mother Clap's house was a regular meeting place for homosexuals. One of the witnesses for the prosecution was the constable Samuel Stephens:

> Stephens: On Sunday night, the 14th November last, I went to the prisoner's house in Field Lane, in Holborn, where I found between 40 and 50 men making love to one another, as they called it. Sometimes they would sit in one another's laps, kissing in a lewd manner and using their hands indecently. Then they would get up, dance and make curtsies, and mimic the voices of women. 'O,Fie, Sir! – Pray, Sir – Dear, Sir, – Lord, how can you serve me so? – I swear I'll cry out. – You're a wicked devil, – and you've a bold face. – Eh, you dear little toad! Come, buss!' – Then they'd hug, and play, and toy, and go out by couples into another room on the same floor, to be married, as they called it. The door of that room was kept by — Eccleston, who used to stand pimp for 'em, to prevent anybody from disturbing them in their diversions. When they came out they used to brag, in plain terms, of what they had been doing. As for the prisoner, she was present all the time, except when she went out to fetch liquors. There was among them William Griffin, who has since been hanged for sodomy; and — Derwin, who had been carried before Sir George Mertins, for sodomitical practices with a link-boy . . . I went to the same house on two or three Sunday nights following, and found much the same practices as before. The company talked all manner of gross and vile obscenity in the prisoner's hearing, and she appeared to be wonderfully pleased with it.

Mother Clap told the court: 'I hope it will be considered that I am a woman, and therefore it cannot be thought that I would ever be concerned in such practices.' She was sentenced to stand in the pillory at Smithfield. She was also fined and sentenced to imprisonment, but she was so battered in the pillory that she died a week later.

CLARENCE, DUKE OF (1864–92) Son of the heir to the throne caught up in the Cleveland Street homosexual brothel scandal. In July 1886 a 15-year-old boy named Arthur Swinscow was arrested carrying eighteen shillings. Asked to explain how a humble Post Office boy came by so much money, he admitted that he worked as a prostitute at the homosexual brothel at 19 Cleveland Street. He told police that among the aristocrats who used the brothel were Lord Arthur Somerset, the Earl of Euston and Colonel Jervois. Somerset, a major in the

Blues and an equerry to the Prince of Wales, hired the solicitor Arthur Newton, a wily manipulator. Newton told the assistant Director of Public Prosecutions that if Somerset was prosecuted he would name the Duke of Clarence, son of the Prince of Wales, as another client. The warning went all the way up to the Prime Minister, Lord Salisbury. Somerset was not prosecuted but was advised to go to France, which he did.

Four boy prostitutes, including Arthur Swinscow, were prosecuted in September 1886 and all were jailed with hard labour. In November 1889 the journalist Ernest Parke named Somerset and Euston in the *North London Press* as the two aristocrats involved in the original allegations, but not mentioned at the trial. Euston sued Parke for libel. His lordship admitted being at the brothel, but said it was a misunderstanding: he thought he was going to see nude women. Parke called witnesses who said they had seen Euston at the brothel. One, John Saul, said Euston was 'not an actual sodomite, but likes to play with you and spend on your belly'. Saul was a prostitute at other brothels, and the judge described him as a 'loathsome object'. Parke was found guilty and jailed for a year with hard labour.

The name of the Duke of Clarence was not raised at the trial. A victim of syphilis and gonorrhoea, he was held in a lunatic asylum and released periodically. He was one of the men suspected of being JACK THE RIPPER.

CLARKE, MARY ANNE Mistress at the centre of a royal scandal. Mary Anne was the mistress of the Duke of York, son of George III, Commander in Chief of the Army and brother of the future Prince Regent. He set her up in a house in Gloucester Place, off Portman Square, with more than twenty servants, including two butlers. This all cost a great deal of money, and while his passion lasted the duke was willing to pay. When his attention strayed, however, towards a Mrs Cary of Fulham in 1807, Mrs Clarke asked for a substantial pay-off: the settlement of her £2,000 debts, the considerable costs of furnishing the Gloucester Place house and an annual allowance of several hundred pounds. When the duke appeared to be giving her the brush-off without paying Mary Anne let it be known that she had been in the habit of recommending promotions for certain officers, that the duke had accepted these suggestions and that large sums of money had changed hands. The opposition Whigs were delighted to press for an inquiry, and the government granted a full hearing before the bar of the House. It was the scandal of the age. Mary Anne told frankly how, to recoup the costs of the Gloucester Place house, she had established a tariff for promotions. This included a price of £2,600 for a majority, and £1,500 for a company. Half-pay officers paid less. She had brought this business to such a level that to remember all the supplicants she had to pin pieces of paper with their names to the bed-clothes.

Pretty Mary Anne made a great impression on the men of the House. On one occasion a note was passed to her saying '300 guineas and supper with me tonight'. The duke denied everything, and Mary Anne had little evidence apart from some ambiguous letters. There was a majority of eighty-two for a resolution saying the duke was innocent, but 196 MPs voted against it, and the duke resigned as Commander in Chief. He was reinstated when his brother George became Regent in 1811. Mary Anne was imprisoned for libel in 1813.

CLATERBALLOCK, CLARICE LA In June 1340 at a time of moral panic over a growing crime wave the city fathers ordered a round-up of 'evildoers and disturbers of the King's peace'. Among the hundreds arrested was the 'common whore' with the very uncommon name Clarice la Claterballock, who was picked up in Bridge ward. It would be interesting to know what speciality accounted for her name.

CLELAND, JOHN (1709–89) Author of the celebrated pornographic novel *FANNY HILL*. Cleland was in the Fleet Prison when he revised the manuscript for publication in 1749. He had been incarcerated for debt after an unsuccessful career as a minor official in India, and said he wrote the book out of boredom. Fanny Hill is a Liverpool girl who comes to London at the age of fifteen and works in a brothel. This gives Cleland opportunities to run the gamut of seduction, flagellation, lesbianism, homosexuality and various sexual aberrations. Despite being immediately banned as pornographic it became a best-seller, but Cleland hardly benefited. He sold the copyright to a bookseller in St Paul's Churchyard for 20 guineas: the bookseller is said to have made £10,000 from it, although from what we know of its sales figures this must be an exaggeration. Cleland was called before the Privy Council, whose president, Lord Granville, asked him how he came to write such a work. Cleland replied that poverty was the spur, and he was awarded £100 a year and a job as a government propagandist. He wrote other novels, and the *Memoirs of a Coxcomb*.

Fanny Hill was frequently republished and just as frequently prosecuted. The future Duke of Wellington took several copies with him to India.

Booksellers went to the pillory and to jail over it. The book enjoyed a new success in 1963 when an unexpurgated edition was seized by the police.

CLIFFORD, BARON DE Edward Southwell Russell was the last peer to be tried by the House of Lords. In December 1935 he was found not guilty of manslaughter after his car was involved in a fatal accident. The right of peers to be tried by the Lords was abolished by the Criminal Justice Act of 1948. More interestingly, Russell married Dorothy Meyrick, a daughter of MRS KATE MEYRICK, the Queen of the Nightclubs in 1920s London. He had given his age as 22 when he was in reality only 19, and was hauled up before the Lord Mayor at Mansion House. He was fined £100 and the Lord Mayor, who must have been a very silly man, told him that he was lucky not to get seven years in prison. The couple separated in the 1950s.

CLINK, THE Prison from which we get the expression 'in the clink'. It stood on the Bishop of Winchester's land in Southwark, and the historian Stow said it was for people who broke the peace on BANKSIDE and in the bishop's brothels there. Later it was used for debtors. It was one of the prisons burned down in the GORDON RIOTS.

COBBETT, WILLIAM (1763–1835) Radical journalist and reformer, jailed in 1810 for libel. He had criticised the flogging of rebellious English militiamen by German mercenaries. He was sent to prison for two years, and like DANIEL DEFOE became a public hero.

COFFEE, IRENE Survivor of a suicide pact who was charged with murder. She and her mother were German Jewish refugees who fled to London in 1937. In 1941, fearing a German invasion, they decided to commit suicide by taking poison. On 18 October police found the mother dead and 29-year-old Irene semi-conscious. She was found guilty, with a recommendation of mercy. Her death sentence was reduced to life imprisonment. *See* SUICIDE

COINING, COUNTERFEITING AND FORGERY Until the late seventeenth century coiners, clippers and counterfeiters were dealt with by fines, the pillory or by having their ears cut off and their noses slashed. In 1697 the Coinage Act, for which SIR ISAAC NEWTON as Master of the Mint claimed responsibility, made coining high treason, a capital offence.

The previous year a forger had been executed, but for the exceptional crime of swindling the Bank of England. Henry Weston, an inveterate gambler, forged the name of a General Tonyn and got away with the fabulous sum of £100,000. Unfortunately he lost the lot in two nights' gambling. He tried to swindle the bank again by getting his mistress to pose as General Tonyn's sister. He attempted to flee to America but was caught on a ship at Liverpool and executed (McLynn, *Crime and Punishment in Eighteenth-Century England*).

Even under the BLOODY CODE forgery was not always dealt with so harshly, however. In 1715 Robert Williams was found guilty of forging a bill of exchange for £60 1*s*. He was sentenced to stand in the pillory twice and fined one mark, which was worth 13*s* 4*d* (Linebaugh, *The London Hanged*). At the same sessions a thief was sentenced to be hanged for stealing a silver tankard and spoon. Perhaps the very rarity of Williams's form of forgery accounts for the leniency on this occasion. Under the Bloody Code forgers and coiners were virtually certain to be hanged.

In the eighteenth century the most basic form of forgery involved using chemicals to change the value written on banknotes. The forger would buy a banknote, often with a face value of £11, and chemically erase all but the initial 'e' of eleven. Then he would write in 'ighty' to make the face value £80.

The Victorian counterfeiter was generally less ambitious: the favourite denominations were £5 and £10. After the notes had been crumpled and soiled to make them look old, they would be passed at horse fairs, markets, hotels and public houses. Specialist forgers cheated sailors by 'personating [them] with intent to receive their wages', forging their tickets and even their wills.

Clipping involved shaving a slice off the edge of a guinea. The edge of the coin would then be filed to restore the milling, and the shavings sold to a coiner. Just to have the special scissors used in clipping was a capital offence.

By the nineteenth century forgery was highly organised. Those who operated it were known as shofulmen, and they were divided into three sections. At the top were the coiners or counterfeiters, the elite group. Below them were the wholesale distributors, who sold the bad money to the third group in the chain, the 'smashers'. The smashers put the coins into circulation. Seven Dials was a centre for distribution, especially the Clock House there. There was a pothouse in Christopher Street, Bethnal Green whose landlord, Cokey Hogan, was also a well-known dealer. The trade was more or less ubiquitous, and all the rookeries had their dealers.

The death sentence for coining and forgery was dropped in the 1830s and a maximum sentence of life imprisonment was substituted. MAYHEW's research (*London Labour and the London Poor*) suggested that this had little deterrent effect. Here is his description of a walk through some of the criminal haunts in the mid-1800s:

> Entering a beer-shop in the neighbourhood of St Giles, close by the Seven Dials, we saw a band of coiners and RINGERS OF CHANGES. One of them, a genteel-looking slim youth, is a notorious coiner, and has been convicted . . . One of them is a moulder; another was sentenced to ten years' penal servitude for coining and selling base coin. A modest-looking young man, one of the gang, was seated by the bar, also respectably dressed . . . looking out, while they are coining, that no officers of justice come near, and carrying the bag of base money for them when they go out to sell it to base wretches in small quantities at low prices. Five shillings of base money is generally sold for tenpence . . .

To get a conviction police needed specimens of the coiner's output, so the coiners usually worked in a top-storey room up a rickety staircase, sometimes with boards removed or obstacles placed to slow down police raiders. The forger needed vital minutes to destroy the evidence in his fire. Police and special agents sometimes had to fight their way in past specially recruited bruisers, savage dogs and traps. *See* JAMES BRENNAN and BOB CUMMINS

COKE, SIR EDWARD (1552–1634) Brutal prosecutor of RALEIGH, ESSEX and the GUNPOWDER PLOTTERS. He carried out the investigation ordered by King James I into the poisoning of Sir Thomas Overbury, the great scandal of the reign. He was also a defender of national liberties against the royal prerogative and an important jurist. From 1620 he led the popular party in Parliament, and was jailed for nine months. In old age he continued to champion civil rights, the Petition of Right (1628) being one of his achievements.

COLDBATH FIELDS PRISON Notoriously severe jail in Islington. Punishments ran the gamut of callous inhumanity from the treadmill – the prison had six – to carrying cannon balls and picking oakum (pulling apart old ships' ropes so that the fibre could be re-used). Prisoners weren't allowed to speak, and they could have only one letter and one visit every three months. It became England's largest prison in the later Victorian period, with about 1,700 inmates in the 1870s. It was demolished in 1885 and Mount Pleasant Post Office was built on the site (Herber, *Criminal London*).

COLLETT, JACK (*c.* 1659–91) Highwayman who carried out his robberies dressed as a bishop. Once he lost his 'canonical habit' at dice, and was forced to 'take a turn or two on the road to supply his present necessities in unsanctifying garments', says the *Newgate Calendar*. However, he had the good luck to hold up the Bishop of Winchester, Dr Mew, and stole not only his robes but about fifty guineas. He was caught breaking into the vestry at St Bartholomew's in Smithfield with an accomplice and was hanged at Tyburn for 'sacriligious burglary'.

COLQUHOUN, PATRICK (1745–1820) Founder of the THAMES RIVER POLICE. Colquhoun was a remarkable Scotsman who already had several successful careers before he arrived in London. Born in 1745, he emigrated to America and prospered as a trader in Virginia before returning to Scotland. He founded the Glasgow Chamber of Commerce and was known as 'the father of Glasgow'. He established himself as a reforming magistrate in London, setting up soup kitchens for the poor and keeping a record of known receivers. He suggested controversially that there was a connection between levels of poverty and crime. His *Treatise on the Police of the Metropolis* advocated a centrally organised police force. He estimated that 115,000 people in the capital were engaged in some sort of criminal activity. Of these, half were prostitutes or 'lewd and immoral women', a figure which is hard to accept since there were fewer than half a million mature women in the city. Colquhoun's figures are important as the first attempt to give a comprehensive picture of the dimensions of the underworld. His suggestion that something like 12 per cent of the population were criminals shows how pervasive crime was. He died in 1820. *See* NUMBERS OF PROSTITUTES

CONDOMS Protective sheaths were first made commercially in the seventeenth century. They were usually made from sheeps' intestines and were used to avoid infection rather than pregnancy. They were uncomfortable to wear but they caught on in court circles and were hailed by the EARL OF ROCHESTER, a crony of Charles II. In 1667 Rochester published a pamphlet entitled *A Panegyric upon Cundums* prophetically praising their efficacy against both disease and pregnancy. '. . . happy is the man who in his pocket keeps a well-made cundum . . .

nor dreads the Ills of Shankers or Cordes or Buboes dire.' As a contraceptive it prevented 'big Belly and the squalling Brat'. He recommended it 'not only for the chaste Marriage Bed but the Filthiest Stews and Houses of Kept Dames'. The famous brothel-keeper MOTHER WISEBOURNE recalled the importation of a gross of 'right Dutch cundums, newly imported from Holland by Mr Mendez the Jew' for the Duke of York. In 1708 a satire said 'Cundums were sold openly in St James's Park, in the Mall and Spring Gardens'. Earlier Pepys wrote that 'cundums could be bought in King Street almost outside the wall of St James Palace'. Some of these may have been made in London: the noted bawd MOTHER DOUGLAS was said to have protected her clients' interests with 'cundums' bought wholesale from J. Jacobs of Oliver's Alley in the Strand. It is interesting that in the late eighteenth century they were known as 'English overcoats': for much of the twentieth century they were called 'French letters' in Britain. James Boswell bought his condoms from MRS PHILLIPS of Half Moon Street (now Bedford Street in Covent Garden). She also sold dildos. Mrs Phillips had been the mistress of the Earl of Chesterfield when she was only 13, and ran through a legion of lovers before opening her sex shop in 1738. The great Georgian bawd CHARLOTTE HAYES was another of her customers, supplying her clients with the 'famed new *Engines*, Implements for Safety of Gentlemen of Intrigue'. Mrs Phillips sold three different sizes of condom, and had an international clientele, or so she claimed. In 1776 she 'hath lately had several orders for France, Spain, Portugal, Italy and other foreign places'. Her equivalent of the discreet barber-shop 'something for the weekend, Sir' went: 'Captains of ships and gentlemen going abroad' could procure 'any quantity of the best goods on the shortest notice'. Later the shop was run by a woman named Perkins, who may have been Mrs Phillips's niece. She advertised 'all sorts of fine machines called cundums' (Burford, *Wits, Wenchers and Wantons*).

Use of condoms slowly grew more widespread. The Victorian diarist known as 'WALTER' used them after getting gonorrhoea several times, but said he detested them. The London Rubber Company, which was making nearly four million a year in 1939, was then given a virtual government monopoly for the duration of the war and production rose to 120 million. The trade name Durex became the generic term for condoms. *See* JAMES BOSWELL

CONTAGIOUS DISEASES ACTS Legislation passed in 1864, 1866 and 1869 which empowered the authorities to detain prostitutes near barracks and dockyards and examine them to see if they had a venereal disease. Syphilis and other venereal diseases were rampant, especially in the Armed Services, and the authorities panicked. By the 1860s almost one third of soldiers, and about one in eight sailors, were being treated for venereal diseases.

Under the 1869 Act police morals squads were set up with powers to stop and detain women they deemed to be 'common prostitutes'. Such women could then be ordered by a magistrate to have an internal medical examination. If infected they could be detained for up to nine months. If they refused the inspection they could also be confined in a hospital for examination and treatment. After that they were subject to regular fortnightly examinations. The police powers were arbitrary. Any woman they chose to label a prostitute was then registered as such. The Acts provoked furious protest campaigns by feminists and moralists, led among others by JOSEPHINE BUTLER and her Ladies' National Association. They objected to women being regulated in deeply personal matters while there was no action against their clients. The Acts were just another example of men's double standards towards prostitutes. 'It did seem hard,' said one imprisoned woman, 'that the Magistrate of the bench . . . had paid me several shillings a day or two before, to go with him' (quoted in Walkowitz, *Prostitution and Victorian Society*). Moralists objected that the acts seemed to condone prostitution. The Acts were eventually repealed and the campaigners took up other 'purist' causes.

CONY-CATCHING Cheating at cards, or more generally, confidence tricks. The Elizabethan playwright ROBERT GREENE, who produced a series of pamphlets on the subject, applies it specifically to cheating at cards in *A Notable Discovery of Cozanage*. The phrase probably originates in prostitutes' cheating, i.e. 'cunny catching'. *See* SWINDLERS

COOPER, LUCY (?–1772) One of the most celebrated of the Great Impures, as the prostitutes of eighteenth-century London were sometimes known. Lucy was a young fruitseller in Covent Garden market, and Elizabeth Weatherby, proprietor of the disreputable Ben Jonson's Head tavern in Russell Street, took her under her wing. It may have been at Weatherby's that Lucy met the ancient debauchee Sir Orlando Bridgeman, who became infatuated with the burgeoning beauty and her quick tongue. The *Nocturnal Revels* indeed says her repartee 'was the greatest attraction she possessed'. Bridgeman's feelings were not reciprocated, but Lucy allowed him to set her up in a 'voluptuous manner' in an elegant house in Parliament Street with her own 'chariot'. Lucy did not want his company, however, and spent many drunken nights at Weatherby's. Her carriage was seen standing outside for forty-eight hours at a time. 'Dissipation was her motto.' She was generous to a fault with Bridgeman's money, entertaining lavishly friends and lovers. Her appetite for drink and sex earned this tribute from Edward Thompson's *The Meretriciad*:

> Lewder than all the whores in Charles's reign . . .
> At famed Bob Derry's where the harlots throng
> My muse has listened to thy luscious song
> And heard thee swear like worser Drury's Punk . . .
> Cit, soldier, sailor or some bearded Jew
> In triumph, reeling, bore thee to some stew.

Bridgeman died in 1764, and Mrs Weatherby the following year. Without her protectors Lucy grew wilder and more drunken. She began frequenting that last resort of low whores, Bob Derry's Cider Cellar in Maiden Lane. One evening two Jews were murdered there, and Lucy was held partly to blame for the violence. She was sent to prison. This may have been the occasion that led the diarist and man-about-town WILLIAM HICKEY and his friends to have a whip-round for her in 1766. 'Tomkyns . . . had that very day received a letter from Lucy Cooper, who had long been a prisoner for debt in the King's Bench [prison], stating that she was almost naked and starving, without a penny in her pocket to purchase food, raiment or coal to warm herself.' Hickey and his friends sent her £50: '. . . this seasonable aid had probably saved the life of a deserving woman who, in her prosperity, had done a thousand generous actions.' She died in poverty in 1772.

COP KILLERS The first policeman of the new force established by Sir Robert Peel in 1829 to be killed on duty was Constable Grantham. On 29 June 1830 he tackled two drunken Irishmen in Somers Town, north London, and was kicked to death. Even before the establishment of the new force policemen were targets. The highwayman Lewis Avershaw was executed in 1795 for shooting a policeman dead and seriously wounding another while resisting arrest. But in the eighteenth century the severity of the law regarding the killing of peace officers might be softened by influence. In 1770 a watchman was

Frederick Guy Browne, guilty of the bizarre murder of a policeman. He shot the officer, then got out of his car and shot out his eyes.

killed on Westminster Bridge in a drunken brawl. The killers, two brothers named Kennedy, were found guilty and then pardoned. Their sister Polly was a prostitute with powerful lovers in the political elite, and she pulled strings. JOHN WILKES and his followers tried in vain to get the pardon rescinded. The political commentator Junius wrote: 'The mercy of a chaste and pious Prince extended cheerfully to a common murderer, because the murderer is the brother of a common prostitute.' There was no mercy for a group of Irishmen who were set on by the police in 1798. In December of that year a detachment of Bow Street Runners with drawn cutlasses burst into a pub where about 30 Irish men and women were drinking and dancing. There was a fight and the leader of the Runners, Duncan Grant, was killed. Although there was clearly no premeditation three of the Irishmen were found guilty of murder and executed. In May 1833 a peaceful meeting in Coldbath Fields, Clerkenwell, calling for universal male suffrage, reacted to police harassment with a barrage of stones. The police lashed out with their truncheons, knocking women and children to the ground. Police Constable Robert Culley was stabbed in the chest and died. A coroner's jury returned a verdict of justifiable homicide. The jury were cheered, and for many years afterwards an annual banquet was held to commemorate the event. In September 1927 two habitual criminals, Frederick Browne and William Kennedy, were driving a stolen car in a country lane near Billericay in Essex when they were signalled to stop by a PC Gutteridge. Browne shot him once, then got out of the car and shot out his eyes. It was later speculated that he may have known of a theory that the eyes of a murdered man hold a photographic impression of his killer. Browne and Kennedy were executed.

In February 1948 PC Nathaniel Edgar was patrolling in the Southgate area of north London. Just after eight in the evening a woman heard three shots on Wades Hill, and found PC Edgar dying at a garage entrance. Edgar had taken the name of the killer before he was shot, and a hunt began for army deserter Donald Thomas. A photograph of Thomas's mistress was published in the press and a Clapham landlady contacted police to say she thought the woman was living in her top floor flat. Police burst into the flat before Thomas had time to draw the Luger pistol he kept under the pillow. The death penalty was suspended at the time, otherwise he would certainly have hanged. Instead he was jailed for life. *See* HARRY ROBERTS and DEREK BENTLEY

CORNELL, GEORGE Gangster murdered by RONNIE KRAY in the Blind Beggar public house in March 1966. He had called Kray 'a fat poof' but there were other reasons for the murder.

CORNELYS, MADAME (?–1779) Proprietor of a fashionable but disreputable establishment in Carlisle House, Soho Square. She was born in the Tyrol and had once been the mistress of CASANOVA, by whom she had a son. She arrived in London in 1763 and after a failed career as a singer she rented Carlisle House where she held highly fashionable and successful recitals, balls and masquerades. These masked balls were fronts for pick-ups, 'the whole Design of the libidinous Assembly seems to terminate in Assignations and Intrigues'. WILLIAM HICKEY describes in his memoirs a visit to her 'truly magnificent suite of apartments . . . So much did it take that the first people of the kingdom attended it, as did also the whole beauty of the metropolis, from the Duchess of Devonshire down to the little milliner's apprentice from Cranbourn Alley'. Although she maintained a high tone and her performances attracted the *haut ton*, fashionable whores always seemed to escape the vigilance of the doormen. As Horace Walpole said, the house attracted 'both righteous and ungodly'. Even her friends in the royal family and Parliament could not shield her for ever, and in 1771 a Grand Jury indicted her for keeping 'a common disorderly house', where she 'does permit and suffer divers loose, idle and disorderly persons, as well men as women, to be and remain during the whole night, rioting and otherwise misbehaving themselves'. (A common disorderly house was another term for a brothel.) Poor Mrs Cornelys was forced to sell off the contents of Carlisle House. She tried other covert forms of brothel keeping, the last being a 'Purveyor of Asses Milk' in Knightsbridge. In 1772 she was committed to the Fleet Prison for debt, and she died there seven years later.

CORRIGAN, MICHAEL (1881–1946) Masterly confidence trickster who sold the Tower of London and London Bridge. In the 1930s and 1940s he had a long successful run, posing as a major and selling prime London real estate to Americans. Among his greatest coups was the Liverpool Street Station Information Booth Swindle. He approached two wealthy Covent Garden fruiterers, brothers Tony and Nick Mancini, in March 1935 and told them that the station's information booth was to be turned into a fruit shop. The Mancinis paid him £18,000 cash in advance rent. The following morning the Mancinis turned up with carpenters and a large supply of wood, ready to transform the booth into a shop. When the staff refused to leave the Mancinis tried to throw them out and a fight started. The police were called.

The major's luck ran out in 1945 when he was arrested in the bar of the Ritz Hotel. With him was the Director of Public Prosecutions, to whom he was trying to sell a pension. Corrigan hanged himself in Brixton Prison, using his tie – a Guards tie, of course.

CORTESI GANG Italian gangsters who split from and then challenged the SABINIS. The Cortesi brothers – Augustus, George, Paul and Enrico – were known collectively as the Frenchies. Initially they claimed a bigger slice of the racing rackets, and the Sabinis agreed. Then another challenge came from some of the Jewish members of Sabini gang, known as the Yiddishers. Concessions were made to them, too, but soon the Frenchies and the Yiddishers united. In an audacious move the new combination hijacked the Sabini protection money from the bookmakers at Kempton Park in the autumn of 1922. After the inevitable reprisals Harry Boy Sabini was convicted for assaulting George Cortesi, and five other gang members were jailed for attempting to murder another of the Cortesi gang. After the BATTLE OF THE FRATELLANZA CLUB the Cortesis were jailed and their challenge ended.

COSTA DEL CRIME Area of Spain's Costa del Sol which attracted British criminals in the 1980s. The main reason, apart from the weather, was the breakdown in 1978 of the extradition treaty between Spain and Britain. The treaty was renewed in 1985, although it did not apply to criminals already in Spain. *See* RONNIE KNIGHT

COSTERMONGERS Generally law-abiding barrow boys who sold fruit, vegetables, fish etc. Their hatred of the police, who harassed them and moved them on, was proverbial. *See* POLICE

COTTINGTON, JOHN (*c.* 1604–59) Former chimney sweep who turned highwayman and robbed the Republican pay wagon of £4,000 (about £300,000 today). Cottington, alias Mul-Sack, was either very lucky or very able. Born at Cheapside, he became a criminal after inadvertently marrying a hermaphrodite. He was a successful pickpocket, and was believed to have tried to rob Oliver Cromwell. He plundered the pay wagon as it was on its way from London to Oxford to pay Cromwell's troops. Later he stole a staggering £6,000 from the office of the Receiver-General at Reading. The *Newgate Calendar* says: 'One time, having noticed that the Receiver-General at Reading was to send up six thousand pounds to London by an ammunition wagon, he immediately contrived to save that trouble, and bring it up to town himself on his own horse. An accomplice was necessary in this undertaking, and he soon found one, by whose assistance he scaled the receiver's house the night before the money was to be carted. The window they got in at was next to the garden, where they left the ladder standing, and came off at the present very well, having bound all the family, to prevent any alarm whereby they might be discovered.'

These sums alone would have made him the most successful of all highwaymen, but after killing a man named John Bridges, with whose wife he had an affair, he fled abroad and stole silver plate worth a further £1,500 from the exiled court of King James

The enormously successful highwayman John Cottingham greeting one of his victims, Lady Fairfax. He got accomplices to stop her coach and, when she got out, offered to accompany her to nearby Ludgate Church. On the way he stole her valuable gold watch, which hung from a chain.

A riotous night at the Shakespeare's Head tavern in Covent Garden in Hogarth's A Rake's Progress, *Plate 3. A posture moll strips ready for her obscene act. The whores are plundering their customers and drinking and quarrelling. Entering the room with a platter is the famous waiter Leathercoat.*

II. He returned to London, hoping to persuade Cromwell to spare him in return for intelligence about the court. He was hanged at Smithfield for the murder of Bridges.

COVENT GARDEN The area was for a long time the centre of the capital's vice and entertainment industries. In the eighteenth century there were public houses in the area where a kind of striptease was performed by 'posture molls'. They 'stripped naked and mounted upon the table to show their beauties' and also offered flagellation. The ROSE TAVERN was called 'that black school of sodom' by the satirical writer Thomas Brown, who said it was a place where men 'who by proficiency in the Science of Debauchery [are] called *Flogging Cullies* . . .'. At the SHAKESPEARE'S HEAD there was a 'WHORES' CLUB' which met every Sunday, presided over by the 'Pimp-master General' JACK HARRIS, author of the famous *List* of whores. There were also 'Mollie houses' and clubs for homosexuals, among them the Bull and Butcher, the Spiller's Head, the Fountain, the Sun and the Bull's Head. Respectable City businessmen would go there to pick up young homosexuals.

Covent Garden swarmed with criminals of all kinds: pickpockets, footpads – violent robbers – fraudsters, even on occasion highwaymen. Many of the nearby courts and alleys were home to thieves and prostitutes, and the rich pickings also attracted criminals from outside the area. According to *The Tatler*, every house in Covent Garden itself 'from cellar to garret is inhabited by nymphs of different orders so that persons of every rank can be accommodated'.

For men of the town and sex tourists there were guides to the charms on offer. The German visitor

J.W. von Archenholz wrote: 'A tavern-keeper in Drury Lane prints every year an account of the women of the town entitled *Harris's List of Covent Garden Cyprians*. In it the most exact description is given of their names, their lodgings, their faces, their manners, their talents and even their tricks. It must of course happen that there will be sometimes a little degree of partiality in these details; however, notwithstanding this, 8,000 copies are sold annually . . .'.

These women, the most celebrated of whom were known as 'Toasts of the Town' and the 'Great Impures', could be met at MOLL KING's coffee house in front of the church of St Paul, WEATHERBY'S, The Shakespeare's Head and The Rose and innumerable other taverns and brothels. These establishments were riotous and dangerous, but were still considered a cut above such houses as Bob Derry's Cider Cellar in nearby Maiden Lane.

A special place in this world of fashionable vice around Covent Garden was held by the bath-houses, or BAGNIOS, in a sense a revival of the medieval stews. They were very expensive but popular.

The area was also known for the many half-starving cheap young whores who lived in the courts and alleys off Drury Lane. WILLIAM HICKEY, the mid-eighteenth century man-about-town whose memoirs give us much valuable information about the *demi-monde*, describes meeting one such while he was still a schoolboy. The girl, not much older than himself, took him by the arm as he strolled under the Piazza and said: 'You are a fine handsome boy and too young to be walking in such a place as this alone, and I'll take your maidenhead.' She took him to her apartment in a filthy tenement in a narrow Drury Lane court, and there, in a 'dirty, miserable bed', he enjoyed what he called his first 'exhibition under a roof'.

Later in the eighteenth century the luxury brothels of Covent Garden were eclipsed by those of St James's, in particular. The centre of gravity of prostitution gradually moved west, but the area continued to be plagued by prostitutes, both street-walkers and women who sought pick-ups inside the theatres.

COWLAND, JOHN (?–1700) Gent who murdered another gentleman in a quarrel over a Drury Lane Theatre orange girl. This story evokes the untamed spirit of the eighteenth century, the rakish life of apparently respectable men and their sexual opportunism. The victim, Sir Andrew Slanning, had the immense income of £20,000 a year. He picked up the orange girl, a species of prostitute of which Nell Gwyn is the most famous example, in the theatre pit. When the play ended, he left with her and was followed by Cowland and some of his friends. Cowland put his arm around the orange girl's neck and Slanning objected, saying the girl was his wife. Cowland knew he was married to 'a woman of honour' and accused him of lying. They drew their swords but were parted, and all agreed to go to the nearby Rose Tavern in Covent Garden, a favourite with eighteenth-century pleasure-seekers of both sexes, to drink wine. As they were going up the stairs, Cowland drew his sword and stabbed Sir Andrew in the stomach. Cowland tried to escape by jumping down the stairs, but was caught. The *Newgate Calendar* says: 'Mr Cowland being found guilty on the clearest evidence received sentence of death, and, though great efforts were made to obtain a pardon for him, he was executed at Tyburn, on the 20th of December, 1700.'

CREAM, DR THOMAS NEILL (1850–92) The Lambeth Poisoner. In 1891–2 four young London prostitutes were poisoned with strychnine, given to them by a client. During the investigation a Doctor Neill complained to a Scotland Yard detective that he was being followed by police who wanted to interview him about the deaths of two prostitutes, Matilda Clover and Louise Harvey. Clover was dead but Harvey wasn't – unknown to the killer, she had thrown away the poison pills he had given her, and was able to identify him. 'Dr Neill' was arrested and turned out to be Dr Cream, who had served a life sentence in the United States for poisoning his mistress's husband. He had probably killed at least three women before that. Bizarrely, during the police hunt he had written to the police pretending to be a private detective, 'A. O'Brien', and offering to solve the case. 'No fee if not successful.' He sent letters demanding money with threats of exposure as the killer to, among others, the wife of Lord Russell. Cream was hanged at Newgate, the hangman later saying that as the trapdoor opened he had said: 'I am Jack the . . .'.

CREMORNE GARDENS Pleasure gardens which opened on a riverside site in Chelsea in 1830. They were typical of such venues used by families for picnics, fireworks, concerts and so on. At night the atmosphere changed. The *Saturday Review* commented that 'none but an idiot' could fail to notice that at dusk the women there were augmented by 'a large accession of fallen [women] characters'. Cremorne fell victim to Victorian values: it lost its licence in 1871, and closed six years later.

Mother Elizabeth Cresswell, the most successful bawd of the seventeenth century. She ran a string of luxury brothels but died in prison.

CRESSWELL, ELIZABETH (*c.* 1625–84) Bawd, considered the most important of the seventeenth century. By July 1658 she was keeping brothels and 'considered without rival in her wickedness'. In 1660, when Charles II was on the throne, Mother Cresswell was at the head of her profession. She had a gift for advertising, boasting of her 'Beauties of all Complexions, from the cole-black clyng-fast to the golden lock'd insatiate, from the sleepy ey'd Slug to the lewd Fricatrix'. She kept a house among the brothels in Whetstone Park by Lincoln's Inn Fields, although her principal place of business was in Back Alley off Moor Lane in Cripplegate – Moorgate Underground Station stands on the site. According to a contemporary, 'His Majesty Charles II personally honoured her with his presence and deigned to inspect her house . . .'. She had other brothels scattered about the city. She became embroiled in the treacherous politics of the time, her lover Sir Thomas Player being a supporter of the Protestant Duke of Monmouth. The authorities struck at Mrs Cresswell, the *Imperial Protestant Mercury* reporting in November 1681: 'The famous Madam Cresswell was on trial . . . at Westminster, convicted after above thirty years practice of Bawdry . . . some of her Does most unkindly testifying against her.' Mother Cresswell later claimed that 'a malignant jury had dispossessed her of her lovely habitation . . . which I have many years kept in Moorfields to the joy and comfort of the whole Amorous Republic'. She was later sent to the Bridewell prison, where she died. She was remembered for her bawdy cry of 'no money, no cunny'.

CRIME Acts or behaviour which violate the criminal law. This law changes from time to time and acts which are crimes at one time are not at another – *see* PROSTITUTION and PORNOGRAPHY. Country folk who were accustomed to collect firewood and trap animals on common land suddenly found with the spread of enclosures that these were criminal acts. Outworkers who manufactured goods in their own homes using materials supplied by their employers and who regarded scraps of surplus material as 'perks' found a society which weighted the law in favour of the property-owning classes treating them as criminals. More and more embezzlement laws were passed, and inspectors were given powers to enter workers' homes. Widespread practice and acceptance of poaching, smuggling, illicit distilling and even wrecking reflected the perceived unfairness of the law.

CRIME CLUBS Criminals formed self-help associations with rules. The best-known was the WHORES' CLUB which met at the SHAKESPEARE'S HEAD TAVERN in Covent Garden. These clubs were democratic and egalitarian and of course, anti-Establishment. JENNY DIVER, the celebrated pickpocket, belonged to such a club. It had four rules or 'articles': (1) Admittance was by consent. (2) No member was to 'presume to go upon any thing by him or herself'. (3) The 'Cant Tongue' was to be spoken. (4) 'A sufficient allowance' was to be paid to any member who was jailed. There was also a 'Hempen Widows' Club' near Black Boy Alley. Its 'articles of confederation' stated: (1) Members were to be prepared to swear anything 'to save each other from being scragged [hanged]'. (2) They should swear that they were substantial householders in order to get bail for members in trouble. (3) An allowance of 7*s* a week was to be made for members in prison (Linebaugh, *The London Hanged*). Looking after members in prison was one of the most important functions of all these clubs, given the appalling conditions facing those without the means to buy food and comforts.

CRIMINAL CONVERSATION Term describing the behaviour of the seducer or lover of an adulterous wife. Until 1857 the wronged husband could sue for damages. Often shortened in newspaper reports to crim. con.

CRIMPING HOUSES Prisons where sailors seized by the press-gangs were held prior to embarkation. During the GORDON RIOTS they were the target of the mob, and their inmates were released.

CRIPPEN, HAWLEY HARVEY (1862–1910) The first murderer to be caught with the aid of wireless. Doctor Crippen was an American who poisoned his wife Cora and buried her in the cellar of their London home. Her extravagance and obsession with a career as a singer for which she had no talent – she used the stage name Belle Elmore – led to money troubles. She may also have been unfaithful. Crippen, a quiet, unassuming little man who was exhausted by his wife's extrovert personality, found comfort in the company of his firm's bookkeeper and typist, Ethel le Neve. After he murdered his wife, Ethel moved into the family home in Camden Town. Crippen told friends that his wife had died in America, but when Ethel began to wear her jewellery they became suspicious and contacted Scotland Yard. On 8 July 1910 Chief Detective Inspector Walter Dew called on Crippen, who immediately admitted that the story of his wife's death was quite untrue, and that he had made it up to avoid a scandal. In fact, he told the police officer, she had left him for another man. Dew and another officer then searched the Camden Town house, found nothing, accepted Crippen's account and left.

Why Crippen decided to flee is unclear. His coolness and forthrightness had convinced Scotland Yard that he was telling the truth. He planned the escape meticulously. He and Ethel were to travel as father and son on the SS *Montrose*, bound for Quebec. Unluckily for Crippen there was a week's delay at Antwerp. Meanwhile Chief Inspector Dew

Dr Hawley Harvey Crippen and his lover, Ethel le Neve, in the dock. He murdered his wife and fled by ship with Le Neve but they were caught with the aid of wireless. Crippen took Ethel's letters to the grave.

called at the doctor's office to tie up some loose ends. When he was told that the doctor had gone away he had the garden and the cellar of the Camden Town house dug up. In the cellar they found the trunk of a woman, covered in lime. There had not been enough water in the mixture for the lime to do its work. A warrant was issued for the arrest of the fugitive couple, and the newspapers took up the story. Even before they arrived on board the *Montrose* Captain Kendall had seen the story. Crippen had shaved off his moustache and hidden his spectacles, but Ethel, although dressed as a man, inadvertently gave them away. Her ill-fitting trousers were held up by two safety pins, her walk was effeminate, her table manners lady-like. And Crippen seemed to dote on his 'son'. On the second day at sea the captain sent a wireless message to the police. Chief Inspector Dew caught a faster liner from Liverpool, and was waiting when the *Montrose* docked on the other side of the Atlantic. Crippen told him: 'I am not sorry. The anxiety has been too much. It is only fair to say that Miss le Neve knows nothing about it. I never told her anything.'

At the trial the prosecution's case was overwhelming, and the jury took less than half an hour to find Crippen guilty. Ethel, who had been charged with being an accessory after the fact, was acquitted.

Crippen's love for Ethel was touching. Three days before his execution, he made a statement reiterating her innocence. 'This love was not of a debased or degraded character . . . Whatever sin there was – and we broke the law – it was my sin, not hers . . . As I face eternity, I say that Ethel le Neve has loved me as few women love men . . .' He was executed at Pentonville Prison on 23 November. He asked that Ethel's letters and photograph be buried with him, and his wish was granted. She married and lived until 1967.

CROCKFORD, WILLIAM Founder in 1827 of the famous gambling club in St James's. He had been a fishmonger and opened the sumptuous club after winning a fortune gambling. It was said he had won £100,000 in a 24-hour gambling session against a group of dandies, including 'Golden Ball' Hughes and Lords Thanet and Granville. The fishmonger had a priceless advantage over these upper-class dupes – a remarkable gift for calculating odds.

CROSSMAN, GEORGE ALBERT Bigamist who kept the body of one of his 'wives' under the stairs. In 1898 he was jailed at the Old Bailey for bigamy, having been through three marriage ceremonies. He was released in December 1902 and within two months 'married' again. A week later he went to the altar with Mrs Ellen Sampson, a widowed nurse. He murdered her and packed her away in a tin trunk under the stairs at 43 Ladysmith Road, Kensal Rise, where he lived with wife No 4. By the time neighbours began to complain of the smell coming from No 43 he had added two more Mrs Crossmans to his tally, setting them up in separate establishments. When police, alerted by the neighbours, called to investigate the smell Crossman fled. He was pursued through the streets and when officers caught up with him in Hanover Road he cut his throat and died on the pavement.

CUMBERLAND, DUKE OF Survivor of an assassination attempt. The Duke was asleep in St James's Palace on 31 May 1810 when the would-be assassin slashed at his head with a sabre. His thick padded nightcap saved him. In the struggle which followed the duke was wounded in the neck, head, hand and arm. He shouted for his valet and the attacker fled from the room. When the guards and servants were roused it was found that a valet named Joseph Sellis was missing. He was found lying dead in his room with his throat cut. He had obviously killed himself, but rumours began that the duke had killed him. Two authors were jailed for libelling Cumberland. One, Josiah Philips, claimed Cumberland had ordered Sellis killed because he had surprised the Duke in a homosexual act with his other valet, Neale. No clear motive for the assassination attempt was found, but it was suggested that Sellis attacked the Duke because he was jealous of the favour shown to Neale.

CUMMINGS, BOB Coiner and body-snatcher involved in the greatest forgery plot of the mid-Victorian years. Cummings had been an engraver but found easier money in the resurrection trade – stealing corpses from graveyards for sale to medical schools. The Anatomy Act of the 1830s ended that racket, and Cummings became a coiner and counterfeiter. At the time engravers of great skill were forging Bank of England notes, usually with a face value of five or ten pounds, but were hampered by a lack of good quality paper. In the 1860s the underworld managed to corrupt workers at the Laverstoke paper mill at Whitchurch in Hampshire, where paper for Bank of England notes was manufactured. Hundreds of sheets of the watermarked paper, suitable for high-value notes, were stolen before the firm noticed a discrepancy in their stocks. They alerted the Bank and a reward of £1,500 was offered. Soon the police were following a Westminster butcher named George Buncher. He was an important part of the plot, and may even have bankrolled it. Officers were secretly listening in when Buncher visited a couple named Campbell at New Cross and discussed selling them some newly forged notes, for which he wanted £200. Police could have rounded up some of the plotters at this stage, but decided to hold off until they could net the master forger as well. It was Cummings, now an elderly man and known in the underworld for his knowledge of counterfeiting, who had put the gang in touch with the forger, a master engraver from Birmingham named James Griffiths. By 1862 Griffiths was producing high-quality forgeries including £50 notes at his workshop in Birmingham. Police followed Buncher when he visited Birmingham, and in October 1862 they swooped, netting most of the gang.

Buncher was arrested in Westminster and Griffiths in Birmingham. Cummings, who was arrested in a street off the Strand, told the detectives who picked him up: 'You needn't hold me, I've nothing about me but a neddy [cosh].' The police had the evidence they needed. Griffiths had been taken in his workshop surrounded by finished and half-finished notes. The sentences were savage: Griffiths was sentenced to penal servitude for life, Buncher got 25 years and another of the gang got 20. Cummings was freed because there was not enough evidence against him.

CUMMINS, GORDON (1914–42) Murderer known as the 'Blackout Ripper'. On 9 February 1942 the body of schoolteacher Margaret Hamilton was found in an air raid shelter in Marylebone. She had been strangled. The following day a former revue actress named Mrs Evelyn Oatley was found naked in a flat in Wardour Street. Her throat had been cut and her genitals mutilated. The next victim was Mrs Margaret Lowe, found dead three days later in her West End flat. She had been strangled and mutilated. Only hours later another victim, Mrs Doris Jouannet, was discovered in a Paddington hotel. She too had been strangled and mutilated. The killer struck again within hours. He grabbed a woman, pulled her into a doorway near Piccadilly and tried to strangle her. He was disturbed by a passer-by and ran off, leaving behind a gas-mask with his service number on it. Police traced it to Gordon Cummins, a 28-year-old RAF cadet. While they were hunting him he attacked a prostitute in her flat, fleeing when she fought back. He was caught and executed in June 1942.

CUMMINGS, MOTHER Bawd and fence who taught young whores to rob their customers at her brothel in St Giles. A notebook in the British Library giving details of fences in 1816 says:

> It appears to be the common practise of this house that when a girl has got in her prey, the more they are intoxicated the more secure, to ascertain the property they have about them, when the girl watches her opportunity to purloin it, leaves the room immediately upon some frivolous excuse and bolts the door on the outside or locks it . . . thereby confining the man who either missing his property or finding the girl not to return, makes to the door, where he commences a knocking, and a woman who is always on the ready on the outside to unbolt it or unlock it, as soon as she thinks proper and by her conduct and language stalls off the robbery by declaring that they not see the girl go away, and that they know nothing of her, and such property Mrs Cummings universally fences, immediately if she is at home, or the next morning as soon as she comes from her residence.

See FENCES

CURLL, EDMUND (1675–1747) The father of English pornographic publishing. He was twice summoned before the bar of the House of Lords for publishing matter about members, and in 1725 he was convicted for publishing obscene books. Curll had the knack of finding an edifying reason for his editions whenever he was in trouble, which was often. In 1719 he published *A Treatise on the Use of Flogging in Venereal Affairs*. He claimed that far from being sexually titillating it was an awful warning to those who might follow the example of a man who had died while being flogged at a Fleet Street brothel. In 1728 he went on trial at the Court of King's Bench in Westminster Hall for publishing *Venus in the Cloister or The Nun in her Smock*, a translation from the French. On that occasion he was fined, but he was soon in trouble again. He was pilloried for *The . . . Late Proceedings at Paris against the Abbé des Rues for Committing Rape upon 133 Virgins . . .* He escaped the usual pelting and battering in the pillory by having a pamphlet circulated among the crowd saying that the book was really a tribute to the late Queen Anne. Curll's translators were said to lie 'three in a bed' at the Pewter Platter Inn in Holborn, and he was known to enjoy the practices described in his books. He was also a publisher of blameless books, although a wit said that his biographies added a new terror to death (Barker and Carr, *The Black Plaque Guide to London*).

CUTPURSE, MOLL (*c.* 1589–1650) Notorious highwaywoman, thief, bawd, fence and forger, alias Mary Frith, alias Mary Markham. In a life truly extraordinary she seems to have tried almost every form of crime, most of them successfully. The *Newgate Calendar* says that during the Civil War when she was already middle-aged she waylaid the Parliamentary General Fairfax and robbed him after shooting him in the arm. She killed two of his servants' horses and attempted to escape, but was caught at Turnham Green and locked up in Newgate prison. She was sentenced to hang but bribed her way out. This is said to have cost her the colossal sum of £2,000.

Moll was born in Aldersgate Street, the daughter of a shoemaker. She was a tomboy:

> A very torn-rig or rumpscuttle she was, and delighted and sported only in boys' play and pastime, not minding or companying with the girls: many a bang and blow this hoyting procured her, but she was not so to be tamed or taken off from her rude inclinations; she could not endure their sedentary life of sewing or stitching; a sampler was as grievous as a winding sheet; her needle, bodkin and thimble she could not think on quietly, wishing them changed into sword and dagger for a bout at cudgels.

When she grew up she took to wearing men's clothes, smoking a pipe – the first woman to do so in England, says the *Newgate Calendar* – and swearing. She was said to have been so ugly that prostitution was out of the question, although she seems to have been married at some stage. She is the heroine of Middleton and Dekker's *The Roaring Girl*, and she made a great noise in the world. Early in 1612, when she was ordered to do penance at St Paul's Cross for some of her numerous crimes, John Chamberlain wrote in a letter:

> The Last Sunday, Moll Cutpurse, a notorious baggage that used to go in men's apparel, and challenged the field of diverse gallants, was brought to the same place, where she wept bitterly, and seemed very penitent; but it is since doubted she was maudlin drunk, being discovered to have tippled of three-quarters of sack before she came to do her penance.

In another play, Nathaniel Field's *Amends for Ladies*, she is berated by one of the characters:

> Hence lewd impudent
> I know not what to term thee, man or woman,
> For nature shaming to acknowledge thee
> For either, hath produced thee to the world
> Without a sex; some say thou art a woman
> Others a man, and many thou art both
> Woman and man, but I think rather neither
> Of man and horse, as the old centaurs were feigned.

It is likely that she appeared on the stage, many years before it was legal for a woman to do so. The *Consistory of London Correction Book* for 1605 records that Mary Frith admitted appearing at the Fortune theatre singing bawdy songs and playing the lute, wearing men's clothes. She was burned in the hand four times, and held in most of London's jails. She was also a very successful receiver of stolen goods, and ran a school at her house in Fleet Street teaching youngsters to steal. As a receiver she exercised some control over the underworld, as the following passage from *The Roaring Girl* suggests. Moll, addressing a cutpurse, says, 'Heart, there's a knight to whom I'm bound for many favours lost his purse at the last new play i' the Swan, seven angels in't, make it good, you're best; do you see? No more.' That admonition has the chilling ring of an underworld ultimatum.

She is reported as saying: 'When viewing the manners and customs of the age, I see myself as wholly distempered, and so estranged from them, as if I had been born and bred in the Antipodes.' She had a good head for business, and her receiving racket was operated on similar lines to that of JONATHAN WILD: for a fee, she would organise the return of stolen goods to their owners. At the time of her death she was prosperous enough to employ three maids. She requested that she be buried upright, but upside down. Over her grave at St Bride's was an impressive marble monument, destroyed in the Great Fire, and engraved with what the *Newgate Calendar* describes as a fine epitaph by Milton. It doesn't read like Milton.

D

DADD, RICHARD (1819–87) Artist, lunatic and murderer. In 1843 Dadd, who was 24 and considered a rising young artist, murdered his father. He spent the rest of his life in asylums for the insane, painting obsessively detailed and crowded fairy fantasies.

DAGOE, HANNAH Burglar who attacked her executioner. Dagoe, a basketwoman at Covent Garden, broke into the home of an acquaintance and stripped it in 1763. She was sentenced to death at the Old Bailey. *The Complete Newgate Calendar* says: 'She was a strong masculine woman, the terror of her fellow prisoners, and actually stabbed one of the men who had given evidence against her.' When the cart taking her to her execution reached Tyburn she struck the executioner violently, dared him to hang her and flung some of her clothes to the crowd so that he would not get them. After the executioner had with difficulty placed the rope around her neck she tied a handkerchief around her face and flung herself from the cart with such violence that she broke her neck and died instantly.

DALY, JOSEPHINE Genial brothel-keeper reckoned by the *Sunday Times* Rich List to be worth more than £7 million. In July 2000 this pensioner of 64 was charged with running a vast north London vice operation based in saunas and massage parlours. Asked to explain where she got the £100,000 in cash found at her home, Daly said she had saved the money from her pension. She also had a white Rolls-Royce, a house in Crouch End worth £1 million and a property empire worth further millions. Women at her parlours had been selling more than massages, but Daly explained that it was difficult to keep an eye on all her business interests. She said she would try to see it didn't happen again. To encourage her she was ordered to forfeit £2 million. Daly, an Irishwoman, had been in the business for more than thirty years and had made many influential friends, including senior police officers. One of her former girls said: 'She never made us feel like shit, and we all knew what we were getting ourselves into. I won't hear a word against her. Josie's the tops.' Wensley Clarkson says in *Gangsters* that there are fears that gangsters will now take over Daly's saunas and massage parlours.

DANDO, JILL BBC television presenter murdered by a stalker. Dando was killed with a single shot on the doorstep of her Fulham home in April 1999. In July 2001 her killer, Barry George, got a mandatory life sentence after Mr Justice Gage told him: 'You have deprived Miss Dando's fiancé, family and friends of a much-loved and popular personality.' George, 41, was convicted on evidence which centred on sightings of him hanging around the area where Dando lived on the morning of the killing. Forensic evidence included a speck of residue from the discharge of the gun used to kill Dando, which was found on his coat, and a fibre that matched his trousers found at the scene. He was a convicted sex offender obsessed by guns, celebrities and the BBC. The jury was not told that George followed or photographed women around Fulham.

DARKY THE COON Jewish gangster, real name ISAAC BOGARD, whose gang clashed with ARTHUR HARDING.

DASHWOOD, SIR FRANCIS (1708–81) Chancellor of the Exchequer, drunk, rake, religious pervert and founder of a hell-fire club whose obscene cavortings became notorious. There had been other hell-fire clubs at the beginning of the eighteenth century, but their depravity caused a national scandal and they were supressed in 1721. Depravity interested Dashwood more than any other aspect of the libertine lifestyle, and in 1750 he set out to revive the hell-fire traditions by hiring the partly ruined Medmenham Abbey near his West Wycombe estate. His own tortured religious impulses amounted almost to mania, and he staged blasphemous and obscene parodies of sacred rituals. The members, many of whom belonged to White's Club, called themselves the Order of Saint Francis. Visitors and members included lords Bute, Sandwich and Melcomb. John Wilkes was an enthusiastic participant. William Douglas, fabulously wealthy and later to be the fourth Duke of Queensberry, long thought to be the wickedest man of the eighteenth century, attended, but was probably too fastidious to perform in public.

They hired the abbey, furnished the cells comfortably, installed a pornographic library including the *Kama Sutra* and a 'prayer book' which instead of prayers listed 365 sexual positions, and set about recruiting upper-class ladies for their sexual orgies. These women wore masks as they surveyed the scene in the candlelight. Only when they were satisfied that no member of their family was unexpectedly present would they reveal their identities. The monks then chose their partners. The sex was public, and the members, mostly middle-aged, overweight and drunk, shouted encouragement to each other, sometimes in Latin or Greek. A tally was kept.

There were said to be doctors and midwives to deal with pregnancies, and children of such brief couplings were called 'the sons and daughters of St Francis'. If the supply of aristocratic nuns showed signs of drying up, or the monks wanted variety, those other 'nuns', the whores of the St James's and Covent Garden brothels, were called upon.

Lesbianism was encouraged, and watched by the whole company. It was said that incest was contrived because sometimes before an orgy all the participants were blindfolded, and a monk might unwittingly make love to his sister, or even his mother. The sight of a naked young girl lying on an altar surrounded by flickering candles rekindled the sex drive of many a jaded habitué of the London brothels, especially if they drank the holy wine from her navel.

One of the bawds who 'brought her Nymphs to participate in the outrageous Orgies' was CHARLOTTE HAYES. Foremost among these nymphs was the lovely Fanny Murray. Among the upper-class women 'nuns' were said to be Frances, Viscountess Fane, Lady Betty Germain and Dashwood's half-sister, Mary Walcott. The intrepid but middle-aged Lady Mary Wortley Montague has been mentioned as a devotee. Some of the most important politicos of the time were involved, although how deeply is not known. Lord Bute was soon to be Prime Minister. LORD SANDWICH, known as Jemmy Twitcher, a sadistic rapist obsessed with defloration, was First Lord of the Admiralty at a time when sea power was vital to Britain's interests. Thomas Potter, son of the Archbishop of Canterbury, was Paymaster-General and Treasurer for Ireland. He was rumoured to be a necrophiliac. JOHN WILKES, defender of democracy, was a fearless critic of the status quo who became Lord Mayor of London. The Chevalier D'Eon, who appeared at different times as a man and a woman, and whose sex was a source of constant speculation among the monks, did not join in the public orgies for obvious reasons. When he died he was found to be a man. This is how HORACE WALPOLE described the order:

> He [Dashwood] and some chosen friends had hired the ruins of Medmenham Abbey, near Marlow, and refitted it in conventual style. Thither at stated seasons they adjourned: had each their cell, a proper habit, a monastic name, and a refectory in common – besides a chapel, the decoration of which may well be supposed to have contained the quintessence of their mysteries, since it was impenetrable to any but the initiated. Whatever their doctrines were, their practice was rigorously pagan: Bacchus and Venus were the deities to whom they almost publicly sacrificed.

The spurious religiosity of the orgies owed much to Dashwood's tortured inner life. When a young man he had 'fornicated his way across Europe' on the Grand Tour, making his way to Rome, where he was deeply affected by the rites of the Roman Catholic church. It was said that at one moment he would be jeering at the trappings of relics and vestments, the next he would be on his knees sobbing. On one occasion he produced a whip in the Sistine Chapel and beat those kneeling in prayer. In the rites at Medmenham he took the role of Christ.

DAVEY, RON Successful pornographer nicknamed Ron the Dustman. Davey had indeed been a dustman with Hammersmith Council. He got into the pornography trade in the 1950s by selling photographs of women members of a nudist club he belonged to. He later recalled that pictures of women wrestling were particularly popular. Davey produced his own wares on primitive printing machines, yet despite the poor quality could not keep up with demand.

DAVIDSON, REVD HAROLD FRANCIS (1875–1937) Parson who saved 1,000 fallen women and was eaten by a lion named Freddy. He caught the habit of saving women when he persuaded a suicidal 16-year-old not to jump into the Thames. In 1905 he got the living at the Norfolk village of Stiffkey but spent most of his time in London saving the fallen. 'I like to catch them between 14 and 20. I believe with all my soul that if Christ were born again in London in the present day He would constantly be found walking in Piccadilly.' He haunted the teashops of Oxford Street, where he thought the pretty waitresses were particularly in danger. He was banned from the shops, and protested to one manageress: 'But what if my bishop invites me here?' She replied: 'The bishop will be served, but you will not.' When he was 45 Davidson met 20-year-old Rose Ellis, a prostitute. Over the next ten years as he fought for her soul there were suggestions that she was his mistress. In 1930 he met a 16-year-old prostitute named Barbara

Harris at Marble Arch. He asked her: 'Has anyone ever told you that you look like the film actress Mary Brian?' He looked after her, and forgave her when she disappeared with a series of lovers, always returning to 'Uncle Harold' when the affairs ended. Some in the village of Stiffkey disapproved of the fact that the rector usually arrived for Sunday services after the congregation had gone home, and objected to the young ladies who stayed at the rectory. The Bishop of Norwich hired private detectives, and Rose Ellis was interviewed. Barbara Harris wrote to the Bishop accusing Davidson of rape and breach of promise. Davidson was called before a consistory court accused of adultery with Rose Ellis and making improper suggestions to waitresses at a Lyons Corner House. He was also charged with 'habitually associating with women of a loose character for immoral purposes'. A photograph of Davidson with a naked 15-year-old created a sensation. He said he had been set up but the girl, Estelle Douglas, said Davidson had told her that he could further her career as a bathing-suit model. He was found guilty and stripped of holy orders.

Before he joined the church Davidson had been an actor, and he now became something of a public performer. He exhibited himself in a barrel on the promenade at Blackpool, attracting crowds so large that he was prosecuted for causing an obstruction. In 1937 at Skegness he began performing with Freddy the lion. He would get into Freddy's cage to denounce the hierarchy of the Church of England. Freddy, normally so docile that he was looked after by an 8-year-old girl, mauled him to death.

His travails had made Davidson famous even before he became a performer. Charabancs would arrive in Stiffkey from all over the country full of admirers who cheered his spirited self-justifications. By and large his parishioners took a tolerant view of his shortcomings.

DAVIES, JOHN Teddy Boy killer who was sentenced to death but reprieved. Davies, 21, was one of a gang of TEDDY BOYS who exchanged insults with apprentice John Beckley and his friend Matthew Chandler on Clapham Common in July 1953. The gang attacked the two friends and someone shouted 'Get the knives out'. Beckley and Chandler jumped on a bus but were dragged off and attacked again. Chandler managed to jump back on the bus, with stab wounds in the groin and stomach. Beckley cried 'Go on then, stab me' and fell dying. Police arrested six youths, four of whom were acquitted of murder but imprisoned for common assault. The jury were unable to agree on a verdict on Davies and another youth. Only Davies was retried, on 19 October 1953. He was alleged to have said to another youth about his knife, 'There is no claret on it.' He was also said to have demonstrated at a coffee bar how he had used the knife, and there were bloodstains in his pocket. He was sentenced to death and appeals to the Court of Criminal Appeal and the House of Lords were dismissed. Twelve days before his execution he was reprieved. *See* RIOTS

DAWSON, NANCY (*c*. 1720–67) Successful actress-whore who had a song written abut her. Nancy was born in Covent Garden to a porter/pimp father and greengrocer mother. Orphaned at an early age, she was put on the stage at Sadler's Wells and was something of a child prodigy, dancing and playing musical instruments. In 1759 she found overnight fame dancing in JOHN GAY's *The Beggar's Opera*. Two years later this vulgar, saucy and greedy little mercenary was celebrated in *The Ballad of Nancy Dawson*, sung to the tune of *Here We Go Round the Mulberry Bush*, once a children's favourite:

> Of all the girls in town
> The black, the fair, the red, the Brown
> That dance and prance it up and down
> There's none like Nancy Dawson.

DEFOE, DANIEL (1660–1731) The author of *Robinson Crusoe* and *Moll Flanders* got into trouble over a pamphlet. In 1703 he was charged with sedition over his satire *The Shortest Way With the Dissenters*. It suggested nonconformists should be massacred. The intention was ironical, as he was himself a dissenter, but the irony was missed and the pamphlet was greeted with wild enthusiasm, one bishop saying he valued it above all works except the Bible. When it was discovered to be a satire Defoe was charged with suggesting the Establishment was insane. He was fined, jailed and pilloried at Cheapside, Cornhill and Temple Bar. The sympathetic mob are said to have pelted him with flowers. To get out of prison Defoe promised the Whigs he would set up a network of pro-government secret agents, who would be unknown to each other, across the country. He went on to establish a successful prototype of the intelligence services. He interviewed and wrote biographies of the criminals JACK SHEPPARD and JONATHAN WILD. He condemned the GIN MANIA, writing in 1728: 'Our common people get so drunk on a Sunday that they cannot work of a day or two following. Nay, since the use of Geneva [gin] has become so common many get so drunk they cannot work at all, but run from one irregularity to another, till at last they become arrant rogues.' His *Moll Flanders* is an unflinchingly realistic tale of a London whore.

D'EON, CHEVALIER (?–1810) Soldier and transvestite. He fled to England from France dressed as a woman after a libel scandal. He became popular in society and passed himself off as a woman, living with another woman for fifteen years, apparently without arousing her suspicions. His sex was nevertheless a constant matter of speculation, and it was said that £20,000 had been wagered on the Stock Exchange on his true nature. He was an interested spectator at the orgies of the Order of St Francis at Medmenham, but was too discreet to perform in public.

The Chevalier D'Eon, whose sexual identity was a source of eighteenth-century gossip. The chevalier attended the orgies of Sir Francis Dashwood's Hellfire Club, but stayed discreetly clothed. After death he was found to be a man.

DEPTFORD FIRE Fourteen young black people died during a house party in 1982. An investigation lasting four and a half years ended without reaching a conclusion, and an inquest returned open verdicts. There were suggestions that the fire was started by racists. In May 2001, after a forensic scientist taking part in a new investigation concluded that the cause was arson, officers from Scotland Yard told the victims' families that they would back calls for a new inquest.

DE QUINCEY, THOMAS (1785–1859) Writer and drug addict. His autobiographical *Confessions of an English Opium Eater* was an early warning about addiction. He also wrote the celebrated essay *Murder considered as one of the Fine Arts*, in which is this splendid example of his wit: 'If once a man indulge himself in murder, very soon he comes to think very little of robbing; and from robbing he next comes to drinking and Sabbath-breaking, and from that to incivility and procrastination.'

DERRICK, SAM Derrick is an interesting example of a penurious eighteenth-century hack. He was probably the author of the *Memoirs of the Bedford Coffee-House*, anonymously published as by 'a Genius'. He coached the actress/whore Jane Lessingham for her first appearance at Covent Garden, which was a triumph, and she repaid him by leaving him for the theatre's proprietor Thomas Harris. She became a successful comedy actress but refused to help Derrick. He was employed by the publisher H. Ranger to edit the famous *Covent Garden List* of whores after JACK HARRIS died, and was then surprisingly appointed to succeed Beau Nash as Master of Ceremonies at Bath. After this sudden rise in status he called on Jane, but her servant said she 'knew no one of that name'. When Derrick forced his way in Jane threatened to call out the Watch. Faithless Jane continued to break men's hearts and purses. She took up with Henry Addington, later Lord Chief Justice and Earl of Sidmouth. She died in 1801.

DESPARD, COLONEL EDWARD (1753–1803) Soldier executed for allegedly plotting to assassinate the king and seize the Tower, the Bank and the Houses of Parliament. He was serving in the army in Honduras when locals accused him of misdemeanours. He returned to England but it was not until two years later that he was told there was no case to answer. By then his career as a soldier was ruined, and he had a sense of grievance. He mixed in radical circles, and intelligence reports of his activities were passed to the government.

Consequently when the Irish rebellion of 1798 broke out he was held in Coldbath Fields prison. After his release in 1800 he and nearly forty soldiers and workmen were arrested at the Oakley Arms in Lambeth when spies reported a plot to murder George III and overthrow the government. Despard was tried for treason, although the Attorney General admitted the story he was putting forward was improbable. Despard's defence counsel called the alleged plot 'a ridiculous scheme'.

> Fourteen or fifteen persons assemble together at a common taproom with no firearms than tobacco pipes, form a conspiracy to overturn a government supported by the unshaken loyalty of many millions . . . by what arms? Not a pike, gun, sword, pistol . . . Yet with these forty or fifty men of buckram, the Tower was to be taken, the Bank was to be seized, the India-house was to be overturned, the king was to be seized in the midst of his guards as he was going to the House of Lords, and the two Houses of Parliament taken most complete possession of.

Among the character witnesses for Despard was Admiral Nelson, who testified that 'no man could have shown more zealous attachment to his sovereign and his country than Despard did'. Perhaps this persuaded the jury to recommend mercy, but the recommendation was ignored and Despard and six others were executed, although they were spared the drawing and quartering usually prescribed for traitors.

Despard died with calm dignity. When he saw the hurdle on which he was to be dragged to the gallows – another part of the execution ritual for traitors – he 'smilingly cried out: "Ha! ha! What nonsensical mummery is this?"' (*Newgate Calendar*). After hanging for half an hour the men's bodies were taken down, their heads cut off and each displayed to the crowd with the words, 'This is the head of a traitor'.

DE VEIL, SIR THOMAS (1783–1846) Notorious corrupt magistrate, predecessor of the FIELDINGS at Bow Street. Among other things he was loathed for his zeal in enforcing the Gin Act. He was just one of the venal 'trading justices' who would accept bribes to drop a charge. Often these bribes would be the favours of a pretty street girl. Nevertheless he brought a new efficiency to law enforcement. De Veil turned part of his house in Bow Street into a kind of court, where cases were heard openly and the public were encouraged to take part as witnesses or observers.

DEVEREUX, ROBERT, 2ND EARL OF ESSEX (1566–1601) Dazzling courtier and favourite of Queen Elizabeth I, executed in 1601. During a quarrel he turned his back on the Queen, and she boxed his ears. She called him 'a rash and temerarious youth', and his subsequent actions proved her right. After being stripped of his dignities he was confined to Essex House in the Strand for a long series of political indiscretions. He broke out with 200 men and rode through the city, hoping to raise support. None came, and he was arrested and tried in Westminster Hall. His friend FRANCIS BACON gave evidence against him, but at least Bacon had warned him of the risks he was running. Essex was executed on Tower Green rather than Tower Hill, the last of many favours the Queen granted him. He died with great dignity.

DEVEUREUX, ARTHUR (?–1905) Chemist's assistant who murdered his wife and twin sons. Deveureux, 24, was living in poverty in Kilburn and wanted a better life for his oldest son, Stanley. He killed his wife and the twins by poisoning them with morphine, put them in a tin trunk and left it at a furniture depository. He moved home and found 6-year-old Stanley a place at a private school. His mother-in-law traced the trunk and had it opened. Deveureux claimed his wife had murdered the twins and committed suicide. 'Imagine my terrible position. My wife had poisoned the twins with morphine belonging to me . . . I was a chemist's assistant, and in a position to get poison . . .' Deveureux was hanged at Pentonville in August 1905.

DIAMOND GEEZERS Term applied to older members of the criminal underworld of whom one approves. Those for whom one has a grudging respect are hard bastards. *See* FRANKIE FRASER

DIMES, ALBERT (1906–72) Anglo-Italian gangster and racecourse thug responsible for the downfall of JACK SPOT. Dimes, originally allied to BILLY HILL, grew up in Little Italy. In May 1941 he was charged with the murder of Harry 'Little Hubby' Distleman, the doorman of the West End Bridge and Billiards Club in Wardour Street, who had been stabbed to death. Another man was hanged for the murder, Dimes being convicted of unlawful wounding. When Jack Spot fell out with Hill and the Italian bookmakers he decided to make an example of Dimes. In August 1955 Spot attacked Dimes at the corner of Frith Street, punching him on the chin. Dimes ran into the Continental Fruit Store on the

Gangster Albert Dimes and his wife. He and Jack Spot wounded each other seriously in a Soho knife fight. He became a kind of Godfather.

corner of Frith Street and Old Compton Street. Spot followed and picked up a small potato knife and stabbed him in the thigh and stomach. The wife of the proprietor, Mrs Sophie Hyams, a friend of Dimes, then hit Spot over the head with a set of scales. This enabled Dimes to grab the knife, and he stabbed Spot, who staggered to a nearby barber's and collapsed.

Spot later told a jury that Dimes had warned him to stay away from race-tracks. He said he had paid £300 for his pitches on the tracks, keeping one for himself and renting the others out. Dimes had told him: 'This is your final warning. I don't want you to go racing any more.' He added that Spot had been making money from the pitches long enough and it was time for someone else to have a go. Spot came off badly in the fight. He had been slashed and stabbed about the head and left arm, and had two wounds in his chest, one of which penetrated a lung. Dimes had been slashed across the forehead and the stomach wound had, a court was told later, 'mercifully just failed to penetrate the abdominal cavity'.

Both men were arrested. Spot said: 'It's between me and Albert Dimes – between us and nothing to do with you.' Dimes was at first more forthcoming. 'You know as well as I do. It was Jackie Spot.' But asked for a formal statement he became vague. 'It was 'a tall man . . . I don't know his name.' At subsequent trials both men were acquitted. Spot's influence had been waning, and the fight and trial marked its end. The crusading journalist DUNCAN WEBB hailed the downfall of Spot, the man he called a 'tinpot dictator'. He wrote that 'the mob' had finally discovered 'what I had known for years – that Spot is a poseur who got away with it by boasting'.

Dimes went into business with FRANKIE FRASER and EDDIE RICHARDSON, supplying fruit machines to night clubs. Just how influential Dimes was is not clear, although some commentators regarded him as a kind of godfather. He met the American *mafioso* Angelo Bruno when he arrived in Britain in 1966 on a trip organised by a New York gambling club, and later visited him in America to discuss installing gaming machines in clubs. Another major crime figure on the gambling trip was Meyer Lansky, one of the founding fathers of American organised crime. Dimes was certainly the arbiter in disputes between rival gangs. When he died of cancer in 1972 the actor Stanley Baker, who got to know him when Dimes gave technical advice on Joseph Losey's 1960 film *The Criminal*, attended the funeral. The Krays sent a wreath with the message, 'To a fine gentleman'. It was destroyed because it was feared it would bring shame on Dimes's family.

DIVER, JENNY (?–1710) Pickpocket of almost legendary skill, heroine of both GAY's and Brecht's *Beggar's Opera*. An Irishwoman, her real name was Mary Young. She was taught how to pick pockets by her countrywoman Anne Murphy in a 'kind of club' near ST GILES. This was a school for pickpockets. The *Newgate Calendar* says:

> She now regularly applied two hours every day in qualifying herself for an expert thief, by attending to the instruction of experienced practitioners; and, in a short time, she was

distinguished as the most ingenious and successful adventurer of the whole gang.

One of the crimes that established her reputation was stealing a ring from a gentleman outside a church in Old Jewry in London as people queued to listen to a popular preacher. Jenny spotted the ring, and held out her hand, which the gentleman took to assist her up the steps. Later he noticed that his ring was missing, but Jenny had slipped away.

She had been taught to read and write and do needlework by her parents, and what was called her 'superior address' was an asset in her new career. She had a costume which made her look pregnant, and she designed false arms and hands which folded across her bulging belly. Sitting in church, looking demure, she could plunder the people on either side by slipping her hands out unseen under her dress. One Sunday evening she seated herself between two elderly ladies in the church in Old Jewry and stole both their gold watches, which she passed to an accomplice. 'The devotions being ended, the congregation was preparing to depart, when the ladies discovered their loss, and a violent clamour ensued. One of the injured parties exclaimed, "That her watch must have been taken either by the devil or the pregnant woman!" on which the other said, "She could vindicate the pregnant lady, whose hands she was sure had not been removed from her lap during the whole time of her being in the pew."' Afterwards Jenny went to a nearby public house, changed her clothes, returned to the church for a later sermon and stole a gentleman's gold watch.

With an accomplice posing as a footman, she robbed the gentry in church, at 'Change Alley, in the theatres, at fairs and tea-gardens. She fleeced a rich young Yorkshireman who fell for her when he saw her at the theatre: Jenny took him to an inn, and as they were about to get into bed Anne Murphy, in the guise of her lady's maid, knocked on the door and said that Jenny's husband had suddenly returned from the country. Jenny told the young man to hide under the bedclothes, then she and her accomplices took his clothes, gold-hilted sword and the rest of his belongings. Her share of the spoils amounted to seventy pounds. Another of her 'lays' involved dressing up expensively and knocking at the door of a great house with an accomplice dressed as a footman. Jenny would pretend to have been taken suddenly ill, and while the people of the house tended to her the accomplice would quickly ransack the house. Jenny would eventually feel better, give the lady of the house her card and invite her to tea. She and her accomplice would leave by coach before the raid had been detected.

She was arrested and transported to Virginia, but got an admirer to pay her passage back to England. She was caught again, transported again, returned again. Inevitably, despite her sleight of hand, wit and charm she was hanged in 1710. As befitted a famous felon, she was allowed to drive to Tyburn in a private coach with her own clergyman at her side, a privilege denied to the great JONATHAN WILD. She died repentant.

DIXON GANG Allies of the KRAYS, although Ronnie Kray in a mad mood shoved a gun into George Dixon's mouth and pulled the trigger. The gun failed to fire and Ronnie later gave Dixon the faulty bullet. 'It's just saved your life,' he told him. 'Wear it on your watch chain as a souvenir.' After the Kray gang was broken up police targeted the Dixons. The police officer in charge of the case, Bert Wickstead, explained that he went after the brothers, George and Alan, 'for the simple reason that they were marching around the East End, boasting that they had taken the place of the Krays'. In July 1972 after a long trial the Dixons and Phillip 'Little Caesar' Jacobs, a successful pub owner, were jailed for assault, extortion and conspiracy. George Dixon and Jacobs each got twelve years, and Alan Dixon nine. After his release George Dixon went into the motor trade and Alan into entertainment.

DODD, DR WILLIAM (1729–77) Clergyman executed for forgery. The case of Dr Dodd was a cause célèbre which involved Samuel Johnson and still intrigues today. Dodd, who had been tutor to the fifth Earl of Chesterfield, was a popular preacher and almost a celebrity. He was also the founder and supporter of several important charities, including the Magdalen, which rescued fallen women. His expensive lifestyle got him into debt – he tried to bribe the Lord Chancellor with £3,000 to obtain a lucrative post – and when he was pressed to pay tradesmen's bills he forged a bond for £4,200 in the name of the earl. He was arrested and from his cell in Newgate appealed indirectly through a noblewoman to Samuel Johnson for help. Johnson wrote a letter in Dodd's name for the prisoner to send to King George III. It was a moving appeal for mercy, in which he said he hoped 'that public security may be established without the spectacle of a clergyman dragged through the streets, to a death of infamy, amid the derision of the profligate and profane; and that justice may be satisfied with irrevocable exile, perpetual disgrace and hopeless penury'. Johnson also wrote to the government making the same point, and a petition calling for mercy was signed by 23,000 and presented to the king. All in vain. The rising god of commerce and the fact that Dodd had put his hand in the purse of a nobleman counted for more than the public clamour. On 27 June 1777 he was driven to Tyburn in his own carriage – an unusual mark of distinction – preceded by a hearse with his coffin. Perhaps the biggest crowd ever to witness an execution, an estimated 100,000, saw him hang.

Johnson, who had no great regard for Dodd, acted for him because he objected to the fact that there was no other punishment than death in such cases, and the whole affair started an agitation, eventually successful, to change the law. Only the king could have saved Dodd, and he was advised against mercy. The PERREAU twins had been executed at Tyburn less than two years before, and the King was reported as saying that if Dodd were pardoned he should have to regard himself as their moral murderer. Lord Mansfield, the LORD CHIEF JUSTICE, was also determined that Dodd should die.

DOG AND DUCK Tavern in St George's Fields, Lambeth, much used by highwaymen. Here aspiring young criminals would go to watch the highwaymen mount up and say goodbye to their 'flashy women'

Sign of the notorious Dog and Duck tavern in St George's Fields, Lambeth, a haunt of highwaymen and other criminals and their 'flashy women'. It dated back at least to 1642. In the eighteenth century it was several times refused a licence, and in 1811 the buildings were demolished.

Girls say goodbye to their soldier boyfriends in Hogarth's The March to Finchley. *The house on the right is Jane Douglas's brothel. She is the pious bawd leaning out of a lower window with her hands clasped in prayer for the safe return of her customers. The cats on the roof indicate a brothel.*

before setting off to rob travellers. It was a favourite resort of whores and their ponces. 'Some of the most beautiful middle-class women of the town, their bullies and suchlike young men, who came there, with no thoughts for the consequences, refresh the thirsty throats of their girls with fiery drinks' (Malcolm, *Anecdotes of the Manners and Customs of London during the Eighteenth Century*). David Garrick in his *Prologue to the Maid of the Oaks* described the riotous goings-on:

> St George's Fields, with taste and fashion struck,
> Display Arcadia at the Dog and Duck;
> And Drury Misses here in tawdry pride,
> Are there 'Pastoras' by the fountain side;
> To frowsy bowers they reel through midnight damps,
> With fauns half drunk and Dryads breaking lamps.

The tavern dated back at least to 1642. It was several times refused a licence in the eighteenth century, and in 1811 the buildings were demolished.

DONAGHUE, ALBERT Thug and stalwart of the KRAY regime. His initiation was violent: Ronnie Kray shot him in the leg and then gave him £15 and a place on his Firm because he hadn't complained. He became a collector of protection money and a bodyguard. He was instrumental in helping FRANK MITCHELL escape from Dartmoor, and later gave evidence against FREDDIE FOREMAN and ALFIE GERRARD for Mitchell's murder.

DOUGLAS, JANE Noted London brothel-keeper, born in Scotland in about 1698 and celebrated by the playwright JOHN GAY as 'that inimitable courtesan'. The *Nocturnal Revels* says that Mother Douglas attracted princes and peers, 'and she fleeced them in proportion to their dignity'. The book says that high-class demi-reps also frequented Mother Douglas's, and mentions the actress Peg Woffington as having 'often sacrificed at the altar of Venus in this chapel . . .' At her brothel uniformed footmen presented the clients with condoms tied with ribbons. Mother Douglas is the buxom woman praying for the safe return of the soldiers at the window of the brothel in Hogarth's print *The March to Finchley*. Hogarth drew her again for his print *Enthusiasm Delineated* of 1761, by which time drink had destroyed her once-elegant figure. The playwright Charles Johnstone described her shortly before her death in that year: 'Her Face presents the remains of a most pleasing sweetness and beauty . . . her body bloated by drink and debauch.' Horace Walpole's correspondent, the diplomat Sir Charles Hanbury-Williams, was less kind: 'A great flabby fat stinking swearing hollowing ranting Billingsgate Bawd . . .'. After her death Mother Douglas's many aristocratic clients could enjoy poignant reminders of the joys of being fleeced by her when her 'fine Old Masters, rich Furniture and costly properties' were sold by auction.

DRAGSMEN Thieves who specialised in stealing luggage from cabs. They would lurk around the large railway stations and the roads leading from them. When they spotted heavily laden cabs they would follow in a light cart and slash the ropes and straps holding the luggage, which would fall into the road and be spirited away.

DRESS LODGERS Brothel keepers were notoriously mean towards their whore-lodgers, but they had justified fears of the girls 'chousing', or absconding without paying their debts. This was particularly so in the case of dress lodgers, girls who were lent fashionable clothes to wear as they sought customers. In return the girls had to take the customers back to their rooms, and pay most or all of their takings to the brothel owner, which meant they could never save enough to buy their own smart clothes. Dress lodgers were naturally tempted to disappear with the clothes, or to take their customers to another house without their landlady knowing.

The brothel keepers sometimes sent servants to keep an eye on the dress lodgers. MAYHEW's colleague Hemyng came across a whore named Lizzie in the Strand who was regularly followed by an old woman in a dirty cotton dress. After being plied with gin this old woman agreed to tell him her story.

She had been a prostitute and was now a servant in a brothel. One of her duties was to watch Lizzie as she sought customers. Lizzie was not a top-rate whore, her dress was too garish for that. She usually attracted men who worked in shops, commercial travellers and impecunious medical students. Occasionally she picked up a clergyman from nearby Exeter Hall. Some nights the two of them tramped the streets in vain. Nevertheless she had good times, and that particular night, the old woman said, Lizzie had three clients in as many hours and had earned forty-five shillings 'for herself'. Seamstresses at the time might be paid as little as three shillings a week.

DREWE, JOHN Art fraudster who flooded the market with fakes. In 1987 he contacted John Myatt, a hard-up artist who advertised in *Private Eye* magazine offering 'genuine fakes' for £150 each. Drewe ordered a work in the style of Marc Chagall. Soon Myatt was pouring out works in the styles of Braque, Klee, Giacometti and others. One 'Giacometti' sold at auction for more than £100,000 but Drewe kept most of the money for himself. To make the fakes more convincing – they were usually painted with ordinary house paints – he carefully concocted provenances for them. This was his major innovation to the technique of selling fraudulent works of art. He became a reader at the Tate Gallery by the simple expedient of donating £20,000 to the gallery's funds. This gave him access to their archives. He inserted photographs and histories of the fake paintings in the archives, thus persuading dealers and connoisseurs who might have been doubtful about a painting's authenticity. He did the same thing at the Victoria and Albert Museum. Dealers were the big losers. One American firm which paid more than £100,000 for a Giacometti became suspicious and hired a specialist firm to check its authenticity. The firm was owned by Drewe, who charged £1,140 for a guarantee that the picture was genuine. By the time Drewe was caught he had made a million. He was jailed for six years and Myatt for a year.

DRIBERG, TOM (1905–76) Labour MP and promiscuous homosexual. For years Driberg got away with behaviour which was illegal. Although his homosexuality was common knowledge he became Chairman of the Labour Party and was ennobled as Lord Bradwell in 1975. In 1942 he entered the Commons after winning a by-election, and was welcomed to Parliament by another well-known homosexual, Sir Henry 'Chips' Channon. In his autobiography Driberg wrote: '. . . Chips kindly showed me round the most important rooms – the Members' lavatories. This was an act of pure, disinterested, sisterly friendship, for we had no physical attraction for each other.' Driberg was invited to some of RONNIE KRAY's homosexual parties. His biographer, Francis Wheen, says that at these parties 'rough but compliant East End lads were served like so many canapés'. LORD BOOTHBY was another guest.

DRUGS *see* following page

DRUITT, MONTAGUE (1840–88) Barrister and sexual pervert suspected of being JACK THE RIPPER. After he drowned himself in the Thames in 1888 the killings stopped, and Sir Melville Macnaghten, assistant commissioner at Scotland Yard, regarded as an expert on the case, said: 'From private information I have discovered that his family thought he was the Ripper, and it was certainly known that he was sexually insane.' Druitt had studied medicine, and the nature of the injuries to the Ripper's victims led many to think the killer was a medical man.

DUBERY, SARAH (?–after 1814) Bawd with a particularly upper-crust clientele. Dubery, who took over CHARLOTTE HAYES's brothel in King's Place, St James's, had foreign ambassadors among her clients and well-known actresses and divas among her beauties. One of these part-time whores was Isabella Wilkinson, a famous rope dancer who performed at Sadler's Wells and Covent Garden. She was the mistress of the Swedish Ambassador, Count Gustav von Nollekens. One night Mrs Dubery promised to introduce the count to a 'new nun'. The count was furious to find that the 'nun' was his Isabella, 'whom he supposed was waiting for him at home as chaste as Penelope . . .' The count's *amour-propre* was restored when Mrs Dubery found him a replacement for the faithless Isabella. Mrs Dubery retired in 1814, 'after a reign of thirty-six years' successful trading'.

Isabella was fond of drink and put on weight, which may account for her eventually breaking her leg. While she convalesced, says the *Nocturnal Revels*, she 'rusticated' at the coffee-houses and bagnios in Covent Garden, where her pick-ups included members of the diplomatic corps, a line of clients she seems to have specialised in. The *Revels* says: ''Tis true her bulk is rather a hindrance to her agility which may in some measure excuse her not being able to get off the ground . . . she still continues to tipple to excess.'

DUDLEY, CAPTAIN RICHARD Incorrigible highwayman, executed in 1708. Dudley, who was educated at St Paul's, was said as a boy to have had 'a natural vicious disposition which baffled all restraint'. When he was 9 he stole some money and ran away from home. Later he ran away again and was found in a brothel with 'two lewd women'. His father enlisted him in the Navy, where he distinguished himself and became an officer. Back on land he joined a gang of thieves and was arrested and sentenced to death. His long-suffering father got him a royal pardon and bought him a commission in the Army. Dudley married a woman whose family paid him £140 a year, but he abandoned her and with his younger brother Will joined a band of robbers. Once again he was caught and once again his father saved him, getting a court to substitute a sentence of transportation for a death sentence. However Dudley and Will, who was transported with him, escaped when their ship stopped at the Isle of Wight. Dudley set off alone and robbed a farmer of his horse and clothes. Later he met a gentleman who was better dressed and mounted, and took his clothes and horse. He gave the man the farmer's horse and clothes, and told him: 'Never say that I robbed you, since according to the proverb exchange is no robbery'. He was reunited with Will and his old gang. For a while they were successful but a reward was offered and they were betrayed by one of their own gang. They were executed and their bodies were conveyed in coffins to their father. At the sight of them he collapsed and died, and was buried in the same grave.

DUELL, WILLIAM Murderer who survived hanging. Duell, who was only 16, raped, robbed and killed a woman named Sarah Griffin. He was hanged at Tyburn in November 1740 and his body taken to Surgeons' Hall to be dissected. While he was being washed it was noticed he was breathing, and he was soon able to sit up. That evening he was taken back to Newgate Prison. He was later transported.

DUELLING This reinforcement of the aristocratic code of honour was a capital offence, but almost never treated as such by juries. If the rules had been obeyed the killer was usually acquitted, or at worst found guilty of manslaughter. Even the rare exceptions did not usually end in executions. In mid-eighteenth century there was the case of Captain Clarke RN who killed another officer, Captain Innis. Clarke used screw-barrel pistols seven inches long, which gave him a distinct advantage over Innis, who used ordinary pocket pistols. The prosecution persuaded the jury that this 'demonstrated an excessive determination on Clarke's part to kill his opponent' (McLynn, *Crime and Punishment in*

Continued on p. 83

DRUGS

In the nineteenth century drugs such as laudanum and opium were freely available, freely enough for the writer DE QUINCEY to experience and describe the torments of addiction in *Confessions of an English Opium Eater*. Conan Doyle could have his hero Sherlock Holmes injecting drugs three times a day without stirring up moral outrage. In 1868 a magazine told of drug-taking in a Chinese 'opium den' in Bluegate Fields, an alley in Shadwell, and two years later Dickens made such a den the centrepiece of his account of the East End in the unfinished *The Mystery of Edwin Drood*. In 1870 Gustave Doré made an engraving of the same opium den for *London: A Pilgrimage*.

Drug-taking became a matter of widespread social concern after the death of a young actress named Billie Carleton in November 1918. Carleton had attended the Victory Ball at the Albert Hall, and the following morning her maid found her dead in bed from cocaine. Although the drug had been given to her by a boyfriend the supplier was a Chinese. There were calls in Parliament for the deportation of all Chinese and attention soon focused on a man known as 'the BRILLIANT CHANG'. He was Chinese and a close friend of Billie Carleton. In March 1922 Freda Kempton, a young dancing teacher, was found dead from a cocaine overdose. Chang had been with her the night before. He told the coroner at her inquest: 'She was a friend of mine but I know nothing about the cocaine. It is all a mystery to me.' He was later deported.

Addicts smoking opium in a drug den in Bluegate Fields. Doré's engraving probably shows the opium den visited by Dickens, and mentioned by him in his unfinished Edwin Drood.

The Chinese drug dealer Brilliant Chang, supplier to the Bright Young Things in the Twenties. After one of his customers died he was deported.

Superintendent Robert Fabian, 'Fabian of the Yard', told in *London after Dark* how in his first week on the beat in Soho an older officer pointed out a man called EDDIE MANNING and warned him to beware of him. 'He's the worst man in London.' Manning was a drug dealer who held what Fabian called 'dope parties' and charged addicts 10*s* (50p) a time for cocaine injections.

The authorities did not yet see drugs as a serious treat. The Drugs Squad had only one car, and as late as 1961 Sir Ronald Howe, head of Scotland Yard's CID branch, wrote: 'In this country drug trafficking presents a very small problem. Englishmen don't take drugs, they prefer Scotch whisky.'

The Sixties 'pop and pot' culture at last made police aware of the widespread use of drugs. The career of HOWARD MARKS as a kind of celebrity dealer in cannabis made the trade seem almost glamorous. The mood had changed by the time the first 'crack factory' in Britain was discovered in Peckham, south London, in August 1988. Crack, a smokable form of cocaine, was already notorious in America for causing almost instant addiction, and drug squad officers had been anxiously anticipating its arrival here. It was known that the drug gave an intense 'high' that lasted only about fifteen minutes, leaving the addict with a craving for more. Crack was introduced to Britain by Yardies, Jamaican gangsters with a deserved reputation for violence.

As the new century loomed the tempo of the Yardie wars became frenetic. From the beginning of 1999 to August 2000 there were twenty-nine drug-related murders in what are called 'black-on-black' attacks in London. In the first seven months of 2000 there were another twenty-three non-fatal shootings, many of them failed murder attempts. On the evening of Monday, 31 July 2000 people queuing outside the Chicago nightclub in Peckham, south-east London, were sprayed with automatic fire by two men standing across the street. Eight people were hit, among them a girl aged 15. Police believe the gunmen had spotted a rival drugs dealer among innocent bystanders and opened fire.

It was this level of terrifying violence that spurred the police to augment its Operation Trident investigation of what is termed black-on-black crime with the formation of a 160-strong squad of detectives. Officers in the squad say they have been able to intercept Yardie killers who are sent to this country 'every two or three months' to carry out killings, often for as little as £500 or £2,000. They have also discovered links between crack dealers in London and others in Liverpool, Manchester, Bristol, Birmingham, Nottingham and Aberdeen.

Eighteenth-Century England) and Clarke was sentenced to death for murder. The King was told that before he died Innis had forgiven Clarke, so he granted a pardon.

Perhaps the most dishonourable duel was that between Lord Mohun and the Duke of Hamilton in 1712. Mohun was a scoundrel who had twice been acquitted of murder. His second, General MacCartney, had been convicted of raping his housekeeper. Having run Mohun through the Duke dropped his sword and tried to help the wounded man. Mohun stabbed him, and they both died.

There was an epidemic of duelling in the eighteenth century. Four prime ministers, Shelburne, Canning, Wellington and Pitt, fought duels. PEEL arranged to fight the Irish nationalist Daniel O'Connell in Ostend but could not find him. JOHN WILKES fought several duels, once being wounded by a man who had been practising his marksmanship assiduously.

If there was any honour in duelling it was shown by Charles James Fox, who was challenged by William Adam over a political insult. Fox refused to fire first, telling Adam, 'Sir, I have no quarrel with you, do you fire.' Adam fired, followed by Fox, who still refused to apologise. Adam fired again and missed, and Fox fired in the air. Only then did he mention that he had been slightly wounded by the first shot.

Humphrey Howarth MP stripped naked in preparation for a duel with Lord Barrymore in 1806. This was to stop particles of clothing infecting any wound, but Lord Barrymore felt it was below his dignity to fight a naked man. Equally absurd duels did go ahead, and some were fatal. Lord Falkland died because while in drink he said to a Mr Powell, who was also drunk, 'What, drunk again tonight, Pogey?' In 1818 a man died not because he had quarrelled with his opponent but because their friends had fallen out. Captain Macnamara killed Colonel Montgomery in 1803 for insulting his dog (Gilmour, *Riot, Risings and Revolution*).

DUGDALE, WILLIAM (1800–68) Indefatigable Victorian pornographer, jailed nine times. His premises in Holywell Street – the centre of London's porn trade until it was demolished to make way for the Aldwych – was the scene of battles with the police and members of the Vice Society. In September 1851 a force of constables led by Inspector Lewis accompanied by men from the Vice Society descended on Holywell Street. They were spotted by Dugdale's look-out, who warned his employer. Those inside the shop locked and bolted the doors, and people in houses and shops nearby emerged and menaced the police and the Society men, whom they regarded as 'miscreants in white chokers, who croak for the safety of Christian England'. The reinforced doors withstood the attack, and after ten minutes Dugdale opened up and said: 'All right Lewis, you can come in now'. Many of the incriminating prints had been burnt while the siege went on but the police took away a large quantity of books, prints, catalogues and plates. Dugdale was jailed for two years.

In another prosecution an agent of the Vice Society gave some idea of their methods:

> I went to the shop two or three times before the day when the sale took place, and bought several innocent publications. On the day in question the prisoner showed me a French print in the window, which I had asked to see. I asked him if he had anything more curious, and he at length invited me to go into the back shop. He then showed me several indecent prints. I asked him the price, and selected two which I produce.

Dugdale had been a radical, and years before had been implicated in the CATO STREET CONSPIRACY. He shared the widespread loathing of the Vice Society, and when he was in the dock in another pornography prosecution he drew a knife and attacked one of its members.

DUVAL, CLAUDE (1643–70) The very epitome of the gallant highwayman. A Frenchman, he accompanied the returning Cavaliers at the restoration of Charles II. As a footman, he had been taught how to ride and shoot to protect his master's coach, and when he was short of money he 'took to the road'. Once his victims were a man and his beautiful young wife. Duval asked for permission to dance with the wife, then helped her out of the coach and danced a minuet with her by the roadside. After he was hanged at Tyburn in 1670 at the age of 27 his torch-lit funeral was attended by hundreds of weeping women. His epitaph at St Paul's Covent Garden read:

> Here lies Du Vall, Reader, if male thou art,
> Look to thy purse, if female, to thy heart.
> Much Havock he has made of both; for all
> Men he made stand, and women he made fall.
> The second Conqueror of the Norman race
> Knights to his Arms did yield, and ladies to
> his face.
> Old Tyburn's Glory, England's illustrious thief,
> Du Vall, the ladies' Joy, Du Vall the ladies'
> Grief.

DWYER'S BETTING SHOP Renowned establishment in St Martin's Lane which welshed. Dwyer's was a well-established business which had a reputation for fairness and punctual settlement and attracted punters big and small. The Chester Cup was then the major handicap race for betting, and when the favourite won in 1851 Dwyer's was in trouble, having accepted a large amount of bets on the winner. Overnight the staff stripped the shop and in the morning punters found an empty shell: they were owed £25,000.

EASTCASTLE STREET RAID The first big robbery in London after the Second World War, organised by the gangster BILLY HILL. He was getting ready to retire, and the £287,000 haul was part of his pension plan. In his memoirs *Boss of Britain's Underworld* Hill wrote that the night before the mail van raid in May 1952 the nine men involved were taken to a flat in the West End and locked in before the briefing on the operation began. Hill's men had been following the van for months and its route was known. Hours before the raid one of the robbers disconnected the van's alarm while the staff were on a tea-break. When the van set out from Paddington Station the robbers followed in stolen cars. In Eastcastle Street near Oxford Street the robbers used their cars to block the road, attacked the crew and stole the van.

They had been expecting to find only between £40,000 and £50,000 and there wasn't enough room in the fruiterer's lorry they had brought to hide all the mailbags. Hill told them to leave thirteen mailbags behind in the mail van. The lorry was driven to Spitalfields market. After keeping it under observation for twenty-four hours to make sure the police had not found it the gang drove it to Dagenham marshes and unloaded it. Although he never admitted being involved, Hill said in his memoirs:

> Walk along Old Compton Street or down Wardour Street, or over the heath at Newmarket on any racing day, or along the promenade at Brighton any week, and ask anyone who thinks they know. Ask them who planned the Big Mailbag Job. The one when £287,000 in freely negotiable currency notes, in hard cash, was nicked, in May 1952, and they'll all tell you, 'We don't know who did it, but we've got a good idea. In any case, we know that Billy Hill planned it. Only he could have done that.'

The mailbag robbery brought unprecedented pressure from the police. Questions were asked in the House of Commons and Sir Winston Churchill himself weighed in, saying the robbers must be caught. Hill wrote: 'All my friends were turned over. My spielers were raided and closed down. Friends of mine going abroad on holidays were turned over by the Customs people. One of my lads even had his car taken to pieces, yet he did not have a criminal conviction. All my telephones were tapped for years afterwards. My mail going through the post was steamed open and read.' There were rumours in the underworld that the police stole some of the abandoned mailbags. Men who had been on the raid claimed they left more mailbags in the van than the police said they found.

EDWARD VII (1841–1910) Monarch with a powerful sex drive. When he was 19 and on army manoeuvres his fellow officers smuggled an actress into his tent. This became known to his parents, Queen Victoria and Prince Albert. When Albert died a few weeks later the Queen believed that grief over Edward's behaviour had shortened his life. Three years later Edward married Princess Alexandra of Denmark. At his coronation there was a special enclosure for his mistresses. It was called the 'Loose Box' and contained the actresses Lillie Langtry and Hortense Schneider, various society beauties and Lady Brooke, the future Duchess of Warwick. When he was nearly 60 he took as mistress the greedy 29-year-old Alice Keppel. She was the great-grandmother of Prince Charles's mistress Camilla Parker-Bowles.

EDWARDS, EDGAR Killer who remarked 'I've been looking forward to this a lot' as he walked to the gallows. On 1 December 1902 Edwards killed grocer John Darby, his wife and daughter in their shop in Wyndham Road, Camberwell. He boarded up the shop and put up a notice saying the business had closed. In the following days he removed the contents of the shop and took them to his home in Church Road, Leyton. Some weeks later he attacked another grocer, who was able to give a description of Edwards. Police found the bodies of his victims buried in his garden. When the judge put on the black cap Edwards, who had tried unsuccessfully to persuade the jury he was mad, said: 'This is quite like being on the stage.' He was executed in March 1906.

EGAN, PIERCE (1772–1849) Successful Regency sporting writer. His *Tom and Jerry* follows the perambulations of two men-about-town. It describes whores besieging the saloon at Covent Garden theatre. Like all his works this book, famous and much admired and plagiarised for many years, is full of facetiousness and slang. He describes how the whores – he uses the euphemism Cyprians –

A scene from Pierce Egan's enormously popular Tom and Jerry. *It's a picaresque journey around the high and low life pleasure haunts of London. Here he captures the easy discourse of Regency men-about-town with customers in an East End tavern.*

surrounded men who visited the saloon unaccompanied by women:

> Tom and Coz had scarcely reached the place for refreshments, when the *buz* began, and they were surrounded by numbers of the gay *Cyprians*, who nightly visit the place . . . The 'Fair MARIA', dressed in a blue riding habit, seated on a chair in the corner, near the recess; and the 'pretty ELLEN', standing behind her, are throwing out 'lures', in order to attract the notice of the Corinthian and Jerry. The 'Old Guy' on the top of the stairs, with his spectacles on . . . is gently tapping, in an amorous way, the white soft arm of 'lusty *black-eyed* JANE': and inviting her to partake of a glass of wine, to which she consents in a most '*business*'-like manner. Indeed, 'Black-eyed Jane' has often publicly remarked, that it is immaterial to her whether it is a DUKE or his *Groom*, so that she receives her compliment. Several Jewesses may also be recognised promenading up and down the Saloon. In the motley group are several Coves of Cases [brothel keepers] and procuresses, keeping a most vigilant eye that none of their 'decked-out girls' [whores who had been provided with their finery by a brothel] brush off with the property entrusted to them for the night; and other persons of the same occupation may be seen closely WATCHING the females belonging to their establishments, that they are not idle, as to the purposes for which those unfortunate girls are sent into the SALOON . . .

ELEPHANT AND CASTLE GANG Important and long-lived south London group. It is said that a fight between one of its leaders, Monkey Benneyworth, and DARBY SABINI led to the latter's rise to prominence in 1920, although the Sabinis were already important racecourse gangsters. It was the centre of resistance to the Sabinis, particularly in alliance with BILLY KIMBER. Brian McDonald in his *Elephant Boys* recalls a clash in 1936 when 'a gang of Italians and Jews raided the Elephant Boys' at the Wellington pub in the Waterloo Road. The Sabinis were by this time led by Darby's brother Harryboy. McDonald's book is a source of much forgotten lore about the Elephant gang and the south London underworld characters of the inter-war and immediate post-war years. His uncle Wag seems to have been leader of the Elephant gang for a while. McDonald doubts whether Benneyworth was ever overall leader of the gang.

ELLENBOROUGH, BARON EDWARD Reactionary Lord Chief Justice. During his tenure, from 1802 to 1818, he opposed moves for the abolition of capital punishment for shoplifting. He also opposed the abolition of the pillory. His death is said to have been hastened by the defiance of a jury which refused his instruction to return a guilty verdict.

ELLIS, JOHN Hangman who committed suicide. Ellis, born in 1874, hanged SIR ROGER CASEMENT, EDITH THOMPSON, DR CRIPPEN and about 200 others. In 1932 he was successful in his second suicide attempt, using a cut-throat razor. He also worked as a barber.

ELLIS, RUTH (1926–55) The last woman to be hanged for murder. Ellis, a night-club manageress, had a tempestuous affair with racing driver David Blakely. At the beginning of April 1955 when she was 28 she had a miscarriage after Blakely allegedly repeatedly struck her in the abdomen. Days later she tried to see Blakely, who was trying to give her the brush-off, at a house in Hampstead where he was staying with friends. She banged on the door and the police were called. On the evening of 10 April she returned, and heard the noise of a party within. Blakely came out and went to a nearby pub with a friend. As he came out again Ellis opened fire with a handgun, firing six shots. Two hit Blakely in the back, one in the thigh and one in the left arm. Another hit a bystander in the hand. Blakely died at the scene. Ellis was taken to Hampstead Police Station and said: 'I am guilty. I am rather confused.' When she was sentenced to death at the Old Bailey she murmured 'Thanks'. Her cause was not helped by her barrister, Melford Stevenson, who decided not to make a closing speech on her behalf. Despite a public outcry she was hanged at Holloway Prison. This sensational crime of passion and its controversial outcome hastened the repeal of the death penalty.

EMPIRE THEATRE Haunt of prostitutes in Leicester Square and target of campaigners for morals. In 1894 one of the latter, a housewife named Laura Ormiston Chant, succeeded in having the theatre shut down briefly. She told a meeting of Middlesex County Council, the licensing authority, that even though she was dressed in her prettiest frock she was accosted by men behind the theatre's circle. She also claimed that a Frenchman had been offended by the words in a comedy sketch, 'I want to see your underwear'. Two Americans had a fit of the vapours over the vulgar songs of Albert Chevalier. Mrs Chant won – the council voted by a majority of 43 not to renew the licence. Opinion was divided. The *Methodist Times* said it was defeat for 'lust and lying', the *Sporting Times* called Mrs Chant 'a nasty-minded busybody'. A theatrical newspaper described her and her backers as 'lachrymose nobodies and childless spinsters . . . merely moody fanatics whose greasy minds see evil in everything'. A stockbroker who had a seat on the council and supported Mrs Chant was thrown into the street by his fellows on the Stock Exchange. The wonder cricketer W.G. Grace formed a league to keep the moralists off the council. Within a week the theatre opened again, and Winston Churchill was one of the enthusiastic patrons. He wrote to his brother: 'Did you see the papers about the riot at the Empire last Saturday? It was I who led the rioters and made a speech to the crowd. My cry was "Ladies of the Empire! I stand for liberty!"'

ESSAY ON WOMAN John Wilkes was incorrectly accused of writing the *Essay*, which was held to be an obscene poem. It was probably written by his fellow debauchee and MEDMENHAM CLUB member Thomas Potter, with notes by Wilkes. It is partly a parody of Pope's *Essay on Man*, and partly an attempt to ridicule one of Wilkes's enemies, Bishop William Warburton. There is a copy in the British Library. Pope's essay begins:

> Awake, my St John! leave all meaner things
> To low ambition and the pride of kings.

The opening lines of the parody are:

> Awake, my Fanny, leave all meaner things:
> This morn shall prove what rapture swiving
>   brings!
> Let us (since life can little more supply
> Than just a few good fucks, and then we die)
> Expatiate free o'er that loved scene of man,
> A mighty maze, for mighty pricks to scan . . .

The Fanny of the opening line is the courtesan FANNY MURRAY, LORD SANDWICH's mistress at the time.

EVANS BROTHERS, THE Highwaymen who released victims of a press-gang. Evan Evans trained as an attorney but became a highwayman with his younger brother Will. Their usual beat covered Mile End and Bow to the Strand. They came across the press-gang on the Portsmouth Road in Surrey, thirty men bound together and guarded by constables. The brothers ambushed the column, tied up and robbed the constables and freed the prisoners. They were caught and hanged together in 1708. *See* HIGHWAYMEN

EVIL MAY DAY Hostility towards prosperous merchants and craftsmen from Europe who had settled in London erupted on 1 May 1517. A mob which included many apprentices was addressed by a rabble-rousing preacher, Dr Beal, at St Paul's Cross. They were led by John Lincoln, a 'disillusioned broker', and their attacks on foreigners' houses and workshops caused such alarm that shots were fired from the Tower and the earls of Surrey and Suffolk led a force of troops to restore order. They took 400 prisoners and Lincoln and other leaders were hanged, drawn and quartered.

King Henry VIII heard the pleas for mercy of the remaining prisoners at Westminster Hall. Queen Catherine went on her knees before Henry to plead successfully for mercy for the female prisoners. Henry was reluctant to spare the remainder, but Thomas Wolsey, the Lord Chancellor, wept and offered personal guarantees for their future good conduct. Henry agreed and the prisoners 'took the halters from their necks and danced and sang'. *See* RIOTS

Cardinal Wolsey was a relentless scourge of whores, yet he kept some at Hampton Court Palace for the use of guests. He persuaded Henry VIII to free Evil May Day rioters.

EXECUTION DOCK Place where pirates were dispatched. Their bodies were supposed to be left hanging at the dock, between Wapping New Stairs and King Henry's Stairs, 'till three tides had overflowed them', according to the historian John Stow. Among those hanged there was CAPTAIN WILLIAM KIDD. The rope broke during his execution in 1701, but he was put back on the scaffold and hanged again.

EXECUTIONS London was the execution capital of Europe, referred to by an eighteenth-century traveller as 'the city of the gallows'. Hanging was not the only form of execution: aristocrats were usually beheaded, and traitors were hanged, drawn and quartered. The victims were first hanged, cut down while still alive and disembowelled. They were then decapitated and quartered, and their body parts were displayed on city landmarks, such as Temple Bar and London Bridge. Heretics were burned at the stake, poisoners occasionally BOILED ALIVE in oil. Deserters, mutineers and spies were sometimes shot.

Gradually these punishments were phased out or modified, and hanging became the preferred method. The Jacobite Lord Lovat, executed in 1747, was the last man to be beheaded with an axe in England. Death by decapitation ended after 1800. The last beheadings were those of the Cato Street conspirators, whose heads were removed with a surgeon's knife after they had been hanged in 1820. The number of capital crimes rose sharply in the eighteenth century. Juries regarded many of the crimes as trivial and were reluctant to convict. In cases of theft, where the death penalty could be imposed for stealing more than a shilling, they often undervalued the goods involved. And conviction did not necessarily lead to execution. Between 1749 and

Traitors' heads on old London Bridge. This was a familiar sight on prominent buildings throughout London. The heads would be picked clean by birds, then the grinning skulls left as a warning.

1758 about 365 people were hanged in London and Middlesex, about 70 per cent of those condemned. In 1808, before the number of capital offences was drastically cut back, there were 804 convictions for capital offences but only 126 executions (Herber, *Criminal London*).

Convicted felons were sometimes hanged near the scene of their crimes. The London historian John Stow vouched for the accuracy of his account of a sixteenth century execution in Aldgate Ward by pointing out that the gallows were erected on the pavement outside his house. Portable gallows were used at Leadenhall, Newgate and Aldgate to hang thirteen apprentice boys after the Evil May Day riots. The first permanent gallows was set up at Tyburn near Marble Arch in 1571. Other places of execution were Kennington Common in the south, Smithfield and, later, Newgate Prison. Pirates were hanged at Execution Dock in Wapping, and traitors were beheaded at Tower Hill. There were gibbets on the marshes on both sides of the river. With the number of capital offences rising from about fifty in the seventeenth century to more than two hundred by 1819 the city sometimes seemed festooned with corpses, and whether this acted as a terrible warning or inured the inhabitants to the sight is a moot point. Eight times a year London's muffled church bells were rung to signify a public holiday for a 'hanging match'. Commenting on the eager expectation with which these were greeted, a visitor observed: 'You would, perhaps, think that they look upon these executions as so many public shows due to the people, and that a stock of thieves must be kept and improved to that end.' Hangings were public spectacles. James Boswell confessed that he never missed a public execution. Many condemned men felt obliged to put on a show of courage. The mob entered into the spirit of things, shouting encouragement to the doomed felons and chanting anti-government slogans. A seventeenth-century ballad said: 'His heart's not big that fears a little rope.' Isaac Atkinson, an Oxford-educated murderer who stabbed the chaplain accompanying him to the gallows, cried out to the audience: 'There's nothing like a merry life and a short one.' In 1717 a condemned man, addressing the crowd waiting to see him executed, said: 'Men, women and children, I come hither to hang like a pendulum to a watch, for endeavouring to be rich too soon.' Hanging days were known as Sheriff's Balls or Hanging Fairs. Hawkers sold food and drink, taverns took drinks out to customers in the streets and ballad sellers peddled cheap copies of the condemned man's last words, real or imaginary. Pickpockets moved through the excited crowds, practising their art. Many in the crowd would be drunk, and the hangman himself was not always sober. One was with difficulty dissuaded from hanging the clergyman who was trying to comfort the condemned.

Many of those who were to die were heroes to the mob. Women wept and threw flowers when the burglar and escaper JACK SHEPPARD went to his execution. JONATHAN WILD, the murderous gangster, was bombarded with stones and dead animals all the way, as was the vicious child killer ELIZABETH BROWNRIGG. Some men died in all their finery. EARL FERRERS wore his wedding suit and rode to his execution in his own landau, a rare privilege. Jack Rann, known as 'sixteen-string Jack' because of the silk strings attached to the knees of his breeches, wore a pea-green suit with a huge nosegay in his buttonhole. Stephen Gardiner wore only a shroud: this could have been a sign of repentance, or more likely it was an attempt to deny the hangman his perquisite of the condemned man's clothes. HANNAH DAGOE fought with the hangman who tried to stop her throwing her clothes to the crowd. At one time the condemned man would climb a ladder with the rope around his neck and jump off. If he lingered on the ladder too long the executioner would 'turn him off'. Later the prisoners stood on a cart beneath the scaffold, often with a clergyman who exhorted them to repent. Some prisoners, including Jack Sheppard, read out a confession. After a decent interval for prayers the hangman put the noose round their necks and the cart moved away. The drop was not usually great enough to break their necks and they were left dangling, dying of slow strangulation. Their friends would rush forward and either try to put them out of their agony by pulling on their legs or attempt to save them by supporting their weight. Because death was slow some men were cut down and saved, such as HALF-HANGED SMITH. Sometimes there were battles between the surgeons' messengers, who tried to take the bodies away for dissection, and the families of the condemned. Another source of conflict was the popular belief that the body or clothes of the deceased, or even the rope used to hang him, had curative properties. In 1797 there was a fracas over the body of the rapist John Briant, during which his head, arms and legs were pulled off. The novelist Samuel Richardson saw a fight over the bodies of the hanged:

> As soon as the poor creatures were half-dead, I was much surprised, before such a number of peace officers, to see the populace fall to haling and pulling the carcasses with so much earnestness, as to occasion several warm rencounters, and broken heads. These, I was told, were the friends of the person executed, or such as, for the sake of tumult, chose to appear so, and some persons sent by private surgeons to obtain the bodies for dissection. The contests between these were fierce and bloody, and frightful to look at.

An important change in the manner of execution was the introduction of the 'drop' at Tyburn in 1759. Instead of being left to die of slow asphyxiation the condemned were killed fairly quickly by dropping through a trapdoor. Earl Ferrers is believed to have been the first man executed by the new method. When the gallows was erected at Tyburn the area was rural. As it became built up the neighbours complained about the riotous behaviour of the spectators. Moralists also objected to the scandalous behaviour of the vast crowds, and it was said that the deterrent effect of public hanging was being eroded. After 1783 the executions were carried out at Newgate and other prisons. The last beheading on Tower Hill was that of the Jacobite LORD LOVAT in 1747. Moving the executions to public spaces outside prisons did little to curb the drunken and obscene behaviour of the vast crowds which still came to watch. When HENRY FAUNTLEROY was hanged for forgery in 1824 the crowd numbered 80,000. The Victorian middle classes were scandalised and pressure forced Parliament to end the public spectacles altogether in 1868, after which executions took place inside prison walls, with only a few officials present. The Victorians drastically reduced the number of capital offences prescribed in the BLOODY CODE. By 1861 there were only four left – murder, treason, piracy with violence and arson in naval dockyards. In 1908 the minimum age for execution was raised from 16 to 18. In 1965 the death penalty was abolished for all crimes other than treason and piracy with violence.

FAHMY, MARGUERITE Wealthy wife acquitted of murder in a sensational trial at the Old Bailey in 1923. She had married an Egyptian playboy, Prince Ali Kamel Fahmy Bey, and soon discovered that he was a cruel and violent homosexual. During a quarrel in their suite at the Savoy Hotel in London she shot him three times. When the night manager went to the room after hearing the shots she told him: 'Oh sir, I have been married six months. They have been torture to me. I have suffered horribly.'

Marguerite was a wealthy widow named Madame Laurent when she met the prince, who at 22 was ten years her junior. She became a Moslem so they could marry. She soon regretted it. There were hints of a homosexual relationship between the prince and his male secretary, and the court was told of the prince's 'vicious and eccentric sexual appetites'. Fahmy claimed she had merely tried to frighten her husband. She said that when they got to their Savoy suite the prince had threatened to kill her. As a precaution she loaded a gun he had given her. As she did so she accidentally fired one shot through a window. The prince tried to attack her and the gun went off again, killing him. She was defended by SIR EDWARD MARSHALL HALL, whose plea to the jury was so clearly racist it brought a diplomatic protest from the Egyptian embassy. Fahmy was found not guilty of murder and manslaughter.

FANNY HILL Much-suppressed novel. John Cleland wrote his *Memoirs of a Woman of Pleasure* in 1749, and it was almost immediately prosecuted as pornography. *See* PORNOGRAPHY

FAUNTLEROY, HENRY (1784–1824) Banker and forger. Fauntleroy began his career as a clerk in his father's bank in Berners Street in 1800. The bank was going through difficult times, and when his father died in 1807 Fauntleroy staved off bankruptcy by secretly selling stocks and shares which belonged to his customers. For a time it worked: the bank became relatively successful, and whenever customers called for their stocks Fauntleroy quickly purchased replacements for them. He also kept up the dividends due on stocks he had already sold.

He acquired some expensive mistresses, large houses, fine furnishings and carriages. At one time he kept a notorious woman of pleasure known as 'Mrs Bang', on whom PIERCE EGAN based his Corinthian Kate. Later he kept a young woman, Maria Forbes, whom he had met while she was still in boarding school. He installed her in a house in Lambeth, settled £6,000 of presumably stolen money on her and when she bore him two children established an atmosphere of domestic harmony around her. He had other mistresses, including the wife of the Somerset Herald.

Then in 1824 the executors of a Lieutenant-Colonel Bellis told Fauntleroy they wanted to hand over their responsibilities to the Court of Chancery. When Fauntleroy objected strongly they became suspicious and went to the Bank of England, where they discovered that most of Bellis's stocks and shares had been sold. Altogether customers' stocks worth £400,000 had been disposed of, using forged powers of attorney. When a police officer came to arrest him Fauntleroy offered him a £10,000 bribe to let him escape. Fauntleroy was hanged outside Newgate in November 1824, watched by an enormous crowd.

FAYED, MOHAMED Egyptian businessman at the centre of the 'cash for questions' scandal. Fayed bought the House of Fraser group in 1985, including the Knightsbridge department store Harrods, after a bitter takeover battle with the businessman 'Tiny' Rowland of Lonrho. Rowland owned *The Observer* and he used it to attack Fayed. Partly in response Fayed appointed the lobbyist Ian Greer of IGA to look after his interests, and Greer introduced him to the Conservative MP NEIL HAMILTON, who was happy to ask questions on his behalf in the Commons. This led eventually to disgrace and bankruptcy for Hamilton, who sued Fayed in a famous libel action and lost. *See* JONATHAN AITKEN

FENCES Middle-men and women who bought stolen goods. IKEY SOLOMONS, on whom Dickens is believed to have based his character Fagin in *Oliver Twist*, is the archetype. Others who played this role which was so essential to the underworld were publicans, pawnbrokers, dealers in all kinds of second-hand goods, costermongers and keepers of low lodging houses. In the seventeenth century fencing was highly organised by criminals such as the great MOLL CUTPURSE. Fences offered information to criminals and helped them dispose of goods abroad if they were too 'hot' to sell in London. In the eighteenth century they organised and bankrolled the plunder of the ships and warehouses on the river.

A notebook in the British Library which once belonged to a Recorder of the City of London and was probably compiled by a police officer, gives a list of receivers in the year 1816. Among them was a Mrs Jennings of Red Lion Market, White Cross Street:

> This is a most notorious fence, and keeps a house of ill fame. She has secret rooms by doors out of cupboards, where she plants or secretes the property she buys till she has got it disposed of. Innumerable boys and girls of the youngest class resort to this house as she makes up more beds than any other house in that part of the metropolis; each room in her house (which is a large one) being divided into various divisions for beds, and the house is thronged every night. She sanctions robberies in her house which are continually committed by the girls on strangers whom they can inveigle into the house and whom the girls will bilk into the bargain, as their flash boys never permit a connection under such circumstances.

Another fence, MOTHER CUMMINGS, was a St Giles bawd and fence in a large way of business. She trained young girls to lure men to her brothel and rob them. Mrs White of Barret's Court, Wigmore Street, who kept an old shoe shop, can only just have subsisted on the brushes, pails and coal scuttles youngsters stole from outside gentlemen's houses and sold to her. An interesting fence was Edward Memmery, a costermonger from Old Pye Street who was also a burglar. He used his horse and cart to sell stolen foodstuffs in the suburbs. His neighbour Robert Charles paid between one and two shillings for a stolen duck or hen and sold them in the suburbs from the back of his donkey.

Women fences sometimes specialised in silk handkerchiefs which were, as we know from Dickens, a staple of the trade. Mrs Diner of Field Lane, Holborn, was particularly brazen:

> Keeps a shop where numbers of silk handkerchiefs hang at the window which she deals in and nothing else, and has lived there eight or nine years in the same way, buying them from pick-pockets of every description, men, women, boys and girls, but chiefly boys, whose practice it is. She has a cockloft through a trap door at the top of her house where she had generally an immense quantity of silk handkerchiefs so brought to her. She is considered a woman of property. The officers sometimes come here, but to no avail, as she takes out the initials or marks, so that the property cannot be identified.

The writer HENRY MAYHEW described a lodging house in Whitechapel's Cat-and-Wheel Alley (later Commercial Street) run by a one-legged Welshman known as Taff. He was the organiser of a gang of child thieves. 'Taff was a notorious receiver of stolen goods,' said one of his lodgers. 'I knew two little boys who brought home six pairs of new Wellington boots, which this miscreant bought at 1*s* a pair; and, when they had no luck, he would take the strap off his wooden leg, and beat them through the nakedness of their rags.'

The plundering of ships and quays on the River Thames, which was eighteenth-century London's most important criminal enterprise, was financed by an army of fences. Among other services, the receivers provided the large sums of cash needed to bribe Customs officers to look the other way.

Petticoat Lane on the boundary of the City was the heartland of the business in stolen goods. Nearby was a large enclosure where the Houndsditch Clothes Exchange was situated. Here many of the stolen goods in London were sold on, particularly clothes. On a dark evening the lamp-lit scene was lively: until recently the scene at Bermondsey Market early on a Friday morning was similar, with antique dealers going from stall to stall and examining the goods by torchlight, and not too many questions were asked if the price was right.

FERNSEED, MARGARET (?–1608) Brothel-keeper and murderer. Her husband was found dead in Peckham Fields near Lambeth, and as Margaret had previously tried to poison him she was arrested and executed in 1608. A pamphlet published in that year, *The Arraignment & Burning of Margaret Ferne-seede for the Murther of her late Husband, Anthony Ferne-seede*, is an important source of information about prostitution in London in the sixteenth century. Like later bawds she would meet wagons bringing young girls to town looking for employment. After they had been seduced they would be forced onto the streets to earn money for her. She also watched married couples for signs of 'any breach of discontent'. She would entice wives who were unhappy with their partners into prostitution, then blackmail them into continuing in vice by threatening to tell their husbands.

FERRARI, CARLO (*c*. 1817–31) Street urchin whose murder helped bring about important changes in the law on dissection. In November 1831 two men named Bishop and May told the porter at the dissecting room at London's King's College that they had the body of a boy of 14, for which they wanted twelve guineas. Something about the appearance of the body made the porter suspicious, and the police were called. There was an inquest, which brought in a verdict of 'wilful murder against some person or persons unknown'. Bishop and May and another man, Williams, were tried at the Old Bailey and found guilty of murdering the boy, who was identified as an Italian named Carlo Ferrari from Bethnal Green. The youngster made his living by showing white mice, and added pathos was given to the case by the fact that his mouse-cage was found in the killers' rooms. The trio were found guilty, May was transported for life and the others hanged. In December 1831 Henry Warburton introduced into the House of Commons a Bill intended to end the sale of bodies. It did away with the use of the bodies of murderers by anatomists, and instead gave them the right to dissect the unclaimed bodies of workhouse inmates. This new and plentiful source made buying from body-snatchers unnecessary.

FERRERS, EARL (1720–60) The only peer to be hanged for murder. Laurence Shirley, the 4th Earl Ferrers, a drunken and violent man whose wife had won a legal separation by Act of Parliament after he kicked her unconscious, developed an irrational hatred for his steward, a man named Johnson. Ferrers learned that in 1760 Johnson had sent Lady Ferrers £50 to live on until she could procure a proper settlement from her husband. Ferrers ordered the man to kneel and shot him. It took Johnson ten hours to die, and Ferrers taunted him in his death agony. He told Johnson's daughter that if her father died, he would support her family on condition they did not prosecute him. During the night he went into the room where Johnson was dying and threatened to shoot him again. When he was arrested he said he was glad he had killed Johnson and would do the same thing again. He was tried by the House of Lords at Westminster Hall and pleaded insanity, conducting his own defence. He was found guilty and petitions to the King for mercy failed. Normally the Establishment could be expected to save one of their own, but they evidently felt that the sacrifice of Ferrers would suggest, against all the evidence, that English justice was impartial. So Ferrers was hanged at Tyburn on 5 May 1760. His request to be beheaded was refused, as was his request to have his mistress with him in prison. So many friends and nobles turned out to see him die – including the Lord High Steward in his state coach, and twelve judges – that the procession to the gibbet took nearly three hours. Ferrers travelled in his own landau and six, wearing his wedding clothes. He tipped the hangman and the chaplain five guineas each. WILLIAM HICKEY, who was a schoolboy at the time, saw him die:

> His lordship was conveyed to Tyburn in his own Landau, dressed in a superb suit of white and silver, being the clothes in which he was married, his reason for wearing which was that they had been his first step towards ruin, and should attend his exit. In compliment to his peerage he was hung with a silk halter, a common cord being covered with black silk, and instead of a cart driving from under him, a stage or platform was erected, upon a trap door on which he stood and on his dropping a handkerchief from his hand, this trap was lowered and he, of course, became suspended. He met his death with fortitude, though many persons said there was a wildness in his eyes and countenance that strongly indicated a deranged mind.

Lord Ferrers was the first man to be executed with the aid of a trapdoor. His body was dissected, but not as drastically as those of common murderers.

FIELDING, HENRY (1707–54) Novelist and playwright, author of *Tom Jones*, and co-founder with his half-brother John of the embryo detective force the BOW STREET RUNNERS. He was appointed chief magistrate of Westminster, and his salary of £550 was paid from a secret fund to avoid suggestions of an official police force. His vision of a force motivated by public spirit rather than profit was not realised in his lifetime, and the Runners became notoriously corrupt (*see* POLICE). He wrote the satirical *Life of Jonathan Wild the Great*. Commenting on the deplorable state of law and order in the wretchedly policed city he wrote:

> Whoever indeed considers the Cities of London and Westminster, with the late vast Addition of their Suburbs, the great Irregularity of their Buildings, the immense Number of Lanes, Alleys, Courts and Bye-places; must think, that, had they been intended for the very Purpose of Concealment, they could scarce have been better contrived. Upon such a View, the whole appears as a vast Wood or Forest, in which a Thief may harbour with as great Security, as wild Beasts do in the deserts of

> Africa or Arabia . . . It is a melancholy Truth that, at this very Day, a Rogue no sooner gives the Alarm, within certain Purlieus, than twenty or thirty armed Villains are found ready to come to his Assistance.

For the poor the Fieldings brought a human face to the practice of justice. The *Covent Garden Journal* reported:

> . . . several wretches being apprehended the night before by Mr Welch, were brought before Mr Fielding and Mr Errigton: when one who was in a dreadful condition from the itch was recommended to the overseers; another, who appeared to be guilty of no crime but poverty, had money given to her to enable her to follow her trade in the market.

Despite his reforming zeal Fielding was a hanger and flogger, believing in the deterrent power of harsh punishments.

FIELDING, SIR JOHN Founder with his half-brother Henry of the BOW STREET RUNNERS. After Henry died in 1754 Sir John continued attempts to establish an honest and efficient force. In 1772 he proposed a General Preventative Plan for an embryo national police force. But when he suggested that High Constables should become full-time criminal investigators he upset the county authorities: his proposals seemed to raise once again the spectre of a professional police force. He had more success with a patrol of mounted officers. He died in 1780 with his dream of an efficient police force unfulfilled, but with the Runners, the forerunner of such a force, well established. His successful bulletin the *Weekly Pursuit*, which gave magistrates all over the country details of stolen goods and suspects, became the *Police Gazette* after 1829.

FINGERPRINTS The first murderer to be convicted with the aid of fingerprints was Alfred Stratton, 22, in 1905. With his younger brother Albert he forced his way into a shop in Deptford and murdered the shopkeeper, Thomas Farrow, and his wife Ann. Alfred's thumb-print was found, and the brothers were hanged.

FINISHES Immoral public houses which attracted upper-class clients after other hostelries had closed for the night. In 1840 the French socialist and feminist Flora Tristan published *Promenades dans Londres* in which she described a visit to one:

> After the play they move on to the 'finishes'; these are squalid taverns or vast resplendent gin-palaces where people go to spend what remains of the night . . . The same friends who accompanied me to the Waterloo Road again offered to be my guides . . .
>
> From the outside these gin-palaces with their carefully fastened shutters seem to be quietly slumbering; but no sooner has the doorkeeper admitted you by the little door reserved for initiates than you are dazzled by the light of a thousand gas lamps. Upstairs there is a spacious salon divided down the middle; in one half there is a row of tables separated one from the other by wooden screens . . . In the other half is a dais where the prostitutes parade in all their finery; seeking to arouse the men with their glances and remarks . . .
>
> Towards midnight the regular clients begin to arrive; several finishes are frequented by men in high society, and this is where the cream of the aristocracy gather. At first the young noblemen recline on the sofas, smoking and exchanging pleasantries with the women; then, when they have drunk enough for the fumes of champagne and Madeira to go to their heads, the illustrious scions of the English nobility, the very honourable members of Parliament, remove their coats, untie their cravats, take off their waistcoats and braces, and proceed to set up their private boudoir in a public place. Why not make themselves at home, since they are paying out so much money for the right to display their contempt . . . The orgy rises to a crescendo; between four and five in the morning it reaches its height.
>
> At this point it takes a good deal of courage to remain in one's seat, a mute spectator of all that takes place. What worthy use these English lords make of their immense fortunes! How fine and generous they are when they have lost the use of their reason and offer fifty, even a hundred guineas to a prostitute if she will lend herself to all the obscenities that drunkenness engenders . . .
>
> For in a finish there is no lack of entertainment. One of the favourite sports is to *ply a woman with drink* until she falls dead drunk upon the floor, then to make her swallow a draught compounded of *vinegar, mustard and pepper*; this invariably throws the poor creature into horrible convulsions, and her spasms and contortions provoke the *honourable company* to gales of laughter and

infinite amusement. Another diversion much appreciated at these fashionable gatherings is to empty the contents of the nearest glass upon the women as they lie insensible upon the ground. I have seen satin dresses of no recognisable colour, only a confused mass of stains; wine, brandy, beer, tea, coffee, cream etc . . . daubed all over them in a thousand fantastic shapes . . . The air is heavy with the noxious odours of food, drink, tobacco, and others more fetid still which seize you by the throat, grip your temples in a vice and make your senses reel: it is indescribably horrible! . . . However, this life, which continues relentlessly night after night, is the prostitute's sole hope of a fortune, for she has no hold on the Englishman when he is sober. *The sober Englishman is chaste to the point of prudery.*

It is usually between seven and eight in the morning when people leave the finish. The servants go out to look for cabs, and anyone still on his feet gathers up his clothes and returns home; as for the rest, the pot-boys dress them in the first garments that come to hand and bundle them into a cab and tell the cabman where to deliver them. Often nobody knows their address; then they are deposited in the cellar and left to sleep in the straw. This place is known as the drunkards' hole, and there they stay until they have recovered their wits sufficiently to say where they wish to be taken.

Kitty Fisher, a famously rapacious courtesan. She boasted she once ate a 1,000-guinea note on a piece of bread, and made impossible demands of her lovers. She spurned the great womaniser Casanova when he offered her 10 guineas, saying she never took less than 50 guineas – about £4,400 today.

FISHER, KITTY (1738–67) Actress-whore who boasted that she ate a 1,000-guinea banknote. According to the German J.W. von Archenholz, Kitty was 'indebted to nature for an uncommon portion of beauty, judgment, and wit, joined in a most agreeable and captivating vivacity'. She was also hard-headed, and despite 'the elegance with which she sacrificed to Venus' kept her mind on business:

The union of so many perfections procured the esteem, and fascinated the desires of those who prefer Cyprian delights to all the other pleasures of life. This lady knew her own merit; she demanded a hundred guineas a night for the use of her charms, and she was never without votaries, to whom the offering did not seem too exorbitant. Among these was the Duke of York, brother to the King; who one morning left fifty pounds on her toilet [dressing table]. This present so offended Miss Fisher that she declared that her doors should ever be shut against him in future; and to show by this most convincing proof how much she despised his present, she clapt the banknote between two slices of bread and butter, and ate it for breakfast.

There is another version of this episode which sets the stakes rather higher. CASANOVA wrote: 'We went to see the well-known procuress Mrs Wells, and saw the celebrated courtesan Kitty Fisher who was waiting for the Duke of — to take her to a ball . . . she had on diamonds worth 5,000 francs . . . she had eaten a banknote for 1,000 guineas on a slice of bread and butter that very day . . .'.

Kitty certainly had expensive tastes. She would demand impossible presents from her lovers, ate fresh strawberries in the depths of winter and for a time slept only with members of the House of Lords. Casanova was with the Earl of Pembroke in St James's Park one day when Kitty passed in her finery. Pembroke told him that he might have her for 10 guineas, but when Casanova offered her this sum she snubbed him, making it clear that her minimum rate was 50 guineas. Reynolds painted her several times, perhaps trying to capture that mysterious X factor that great courtesans are supposed to have: he didn't succeed.

FITCH, HERBERT Police bodyguard to royals, including Edward VII. In his book *Memoirs of a Royal Detective* he described how before a foreign monarch visited Britain the route would be meticulously searched. Plain-clothes officers would drink in working-men's clubs, listening for any hint of a plot. One undercover officer who spoke French, German and Yiddish posed as a cobbler and lived in the slums of the East End, spying on supposedly dangerous anarchists. When his turn came to act as a bodyguard to a member of the royal family he would tell his East End friends that he was going into hospital.

FLAGELLATION A very English practice, much commented upon by foreigners. The MESSINAS' prostitute MARTHE WATTS was surprised when she arrived in London at the number of men who wanted her to thrash them.

Sarah Potter was a noted Victorian brothel-keeper and flagellant. At various times she had establishments, including brothels specialising in flagellation, in Castle Street off Leicester Square, Wardour Street, Albion Terrace off the King's Road, Howland Street off Tottenham Court Road, the Old Kent Road and eventually, in Lavinia Grove, King's Cross. She was arrested in 1873 and a pamphlet gave the following account of her business:

> . . . under the auspices of the Society for the Protection of Females, seizure was made at the then notorious 'Academy' of Sarah Potter, alias Stewart, in Wardour Street, and a rare collection of Flagellation appurtenances taken to the Westminster Police Court when the general public for the first time became aware that young females were decoyed into Stewart's School of Flogging, to undergo the ordeal of the birch from old and young Flagellists, for the benefit of the woman Stewart. These curious specimens of her stock-in-trade consisted of a folding ladder, with straps, birch rods, furze brooms and secret implements, for the use of male and female.
>
> Her method of conducting business was to get hold of young girls, board, lodge and clothe them, and in return they were obliged to administer to the lusts of the patrons of the boarding-house. They were flogged in different ways. Sometimes strapped to the ladder, at others they were flogged round the room – at times they were laid on the bed. Every device or variation which perverted ingenuity could devise was resorted to to give variety to the orgies, in return for which the mistress of the house was paid sums varying from £5 to £15. The profits of this school enabled Stewart to keep a country house and a fancy man, to the great scandal of the community.

The case against Mrs Potter/Stewart was brought by a girl of 'about fifteen', Agnes Thompson, at the instigation of the Society for the Protection of Females and Young Women. Agnes said that a year previously she had gone with a man to a house where he had 'effected her ruin'. Since then she worked for Mrs Potter at the Albion Terrace address. She said: 'I was flogged by gentlemen with birch rods. I was beaten on my naked flesh.' She described an occasion when she was whipped by a man called 'Sealskin' and another known as 'The Count'. During this ordeal she had been tied to the ladder which was produced in court.

Two other girls, Catherine Kennedy, who was 17, and Alice Smith, described in a report in *Lloyd's Weekly London Gazette* as 'a young woman of considerable personal attractions', told of similar floggings. Smith said she was not paid for her services. Mrs Potter was found guilty and sent to prison. She died in 1873 and her grave in Kensal Green Cemetery has a handsome tombstone.

The great Victorian expert on erotology HENRY SPENCER ASHBEE provides a list of Victorian flagellation brothels in his *Index Librorum Prohibitorum*. There was Mrs Lee's in Margaret Place, Regent Street, Mrs Shepherd of Gilbert Street, Mrs Phillips of Upper Belgrave Place and of course Mrs Potter.

Many got their taste for flagellation at public schools. The most enthusiastic flogger in Eton's history was Dr John Keate. A diminutive fury with the birch, which at five feet was almost as long as he was tall, he even chastised candidates for confirmation. When one boy protested Keate declared: 'You are only adding to your offence by your profanity and lying.' Yet Gladstone recalled that at a dinner in 1841 to commemorate four centuries of the school, Keate was cheered to the echo by former pupils he had tormented. 'The roar of cheering had a beginning, but never knew satiety or end. Like the huge waves of Biarritz, the flood of cheering continually recommenced; the whole process was such that we seemed to have lost all our self-possession . . .' *See* THERESA BERKLEY and MARY WILSON

FLASH HOUSES Low lodging houses or brothels, often associated with public houses. They were central to the criminal enterprise in the eighteenth and early nineteenth centuries. Criminals used them to eat and sleep, to plan robberies, to exchange information, to recruit new gang members, to dispose of or acquire stolen goods. Most experts agreed that 'flash houses' were responsible for much juvenile crime. Boys mixed there with mature thieves and prostitutes and girls of their own age, who were often their mistresses. Henry Grey Bennett, chairman of the 1816 Select Committee on the Police, accused the police of taking bribes for keeping the activities of the flash houses secret from the magistrates, and he named some of the more notorious houses. There was the Black Horse in Tottenham Court Road, frequented by thieves such as Huffey White and Conkey Beau. The landlord, Blackman, 'has been considered a thief for fifteen years . . . there is not a regular flash-house in London that is not known to the officers of the police, from the Rose in Rose-street, Long Acre, kept by Kelly, which he kept long with impunity, to the Bear, opposite to Bow-Street office, the infamous character of which is notorious, and which unites the trades of brothel and public-house.' Grey Bennet's efforts at reform were defeated by a combination of police corruption and the vested interests of the brewers.

These lodging-houses abounded all over the country, but were particularly numerous and scandalous in London. In 1851 the Common Lodging House Act was passed in an attempt to control them. Police were given powers to inspect and close them if they failed to reach an elementary standard of decency and cleanliness. Hundreds were closed, and the remainder put their prices up to meet the costs of the new standards. Some of the poor were thus made homeless because they could not afford to pay.

FLEET MARRIAGES Clergymen imprisoned in the Fleet prison claimed they had the right to conduct marriages as the area was outside the

A Fleet wedding in the early eighteenth century. Bogus clergymen claimed the right to marry couples in the area around the Fleet Prison. The practice, which caused much legal confusion about wills and debts, was ended by the Marriage Act of 1753. After that couples would go to Gretna Green.

jurisdiction of the Bishop of London. Several local taverns in Fleet Street claimed the same privilege. There was a surprisingly large demand for their services from people who did not want their marriage registered in the normal way. Almost 3,000 marriages were performed in the four months ending in February 1705. Fleet marriages were valid and cheap compared to conventional weddings, which were heavily taxed. Bigamists could see to it that their marriages were not registered at all, and marriages which had never taken place were recorded. Women would marry insolvent debtors to cancel their own debts. Heiresses who had been drugged or intoxicated could be taken there and married for their money. One of those who performed the ceremonies was a 'Dr Gaynam', a bogus clergyman who was really a watchmaker. He was known as 'the Bishop of Hell'.

The implications for inheritances and debts were grave. A Marriage Act was passed in 1753 to put a stop to Fleet marriages by ruling that only church weddings were valid. It also made marriage of persons under 21 invalid without parental consent. This started the era of the Gretna Green marriage. Some time later as wrangles about inheritances continued the government bought some of the Fleet marriage registers.

FLEET PRISON First recorded in 1170, although it was probably older. It was eventually London's main debtor prison, notorious for the rapacity of the Keepers. Prisoners paid for their accommodation. Moses Pitt, imprisoned for debt, revealed in his *Cry of the Oppressed* in 1691 that the Keeper charged him £2 4*s* 6*d* for being housed on the 'gentlemen's side', although the fee should have been only 4*d*. The weekly charge was another 8*s* instead of 2*s* 4*d*. When he ran out of money he was sent to the dungeon. He said his companions there were 'so lowsie that as they either walked or sat down you

Prisoners exercise in the yard of the Fleet Prison. This genial scene belies the true nature of the Fleet. Inmates were fleeced by the warders, and it became known as the biggest brothel in Britain because women prisoners sold sex to improve their conditions. It was the main prison for debtors.

might have picked lice from their outward garments'. One Keeper in the early eighteenth century paid £5,000 for the office, an immense sum which he confidently hoped to recoup through extortion. In 1726 a Parliamentary committee found that the Keeper at that time, Thomas Bambridge, was guilty of 'great extortions, and the highest crimes and misdemeanours'. Bambridge was tried for murder, but acquitted. He was also cleared of stealing jewellery from a prisoner, Elizabeth Berkeley. He was removed from office, and cut his throat twenty years later. Because women inmates sold sex to improve their conditions the prison was known as the biggest brothel in England. Numerous attempts were made to reform it, without success. It was demolished in 1846. Famous prisoners included the poets John Donne and the Earl of Surrey.

FLETCHER, YVONNE Young policewoman murdered by a Libyan gunman. Fletcher was on duty outside the Libyan embassy in St James's Square during a small protest demonstration in April 1984. A gunman fired from the first-floor window of the embassy, killing the 25-year-old policewoman. Her fiancé, a police constable, was just yards away. There was a ten-day siege of the embassy before the staff, who were covered by diplomatic immunity, were escorted to Heathrow for a flight to Tripoli.

FLYING DUSTMEN, THE This fascinating case before Middlesex Sessions in September 1812 revealed the value of coal ashes taken from houses. A Mr Lacock had paid the parish of St Mary, Islington, the 'enormous sum' of £750 a year for the contract to gather this item of household refuse. Charles Fox, one of a group of rogue refuse collectors known as 'flying dustmen', stole some of the ashes, and, when caught in the act by one of Lacock's carters in King Street, Islington, with a basket of ashes on his head, which he emptied into a cart that was standing at the door, swore that all the men in Islington should not stop him. He struck the carter several times before escaping, but was arrested. He was sentenced to three months' imprisonment for assault. The value of the 'dust', an important feature in Charles Dickens's *Our Mutual Friend*, was so puzzling that the *Newgate Calendar* felt it necessary to give an explanation for 'country readers'.

> Country readers could hardly suppose that a man gave £750 a year, and employed several carts and a number of men, to empty his neighbours' dust-tubs, wherein all manner of filth was thrown. Yet this was the case in every parish in and about London, the officers giving the contract to the best bidder, and to obtain which there was sometimes as great a struggle as to get elected churchwarden. Lacock cleared a few hundreds a year by his contract. In a part of his extensive premises he employed several score of poor women and children to sift the ashes. First they produced cinders, which sold for about half the price of coal, to forges, kilns, etc. The next siftings, becoming each finer than the last, were used as manure, and in the making of lime, brick, etc. Thus the collecting of house ashes, which formerly the inhabitants were obliged to pay people to take away, produced a clear income, sufficient of itself for the decent maintenance of a family. The regular dusty squad, fired with indignation at this usurpation of their rights and privileges, and fearing a forestalling of their Christmas presents, issued the following cautionary handbill to their employers:
>
> 'To the worthy inhabitants of St Mary, Islington. Ladies and Gentlemen,
>
> We, the regular dustmen of this parish, humbly present our respects to you, and beg that you will not give your Christmas Box but to such men as deliver one of these bills, and show a medal with the following inscription :-
>
> William Duke of Cumberland, Battle of Culloden, with a badge,'R. Lacock, No. I and 2, Islington.'
>
> Men having been found going about dressed like dustmen, under false pretences to defraud the regular men of what little you may please to bestow. Please not to deliver this bill to anyone. John Smith and John Waling'

FOOTPADS Violent robbers. Because they had to escape on foot they were likely to maim or even kill their victims. They were going to hang anyway if they were caught. The Carrick gang, rounded up by JONATHAN WILD in the 1720s, consisted of about fifteen men. Other gangs were usually smaller.

Footpads were more feared than highwaymen, who could escape easily and were consequently less homicidal. One tactic of the footpads was to attack a coach when it was forced to slow down, because of a steep hill or because the road narrowed. In June 1772 a coach carrying a Mr Fry and six young ladies was held up as it slowed down to cross Richmond Bridge. To stop it the footpads fired through the coach window, grazing a woman's ear and blowing away her earring. The gang, who got away with four guineas on that occasion, had held up two post-chaises from Richmond two days earlier. The gang of footpads led by Obadiah Lemon used fishing rods to hook hats and wigs out of passing coaches. Coach owners then fitted a kind of grille to the windows. So the Lemons took to jumping on to the back of coaches, cutting a hole in the roof and stealing the valuables through it.

FOREMAN, FREDDIE Important and influential leader of a gang of south London robbers, and ally of the KRAYS. In January 2000 he confessed in an ITV programme to the murders of FRANK MITCHELL and a small-time crook named Ginger Marks, whose disappearance had long fed the rumour machine of the underworld. Foreman told how he had used a small boat which was part of a smuggling operation he ran from Newhaven in Sussex to dump the bodies, weighted and trussed in chicken wire, in the busy shipping lanes of the English Channel. Foreman also filled in gaps in the chronicle of the KRAYS, and admitted that he intimidated witnesses who saw Ronnie Kray kill GEORGE CORNELL.

Foreman, known as The Mean Machine, was born in 1932. He began his life of crime as a petty thief just after the war. There was a ready market for stolen electrical goods such as refrigerators and radios. He met Charlie Kray whom he described as 'a good fence'. From petty crime he moved on to payroll robbery. He describes in his autobiography *Respect . . . The Managing Director of British Crime* a payroll van robbery in which one of his team was shot through the head by a guard in the back of the van. The man was taken to a compliant doctor, but it was too late to save him. He too ended up in the sea. Foreman was sentenced to ten years in prison for being an accessory in the MCVITIE murder. In 1989 he was jailed for nine years for his part in what was then Britain's biggest cash robbery, the £7 million Security Express raid in 1983. He became one of the British fugitives on Spain's Costa del Sol, but the Spanish police drugged him and put him on a plane back to Britain. When his autobiography was published there was a champagne launch at London's Café Royal, attended by celebrity gangsters. The actress Barbara Windsor, former wife of RONNIE KNIGHT, was also there.

Foreman's appropriation of the title Managing Director of British Crime is interesting. It is clear he has been a major criminal for a long time. NIPPER READ, the senior police officer instrumental in bringing down the Krays, admitted in a TV programme that when he went after the Krays he didn't realise how important Foreman was, and he believed that the south London gangster should have been given a thirty-year sentence along with his allies. Although now in his seventies Foreman is seen as one of the few criminals capable of standing up to the ADAMS FAMILY. It is said that after one of that family cut off his son's ear Foreman threatened to start an underworld war, and the Adamses took the threat seriously enough to attend peace talks.

FOREST, JOHN (?–1538) Martyr who preached against HENRY VIII's divorce from Catherine of Aragon. His burning at the stake at Smithfield on 22 May 1538 was meticulously planned. Thomas Cromwell was just one of the high officers of state who were present. A wooden holy relic, said to be capable of destroying a forest by fire, was brought to London and broken up to add to the flames. This pun may have pleased Cromwell. Forest was suspended over the flames on a kind of bed made of chains, and slowly roasted.

FOTHERINGHAM, PRISS (?–after 1663) Exhibitionist bawd who specialised in the 'chuck game'. Priscilla or Priss Carsewell is first heard of at the Middlesex sessions in July 1658 when she was charged with theft. She was sentenced to be hanged but was granted a conditional pardon by the new Lord Protector, Richard Cromwell. She married into the brothel-keeping family of the Fotheringhams. Her husband Edmund was her pimp and at least ten years her junior.

He beat her and gave her a venereal disease, so she took his money and ran off with a sword cutter. When the money was gone, she returned, and Edmund had her committed to NEWGATE PRISON, where she spent about a year. There she met the brothel-keepers DAMARIS PAGE and MOTHER CRESSWELL. Then as now, prisons were universities of crime, and Priss had the best tutors. She also met there her chronicler, JOHN GARFIELD.

As a whore Priss specialised in a particularly successful money-spinner known as 'chucking' or 'the chuck game'. One of her early chroniclers reported: 'Priss stood on her head with naked Breech and Belly while four Cully-Rumpers chucked in sixteen half-crowns into her *Commoditie*.' She performed this feat several times a day to acclaim from a crowd of enthusiastic fans. It made her brothel, the Six Windmills in Chiswell Street, Cripplegate Without, popular with customers from nearby taverns and also from far wider afield.

Priss died wealthy about 1668, probably in her middle fifties. Although she must have been a fit, even athletic, woman to have performed the 'chuck ceremony' several times a day when younger, she was later much afflicted by disease. Garfield wrote in 1663 that she was 'now overgrown with age and overworn with her former all-too-frequent embraces'. Her husband was also dying, 'rotten with syphilis'.

FOWLER, NELLY High-class whore Gladstone attempted to save. She wrote of him: 'The Prime Minister actually called to see me. He is not at all as stern as they all say he is, but most well-mannered, kind and considerate, and indeed, a wonderful figure of a man, so very, very handsome, that one longs to stroke that magnificent head.' Other whores were less reverential, referring to the great statesman as 'old glad-eye'. D. Shaw, author of *London in the Sixties*, wrote of Nelly and other mid-Victorian temptresses:

> The ladies who frequented Mott's, moreover, were not the tawdry make-believes who haunt the modern 'Palaces' but actresses of note, who if not Magdalens [prostitutes] sympathised with them; girls of education and refinement who had succumbed to the blandishments of youthful lordlings, fair women here and there who had not yet developed into peeresses and progenitors of future legislators. Among them were 'Skittles' [the courtesan], celebrated for her ponies, and sweet Nelly Fowler, the undisputed Queen of beauty in those long-ago days. This beautiful girl had a natural perfume so delicate, so universally admitted, that love-sick swains paid large sums for the privilege of having their handkerchiefs placed under the Godess's pillow, and sweet Nelly pervaded – in spirit if not in the flesh – half the clubs and drawing rooms of England.

FRASER, FRANKIE Veteran gangster and hard man also known as 'Mad Frankie'. He got his nickname by successfully pretending to be mad to avoid serving in the forces during the Second World War. He was a member of the BILLY HILL and RICHARDSON gangs and a veteran of the struggle between Hill and Jack Spot for control of the West End. In 1956 he was jailed for seven years for an attack on Spot. After the fight in MR SMITH'S CLUB Fraser was acquitted of murder but convicted of affray. He was sentenced to five years' prison. He got another five years for leading the 1969 Parkhurst jail riots. He claimed he also got what he called a 'thorough beating' from prison officers, and needed sixty stitches in his head. In 1991, free once more, he was gunned down outside the Turnmills night club in Clerkenwell. He lived to tell the tale. 'The bullet was a .22, it came in by my right eye, went all round my face under my nose and lodged by my left eye. But it was good fun, good action, it makes a good night's drink, after all.' The ADAMS BROTHERS from north London were rumoured to be behind the shooting. In a startling example of gangster chic Fraser later became, in his eighties, a much-interviewed celebrity and chat-show guest.

FRY, ELIZABETH (1780–1845) Quaker and prison reformer. She began her campaign in 1812, when she was in her thirties, with a visit to NEWGATE PRISON. About three hundred women and their children were crammed into two cells and two wards. Some of the women were dirty and drunken, some dangerous. Jail fever was a constant threat. To Fry, brought up in a prosperous, loving and devout family, it must have seemed truly infernal. Nevertheless by 1816 she and some friends were regular visitors, and were accepted by the women convicts as worthy of respect and even love. Her aims included separation of the sexes, classification according to the nature of the crime committed, provision of work and education. She was so successful that her work was widely copied abroad. She also improved care in hospitals and the treatment of the insane. Henry Grey Bennett, chairman of the 1816 Select Committee on the Police, who himself wanted to fight crime by reforming the prisons, paid tribute to her:

> I visited Newgate in the beginning of the month of May 1817, and went round, first, the female side of the prison: I had been there a few weeks before, and found it, as usual, in the most degraded and afflicting state; the women were then mixed all together, young and old; the young beginner with the old offender; the girl, for the first offence, with the hardened and drunken prostitute; the tried and the untried; the accused with the condemned; the transports [those sentenced to transportation] with those under sentence of death; all were crowded together, in one promiscuous assemblage; noisy, idle and profligate; clamorous at the grating, soliciting money and begging at the bars of the prison, with spoons attached to the ends of sticks. In little more than one fortnight the whole scene was changed, through the humane and philanthropic exertion of Mrs Fry, the wife of a banker in the city, assisted by others of the Society of Friends . . .

FUCHS, KLAUS (1911–88) Spy who gave the secrets of the atom bomb to the Russians. Fuchs, a German Quaker refugee from Nazi Germany, first worked with Russian spies in London. In 1943 he was sent to work on the project to build the first atomic bomb at Los Alamos in New Mexico, and was in an ideal position to provide the Russians with details of its construction. In 1946 he returned to England and worked at the atomic centre at Harwell. The arrest of other spies cast suspicion on Fuchs, and in 1950 he was persuaded to confess. He was jailed for nine years for spying, and after his release in 1959 went to East Germany, where he was given an important role in their nuclear research industry.

FUMBLE, LORD The Earl of Harrington's nickname may have derived from his sexual preferences. Certainly William Stanhope and his wife were renowned for their vices. In 1773 *The Westminster Magazine* called him 'a person of the most exceptional immorality'. The *Town and Country Magazine* said he was 'as lecherous as a Monkey'. The magazine listed some of his lovers, starting with the corpulent opera singer Signora Caterini Galli, then Kitty Brown who had 'a fair complexion, brilliant blue eyes . . . with small, pouting Bubbies'; then he had a brief fling with the greedy KITTY FISHER, who boasted of eating a 1,000-guinea banknote. She was succeeded by another actress, Mrs Houghton. When the Duke of Dorset died the earl took on his mistress, Jane Courteville, only to see her fall for 'the corpulent charms' of the bawd Mrs Rushton of King Street. At one stage he had a harem in his mansion, 'which comprised a Negress in a feather'd Turban, a young girl in pseudo-classical dress, another [dressed] as a Country-wench, as well as a Mandolin-player . . .' After his affair with a Miss Lisle, the widow of a military hero, who had become a whore, the *Town and Country Magazine* said this of the earl and his wife: 'His Lordship is an impotent Debauchee and his Lady a professional *Messalina* [the cruel and debauched wife of the Roman emperor Claudius] who has little cause to be jealous – she would rather be inclined to laughter at this *liaison*.' Lady Harrington had a weakness for both sexes. When her lesbian lover Elizabeth Ashe deserted her for a diplomat she was 'quite devastated . . . her character had been demolished by this desertion'. Ashe, one of the many actress-whores of the time, was twice married and had many lovers. After she died at the age of 84 Horace Walpole observed that she had 'a large collection of amours' (Burford, *Royal St James's*).

GANGS After the heyday of the organised underworld in the seventeenth and eighteenth centuries the following century threw up little in the way of hierarchical gangs until the arrival of waves of immigrants from eastern Europe. In the late nineteenth and early twentieth centuries the geography of the underworld changed. Mass immigration drove some prosperous East End criminals south of the river to what were seen as socially better areas. They included successful confidence tricksters, safe-breakers and high-class thieves 'who regarded themselves as the aristocrats of the underworld'. The overcrowding in the East End also forced out lesser criminals such as forgers, racecourse thugs and particularly housebreakers and pickpockets. This criminal diaspora spawned new gangs, who in the 1920s and 1930s clashed with gangs from north of the river, including the SABINIS. The south London teams included Monkey Benneyworth's ELEPHANT GANG. It is said that a fight with Benneyworth led to Darby Sabini's rise to power. The south London gangster had attacked a barmaid in Sabini's favourite pub, the Griffin in Clerkenwell, tearing off her dress. Although Benneyworth was a much bigger man Darby Sabini thrashed him, knocking him out and breaking his jaw and cheekbone. Benneyworth later returned with his Elephant Gang but was driven out by Sabini and a crowd of young Italians.

The bombing of the East End and other areas with strong criminal traditions in the Second World War also dispersed some criminal families. 'Until they were destroyed by Hitler's bombs, there were still London streets, such as CAMPBELL ROAD near Finsbury Park, Edward Square and Bemerton Street in Islington, Wilmer Gardens and Essex Street in Hoxton, and parts of Notting Dale, which were virtually no-go areas as far as the police were concerned (Murphy, *Smash and Grab*).

Many London gangs of the mid-twentieth century would probably have been forgotten if the gangster BILLY HILL had not listed them in his autobiography *Boss of the Underworld*. Writing about the struggle for supremacy with the WHITE GANG in the West End he wrote of a grand coalition of criminals from London and surrounding districts:

> I saw a chance to clean up the West End. So the Elephant mob came my way, and over the bridge from South London with them came the teams from Brixton and Camberwell and Southwark and Rotherhithe. From Shepherd's Bush and Notting Hill the burglars came, and the King's Cross gang and the Holloway team joined in. The Paddington and Kilburn lot fell in behind as well. Then the other mobs from down East said they wanted to join us. Timber Jim and Wooden George from Ilford came along with their team. Bugsy Reilly brought the Upton Park mob along. A handy gang from Dagenham turned up. Then Fido the Gipsy from Essex joined in. If necessary Fido could have brought along 1,000 gipsies with him to settle this argument.

GARFIELD, JOHN Author of the guide to London harlotry *The Wand'ring Whore* (1660–3). While serving a sentence in Newgate Prison he wrote another guide with the subtitle *The Unparalleled Practices of Mrs Fotheringham*. PRISS FOTHERINGHAM was one of the great bawds of the age, and Garfield also lists other famous contemporary bawds: there were MRS CRESSWELL, Betty Lawrence, Mrs Curtis, Mrs Smith, Mrs Bagley, and MRS PATIENCE RUSSELL. There is no mention of MRS HOLLAND of the Holland's Leaguer, who was presumably long dead. Another edition lists about two hundred whores, who would have paid for these advertisements.

GARNISH Money extorted from prisoners by their jailers. Prisoners were fleeced, having to pay for the very necessities of life. The jailers paid high prices for their positions, and recouped it by extorting money for food, candles, heat, drink, cleaning, sex, visits and fresh air. Those unable to pay or whose money was all gone were thrown into clammy, dark and pestilential dungeons, where the lice cracked underfoot. In 1702 a report on conditions in Newgate stated:

> We do find that the prisoners in the common side of the prison . . . pretend to demand money of every new prisoner that comes in, under the notion of garnish money, which was formerly but 9*s*. and is now advanced to 17*s*. . . . if any prisoner comes in and has not wherewith to pay the garnish money he or she is presently conveyed into a place they call Tangier, and there stript, beaten and abused in a very violent manner.

GARROTTERS An outbreak of violent street robberies in the early 1860s caused a panic. Garrotting probably started more or less unnoticed in east London and after being perfected there was used in the west, where it became news. This 'lay' was worked by teams of at least three – two to rob the victim and a third, perhaps a woman, to act as look-out. The garrotter would attack the victim from behind using a rope, cloth, stick or just his powerful forearm around the throat to half-strangle him and pull his head back. His accomplice then robbed him. It was all over in seconds.

In July 1862 an MP named Pilkington was garrotted and robbed as he walked from Parliament to his club in Pall Mall. That same night Edward Hawkins, a distinguished antiquary who was in his eighties, was attacked between St James's and Bond Street. In November a woman described as 'respectable looking' stopped a jeweller in the street, and her hidden companions then garrotted him. His throat was crushed, and he died several days later. In another attack the victim, a gunsmith, had his hand so badly mangled it had to be amputated and he too died.

Anti-garrotting societies were set up and soon no suspicious-looking character wearing a loose scarf was safe from being dragged to a police station and denounced. In July 1863 legislation known as the 'garrotting Act' was passed. Offenders could be flogged, with the punishment inflicted in instalments to allow the men to recover between floggings, which made it more terrifying. Men were known to collapse in the dock when the sentence was passed. The attacks died out as suddenly and mysteriously as they had begun.

GATEWAYS CLUB, THE Lesbian drinking den made notorious by the film *The Killing of Sister George*, which was partly filmed there in 1968. The club, in Bramerton Street just off the King's Road in Chelsea, was run by Gina Ware and her husband Ted. They married when the beautiful Gina was 31 and Ted 56. Later a trouser-wearing woman known simply as Smithy became part of the Wares' household, and worked as a barmaid in the club. Before the Wares turned the club into a women-only venue it had attracted bookies and tarts, gangsters such as JACK SPOT and the poet Dylan Thomas. *The Killing of Sister George*, which depicted sex between women at a time such things were simply inconceivable in polite circles, brought the club unwanted publicity. In 1971 it was picketed by members of the Gay Liberation Front, who chanted 'Out of the closets, into the streets'. They objected to the covert lesbianism of which the club was a bastion. Nevertheless the club, which opened in 1944, didn't close until 1985.

GAUL, JOHN Wealthy Soho pimp who hired killers to murder his estranged wife. In January 1977 Barbara Gaul was shot dead outside the Black Lion Hotel at Patcham, near Brighton. He husband had hired brothers Roy and Keith Edgeler to kill her because he feared she was about to disclose business secrets which could harm him. Gaul had been fined £25,000 in October 1962 for living off prostitution. He was leasing flats to prostitutes for £20 a week, although only £8 8*s* was entered in the rent book. The Edgeler brothers, who were jailed for life, refused to name Gaul, who had fled to Malta. He defied attempts by Surrey police to extradite him, and died in Italy in 1989. Keith Edgeler said he had not been paid for the killing.

GAY, JOHN (1685–1732) Playwright and poet who wrote *The Beggar's Opera*. This hugely successful play was ostensibly about JACK SHEPPARD and JONATHAN WILD, but was also a thinly disguised satire on the corruption of the prime minister ROBERT WALPOLE. Gay met Wild at Windsor races in 1719, and Wild 'discoursed with great freedom on his profession, and set it in such a light, that the poet imagined he might work up the incidents of it for the stage'. The first performance was given at Lincoln's Inn Fields in 1728. The play ran for sixty-two nights, a record for the time, and the theatre owner, John Rich, packed the audiences in, even having nearly a hundred seated on the stage itself. It was said the play made Gay rich and Rich gay.

There was a debate, prefiguring the modern debate about violence on television, about the effects on susceptible young men of seeing *The Beggar's Opera*. Highwaymen would sometimes claim that they had been corrupted by seeing the play, and the FIELDINGS, among others, claimed it was likely to deprave and corrupt. Sir John Fielding tried to have it suppressed in the 1770s.

GEORGE III (1738–1820) Monarch who survived several assassination attempts. The first was by Margaret Nicholson, a domestic servant, on 2 August 1786. As the king alighted from his coach at St James's Palace to attend a levee Nicholson approached, holding out a piece of paper which he assumed was a petition. She suddenly produced a knife and lunged at him. The blade scarcely damaged his waistcoat, and the King was unhurt. He called out to onlookers who had grabbed Nicholson: 'The poor creature is mad. Do not hurt her. She has not hurt me.' He gave instructions that no one should tell the Queen what had happened until the levee was over. He showed similar sang-froid on 29 October 1795 when a mob surrounded his coach shouting 'Peace and bread! No war! No war! Down with George!' A shot of some kind pierced the window by the King's side and passed through the coach. The King rebuked one of his noble passengers. 'Sit still, my lord. We must not betray fear whatever happens.'

There were two further attempts on his life on 15 May 1800. At a review of the Foot Guards in Hyde Park, a bullet struck a man standing near the King. When it was suggested to the King that the princesses should be sent away he replied: 'I will not have one of them stir for the world.' That evening at Drury Lane Theatre a deranged former soldier, James Hadfield, fired a pistol at the King. The bullet struck a pillar in the royal box. He turned to reassure the Queen: 'It's only a squib. We will not stir. We'll stay the entertainment out.' When the play ended the King followed his usual practice of taking a nap before the start of the following farce.

GEORGE IV (1762–1830) Licentious king who as a young man gambled, whored and incurred enormous debts. Burford tells in *Royal St James's* of 'cold and overt betrayal', of the Prince visiting the fashionable brothels of King Street and King's Place, in the company of the Whig leader CHARLES JAMES FOX and other raffish friends. There is a caricature of the Prince being dunned by brothel-keepers who are holding up itemised bills, including £1,000 for 'first slice of a young tit only 12 years' and £1,000 for 'uncommon diversions'. At the edge of the crowd a young girl holds a paper asking for payment for her lost maidenhead. The Prince and his brother the Duke of Clarence were said to be regular visitors to Mrs Windsor's brothel in King's Place. He and another brother, the Duke of Cumberland, were guests at the wealthy bawd CHARLOTTE HAYES's Epsom mansion. In later life, when he had become so gross he needed a hoist to mount his horse, he preferred middle-aged and ample aristocrats. He had wit and taste, but the nation had to pay far too high a price for his contributions to collecting and architecture.

GERALD, QUEENIE Brothel-keeper with an establishment in the Haymarket. When it was raided by police in June 1913 Queenie was in the bathroom with two girls, aged 17 and 18, who were said to be 'almost nude'. Queenie, an attractive 26-year-old, said she was giving the girls a bath. Police found letters from men, a revolver, a whip, a cane, some photographs and rather a lot of money – more than £200. Queenie pleaded guilty to living on immoral earnings and was sent to prison for three months. There were rumours of white slavery, that virgins were being procured for wealthy men. Keir Hardie, the Labour MP, harassed the Home Secretary, the Pankhursts weighed in, and eventually the affair was aired in the Commons. Queenie was still in business in the Twenties.

GERMAN PRINCESS, THE (1642–73) Title assumed by Mary Carleton, bigamist, confidence trickster, thief and playwright executed for illegally returning from transportation. She claimed to be the daughter of a German, Lord Holmstein, but really came from the family of a musician in Canterbury. After being acquitted of bigamy at Maidstone Assizes she went to Cologne, where she cheated a rich gentleman out of a fortune in jewels by promising to marry him. Instead she returned to London and claimed she was the daughter of a prince of the Holy Roman Empire who had banished her for marrying without his consent, and then had her husband executed. She married a man named Carleton, was tried for polygamy but again acquitted for lack of evidence. She became an actress and was taken up by a gentleman who showered her with gems and money. When she grew tired of him she stripped his house of valuables and moved out. She wrote a play, *The German Princess*, about her exploits, and appeared in it herself. She launched herself with aplomb on a varied career of crime, cheating tradesmen and operating various scams, including a variant of the BADGER GAME. She invited a young barrister to her rooms in Holborn to advise on her financial affairs. While they talked a servant entered and said Mary's husband had arrived. Mary persuaded the lawyer to hide in a cupboard. He was discovered by her outraged 'husband' who drew his sword and threatened to defend his honour by killing him. The terrified lawyer was thankful to buy his way out for £100. Later Mary was arrested for stealing a silver tankard and transported to Jamaica. She returned illegally after two years and married a wealthy Westminster apothecary, whom she soon left, having robbed him of £300. She was arrested after the Keeper of the MARSHALSEA PRISON recognised her while searching her lodgings near St George's Fields for stolen goods. She unsuccessfully PLEADED HER BELLY and was executed at Tyburn.

GERRARD, ALFIE Hitman, one of the murderers of FRANK MITCHELL. He reportedly died of alcoholism, although FREDDIE FOREMAN says the cause of death was gluttony. His son NICKY 'SNAKEHIPS' GERRARD was also a hitman.

GERRARD, NICKY Hitman known as 'Snakehips'. Son of ALFIE GERRARD. Hired by RONNIE KNIGHT to kill TONY ZOMPARELLI. When Zomparelli was released from prison after serving a sentence for killing Knight's brother Snakehips was waiting. As Zomparelli played a pinball machine in a Soho amusement arcade on 4 September 1974 Snakehips fired four bullets into the back of his head. It is believed Snakehips may have carried out as many as a dozen contract killings. Police say in 1970 he shot dead Andre Mizelas, 48, owner of the Andre Bernard hairdressing chain, as he drove in Hyde Park. Mizelas, whose clients included the actress Julie Christie and the Queen's great-aunt, Princess Alice, Countess of Athlone, was murdered over a debt. Snakehips, who was paid £5,000 for the killing, was himself murdered in 1982 as he left his daughter's eleventh birthday party. Two men in balaclavas cut him down with shotguns. One theory about the killing was that he had become too violent even for the gangland bosses who hired him. A criminal who knew him said: 'When you've got a mad dog in the family, it's sad but you've got to put him down.'

GHOST SQUAD A secret group of undercover officers serving with the FLYING SQUAD. The group was set up in January 1946 and disbanded four years later. They were known as the Ghost Squad because the identities of the thirty or so officers were a secret and they never appeared in court. Although they claimed that they arrested 780 criminals and seized stolen property worth £300,000 their payouts to informers totalled a surprisingly high £20,000.

GIBB, JANE Mad prostitute who became the target of popular hatred and hysteria. Gibb had been in trouble for robbing customers violently. In 1799 she murdered one of them, and was obviously deranged at her trial, as the *Newgate Calendar* makes clear:

> During the whole time of her giving evidence, she appeared to be in a violent passion: she frequently darted looks of fury and rage . . . her language was extremely low and vulgar; and the very tone of voice in which she delivered herself was disgusting. She seldom attended to the questions that were put to her, but poured forth a heap of words without much connection or meaning . . .

For some reason the whole population seemed to take against her. She was taken to the Bridewell, where the other prisoners threatened to beat her. As she was taken to and from court for further hearings crowds tried to lynch her. The Watch were called out to protect her. The *London Chronicle* reported in December 1799 that in Bedford Square the mob tore all the clothes off her back before the constables could rescue her. She was eventually sent to Bedlam.

GIN MANIA Craze for the drinking of cheap spirits which afflicted London's poor from the 1720s to the 1750s. Gin drinking was introduced from Holland by Dutch followers of William III. The government encouraged it: Parliament was dominated by gentlemen farmers, the country was producing a glut of grain and distilling it into gin was vastly profitable. Taxes on gin were reduced. The duty was only 2*d* a gallon, sellers didn't need a retail licence and soon the drink was being sold in thousands of premises of varying degrees of respectability – in 1725 there were 6,187 in the capital excluding the City and Southwark. By contrast, the vastly bigger London of 1945 had only 4,000 pubs.

Gin was cheap – 'Drunk for a Penny, Dead Drunk for two pence, Clean Straw for Nothing' was the boast of the gin shops. Most of the distilling of gin took place in London, and most of the drinking. Among the poor, almost everyone drank it – men, women and children, even infants. It was used as an anaesthetic to silence starving children. It was a food substitute for their starving parents. The drink's vile taste and lethal potency – it was sold at the strength it came from the still, much stronger than the gin sold today – were disguised by heavy sweetening with sugar and flavouring with cordials.

The results were appalling. Judith Defour fetched her 2-year-old child from a workhouse where it had been given new clothes. She strangled it, sold the clothes for 1*s* 4*d*, left the naked body in a ditch at Bethnal Green, split the money with the woman who had suggested the crime and spent the rest on gin.

People reeled about the streets or collapsed in gutters at all hours of the day and night. In the middle of the day men, women and children lay stupified in the streets in slum areas such as St Giles and Whetstone Park. Inside the gin shops unconscious customers were propped up against the walls until they came round and could start again. The liquor was ubiquitous: the outlets included street stalls, back rooms in private houses and cellars as well as the regular gin shops. In 1743 eight million gallons of the fiery spirit were consumed, according to official estimates, but some thought the figure was as high as nineteen million gallons. And by far the greatest part of it went down the throats of the poor of London. The novelist and magistrate HENRY FIELDING, in *Inquiry into the Causes of the Late Increase of Robbers*, wrote:

> A new kind of drunkenness, unknown to our ancestors, is lately sprung up amongst us, and which, if not put a stop to, will infallibly destroy a great part of the inferior people. The drunkenness I here intend is that acquired by the strongest intoxicating liquors, and particularly by that poison called Gin; which I have great reason to think is the principal sustenance (if it may be so called) of more than a hundred thousand people in this metropolis. Many of these wretches there are who swallow pints of this poison within the twenty four hours; the dreadful effects of which I have the misfortune every day to see, and to smell too. But I have no need to insist on my own credit, or on that of my informers; the great revenue arising from the tax on this liquor, (the consumption of which is almost wholly confined to the lowest order of people) will prove the quantity consumed better than any other evidence.

Hogarth's Gin Lane *shows the disorder and misery Gin Mania caused. It is set in the slum of St Giles, where many of the houses were gin shops. Gin was cheap –'Drunk for a Penny, Dead Drunk for two pence, Clean Straw for Nothing' – and was used to numb the pangs of hunger.*

Particularly disturbing was the extent to which women were 'habituated' to gin. 'We find the contagion has spread among [women] to a degree hardly possible to be conceived,' reported a committee of the Middlesex magistrates in 1736. 'Unhappy mothers habituate themselves to these distilled liquors, whose children are born weak and sickly, and often look old and shrivelled as though they had numbered many years; others, again, give [gin] daily to their children, whilst young, and learn them, even before they can go [walk] to taste and approve of this great and certain destroyer.'

The government made clumsy efforts to curb the gin mania it had created. In 1729 following a campaign for restriction led by the Middlesex magistrates a licence fee of £20 for retailing spirits was imposed, and the spirit duty was raised from 2*d* to 5*s* a gallon. These measures were found to be unworkable and repealed in 1733, a move which was followed by another wave of drunkenness and disorder. This in turn led to the more draconian 'Gin Act' of 1736 requiring a £50 licence for retailing.

There was rioting, an explosion in Westminster Hall and threats to the life of the Master of the Rolls, Joseph Jekyll, seen as the chief initiator of the Act. Five informers under the Gin Act were stoned to death, one of them in New Palace Yard. A particular hate figure was the magistrate SIR THOMAS DE VEIL, loathed among other things for his attempts to implement the Gin Act. In William Hogarth's print *Night* a figure which would have been clearly recognisable to contemporaries as Sir Thomas has the contents of a chamber pot poured over his head. This refers to a story that Sir Thomas was one day sampling gin, only to find that an ill-wisher had replaced it with urine. In January 1738 a mob besieged his house in Frith Street, threatening to burn it and kill his informers.

Popular violence effectively killed the law, and in seven years only three of the expensive licences were paid for. The law spawned a horde of informers: in a period of less than two years there were 12,000 cases, and nearly 5,000 convictions. The public took its revenge by hunting down the informers, a number of whom were murdered.

The rage for gin seemed to subside gradually. In 1751 some gin-shops were suppressed, and the increase in taxes was eventually so effective that in 1757 an observer commented: 'We do not see the hundredth part of poor wretches drunk in the street since the said qualifications.'

GLADSTONE, WILLIAM EWART (1809–98) Statesman with a weakness for reforming prostitutes. Among those he tried to reclaim was SKITTLES, otherwise Catherine Walters. Cynics pointed out that he tried to redeem only the beautiful. Of one, Elizabeth Collins, by whom he was clearly infatuated, he wrote in July 1852: 'Half a most lovely statue, beautiful beyond measure.' The MP Henry Labouchere said: 'Gladstone manages to combine his missionary meddling with a keen appreciation of a pretty face. He has never been known to rescue any of our East End whores, nor for that matter is it easy to contemplate him rescuing any ugly woman, and I am quite sure his conception of the Magdalen is of an incomparable example of pulchritude with a superb figure and carriage.' When he was caught kissing Mrs Cornwallis West, a woman celebrated merely for being a beauty, it seemed to some to confirm his hypocrisy. The prostitutes mostly took a fairly cynical view of his activities, calling him 'Old Glad Eye'. He fought a long-running battle against the brothel-keeper MRS JEFFRIES, known as the wickedest woman of the age.

GOADBY, JANE (flourished 1751–79) Innovative madam, credited with introducing the sumptuous French style to London brothels about 1750. She had been to Paris to see what that city had to offer, opened a house in Berwick Street, Soho, and 'catered to all tastes, at the most exclusive prices'. Only the most beautiful and refined whores were engaged, and they were medically examined first. A physician was retained to carry out weekly examinations. The girls were dressed in fine French silks and lace. Mrs Goadby 'brought an air of refinement into brothel-keeping'. The *Nocturnal Revels* says that in 1779 she was still 'laying in good stocks of clean goods warranted proof for the races and watering places during the coming summer', but she retired soon afterwards with a fortune and a fine country house. There were others to follow her lead. The new brothels were called seraglios, nunneries, abbeys, temples and cloisters, and the girls were sometimes known as nuns. One of the girls who graduated from her Berwick Street establishment was ELIZABETH ARMISTEAD, later wife of the Whig leader Charles James Fox.

GODDARD, SERGEANT GEORGE Crooked officer responsible for policing the West End clubs in the 1920s. It took a long time for fellow officers to notice that Goddard, who earned £6 15*s* a week, drove an expensive car, lived in a large house and had numerous bank accounts and safe-deposit boxes. He had been extorting money from the club owners, including 'Night Club Queen' KATE MEYRICK. Goddard was tried and explained that he had been lucky with bets on the horses. He had also made £2,000 from foreign-exchange dealing and £4,000 from selling 'Empire Rock' at the British Empire Exhibition of 1924. Not surprisingly he was found guilty of 'corruptly receiving money'. He was fined £2,000 and sentenced to eighteen months' hard labour. When he was released he spent a prosperous retirement in the country. Mrs Meyrick was less fortunate. Shortly after finishing one of her spells in Holloway for running illegal clubs she was charged with bribing Goddard, and got fifteen months' hard labour.

GODDARD, RAYNER (1877–1971) Reactionary Lord Chief Justice, in office from 1946 to 1958. He fought moves to abolish the death penalty: he thought murderers should be 'destroyed', and was in favour of executing murderers who were insane. He treated psychiatrists with contempt. His behaviour during the trial of DEREK BENTLEY helped the campaign for abolition.

GODFREY, SIR EDMUND BERRY (1622–78) Justice of the Peace who was murdered while he investigated TITUS OATES's allegations of Catholic plots. In 1678 Berry interrogated Oates and later said he believed his own life was in danger from Catholics. On 12 October he disappeared and five days later his body was found in a ditch on Primrose Hill. He had been strangled and then stabbed with his own sword. A Catholic, Miles Prance, who had been tortured, gave evidence before Parliament in December that he was the look-out when Godfrey was murdered in Somerset House. He named the killers as Robert Green, Henry Berry, Lawrence Hill and two Catholic priests, Gerald and Kelly. The first three were tried in February 1679 and hanged. Their innocence is widely accepted. *See* TITUS OATES

GODFREY, ELIZABETH Prostitute executed for murder in 1807. Godfrey took a man back to her room in a Marylebone lodging house on 23 December 1806. He accused her of robbing him and after a row another lodger, Richard Prince, called out the Watch. Godfrey was held overnight in the Watch house. On Christmas Day she knocked on Prince's door and stabbed him in the eye with a knife. Asked why she had done it she said: 'It served him right.'

GOLDSMID BROTHERS, THE Two Jews who scaled the heights of City success and then committed suicide. They were the sons of a Dutch merchant who settled in London. The brothers went into business together in the 1770s and quickly became dominant figures in various lines of business – dealing in funds, broking, loan contracting etc. They became friends of the royal family and generous philanthropists. They both acquired splendid country houses. However one of them, Benjamin, became fat, gouty and melancholic and in 1808 he hanged himself with a silk cord. His brother Abraham was badly affected: in 1810 he was knocked down by an ox in Lombard Street and by September with business and psychological pressures growing he was showing clear signs of strain. On the evening of the last Thursday in September he played 'a distracted game of cards' at his country home and the next morning he shot himself in the grounds (Kynaston, *The City of London,* Vol. 1).

His death caused consternation in the City, to the annoyance of WILLIAM COBBETT. His *Weekly Political Register* thundered:

> All this for the death of a Jew merchant! The *king* and the *heir apparent* to be informed of it by a royal messenger! And, is it really true, that this man's having shot himself made the citizens of London almost forget everything else? Is it really true, that such an event put business nearly at a stand? Is it really true, that it produced an effect equal to *peace* or *war* suddenly made? And is it true; is there truth in the shameful fact, that a Jew Merchant's shooting himself produced *alarm* and *dismay* in the capital of England, which is also called, and not very improperly, perhaps, the emporium of the world?

GOLDSTEIN, LILLIAN (1898–1976) The 'Bob-Haired Bandit', partner and driver for motor bandit RUBY SPARKS in the 1920s. She came from a respectable Wembley Jewish family. She worked as a dressmaker until an unhappy love affair with a married man made her take to crime. She drove the car while Sparks carried out smash-and-grab raids and burglaries. Nutty Sharpe of the Flying Squad said of her: 'She usually drove a big Mercedes car. Sitting at the wheel with her man's raincoat collar turned up around her close-fitting little black hat, there wasn't much of her to see.' Of her legendary skill as a driver he said: 'She could whiz that great long tourer about with the skill of an artist.' Newspapers described her as 'a girl bandit with dark bobbed hair, a small innocent-looking face and an active and intelligent brain'.

In 1927 she and Sparks were arrested and charged with robbery. She was acquitted but he got three years. In 1939 Sparks was jailed for five years. Goldstein was convicted of harbouring him after he escaped from Dartmoor, and sentenced to six months' imprisonment. She served only three weeks. The judge then released her, saying she had 'followed a natural womanly instinct in trying to succour and protect this man, with whom you had intimate relations over a period of years'. Lilian later told Sparks she had 'had enough of this bandit queen lark' and went back to Wembley Park for good.

GONSON, SIR JOHN Magistrate who was a scourge of prostitutes in the eighteenth century. *See* MOTHER NEEDHAM and KATE HACKABOUT

GORDON RIOTS The riots which raged for a week in June 1780 were the most destructive of the eighteenth century. They were fomented by the young Lord George Gordon, an opportunist MP who saw the Catholic Relief Act of 1778 as a chance to further his career. The Act, intended to improve the civil rights of Catholics, was unpopular in London, and on 2 June Gordon harangued a vast crowd of perhaps 60,000 protesters at St George's Fields. They set off towards Westminster where, encouraged by Gordon, they terrorised the politicians. That night they destroyed the Sardinian embassy and ransacked the Bavarian embassy. Over the following days Catholic chapels, houses, shops and taverns were attacked and Irish areas terrorised. Gordon had lost control of the mob, which destroyed NEWGATE PRISON and the Bow Street police office, broke open the New Prison and Clerkenwell Bridewell, burned the FLEET and KING'S BENCH Prisons, attacked the Bank of England, threatened Parliament and Lambeth Palace and set fire to the Catholic Thomas Langdale's gin distillery, a blaze in which some of the looters perished.

The Lord Mayor had 'pursued a policy of benign non-intervention' (Inwood, *A History of London*). Now the City Militia and the Honourable Artillery Company were called out, and about 10,000 troops were brought into the city and given orders to fire on the rioters. At least 300 rioters were left dead and dying, 450 were arrested, 25 were hanged and a further twelve jailed. The policy of hanging criminals near the scene of the crime meant gallows were set up all over London: at Tower Hill, Bishopsgate, Bow Street, Holborn Hill, Bethnal

A prostitute and her servant gloat over the spoils of a night's whoring in Plate 2 of Hogarth's A Harlot's Progress. *Unseen by her, the magistrate Sir John Gonson, scourge of whores, has come with his posse to arrest her. This is the point of no return: ahead lie prison and death.*

Green, Whitechapel, Moorfields, Old Street, St George's Fields, Bloomsbury Square and the Old Bailey. Many of those hanged were little more than children. Seventeen were under 18 and three were not yet 15. Horace Walpole commented: 'The bulk of the criminals are so young that half a dozen schoolmasters might have quashed the insurrection.'

The targets of the mob are interesting. Although Gordon had used anti-Catholic feeling to whip up the riots, and some Catholic chapels, houses and schools were attacked, none of the city's 14,000 Catholics was killed. The symbols of law became the main focus of the mob's fury: eight prisons, the homes of judges – that of LORD MANSFIELD, the Lord Chief Justice, was ransacked – about twenty crimping houses (where pressed sailors were held) and spunging houses for debtors. The poet and visionary artist William Blake took part in the destruction of Newgate Prison 'and saw the burning of this, London's Bastille, as a real and symbolic act of liberation' (Inwood, *A History of London*). JOHN WILKES, the radical whose antics had long kept the London mob in a ferment, joined his fellow Common Councillors in taking up arms to defend the Bank of England.

Gordon was tried for high treason but acquitted. He later became a Jew, Israel Abraham George Gordon. In 1787 he was convicted of a libel on Marie Antoinette and imprisoned in NEWGATE, where he died of jail fever.

The recriminations that followed the riots led to Lord Mayor Kennett being forced from office. He had refused to allow the military to fire on the rioters while they were burning Newgate. Magistrates were also criticised for being reluctant to authorise the use of firepower. *See* RIOT ACT

GOULD, MRS HANNAH (flourished 1742–79) Bawd with social pretensions. The *Nocturnal Revels* says Mrs Gould's brothel in Russell Street was second only to MOTHER DOUGLAS's in importance. She tried to maintain a high tone: 'This lady plumed herself much upon being the gentlewoman; she despised every woman who swore or talked indecently, nor would she suffer drunken females.' Her lover was a 'certain notary public of Jewish extraction' for whom, the *Nocturnal Revels* says, she had a great passion 'on account of his *uncommon parts* and *great abilities*'. Burford and Wotton identify him as the notary public Moses Moravia (*Private Vices, Public Virtues*). Her establishment, which catered for wealthy bankers and merchants, was exceptionally well run and orderly, and also exceptionally expensive. The clients would sometimes arrive on Friday after a hard week in the City and stay until Monday morning, when they would return refreshed to their toil. The unfortunate Moravia was jailed for trying to defraud an insurance company and died in poverty in 1767, Mrs Gould having presumably dropped him.

GRAHAM, DR JAMES (1745–94) One of the greatest quacks in the golden age of quackery. Proprietor in the 1780s of the Temple of Health and Hymen off the Strand, where was located his Grand Celestial Bed, which promoted long life and sexual rejuvenation. The bed was supported by forty pillars of glass, and could be hired by couples desperate for children. Graham guaranteed that they would produce an heir. Among his assistants was the twentyish Emma Hart, known to history as Lady Hamilton, Nelson's mistress. At Graham's she was known as Hygieia, Goddess of Health. To demonstrate the powers of mud baths she and Graham would immerse themselves up to their chins in the ooze, he in an enormous wig and Emma with her hair festooned with flowers and feathers. Graham would sit on a Celestial Throne to deliver 'very celebrated' lectures. He sold the usual nostrums, with fancy names such as Imperial Pills and Nervous Aethereal Balsom. Graham became a religious fanatic and went mad. He was confined in a lunatic asylum and died in 1794.

GRAHAME, KENNETH (1859–1932) Author and survivor of a murder attempt. In 1903 a young man walked into the Bank of England and asked to see Grahame, who worked there. He handed Grahame a roll of paper tied at one end with white ribbon and at the other with black. When Grahame untied the black ribbon the man drew a revolver and fired several shots at him. He was slightly wounded. The young man, an engineer named George Robinson, was arrested, and explained that he had decided to kill Grahame if he opened the black ribbon first. At his trial it was disclosed that he had become insane after being bitten by a dog. He was locked up and five years later Grahame wrote *The Wind in the Willows*.

GREAT TRAIN ROBBERIES *see* following page

GREENE, ROBERT (1560?–92) Playwright whose works give us important information about the Elizabethan underworld. Greene described the tricks of the pickpockets who infested old ST PAUL'S CATHEDRAL, and the arts of the CONY-CATCHERS.

GREGORY, MAUNDY (1877–1941) Political fixer and seller of honours. In the 1920s when he was the editor of the *Whitehall Gazette* Gregory established a tariff for honours: £10,000 for a knighthood, £30,000 for a baronetcy and £100,000 or more for a peerage. In 1925 the Honours (Prevention of Abuses) Act should have put men like Gregory out of business. However, through his contacts he would find out who was going to be honoured. As these people would have no prior knowledge of the matter Gregory would contact them and offer to get them the honour for a price. John Davidson, chairman of the Conservative Party decided to put a stop to the racket. He got a colleague to worm his way into Gregory's confidence, and so found out who his clients were. Davidson made sure that none of these people got a title. Gregory offered a title to a retired naval officer, who went to the police. Gregory was charged with fraud. There were fears that he would tell tales, and the Conservatives approached the Labour Prime Minister, Ramsay MacDonald, with a plan to pay Gregory hush money. They suggested that the philanthropist Sir Julian Cahn should be made a baronet, for which he would pay £30,000. The money could be given to Gregory and he would go into permanent exile in France. MacDonald was reluctant to go along with this, but he knew that prominent Labour figures were also involved in the titles racket, and that Gregory might name them. 'The dunghill', he concluded, 'had to be cleared away without delay.' Gregory served two months in Wormwood Scrubs and was then whisked away to France, where he died in hospital in 1941, without revealing what he knew.

GUERIN, EDDIE (1860–1931) Robber, escaper and putative cannibal. In 1901 Guerin, who was born

Continued on p. 114

GREAT TRAIN ROBBERIES

The first Great Train Robbery, in 1855, in which a gang stole a quarter of a ton of gold from the London to Folkestone express, far surpassed the later raid in ingenuity and daring. EDWARD AGAR, the leader of the robbers, was already a successful burglar before the raid. He was told by William Pierce, who had been sacked by South-Eastern Railways in 1850, that gold bullion was being sent from London to Paris. Over a long period Agar and Pierce painstakingly built up a picture of the shipments: the coins and gold ingots were packed into metal-bound chests, sealed with the merchants' wax stamps and packed into one of the latest Chubb safes, which was then locked. There were two locks on the safe, and the two keys were held by two different officials. The safes were then loaded on to the guard's van of the South-Eastern's Folkestone express. At Folkestone there were also two keys, one held by the railways superintendent, the other locked in a cupboard in an office on the harbour pier. When the train reached Folkestone the safe would be taken out and opened, and the bullion chests weighed to check that the weight was exactly the same as when they left London. The bullion chests were then loaded onto a paddle steamer bound for Boulogne. When they arrived they were again weighed, and taken by train to Paris.

At first Agar felt that the robbery was beyond them. It was his young mistress, Fanny Kay, who proved the catalyst. She had been a barmaid at Tonbridge station in Kent, and knew various employees of the South-Eastern. Among them was James Burgess, a guard on trains from London to Folkestone. The last of the conspirators was William Tester, a well-educated young man with a monocle. He was assistant to the superintendent in the traffic department at London Bridge.

With his new accomplices Agar set about getting hold of the two safe keys so that he could make wax impressions of them. In the spring of 1854 he went to Folkestone to study the procedure for opening the safe when it arrived on the express. He discovered that sometimes the safe contained not bullion but packets of other goods for delivery locally in Folkestone. On these occasions the safe might be locked with only one key: the other, held by the superintendent of the railway, would not be needed.

Then the robbers had an extraordinary piece of luck. One of the keys at Folkestone was lost, and the safes were sent back to Chubbs to have new locks and new keys. William Tester was given the job of liaising with Chubbs.

When the safes and keys were ready Chubbs notified Tester. Agar hired a room at a public house in Tooley Street, near London Bridge station, and Tester brought him the keys. Agar pressed them into tins of wax and returned them. The whole thing had taken a matter of minutes. The keys were returned to London Bridge station. Only then did Agar realise that Tester, instead of bringing him two different keys had brought him two copies of the same one. They were almost back where they had started, but Agar refused to give up. Once more he turned his attention to Folkestone. He went to the pier where he knew a copy of the second key was kept in a locked cupboard in the railway office. Although staff were supposed to man the office at all times, they sometimes left it locked but empty for about ten minutes while they met the ferry.

Agar waited until the staff were out and made an impression of the lock on the main office door. With this he made a key. Next he sent himself a parcel by the South-Eastern Railway to be collected at Folkestone. When it arrived, he went to the office on the pier to collect it. John Chapman, the railway official in charge of the office, opened a wall cupboard with a key he kept in his pocket. From the cupboard he took the all-important safe key, and went out to open the safe, leaving the cupboard key in the lock. While he was away Agar took an impression of the cupboard key.

Agar returned to London, made a copy of the cupboard key and contacted Pierce. Some weeks later they went to Folkestone. This time Pierce, dressed in a railway uniform, entered the railway office while the staff were out meeting the ferry and got the safe key from the cupboard and took it to the waiting Agar, who made impressions from it. By the time the staff returned the key was back in the locked cupboard.

By May 1855 the gang were ready. On the 15th while Agar watched, Burgess walked onto the forecourt of London Bridge station and gave a prearranged signal: it meant that the train was carrying bullion that night. Burgess let Agar into the guard's van and as the express sped from London Bridge station towards Folkestone he opened the safe, removed the gold, replaced it with exactly the same weight of lead shot, then resealed the safes with home-made seals. When the train stopped at Redhill some of the gold was passed to an accomplice on the platform. At Folkestone Agar and Burgess left the train with the remainder. The safes were weighed on the quayside, found to be the correct weight, and shipped to France. The theft was not discovered until they were opened in Paris.

To help dispose of the gold Agar recruited JEM SAWARD, a successful Queen's Bench defence counsel known to his clients as 'Barrister Saward' who was also a highly successful criminal. For eighteen months the authorities had no leads, and the gang enjoyed their fortune. Then Agar's estranged girlfriend, who had been cheated by another member of the gang, went to the police. When the trial opened at the Central Criminal Court in January 1857 Agar, who by this time was in prison for another offence, gave evidence for the Crown and was not charged. Two other members of the gang got fourteen years' transportation, another the light sentence of only two years because of a technicality.

On 8 August 1963 a gang used a false signal to stop the night train from Euston to Glasgow at Sears Crossing in Buckinghamshire. They coshed the driver, Jack Mills, separated the mail van from the rest of the train, broke in and stole 120 mail bags containing about £2,600,000. It was the biggest cash robbery in history.

The raid had been meticulously planned, largely by BRUCE REYNOLDS, a fairly successful robber and a glamorous figure who drove an Aston Martin and had contacts throughout the London underworld. The gang had been given vague details of cash shipments on mail trains by a mysterious Irishman. It was Reynolds who turned these into a workable blueprint and put together the team for the raid. His second-in-command was Gordon Goody, a giant of a man with 'Hello Ireland' and 'Dear Mother' tattooed on his biceps. He shared Reynolds's love of the good life. The others included CHARLIE WILSON, a bookie and former protection racketeer; Buster Edwards, a club-owner and small-time crook; Jimmy White, an ex-paratrooper who had already worked with Reynolds; Tommy Wisbey and Bob Welch, who had been involved in earlier train robberies on the Brighton line with some of the other gang members; Jimmy Hussey, a man with a string of convictions for theft and violence; Roger Cordery, an expert on trains and signals; Roy James, a getaway driver who needed money to get into Formula One racing: John Wheater, a solicitor and his clerk, Brian Field; and Leonard Field, no relation, a florist. Then there was RONNIE BIGGS, an incompetent crook. There are also believed to have been others who were never caught. Police believe the hapless Billy Boal was also involved, although the others all denied it. He was to die in prison.

After the raid the gang drove to their hide-out, Leatherslade Farm, about twenty-seven miles away. The money was divided up. The gang had planned to clean the farm thoroughly, and in fact they left very little evidence. But there were about fifteen men in the gang, and some prints were left – on a sauce bottle, on a saucer of milk put out for a cat and on a game of Monopoly. When the robbers saw a small plane circling the area they panicked. Carrying suitcases filled with money they fled.

By 13 August the police had found the farm and the mail bags. Soon they found the prints of James, Hussey, Edwards and Wilson among others. Tommy Butler, head of the Flying Squad and a veteran of the BILLY HILL and JACK SPOT campaigns, was put in charge of the investigation.

Boal and Roger Cordery were arrested in Bournemouth when they tried to rent lodgings from the wife of a police officer. A large sum of money was found in their car. A Dorking couple on a motorcycle who stopped in a wood found a suitcase full of cash. They alerted the police who found another bag. The total amount in the two bags was £100,000. In one of the suitcases was a receipt from a German hotel in the name of Field. This was Brian Field, the solicitor's clerk.

Jimmy White's caravan at Box Hill in Surrey was raided and £30,000 was found. One after another, the gang were rounded up. The trial began at Aylesbury on 20 January 1964. Biggs, Wilson, Wisbey, Bob Welch, Jim Hussey, James and Goody got thirty years each. Lennie and Brian Field each got twenty-five years. Cordery, who pleaded guilty, received twenty years and Boal twenty-four. Boal died in prison. Wheater got three years. Reynolds, who was not arrested until later, got twenty-five years.

Only £400,000 of the stolen money was recovered. The robbers themselves did not have much time to enjoy it. Some of them escaped and found life on the run expensive. Others were cheated by the people they entrusted the money to while they served their sentences.

Brian Field had his twenty-five year sentence reduced to five years for receiving. He died in a road accident. Edwards, who had escaped to Mexico with Reynolds, gave himself up in 1966 and got fifteen years. He suffered from depression and hanged himself near the flower stall he kept at Waterloo Station. Wilson, who escaped from Winson Green prison in Birmingham and made his way to Canada, opened his door one day in January 1968 to find Tommy Butler and fifty Royal Canadian Mounted Police officers standing there. After serving his sentence he was murdered in Spain.

Reynolds left Mexico for France and then Torquay. On 8 November 1968 he opened the door to find Butler, who had stayed on at Scotland Yard to track down those train robbers who were still free, standing there. Butler: 'Hello Bruce, it's been a long time.' Reynolds: 'C'est la vie.' After serving his sentence he lived in a flat at Croydon and wrote his memoirs, *Autobiography of a Thief*. Ronnie Biggs, the least of the robbers, escaped from Wandsworth Prison in July 1965 and eventually arrived in Brazil. Old and sick, he returned to Britain in 1999 and was arrested.

in London in 1860, was sent to the Île du Salut off Devil's Island for robbing American Express in Paris. He escaped and made his way back to London, where his reputation was enhanced by the belief that in order to survive he had eaten the two men who escaped with him. He was arrested on a French warrant after his former mistress, a prostitute known as CHICAGO MAY, betrayed him. He successfully fought attempts to extradite him on the ground that he was born in England. He was ambushed and shot outside Russell Square underground station by Chicago May and her lover Charlie Smith, otherwise known as Cubine Jackson. Smith was jailed for life for the murder attempt, and Chicago May for fifteen years. In old age Guerin bemoaned 'the young thieves of today who have no skills or code of conduct'.

GUINNESS SHARE SCANDAL, THE In 1990 four noted City figures were charged with illegally supporting the price of shares in the Guinness brewing conglomerate during a takeover battle. Former Guinness chairman Ernest Saunders got five years for conspiracy and three and a half years for false accounting but was released after ten months because of what his doctors described as a form of dementia. He later started a second successful City career. Sir Jack Lyons, Gerald Ronson and Anthony Parnes were also given jail sentences. Lyons, 74, escaped jail because of ill-health but was stripped of his knighthood and fined £3 million. Ronson was fined £5 million. The trial lasted 112 days and cost around £7.5 million, making it the most expensive court action in British legal history to that time.

GULLY, JOHN Prize-fighter and crooked racehorse owner who became an MP. Gully, British heavyweight boxing champion from 1806 to 1808, is reputed to have been released from NEWGATE PRISON to fight the Game Chicken in 1808. His scandalous and successful career on the turf made him wealthy. In 1832 his horse St Giles won the Derby after all the other horses had been 'pulled' or 'made safe' by agreement among the owners. Gully was said to have won £50,000 on St Giles. When another of his horses, Margrave, won the St Leger through a similar fix his winnings are thought to have been more than £30,000. He had twenty-four children and was MP for Pontefract in the 1830s.

GUNPOWDER PLOT, THE Ambitious plan to kill the king, queen, heir to the throne and the entire government and replace it with Catholics. A group of Roman Catholic dissidents led by Robert Catesby planned to blow up the Palace of Westminster on 5 November 1605, when King James I and the Queen would be present at the State Opening of Parliament. Catesby was a reckless extremist whose family had suffered for their faith with fines and imprisonment. He brooded on these wrongs, and with his fellow plotters gradually refined the scheme. They acquired a large amount of gunpowder, rented a house near the Houses of Parliament and began digging a tunnel underneath it. The tunnel filled up with water and was useless, but they were then able to rent a cellar directly under the House of Lords. There they heaped up thirty barrels of gunpowder and waited for the State Opening. The deluded plotters believed they could themselves form a government and thus achieve toleration for Catholics. A key figure in the plot was Guy Fawkes, a Catholic convert, a Yorkshireman who had distinguished himself in the armies of Spain. He had already been involved in various plots, and was courageous and resourceful. He was the man chosen to ignite the enormous bomb.

Guy Fawkes and the Gunpowder Plot conspirators. They were disaffected Catholics who aimed to blow up Parliament and form a government. The plot was betrayed and Fawkes discovered with the explosives. Catesby, the leader, died fighting: Fawkes was terribly tortured and then executed.

The plot was betrayed. On the evening of 26 October the Catholic Lord Monteagle received a letter from his brother-in-law, Francis Tresham, who was involved, warning him not to go to the State Opening. Monteagle told Robert Cecil, the chief minister, and Fawkes was discovered hiding in the cellar. He was carrying the slow matches and touchwood necessary to ignite the gunpowder. Fawkes was taken to the king and told him that 'a desperate deed requires a desperate remedy'. He named his fellow conspirators, but only after three days of 'the uttermost torture'. Catesby had left London on 2 November for the west Midlands, where he hoped to raise a revolt. After the arrest of Fawkes he was hunted down and died fighting at Holbeche in Staffordshire with three other conspirators. He was holding an image of the Virgin. Eight plotters were executed in January 1606. Among them was Fawkes, who had been stretched on the rack and could not climb the scaffold unaided. The plot affected King James I's nerves so badly that he refused to dine in public and became something of a recluse. When some youths fired a cannon in Gray's Inn Fields, the king, who was sleeping in Whitehall Palace a couple of miles away, sat up in bed and shouted 'Treason'.

GWYN, NELL (*c.* 1650–87) Orange girl who became Charles II's mistress. She was born about 1650 in London; her mother, who was often drunk on cheap brandy, kept 'something very close to a bawdy house'. Before she found employment at the King's Theatre as an orange girl, Nell sold fish in the streets and worked as a servant in a brothel. She became the mistress of the leading actor Charles Hart, who trained her to be an actress. PEPYS, who saw her in John Fletcher's *The Humorous Lieutenant* in January 1666, wrote in his diary that 'Nelly, a most pretty woman', had acted the part of Celia that day 'and did it pretty well'. She was at her best in comedy. Pepys wrote of her in Dryden's *The Maiden Queene*: 'there is a comical part done by Nell . . . so great performance of a comical part was never, I believe, in the world before as Nell do this . . .'. He was not convinced by her acting in tragic roles, and indeed she seems to have been an untroubled extrovert.

There are many pictures of Nell, in words and paint. Sir Peter Lely's coquettish nude portrait of the recumbent beauty shows her long chestnut hair, inviting hazel eyes, fine breasts and unabashed sexuality. It cannot even hint at her ready wit and charm, sense of fun and total lack of pretension. Her

Nell Gwyn, the orange girl who became the mistress of King Charles II. Bishop Burnet called her 'the indiscreetest and wildest creature that ever was in court, [who] *continued to the end of the king's life in great favour, and was maintained at a vast expense'.*

time as an orange girl had equipped her to look after herself in a man's world, with a gift for instant repartee and a sometimes wounding sarcasm. The king saw her act, and although still embroiled with LADY CASTLEMAINE and two actresses he interrupted these affairs for a liaison with Nell. Her first son by Charles was born in 1670. This was virtually the end of her stage career. She moved into Pall Mall, where she had another son by the king in 1671. Bishop Burnet wrote:

> . . . Gwyn, the indiscreetest and wildest creature that ever was in court, continued to the end of the king's life in great favour, and was maintained at a vast expense. The Duke of Buckingham told me, that when she was first brought to the king, she asked only five hundred pounds a year: and the king refused it. But when he told me this, about four years after, he said she had got of the king about sixty thousand pounds. She acted all persons in so lively a manner, and was such a constant diversion to the king, that even a new mistress could not drive her away. But after all he never treated her with the decencies of a mistress, but rather with the lewdness of a prostitute; as she had been indeed to a great many: and therefore she called the king her Charles the third, since she had formerly been kept by two of that name.

She had to compete for the king's affections with the French duchess Louise de Kéroualle. Sarcasm was one of her weapons. In a letter Madame de Sévigné quotes Nell talking about Kéroualle's pretentiousness:

> The duchess, says she, pretends to be a person of quality: she says she is related to the best families in France: whenever any person of distinction dies, she puts herself into mourning. If she be a person of such quality, why does she demean herself to be a courtezan? She ought to die with shame. As for me, it is my profession: I do not pretend to be anything better.

When her coach was stopped in Oxford by an angry mob who mistook her for Louise, Nell put her head out of the window and called out, 'Pray, good people, be civil – I am the *Protestant* whore.' When Louise unwisely bandied words with her, Nell crushed her. On one occasion Nell appeared at Whitehall richly dressed, and Louise, who had been made Duchess of Portsmouth, said, 'Nelly, you are grown rich, I believe, by your dress. Why woman, you are fine enough to be a queen.' Nell replied, 'You are entirely right, madam, and I am whore enough to be a duchess.'

Charles died in 1685 and was succeeded by his brother as James II. Nell, a brilliant mimic, had often made him the butt of her wit, and nicknamed him 'dismal Jimmy'. But Charles's last words had been 'Let not poor Nelly starve'; and eventually James granted her £1,500 a year for life, as well as paying off all her debts. Nell had made strenuous efforts to get King Charles to ennoble their first son, Charles. She would ostentatiously call her son 'you little bastard' and when the king remonstrated, would reply: 'Why, I have nothing else to call him.' Charles took the hint and, although he bestowed no titles on Nell, he made the boy Duke of St Albans.

After the king had died Nell lingered on for two years, in increasingly poor health and in the end partly paralysed. Some attribute this to venereal disease caught from the king. There is no evidence for this, although the king did give VD to Louise de Kéroualle. Nell died in November 1687, aged about 37.

GYPSIES Much persecuted and demonised group. The first gypsies reached England in the sixteenth century and the persecution began almost at once. An *Act Concerning Egyptians* in 1530 states:

> For as much afore this time diverse and many outlandish people calling themselves Egyptians, using no craft nor fact of merchandise, have come into this realm and gone from shire to shire and place to place, in great company and used great subtle and crafty means to deceive the people, bearing them in hand, that they by palmistry could tell men's and women's fortunes, and so many times by craft and sublety have deceived the people of their money, and also hath committed many and heinous felonies and robberies to the great hurt and deceit of the people they have come among.

The gypsies were ordered to leave the country within sixteen days. However at first little seems to have been done to expel them, and six years later HENRY VIII's chief minister Thomas Cromwell complained that local officials 'do permit them to linger and loiter in all parts, and to exercise all their felonies, falsehoods and treasons unpunished'. He ordered that gypsies were to be taken to the nearest port and expelled. Any who refused were to be summarily executed. But a pamphlet published in 1614 points out that, despite all the executions, 'still they wandered as before, up and down, and meeting once a year at a place appointed; sometimes at the Devil's Arse in the Peak Derbyshire, and at otherwhile at Ketbrooke by Blackheath, or elsewhere as they agreed still at their meeting'. The situation was complicated after the first decades of persecution by the presence of native-born gypsies. Just being in the company of gypsies was an offence: in 1782 a girl of 14 was hanged for it.

Gypsies and areas where they settled in numbers, such as Notting Dale, continued to be disreputable, so much so that when beggars from eastern Europe arrived in the capital at the turn of the twenty-first century some newspapers were happy to call them gypsies.

HACKABOUT, KATE A notorious street prostitute whose highwayman brother Francis was hanged in April 1730. Two months later Kate was arrested in one of SIR JOHN GONSON's raids. The *Daily Post* reported:

> Eleven men and Women were at the same Time brought before the Justices; but seven of them being young Sinners, and never in Bridewell before, were discharged, upon their seeming Penitence and Promise of Amendment; and the remaining four were committed to Bridewell in Tothill Fields to hard Labour. Three of them were taken at Twelve and One o'clock, exposing their Nakedness in the open Street to all Passengers, and using the most abominable filthy Expressions; the fourth was the famous Kate Hackabout (whose brother was lately hanged at Tyburn) a woman noted in and about the Hundreds of Drury, for being a very termagant, and a Terror not only to the Civil Part of the Neighbourhood by her frequent Fighting, Noise, and Swearing in the Streets in the Night-Time, but also to other Women of her own Profession, who presume to ply or pick up Men in her District, which is half one side of the Way in Bridges Street.

Hogarth calls his innocent young country girl arriving in London at the start of his series of engravings *The Harlot's Progress* Hackabout. She becomes the harlot of the title.

HACKMAN, JAMES (1751–79) Clergyman and murderer. Hackman had an affair with Martha Ray, mistress of John Montagu, EARL OF SANDWICH and First Lord of the Admiralty. It began in 1774 when Hackman was a young army officer. On a recruiting drive he was invited to dine at Sandwich's home near Huntingdon, and met Martha. She was in her thirties, had been Sandwich's mistress for nineteen years and had borne him nine children. Hackman asked Martha to go away with him. At first she seemed to accept this proposal but then refused. In 1779 Hackman left the army and was ordained a deacon. When it became clear to him that Martha would not change his mind he waited for her outside the Theatre Royal in Covent Garden. As she stepped into her coach he shot her in the head, then shot and wounded himself with a second pistol. At his trial he claimed he had intended to commit suicide in front of her, and shot her after giving way to a sudden impulse. The jury believed that the fact he was carrying two pistols meant he always intended to murder her. Sandwich offered to intercede for him but Hackman refused, saying he wanted to die. He was hanged at Tyburn on 19 April 1779.

HAGGERTY AND HOLLOWAY Murderers whose executions attracted such a crush of spectators there was a panic and many died. Owen Haggerty, John Holloway and Benjamin Hanfield waylaid a merchant named John Steele on Hounslow Heath in November 1802. Hanfield, who later gave evidence against the other two, claimed he ran off as Holloway began to batter Steele with a bludgeon. Steel's body was found in a ditch. He had a fractured skull and many other wounds, and he had been robbed. Although a reward was offered the investigation made no progress. Then about four years later Hanfield was convicted at the Old Bailey of theft. While he waited for transportation he became ill, and thinking he was dying, confessed to the murder, naming Haggerty and Holloway. They were hanged outside Newgate on 23 February 1807. A crowd of 40,000 had gathered, and in a panic at least thirty-six people were trampled to death.

HALF-HANGED SMITH Housebreaker John Smith was hanged at Tyburn on Christmas Eve 1705. When he had been hanging for a quarter of an hour a reprieve arrived, and he was cut down. He was still breathing, and recovered, surviving even the bleeding and other medical treatments of the time. He recalled being

> sensible of very great pain occasioned by the weight of his body, and felt his spirits in a great commotion, violently pressing upwards; that having forced their way to his head, he saw a great blaze or glaring light, which seemed to go out at his eyes with a flash, and then he lost all sense of pain. After he was cut down, and began to come to himself, the blood and spirit forcing themselves into their former channels put him, by a sort of pricking or shooting, to such intolerable pain that he could have wished those hanged who cut him down.

He had not learned his lesson, however, and faced trial on capital charges twice more. The first time he was acquitted, and the second he was saved by the sudden death of the prosecutor.

HALF-PRICE RIOTS Violent protests which followed the decision to abolish cut-price admission to theatres after the second act. Poorer playgoers regarded this long-established concession as a right, and when David Garrick and John Beard withdrew it at Drury Lane and Covent Garden in 1763 the theatres were wrecked. The essayist Charles Lamb led an interesting riot when his own farce *Mr H* was staged at the Drury Lane theatre. Lamb had packed the house with his own supporters in an attempt to stop rivals causing trouble. Shortly after the curtain went up Lamb decided he'd seen enough, and that his play was feeble. Jumping up and down on his hat he cried out 'An outrage! A nausea! Ring down the curtain!' He was an immoderate drinker.

HALL, SIR EDWARD MARSHALL (1858–1927) Outstanding defence lawyer, called to the Bar in 1888. He succeeded in winning acquittals in cases where the guilt of the defendant seemed obvious, including that of MARGUERITE FAHMY. Another sensational acquittal was that of Robert Wood, a young artist accused in the CAMDEN TOWN MURDER trial. There were cases where even his brilliance could not save his clients: these included George Joseph Smith, the BRIDES IN THE BATH murderer.

HAMILTON, LADY EMMA (*c*. 1765–1815) Mistress of Lord Nelson. She was born Emma Lyon in Cheshire. Before she met the great naval hero she had a varied amorous career which included children by a navy captain and a baronet. She advertised her charms by posing in London as Hygieia in the 'Temple of Health' of the famous quack JAMES GRAHAM. Emma became the mistress of the Hon Charles Greville and then married his uncle, Sir William Hamilton. They lived at Naples, where she was on intimate terms with Queen Maria Caroline. Nelson met her in 1791 and later she gave birth to their daughter, Horatia. After Nelson's death she squandered the money her husband had left her. Three years before her death in 1815 she was arrested for debt. The DUKE OF QUEENSBERRY, Old Q, sent her money and left her more in his will.

Sir William Hamilton, a lover of classical art, had seen in her the epitome of ideal beauty, and he had encouraged her to put on public performances in which she posed in what were thought to be classical attitudes, based on Greek art. Goethe was captivated:

Nelson's mistress, Emma Hamilton. Before they met she had various amorous adventures and several children. She liked to dance and pose in classical attitudes, scantily and loosely clad.

'She lets down her hair, and with a few shawls gives so much variety to her poses, gestures, expressions etc that the spectator can hardly believe his eye . . . in her he has found all the antiquities, all the profiles of Sicilian coins, even the Apollo Belvedere.'

HAMILTON, KATE The most celebrated of London's disreputable night houses in the 1850s and 1860s was the Café Royal in Princess Street, Leicester Square, known after the woman who ran it as Kate Hamilton's. Only high-class whores were allowed in to mix with the wealthy clientele. Kate weighed twenty stone 'with a countenance that had weathered countless convivial nights'. D. Shaw in *London in the Sixties* describes her as 'shaking with laughter like a giant blancmange' as she sat all night with her favourites drinking champagne. Her bodice was always cut low, and she herself cut a tremendous figure ensconced on a platform above the fray, her powerful voice keeping order. High-class night houses such as Kate's made their money by selling food and drink at outrageous prices – champagne and moselle at twelve shillings a bottle.

MAYHEW's *London* says that Kate was so selective – only men prepared and able to spend five or six pounds, or even more, were admitted – 'these

A bloated Kate Hamilton, seated with her cronies on a dais, presides at her night house, one of the most famous of Victorian resorts for the fast set. Only the better class of whore was admitted.

supper rooms are frequented by a better set of men and women than perhaps any other in London'. Not even Kate's was immune to raids by the police, although generous bribes probably ensured no harm came of them. Shaw's *London in the Sixties* describes what happened when a raiding party was spotted: 'An alarm gave immediate notice of the approach of the police. Finding oneself within the "salon" during one of these periodical raids was not without interest. Carpets were turned up in the twinkling of an eye, boards were raised and glasses and bottles – empty or full – were thrust promiscuously in; everyone assumed a sweet and virtuous air and talked in subdued tones, whilst a bevy of police, headed by an inspector, marched solemnly in and having completed the farce, marched solemnly out. What the subsidy attached to this duty, and when and how paid, it is needless to inquire.' Kate's was one of a chain of night houses and brothels run by a Jewish syndicate headed by DAVID BELASCO.

HAMILTON, NEIL MP most tainted by the 'cash for questions' scandal in the 1990s. A right-wing Tory when he entered Parliament in the 1983 election, he was witty and rancorous and ably assisted by his formidable wife Christine. He won a libel action against the BBC in 1986 over a *Panorama* programme about extreme right-wingers in the party. His outside interests brought in a good income, and he had a reputation for enjoying hospitality. The couple stayed for a week at the Paris Ritz in September 1987 with the owner, MOHAMED FAYED, paying the bill. The accommodation would have cost £1,482, and extras – including generous use of the minibar and restaurant – would have cost £2,120. Even Fayed was moved to complain. In 1994 Fayed claimed that he had also given Hamilton £28,000 in cash. The MP would turn up regularly for his cash-stuffed brown paper envelopes. Hamilton denied this but in December 1999 a libel trial jury found that he had been corrupt. No doubt they were swayed by the revelation that he demanded £10,000 from Mobil Oil for an abortive Finance Bill amendment in 1989.

HAMMERSMITH GHOST, THE At the beginning of the nineteenth century the inhabitants of Hammersmith were being pestered by a ghost. An excise officer named Francis Smith took it upon himself to rid the area of this nuisance. On the night of 3 January 1804 he went out with a gun and confronted Thomas Millwood, a bricklayer who happened to be wearing the white smock of his trade. Smith shot him dead and then realising his terrible mistake, asked to be arrested. He was condemned to death for murder at the Old Bailey although the jury said he should have been charged with manslaughter. There was a general feeling that Smith had merely been unlucky, and a year's imprisonment was substituted for his death sentence.

HANGMEN *see* following page

HANKEY, FREDERICK (*c*. 1825–82) Ingenious smuggler of pornography, based in Paris. Hankey, whose brother was an important official in the Bank of England, was thought by his friends to be an erotomaniac. 'When Hankey's bookbinder proved refactory, Hankey provided him with access to young girls, and in doing so ruined the man's marriage' (Pearsall, *Worm in the Bud*). He asked the explorer Sir Richard Burton to get him the skin of a Negress. He and a friend took two girls to a public execution, so that they could have intercourse during the event. He used couriers to smuggle pornography back to London, including someone in the Foreign Office who used the embassy bag. His cousin Arthur's valet was another courier, but the best of all was Mr Harris, manager of Covent Garden. Hankey said: 'He is not only devoted to me but a very good hand at passing quarto volumes as he has done several times for me in the bend of his back.'

HANRATTY, JAMES (*c*. 1936–62) Small-time criminal controversially executed for the murder of Michael Gregsten at Dead Man's Hill near Bedford in August 1961. Later confirmation of his guilt, based on new DNA testing techniques, has not dispelled some people's doubts about the case.

Gregsten was sitting in a car at Dorney Reach, near Maidenhead, with his lover Valerie Storie when a man tapped on the window. Gregsten opened it and the man pointed a gun at him, then got into the car. After making him drive to Dead Man's Hill the man shot Gregsten dead, then raped and shot Valerie Storie five times. She lived but was paralysed. The revolver used in the crime was found on a bus at Peckham.

Two weeks later cartridge cases fired in the same gun were found at a hotel in Maida Vale. Police picked up Peter Alphon, who had stayed at the hotel after the murder. Valerie Storie failed to pick him out at an identity parade. Police then picked up Hanratty, a petty criminal who had stayed at the hotel on the night before the murder. Storie picked him out at an identity parade. He was tried and hanged at Bedford prison in April 1962. Alphon later confessed repeatedly to the crime. His obvious mental instability did nothing to quell unease about the case. Several people supported Hanratty's alibi that he was in Rhyl at the time of the murder.

In March 2001 Hanratty's remains were exhumed so that a DNA sample could be taken for analysis. Forensic experts matched it to two samples from the crime scene. A year later, the Court of Criminal Appeal ruled that Hanratty's conviction was sound and there were no grounds for a posthumous pardon.

HARDING, ARTHUR Gangster whose memoirs are an invaluable guide to the East End underworld around the beginning of the twentieth century. His lifetime spans the era of the razor gangs, the racecourse wars, and finally the KRAYS and the RICHARDSONS. He was born in 1886 in THE NICHOL, the district called the Jago in Arthur Morrison's novel *A Child of the Jago*, which was published in 1896. The Nichol was virtually a no-go area for the police. Harding's gang fought a feud with criminals led by a Jewish gangster and pimp named ISAAC BOGARD, who was dark-skinned and known as DARKY THE COON. Darky dressed like a cowboy and carried a big pistol in his belt – carrying guns was not illegal at the time. After a series of shootings and beatings Harding's gang tried to murder Darky and his men as they left Old Street Magistrates Court. The Harding gang were ambushed by the police. Today it is almost inconceivable that gangsters would attempt to murder men in a police court, but Harding was sentenced to only twenty-one months' hard labour, with another three years' penal servitude to follow. Harding continued as an East End 'terror' who occasionally clashed with more important gangsters, including the SABINIS. He was later a dealer in second-hand clothes and knew Charles Kray, the twins' father, who made a good living buying old clothes and gold.

HARMAN, THOMAS Magistrate and author of a book on vagrants printed in 1567. Harman gives us much valuable information on itinerant criminals, including BAWDY BASKETS and their protectors, the 'upright men', all-purpose criminals who formed an underworld elite. One of his anecdotes is worth recounting at length, because Harman was personally involved. While he was working on the

Continued on p. 124

HANGMEN

When prisoners were still branded, whipped and tortured it was usually the hangman who administered the punishment. They were often brutal sadists who were themselves criminals, and several ended their lives on the scaffold. The first hangman for whom records exist, Cratwell or Gratnell, was hanged at Clerkenwell in 1538 for robbery. The Earl of Essex saved a hangman named Derrick who had been condemned for rape, only to have his own head struck off by Derrick in 1601.

Another hangman, Edward Dennis, was condemned for his part in the GORDON RIOTS. He pleaded that his son should be allowed to succeed him as common hangman, and rather than have son hang father the authorities pardoned Dennis. He executed more than thirty fellow rioters. He also hanged MARY JONES and the clergyman DR DODD. He continued to serve as hangman until 1786, when he was presented with an official robe by the Sheriffs of London. He promptly sold it.

JACK KETCH, perhaps the most infamous of the hangmen, put to death more than 200 of the Monmouth rebels, then bungled the execution of the Duke of Monmouth in 1685. The duke had handed him six guineas, and promised him more if he made a clean job of it. The duke pointed out that the axe was blunt, and after the first stroke he got to his feet and remonstrated with Ketch. The horror continued with Ketch hacking at the duke's neck. At one stage he flung the axe on the ground. 'God damn me, I cannot do it,' he said. Finally after many strokes of the axe he had to use a knife to detach the head. Ketch was sacked soon afterwards, and his name became a term of contempt for the hangman. He was recalled to hang his successor, Pascha Rose, who had been convicted of burglary.

Among the hangmen to bear the alias Jack Ketch was John Price, executioner in 1714–15, who began his career of crime as a pickpocket with a gang of gypsies. He later joined the merchant navy

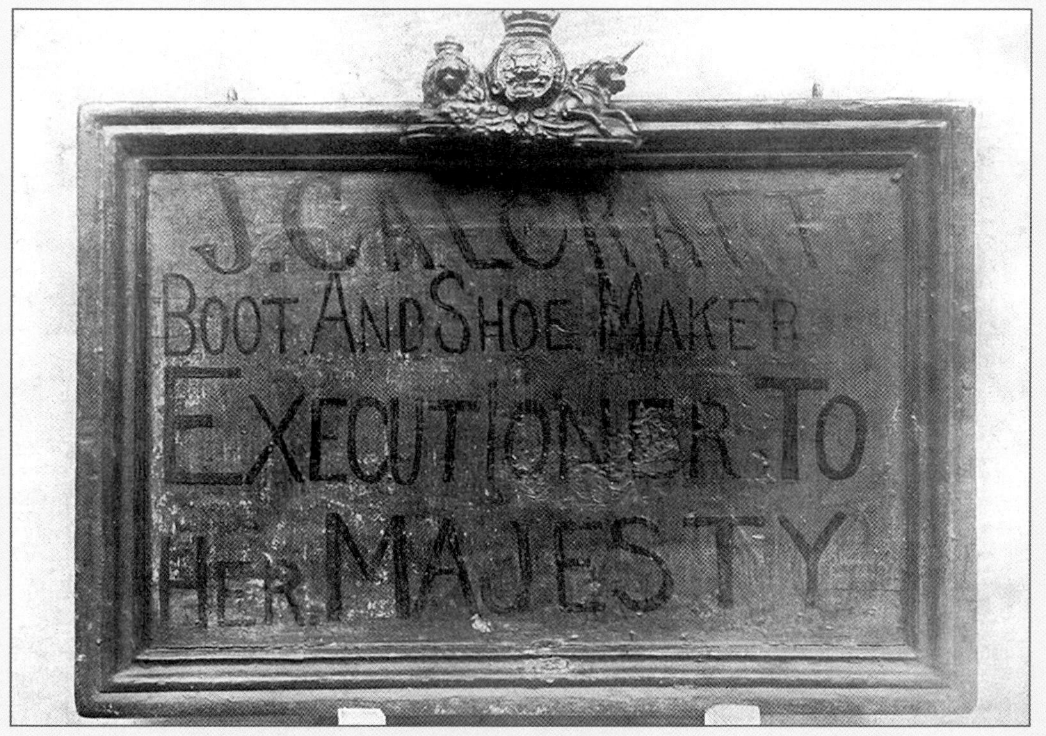

Sign at the executioner William Calcraft's shop. He was drunken and incompetent. Dickens remonstrated after seeing Calcraft hang the Mannings: 'Mr Calcraft should be restrained in his unseemly briskness, in his jokes, his oaths and his brandy.'

and was caught picking the pockets of his fellow sailors. For this he was whipped, pickled in brine and keel-hauled. After further crimes he became hangman for Middlesex. One drunken night he attacked a woman pie seller. When she resisted his advances he battered her and gouged out one of her eyes. She died in agony four days later. This Jack Ketch was executed in 1718.

Other executioners should have hanged, but their services were considered too valuable. John Thrift, executioner from 1735 to 1752, was pardoned after being found guilty of murder. He had stabbed a man in a quarrel, and a when a crowd besieged his house shouting 'Jack Ketch, Jack Ketch' he ran out and killed one of them with a sword. He was reprieved, and even restored to the job of hangman. His violent outburst was uncharacteristic: Thrift was a kind-hearted man who seems to have hated his job. He almost broke down while beheading and disembowelling nine Jacobite rebels in 1746. Later that year he was so overcome when he prepared to behead another Jacobite, Lord Kilmarnock, that he fainted, and Lord Kilmarnock had to comfort him. He was the executioner of the Jacobite LORD LOVAT in 1747. He also hanged the celebrity highwayman JAMES MACLAINE. Thrift had bad dreams about people he had executed, and died soon after his reprieve. His successor John Turlis was promoted after he was caught stealing. Rather than hang him the authorities found it expedient to make him hangman of Surrey as well as the City of London. Jack Hooper was known as the 'Laughing Hangman' because he sought to cheer up his victims with jests and quips. Even he could not comfort the forger Japhet Crook, alias Sir Peter Stranger, who had been sentenced to have his ears cut off and his nose slit and seared with a red-hot iron before beginning his prison sentence. Hooper cut off his ears, holding them up to the crowd. Then he slit Crook's nose and applied the iron. The pain made Crook leap from his chair. Colin Wilson says he recovered sufficiently to drink himself insensible before being taken away to start his sentence. Hooper hanged the murderer SARAH MALCOLM and was saddened because he thought she was probably innocent. Hooper's predecessor, Richard Arnett, who executed JACK SHEPPARD and JONATHAN WILD, seems to have needed drink to get through the ordeal of executions. He was so late for his first hanging that the crowd threw him into a horse pond. He was confused by drink at another execution and was with difficulty prevented from hanging the Newgate chaplain.

There have been several families of executioners, what Shakespeare referred to as 'hereditary hangmen'. Richard Brandon, who almost certainly beheaded CHARLES I, was the son of the executioner Gregory Brandon of Whitechapel. Gregory Brandon was convicted in 1611 of manslaughter. He pleaded BENEFIT OF CLERGY and was branded on the thumb. Richard Brandon was himself a criminal, having been held in Newgate Prison in 1641 for bigamy. He was released later that year and executed the Earl of Strafford, followed by Archbiship Laud in 1644. The Pierrepoints were related hangmen in the twentieth century. Three members of this family – Henry, his brother Thomas and Henry's son Albert – were executioners for a total of more than 50 years.

Some hangmen tried to make the execution as quick and painless as possible. Not so William Calcraft, a notorious Victorian executioner, who added bizarre drunken antics to his bungling incompetence. Dickens was moved to observe, after seeing Calcraft hang the MANNINGS: 'Mr Calcraft should be restrained in his unseemly briskness, in his jokes, his oaths and his brandy.' Calcraft, who did the job for forty five years and in 1832 hanged a boy of nine for setting fire to a house, used too short a rope to ensure a swift death. As his victims squirmed at the end of the rope he would jump onto their backs or pull on their feet to hasten their deaths. His successor, William Marwood, said: 'Old Calcraft strangled 'em . . . I execute 'em.' Marwood devised the long drop, which usually killed the condemned more or less instantly. He was the executioner of HENRY WAINWRIGHT in 1875, CHARLES PEACE in 1879 and GEORGE LAMSON in 1882, as well as more than 160 others.

Hangmen in the twentieth century were certainly more efficient. Albert Pierrepoint, who was an executioner from 1931 to 1956 and hanged many murderers including RUTH ELLIS, the last woman to die on the scaffold in Britain, reckoned it took a maximum of twenty seconds for a prisoner hanged by him to die. 'I hanged JOHN REGINALD CHRISTIE, the Monster of Rillington Place, in less time than it took the ash to fall off a cigar I had left half-smoked in my room at Pentonville.' Pierrepoint hanged more than 400 people. In 1956 he resigned and campaigned against capital punishment. 'I have come to the conclusion that executions solve nothing, and are only an antiquated relic of a primitive desire for revenge which takes the easy way and hands over the responsibility for revenge to other people.' His successor, Harry Allen, was a life-long supporter of hanging. In 1983 he said 'Since the rope was scrapped discipline has gone right out of the window'.

proofs of a book at his lodgings in Whitefriars a 'counterfeit crank' came to his door and asked for alms. He was a frightful sight, his face covered in blood, his wretched clothes with mud. Harman asked him what was the matter, and he replied: 'Ah good master, I have the grievous and painful disease called the falling sickness.' He claimed he had been having epileptic fits for years, and had been in Bedlam. His name was Nicholas Jennings.

Harman was suspicious and had Jennings followed. Two lads watched him as he begged at the Temple. He then went into a field behind Clements' Inn, where he daubed his face with fresh blood from a bladder he carried. Harman's men followed Jennings to Newington, where they had him arrested. They forced him to wash and to show how much money he had. It amounted to the largish sum of fourteen shillings. Jennings was then stripped and revealed to be a handsome man with flaxen hair. Somehow he managed to escape naked into the night.

Some time later, on New Year's Day, Harman's printer saw Jennings at Whitefriars. He was now dressed as a gentleman. The printer had him arrested, and they found his lodging to be well-furnished. He was put in the pillory at Cheapside where he had to alternate between his beggar's rags and his finery. He was then tied to a cart and whipped all the way to his front door. Finally he was given a spell in Bridewell Prison before being released on condition he reformed (Salgado, *The Elizabethan Underworld*).

A gallant propositioning a whore by the Piazza in Covent Garden, the centre of the sex industry.

HARRIS, JACK (*c.* 1710–65) Author of a list of prostitutes, the *List of Covent Garden Ladies or the New Atlantis*, which had the sub-title *Containing an exact description of the Persons, Tempers and Accomplishments of the several Ladies of Pleasure who frequent COVENT-GARDEN and other Parts of the Metropolis*. It gives their addresses, prices and specialities. Harris began selling hand-written lists in the 1740s, and by the time of his death in 1765 sales had reached 8,000 printed copies a year. Not all the descriptions are flattering, but the list launched many young women into fame and fortune, including one of the most famous of all eighteenth-century courtesans, FANNY MURRAY.

Jack Harris is believed to have been head-waiter at the SHAKESPEARE'S HEAD tavern in Covent Garden, although his various rackets must have made him wealthy. He had agents all over London seeking out new faces for his *List*, every stage coach and wagon would be met, and once a year he went to Ireland, where he said the girls were among his most beautiful recruits. He was proud he was responsible for seeing that London was so well-stocked with fine whores, whom he had taught himself to become 'perfect adepts'. For inclusion in the *List* he charged the whores a fifth of their income, and set up a kind of trade union, THE WHORES' CLUB, one of whose main functions seems to have been collecting his fees.

His style is playful and full of *doubles entendres*. He writes in a seafaring vein of a Miss Devonshire of Queen Anne Street: 'Many a man of war has been her willing prisoner, and paid a proper ransom; her port is said to be well-guarded by a light brown *chevaux-de-frieze* . . . the entry is rather straight; but when once in there is very good riding . . . she is ever ready for an engagement, cares not how soon she comes to close quarters, and loves to fight yard arm and yard arm, and be briskly boarded.' Some entries are more frankly pornographic. This is Miss Wilkinson of 10 Bull and Mouth Street:

> . . . a pair of sweet lips that demand the burning kiss and never receive it without paying interest . . . Descend a little lower and behold the semi snowballs . . . that want not the support of stays; whose truly elastic state never suffers the pressure, however severe, to remain but boldly recovers its tempting smoothness. Next take a view of nature *centrally*; *no folding lapel*; no *gaping orifice*; no *horrid gulph* is here, but the *loving lips* tenderly kiss each other, and shelter from the cold a small but easily stretched passage, whose *depth* none but the *blind boy* has liberty to fathom . . .

He says of a Miss Johnson of Goodge Street: 'She has such a noble elasticity in her loins that she can cast her lover to a pleasing height and receive him again with the utmost dexterity.' Harris also tells us that Lord Chesterfield, urbane writer of the famous *Letters*, liked to have his eyelids 'licked by two naked whores'.

After Harris died hack writers were employed to keep the *List* going. The later editions make it clear that Covent Garden was no longer the main focus of high-class harlotry, as many of the women have addresses elsewhere. In 1795 two booksellers were jailed for publishing Harris's *List*.

HARRIS, LEOPOLD (1893–1974) Insurance assessor and arsonist. Harris joined his family's firm of assessors and found himself in an ideal position to pursue a life of fraud. He put together a team of crooks and carried out a series of insurance swindles. For example, he set up the Franco-Italian Silk Company, then burnt it to the ground. The stock was worth £3,000 but as assessor to the company that had insured it Harris was able to arrange a payout to himself of £15,000. When he was caught in 1933 it was estimated that his false claims had brought payouts of a quarter of a million pounds. After his release from jail Harris rejoined the family firm and made it successful.

HASTINGS, LADY FLORA Tragic figure falsely accused of scandalous behaviour by QUEEN VICTORIA. Lady Flora had been lady-in-waiting to Victoria's mother, the Duchess of Kent. She earned Victoria's dislike by working closely with Sir John Conroy, Comptroller of the duchess's household, whom the queen detested. At Christmas 1838 Lady Flora, who was 27, felt unwell and consulted the queen's physician Sir James Clark. Sir James could not help noticing that Lady Flora's figure looked unusually full for an unmarried woman, and speculated unwisely to one of the queen's ladies that she might be pregnant. The queen got to hear of this and, remembering that Flora had travelled alone with Sir John Conroy in a post-chaise, jumped to the wrong conclusion. She wrote in her journal: 'We have no doubt that she is – to use the plain words – with child.' She referred to Conroy: 'The horrid cause of all this is the Monster and Demon incarnate . . .' The queen insisted on Lady Flora being medically examined. Two doctors testified that she was not pregnant. Victoria did not insist that Sir James Clark resign, instead letting him know that she thought a private apology would be sufficient. News of the affair got out and there was a public scandal. Flora's brother Lord Hastings wrote to the *Morning Post* to clear her name. Four months later Lady Flora died and the cause of the swelling was revealed: she had incurable liver disease.

HASTINGS, WARREN (1732–1818) British administrator in India accused of 'high crimes and misdemeanours'. Hastings made a fortune of £80,000 as Governor General of Bengal. When he returned to England in 1784 with the spoils he was accused of corruption. After a trial at the bar of the

Warren Hastings, who made a fortune while Governor General of Bengal and was later accused of 'high crimes and misdemeanours' in the House of Lords. After a seven-year trial he was cleared of corruption.

House of Lords lasting *seven years* he was acquitted on all charges. However, his fortune was gone, eaten up by legal expenses. The East India Company gave him a generous pension and he spent his declining years living as a country gentleman.

HATRY, CLARENCE (1888–1965) Businessman and forger who caused a major City crash. Hatry had a background in business, having failed to save the family silk merchant's he inherited when it was already in difficulties. He went bankrupt for the first time in 1909 when he was 21. He bounced back and in 1914 bought the City Equitable Insurance Company for £60,000, later selling it for £250,000. He acquired all the appurtenances of wealth, large homes, the world's second biggest yacht and racehorses. His companies had a turnover of £12 million a month. In 1928 he needed £3 million to take over companies which later became British Steel and finding he didn't have it, he forged share certificates. When the fraud was discovered his companies were found to have a deficit of £132 million. He was jailed for fourteen years, and emerged to start again and be made bankrupt again. At the time of his death in 1965 he was again, ever optimistic, building up a business.

HAWKHURST GANG The most bloodthirsty of the eighteenth-century smuggling gangs which supplied London with cheap commodities. From their base in the village of Hawkhurst near Hastings their network spread out over five counties. The Hawkhurst gang fell out with smugglers in the nearby village of Goudhurst over some contraband tea. The Goudhurst leader, John Sturt, had been a sergeant in the army, and soon he was training the villagers for defence. The leader of the Hawkhurst gang, Thomas Kingsmill, who had already with the help of ninety-two men and a pack of vicious dogs routed the people of Folkestone, led his men in an attack on Goudhurst. They captured one of the Goudhurst villagers, took him back to Hawkhurst and tortured him until he revealed details of the village's defences. The man was then sent back to Goudhurst with a warning that the smugglers would return on 20 April 1747 and burn the village to the ground, slaughtering every man, woman and child.

The smugglers duly arrived and attacked. They were met by a volley from the defenders, and in the ensuing firefight Kingsmill's brother George was shot dead with another of the smugglers, and many more were wounded. The Goudhurst men chased the smugglers back to Hawkhurst.

Later that year the Hawkhurst gang carried out their most audacious exploit: they raided the Custom House at Poole Harbour under the guns of a Royal Navy ship and made off with a huge cargo of tea.

A shoemaker named Daniel Chater, who had seen the smugglers as they returned in triumph through Fordingbridge, turned informer, and an elderly Customs man, William Galley, was told to escort him to a Sussex magistrate. When they stopped to eat at the White Hart at Rowland's Castle the landlady, who was sympathetic to the smugglers, contacted the local branch of the Hawkhursts. Soon some of the smugglers arrived at the inn and after getting them drunk, took Chater and Galley prisoner. After beating them they tied them to their horses and took them to a park, whipping them all the way. By 2 a.m. Galley was almost dead. The smugglers cut off his nose and testicles, and buried him, possibly while he was still alive. Chater was kept chained up in a shed for three days, then he was half-choked with a rope and thrown down a well. Boulders were thrown down on him.

There were thought to be connections between smugglers and the Jacobites, and the fanatical anti-Jacobite Duke of Richmond pursued the killers. He established a special commission so that reliable judges could be brought from London, rather than trust the local justices to try the killers of Chater and Galley. He also offered large rewards for information.

One of the killers was eventually arrested for another crime, and turned informer. Soon seven of the gang were arrested and executed. Then Kingsmill and four more of the gang were caught. Their trial at the Old Bailey was told that the Poole raid was 'the most unheard of act of villainy and impudence ever known'. After their execution their bodies were exhibited on gibbets.

Richmond's two-year campaign broke the gang. He died in 1750, having had thirty-five Hawkhurst men executed: another ten escaped the noose by dying in prison. What remained of the gang made a last stand in 1751. In a pitched battle with the army the gang's last leader was taken.

HAYES, CATHERINE (1690–1726) Murderer whose burning at the stake was bungled. In March 1725 a watchman found a severed human head on the foreshore of the Thames near the spot where the old Tate Gallery now stands. It was displayed on a pole in the churchyard of St Margaret's, Westminster, in the hope that someone would identify it. When it began to rot it was put in a jar of spirits to preserve it. Some people thought it might be a Mr Hayes, who had lived with his wife in Tyburn Road (now Oxford Street). Hayes, a wealthy moneylender, had vanished, and his friends were looking for him. Catherine Hayes said her husband had gone to Portugal after killing a man, but she and two of her lodgers, Thomas Billings and Thomas Wood, who were both her lovers, were arrested. She was shown the head, which she identified as her 'poor husband' and kissed the jar. The head was taken out and she kissed that too, and asked if she could have a lock of the hair. Then she fainted. The performance was in vain. Wood, the more timid of the killers, who was probably still a teenager, confessed. He said that Catherine Hayes had told him that her husband was an athiest, and that 'it would be no more sin to kill him than to kill a dog'. Faced with the confession Catherine and Billings also admitted murder. She had offered them part of the £1,500 she expected to inherit on her husband's death. One night at the beginning of March she, her husband and the two lodgers had been drinking. Mr Hayes, who had been challenged to drink six bottles of wine, fell asleep and the lodgers killed him with a hatchet. They cut off his head and threw it into the river, expecting the tide to take it away. Unfortunately for them the tide was coming in. After the murder Catherine Hayes tried to collect all the money owed to her husband, and generally behaved with great coolness. All three were sentenced to death, Mrs Hayes to be burned at the stake because she was guilty of petty treason – the killing of her lord and master. They were all sent to Newgate to await execution, and when Billings and Catherine met in the chapel there they held hands, and she rested her head on his shoulder.

Wood died of jail fever at Newgate, Billings was hanged at Tyburn. Mrs Hayes was chained to a stake near the gallows and the hangman, Richard Arnet, prepared to strangle her with a rope before burning her body, the customary method of dispatching women sentenced to die at the stake. He lit the fire too soon and was driven back by the flames before he could garrot Hayes. Her death agony was long and horrifying. She screamed and tried to push the burning faggots aside. An account of the burning says 'she survived amidst the flames for a considerable time, and her body was not perfectly reduced to ashes in less than three hours'. *See* BURNING AT THE STAKE

HAYES, CHARLOTTE (*c.* 1725–1812) The most important brothel-keeper of early Georgian times, born in a Covent Garden slum. She lived on into the next century, dying in her eighties after a long career of innovation which included a 'Cyprian Fete' at which gentlemen 'of the highest breeding' first watched athletic young men copulating with nubile whores and then joined in themselves.

Early in her career Charlotte was imprisoned in the Fleet debtors' prison and there met and fell in love with an Irish con-man, Dennis O'Kelly. Together they experienced wild swings of fortune. Charlotte set up a brothel while in prison and used the proceeds to start O'Kelly on a career which would see him become a wealthy colonel of militia and owner of the Duke of Chandos's estate, Canons, at Edgware. At least as important from the social point of view was his ownership of the wonder horse Eclipse, which never lost a race. This was an entrée to the highest levels of society, and friendship with the Prince of Wales.

The couple were freed in an amnesty in 1760, and the following year Charlotte set up her first luxury brothel, a 'Protestant Nunnery', in Great Marlborough Street. O'Kelly's racing connections helped bring in aristocratic devotees of the turf – the dukes of Richmond and Chandos, the earls of Egremont and Grosvenor among others. Charlotte decided she needed to be even closer to the court, and in 1767 opened another brothel at No. 2 King's Place. The *Town and Country Magazine* called her 'a living saint' and said she should be canonised because she could 'make old Dotards believe themselves gay vigorous young fellows, and turn vigorous young men into old Dotards'.

Charlotte kept her nuns, as the girls were known, in a kind of benign servitude. Like other bawds of the time, she charged them so much for jewellery, rich clothes, food and lodging that they were always in debt to her. Their best hope was to find a wealthy husband who would buy them out. Girls who graduated from her brothels to become famous independent whores included Kitty Fredericks, the 'veritable *Thais* amongst the *haut ton*, the veritable *Flora* of all London', and Frances Barton, who turned into the actress Frances Abington, famous alike for 'so often exposing her lovely naked bosom to the gaze of lascivious leering gentlemen' and for her rich and varied love life.

The memoirist and man-about-town WILLIAM HICKEY visited 'that experienced old Matron Charlotte Hayes in her *House of Celebrity* in King's Place'. In 1776 she was committed to the MARSHALSEA PRISON for debt. Dennis came to her rescue. He died in 1788 aged 67, leaving her £400 a year for life and much else besides, including his parrot Polly, which reputedly could sing the whole 104th Psalm. In 1798 Charlotte, still living at

Canons, was again in a debtors' prison because of her extravagance. Dennis's nephew bailed her out and paid all her debts in return for her making over all her assets to him. She is last heard of in 1811 at Canons, and died soon afterwards.

HEADLESS MAN SCANDAL In 1963 Lord Denning, Master of the Rolls, was appointed to carry out an inquiry into the security implications of the PROFUMO SCANDAL. In the course of his inquiry he investigated rumours of naked orgies in high places. One concerned a cabinet minister said to attend the orgies dressed only in a small apron, another the identity of the 'Headless Man' who featured in the divorce of the DUCHESS OF ARGYLL in 1963. During the divorce hearings the jury had been shown photographs of the duchess, wearing only three strings of pearls, fellating someone. Because little could be seen of him but his penis he was known as 'the Headless Man'. There was much speculation as to his identity and many people believed he was the Tory minister Duncan Sandys. In *The Denning Report*, published in October 1963, Denning wrote:

> There is a great deal of evidence which satisfied me that there is a group of people who hold parties in private of a perverted nature. At some of these parties, the man who serves dinner is nearly naked except for a small square lace apron round his waist such as a waitress might wear. He wears a black mask over his head with slits for eye-holes. He cannot therefore be recognised by any of the guests. Some reports stop there and say nothing evil takes place. This may well be so at some of the parties. But at others I am satisfied that it is followed by perverted sex orgies: that the man in the mask is a 'slave' who is whipped: that guests undress and indulge in sexual intercourse one with the other: and indulge in other sexual activities of a vile and revolting nature. My only concern in my inquiry was to see whether any minister was present at these parties: for if he were, he would, I should think, be exposing himself to blackmail.

The whole thing seems incredible now. To clear Duncan Sandys Denning had the minister's penis examined by a Harley Street consultant. It was later revealed that the 'Headless Man' was the film actor Douglas Fairbanks Junior.

HEATH, NEVILLE (1917–46) Whip-wielding sadist who killed two women. In June 1946 the body of 32-year-old Margery Gardner was found in a hotel room in Notting Hill. She had been suffocated and her body sexually mutilated. There were also seventeen whip marks on her face and body. Heath, a former RAF officer, was known to have stayed at the hotel and police issued a statement saying they thought he could help with their inquiries. He wrote a letter to the officer in charge of the case saying that he had come back to the hotel and found the body of Mrs Gardner: 'I realised that I was in an invidious position . . .' He gave a description of a man he claimed she had been with. Heath added: 'The personal column of the *Daily Telegraph* will find me, but at the moment I have assumed another name.' He booked into the Tollard Royal Hotel in Bournemouth using the name Group Captain Rupert Brooke. A young woman, Doreen Marshall, was reported missing, and the manager of the Tollard asked Heath if a girl he had dined with might not be Miss Marshall. 'Oh no, I have known that lady for a long while,' he replied. However shortly afterwards he rang the local police and said he might be able to help. He went to the police station and told how he had indeed dined with Miss Marshall, and afterwards went for a walk with her. They had parted after the walk. Heath's photograph had been sent to all police

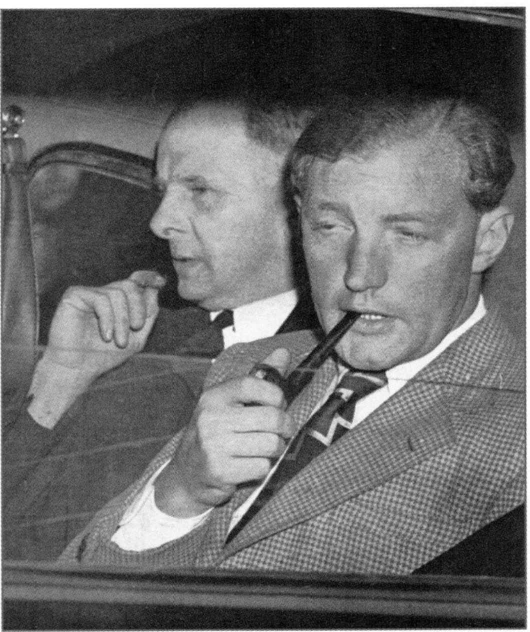

Neville Heath, a sadist who killed two women and mutilated their bodies. He was executed in 1946. Heath, a former RAF airman, said before he was hanged: 'It's just another op. Only difference is that I know I'm not coming back from this one.'

stations, and one of the officers noticed the strong resemblance of Brooke to the wanted man. Heath was arrested, and shortly afterwards the body of 21-year-old Miss Marshall was found concealed in a ravine about a mile and a half from the Tollard. She had been terribly mutilated. It seemed the murderer stripped naked before attacking her, as there was no blood on his clothes.

At his trial at the Old Bailey Heath did not give evidence. His counsel told the jury: 'You would probably not believe a word he said if he were called.' Before he was executed at Pentonville Prison in October 1946 Heath said, referring to his service as an RAF pilot, 'It's just another op. Only difference is that I know I'm not coming back from this one.'

HEATHROW RAID For many years Heathrow Airport was notorious as a focus for crime – 'Thief Row'. In 1948, however, when JACK SPOT's gang planned an ambitious robbery there, the airport was still being built. Sammy Josephs, a Jewish thief associated with the Spot gang, learned that valuable cargoes were kept overnight in warehouses at the airport. He told Spot, and soon plans were being made to steal nearly one million pounds' worth of bullion and other valuables.

The planning was meticulous. Members of the robbery team went on guided tours of the airport, parcels were sent from Ireland and Josephs and another member of the team, Franny Daniels, were able to check out the Customs shed as they collected them. On the night of 24 July the team were in place and the raid began.

The raiders had drugged the tea of the BOAC staff but police, who had been tipped off, had taken the place of the BOAC men. When the ten raiders, armed with coshes and iron bars, entered the warehouse they saw men in BOAC uniform apparently drugged, and tied them up. They began to open the safe. Suddenly officers from the Flying Squad who had been waiting in the shadows were swarming around them. In what became known as the Battle of Heathrow the Spot mob came off worst. Eight of the robbers, bloody and battered, were arrested. Two others got away. Teddy Machin, fabled chiv man, fell into a ditch as he fled, and was knocked unconscious by his fall. He woke after the police had left and staggered away to safety. Franny Daniels hid under one of the Black Marias which were taking his comrades off to police stations. When it drove away he clung to the chassis. The Black Maria was driven to Harlesden police station, and Daniels was able to escape. The eight men, who appeared in court wearing bandages and slings, got from five to twelve years' penal servitude, long sentences for the time. The judge, Sir Gerald Dodson, told them: 'A raid on this scale profoundly shocks society. You went prepared for violence and you got it. You got the worst of it, and you can hardly complain.'

HENRY VIII (1491–1547) Syphilitic king who suppressed the brothels on Bankside. He and Cardinal Wolsey organised periodical crackdowns on vice, yet the cardinal reportedly had an inscription over one of the doors at Hampton Court saying: 'The rooms of the whores of my Lord Cardinal', and Henry was also said to have had such a room. Henry died in 1547 'in agony of syphilitic periostitis in a stupor' at the age of 55. His vast carcass was placed in a lead coffin and carried to Syon House, where, according to a contemporary account, the coffin split and the rotten corpse leaked fluid: '. . . the pavement of the church was wetted with Henry's blood. In the morning came plumbers to solder the coffin, under whose feet was seen a dog creeping and licking up the King's blood.' Some years before a friar preaching in Greenwich Church had told the king that when he died dogs would lick his blood.

Henry VIII, who may have died of syphilis, was hard on others' weaknesses. He made buggery a capital offence and decreed branding in the face for whores who mixed with his soldiers.

HERVEYS, THE Several generations of this aristocratic family have produced people who have been mad, bad, or amusing to know. Mary Wortley Montague said 'When God created the human race he made men, women – and Herveys'. Lord Hervey of Ickworth (1696–1743) had a wife, eight children, mistresses and a male lover named Stephen Fox. He evicted his wife and children from his London home so Fox could live there. Hervey approved when Fox married a girl of 13. His shameless bisexuality eventually led to him being ostracised. A later Hervey, Frederick, Earl of Bristol and Earl-Bishop of Derry (1730–1803), lived a scandalous life in Italy, noted for his 'freedom of conversation' after dinner. After he spent a spell in prison there a young Irish woman saw him out with some whores. She wrote: 'He was sitting in his carriage between two Italian woman, dressed in a white bed-gown and night-cap like a witch and giving himself the airs of an Adonis.' When he died the crew of a ship refused to take the remains of a Protestant bishop back to England, and he was smuggled home labelled as an antique statue. His daughter, Lady Elizabeth Foster (1759–1824) was the friend of Georgiana, profligate wife of the Duke of Devonshire. They had a *ménage-à-trois* and Elizabeth bore the duke two illegitimate children before becoming his second wife in 1809. Victor Hervey (1915–85), the 6th marquess, was an eccentric journalist and gun-runner. By experimenting he was able to assure his readers that a rank of taxis would buckle like a concertina if a car was driven into them. He failed as a gun-runner during the Spanish Civil War and was given a three-year prison sentence for robbery.

All this was merely a rehearsal for the life of John Augustus Hervey, the 7th marquess, who was born in 1954. While his father was alive he lived as a tax exile in France on a £4 million family trust. When his father died he moved into the family home at Ickworth, Suffolk where he and his friends consumed prodigious amounts of drugs and indulged in reckless midnight sport with guns. A helicopter brought in the drugs by night and also young men, whose company the marquess preferred. He was arrested for dealing in heroin and cocaine and spent a year in prison. When he died at the age of 44, having gone through a fortune of £16 million, the cause of death was 'multi-organ failure attributable to chronic drug abuse'.

Lady Victoria Hervey, daughter of the 6th marquess, born in 1979, appears frequently in gossip columns.

HICKEY, WILLIAM (1749–1830?) Eighteenth-century memoirist who left a lively picture of the demi-monde of London. In their way his *Memoirs* are as frank about the author's weaknesses as those of PEPYS or BOSWELL. In his case the weaknesses were for wine and women. He was frankly carnal and fun-loving, quite unable to resist the company of pretty girls or the sound of a pulled cork. His self-portrait catches the racy side of London in the age of George III, when vice was more self-confident and flagrant than before or since. Hickey knew a good many of the city's whores and brothels. He mentions WEATHERBY'S disreputable coffee house in Russell Street in 1768, and visits to MRS CORNELYS's and CHARLOTTE HAYES's establishments. His father sent him to India to put him beyond temptation.

HICKORY PUCKERY Fraud involving collusion between eighteenth-century importers of tobacco and the officials who weighed the cargoes. Micajah Perry, grandson of the founder of a London tobacco dynasty, was a noted practitioner. He was a leading banker in New York and Pennsylvania as well as a magistrate at Guildhall and the Old Bailey. By 1720 his tobacco revenues were falling, so he 'defrauded the King's Revenue by more than half by colluding with the Thames landwaiters to short-weight his imports . . . thereby reducing his duty' (Linebaugh, *The London Hanged*). If the tobacco was re-exported the process was reversed – the weight was overstated, so increasing the tax drawback Perry was entitled to. This was known as Puckery Hickory. While people were being hanged for trivial offences Perry became an alderman of the City and a member of the Board of Trade and Plantations. His son became Lord Mayor of London.

HIGGINS, BOB Senior detective who investigated some of London's criminals during thirty-two years with the Metropolitan Police. It was Higgins who caught GORDON CUMMINS, an RAF trainee who revived memories of JACK THE RIPPER by the way he murdered four women in early 1942. Higgins regarded him as 'by far the most vicious killer I encountered, or, in fact, ever heard about in the whole of my police career'. He helped to recapture RUBY SPARKS, the motor bandit, after he escaped from Dartmoor, and HARRY JENKINS, a gangster and killer. In 1958 he wrote his autobiography, *In the Name of the Law*.

HIGHWAYMEN *see* opposite page

HILL, BILLY (1911–84) The self-styled Boss of Britain's Underworld, one of the dominant figures in

Continued on p. 132

HIGHWAYMEN

Throughout the eighteenth century the roads around London, and sometimes the streets and parks of the city itself, were plagued by the so-called 'gentlemen of the road'. Some took to the roads because of bankruptcy or gambling debts, or because they were from that stratum of society bred to polite living without the means to sustain it: thus some were the sons of parsons. Others were soldiers disbanded at the end of military campaigns. A surprising number had been butchers' apprentices, a trade which gave them knowledge of the routes drovers took to London. These drovers and their animals were frequent targets.

The most notorious of the highwaymen was DICK TURPIN, who was born in 1706, the son of an Essex farmer. Turpin was immortalised in Harrison Ainsworth's *Rookwood*, which paints a romanticised and inaccurate picture both of the man and the way of life. Turpin was in fact a vicious and ruthless criminal.

Highwaymen would arm themselves to the teeth, carrying as many as seven pistols. Some wore black masks over their eyes and silk handkerchiefs over their faces.

The highwayman's reputation for courtesy and gallantry was sometimes justified, sometimes not. They might beg to be excused for being forced by necessity to rob, and some showed chivalry towards women, refusing to search them or returning objects of sentimental value. CLAUDE DUVAL, a seventeenth-century highwayman, took gallantry to extremes. Once his victims were a man and his beautiful young wife. Duval asked for permission to dance with the wife, then helped her out of the coach and danced a minuet with her by the roadside. After he was hanged his torch-lit funeral was attended by hundreds of weeping women.

The *Weekly Journal* of August 1723 tells of a highwayman who took a man's watch, then agreed to return it to him for two guineas. The victim suggested they ride to his home, where he would get the money. They rode to the man's home, the money was handed over and 'after the drinking of a bottle of wine, with mutual civilities they took leave of each other.' On Wimbledon Common a highwayman demanded that a young married woman hand over a ring. When she said she would 'sooner part with life', he replied: 'Since you value the ring so much, madam, allow me the honour of saluting the fair hand which wears it, and I shall deem it a full equivalent.' The lady stretched forth her hand through the coach window, the highwayman kissed it and departed.

The courage of the highwaymen was legendary. Dick Turpin at his execution did not wait for the hangman to move the cart away from under him, but flung himself off. Another highwayman, the celebrated JAMES MACLAINE, kicked off his shoes and jumped into the air with the noose around his neck, holding his knees to his chest to increase the force of the 'drop' and hasten his death.

MacLaine held up HORACE WALPOLE in Hyde Park in 1752: his pistol went off accidentally, and the bullet grazed the great aesthete's head. MacLaine, a country parson's son, lived in 'splendour', according to the account of his career in the 1764 *Select Trials*. His apartment in the fashionable area of St James's where he lived with his mistress was maintained on the proceeds of nightly hold-ups.

John Rann, known as 'Sixteen-string Jack' because of the silk strings he attached to the knees of his breeches, also put on a show for the mob when he was executed in 1774. Rann was a dandy, and made his final appearance in a new pea-green suit, a ruffled shirt and a hat surrounded with silver rings. In his buttonhole he wore a huge nosegay. The night before his execution he was allowed to entertain seven girls in his cell.

With a large section of the disaffected populace sympathetic to their cause, highwaymen found London an ideal place to work and hide. They needed safe houses to operate from – taverns, inns and stables. They also needed FENCES or receivers and here men like the bounty hunter and fence JONATHAN WILD were vital.

Among the safe houses were the Blue Lion in Gray's Inn Lane and the Bull and Pen in Spa Fields. St George's Fields between Southwark and Lambeth had many havens, including the notorious DOG AND DUCK, the Shepherd and Shepherdess, Apollo Gardens and the Temple of Flora. Young boys used to go to the Dog and Duck to watch the highwaymen mount up and say goodbye to their 'flashy women' before setting off to prey on travellers on the highways.

Jonathan Wild, the self-styled Thief-Taker General, broke up the major gangs of highwaymen in London: he also pursued some of the more famous solo operators. One of these was Benjamin Child, a womaniser and gambler who truly lived up to the romantic image of his profession. He made a fortune from his crimes, and left over £10,000 in his will. One of his exploits was to use part of his loot to free all the debtors in Salisbury jail. There is no direct evidence that Wild caught Child, but John Hawkins, a highwayman who was one of Wild's victims, swore that he would be avenged on the man who had impeached Child, and it was widely believed that he was referring to Wild.

Wild proved his courage and ruthlessness many times, none more so than when he arrested James Wright, a member of the Hawkins gang. In 1720 he captured Wright by 'holding him fast by the chin with his teeth, till he dropped his firearms, surrendered and was brought to Newgate'. Wright was acquitted and went back to his old trade of hairdressing.

The numbers of highwaymen usually increased sharply with the ending of military campaigns, as soldiers and sailors, many of whom had been pressed into service, were disbanded. But towards the end of the eighteenth century their numbers went into sharp decline. An important factor was the growing expertise of the BOW STREET RUNNERS, the police force founded by the FIELDING brothers.

The last mounted highway robbery took place in 1831. Frank McLynn, in *Crime and Punishment in Eighteenth-Century England*, gives several reasons for the decline of the highwayman. He quotes George Borrow's *Romany Rye* where an ostler declared that the authorities' refusal to license public houses like the Dog and Duck, known haunts of the criminals, was a factor. Another, said the ostler, was the enclosure system that destroyed many of the wild heaths the highwaymen favoured for their hold-ups. Third was the coming of the Bow Street Runners and the permanent mounted patrol operating out of London. To these McLynn adds the spreading suburbs and improvement in roads. And finally the role of money: bigger rewards and the growth of the banking system, which ensured people did not have to carry large amounts about with them when they travelled, meant the highwaymen had had their day.

London crime after the Second World War. He was born into a noted criminal family in Seven Dials near Leicester Square in 1911. His father spent time in prison for assaulting the police, and his mother was a receiver. His brother Jimmy was a pickpocket, his sister MAGGIE, known as the Queen of the Forty Elephants, was a successful hoister or shoplifter.

Hill's main strength was as a planner and organiser of major robberies, but he was ruthless and vicious enough to win control of much of the West End, with its important clubs and gambling rackets, from the WHITES. They had seized control after the Anglo-Italian SABINI GANG were interned as enemy aliens at the beginning of the Second World War. In his ghosted autobiography *Boss of Britain's Underworld* Hill suggested there was an epic confrontation between the Whites and a coalition led by himself and the Jewish racecourse gangster JACK SPOT. The affair is encrusted with gangland legend but the veteran Hill enforcer MAD FRANKIE FRASER remembers little more than a brawl and one of the other gang's leaders, Harry White, hiding under a table. The Hill–Spot coalition later broke down to the sound of cracking bones and breaking glass. Their rivalry, a kind of semi-comic opera played with real guns and knives, kept newspaper

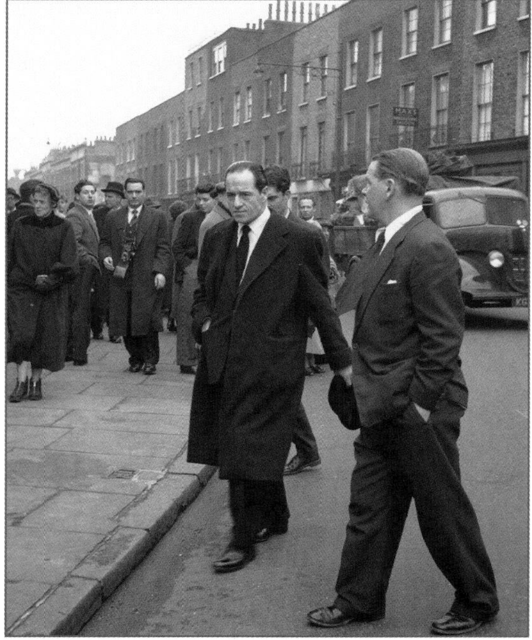

The gangster Billy Hill (holding hat) at a gangland funeral in 1957. He ruled London's underworld more or less unchallenged for some years.

Gangland figures celebrate the publication of Billy Hill's autobiography Boss of Britain's Underworld *in Gennaro's in Soho. Hill is fourth left, and behind him are Ruby Sparks and Frankie Fraser.*

readers entertained during the otherwise largely colourless post-war years.

By the beginning of the Second World War Hill was leader of a versatile gang of smash-and-grab raiders, burglars and hard men, well-placed to take advantage of the opportunities wartime disruption offered. His team was so successful that he claimed many young villains wanted to work with him and he had to put them on a rota. The blackout and the fact that the youngest and fittest policemen had gone into the armed services meant that a new line, breaking into post offices around London and cracking their safes, was ridiculously easy. Hill says in his autobiography that he was taking an average of £3,000 a week from these raids.

After the showdown with the Whites in July 1947 there was an unprecedented period of peace in the underworld. Hill called the years 1950 and 1951 'peaceful and profitable . . . The truth was we had cleared all the cheap racketeers out'. In 1952 he organised the £287,000 mailbag robbery in EASTCASTLE STREET.

After the alliance with Spot broke down Hill attributed their falling out to Spot's jealousy. Spot certainly behaved recklessly, not realising that he had grown middle-aged and soft. He formed an alliance with the KRAY TWINS, the up-and-coming East End gangsters, but before the all-out gang war the twins wanted could break out both Spot and Hill retired.

Hill went to Spain, saying he had had enough. He had become a minor celebrity. The launch of his book, *Boss of Britain's Underworld*, had been attended by the publicity-hungry and wealthy Lord and Lady Docker: Hill had organised the return of Lady Docker's stolen jewels. Hill became a kind of criminal elder statesman, visited by travelling gangsters in Spain and making occasional trips to London, where he turned up at clubs run by the Krays. The twins were pleased with this apparent endorsement of their plans for universal hegemony, and Hill took the opportunity to hob-nob with Lady Docker and go gambling with property racketeer PETER RACHMAN and his mistress MANDY RICE-DAVIES, one of the girls in the PROFUMO scandal. He returned permanently to England in the early seventies and ran a night-club at Sunningdale. When he died in 1984 Jack Spot called him 'the richest man in the graveyard'.

HILL, MAGGIE Sister of the gangster BILLY HILL. She was a successful shoplifter, known as the Queen of the Forty Elephants. Some thought this referred to her known contacts around the Elephant and Castle in south London, but one commentator said it derived from her gang of giant women shoplifters who were capable of beating up young tearaways and frightening shopkeepers into silence as they made off with armfuls of goods. The daughters of these fearsome women continued the tradition. The gangster FREDDIE FOREMAN tells in his autobiography, *Respect*, how he teamed up with the gang, by then known as The Forty Thieves, when he was 18: 'My job was to graft with girls like Mae Mae Cooper, Annie Revel and Nellie Donovan, and make sure they got away after shoplifting from top stores like Harrods. You would bump into the guy who was going to give them a pull, or give him a right-hander if he got too clever.'

HIND, CAPTAIN JAMES (*c.* 1618–52) Highwayman who tried to hold up Oliver Cromwell. After the execution of Charles I, Hind vowed to prey on Republicans, and, happening to come across Oliver Cromwell as he made his way towards London, he and an accomplice stopped his coach. Cromwell's guard of seven soldiers overwhelmed them, the accomplice was taken and Hind escaped with difficulty. His next Republican victim was the puritan clergyman Hugh Peters, later executed for his presumed complicity in the death of the King. Hind robbed him of 'thirty broad-pieces of gold', his coat and cloak. He held up John Bradshaw, president of the court that had condemned the King, near Shaftesbury in Dorsetshire, and harangued him. He said he would leave him to the pangs of his own conscience 'till Justice shall lay her iron hand upon thee, and require an answer for thy crimes in a way more proper for such a monster, who art unworthy to die by any hands but those of the common hangman'. He did not spare Bradshaw's purse. The last of his regicide victims was Colonel Thomas Harrison, who was executed after the Restoration. Hinds fled to London, but was betrayed and condemned for high treason. He was hanged, drawn and quartered in September 1652, aged 34.

HINDS, ALFIE (1917–91) Jail breaker who gained his release by suing for libel. Hinds, a career criminal with a formidable intellect, was convicted in 1953 of stealing jewellery and cash from Maples store in London. The evidence was thin but the jury took only half an hour to find him guilty. The judge, LORD GODDARD, jailed him for twelve years, calling him a most dangerous criminal. In 1955 Hinds escaped from Nottingham Prison and began a campaign, largely through the Press, to get a retrial. He was arrested in Dublin 245 days later. During his trial for prison breaking he defended himself, and displayed a formidable knowledge of the law, a fact acknowledged by the trial judge. He made further escapes, and continued to seek a retrial. In 1961 when he was held in Parkhurst Prison on the Isle of Wight he needed a solicitor to help with his application for a writ of habeas corpus. A local solicitor, Percy Rolf, took up the case. He helped Hinds bring a libel action against Chief Superintendent Herbert Sparks, who had arrested him in 1953. Sparks had written a series in the *Sunday Pictorial* under the headline: 'The Iron Man tells how he tricked the King of Escapers'. Hinds persuaded the jury that his conviction was wrong, and was immediately released on licence by the Home Secretary. He was still refused leave to appeal to the House of Lords against the original sentence. He retired to Jersey, became a businessman and secretary of the Channel Islands branch of the Mensa Society for people with high IQs. The law was changed so that a libel suit could not be brought against police on the basis of a wrongful conviction.

HITMEN The underworld's anonymous assassins. ALFIE GERRARD was a comparatively rare example of a hitman in the 1960s. It wasn't until the 1990s that professional killers became fairly common in the capital. Hitmen were used by both sides in a gang war that broke out in south London in the early 1990s between the ARIFS and the BRINDLES. The feud, which has cost nine lives, included the attempted assassination of Tony Brindle by Irish terrorist gunman Michael Boyle. Boyle, who was said to have been paid £25,000 to kill Brindle, was one of several nationalist and Loyalist Irish gunmen specially imported for gangland hits in London.

With the new century just months old concern at the growing number of contract killings in Britain – estimated at about thirty a year – led police to compile a register of convicted and suspected contract killers, and their techniques.

Police estimate that up to twenty hitmen are operating out of the south-east, charging between £1,000 and £20,000 for a murder. Jason Bennetto wrote in *The Independent* on 31 May 2000: 'One infamous London hitman, known as Mad Georgie, is said to be behind 23 murders. He is credited with thinking up the motorbike hit in which two men, whose crash helmets cover their faces, use a powerful off-road scrambler motorcycle.The killers will speed up to their target, and the pillion rider will jump off, shooting his victim with a handgun or sawn-off shotgun. The two men then flee on the motorcycle, taking a predetermined route.' Gangs are thought to employ Yardie gunmen to get rid of rivals. *See* SOLLY NAHOME

HOLLAND, ANNE (?–1705) Beautiful thief who had a varied life of crime. She used many aliases, including Jackson, Goddard and Charlton. Her lovers and husbands included the highwayman James Wilson. With another of her husbands, Tristram Savage, who was dressed as a woman, she robbed the astrologer Dr Trotter at his home in Moorfields. First they asked Trotter to tell Anne's fortune and while he consulted his astrological charts Savage produced a pistol and tied up the old fraud. The couple stole a gold watch, cash and other valuables. Anne was executed at Tyburn in 1705.

HOLLAND, ELIZABETH (flourished 1597–1632) Bawd who kept the most luxurious brothel in London in the early seventeenth century. Holland, who was born towards the end of Queen Elizabeth's reign, had been a successful and enthusiastic harlot before deciding to be 'no more a bewitching whore but a deceiving bawd . . . the sins of others shall maintain her sin'. She opened her first establishment in Duke Humphreys Rents in the City and set new standards of luxury and rapacity. The brothel was a success, being 'crammed like Hell itself where wicked creatures lay bathing themselves in Lust', according to her anonymous biographer of 1632. The food was particularly good, and 'the visitants came flocking so fast that her kitchen was ever flaming'. Her rivals persuaded the authorities to move against her, and she found herself in another kind of Hell, Newgate Prison. Before her trial she escaped with the help of friends in high places. The freedom from City regulations drew her to the red-light district of Bankside, where she was advised that the Paris Gardens Manor House, then a deserted ruin, might suit her. It was a moated mansion with a gatehouse, drawbridge and other buildings within fields with water-filled ditches spanned by small bridges. About 1600 Mother Holland acquired it and turned the gardens into a pleasant backdrop for dalliance. There were walks with trees and shrubberies, prefiguring the pleasure gardens at Vauxhall and Ranelagh. She provided the best food and wine, and the prettiest and most accomplished women for her customers, among whom were King James I and his favourite, George Villiers, Duke of Buckingham. All agreed with her catchphrase 'This Chastitie is clean out of date'.

A tribute to the sumptuousness of the interior was the local nickname for the water-girt mansion, which was still known as 'the Nobs' Island' fifty years later. If the food and drink were exceptional, so were the prices. London probably never produced a more rapacious bawd than Elizabeth Holland. She would greet each guest in person, as much to ascertain their financial status as to inquire about their special wishes. There was no credit: anyone temporarily embarrassed financially would not be admitted, however exalted. She stood for no rowdy or violent behaviour, such as ill-treating the girls.

For thirty years the Leaguer was the most famous brothel in London. Its exclusiveness and efficiency, the quality of the whores and the food and drink and its formidable owner – described as a small woman, still beautiful – ensured its success. But Mother Holland had made enemies, and when James I died and was succeeded by Charles I, who ordered the suppression of brothels, they saw their chance. Discipline also seems to have been breaking down at the Leaguer. The parties grew noisier and rowdier, the girls less genteel and ladylike. The pamphleteer Daniel Lupton expressed some of the concern when he wrote about 1630:

> . . . this may be better tearmed a foule Denne than a Faire Garden . . . heeratte foule beasts come to itt and as badde and worse keepe it; they are fitter for a Wildernesse than a Cittee: idle base persons . . . the Swaggering Roarer, the Cunning Cheater, the Rotten Bawd, the Swearing Drunkard and the Bloudy Butcher have their Rendezvous here.

In December 1631 a troop of soldiers was sent to close down the Leaguer. The story goes that Mother Holland first enticed them onto the drawbridge, then suddenly dropped it downwards so that the men were plunged into the stinking moat. As they floundered about in the slime her jeering whores pelted them with missiles and poured the contents of their chamber pots on their heads. The soldiers regrouped several times but were repulsed and eventually withdrew in disarray.

A larger force was later sent but it too was repulsed. It was this 'beleaguering' of Mother Holland's fortress which may have earned it the name the Leaguer. The whores' victory was short-lived, however; by the following year the Leaguer was successfully closed down. That is the last we hear of Mother Holland and her girls, but the house kept the name. On a map of 1746 it is called Holland Leger. Today Hopton Street runs through the site.

HOLLAND, NAN An expert in the simple 'service lay', which entailed hiring herself out as a servant and then stealing from her master. It was said she could 'wheedle most cunningly, lie confoundedly, swear desperately, pick a pocket dexterously, dissemble undiscernibly, drink and smoke everlastingly, whore insatiably and brazen out all her actions impudently'.

HOMOSEXUALITY This was made a capital crime in 1533. Convictions were rare as it was difficult to prove, but it aroused strong official and popular horror and loathing. After most countries on the continent decriminalised homosexuality the pace of executions increased in England until they were running at about two a year. Juries were reluctant to convict. Only if 'penetration' was proved would the death penalty be imposed. Mostly the juries would decide that homosexual acts were common assaults, meriting a fine. However, those who were convicted and condemned were most unlikely to be reprieved. The punishment of the VERE STREET COTERIE in 1810 showed society at its most vindictive.

There was plenty of evidence of homosexual activity. A mollies' house opposite the Old Bailey dated from 1559, and the men reportedly addressed each other as 'Madam' or 'Ladyship'. In 1661 another homosexual brothel was the Three Potters in Cripplegate Without. The Fountain in the Strand was a known haunt of homosexuals throughout the eighteenth century. There was a male brothel in Camomile Street, Bishopsgate – the manager was known as the Countess of Camomile. In 1570 Sir Thomas Gresham's Bourse, which later became the Royal Exchange, was opened and the area soon became the haunt of prostitutes and catamites, the latter attracting customers among the City's rich merchants. In May 1726 the *London Journal* wrote of twenty 'Sodomitical Clubs' where 'they make their execrable Bargains, and then withdraw into some dark Corners to perpetrate their odious Wickedness'. These 'clubs' included MOTHER CLAP's in Holborn, where there were beds in every room with 'commonly thirty to forty Chaps every night – and even more – especially on Sunday Nights'. The Talbot Inn in the Strand was another haunt, as were even the 'Bog-Houses' of Lincoln's Inn.

The writer Ned Ward complained in the *London Spy* in 1700 about the antics of male prostitutes at the Fountain, a tavern in Russell Square. Dressed as women, they would enact mock childbirths using a doll, which would be 'Christened and the Holy Sacrament of Baptism impudently Prophan'd'. Ward later wrote about these members of the 'Mollies' Club': 'There is a curious band of fellows in the town who call themselves "Mollies" (effeminates, weaklings) who are so totally destitute of all masculine attributes that they prefer to behave as women. They adopt all the small vanities natural to the feminine sex to such an extent that they will try to speak, walk, chatter, shriek and scold as women do, aping them as well in other respects.'

There were 'mollies' in high places, of course. In February 1685 Henry, Duke of Grafton killed the notorious Jack Talbot, younger brother of the Duke of Shrewsbury, in a duel. Grafton had objected to some remarks Talbot had made about Princess Anne and her husband. A contemporary satire described Talbot as:

> Thrice fortunate Boy
> Who can give double-Joy
> And every Turn be ready;
> With Pleasures in Store
> Behind and Before
> To delight both My Lord and My Lady.

There was 'a tremendous upsurge in sodomy' around the beginning of the eighteenth century, and in 1707 a raid on a 'Sodomites' Club' in the City caused a great scandal. About forty men were arrested, including the respected Cheapside mercer Jacob Ecclestone, who later committed suicide in Newgate. Another respected City figure, the Cheapside draper William Grant, hanged himself there, and the curate of St Dunstan's-in-the-East, a Mr Jermain, cut his throat with his razor, as did another merchant, a Mr Bearden. Several others also committed suicide before the case came to trial. All these men frequented the alleys around the Royal Exchange. The favourite meeting place was Pope's Head Alley. In nearby Sweetings Alley the 'breeches-clad bawds' congregated.

In October 1764 *The Public Advertiser* reported that: 'A bugger aged sixty was put in the Cheapside Pillory . . . the Mob tore off his clothes, pelted him with Filth, whipt him almost to Death . . . he was naked and covered with Dung . . . when the Hour was up he was carried almost unconscious back to Newgate.'

Some used the reaction against the upsurge in sodomy to blackmail innocents. In September 1724 a young man walking in the streets was accosted by a man who seized him and cried out, 'A sodomite! A sodomite!' The terrified young man was advised by a passing gentleman, in reality an accomplice, to give the blackmailer five or six guineas, but protested that he did not have the money. The two older men then followed him to the place where he worked, hoping to get money, but were driven off by one of the young man's colleagues, who drew his sword. The blackmailers ran off, 'leaving the boy prostrate with shock'. In January 1725 two men were found guilty of a similar attempt at blackmail, and were sentenced to 'two hours on Tower Hill Pillory, two hours on the Cheapside Pillory, a fine of Twenty pounds and six months in Newgate'.

George Skelthorpe, who was executed in 1709, used to pick up 'Sodomites' at a public house in Covent Garden and go with them to 'a by-place thereabouts to commit their foul acts'. He would grab them, threaten to take them before a justice 'by which means he got a great deal of money at several times . . .'

Some men got off very lightly. In 1722, a year in which there was a spate of prosecutions, John Dicks picked up a young boy and took him to ale-houses where he got him drunk. He buggered the boy in the yard behind the Golden Ball in Fetter Lane. When a pot-boy who heard the commotion went to see what was going on Dicks attempted to bugger him as well, and the landlord caught him 'in the very act of buggery'. Dicks pleaded with the landlord not to report him, 'for if you swear against me you swear away my life'. Dicks was found guilty of attempted sodomy, fined twenty marks, stood in the Temple Bar pillory for an hour and sent to Newgate for two years.

Women whores protested at all this unwanted competition:

How Happy were the good old English Faces
'til Mounsieur from France taught PEGO a Dance
to the tune of Old Sodom's Embraces.
But now WE are quite out of Fashion.
Poor whores may be NUNS, since MEN turn their GUNS
And vent on each other their Passion.
But now, we find to our Sorrow we are over-run
By the Parks of the BUM
and Peers of the Land of Gomorrah!

In 1726 the Societies for the Reform of Manners succeeded in closing down more than twenty mollies' houses, including MOTHER CLAP's. One young catamite, Edward Courteney, told of the goings-on at another mollies' house, the Royal Oak in Pall Mall. He said there were several rooms at the back of the tavern which were used by homosexuals who acted as married couples. The landlord had 'put the bite on him' to go with a country gentleman who promised to pay him handsomely. He 'stayed all night but in the morning he gave me no more than a sixpence'.

A 'club of paederasts' used to meet in the Bunch of Grapes in Clare Market. When they appeared before Bow Street magistrates eighteen were wearing women's clothes. Although they were found not guilty for lack of evidence, they had to run the gauntlet of a large crowd which gathered outside the courtroom. Handcuffed together, they could do little to protect themselves from a storm of stones and filth hurled by these vindictive spectators. In 1764 a homosexuals' club for Footguards was discovered, and sixteen soldiers were charged. Buggery in the armed forces was usually punished with death.

The Criminal Law Amendment Act of 1885 made almost any sexual contact between males a serious criminal offence, and also opened the way to blackmail. It was called a 'blackmailer's charter' at the time, and men who could face prison if convicted of what had hitherto been overlooked were now open to extortion.

The last two men to be hanged for buggery were John Smith and James Pratt in 1835, and it was not until 1861 that the death penalty for buggery was abolished. The Wolfenden Report of 1957 led to changes in the law which made homosexual acts between adult men legal if they took place in private. (Homosexual acts between women have never been illegal.) This ended the scandal of police officers hanging round public toilets in the hope of catching homosexuals in the act, or even enticing them. The toilets at Leicester Square and Falconberg Mews, Westminster, were among many others notorious for this police activity.

HOTTEN, JOHN CAMDEN (1832–1907) Publisher of expensive pornography for well-heeled Victorians. He was the publisher of such works as *Lady Bumtickler's Revels* and *Madam Birchini's Dance*. With the aid of the blackmailer CHARLES AUGUSTUS HOWELL he hoped to get the poet Algernon Charles Swinburne to produce suitable material. Swinburne was the author of the splendidly subversive 'La Soeur de la Reine', about Queen Victoria's twin sister, a Haymarket prostitute. The Queen herself is seduced by William Wordsworth after a suggestive reading of his poem *The Excursion*. Her rampant sexual demands can afterwards be satisfied only by Lord John Russell and 'Sir Peel'. Hotten did not have the nerve to have such works printed, and they circulated privately.

HOWARD, CATHERINE Fifth wife of HENRY VIII, executed for adultery in 1542. She was aged about 19 when she was sent to the Tower. On the way she saw the heads of her lovers Francis Dereham and Thomas Culpepper on spikes at London Bridge. Told on 12 February that she was to die the next day she asked that the block be brought to her cell so that she could practise laying her head on it. Although she had not always behaved responsibly her speech on the scaffold had quiet dignity: 'If I had married the man I loved instead of being dazzled with ambition, all would have been well. I die a queen, but I would rather have died the wife of Culpepper.'

HOWARD, JOHN (1726–90) Prison reformer after whom the Howard League for Penal Reform is named. While travelling in Europe he was imprisoned by the French. Later he campaigned for better conditions in British prisons. In 1774 this led to Acts being passed giving fixed salaries to jailers and laying down standards for cleanliness. He died of typhus, caught while visiting a prison in Russia, in 1790.

HOWARD, THOMAS, DUKE OF NORFOLK (1536–72) Catholic peer executed for plotting against Queen Elizabeth I. He was drawn into the plot masterminded by the Florentine banker Roberto Ridolfi to murder the queen and replace her with Mary Queen of Scots. *See* TOWER OF LONDON

HOWELL, CHARLES AUGUSTUS (1837–90) Blackmailer who dug up the body of Dante Gabriel Rossetti's wife. Howell ingratiated himself with members of the artistic Pre-Raphaelite circle and then attempted to blackmail them. Rossetti's wife Elizabeth died in 1862 after taking an overdose of laudanum. Rossetti had his unpublished manuscripts buried with her. Seven years later he changed his mind and wanted to retrieve them. Howell performed this service, hoping this would put Rossetti in his power. His usual technique was to write to his victims, getting them to disclose secret sexual obsessions by pretending to share them. He would paste their letters into a scrapbook, then say he had been obliged to pawn the scrapbook for a large sum of money. Unfortunately the money was now spent, but if the correspondent would lend him a similar sum he would be able to redeem the scrapbook before the pawnbroker sold it. It seems the victims usually paid this 'loan'. He accompanied Algernon Charles Swinburne to homosexual brothels, and teamed up with the publisher JOHN CAMDEN HOTTEN to get the poet to write pornography. Naturally his blackmailing made enemies, and in 1890 Howell was found dead in a Chelsea gutter with his throat cut and a half sovereign between his teeth – the mark of a blackmailer.

HULKS Decrepit old warships used as floating prisons. They were introduced as temporary prisons in 1776, although they continued to be used well into the nineteenth century. They quickly became stinking, pestilential death traps, crawling with vermin and home to a wide range of deadly and unpleasant diseases – typhus and cholera perhaps the worst. The regime was even tougher than prison. The convicts were given a restricted diet and put to public work at the arsenal at Woolwich, the quarries at Portland or the dockyard at Portsmouth. MAYHEW wrote of the early days of the hulks, when 700 men were crowded together on the *Justitia* in the Thames: 'The state of morality under such circumstances may be easily conceived, crimes impossible to mention being commonly perpetrated' (Mayhew and Binney, *The Criminal Prisons of London*). He was referring to the homosexual rape of young prisoners. Venereal disease was even more widespread than in the outside world.

The diet on the hulks, for men doing hard manual labour for long hours, was inadequate. The day started at 5.30 a.m. with a pint of cocoa and a 12-ounce piece of dry bread. Then the men would be ferried ashore to work, breaking granite, clearing drains, building roads, scraping the rust off shells. They were ferried back to the hulks for the main meal of the day at 11.30. This consisted of a pound of potatoes and some boiled meat, which was often rotten, and six ounces of bread. Then it was back to work until 5 p.m., when they would return to the hulks for supper, which was a pint of gruel and bread. The diet for those on a punishment regime was a pound of bread per day, and water.

Some men managed to escape with the help of free labourers who would hide clothes for them somewhere in the arsenal. Others escaped from the hulks. In 1776 five prisoners on the *Justitia* seized the officers' weapons and locked up the warders. They then escaped in a boat brought alongside by friends. Two of them were killed in the ensuing pursuit, and another two recaptured. Among other escapes around the same time, twenty-two men forced their way into the captain's cabin and took pistols and swords. They then rowed to the north bank of the river and freed themselves from their chains with tools they took from a blacksmith's. A unit of sailors caught up with them at East Ham and in the fire-fight which followed one of the prisoners was killed and three recaptured. The others fled into Epping Forest, and a few managed to remain free. The rest were recaptured over the following months, and hanged.

In 1778 thirty-six convicts rushed the warders on one of the hulks and when the crew opened fire one of them was killed and eighteen wounded. The hopelessness of such attempts was no deterrent. They probably felt that if they stayed they would soon die anyway. During one two-year period 176 prisoners out of a total of 632 on the hulks died – more than a quarter. At a Parliamentary inquiry the director of the project, Duncan Campbell, had to admit that when men were being transported to America 'upon an average of seven years, the loss of convicts in jail and on board will be one seventh'.

PATRICK COLQUHOUN, founder of the Thames River Police, was one of many who spoke out against the hulks, calling them 'seminaries of profligacy and vice' which 'vomit forth at stated times upon the public a certain number of convicts, who having no asylum, no home, no character, and no means of subsistence, seem to have only the alternative of joining their companions in iniquity and of adding strength to the criminal phalanx'. Yet the hulks, intended originally as a temporary measure, continued in use until July 1857 when the last of them, the *Defence*, was destroyed by fire at Woolwich.

HUME, DONALD Small-time crook who murdered car dealer, gun-runner and super-spiv Stanley Setty in 1949. They had been partners, Hume supplying Setty with stolen cars and finding customers for his forged petrol coupons. He invited Setty to his flat and stabbed him to death with a German SS knife. It was never clear why, although Setty had been unkind to Hume's dog. Hume stole some money he found on the body, then cut it up and dumped it in the sea off the Essex marshes from a small aircraft. Hume was tried for murder and acquitted after he claimed unidentified gangsters paid him to dump the body, but jailed for twelve years as an accessory. He was released in 1958 and told a newspaper that he really had murdered Setty. He went abroad and after spending the £2,000 he got for his story decided to return to London to rob a bank. In August 1958 he took two 'pep' pills and went to the Midland Bank in Boston Manor Road, Brentford. During the raid he shot and wounded a cashier before fleeing with £1,500. In November he raided the same bank, seriously wounding the manager and escaping with £300. This time he went to Zurich, leaving behind on a train a raincoat with a name-tag with one of his known aliases. In Zurich he tried to rob a bank, wounded a cashier and then shot dead a taxi-driver.

He was jailed for life, and after sixteen years in a Swiss prison he was found to be insane and transferred to Broadmoor. While he was in prison his wife Cynthia, a former night-club hostess, divorced him. She married the investigative journalist DUNCAN WEBB.

HUMPHREYS, JIMMY Soho strip club owner and pornographer who caused the downfall of the Obscene Publications Squad, known as the Porn Squad. In the 1960s Humphreys and other Soho pornographers were paying police large sums of money to be allowed to operate. He and his wife Rusty, a former dancer, used to entertain the corrupt officers lavishly. They would invite them to their holiday home in Ibiza, where the police would relax with girls from the strip clubs. Among the senior officers involved were Commander Wally Virgo of the CID, Bill Moody, head of the Porn Squad, and Commander Ken Drury, head of the Flying Squad.

In one deal Humphreys agreed to pay the police an initial £14,000 and £2,000 a month for permission to sell obscene books from his Soho premises. As part of the deal he had to take the vice racketeer BERNIE SILVER as a partner. Humphreys recorded all this in a series of diaries which were later handed to the police.

In February 1976 Drury, Virgo, Moody and others were arrested in a series of dawn raids. Humphreys, who was serving a jail sentence at the time, was given a royal pardon in 1978 for his part in this coup, and released. He and Rusty left the country and he became a bookmaker in Mexico and Florida. By the 1990s they were back in England, renting flats to prostitutes. It is said that Rusty occasionally acted as a 'maid' for the women. In summer 1994 they were both jailed for eight months.

After the trials the Obscene Publications Squad was disbanded and its role was taken by a squad of uniformed officers. *See* PORNOGRAPHY

HUNT, LEIGH (1784–1859) Poet and essayist, jailed with his brother John in 1813 for criminal libel against the Prince Regent. In their Sunday paper *The Examiner* they had described him thus: 'This Adonis in loveliness is a corpulent man of fifty . . . a libertine over head and ears in debt and disgrace, a despiser of domestic ties, the companion of gamblers and demireps, a man who has just closed half a century without one single claim on the gratitude of his country or the respect of authority.' They were each jailed for two years and fined £500. In jail Leigh Hunt continued to edit *The Examiner*, which was a leading Liberal paper and attracted contributions from Byron, Keats, Shelley, Moore and Lamb.

I

INCE, GEORGE (1940–) Robber and victim of mistaken identity. In May 1973 Ince was accused of murdering Muriel Patience at the Barn Restaurant in Braintree, Essex. His lawyer claimed that at the time of the murder Ince had been in bed with with a Mrs Dolly Gray. This turned out to be Dolly Kray, wife of the KRAY twins' brother Charles. Ince was acquitted and another man was later convicted of the murder. Because of the Ince case and others the Court of Appeal later laid down new guidelines on identification evidence.

INFORMERS OR GRASSES Vital source of information for the police. All successful policemen, from JONATHAN WILD on, have depended on underworld tip-offs. When the Metropolitan Police force was founded in 1829 officers were forbidden to mix with criminals, a policy that soon had to be changed. 'The memoirs of successful Scotland Yard detectives like Peter Beveridge, John Gosling and Robert Fabian stress that the detective is only as good as his network of informers' (Murphy, *Smash and Grab*). Because of the rewards system the police themselves inevitably became corrupt. For the informer the danger is of mutilation or death. In the interwar years he would have his face slashed with a long cut ending at the mouth: the 'mark of the nark' which would brand him as an informer and a man to steer clear of. In today's underworld informers are usually silenced for ever. *See* BERTIE SMALLS

IRELAND, COLIN Sadist who murdered five men in three months. Ireland's first victim was Peter Walker, a 44-year-old theatre director found suffocated in his flat on 8 March 1993. The previous evening he had gone to a gay pub in Earl's Court. There he met Ireland, a heterosexual who picked up men by pretending to be a homosexual sado-masochist. He would torture them, get their cash withdrawal cards and PIN numbers and kill them. His other victims were Christopher Dunn, killed on 28 May after being tortured with a lighter; Perry Bradley III, son of an American Congressman, found on 4 June having been whipped and strangled; Andrew Collier, found on 7 June, after being beaten and strangled, and chef Emanuel Spiteri on 12 June. Police found a CCTV picture of Ireland and Spiteri leaving a cash-point machine. After they circulated it Ireland surrendered. Ireland, who had been twice married and denied being a homosexual, said: 'I was a thin lanky little runt – always getting the worst of it. It was building up in me, a general dislike of people.'

IRELAND, WILLIAM (1777–1835) Forger who confounded the Shakespeare experts. In February 1795 some manuscripts purporting to be by Shakespeare were displayed by a bookseller named Samuel Ireland at his home in Norfolk Street, off the Strand. They had been discovered by his son William, who was eighteen at the time, in the house of a gentleman he had met. They included early drafts of *Hamblette* and *Kynge Leare* and love poems to 'Anna Hathereway'.

Seventeen literary scholars examined them and pronounced them genuine. The Prince of Wales came to gawp, and Boswell sank to his knees and kissed them. He 'thanked God he had lived to see them'.

Richard Brinsley Sheridan was looking for a sensation to revive the fortunes of his Theatre Royal in Drury Lane, and he decided to stage one of the plays, *Vortigern*. It was about a fifth-century English chieftain in love with his own daughter. Doubts about the authenticity of the text began to emerge: the great actress Mrs Siddons refused to appear in it, and John Kemble, who was cast as Vortigern, also had grave doubts. The performance went ahead, and as it progressed the audience became restive. When Kemble spoke the climactic line 'And when this solemn mockery is o'er . . .' there was laughter. After much pressure William Ireland confessed that he had forged the manuscripts, using old paper and ink got up to look right. He had planned to write a complete cycle of royal plays on all the kings and queens not covered by Shakespeare. He disappeared into obscurity, dying in 1835. He had remained proud that he had fooled the experts.

J

JACK THE RIPPER *see* following page

JACK THE STRIPPER MURDERS A series of prostitute murders in the 1960s. The body of Hannah Tailford was found in the Thames near Hammersmith Bridge on 2 February 1964. Tailford, who was 30, was naked except for her stockings, which were around her ankles. Her pants were stuffed into her mouth and her face was bruised. There was a suggestion that she was blackmailing a client. Her flat had been fitted up as a photographic studio. On 8 April the body of Irene Lockwood was found in the river at Duke's Meadow. She had been strangled, and again blackmail was suggested as a motive.

The next victim was Helen Barthelemy, found near the river at Brentford on 24 April. There were traces of paint spray on the body, a fact of growing significance in the investigation. On 14 July Mary Fleming was found near a garage in Chiswick. There were traces of paint on the body of the mother of two. Like all the other victims she was under five feet three inches in height. On 25 November the body of another prostitute, Margaret McGowan, was found in a car park near Kensington High Street. Again there was paint on the body. On 16 February 1965 the body of Bridie O'Hara was found behind a shed near Westfield Road, Acton. Although other murders were later tentatively linked to the Jack the Stripper series O'Hara was probably the killer's last victim.

Police linked the paint to a paint-spray shop at Acton. There appeared to be a break-through when a man who lived in south London killed himself in June 1965, leaving a note saying he was unable to stand the strain any longer. Police, who believed he was the killer, never named him, but journalist Brian McConnell said in his book *Found Naked and Dead* that he was an ex-policeman who had a lifetime obsession with prostitutes. It was also suggested that the killer was the former world light-heavyweight boxing champion FREDDIE MILLS, who was found shot dead in a car in Soho, but police denied this.

JACKSON, REVD WILLIAM (1737–95) Vicious libeller and spy. Jackson, who was an Oxford-educated Irishman, became embroiled in the affair of the DUCHESS OF KINGSTON, who was charged with bigamy in 1775. The duchess hired Jackson, editor of the *Public Ledger*, to defend her, particularly against the playwright Samuel Foote, who planned to lampoon her in a new comedy, *A Trip to Calais*. Jackson belaboured Foote in his paper, and traced a former servant of Foote's who was prepared to give evidence that the playwright had indecently assaulted him. Foote was tried, and the judge told the jury that there was a conspiracy against the playwright. He was acquitted but the affair had affected him so badly that he died within the year.

The duchess was found guilty of bigamy and went to St Petersburg, where she became friendly with Catherine the Great. Jackson followed and joined her there briefly, returning to England with what was described as 'a considerable sum of money as a final reward for his services'. When the money ran out he announced his death in the newspapers in 1788 and went to France to escape his creditors. He became a revolutionary and in 1794 returned to England as a French spy. He went to Dublin to stir up trouble and was arrested and charged with treason. He refused bribes to name co-conspirators, and killed himself in the dock with a massive dose of arsenic. The *Morning Chronicle* described him as 'the libelling, lying, swearing, drunken King's Bench parson'.

JACOBY, HENRY Pantry boy executed for murder. Jacoby was 18 and had recently started work at the Spencer Hotel in Portman Street in March 1922. He decided to rob one of the guests, Lady White, widow of the former chairman of the London County Council. He went into her room, shone a torch and she woke with a scream. Jacoby hit her several times with a hammer he had found in a toolbag in the basement. He fled in panic but had the presence of mind to wash the hammer and return it to the toolbag. The police had no clues but Jacoby finally volunteered a confession. Strenuous efforts were made to save him, but he was even refused a Christian burial.

JEFFREYS, GEORGE (1648–89) The most notorious 'hanging judge'. He had shown himself to be a willing tool of the state, active in the Popish Plot prosecutions. He was appointed Chief Justice of the King's Bench in 1683 and was raised to the peerage by James II two years later. His savagery at the West Country trials of Monmouth's followers earned the hearings the title of 'the Bloody Assizes'. He sentenced 74 men to be executed in Dorset, 233 to be

Continued on p. 143

JACK THE RIPPER

The fascination of the Whitechapel Murders has endured while more prolific serial killers have been forgotten. The interest lies mainly in speculation about the identity of the murderer, which will probably never be known. Jack killed at least six women, all within one square mile in a three-month period in 1888. All but one were prostitutes, all had their throats cut and were mutilated with a knowledge of human anatomy that led the police to suppose that the murderer had some surgical training.

Writers and social investigators were beginning to awaken the Victorian conscience about the problems of the East End. In 1870 Dickens had made a real opium den in Bluegate Fields, Shadwell, the focus of his unfinished *The Mystery of Edwin Drood*, and Gustave Doré made an engraving of the same den two years later for *London: A Pilgrimage*. Walter Besant's East End novel *All Sorts and Conditions of Men* of 1882 was followed by those of Arthur Morrison and Israel Zangwill, among others. The year after the Ripper killings the first part of Charles Booth's seventeen-volume investigation of London poverty and vice, *Life and Labour of the People in London*, was published. Its title was *East London*. In this atmosphere of heightened awareness and anxiety, the Ripper murders were sensational. The fact that all the killings were committed within 500 yards of Whitechapel High Street, 'where the wealth of the City met the poverty and mystery of the East End', added to the sense of mystery and menace.

The first woman to die was Martha Turner, 35. She was stabbed again and again at George Yard Buildings off Whitechapel Road, on 7 August. The Ripper struck again on 31 August, killing Mary Ann Nicholls, a 42-year-old prostitute. She was found lying on the pavement of Buck's Row. She had been staying in a room in Flower and Dean Street, long notorious for its prostitutes. She is said to have told the lodging-house keeper: 'Don't let my doss, I'll soon be back with the money. See what a fine new bonnet I've got,' although this remark has also been attributed to another of the Ripper's victims.

Eight days later 47-year-old Annie Chapman was killed half a mile away in Hanbury Street. She had been married to a veterinary surgeon but her drinking ruined the marriage. Her death, and the Press attention the murders now received, started a panic. The murderer struck twice on the night of 30 September, first butchering Elizabeth Stride, 44, in the back yard of a working men's club in Berner Street. She had turned to drink and prostitution after her entire family died when the pleasure steamer *Princess Alice* sank in the Thames. Early next morning the horribly mutilated body of Catherine Eddowes, 43, was found in Mitre Square. She had been released from police custody the previous night after being taken in for drunkenness.

There was a break of five weeks before the last murder. On 9 November Mary Kelly took the Ripper back to her squalid room in Miller's Court, off Dorset Street. Kelly, a 24-year-old widow, lived there alone. The rent collector found parts of her body strewn about the room.

The killer sent taunting letters to the police. More than six hundred plain-clothes officers were drafted in, without success. Public confidence in the police fell. The Police Commissioner, SIR CHARLES WARREN, resigned, not before he had been chased across Tooting Common by the bloodhounds he was training to help him catch the Ripper. There have been many suspects, before and since. Perhaps the most credible is an unsuccessful barrister name MONTAGUE JOHN DRUITT, who committed suicide in the Thames about a month after the last of the Ripper murders. He came from a medical family and may even have studied medicine himself.

Among the groups suspected – they included doctors, butchers and foreigners – were the Jews. There were minor disturbances, and popular hostility against Jews might have turned into something much more serious had not a policeman had the sense to erase a chalked message, believed to have been left by the Ripper, implicating the 'Jewes' in the fifth killing. It was pointed out that National Vigilance Association campaigns leading to the closure of brothels and the dispersal of prostitutes had forced destitute whores in the most dangerous parts of the city to trade sex in dark alleys and the most squalid doss houses.

hung drawn and quartered in Somerset, and a further 800 to be transported. He harangued the court with remarks such as 'There is not one of these lying, snivelling, canting Presbyterians but, one way or another, had a hand in the rebellion.' He boasted of having sent more traitors to the gallows than all his predecessors since the Conquest. James made him Lord Chancellor but when the king fled the country Jeffreys was sent to the TOWER, where he died.

JEFFRIES, MARY Victorian brothel owner and enemy of the campaigning journalist W.T. STEAD. Jeffries, once described as the wickedest woman of the century, had started her career as a prostitute at the exclusive establishment of Madame Berthe in the 1840s. Berthe's was an old-fashioned house which had not moved with the times and provided straightforward commercial sex. Mrs Jeffries, who wanted to cater for the full gamut of perversions, saw the possibilities and with finance provided by wealthy clients opened an establishment in Church Street in Chelsea which catered to the latest tastes in sexual matters. Soon she was running four houses in Church Street – numbers 125, 127, 129 and 155. There was also a brothel which specialised in flagellation at Rose Cottage, Hampstead. In all she had eight brothels. Among her clients were the King of the Belgians and what she described as 'patrons of the highest social order'.

Benjamin Scott, Chamberlain of the City of London and chairman of the London Committee for the Exposure and Suppression of the Traffic of English Girls for the Purposes of Continental Prostitution, wanted to prosecute Jeffries. There was an unlikely story that she had a 'white-slave house' by the river at Kew, and that drugged girls were sent abroad in closed coffins with air-holes in the lids. A charge which had real substance, that she kept brothels for the nobility, was regarded by the Assistant Commissioner at Scotland Yard as 'highly improper': he refused to prosecute. Instead on 16 April 1885 she was charged with keeping a disorderly house.

When the case against her was heard in May 1885 Mrs Jeffries arrived at court in a carriage provided by a member of the House of Lords. She was fined £200 and ordered to find £200 as surety. A titled Guards officer stood surety for her, and before the day was over she was back in business. When Stead stood trial she was seen handing out rotten fruit for crowds outside the courthouse to throw at him.

JENKINS, HARRY Murderer who escaped the noose once but was executed for a later killing. Jenkins, a member of the ELEPHANT AND CASTLE GANG, and two other armed men, Christopher Geraghty and Terence Rolt, tried to rob a jeweller's in Charlotte Street, W1 in April 1947. The staff resisted and set off the burglar alarm, and the three fled. A motorcyclist, Alec de Antiquis, 34, was shot as he tried to stop them. His last words as he lay dying were 'I did my best'. A photograph of de Antiquis lying in the road was published by newspapers around the world. The robbers were traced by Robert Fabian, 'Fabian of the Yard'. Jenkins had a record of assaults on the police and was known as 'The King of Borstal'. In fact he had been released from Borstal, a corrective training establishment for young offenders, only a week earlier. Geraghty had twice escaped from Borstal with Jenkins. It was he who shot de Antiquis. He and Jenkins were hanged in September 1947. Rolt, who was only 17 and too young to hang, was detained during His Majesty's pleasure. Nearly three years earlier Jenkins and two other men had taken part in another jewellery raid in which a man was killed. As the trio were making their getaway from the jeweller's in Birchin Lane in the City, a retired navy captain named Ralph Binney stood in front of their car with his arms outstretched. The driver, Ronald Hedley, did not stop and Binney was dragged for over a mile. Hedley was sentenced to death, reprieved, and served nine years in prison. The third member of the gang, Jenkins's brother Thomas, got eight years. Witnesses failed to identify Harry Jenkins and he was not charged.

JEW BILL Short-lived measure killed off more by the threat of unrest than any serious violence. The Bill enabled Jews to be naturalised by Act of Parliament without taking the sacrament. The aim was to reward Jews who had been helpful to the government during the 1745 Jacobite rising and afterwards. It passed through the Lords and Commons practically unnoticed in 1753. Then, Ian Gilmour says in *Riot, Risings and Revolution*, as it waited for the king's assent 'intense public clamour' broke out.

In so far as the agitation was anti-semitic it was religious, not racial. There were also elements of economic interests and familiar London anti-emigrant sentiments. Apart from a minor scene in a theatre there were no attacks on Jews or their property. But grotesque fears, real or pretended, were expressed: Judaism would become the fashionable religion, thus endangering the livelihoods of butchers; it would lead to a general naturalisation of Jews; it would produce a swarm of foreigners. In November the government moved to repeal the measure which had been enacted only in June.

The issue continued to reverberate during the subsequent general election. Gilmour quotes a satirical account of the controversy in one constituency:

> I was present in — where the election is coming on . . . The town . . . is divided into two parties, who are distinguished by the appellation of *Christians* and *Jews*. The Jews, it seems, are those who are in the interest of a nobleman who gave his vote for passing the Jew Bill, and are held in abomination by the Christians. The zeal of the latter is still further inflamed by the vicar, who every Sunday . . . preaches up the pious doctrine of persecution . . . Sir Rowland swears that his lordship is actually circumcised, and that the chapel in this nobleman's house is turned into a synagogue. The knight has never been seen in a church, till the later clamour about the Jew Bill; but now he attends it regularly every Sunday, when he devoutly takes his nap all the service . . . Every Saturday he has a hunt, because it is the Jewish Sabbath; and in the evening he is sure to get drunk with the vicar in defence of religion . . . (Gilmour, *Riot, Risings and Revolution*)

JOAD, CYRIL (1891–1953) Philosopher who cheated on a train fare. Joad was a member of the panel of the popular radio programme *Brains Trust*, remembered for his catchphrase 'It all depends what you mean by . . .'. He was caught travelling without a ticket on a train, and convicted of defrauding the Great Western Railway of 17*s* 1*d*. When it was revealed that it was not his first such offence he was fined £2 with costs of 25 guineas. The case ended his radio career. He was the author of more than forty books, turning to religion with his last, *Recovery of Belief*, having been an atheist.

JOHNSON, WILLIAM (?–1714) Highwayman who shot a prison turnkey in court. Johnson called at the Old Bailey to see his friend Jane Housden, who was being tried for coining. He tried to speak to her but Spurling, the head turnkey at Newgate, told him he must wait until the trial had ended. Spurling was a known prison bully and criminal, and Johnson drew a pistol and shot him dead, to shouts of encouragement from Housden. The judges adjourned Housden's trial for coining and instead immediately tried her and Johnson for murder. They were hanged in September 1714 in the yard of the Sessions House.

JONES, CATHERINE Bigamist acquitted because her second husband was a hermaphrodite. Jones appeared at the Old Bailey in September 1719 and readily admitted that she had married again while her husband was abroad. However she claimed the second marriage was illegal because the groom, Constantine Boone, was a hermaphrodite 'and had been shewn as such at the Southwark and Bartholomew fairs', in the words of the *Newgate Calendar*. 'To prove this a person swore that he knew Boone when a child, that his (or *her*) mother dressed *it* in girl's apparel, and caused it to be instructed in needlework, till it attained the age of twelve years, when it *turned man, and went to sea*.' Boone appeared in court and admitted being a hermaphrodite, and witnesses gave evidence that he had more female than male characteristics.

JONES, CONSTANTIA Prostitute executed in 1725 for robbing her client. Jones, a 30-year-old 'three-penny upright', had been in Newgate twenty times. The client told a jury: 'As I stood against the wall, the prisoner came behind me, and with one hand she took hold of — and the other she thrust into my breeches pocket and took my money.' Clients who went to court with claims that they had been cheated by whores usually won (Linebaugh, *The London Hanged*).

JONES, ELIZABETH Girl who went on a wartime crime spree. In October 1944 when Jones was 18 and a striptease artist living in Hammersmith she met American army deserter Karl Hulten in a cafe. They were both fantasists who saw themselves as a gangster and his moll. Driving about in a stolen army truck they attacked and robbed pedestrians and cyclists. They threw one woman into the Thames after Hulten had battered her with an iron bar. On 7 October 1944 they hailed a taxi driven by George Heath. Hulten shot the cabbie dead and stole nineteen shillings – less than a pound. On 10 October Hulten was arrested in the Fulham Palace Road with the gun in his pocket. Jones was arrested after telling a policeman friend who said she looked pale: 'If you had seen someone do what I have seen you wouldn't be able to sleep at night.' They were sentenced to death in January 1945 and despite an appeal from the American ambassador Hulten was hanged. Jones was reprieved because of her youth and released in 1954.

JONES, JANIE Madam jailed for keeping an amusing stable of prostitutes. Jones was an exhibitionist who drove round London in a pink

Rolls-Royce. She held parties where guests watched through a two-way mirror while other unsuspecting guests had sex with one of her girls. In 1966 she was charged with blackmail, and as in subsequent trials her accuser was allowed to hide his name behind a letter of the alphabet. Mr A claimed Jones had threatened to tell his wife about his exploits – he had sex with Jones's girls Tania, Maureen, Nina, Janice, Tessa and Chrystal – unless he paid her £1,200. Mr A, who described himself as 'nominally a sadist', had hoped some of the girls would get into a pool and disport themselves like fish. Jones was acquitted. A month later she was arrested for running a brothel. Police told how they watched the goings-on in her flat from the balcony of a house opposite. There was no house opposite. The case collapsed. In June 1971 the *News of the World* exposed a sex scandal at the BBC. The newspaper said Jones was tricking her girls into having sex with producers and disc jockeys, believing that they were auditioning for radio and TV. Two years later Jones was tried at the Old Bailey on a variety of charges, which included blackmailing a peer referred to as Lord Y. Jones's girls told the court that Lord Y carried a teddy bear and liked them to dress as schoolgirls. Jones was found not guilty of blackmail, but given the astonishing sentence of seven years in prison for controlling prostitutes. The judge, Alan King-Hamilton, said she was the most evil woman he had ever sentenced. In 1987 *Private Eye* alleged that King-Hamilton had been a client of the noted dominatrix LINDI ST CLAIR.

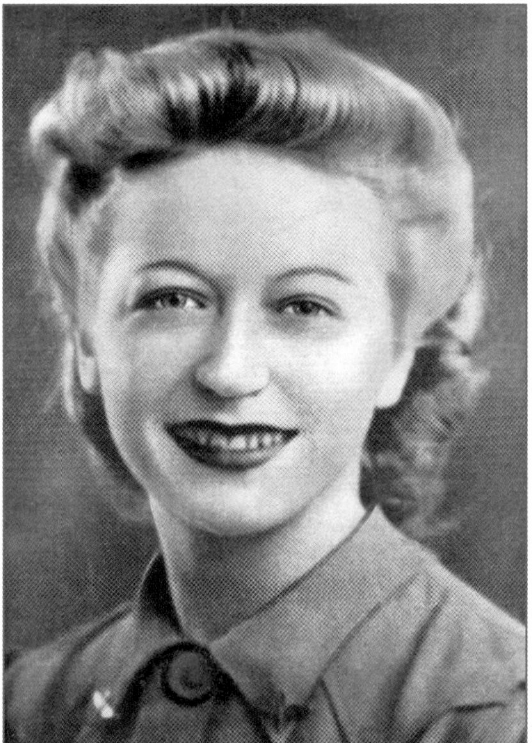

Elizabeth Jones, teenage striptease girl who went on a wartime crime spree. In 1944, when she was 18, her American army deserter boyfriend Karl Hulten shot a cabbie dead and robbed him. Hulten was executed, Jones was reprieved because of her age.

JONES, MARY The particularly heartless hanging of this pretty young shoplifter in 1770 was referred to by Dickens in *Barnaby Rudge*. Mary Jones was eighteen and the mother of two small children. Her husband was press-ganged and she was left penniless and turned out onto the streets. She took some cloth from the counter of a shop in Ludgate Street and put it under her cloak: when the shopkeeper saw her she put it back on the counter. Her defence was that 'she had lived in credit, and wanted for nothing, till a press-gang came and stole her husband from her; but since then she had no bed to lie on; nothing to give her children to eat; and they were almost naked; and perhaps she might have done something wrong, for she hardly knew what she did.' The parish officers spoke up for her, but the shopkeepers in Ludgate Street complained that there was too much shoplifting in the area, and objected to the woman being shown mercy. '. . . and this woman was hanged for the comfort and satisfaction of shopkeepers in Ludgate Street. When brought to receive sentence, she behaved in such a frantic manner, as proved her mind to be in a distracted and desponding state; and the child was sucking at her breast when she set out for Tyburn.' When Sir William Meredith told her story in the House of Commons some of his colleagues were in tears.

JOYCE, WILLIAM (1906–46) Wartime traitor known as 'Lord Haw-Haw'. Joyce was born in New York but in 1922 his family emigrated to England. He joined SIR OSWALD MOSLEY's British Union of Fascists in 1933 and acquired a British passport. He was expelled from the BUF and formed his own Hitler-worshipping British National Socialist Party. He went to Germany and during the war broadcast a stream of propaganda and threats against Britain. He was captured and tried at the Old Bailey in 1945. His British passport didn't run out until 1940, by which time he had been broadcasting for the Germans for nine months, and so he was executed.

Janie Jones (left) and a friend make an impression at a London film premiere. Janie, essentially a harmless fun-lover, was given the astonishing sentence of seven years for controlling prostitutes.

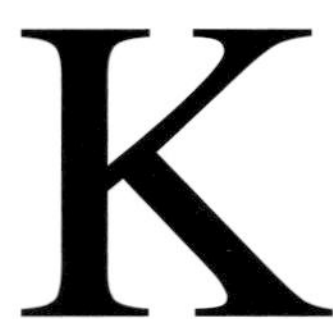

KAGAN, LORD JOSEPH (1915–95) Businessman friend of Labour Prime Minister Harold Wilson who was jailed for financial dishonesty. Kagan held the patent for Gannex raincoats, lightweight waterproofs of which Wilson was inordinately fond. Kagan was generous to Labour Party funds and was created a life peer in Wilson's resignation honours in 1976. He astutely moved into denim as Gannex became less popular. In 1978 he was charged with theft and defrauding the taxman. He fled abroad, but was betrayed by a disgruntled mistress. He was returned to Britain and was sentenced to ten months in jail and a large fine for theft and false accounting. He described his time in prison as 'fascinating' and after his release returned to the House of Lords, saying 'I do not feel disgraced in any way'.

KAGGS FAMILY Subtle and successful Victorian confidence tricksters. The father, John Kaggs, had been a butler, and run away with the daughter of an employer. Their eldest daughter, Betsy, was central to their success. She would call at the London house of a carefully selected lady known for her charity, and introducing herself as the daughter of a crippled army officer reduced to poverty, offer her few possessions for sale. The idea was to lure the lady to the Kaggs home, where a touching scene had been prepared. Mr Kaggs, apparently mortally ill, lay in bed in a garret. This gave the impression that the family lived in the attic whereas in fact they occupied the whole house. Mr Kaggs, the visitor would be told, had been wounded in the Peninsular War. He had later been cheated out of his money by a share broker. By the bed were medicine bottles and a Bible. One of the Kaggs daughters was dressed as a nurse, the younger children in black.

After a while word spread in charitable circles about the family, and with their income dwindling they decided to emigrate. An advertisement in *The Times* told of a 'poor but respectable family' who needed a small sum of money to emigrate to Australia, and offering the highest possible character references. This was so successful that the family were able to stay a further two years in London before departing for Australia.

KEATING, TOM (1917–84) Art restorer and forger of paintings. In 1976 an art expert suggested that a painting sold at auction for £9,400 as the work of the watercolourist Samuel Palmer was a forgery. Keating not only admitted painting pastiches of Palmer but claimed that there were some 2,500 fakes by him in circulation. As it became clear that the greed and gullibility of art dealers and experts knew almost no bounds Keating became a popular figure with the public, and his fakes, or 'Sexton Blakes' as he called them, found ready buyers. He made popular television programmes showing him copying famous paintings. In 1979 he went on trial at the Old Bailey for forgery but the trial was stopped because he was in poor health. After his death in 1984 there was a major sale of his work which achieved the respectable total of £274,000.

KEELER, CHRISTINE (1941–) Model and showgirl at the centre of the PROFUMO AFFAIR. She left home when she was 16 and found work in London at Murray's Cabaret Club. There she met and became friends with two people also involved in the affair, the model Mandy Rice-Davies, who became a close friend, and the society osteopath and artist Stephen Ward, who had wealthy and aristocratic patients. She was staying with him in a cottage on Lord Astor's Cliveden estate when she met John Profumo, the Minister for War. They began a brief affair. Keeler's other lovers included Captain Ivanov, the Russian Naval Attaché. Profumo resigned in 1963 after admitting lying to the House of Commons about the affair. Ward became the other main victim of the affair, prosecuted for living off the immoral earnings of Keeler and Rice-Davies. He committed suicide while still on trial. It seems clear now that Ward was not guilty. In fact he gave the girls more money than they ever gave him. Keeler never found her feet again. Her 1989 autobiography, *Scandal*, was successfully filmed, and she later plaintively updated it. She had two failed marriages and two sons.

KELLEY, EDWARD Associate of the eminent seventeenth-century mathematician, astronomer and alchemist Dr John Dee. Dee appears to have been honest, but Kelley was not. An ex-apothecary, he had been in the pillory for digging up graves and had his ears cropped for coining. He was also a necromancer. Together they achieved Europe-wide renown. When they were staying at the court of the Emperor Rudolf in Prague in 1588 Kelley, who acted as Dee's crystal-gazer, was helped by spirits to discover some books which Dee had burned weeks earlier. The spirits told him that he and Dee were to

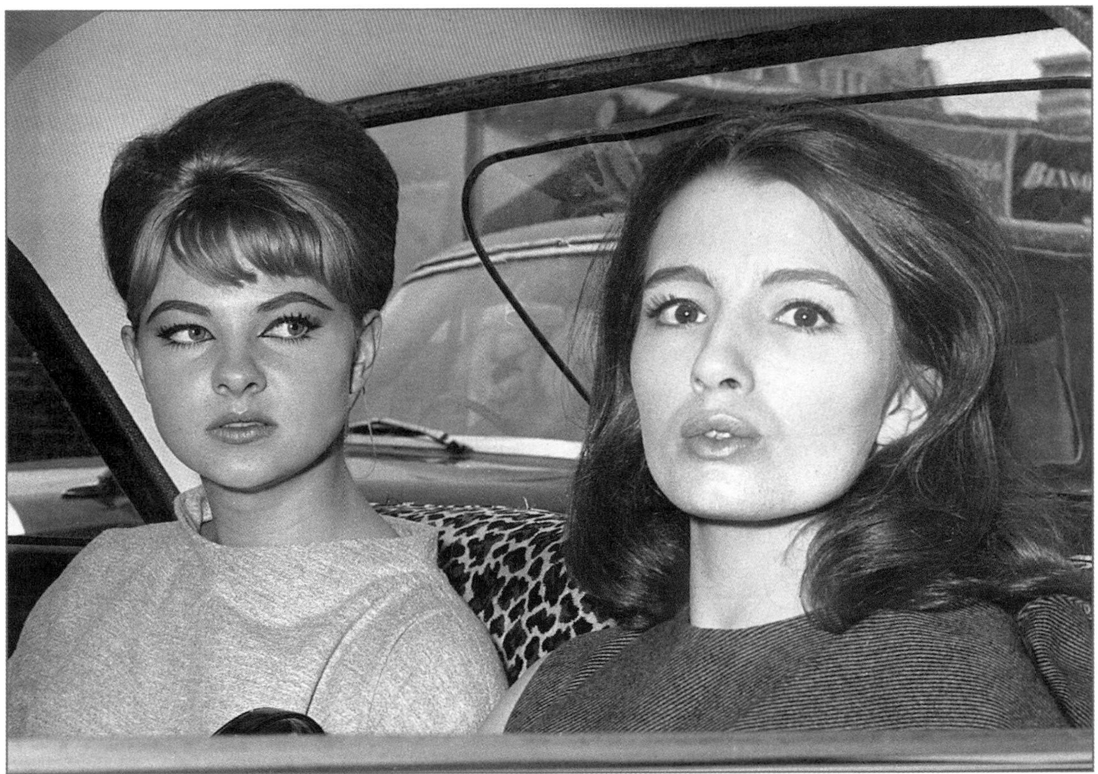

Christine Keeler (right) and Mandy Rice-Davies, two women who in different ways epitomised a louche world of clubs and casual sex.

share their wives. It was believed that the two men had discovered the philosopher's stone, and witnesses saw Kelley turn base metal into gold. In 1588 the pair were invited back to England to work these wonders for the benefit of the state, and Dee returned. Kelley, judged by the emperor too valuable to lose, died five years later after breaking his legs while trying to escape.

KESSEL, MAX Vice czar in inter-war London. In 1936 he was shot dead by a Frenchman, Marcel Vernon, and his body dumped in a ditch at St Albans. Vernon had escaped from Devil's Island, and after being found guilty of Kessel's murder and deported to France he was returned there. His trial led to new speculation about white slavery. Vernon ran an extensive prostitution racket abroad with bases in South America, the US and Canada, in addition to his Soho establishments. His trial was told of young women being lured abroad with promises of jobs only to be tricked or forced into prostitution. The worst fears of the Victorian purity campaigners seemed to have been justified. But a best-seller published in 1934, Henri Champly's *The Road to Shanghai*, gave an altogether different impression. Champly believed that most of the women went willingly and knew exactly what awaited them. They went in search of adventure and fortune, leaving a depressed labour market at home for at least the chance of steady earnings and perhaps marriage to a wealthy client. Once again the white slave trade seemed to be a chimera. *See* W.T. STEAD

KETCH, JACK (?–1686) Most famous of all the hangmen. He bungled the execution of the Duke of Monmouth, who rose from the block to remonstrate with him. After he was sacked London hangmen were popularly known as Jack Ketch. *See* HANGMEN

KIDD, CAPTAIN WILLIAM (*c.* 1645–1701) Pirate hanged at Execution Dock in 1701, the victim of a high-level cover-up. Kidd had originally been commissioned by the government to hunt down pirates. He had also been given a secret commission by Lord Bellomont, governor of New York, acting on behalf of a syndicate of powerful politicians and the king, to seize ships and share the booty. Among his victims were two Armenian ships which were under French protection. Since Britain was at war with France this should have made them fair game, but the East India Company accused Kidd of piracy, and when news of the syndicate leaked out it was decided Kidd should be sacrificed. He was arrested and examined by the House of Commons. To justify himself he handed over the French passes carried by the Armenian ships. He was held in Newgate for two years and then tried at the Old Bailey. The passes had vanished, and the court decided they had never existed (they have now been found at the Public Record Office at Kew). When Kidd was strung up the rope broke, but he was re-hanged. *See* EXECUTION DOCK

KIMBER, BILLY Leader of a Birmingham racecourse gang known as the Brummagem Boys, for a time the dominant force in the racecourse wars. Around 1910 he controlled many of the racecourses in southern England. Before the SABINI GANG established dominance over the southern courses he brought a kind of order to the exploitation of the bookies there, forcing them to pay into what Brian McDonald in *Elephant Boys* calls a 'mutual fund'. Apparently the bookies were happy to pay because Kimber drove away the unruly freelance thugs. He fought a long battle for supremacy with the Sabinis and lost. After being shot by the Sabini ally ALF SOLOMONS Kimber confined his activities to the northern courses. He came from south London and was loosely allied to the ELEPHANT GANG. He was far from being a mindless thug. Chief Inspector Tom Divall of Scotland Yard, who was saved by Kimber from being beaten up, called him 'one of the best' and recalled his 'soothing and tactful way of speaking'. Murphy (*Smash and Grab*) says that this attribute came in useful at the 1919 St Leger meeting at Doncaster. Racegoers were infuriated when some of the bookies welched, and it was Kimber who calmed them down. He was later employed as a manager at Wimbledon greyhound stadium.

KINCHIN LAY, THE This despised form of street crime, which involved stealing from children, was practised mainly by women. This is how Fagin described it in *Oliver Twist*:

> The kinchins, my dear, is the young children that's sent on errands by their mothers, with sixpences and shillings; and the lay is just to take their money away – they've always got it ready in their hands – then knock them into the kennel [gutter] and walk off very slow as if there's nothing else the matter but a child fallen down and hurt itself.

There were many variants. Some of the women specialised in stealing packets from little shop messengers – milliners' apprentices with parcels of expensive silk were a favourite target. Then there was 'skinning', luring children to some quiet spot where they could be stripped of their clothes and shoes. This 'lay' produced its best results in the winter, when the children would be wearing extra clothes.

KING, MOLL Proprietor of a riotous coffee house in Covent Garden. In the 1720s and 1730s the coffee house, named after her, was the most important meeting place for the worlds of fashion, harlotry high and low, crime and bohemian intellectualism, the haunt of 'bucks, bloods, demireps and choyce spirits of all London'. Located in the wooden shacks which ran along one side of the Piazza, it was never a brothel, although it was certainly disorderly. Gullible men who had too much to drink might awake to find themselves with a large bill for breaking the crockery – a supply of broken crockery was kept hidden for this confidence trick.

As a young girl Moll had been a street fruitseller in Covent Garden market, loved for her good looks and peculiar sweetness of temper. She lost both eventually,

Moll King, proprietor of a famous coffee house in Covent Garden. It was the venue for society high and low and, although never a brothel, was riotous.

as *The Life and Character of Moll King* of 1747 makes clear. Among her friends were celebrated whores, including SALLY SALISBURY, the most famous of her time. Moll married another street seller, Tom King. They went into business in a small way selling coffee at a penny a dish in 'a little hovel' in front of the church of St Paul. Their shop soon expanded, becoming a magnet for 'young rakes and their pretty misses . . . Every swain, even from the Star and Garter to the coffee house boy, might be sure of finding a nymph in waiting at Moll's Fair Reception House, as she was pleased to term it, and the most squeamish beau, surely, could not refuse such dainties and the very sweetest too that ever Covent Garden afforded.' The Kings became so wealthy that Tom bought an estate at Haverstock Hill on the way to Hampstead and built 'a very genteel country house'. In fact it was a row of houses, which still exists. Tom drank himself into a decline and died at his country house in 1739. Moll carried on, growing wealthier, more drunken and imperious until she was imprisoned for thrashing a young customer. She was fined the enormous sum of £200 and sent to the King's Bench prison until she paid up. She refused, saying the fine was excessive, and was sent to Newgate to cool off. For three months she negotiated with the High Bailiff, and eventually got the fine reduced by half. She died in 1747.

KING'S MESSENGERS A police force directly under the control of the Privy Council. Although they were a political force responsible for rooting out treason, they had a wider remit, as coining and counterfeiting were also treason.

KING'S PLACE BROTHELS Establishments in the heart of the fashionable West End, renowned in the eighteenth century for luxury and style. The great bawd CHARLOTTE HAYES kept a brothel here, as did BLACK HARRIOTT and SARAH DUBERY among others. Some idea of the prices in a such brothels in the middle of the eighteenth century can be gained from the price-list of Charlotte Hayes's extremely successful establishment. She called it a 'cloister', and her girls were nuns and 'choice merchandise'. The following is a contemporary list of her charges. Although the style is facetious, the prices are believed to be accurate. Some of the customers' names are aliases for real people.

> *Sunday the 9th January*
>
> A young girl for Alderman Drybones. Nelly Blossom, about 19 years old, who has had no one for four days, and who is a *virgin* — 20 guineas
>
> A girl of 19 years, not older, for Baron Harry Flagellum. Nell Hardy from Bow Street, Bett Flourish from Berners Street or Miss Birch from Chapel Street — 10 guineas
>
> A beautiful and lively girl for Lord Sperm. Black Moll from Hedge Lane, who is very strong — 5 guineas
>
> For Colonel Tearall, a gentle woman. Mrs Mitchell's servant, who has just come from the country and has not been out in the world — 10 guineas
>
> For Dr Pretext, after consultation hours, a young agreeable person, sociable, with a white skin and a soft hand. Polly Nimblewrist from Oxford, or Jenny Speedyhand from Mayfair — 2 guineas
>
> Lady Loveitt, who has come from the baths at Bath, and who is disappointed in her affair with Lord Alto, wants . . . to be well served this evening. Capt. O'Thunder or Sawney Rawbone — 50 guineas
>
> For his Excellency Count Alto, a fashionable woman for an hour only. Mrs O'Smirk who comes from Dunkirk Square, or Miss Graceful from Paddington — 10 guineas
>
> For Lord Pyebald, to play a game at piquet, for *titillatione mammarum* and so on, with no other object. Mrs Tredrillo from Chelsea — 5 guineas

It is interesting that Lady Loveitt – identified by Burford as the nymphomaniac Lady Sarah Lennox – has to pay the highest price.

KINGSTON, DUCHESS OF (1720–88) Beauty tried in the Great Hall of Westminster for bigamy. Elizabeth, Duchess Dowager of Kingston, was previously Elizabeth Chudleigh, a Maid of Honour to the Princess of Wales. She was courted by the Duke of Hamilton who promised to marry her when he returned from the Grand Tour. However while he was away she met and married the noted philanderer Lieutenant Augustus Hervey RN in 1774. They kept the marriage secret because otherwise Elizabeth would have lost her position in the royal household and her £400 a year salary. After the ceremony Hervey sailed away to a life of further sexual encounters. Elizabeth too had a good time. In 1749 at the Venetian ambassador's ball at Somerset House she wore a costume which revealed all. (She continued to display this kind of exhibitionism even when she joined the aristocracy.) Mrs Elizabeth Montague wrote: 'Miss Chudleigh's undress was remarkable . . . The Maids of Honour were so offended they were lost for words.'

She became the mistress of the wealthy and elderly Duke of Kingston, and in March 1769 they married. She had convinced herself that the marriage ceremony she and Hervey had gone through was 'such a scrambling shabby business and so much incomplete' it was not really a wedding. Hervey remained silent. The duke died in 1763. There had been society gossip about the legality of the marriage and the eldest of his heirs, who had been disinherited, challenged the will and the marriage itself. Hervey had recently succeeded to the title of Earl of Bristol, so if Elizabeth lost she was still Countess of Bristol. Instead of mounting a defence she treated the court with contempt, ranting at her peers for their insolence. She was found guilty, and the Attorney General tried to have her burned in the hand. However, strings were pulled and even this punishment was waived. The judges ordered her not to leave the kingdom, but she went to France and eventually Russia, where she became the friend of Catherine the Great. She died in Paris in 1788. Horace Walpole commented: 'So all this combination of knavery receives no punishment but the loss of the duchy.' Elizabeth, who became Countess of Bristol in 1777, was illiterate.

Augustus Hervey's conquests included many foreign aristocrats he met while a captain in the Royal Navy. Back in England he was for a time the lover of the rapacious KITTY FISHER but in 1770, when he was Earl of Bristol, he settled down with the humble beauty Mrs Mary Nesbitt.

KNIGHT, RONNIE (1934–) Flamboyant criminal who more or less invented the Costa Del Crime. Knight was born in Hoxton, east London. His brother David was stabbed to death in the Latin Quarter Club in Soho in May 1970 by Alfredo 'Italian Tony' Zomparelli. Knight later said that he went after Zomparelli 'like a lion after a wart hog'. In September 1974 Zomparelli was shot dead while playing a pinball machine in the Golden Goose amusement arcade in Old Compton Street. Six years later Knight was arrested for the murder. A hitman named George 'Maxie' Bradshaw claimed Knight had paid him £1,000 to help carry out the murder. Bradshaw was jailed for life but Knight and the other assassin, NICKY GERRARD, known as 'Snakehips', who fired the shots, were cleared. Knight declared: 'I knew I was innocent. Gawd love me, I was being set up. Framed. As large as life.' Knight, who cannot be tried a second time for the killing, later told in a book how Snakehips had phoned him in a club after murdering Zomparelli. 'Ronnie, it's done. Are you covered?' Knight says he replied: 'Don't worry, I've got so many witnesses here there ain't a court big enough to hold them.' With his brother Johnny, Ronnie Knight had been buying land near Fuengirola in Spain. In 1975 they moved into a house they had built there. He later described the area as 'paradise found'. The attractions of Spain to British criminals on the run were obvious from the late 1970s onward. The extradition treaty with Britain broke down in 1978 because of the political impasse over Gibraltar, and there were opportunities to develop the local drugs and smuggling rackets. After the Knights moved in the Marbella area attracted other British criminals, and it became known in the tabloid newspapers as the Costa Del Crime. Among the new arrivals were south London gang leader FREDDIE FOREMAN, Ronald Everett, once a close friend of the KRAY twins, John James Mason, who had been cleared of the £8 million Bank of America robbery in Mayfair in 1976, and Clifford Saxe, at one time the landlord of the Fox pub in Kingsland Road, Hackney, where the robbery is said to have been planned. They were wanted by police in connection with the 1983 Shoreditch Security Express robbery, for which Ronnie's brothers Johnny and Jimmy were eventually jailed. In 1994 Ronnie voluntarily flew back to England where he was jailed for seven years for handling £314,813 from the robbery. He served four years of the sentence. In July 2000 he was fined £200 for shoplifting at a Waitrose supermarket in Brent Cross, North London. Knight, 66, admitted stealing groceries worth £39.74, although he had £270 in cash. He told magistrates at Hendon, north London: 'I am so sorry that I have done this. I hope the children still want me.'

KNIGHTSBRIDGE SAFE DEPOSIT RAID In April 2000 Italian police stopped a stolen Lancia car near Ascoli, east of Rome. When they tried to arrest the two men inside there was a struggle and one was shot dead. The dead man was Valerio Viccei, the mastermind of Britain's biggest robbery, the Knightsbridge safe deposit raid of 1987 in which between £40 million and £80 million was stolen. The true figure will never be known, because much of the loot had been hidden in the safe deposit by gangsters, who are not likely to make a claim. Viccei, 45, was still serving a 22-year jail sentence for the crime, having controversially been moved to a top-security prison in Italy after serving only five years in a British jail. The authorities at Pescara in southern Italy allowed him out on day release, and police believe he was using his free time to plan another robbery. In a newspaper interview not long before his death Viccei, who was nicknamed the Italian Stallion because of his success with beautiful women, claimed he was going straight and was a 'successful businessman'. Viccei pulled off a string of robberies on banks in London, including Coutts in Cavendish Square, and kept the proceeds in the Knightsbridge Safe Deposit Box Centre, opposite Harrods. He met the managing director of the centre, 31-year-old Parvez Latif, and wooed him over champagne and expensive meals. Latif, who was heavily in debt, was dazzled by Viccei's playboy lifestyle, his Ferrari Testarossa and taste for pure Colombian cocaine. Gradually Latif was drawn into the plot to loot the deposit centre. On Sunday 12 July 1987 Latif stuck a notice to the door: 'We apologise to all our customers for any inconvenience caused to them during the improvements to our security system. Business as usual from tomorrow. Thank you.' Viccei, who had put together an international team of robbers, rang the bell, which was answered by Latif. Because the deposit's guards were not part of the plot both Viccei and Latif had to keep up an elaborate charade. Viccei and his team pretended they were customers, and once inside Viccei pulled out a gun. Other members of the team then arrived and together they attacked the steel deposit boxes with power drills and sledge hammers. Viccei filled the bath tub of their hide-out with cash and jewels, and the floor of the room was also covered in jewels. There were also drugs and antiques.

Viccei had cut his hand during the robbery and left bloody fingerprints, which were identified. He was arrested in a traffic jam at Marble Arch in his Ferrari.

KRAY BROTHERS Violent twin gangsters who briefly seemed likely to exercise total hegemony over the whole London underworld. They achieved local control in the East End in the 1950s before moving into the protection, drinking clubs and gambling rackets of the West End. Allied to the NASH family of north London, and FREDDIE

The Kray twins with their parents. They used violence as an instrument of policy, and courted the limelight to a greater extent than gangsters before or since. They modelled themselves on American mafiosi.

FOREMAN of south London, they were opposed principally by the RICHARDSONS. Ronnie Kray, a homosexual psychopath, was jailed for three years in 1956 for attacking a man with a bayonet. While he was in Winchester prison he was certified insane. His twin brother Reggie switched places with him and Ronnie walked out, but eventually he was so obviously insane Reggie sent him back to prison to be cured. By 1959 when he was released he had apparently recovered, but in reality had long periods of extreme paranoia when he made lists of those who would 'have to go'. The twins put together the gang known as The Firm, which included financial advisers Leslie Payne and Freddy Gore and thugs such as Connie Whitehead, ALBERT DONOGHUE, Ian Barrie, and 'Scotch Jack' Dickson. Freddie 'the Mean Machine' Foreman, a south London gang leader and robber who was to have a long career in crime, was another henchman. The twins' older brother Charles, also a criminal but more of a fixer than a gangster, was loosely allied to the gang.

In 1960 the property racketeer PETER RACHMAN, who was paying protection money to the twins, tipped them off about a gambling club, Esmeralda's Barn, in Wilton Place off Knightsbridge. Rachman believed, rightly, that the owner would cave in if threatened by gangsters. The Krays got a controlling interest in the club for £1,000. This was one of their biggest coups: at its most prosperous the club netted them £40,000 a year. They became involved in LONG-FIRM FRAUDS. In 1962 they cleared more than £100,000 from these frauds alone. In his memoirs *The Brotherhood*, their financial adviser Leslie Payne reckoned that in the mid-1960s between a third and a half of all the illegal gaming clubs in London were paying the Krays protection money. They expanded outside London, forming an alliance with the leading gang in Glasgow and taking over clubs in Birmingham and Leicester. Links they formed with the Mafia grew more important as the Americans became interested in investing in London gambling clubs.

On 9 March 1966 Ronnie Kray shot and killed GEORGE CORNELL, a member of the South London Richardson gang, in the Blind Beggar pub on the Mile End Road. Cornell had called Ronnie a 'fat poof' but there were other reasons for his execution. Cornell was allied to the Richardsons, and tensions between the two gangs was growing. Then the twins kept a long-standing promise by springing FRANK MITCHELL, the so-called Mad Axeman, from Dartmoor prison. When he became a nuisance they had him murdered. Finally Reggie murdered JACK 'THE HAT' MCVITIE, a drunken criminal who had failed to fulfil a contract to kill Leslie Payne. The twins' violence made other members of The Firm fear it could be their turn next, and several of them agreed to give evidence. In July 1968 both twins were sentenced to life imprisonment for murder, with a recommendation that they should serve at least thirty years. They were 35.

In March 1995 Ronnie Kray died in BROADMOOR. Charley died in April 2000. Reggie died in October 2000, having been released on compassionate grounds because of bladder cancer. The twins' lavish and histrionic gangster funerals through the East End were surely the last of their kind. Today's gangsters tend to agree with Al Capone that the limelight brings grief.

KYD, THOMAS (1558–94) Playwright tortured in prison. Kyd, author of the sensationally violent *Spanish Tragedy*, was arrested in 1593 after atheistic works were found in his rooms. He protested that they belonged to his friend CHRISTOPHER MARLOWE, but he was sent to the Bridewell prison, where he was 'put to the torture'. He died in poverty the following year.

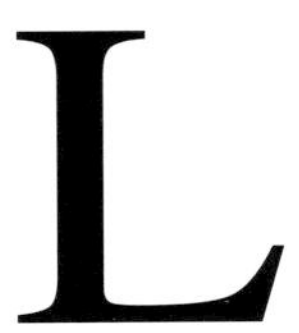

LADY CHATTERLEY'S LOVER D.H. Lawrence novel at the centre of a sensational pornography trial. The authorities hoped the 1960 trial of Penguin Books over their reprint of *Lady Chatterley* would set limits to the onward march of obscenity. Instead it helped open the way for the porn revolution. Penguin amassed an army of distinguished writers and critics prepared to testify that the book was important and that the passages labelled obscene were justified. The prosecution struggled to find any witnesses for their case. Some of the experts they approached refused, and instead gave evidence for the defence. There was an air of unreality about the prosecution. The Q.C. Mervyn Griffith-Jones, who would later prosecute in the trial of Stephen Ward, asked the jury: 'Is it a book you would even wish your wife or your servants to read?' In an effort to shock the jury he listed the number of 'fucks', 'fucking' and other vulgar words, even 'arse' and 'shit'. A liberal bishop called by the defence said that Lawrence had tried to portray sexual intercourse as 'an act of holy communion'. When the jury threw out the case there were cheers in court.

LAMB, MARY Writer and murderer, co-author with her brother Charles of *Tales from Shakespeare*. In 1796, insane, she stabbed her mother to death with a table knife. Charles, the essayist and critic, devoted the rest his life to looking after Mary, who was released into his care.

LAMBOURNE, LADY MARGARET Woman who tried to assassinate Queen Elizabeth I. Lady Margaret sought revenge for the beheading of Mary Queen of Scots in 1587. She dressed as a man and concealed two muskets under her greatcoat, one to kill the queen with and the other herself. As she approached the queen in her garden one of the muskets accidentally went off, killing a peacock, and she was overpowered. She told Elizabeth that she was motivated by love, and the queen replied: 'So, you have done your duty. Now, what do you think my duty is?' 'You must pardon me,' said Lady Margaret. The queen agreed.

LAMBTON, LORD ANTHONY CLAUD FREDERICK (1922–) Tory politician caught in a sex trap. Lord Lambton, a junior Defence Minister, was in the habit of visiting call-girls. He particularly favoured Norma Levy, an ex-dancer with an apartment in Maida Vale. Journalists used a two-way mirror in Levy's bedroom to photograph Lambton with Norma Levy and a woman called Gina. The paper involved did not use the story, but Norma Levy mentioned the affair to the owner of a Regent Street club who contacted senior Tories. Lambton resigned and went to live in his Italian villa, where he wrote novels. He summed up his attitude to the affair when he said in a TV interview: 'Surely all men visit whores?'

LAMPLUGH, SUZY Estate agent who disappeared in 1986 and is believed to have been murdered. She had gone to meet a client who gave his name as Mr Kipper to show him around a house in Fulham. In 1994 she was officially declared dead. Police were convinced there was a link with convicted murderer and rapist John Cannan, but had no evidence. He had been released from prison three days before Miss Lamplugh vanished. He denies being her killer. In 1989, when he was in his thirties, he was jailed for life for the murder of a 29-year-old woman.

LAMSON, DR GEORGE (1850–82) Doctor who murdered his brother-in-law for money. Lamson worked as a medic during the Siege of Paris in 1871 and in 1876–7 was a volunteer army surgeon in Serbia and Romania. During the Balkans campaigns he became a morphine addict. Back in London in 1876 he married a ward in Chancery and quickly spent her small fortune. He inherited another £700 when his brother-in-law died – he later denied killing him – and bought a medical practice in Bournemouth. This failed, and he began to forge cheques. He decided that murdering his wife's other brother was the only way out. This brother, Percy John, 18, lived at a private school at Wimbledon. With his sister he was heir to a modest fortune. He was an invalid and was not expected to live long, but Lamson could not wait. On 3 December 1881 Lamson visited him and gave him some cake. Shortly after Lamson left Percy John died in agony. The school doctors believed he had been poisoned, but at the time there was no scientific way of detecting the poison used, aconitine. However, the chemist who had sold Lamson the poison read the story in the newspapers and contacted the police. Efforts were made to save Lamson but after two stays of execution he was hanged in April 1882. Shattered by withdrawal symptoms, he had to be carried half-conscious to the scaffold.

LAW, JOHN (1671–1729) Innovative economic thinker who spent time in a London prison for killing a man in a duel. Law, the son of a Scottish moneylender, was born in Edinburgh in 1671. He moved to London and killed a man named Beau Wilson in a duel over a Mrs Lawrence. He fled to Amsterdam and studied banking. He became an advocate of the use of paper money as a stimulus to trade and industry, and in 1708 suggested to the French Regent, the duc d'Orleans, setting up a national bank to issue paper money. He was allowed to set up a private bank and soon began selling shares. To augment the bank's inadequate gold reserves he was also granted monopolies on land in Louisiana and the Canadian fur trade. What followed was like the slightly later SOUTH SEA BUBBLE scandal in London. Vast crowds clamouring for shares besieged Law's office. He sat at a desk with a huge pile of shares and exchanged them for gold. Those who managed to reach the front of the queue found that once outside they could sell their shares for an immediate profit. The more astute investors realised the situation could not last. A run on the bank by small investors threatened to overwhelm it, and Law announced that he would not change more than a 100-livre note per person. This made matters worse and he fled. In 1721 he returned to England. His hopes of being invited back to France were not realised, although the Regent remained friendly and granted him a pension. When Law asked him how he had dealt with the aftermath of the financial disaster the Regent replied: 'I disposed of it by making a bonfire of the documents.' Law died poor in Venice in 1729.

LAWRENCE, STEPHEN Student whose murder by white racists led to wide-ranging criticisms of the police. Stephen, a black student, was 18 when he was stabbed by a gang of youths in 1993 in Eltham, south-east London. An inquest found that he had been the victim of 'a completely unprovoked racist attack by five white youths'. Neil Acourt, his brother Jamie, David Norris, Gary Dobson and Luke Knight were arrested but the case never reached court. A private prosecution by Stephen's parents also failed. The Macpherson report into the case branded the Metropolitan Police 'institutionally racist' and was critical of the initial police investigation. In July 2002 two of the suspects, Neil Acourt and David Norris, were convicted of racially abusing a black policeman. Woolwich Crown Court was told that Norris, a passenger in a car driven by Acourt, shouted 'nigger' and hurled a drink container at the off-duty officer. The pair were jailed for eighteen months.

LAY Underworld slang for a criminal plan or means of livelihood. The 'crack lay' was housebreaking, the 'dub lay' was gaining entry by the use of keys. *See* KINCHIN LAY

LEARY Boy gang leader whose story gives us an insight into the lives of young Regency street criminals. The 1816 parliamentary committee on the police heard that he had been described by the chaplain of Newgate as 'an extraordinary boy'. Grey Bennet, the committee's chairman, was obviously struck by the boy's manner. He was Irish, about 13 years old, 'good-looking, sharp and intelligent, and possessing a manner which seemed to indicate a character very different from what he really professed'. Bennet saw him in Newgate when he was under sentence of death for stealing a watch, chain and seals.

> He had been five years in the practice of delinquency, progressing from stealing an apple off a stall to housebreaking and highway robbery. He belonged to the Moorfields Catholic School, and there became acquainted with one Ryan . . . by whom he was first instructed in the various arts and practices of delinquency; his first attempts were at tarts, apples etc., then at loaves in bakers' baskets, then at parcels of halfpence on shop counters, and money-tills in shops; then to breaking shop windows and drawing out valuable articles through the aperture; picking pockets, housebreaking etc. etc.; and Leary has often gone to school the next day with several pounds in his pockets as his share of the produce of the previous day's robberies; he soon became captain of a gang, generally known since as Leary's gang, with five boys, and sometimes more, furnished with pistols, taking a horse and cart with them; and if they had an opportunity in their road, they cut off the trunks from gentlemen's carriages . . . He has been concerned in various robberies in London and its vicinity; and has had property at one time amounting to £350; but when he had money he either got robbed of it by elder thieves who knew he had so much about him, or lost it by gambling at flash-houses, or spent it among loose characters of both sexes. After committing innumerable depredations, he was detected at Mr Derrimore's at Kentish Town, stealing some plate from that gentleman's dining-room, when several other similar robberies coming against him in that

> neighbourhood, he was, in compassion to his youth, placed in the Philanthropic [a home run by the Philanthropic Institution]; but being now charged with Mr Princep's robbery, he was taken out therefrom, tried, convicted and sentenced to death, but was afterwards respited and returned to the Philanthropic. He is little and well-looking; has robbed to the amount of £3,000 during his five years career.

Leary had been in and out of every prison in London, including Newgate two or three times. Finally he was transported for life. While he was in Newgate he refused to attend the school set up by the chaplain, preferring the company of the older criminals.

LEIGHTON, DR ALEXANDER Scottish cleric mutilated for crossing Archbishop Laud. Leighton opposed Laud's attempt to impose liturgical changes on the church in England and Scotland. He wrote a pamphlet in 1624 describing bishops as men of blood. Laud had him arrested and he was convicted by the Court of Star Chamber of sedition. One of his ears was cut off, his nose was slit, he was pilloried, branded, whipped, fined and imprisoned. When he was released eleven years later he was blind and deaf and could scarcely crawl.

LESBIANISM Known as 'the game of flats' in the eighteenth century, this has never been a crime. Women have, however, been jailed for marrying other women while pretending to be men. Mary Hamilton, who dressed as a man, married fourteen women and in each case left them shortly afterwards. She was caught after the fourteenth, and her latest 'wife' said she had always believed that Hamilton was a man. Hamilton, who used a dildo to fool the women, was whipped through the streets.

Ann Morrow was sentenced to the pillory and three months in jail after marrying three different women. In the pillory at Charing Cross in 1777 she was blinded in both eyes by missiles. Those pelting her were mostly women.

LEVERSON, RACHEL Blackmailer and confidence trickster. Her beauty parlour in Bond Street – slogan Beautiful for Ever – was the backdrop to her frauds on ageing and susceptible women in the 1860s. Despite styling herself 'Madame Rachael', Sarah Rachel Leverson was an illiterate working-class Jewish woman who hailed from Lancashire. She is described in Shaw's *London in the Sixties* as a 'bony and forbidding looking female with the voice of a Deal boatman and the physique of a grenadier'. She had tried fortune-telling, selling old clothes and fish and had perhaps been a prostitute before going into the beauty business.

The wife of a City broker who had indulged in some expensive beauty treatments found, when she emerged from Mrs Leverson's Arabian Baths, that her diamond rings and earrings had vanished. When she complained Madame Rachael threatened to tell her husband that she had gone to the baths to meet a lover. The couple took legal advice. Their lawyer told them that if they prosecuted Madame Rachael she would use the legal process to destroy the woman's character. The couple dropped the case.

Madame Rachael was making a good living from her rackets, with a house in Maddox Street in Mayfair, a coach and pair and a box at the opera, for which she paid £400 for a season. Then she cheated a foolish widow named Mary Tucker Borrodaile of her entire £5,000 capital. Mrs Borrodaile agreed to pay £1,700 for beauty treatments. On one occasion when she was in the Arabian Baths she caught a glimpse of a middle-aged bachelor, Lord Henry Ranelagh. Lord Henry also caught a glimpse of her in the bath, and was captivated. He was determined to marry her, and Madame Rachael was to be the go-between. For the moment they would communicate by letter, as he expected objections from his family to him marrying somebody of lower social status.

Poor Mrs Borrodaile was taken in, and soon she had parted with all her money to Mrs Leverson via 'Lord Ranelagh', who said he was temporarily short of cash. Mrs Borrodaile's relatives intervened, and Madame Rachael was prosecuted for fraud in the Central Criminal Court in September 1868.

Sergeant Ballantine, who prosecuted, described Mrs Borrodaile as 'a skeleton encased apparently in plaster of Paris, painted white and pink, and surmounted with a juvenile wig'. She was the butt of much crude humour – one newspaper described her as a 'senescent Sappho' – and she was laughed at in court. The defence made it seem that Mrs Borrodaile was simply a silly old woman seeking to gratify desires that should have died down long ago. The first jury could not reach a decision, but a month later a second trial ended with Madame Rachael being sent to penal servitude for five years.

She was released in 1872 and incorrigibly set up in the beauty business again, near her old premises. Six years later a young woman accused her of stealing necklaces she had left as security for beauty treatments, and she was sent to jail again, where she died in 1880.

LEY, THOMAS Jealous lover whose obsession led to murder. Ley had been Minister for Justice in New South Wales, but the suspicious deaths of two business associates and a bribery scandal ended his political career. He returned to England in 1929, followed by his former mistress, Mrs Maggie Brook. In 1946 she went to live in Wimbledon with her daughter and son-in-law. Although Mrs Brook was now 66 Ley phoned her and accused her of having sex with her son-in-law. He drove to Wimbledon and insisted on her going with him to his house in Knightsbridge Court.

Next Ley, who was clearly insane, became convinced that Mrs Brook was having an affair with a barman named John Mudie, whom she had met only once. Mudie was lured to a house in Beaufort Gardens by Ley and two accomplices, tied up and strangled. The body was dumped in a chalk pit.

The killers were quickly arrested, and Ley and one of his accomplices stood trial at the Old Bailey in March 1947. They were sentenced to death. In May Ley was declared insane after being examined by specialists. A month later he died of a seizure in Broadmoor. His accomplice was reprieved and sentenced to penal servitude for life.

LLOYD GEORGE, DAVID (1863–1945) Statesman involved in the scandalous sale of honours. The racket was not new, but the flagrant exploitation of the system under Lloyd George when he was Prime Minister after the First World War was staggering. The scale of charges ranged from £10,000 for a knighthood to £50,000 for a peerage. In less than four years more than 1,500 knights were made, and twice as many peerages and baronetcies as in the previous twenty years. Unfortunately for Lloyd George his agent, the egregious MAUNDY GREGORY, was so greedy he sold honours to criminals, including Sir John Drughorn, who had been convicted in 1915 of trading with the enemy. In 1925 the Honours (Prevention of Abuses) Act outlawed the practice.

LOCKE, JOHN (1632–1704) Philosopher who held that the government 'had no other end but the preservation of property'. He was commissioner of appeals for a period until 1704. His philosophy is characterised by tolerance and common sense.

LONG-FIRM FRAUD A simple but effective way of making a lot of money quickly. A bogus company is set up and premises acquired. Goods are ordered, sold and the suppliers paid. This goes on for months. Then, when the suppliers' confidence has been won, a much larger order is placed and the firm and the goods vanish. The RICHARDSONS refined this racket: the premises and goods were insured, the goods sold and the premises torched. Insurance would then be claimed.

LOPEZ, RODRIGO Physician to Queen Elizabeth I, who had him executed in 1594. Lopez, a Portuguese Jew, arrived in England in 1559. He was so successful as a doctor that he became the first house physician at St Bartholomew's Hospital, and numbered Leicester and WALSINGHAM among his patients. In 1586 he became physician to the queen, who held him in high regard. However he made an enemy of the Earl of Essex, who accused him of being involved in a Spanish plot to murder the queen. Lopez seems to have had some knowledge of the plot, but by no means sympathised with it. Essex had one of Lopez's servant arrested and tortured. On evidence thus extracted Lopez was arrested. After hesitating for three months the queen signed his death warrant. At Tyburn he declared that he 'loved the Queen as well as he loved Jesus Christ'. Because he was a Jew this caused 'no small laughter in the standers-by'.

LOVAT, LORD (*c.* 1667–1747) The last peer to be executed for high treason, and the last man to be beheaded in England. Lovat, a scheming Jacobite executed for his part in the '45 rebellion, exclaimed 'God save us!' when he saw the enormous crowd which had come to see him die on Tower Hill in 1747. When one of the spectators' stands collapsed, killing several people, Lovat said: 'The more mischief, the better sport.'

LOWSON, SIR DENYS (1901–75) Crooked financier and insider dealer. By the age of 30 Lowson was worth £200 million. Some idea of how he achieved this was given in the *Investor's Chronicle* in 1972 when they showed how he and his friends had used inside knowledge of a takeover to make millions. They bought shares in the National Group of Unit Trusts at 62p each and sold them six months later for £8.67 each. Sir Denys, who managed the trusts, made £5 million. After the government announced that the Department of Trade would conduct an investigation Sir Denys promised to return the £5 million. He never did. When the authorities began to close in Sir Denys left on a round-the world cruise. He returned to England to die in April 1975. Hours before his death warrants for his arrest were issued.

Lord Lovat, the Jacobite executed in 1747. Hogarth has caught the wily old schemer perfectly. A stand collapsed at his execution, killing several spectators. 'The more mischief the better sport', he commented.

LUCAN, LORD (1934–?) Vanished English aristocrat, gambler and, almost certainly, murderer. In 1974 Richard John Bingham, Earl of Lucan, disappeared after battering and killing Sandra Rivett, his children's nanny, at his wife's Belgravia home. He is believed to have mistaken her in the dark for his estranged wife Veronica. He attacked his wife too before driving to the home of a friend. His car was found at Newhaven, but he was never seen again. It emerged that Lord Lucan, who had lost a custody action over his children, had large gambling debts. Gambling friends vouched for his good qualities, and John Aspinall, owner of a club where Lucan lost a lot of money, said of Lady Lucan to the *Sunday Times*: 'If she'd been my wife I'd have bashed her to death years before.' Police found recordings of Adolf Hitler in Lucan's flat. In 1975 a coroner's jury decided he had murdered Rivett.

LUKER, ELIZABETH Playgoer who started a disastrous riot. In 1789 she was with a group who went to see a performance at Sadler's Wells Theatre. Her companions had been drinking and began an argument with another section of the audience. Luker, who was about 30, cried out to her friends, 'Fight, fight!' This was misheard throughout the theatre as the alarm 'Fire, fire!' and in the ensuing panic eighteen people were trampled to death. Luker was jailed for fourteen days, the magistrate regretting that it could not be longer.

LUTTRELL, COLONEL JAMES (1725–92) Obscure politician and debaucher of under-age girls. He stood against JOHN WILKES when the latter campaigned for the fourth time to be MP for Middlesex in 1774. Luttrell, who was already an MP, was a violent womaniser. He kidnapped a girl of eleven, seduced her and bribed witnesses to say she was a prostitute. He went to one of MRS CORNELYS's famous masques dressed as a corpse carrying a coffin with an inscription saying he had died of venereal disease which he caught from Mrs Cornelys. That lady had been the mistress of better men, notably CASANOVA, and she wasn't amused. When his father, Lord Irnham, challenged him to a duel Luttrell refused because 'Lord Irnham is not a gentleman'. Wilkes won the election by a huge majority but the House declared Luttrell the winner.

LYON, ELIZABETH Mistress of the burglar and jailbreaker JACK SHEPPARD. She helped Sheppard escape from prison, and later betrayed him to JONATHAN WILD. She was found guilty of a felony and transported. Also known as Edgeworth Bess.

M

MACCLESFIELD, EARL OF In May 1725, the same month that JONATHAN WILD was tried and hanged, another trial took place – that of Thomas Parker, Earl of Macclesfield. Lord Chancellor in Walpole's administration and a close friend of King George I, Macclesfield was accused of accepting bribes and embezzling more than £100,000 of Chancery funds – about £3,000,000 in today's money. He was fined £30,000 – the king promised to make good his loss out of the Privy Purse in £1,000 instalments, but died after only one payment – and the press and the government's opponents made much of the parallels between the cases, and between the methods of the great criminal, Wild, and the great statesman, Walpole.

MCKAY, MURIEL First woman to be kidnapped for ransom in England. Mrs McKay, wife of a newspaper executive, disappeared in December 1969 from her home in Wimbledon. When her husband returned home from the office of the *News of the World*, where he was acting chairman in the absence of Rupert Murdoch, he found the house had been ransacked. The following day a caller claiming to be 'M3 – the Mafia' asked for a ransom of a million pounds. Mr McKay called in the police and they arranged to drop a suitcase full of banknotes – most of them fakes – at an agreed spot. The kidnappers became suspicious and the handover never took place, but the police spotted a blue Volvo on two occasions and traced it to Arthur Hosein, a 33-year-old tailor who ran a smallholding at Stocking Pelham, Hertfordshire, with his brother Nizamodeen. No body was ever found but the police discovered that Nizamodeen had visited County Hall to get the number of Mr McKay's office Rolls-Royce. The brothers, who apparently mistook Mrs McKay for Mrs Murdoch, were jailed for life.

MACLAINE, JAMES (1711–50) Highwayman who almost shot HORACE WALPOLE. Maclaine wasted an inherited fortune, then the £500 he received as a marriage settlement. When his wife died he assumed the lifestyle of a gentleman in an effort to find another rich wife. His money ran out and he became a highwayman, using his considerable criminal income to live in style, even staying at White's Club. His partner, a Scottish apothecary named Plunkett, also aped the gentleman. At Maclaine's trial in 1750 Lady Caroline Petersham spoke for him. She was among those who later visited him in prison, as were members of White's Club. Many women wept when he was sentenced to death. While he was being held in Newgate awaiting execution about 3,000 people paid to see him on a single day. Horace Walpole, to whom MacLaine apologised for the accidental shooting, wrote:

> The first Sunday after his condemnation 3,000 people went to see him. He fainted away twice with the heat in his cell. You can't conceive the ridiculous rage there is of going to Newgate, and the prints that are published of the malefactors and the memoirs of their lives and deaths set forth with as much parade as – as Marshal Turenne's – as we have no generals worth making a parallel.

See HIGHWAYMEN

MCNAGHTEN RULES In 1843 Daniel McNaghten murdered Edward Drummond, private secretary to the Prime Minister, SIR ROBERT PEEL. McNaghten, who was suffering from delusions of persecution, mistook him for Peel. He was acquitted on the ground of partial insanity. Disquiet about the case led to the establishment of the McNaghten Rules on the criminal responsibility of the insane. They stated that it must be proved that at the time a crime was committed the accused was suffering such impairment of reason that he did not know the nature of the act, or that he was doing wrong; also that everyone is to be presumed sane unless the contrary can be proved. The Homicide Act of 1957 tidied up the rules by recognising the plea of diminished responsibility.

MCVICAR, JOHN Former armed robber and prison escaper. His escape from Durham jail in 1968 brought him nationwide notoriety, but his criminal career was less than auspicious. 'As a criminal I have been a lamentable failure. Whatever money I earned by crime I could have earned as a labourer in half the time I spent in prison . . .' He found punditry in print and on television much more lucrative. 'The professional criminal wants respect, prestige and the recognition of those who subscribe to his own need of machismo.' He says he was threatened by emissaries of the Adams gang after he had written about them.

MCVITIE, JACK 'THE HAT' (?–1967) Incompetent criminal murdered by REGGIE KRAY.

He accepted £100 from the Kray twins for a contract but failed to carry out the killing. He kept the money and also, in his cups, boasted of ripping off the twins and issued threats against them. Facing death, he was told by Ronnie to 'be a man'. McVitie replied: 'I'll be a man, but I don't want to die like one.' *See* KRAY TWINS

MALCOLM, SARAH (1711–33) Triple murderer drawn in the death cell by William Hogarth. Malcolm was a laundress in the Temple. Among her employers was wealthy Mrs Lydia Duncombe, who was nearly 80. Malcolm entered her home in February 1733 and took money, silver and other valuables. Afterwards the bodies of Mrs Duncombe and her two woman servants were found. Mrs Duncombe and one of the servants had been strangled, the other's throat had been cut. A bloody tankard was found in Malcolm's lodgings. She admitted robbery but denied murder, saying she had kept watch while another woman and two brothers committed the crimes. She was hanged near Fetter Lane at the age of 22. Hogarth was clearly interested in the young murderer and made two portraits of her. He said her face showed she was 'capable of any wickedness'. It was believed Malcolm, who had a lover whom she wanted to marry, carried out the robbery to provide a dowry.

Sarah Malcolm, the triple murderer hanged in 1733, when she was 22. She was drawn in the death cell by William Hogarth, who said her face showed that she was 'capable of any wickedness'. The hangman thought she was innocent.

MALORY, SIR THOMAS (?–1471) The shadowy author of *Le Morte d'Arthur* is reputed to have been a rapist and outlaw. Malory, who died in 1471, is said to have led a band of outlaws who stole cattle and robbed from monasteries. He was accused of twice breaking into the home of one Hugh Smyth in 1450 and 'feloniously raping' Smyth's wife Joan on each occasion, as well as stealing a large sum of money. He wrote *Le Morte d'Arthur* in prison.

MALTBY, CECIL Murderer who kept his lover's body in the bath for months. Maltby shot his lover Alice Middleton three times in the back in August 1922. When police broke into the flat in Park Road, Regent's Park five months later he shot himself. They found Mrs Middleton's body wrapped in a sheet in the bath, and a note nailed to the bedroom door: 'In memory of Alice H Middleton who committed suicide . . . darling why did you do it? Everybody loved you. I cannot live without you. When I can brace up my courage shall soon be with you – Cecil Maltby.'

MANNING, EDDIE Early example of a drug dealer. Manning, a Jamaican, was jailed for sixteen months in 1920 for shooting three men in the legs in Cambridge Circus. One of them had punched and insulted an actress friend of Manning's. In 1922 a drug addict named Eric Goodwin died from a heroin overdose at Manning's house. Manning was arrested carrying cocaine and opium in Primrose Hill in north London. He had a silver-topped cane which had a secret compartment for drugs. He died in prison. The detective Robert Fabian wrote: 'We strongly suspected Eddie was giving dope parties in various parts of London, and injections of cocaine at 10*s* a time . . . He had his own team of strong-arm villains – both white and coloured boys who were usually full of drugs – and kept a profitable sideline in protecting prostitutes.'

MANNINGS, THE Murderous couple who robbed and killed Mrs Manning's lover in 1849. Maria Manning was born in Switzerland and arrived in England as maid to a Lady Blantyre. On the voyage she met an Irishman named Patrick O'Connor, and they were attracted to each other. Once in England, however, she met and married a petty crook named Frederick Manning, who claimed he expected to inherit property from his mother. With Maria's money they bought an inn in Taunton, Somerset. They were both arrested over a robbery, but released for lack of evidence. They went to London and opened a beer shop in the Hackney Road. Mrs

Manning, who had become disillusioned with her marriage, met O'Connor again and ran away with him. Her husband traced her to Bermondsey in south London. The couple lived together again, but O'Connor continued to be Maria's lover with Manning's agreement. Manning had discovered that O'Connor was wealthy. When O'Connor made a will in Maria Manning's favour his fate was sealed. He had refused to lodge in the Mannings' house, and Maria feared that he was growing tired of her. She invited O'Connor to dinner, and he was not seen alive again. Friends reported him missing, and police forced their way into the Mannings' house. The couple had fled, and O'Connor's corpse was found under a flagstone in the kitchen. Mrs Manning had shot him in the head, and her husband then battered him with a chisel. 'I never liked him much,' he said to his wife. In court the Mannings blamed each other. When she was sentenced to death Mrs Manning screamed 'Base and shameful England'. They were hanged on the roof of Horsemonger Lane prison in 1849. Still deeply in love with her, Frederick Manning had tried to see Maria as they awaited execution, but she said she would agree only if he made a statement clearing her. The drunken behaviour of the crowd at the executions shocked Dickens, who was present. He felt 'for some time afterwards almost as if I was living in a city of devils'.

> I believe that a sight so . . . awful as the wickedness and levity of the immense crowd collected at that execution could be imagined by no man. The horrors of the gibbet and of the crime which brought the wretched murderers to it faded in my mind before the atrocious bearing, looks and language of the assembled spectators.

MANSFIELD, LORD (1705–93) Unpopular Lord Chief Justice, whose home was ransacked by the GORDON RIOTERS. His opposition to a reprieve was one of the factors in the refusal to spare the clergyman DODDS. He reversed the outlawing of WILKES on a technical point.

MAPLETON, PERCY Short-story writer and journalist who murdered a man on a train. In June 1881 he stabbed and shot coin dealer Frederick Gold on a London to Brighton train, then threw the body out of a window. In their hunt for him, police issued a picture of a wanted man for the first time. When he was arrested police found rare coins in his lodgings. He was hanged in November 1881.

MARK, SIR ROBERT Reforming chief of the Metropolitan Police. Appointed Commissioner in 1972, he told a meeting of the CID 'that they represented what had long been the most routinely corrupt organisation in London, that nothing and no one would prevent me from putting an end to it and that if necessary, I would put the whole of the CID back into uniform and make a fresh start'. In 1978 officers from outside London were brought in to investigate allegations of corruption against London detectives. At first Operation Countryman promised much. The team compiled a list of seventy-eight Met officers and eighteen from the City of London against whom there were allegations of various kinds of corruption. But obstruction within the force stopped any real progress, and in 1982 the operation was wound up.

MARKOV, GEORGI (?–1979) BBC broadcaster almost certainly murdered by the Bulgarian secret service. Markov, a refugee from Bulgaria whose broadcasts riled the Communist government of his native country, was stabbed in the right thigh with a poisoned umbrella tip in the Strand in September 1979. The killer, who had been waiting at a bus-stop, apologised to Markov and then caught a passing taxi. At first Markov did not realise exactly what had happened but he later felt ill and was taken to hospital. He died four days later on 11 September. During a post-mortem examination a tiny pellet was found in his thigh. It had been filled with the poison ricin.

MARKS, HOWARD (1945–) Celebrity drug smuggler and all-round charmer born in Wales. He was recruited by MI6 in the hope that his charm and good looks would persuade women at the Communist Czechoslovakian embassy to part with secrets. He had begun to deal in cannabis while a student at Oxford, and he was arrested in the U.S. when drugs were found in rock music equipment his team had imported. Marks was extradited to Britain where he was granted £20,000 bail. In April 1974 a man who claimed to be from the Customs and Excise called at his rented house in Oxford and took him away, and he vanished. From a hide-out on the Isle of Dogs in East London he began to travel the world setting up drug deals. He returned to Britain from time to time, and although apparently taking little care to hide proved elusive as far as the authorities were concerned. In October 1977 he was back in Wimbledon for the birth of his second daughter and he also visited the Nashville pub in Hammersmith, where he sang Elvis Presley songs. At the same time he was smuggling up to 30 tons of cannabis a time into the United States and Canada. Eventually police forces from America, Canada, Great Britain and Spain combined to end what was the most successful career of any independent drug smuggler. They were helped by Lord Moynihan, crooked brother of a Tory minister, who taped conversations with Marks about plans to establish a cannabis plantation in the Philippines. At Palm Beach Federal Court in Florida Marks pleaded guilty to cannabis importation charges, and was sentenced to twenty-five years, reduced on appeal to twenty. He was sent to the penitentiary at Terre Haute, Indiana, where he taught some of the world's toughest criminals English grammar and philosophy. He was released in 1995 after seven years on the ground of good behaviour. Despite the huge deals he was involved in and the enormous amounts of money involved, he said he made only \$2–\$3 million, and that he had spent it all. His autobiography *Mr Nice* was a best-seller, and he is a popular lecturer on the decriminalisation of soft drugs.

MARLOWE, CHRISTOPHER (1564–93) Playwright and murder victim. The author of *Dr Faustus* and *The Jew of Malta* led a troubled and violent life. In 1589 he was held in Newgate prison for his part in the death of a man in a street brawl. He was deported from the Netherlands for attempting to pass forged gold coins and in 1593 he fell foul of the Privy Council for being an atheist. He spent most of the day he was murdered, 30 May 1593, drinking with two disreputable companions in Eleanor Bull's tavern on Deptford Strand. One of them, Ingram Frizer, claimed Marlowe attacked him with a knife. In the struggle Marlowe was stabbed in the eye. A jury returned a verdict of self-defence. Some historians believe he was murdered on the orders of SIR FRANCIS WALSINGHAM, who was Frizer's employer.

MARSHALSEA PRISON Charles Dickens's father was held for debt in the Marshalsea in Southwark in 1824. In *Little Dorrit* Dickens describes it as 'partitioned into squalid houses standing back to back . . . hemmed in by high walls duly spiked at the top'. The original Marshalsea on a site nearby dated from the fourteenth century. It was one of the prisons destroyed by WAT TYLER in 1381. Although the rebuilt Marshalsea was used to house both Catholics and Protestants during the Reformation it later became largely a debtors' prison. One of the Keepers, William Acton, was tried for murder in 1729. To amuse some visitors he had a prisoner named Thomas Bliss subjected to various tortures. Thumbscrews, an iron skullcap and an iron collar were tried on the wretched man, who died soon after. Acton was also tried for three other murders. He was acquitted.

MARY CUT-AND-COME-AGAIN (?–1745) Ballad singer and pickpocket, real name Mary White. She was executed for stealing an apron worth 6*d*. When the Watchmen arrested her she pulled out her breasts and 'spurted the milk in the fellows' faces, and said damn your eyes . . . do you want to take my life away?' Defiant to the end, she kicked the prosecutor at her trial and spat on the judge's seat. The ORDINARY or chaplain of Newgate said of her: 'She was queen of the blackguards, pilferers, and ballad singers, universally known amongst them, and partaker in most of their villainies: she acquired the cant name by which she stood indicted for her dexterity in cutting off women's pockets.'

MAURICE OF LONDON Bishop noted for his sexual appetite. He became William the Conqueror's chancellor, and Bishop of London in 1086. He was an efficient public servant, and lavishly rebuilt St Paul's Cathedral. To monkish remonstrations about his pursuit of women he replied that sexual satisfaction was essential to his health.

MAXWELL, ROBERT (1923–91) Publisher, self-publicist, sometime politician and fraudster. A self-educated war hero, Maxwell succeeded in building a major publishing empire with interests around the world. This was all the more surprising after a DTI inquiry into his business affairs in 1971 concluded that 'notwithstanding Mr Maxwell's acknowledged abilities and energy, he is not . . . a person who can be relied on to exercise proper stewardship of a publicly quoted company'. His greatest success was the takeover of the Daily Mirror group of newspapers in 1984. As his empire expanded he resorted to siphoning large sums from his companies and their pension funds to finance new purchases. With his companies more than £2 billion in debt he fended off criticism and investigations with libel writs, threats, illegal share support schemes and a Byzantine tangle of alliances and share swops. When he died mysteriously at the age of 68 – he disappeared from his luxury yacht in 1991 and his body was found in the sea off the Canary Islands – the empire was found to be bankrupt and his family lost control of it. His sons Ian and Kevin successfully defended court actions over the affair. Maxwell is remembered at the *Mirror* for landing by helicopter on the roof of his high-rise HQ and pissing over the edge, saying: 'That's what I think of my readers.'

MAY, ALAN NUNN Traitor jailed for ten years in 1946 for betraying the country's atomic secrets to the Russians. Nunn May, a physics lecturer at London University, had given the Russians, who were trying to build their own bomb, microscopic samples of uranium. In return he got a few dollars and two bottles of whisky.

MAYHEW, HENRY (1812–87) Writer and pioneering social observer. His influential *London Labour and the London Poor* (4 vols), based on interviews, is a classic which gave voices to a stratum of the population otherwise lost to history. He was also the author of novels and plays. With Mark Lemmon and others he founded the humorous magazine *Punch*.

MEFF, JOHN (?–1721) Victim of the Thief-Taker General JONATHAN WILD. Meff, who was hanged in London at the age of 40, had a remarkable life. The son of French Huguenot parents, he was apprenticed to a weaver but became a thief. He had been sentenced to hang in 1717, but bailiffs served a writ for debt on the hangman before he could carry out the sentence. The mob waiting to see the execution pounced on the hangman, and 'beat him to death'. Meff was reprieved, and transported to America. On the voyage out his ship was captured by pirates, who included the women Anne Bonny and Mary Read. Most of the transported felons agreed to throw in their lot with the pirates but Meff refused, and was marooned on a desert island. He found a canoe, and made his way to the American mainland. He later returned to England, became a thief again and was captured and imprisoned in Newgate. He escaped with the aid of a bricklayer and fled to Hatfield, where he fell into the hands of Wild, who turned him in to the authorities in return for 'a very handsome sum'. 'Departing this "restless and tumultuous world" Meff hanged conscious of the "misfortunes" of his life.'

MELBOURNE, VISCOUNT (1779–1848) Statesman and husband of Lady Caroline Lamb, Byron's lover. In 1836 a magistrate named George Chapel Norton brought an action for CRIMINAL CONVERSATION or adultery against Melbourne, who was Prime Minister. Norton's beautiful wife Caroline, author of many novels, knew Melbourne, and he would frequently call on her. If she was out he would leave brief notes, such as 'I will call at about half-past four or five – Yours, Melbourne'. Norton was a wife beater and there was little sympathy for him. His witnesses made a poor showing, one, a coachman, admitting that on one occasion when he had driven the Nortons to a ball he had been so drunk he was arrested. He also admitted that Norton had given him £10 to appear as a witness. The jury cleared Melbourne, but *The Times* wrote: 'Lord Melbourne has been acquitted by the verdict of the jury, against the laws of God and man.'

MESSINA BROTHERS Five Sicilians who dominated vice in the West End for twenty years from the 1930s. They brought a ruthless efficiency to the business of vice, ruling by terror and amassing considerable wealth. Under their guidance prostitution became big business for the first time since the eighteenth century, but without the sense of style and fun of the earlier period.

Eugenio or Gino arrived in London in 1934, followed later by his brothers Carmelo, Alfredo, Salvatore and Attilio. The campaigning journalist DUNCAN WEBB, who launched a crusade against the Messinas in the pages of *The People* newspaper, wrote: 'By bribery and corruption they organised marriages of convenience both in Britain and abroad to enable their harlots to assume British nationality. They ruled their women by persuasion, threat or blackmail and the use of the knife and the razor. They ruled the streets of the West End by similar methods. Indeed, so terror-stricken did the underworld become at the mention of the word "Messina" that in the end they found little difficulty in building up their vast empire of vice.' The prostitute and madam MARTHE WATTS, who became the mistress of Gino Messina, said that during the war 'London became filled with British and Allied troops and with war workers away from home. Time was short, money was loose, morals were out'. Watts said that she earned £150,000 for Gino Messina between 1940 and 1955.

It was Webb who brought the Messinas down. On 3 September 1950 *The People* named the 'four debased men with an empire of crime which is a disgrace to London'. At that stage the brothers owned properties that operated as brothels in Shepherd Market, Stafford Street, Bruton Place and New Bond Street, all in the West End. Scotland Yard set up a special task force to break the brothers. They eventually all fled abroad. Eugenio, Carmelo and Alfredo ran the vice empire from Paris until November 1953 when Eugenio was kidnapped and his brothers had to pay a ransom of £2,000 to get him released. Eugenio and Carmelo moved to Brussels but were soon in trouble. They had been sending Belgian girls to Britain to staff their brothels, and they were arrested there in 1955 in possession of loaded revolvers.

REPERTOIRE SPECIALISTES . REPERTOIRE SPECIALISTES . REPERTOIRE SPECIALISTES

14474.40

MESSINA

Eugène.

Section : WHITE SLAVE TRAFFIC

Born on 26th June 1908 in Alexandria (Egypt)
Nationality : British.
Profession : claims to be a merchant in precious stones.
married to ASTIER Andrée.

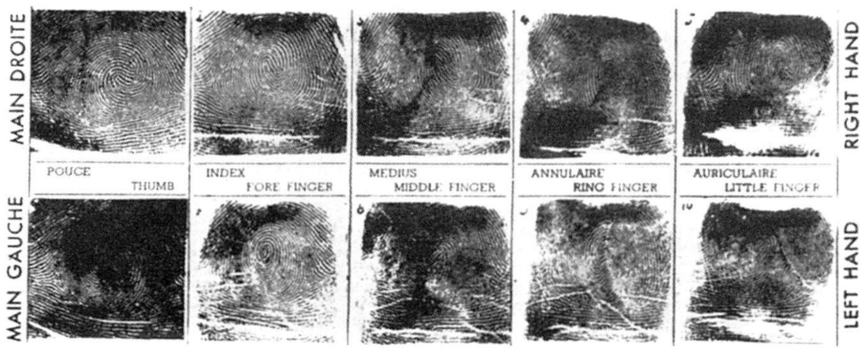

Description :
height 5'9"
hair dark auburn
eyes brown
strong build.

Previous condemnations :
Belgium and Great-Britain : 3 condemnations. Has been the object of an enquiry in Belgium on white slave traffic (no results).

Accomplices : MESSINA Andrée, née ASTIER - MESSINA Salvatore - MESSINA Alfrrdo, born on 2nd August 1901 in Malta.

Present residence : Great Britain.

I.C.P.C. PARIS
November 1947.

N° 119 a 47

The police record sheet on the vice racketeer Eugenio Messina. He and his brothers ruled a vicious West End vice empire from the mid-1930s until the 1950s.

Eugenio was jailed for seven years. Carmelo, who was now in poor health and had not long to live, was deported. He moved first to Ireland and then entered England using a false passport. In October 1958 he was arrested as an illegal immigrant, jailed for six months and then deported to Italy, where he died six months later at the age of 43.

In 1959 Attilio was tried for living on the immoral earnings of Edna Kalman. The trial heard how Attilio seduced women into prostitution. Kalman told how he first picked her up in his car. He then used a campaign of fairly subtle flattery and promises to persuade her to go on the streets. She went to live with him, and he seems to have suggested that they would eventually marry. Another witness, who was not named in court, said he told her: 'Eventually you will have your own flat and entertain a few very rich, well-known and influential people.' Another girl told the court: 'For the first time in my life I felt that someone wanted me. His voice was so soft, so ingratiating, I said to myself after our first meeting: "This is a gentleman."'

After the women became prostitutes the tone changed. There were beatings and threats. Mrs Kalman was told that her face would be slashed if she tried to get away. When she became sick and exhausted and her doctor told her to take a month's rest Attilio said this was 'rubbish' and ordered her back onto the streets. He shouted at her: 'I'm tired of this. I could get a seventeen-year-old who would work harder and I could sleep with her as well.' Attilio was sentenced to four years' imprisonment. The Messinas were finished.

METYARDS, THE Mother and daughter hanged for murdering servant girls. Sarah Metyard was a milliner who treated foundling children in her care with fiendish cruelty. In 1758 five girls were sent to work at her home in Bruton Street, among them Anne Naylor and her younger sister. Anne was a sickly child and Mrs Metyard found her work unsatisfactory. The child was beaten and her hands were tied behind her back to a door handle so that she could not sit down. She was kept like that for three days without food. When she was finally allowed to lie down she died.

Mrs Metyard and her daughter, also called Sarah, locked the attic in which the body lay and told the other girls that Anne had run away. Anne's sister saw that the dead girl's shoes and clothes were still in the house. When she pointed this out the Metyards strangled her.

Four years later Mrs Metyard's daughter left with a lodger named Rooker and became his mistress. Her mother pursued Rooker from address to address and shouted abuse through the door. When Rooker invited her into his house in Ealing, hoping to reason with her, she attacked her daughter. After she left her daughter told Rooker about the killings. Rooker believed young Sarah would not be prosecuted because of her age, and alerted the authorities, but the Metyards were tried together and executed at Tyburn in July 1768.

MEYRICK, KATE (1877–1933) 'Nightclub Queen' of the twenties. Kate, famous as the first woman in Ireland to ride a bicycle, was abandoned by her doctor husband, leaving her at the end of the First World War with eight children to support, including two sons at Harrow and four daughters at Roedean. She had never been in a nightclub before she became co-manager of Dalton's in Leicester Square, a frequent target for the police because of its reputation as a pick-up point for prostitutes. She went on to open dozens more, including the 43 Club in Gerrard Street, famous for attracting bohemians such as the artists Augustus John and Jacob Epstein and the writers Joseph Conrad and J.B. Priestley as well as gangsters and aristocrats. Others included the Folies-Bergère in Newman Street, the Little Club in Golden Square, the Manhattan in Denman Street and the Silver Slipper in Regent Street. DORA, the Defence of the Realm Act, which prohibited the sale of alcohol after 10 p.m., was still in force, and her clubs were frequently raided. Eventually fines gave way to periods of imprisonment and with her health breaking down she promised to retire.

Her clubs were plagued by gangsters, particularly members of the SABINI GANG and their racetrack rivals. They demanded free drinks and sometimes staged shootouts. Kate said: 'An evening-dress constituted no guarantee at all of its wearer's credentials: a party of apparently quite decent men might easily – only too often did – turn out to be one of the numerous gangs of bullies or racecourse terrorists who held sway.' She died at the age of 56, her health broken by periods in prison. When she died dance bands in the West End fell silent for two minutes as a tribute. Some of her children married into the aristocracy. She wrote readable memoirs, *Secrets of the 43*.

MILLER, SIR ERIC (1921–77) Tycoon who was too generous to his friends. After Miller, chairman of Peachey Property Corporation, shot himself to escape fraud charges in 1977 the full extent of his generosity emerged. REGINALD MAUDLING, once Tory Chancellor of the Exchequer, was given a

Kate Meyrick, queen of the nightclubs in the Twenties. She ran a series of London clubs, and was jailed several times. Her clubs were plagued by gangsters, including the Sabinis. When she died, dance bands in the West End fell silent for two minutes as a tribute. Her daughters married into the aristocracy.

mansion flat for a rent of £2 a week. Harold Wilson, former Labour Prime Minister, got a surprise farewell party at a cost to Peachey of £3,000. Bobby Moore, the England soccer captain, got £45,000 repairs to the house Miller had already given him. Miller had not stinted himself, owning a £700,000 house, private helicopter, executive jet, Rolls-Royce and two Ferraris. His son's Bar Mitzvah, for which he flew a planeload of guests to Israel, cost Peachey £250,000.

MILLS, FREDDIE Former world boxing champion found shot dead in his car in Soho in July 1965. At first it was thought that Mills had been murdered, and it was suggested that the KRAYS had him killed because he owed them money. Then the owner of a rifle found beside Mills in the car was traced and said the boxer had borrowed it for a fancy-dress party. Among the many theories about Mills's suicide was the suggestion that he was the killer in the JACK THE STRIPPER prostitute murders.

MISTER SMITH'S Drinking club at Catford in south London where the RICHARDSON GANG fought a disastrous gun and fist fight with a local gang, the Hawards. The clash ended the Richardsons' reign of terror.

MITCHELL, FRANK (1933–67) Minor criminal known as the Mad Axeman, murdered on the orders of RONNIE KRAY. Mitchell, an inadequate who spent long spells in prison, was sprung from Dartmoor by the Krays. They found him a hide-out and a mistress. He wanted the authorities to give him a date for release. He was a muscular young giant, prone to violent rages, and when he became troublesome Ronnie Kray had him murdered by FREDDIE FOREMAN and ALFIE GERRARD.

MOHOCKS Upper-class thugs who murdered and maimed for amusement. In March 1712 five Mohocks, 'peers and persons of quality', were involved in a scuffle in a tavern in the Strand. During it the landlady was killed. 'The gentlemen laughed and ordered that she should be added to their bill.' Queen Anne, who was not amused, ordered an inquiry and the High Constable who had released the five from custody was sacked. At a subsequent trial they were all acquitted. The queen then offered a reward of £100 for information about people causing 'great and unusual riots and barbarities', but the outrages continued. Other Mohocks attacked innocent men and women in the streets at night, raping, slitting noses, cutting off ears and rolling people downhill in barrels. The writer L.O. Pike described the antics of 'the roisterers who made night hideous in the eighteenth century. The "Mohocks", the "Nickers", the "Tumblers", the "Dancing Masters" and the various bully-captains . . . If they met an unprotected woman, they showed they had no sense of decency; if they met a man who was unarmed or weaker than themselves they assaulted and, perhaps, killed him.' The Sweaters would surround a victim and prick his buttocks with swords as he tried to flee. The Bold Bucks specialised in rape. If they could not find victims in the streets they would enter houses and drag out screaming women. They would first drink so much 'they were quite beyond the possibility of attending to any notions of reason or humanity' (Hibbert, *The Roots of Evil*). Some historians have doubted whether these thugs really existed or were a media invention. Possibly their activities have been exaggerated.

MOLESWORTH, LADY Victim of an arson attack. In May 1763 her house in Brook Street was destroyed by fire. Lady Molesworth, her brother, two daughters and three servants died. The cause of the fire was a mystery. Eighteen years later a trunk which a servant of Lady Molesworth had sent to a friend in Ireland was opened, and found to be full of silver with the Molesworth crest. The servant was arrested and admitted starting the fire to cover the theft of the silver.

MONSTER, THE Mystery attacker who stabbed and slashed women in London in 1789–90. The well-dressed man was said to have charming manners. He invited women to smell a nosegay he was carrying, but hidden in it was a spike which he jabbed in their faces. He also slashed the breasts, buttocks and thighs of his victims. In the widespread publicity surrounding the affair he came to be known as The Monster.

One of his victims was Ann Porter, who was attacked as she walked in St James's Street with her sister one night in January 1790. She felt a blow, turned to see a man crouching nearby and fled with her sister. When she reached home she found a deep wound, nine inches long, in her thigh. Some months later she saw a man in a park whom she identified as her attacker. He was Rhynwick Williams, who worked for a maker of artificial flowers. Colleagues testified that he was at work at the time Ann Porter was attacked, but seven other women identified him as their attacker. Williams was sentenced to two years in Newgate, and the attacks ceased. But there were many who felt the wrong man had been punished, particularly as some women said that their attacker had been much better educated than Williams.

MOODY, JIMMY Murdered gangster who took part in a daring prison breakout. Moody was involved in the shootout at MR SMITH'S CLUB at Catford in 1966 which ended the reign of the RICHARDSON GANG as overlords of south London crime. He had helped carry wounded Richardson henchman FRANKIE FRASER away. Moody was acquitted of taking part in the fight, and joined a successful gang of security van raiders. For a time he hid out in a lock-up garage which he furnished comfortably. When he was finally arrested he was charged with crimes involving £930,000 and sent to Brixton prison to await trial.

His brother smuggled in tools and hacksaw blades, and together with his cellmates Gerard Tuite, an IRA bombmaker, and Stanley Thompson, he loosened bricks in the cell wall. On 16 December 1980 they escaped through the hole. For thirteen years Moody managed to stay out of the news and out of prison. He may have been living quietly on the money he stole as a security van raider, or he may have been an underworld hitman. The latter would explain what happened next. On 1 June 1993 he was drinking at the Royal Hotel in Hackney when a leather-jacketed man entered the bar and ordered a pint of lager. He then turned towards Moody and shot him four times, cursing as he did so, before escaping in a stolen car. It was widely believed that Moody had taken part in a murderous feud between the BRINDLE and ARIF families, and that he had been involved in the killing of David Brindle.

MOODY, DETECTIVE CHIEF SUPERINTENDENT WILLIAM (1931–) Corrupt detective largely responsible for the downfall of the Obscene Publications Squad. In February 1976 Moody was arrested with dozens of other officers and accused of taking bribes from Soho pornographers. At their trial the judge estimated that Moody and Commander Wally Virgo of the CID had between them taken

£100,000 from the pornographers, 'a scale which beggars description'. Virgo and Moody were each sentenced to twelve years in prison, although Virgo was freed after ten months. *See* PORNOGRAPHY

MORALS POLICE The First World War saw the introduction of patrols composed of women to police public morality. Two different organisations, the Women Police Volunteers and the Women's Patrols, roamed parks and cinemas, warning copulating or passionate couples and witnessing police arrests of homosexuals caught in the act. Results were mixed. Patrolwomen who saw two men indulging in fellatio in Hyde Park were said to be 'not only willing but anxious' to give evidence in court. On the other hand, two patrolwomen who saw a corporal copulating with a woman clerk from Harrods in the same park refused to appear in court. The women's patrols also enforced curfews for girls, and had powers to search women's houses for enlisted men and put a stop to private drinks parties. They were active in the vicinity of army camps where they sought to restrain young girls suffering from 'khaki fever'.

MORE, SIR THOMAS (1478–1535) Statesman and scholar, born in London. He was appointed Lord Chancellor on Wolsey's fall in 1529, but resigned in 1532 because of his opposition to HENRY VIII's break with the Roman Catholic Church. He refused to recognise Henry as head of the English Church and was executed for treason.

MORRISON, STEINIE (?–1921) Small-time crook who died in prison after what was almost certainly a miscarriage of justice. Morrison was sentenced to death at the Old Bailey in 1911 for the murder of Leon Beron, despite a sympathetic summing up by the trial judge. He was later reprieved. The trial took place in a highly charged atmosphere, anti-semitism mixing with police desire for revenge after events leading up to the recent SIEGE OF SIDNEY STREET had left three officers dead and two wounded. Some of those involved were Jews, as were Beron and Morrison.

Beron's body was found on Clapham Common on 31 December 1911. He had been killed by blows to the head, and after death he was stabbed three times in the chest. There were S-shaped scratches on his face, which was covered by a silk handkerchief. His gold watch and chain was missing. Beron had a small income from property, but probably relied on receiving and being a police informer. Chief Detective Inspector FREDERICK WENSLEY knew both Beron and Morrison, and when he discovered that the two men had been together in the East End on the night of the murder he arrested Morrison. The trial in March 1912, which lasted nine days, turned on whether Morrison would have been able to get to the Common and back in a certain time. The judge was unconvinced by the evidence of three cab drivers who came forward after the offer of a small reward. There was a lot of contradictory and confusing evidence, much of it irrelevant. In the hysterical atmosphere Morrison's counsel, Edward Abinger, made a serious error of judgment – he attacked the character of a prosecution witness. The Criminal Evidence Act of 1898 allowed defendants to go into the witness box to speak on their own behalf. It also ensured that a defendant's criminal record would not be revealed to the jury. However, this was conditional on the defence not attacking the Crown witnesses. Morrison had been caught out in a string of lies to the court. Now the prosecution revealed his long career in crime. Despite the unreliability of the Crown's identity evidence – a fact the judge pointed out – the jury rejected Abinger's suggestion that Beron was a police spy and was killed in revenge by Russian anarchists. Although an acquittal had been widely expected they took only thirty-five minutes to find Morrison guilty.

When the judge ended the death sentence with the traditional words 'And may the Lord have mercy on your soul' Steinie cried out: 'I decline such mercy. I do not believe there is a God in heaven either.'

Steinie was tall and handsome, much loved by women, unsuccessful and deluded. He never accepted the guilty verdict and in the end, appealed on four occasions for the original death sentence to be carried out. He went on a series of hunger strikes and died in prison in January 1921. He had told the chaplain in Dartmoor: 'The man who killed Beron is no doubt a man who is exactly my double, but about four inches shorter. He met me in the East End of London one afternoon. He stopped me with a look of astonishment on his face and said, "Who the hell are you?" I said to him, jokingly, "It is singular that there should be two such good-looking men." He replied: "You may be damned sorry for it one day." He then told me that he was associated with some foreign secret society, and asked if I knew anything about them. I said, "No, and I don't want to."'

MOSLEY, SIR OSWALD (1896–1980) Political extremist who led the British Union of Fascists. Few men can have shown more promise or been as blessed by fortune. He was educated at Winchester and Sandhurst, served with distinction in the First World War, became MP for Harrow, had a post in the

1929 Labour Government and married Lord Curzon's daughter. After a visit to Mussolini's Italy he joined the BUF and as its support began to wane sought confrontation with the Jews of the East End. It was during a provocative demonstration in Cable Street that Jewish gangster JACK SPOT claimed he knocked out Mosley's bodyguard, although it seems unlikely. Mosley and his second wife Diana Mitford were detained for three years during the Second World War as a danger to the state. After their release in 1943 Mosley went back into politics but his Union Movement party was a flop. In the 1955 General Election he lost his deposit at North Kensington. He died in 1980.

MOTHER In the eighteenth century London's female brothel-keepers were usually known as Mother. The keeper of a homosexual brothel in Smithfield was known as MOTHER CLAP. *See* MOTHER NEEDHAM, MOTHER WISEBOURNE

MOTTS The Portland Rooms, known as Motts, was a luxurious Victorian dancehall where the most expensive courtesans sought customers between midnight and four or five in the morning. Gentlemen not wearing dress coats and white waistcoats were refused admission. Shaw's lively memoir of the mid-nineteenth-century capital, *London in the Sixties*, sets the scene:

> The ladies who frequented Motts, moreover, were not the tawdry make-believes who haunt the modern 'Palaces' but actresses of note, who if not Magdalens [prostitutes]

Mother Windsor, a veteran bawd, confronts the doddery old rake the Duke of Queensberry. Two of her girls support the Duke, long thought to be the wickedest man in Europe. He was a generous patron of whores.

> sympathised with them; girls of education and refinement who had succumbed to the blandishments of youthful lordlings, fair women here and there who had not yet developed into peeresses and progenitors of future legislators. Among them were 'SKITTLES', celebrated for her ponies, and sweet Nelly Fowler, the undisputed Queen of Beauty in those long-ago days. This beautiful girl had a natural perfume so delicate, so universally admitted, that love-sick swains paid large sums for the privilege of having their handkerchiefs placed under the Goddess's pillow, and sweet Nelly pervaded – in spirit if not in the flesh – half the clubs and drawing rooms of England.

MUGGING The crime and the word are ancient, but had been all but forgotten until an outbreak in the 1970s. Muggers were doing essentially what the FOOTPADS and GARROTTERS of the past had done. Police in the capital have been under constant pressure to reduce the level of muggings, which have aroused a disproportionate degree of fear, since most victims are not harmed and the amounts stolen are usually small. The arrival of the mobile phone, which distracts the user, has brought easy picking for young muggers.

MULLINS, DODGER East End thug and racecourse bully. BILLY HILL described how he cut up two young toughs who attacked the elderly Dodger:

> One afternoon I was in one of these Soho clubs having a drink and thinking about tomorrow when I went to the toilet. When I opened the door I saw two young tearaways from over the water belting the life out of my old friend Dodger Mullins with an iron bar. In his time Dodger had been a twenty-four carat villain. He was well into his sixties now . . . We all liked Dodger . . . Now two young tearaways were reaching for the crown of glory in being able to say they had beaten the life out of Dodger . . . I got out my chiv and gave one tearaway my favourite stroke, a V for Victory sign on his cheek. Then I cut the other monkey to ribbons . . .

In spite of what Hill says by no means everyone liked Dodger. When he got tired of a girlfriend he pushed her out of a moving car and broke her back (Murphy, *Smash and Grab*). Brian McDonald quotes a gangland character talking about Mullins:

> He had a gang which terrorised East End shopkeepers, mostly for free meals, smokes and booze. He never paid for anything. His uncouth presence on racecourses had been curtailed by BILLY KIMBER, because he openly threatened bookies and punters and ran pickpocketing binges where so many people were robbed that on one occasion it led to a riot (McDonald, *Elephant Boys*).

Mullins upset the powerful SABINI bookmaker ALF SOLOMON by encroaching on one of his rackets, but nevertheless outlasted the Sabini era.

MUNBY, ARTHUR (1828–1910) Poet, diarist, civil servant and indefatigable investigator of the lives of working-class women. Munby tells the story of Sarah Tanner, whom he first knew in about 1854 when she was 'a maid of all work' to a tradesman in Oxford Street. This was before she became a prostitute. He described her as 'a lively honest rosy-faced girl, virtuous and self-possessed'. When he met her a year or so later in Regent Street she was dressed in finery that could mean only one thing. '"How is this?" said I. Why, she had become tired of service, wanted to see life and be independent; and so she had become a prostitute, of her own accord and without being seduced. She saw no harm in it; enjoyed it very much, thought it might raise her and perhaps be profitable.' Sarah took it seriously as a profession, learning to read and write 'in order to fit herself to be the companion of gentlemen'.

Over the next few years Munby saw Sarah from time to as she solicited on the streets, and usually stopped for a chat. 'She was always well but not gaudily dressed, always frank and rosy and pleasant; and never importunate; nor did I ever hear her say a vicious word . . . '

He did not see her again until 1859, and another transformation had taken place. She was now dressed 'quietly and well, like a respectable upper servant'. Sarah had saved enough over three years of prostitution to open a coffeehouse, the 'Hampshire Coffee house over Waterloo Bridge' (Hudson, *Munby, Man of Two Worlds*).

> Now here is a handsome young woman of twenty-six, who, having begun life as a servant of all work, and then spent three years in voluntary prostitution amongst men of a class much above her own, retires with a little competence, and invests the earnings of her infamous trade in a respectable coffee house . . .

Surely then this story is a singular contribution to the statistics of the 'Social Evil' and of female character and society in the lower classes.

MURDER ACT OF 1752 This Act aimed to increase the deterrent effect of hanging by decreeing that the bodies of executed murderers should be handed over to the surgeons for dissection. The Act also gave judges the power to order hanging in chains for the bodies of the condemned. *See* EXECUTIONS

MURRAY, FANNY (1729–1778) Noted courtesan who became the chief 'Toast of the Town' in the middle of the eighteenth century. She achieved fame and adoration exceptional even in that age of celebrity whores. A gallant who drank champagne from her slipper sent it to a noted chef to be turned into a dish on which he and his friends feasted.

She had been whoring for four years with limited success when JACK HARRIS included her in his famous *List*. What followed showed the power of advertising.

Fanny was born in 1729 in Bath, where her father was a poor musician. According to the anonymous *Memoirs of the Celebrated Miss Fanny Murray* published in 1759 she was orphaned at the age of twelve, and became a flower-seller in the Rooms. Her first seducer when she was a very young teenager was the rake Jack Spencer, who gave her 'a few tawdry gifts' before abandoning her. After several affairs – including one with Beau Nash, Bath's arbiter of taste, who was in his sixties – Fanny left for London. She lodged with a Mrs Softing who introduced her to randy old men, one of whom gave her a snuffbox with £40 in it. She quarrelled with Mrs Softing who threw her out, and she became a common prostitute. 'What must be the ultimate end of such variegated concupiscence? Infection.' Fanny had her first dose of the pox, she needed expensive treatment and she had no money. She had to pawn her clothes, the surgeon's last fee being produced by her last gown. At this low ebb in her career her new landlady mentioned that a procuress in Old Bailey was looking for 'any clean fresh country goods' to replace girls who had been imprisoned in Bridewell. The results of her first week's efforts were earnings of £5 10*s* 6*d*, and expenditure of £5 10*s*. Fanny's problem, like that of many other whores, was that she had to hire her clothes at exorbitant rates from her bawd. That woman took all her money and was constantly threatening to have her imprisoned for debt if she didn't earn more. She managed to save and conceal

Fanny Murray, the most celebrated Toast of the Town in the second half of the eighteenth century. An admirer once had her slipper cooked and served up as a meal. She became a respectable housewife.

seven guineas from her earnings, and with this money she fled the brothel and took up with some of her upper-class former lovers. Her luck had changed, and soon 'she had so much business, all in the private lodging, ready-money way, that she could not possibly drive so great a business entirely on her own bottom . . .' Fanny took an apprentice, and her business was so flourishing that it soon attracted the attention of Harris, publisher of the *List of Covent Garden Cyprians*. 'Mr Harris, the celebrated negotiator in women, applied to get her enrolled upon his parchment list.' The *Memoirs* shows to what an art Harris had raised his pimping operation. 'The ceremony was performed with all the *punctilios* attending that great institution.' Fanny, was examined by a surgeon to prove she was free of venereal disease, and a lawyer was on hand as she signed the solemn agreement to pay Harris a fifth of her earnings, and also to hand over twenty pounds if she lied about the state of her health. This is how Harris described her:

> Perfectly sound in Wind and Limb: a fine Brown [brunette] Girl rising nineteen years

> next Season. A good Side-box Piece – will show well in the Flesh Market – wear well – may be put off for a virgin any time these twelve months – never common this side Temple Bar, but for six months. Fit for High Keeping with a Jew Merchant – NB a good premium from ditto – then the run of the house. And if she keeps out of the Lock [the VD hospital] may make her Fortune and ruin half the Men in town.

This ambiguous advertisement worked, and Fanny became the acknowledged Top Toast, although at first she charged a minimum of two guineas, which was very low. Another whore in Harris's *List*, Poll Davis of Manchester Square, was said to charge a minimum of ten guineas and half a crown for her servant. Slightly later in the century the Honourable Charlotte Spencer was charging a minimum of £50 per night. No doubt Fanny soon raised her prices. She was among the more classy whores who became sought-after models for some of the leading painters. The well-known rake Richard Rigby said of her that she was now 'followed by crowds of gallants . . . it would be a crime not to toast her at every meal'. There is a story that one of her temporary lovers having one evening drunk champagne from her slipper at the Castle tavern in Henrietta Street, asked the chef to cook and serve it. The chef minced the slipper, cooked it in butter and served it garnished with its wooden heels thinly sliced.

Fanny became the mistress of the wealthy Sir Richard Atkins, who set her up in a fine house at Clapham. When he died Fanny, who was only 27, was arrested for debt. John Spencer, the son of her first seducer, came to her rescue, paid her debts and gave her an annual allowance of £200. There was a suggestion that he was responding to her threat to publish her memoirs. She married the actor David Ross and became a respectable housewife, dying, much loved by her many noble friends, in 1778.

NAHOME, SOLLY Diamond merchant and financial adviser to the ADAMS family. Nahome was gunned down outside his London home in December 1998 by a man on a motorbike. He laundered the Adams's illegal drugs millions into diamonds and off-shore accounts, or used them to finance property deals.

NAPLES, JOSEPH Bodysnatcher who left a revealing diary. Naples, a former sailor in the Royal Navy who saw action at the Battle of Cape St Vincent, was a member of the BOROUGH BOYS GANG. His diary, kept in the Library of the Royal College of Surgeons, covers the year 1811. Entries for the end of November include:

> Thursday 28th. At night went out and got 3, Jack & me Hospital crib, Benjn, Danl and Bill to Harpers, Jack & me 1 big Gates, sold 1 Taunton Do St Thomas's.
> Friday 29th. At night went out and got 3, Jack, Ben & me got 2, Bethnal Green, Bill & Danl. 1 Bartholow. Crib opened; whole at Bartw.
> Saturday 30th. At night went out and got 3 Bunhill Row, sold to Mr Cline, St Thomas's Hospital.

This shows that on successive nights the gang got three bodies. The surgeons at Bart's and St Thomas's, including a Mr Cline, were good customers. *See* BODY SNATCHING

NASH GANG, THE North London crime family, allies of the KRAYS. The six Nash brothers – Billy, Johnny, Jimmy, Ronnie, George and Roy – came from Islington. They achieved notoriety in 1960 after the Pen Club killing. At the time the *Sunday Pictorial* called them 'the wickedest brothers in England'.

The Nashes took the classic route to criminal self-sufficiency if not riches, starting out by extorting protection money from small businesses and then moving into clubs. In the early 1960s it was estimated that Johnny Nash, the second oldest after Billy, had twenty clubs under his protection. The family were friends of both the Krays and the RICHARDSONS.

On 7 February 1960 Jimmy Nash was in the Pen Club in Spitalfields with his girlfriend and two men friends. A fight broke out and the club's owner, Billy Ambrose, who was on leave from a prison sentence, was shot in the stomach when he tried to intervene. Selwyn Cooney, who ran the Cabinet Club in the West End for BILLY HILL, was shot twice in the head. His body was carried out and laid on the pavement outside. Ambrose drove himself to hospital. Jimmy Nash was charged with murder. More than thirty people had been drinking in the club at the time of the shooting, but only four could remember seeing anything. They took a considerable risk. The two main witnesses, a man and his girlfriend, were slashed with razors and had to be given police protection. The woman was attacked while in her bath. During Jimmy Nash's trial the public gallery was full of ferocious gangsters, including the Kray twins and members of the Billy Hill gang. Nash, who admitted punching Cooney but denied murder, was jailed for five years for grievous bodily harm. The *Sunday Pictorial* commented: 'As far as the law is concerned, all that happened to Cooney is that he leaned on a bullet that happened to be passing.' The trial relegated the Nashes to the second rank of gangsters.

Billy Nash, writing in the *Sunday Pictorial*, said he and his brothers would quit the rackets if they could. 'We have the toughest reputation in London. That means there are fools all over London who would like to take us and make their names.'

NAYLOR, JAMES Quaker preacher who was punished for blasphemy. Naylor, who claimed to be the Messiah, was examined before Parliament in 1656 and sentenced to be pilloried, whipped through the streets and then pilloried again. His tongue was also pierced through with a hot iron and he was branded in the forehead with a B for blasphemer. After this ordeal he was held in Bridewell until 1659.

NEEDHAM, MOTHER (*c.* 1660–1732) Vicious bawd whose brothel was in Park Place, St James's, the centre of high-class bawdry, much patronised by the court. Even in middle age she was considered striking, Hogarth describing her as 'the handsome old Procuress ... well-dressed in silk and simpering beneath the patches on her face . . .' She is the bawd propositioning a pretty country girl in Plate 1 of Hogarth's *A Harlot's Progress*. She treated her girls little better than slaves. They were forced to hire their clothes from her at outrageous prices, and if they couldn't pay were harried to improve their work rates. If they still weren't earning enough for their

A procuress chats up a naive young country girl who has come to town in a wagon in Plate 1 of Hogarth's A Harlot's Progress. *This is a portrait of the vicious bawd Mother Needham. The man on the right is the rake Colonel Francis Charteris, one of the most debauched characters of the age.*

keep they might be bundled off to the debtors' prison and left there to rot until they agreed to her terms. When they were too old or diseased she threw them out.

Mother Needham got her girls from various places, including, apparently, auctions. In October 1784 *The Rambler* magazine carried this advertisement: 'TO BE SOLD by Inch of Candle at Mrs Kelly's Rooms several Orphan Girls under sixteen imported from the Countrey & never shewn before. Gentlemen of sixty-five and over are invited.' She was well-known for picking up country lasses just come to town. The essayist Richard Steele wrote in *The Spectator* in January 1712 about a visit he had made to the Bell Inn in Cheapside: 'But who should I see there but the most artful Procuress in the Town examining a most beautifull Country girl who had just come up in the same Waggon as my Things . . .' The girls would have been impressed by this handsome and well-dressed woman and her promises. Only later would they experience her temper and vicious tongue. The *Dunciad* says:

> Try not with Jests obscene to force a Smile
> Nor lard your Words with Mother Needham's style!

It was at Mother Needham's that SALLY SALISBURY, who had moved on after MOTHER WISEBOURNE's death, stabbed her lover. Needham's brothel was patronised by the nobility, particularly the Duke of Wharton and his cousin, COLONEL CHARTERIS. She is believed to have arranged for Anne Bond to become Charteris's servant, and this may have led to her arrest in March 1731 by the magistrate Sir John Gonson, a well-known scourge of prostitutes and procuresses. She was sentenced to the pillory where, perhaps because of her friends in high places, she was allowed to lie face down and so protect her face. The *Daily Advertiser* reported that, 'notwithstanding which evasion of the Law and the diligence of the Beadles and a number of Persons who had been paid to protect her she was so severely pelted by the Mob that her life was despaired of . . .' The *Daily Courant* reported that 'at first she received little Resentment from the Populace, by reason of the great Guard of Constables that surrounded her; but near the latter End of her Time she was pelted in an unmerciful manner'. Several recent authorities say she died of her injuries, but the *Grub Street Journal* reported that 'Elizabeth Needham *alias* Bird *alias* Trent' was one of a number of brothel-keepers tried on 14 July and was committed to Newgate. She seems to have died shortly afterwards, for in September a broadsheet entitled *Mother Needham's Elegy & Epitaph* commented:

Ye Ladies of Drury, now weep
Your Voices in howling now raise
For Old Mother Needham's laid deep
And bitter will be all your Days.

NEWGATE CALENDAR Record of the trials and executions of notorious criminals. It was first published about 1774. There were later series which took the record into the nineteenth century. The tone is relentlessly moralising.

NEWGATE PRISON The Old Bailey or Central Criminal Court is built on the site of this ancient prison in Newgate Street. There had been a prison there since at least the twelfth century. Its inmates comprise a celebrity roll-call of London organised crime, besides a great many petty criminals executed for trivial crimes, religious martyrs and murderers.

The prison was sometimes known as 'The Whit' after the Lord Mayor Richard Whittington, whose executors refurbished the ruinous building in the

Condemned prisoners pray round a symbolic coffin in the chapel at Newgate Prison. Members of the public have come to gawp. The preacher is the hated Ordinary, or chaplain. He would write down the prisoners' confessions and sell them at their executions. If prisoners refused to cooperate, he would make the confessions up.

Prisoners exercise in Newgate under the stern gaze of their guards. Every aspect of prison life, especially the food, was made as unpleasant as possible. This was truly the heart of darkness in Victorian England.

fifteenth century. It was burned down in the Great Fire of 1666 and a new building, of imposing magnificence, was finished in 1672. The splendid facade belied the squalid interior. The prison was a filthy death trap. In 1719 Captain Alexander Smith wrote: 'Newgate is a dismal prison . . . a place of calamity . . . a habitation of misery, a confused chaos . . . a bottomless pit of violence, a Tower of Babel where all are speakers and no hearers.' Jail fever was rife, and about thirty of the inmates died each year. The smell was appalling, and people passing outside the gateway covered their noses. Another reason for avoiding it was the prisoners who urinated from windows in the upper storeys or threw the contents of chamber pots into the streets.

Yet for those with hard cash – known as rhino – almost anything might be bought, including sex. 'A Free and Easy Club with by-laws to promote tumult and disorder organised drink and hops for singing and dancing. One of the strong drinks brewed in the Whit, a place as noted for the variety of its potions as the irony of its expressions, was called South Sea. The gin brewed in Newgate was called Cock-my-Cap, Kill-Grief, Comfort, Poverty, Meat and Drink

Newgate Prison, described as 'a prototype of Hell' and 'a bottomless pit of violence'. Inmates included Jonathan Wild and Jack Sheppard, and Lord George Gordon, instigator of the riots during which the prison was wrecked. Today the Old Bailey stands on the site.

Newgate Prison ablaze during the Gordon Riots in 1780. The rioters stormed the prison, freeing the inmates and piling up the furniture to start fires. The keeper had to flee with his wife and daughter over the roof as the mob began to storm the buildings. The prison was later rebuilt, but was demolished in 1901.

or Washing and Lodging.' The keeper and his turnkeys made fortunes from the sale of alcohol, and also from the sale of almost anything necessary to life: candles, food, water, heat. Those with no money were cast into the Stone Hold, a stinking subterranean cavern 'into which no daylight can come'. There were no beds. For many it was an unauthorised death sentence.

The petty criminal JACK SHEPPARD, the most famous jail escaper of all time, made a mockery of the prison's security. In 1724, in the greatest of all his escapes, he broke out despite having been handcuffed, manacled and chained to the floor. Other escapers used the sewers. In 1731 six prisoners who broke through a dungeon floor braved the nauseating filth of the sewer beneath. Two of them were drowned and their skeletons were found later, but the others escaped. The robber Daniel Malden escaped from the condemned cell in 1737 and made his way to freedom through a sewer. He fled to Europe but returned, was recaptured and hanged. JONATHAN WILD, the Thief-Taker General who was executed in 1725, was held here during his trial. Other noted inmates included TITUS OATES and DANIEL DEFOE.

The prison was one of the main targets of the mob during the GORDON RIOTS. They first demanded the release of the prisoners. The keeper refused, then had to flee over the roof with his wife and daughter as the mob began to storm the buildings. The mob piled up all the furniture, together with doors, floorboards and a collection of pictures, against one of the walls and set them alight. They then freed all 300 prisoners, including four footpads who were to be executed next day. The poet George Crabbe said he never saw 'anything so dreadful'. The prisoners were conducted through the streets in their chains. The building was burned out. A new building was finished in 1783, in time to receive as a prisoner LORD GEORGE GORDON, instigator of the riots.

From1783, when executions at Tyburn were ended, hangings took place in the open space outside the prison door. These attracted vast crowds: in 1807 alone thirty people were crushed to death. In 1868 the prison got an execution shed in one of its yards. From then on only officials and invited guests could attend executions. Newgate was demolished in 1901 after its fixtures and fittings had been auctioned off. The scaffold was moved to Pentonville prison, which became the main centre for executions north of the Thames.

As well as the Whit, the underworld had many other names for Newgate, among them the Sheriff's Hotel, the Stone Tavern, the Nark and the Quod. 'Quoded' meant being imprisoned.

NEWTON, SIR ISAAC (1642–1727) Great physicist who was also a successful Master of the Mint. Newton claimed credit for the Coinage Act of 1697 which made counterfeiting high treason, for which the punishment was death. As Warden and Master he spent fifty days a year prosecuting clippers and coiners. The government had itself debased the coinage – in 1697 half-starved sailors in the Navy had rejected £10,000 in shillings and sixpences sent by the government to pay off the fleet because the money was unsound. 'Clipping, coining and counterfeiting threatened the stability of the kingdom' (Linebaugh, *The London Hanged*). In this difficult situation Newton proved to be a brilliant administrator. However, he was not so astute with his own money: he lost a fortune in the SOUTH SEA BUBBLE.

NGARIMU, TE RANGIMARIA The first female hired killer in Britain. Ngarimu, a Maori, was hired by another New Zealander, Keith Bridges, and Paul Tubbs, to kill their business partner in 1992. They claimed the victim, Graeme Woodhatch, had cheated them out of £50,000 in the roofing business they ran. Bridges met Ngarimu when she was working as a barmaid in London in the 1980s. He offered her £7,000 to kill Woodhatch. Ngarimu, who wanted to buy a mobile home, accepted. On 24 May 1992 Woodhatch was making a phone call at the Royal Free Hospital at Hampstead where he had been operated on for piles when Ngarimu shot him twice in the head and twice in the body. She then caught a flight back to New Zealand, leaving the gun and the clothes she had been wearing at Bridges's flat in Camden Town.

The police finally traced Ngarimu and she returned to London, having undergone a religious conversion. Her evidence helped convict Tubbs and Bridges, who both got life imprisonment after a trial which began in May 1994. During the trial Bridges was shot in the chest and leg while walking in Ruislip, and proceedings were held up until he recovered. Ngarimu, who was 27 at the time of the murder, was given a life sentence.

THE NICHOL Rough area of the East End where the gangster ARTHUR HARDING was born in 1886. The district is called the Jago in Arthur Morrison's novel *The Child of the Jago*, which was published ten years later. It was bounded by High Street Shoreditch and Hackney Road on the north and Spitalfields to the south. Harding later told the author Raphael Samuel, whose *East End Underworld* is based on Harding's dictated memoirs: 'The Nichol was something of a ghetto. A stranger wouldn't chance his arm there . . . The whole district bore an evil reputation, and was regarded by the working-class people of Bethnal Green as so disreputable that they avoided contact with the people who lived in the Nichol.' The Nichol was swept away in the late nineteenth century slum clearances. In the 1890s it was replaced by the Boundary Street Estate, the first of the London County Council developments.

NICKELL, RACHEL Mother stabbed to death on Wimbledon Common in July 1992. Nickell, who was 23, was sexually assaulted and stabbed 49 times. Her 2-year-old son Alex was thrown into the undergrowth. Police used a young policewoman to try to entrap their main suspect, Colin Stagg, into incriminating himself. When the case reached the Old Bailey the judge criticised this police tactic and the prosecution withdrew its case.

NILSEN, DENNIS Civil servant and mass murderer. He invited men back to his flat in Muswell Hill, got them drunk and strangled them. When an engineer was called to the house in February 1983 to investigate a blocked drain he found human flesh. Various bits of bodies were found around the flat, including two heads and a skull. Nilsen had removed the flesh from the skull by boiling it. He explained that he had killed 'for company'. By the time he was caught he had murdered fifteen men.

NOTTING HILL RIOTS Britain's first serious race riots. There had been minor riots against blacks in Stepney in 1919, Deptford Broadway in 1949 and Camden Town in August 1954. The Notting Hill attacks were on a much larger scale. They began with a series of isolated assaults on blacks in West London in the summer of 1958. On Sunday 24 August nine young whites, mainly from Notting Dale and the White City Estate, went 'nigger hunting' in a car. Armed with a knife, a chair leg and other improvised weapons they carried out a series of assaults in which three West Indians were seriously hurt. The Notting Hill Riots began a week later, after the pubs closed on

Saturday 30 August. Black people and their homes were attacked and there were attempts by drivers to run down blacks in the streets. TEDDY BOYS were a significant factor in the riots. Mobs roamed the streets, and crowds of up to 400 whites attacked West Indian houses in Bramley Road, Lancaster Road and other streets in Notting Dale. The following weekend there were further attacks, mainly in Bramley Road and other streets near Latimer Road Underground Station. For four days white mobs of up to 700 terrorised blacks by attacking their homes or chasing them through the streets. Agitators from SIR OSWALD MOSLEY's Union Movement stirred up trouble, and gangs armed with milk bottles, iron bars, bicycle chains, knives and petrol bombs prowled the streets looking for victims. A black student named Seymour Manning who had been attacked by three whites in Bramley Road rushed into a greengrocer's. The shopkeeper's wife confronted the trio and with another housewife and a teenage boy kept what was now a growing crowd at bay until the police arrived. The mob shouted 'Lynch him'. After the police had brought the riots under control the nine 'nigger hunters' were each jailed for four years.

NOYE, KENNETH Murderer and gangster, one of the most successful and notorious of the post-KRAY era. In May 1996 he was involved in a 'road rage' incident on the M25 in Kent. During it he stabbed to death Stephen Cameron, a 25-year-old electrician. Although he went on the run and evaded justice for two years, it was effectively the end of a spectacular criminal career.

Noye had already rebuilt that career after being found not guilty of murdering a police officer whom he stabbed to death, and then serving a long jail sentence for laundering gold from the £26 million BRINK'S-MAT ROBBERY. Noye came from ranks of the lower middle class, unlike most of the south London villains who were his first accomplices. Kathy McAvoy, wife of the Brink's-Mat robber 'Mad' Micky McAvoy, said: 'Noye wasn't from south London, he was from the suburbs and that's just not the same. Noye wasn't the real thing and he knew the rest of us thought that.'

Noye was born in Bexleyheath, Kent, in May 1947. His father James was a Post Office engineer. After school he became involved in petty crime, receiving and smuggling, and spent time in BORSTAL. He met his future wife, Brenda Tremain, a legal secretary, at the lawyer's chambers where he had gone for advice after a brush with the police.

He began to mix with the aristocracy of crime, the KRAYS, RICHARDSONS, FRANKIE FRASER and others. Ostensibly he was a respectable businessman, living with Brenda and their two sons in a mansion in Kent and dealing in cars, property and timeshares. Behind this front he had moved into a higher league of crime, becoming a fence and armourer to the underworld and providing services like money laundering that the major robbers were not capable of organising for themselves.

His first fortune was made in gold smuggling. He would import gold illegally and make huge profits by evading the VAT due when it was sold. The gold was coming in from Africa, Kuwait and Brazil. It has been estimated that between 1982 and 1984 he made more than £4 million.

Noye's interest in gold and the ways it could be moved around the world and illegally traded was invaluable to the underworld after the Brink's-Mat robbery at Heathrow airport in November 1983. The robbers included some major figures from London's underworld, among them BRIAN 'THE COLONEL' ROBINSON, John 'Little Legs' Lloyd and 'Mad' Micky McAvoy. They turned to Noye with his proven record as a fence to launder the three tons of gold ingots.

In January 1985 Noye confronted a man in a balaclava in the garden of his home at West Kingsdown. There was a struggle and Noye stabbed the masked man ten times. Noye says he asked the dying man who he was and he gasped out: 'SAS . . . on manoeuvres.' The masked man was a policeman, Constable John Fordham, who had been taking part in a stake-out of the Noye home. Police suspected Noye and another man in the house at the time, Brian Reader, of being involved in the gold robbery. Noye and Reader were charged with murder. Noye said of the moment he confronted PC Fordham: 'I just froze with horror. All I saw when I flashed my torch on this masked man was the two eye-holes and the mask. I thought that was my lot. I thought I was going to be a dead man. As far as I was concerned I was fighting for my life.' In 1986 when he faced a jury at the Old Bailey he pleaded self defence and they believed him: although the prosecution had told the jury how Noye had plunged his knife up to the hilt in the unarmed officer's body ten times, he and Reader were acquitted of murder.

Noye's house was searched and police found eleven bars of gold and copper coins which could be used in melting down the precious metal. He was tried with six others on charges including disposing of the gold. Found guilty, he was given the maximum sentence of fourteen years for handling stolen goods. After the verdict he shouted to the jury: 'I hope you all die of cancer.'

He had handed back nearly £3 million of the Brink's-Mat loot to avoid having his home seized, and with new contacts he decided drugs were the quickest way of recouping his losses. At Swaleside prison he met Pat Tate, a drug dealer from Essex. Tate persuaded him to invest £30,000 in an ecstasy shipment, and he made a quick profit. In December 1995 Tate was shot dead with two other men in a Range Rover parked in a country lane near Chelmsford, Essex. Another of Noye's associates, car dealer Nick Whiting, was abducted from his showrooms in West Kingsdown by an armed gang in 1990. His body was found on Rainham Marshes in Essex. He had been stabbed nine times and shot twice with a 9mm pistol.

Thanks to his expertise in corrupting officials Noye escaped arrest for another drug plot. While he was finishing his sentence at Latchmere he had become involved in a cocaine deal with the Miami Mafia. He was tipped off that he was under surveillance by the US Drugs Enforcement Agency. The tip came from John Donald, a detective with the National Criminal Intelligence Service, who was jailed for eleven years in 1996 for corruption.

After he had served his Brink's-Mat sentence he went to northern Cyprus, where he met fugitive tycoon Asil Nadir, the former Polly Peck boss who is wanted in Britain on fraud charges. Noye invested in a time-share development on the island, and discussed other business deals with Nadir.

Then he got involved in a plot to swindle £1 billion from cash-dispensing machines. His partners included 'Little Legs' Lloyd. The plot collapsed and Noye's partners were arrested and sent to prison. Frustrated police could not arrest Noye because they lacked the evidence. There was speculation that once again, he had been tipped off just in time.

Other criminals Noye has been linked with include TOMMY ADAMS of the powerful north London crime family. They were filmed together by police investigating the handling of the Brink's-Mat gold. His close friend Micky Lawson was cleared of handling that gold, but during the trial of Detective Sergeant Donald, the corrupt National Criminal Intelligence Service officer, the court was told that Noye and Lawson were behind 150-kilo cocaine shipments from the US.

In April 1996 Noye was back in Cyprus, this time accompanied by his mistress Sue McNichol-Outch. He visited Asil Nadir before returning to Britain. A month later Noye's Land Rover Discovery pulled in front of Stephen Cameron's van. Stephen's fiancée Danielle Cable saw Noye pull a knife and stab Stephen to death before driving off in his Land Rover. Later he turned up in Spain, and using a passport in the name of Alan Edward Green he settled in Atlanterra, between Cadiz and Gibraltar.

By 1998 Noye had settled into a £330,000 villa. He had acquired a new girlfriend, Mina al-Taifa, who has Lebanese-French blood, but Sue McNicholl-Outch also came to stay from time to time. Despite his great wealth Noye needed money, because it was too dangerous to take cash from his various accounts as police were monitoring them. He linked up with a marijuana smuggler in Gibraltar and reportedly made £1 million.

Noye's wife Brenda visited him, and it was one of her visits in 1998 which helped police to pinpoint where he was staying. Two Kent police officers travelled to the Atlanterra area and spotted Noye riding his 600cc Yamaha trail bike along a coast road. Danielle Cable was then taken to the town and identified Noye as he sat in a restaurant with Mina. He was arrested by Spanish police.

There are misgivings among senior officers about Noye's links to the Freemasons. In the late 1970s he joined the Hammersmith Freemasons' Lodge in West London, having been sponsored by two police officers. He eventually became master of the lodge.

NUMBERS OF PROSTITUTES There are vastly fewer prostitutes in today's London, although it is difficult to get precise numbers for past centuries. Estimates about the middle of the nineteenth century varied between 5,000 and 220,000. Paula Bartley says in *Prostitution: Prevention and Reform in England 1860–1914* that in the 1860s some people suggested that there were half a million prostitutes in England, yet police statistics suggested that the figure was around 30,000. The police figures were based on prosecutions, which were low. As Bartley points out, the discrepancies could also be explained by the different ways the figures were compiled. COLQUHOUN, who thought the total in London in 1800 was around 50,000, included 25,000 unmarried women 'who cohabit with labourers and others without matrimony', which wouldn't meet our definition of prostitution today, although presumably some of these women were also prostitutes. J.B. Talbot, secretary of the deeply puritanical London Rescue Society, reached the conclusion that there were 80,000 prostitutes in the capital. This was based on his own observations 'and the evidence of eight different investigators'. This figure came to be widely accepted, although there was little hard evidence for it.

HENRY MAYHEW was another expert witness who believed the figure of 80,000 prostitutes. He wrote that in 1857 'according to the best authorities' there were 8,600 prostitutes 'known to the police', but felt that this figure 'scarcely does more than record the circulating harlotry of the Haymarket and Regent Street'.

The doctor and writer William Acton, an authority on the subject, did not agree, although he suggests that the true total was far in excess of the lower estimates. In his book *Prostitution*, published in 1857, he wrote:

> I can merely give a few of the more moderate [estimates] that have been handed down by my predecessors. Mr Colquhoun . . . rated them at 50,000 some sixty years ago. The Bishop of Exeter spoke of them as reaching 80,000. Mr Talbot . . . made the same estimate. The returns on the constabulary force presented to Parliament in 1839, furnished an estimate of 6,371 – viz., 3,732 'known to the police as kept by the proprietors of brothels', and 2,639 as resident in lodgings of their own, and dependent on prostitution alone for a livelihood. It was estimated by the Home authorities in 1841, that the corresponding total was 9,409 – which, I hardly need point out, does not include the vast numbers who regularly or occasionally abandon themselves, but in a less open manner . . .
>
> The police have not attempted to include the unnumbered prostitutes whose appearance in the streets as such never takes place; who are not seen abroad at unseemly hours; who are reserved in manners, quiet and unobtrusive in their houses and lodgings, and whose general conduct is such that the most vigilant of constables could have no pretence for claiming to be officially aware of their existence or pursuits.

There were attempts to establish exactly how many prostitutes there were in London in the early nineteenth century. In 1817 the London Guardian Society, set up to preserve public morals and reform prostitutes, reported to the Parliamentary Committee on the State of the Police the results of its survey of prostitutes in parts of the city. These were startling. In three parishes – St Botolph without Aldgate, St Leonard's, Shoreditch, and Saint Paul's, Shadwell – there were 360 brothels and 2,000 prostitutes in a population of 59,050. Saint Paul's, Shadwell alone had 200 brothels and 1,000 prostitutes out of 9,855 inhabitants and 1,082 houses. Nearly a fifth of the houses in the parish were brothels.

In Stepney, four streets abutting on the Commercial Road had sixty-five brothels and 194 prostitutes. Southwark's parish of St George the Martyr had 370 prostitutes, and Lambeth, which housed many of the women who plied their trade in Vauxhall Gardens, had 1,176 brothels and 2,033 prostitutes. In the City, there were twenty-two brothels housing 150 prostitutes 'in the vicinity of New Court'. At Westminster Abbey the Almonry was a haunt of whores. Another area infested with brothels was the borough of Southwark. The Police Committee heard evidence that among the reasons were the area's theatres and circus, the three nearby bridges to the City and the fashionable parts of town, and the 'great numbers of small houses lately built in that parish, which are particularly suited for such occupants.'

In 1840 the French socialist and feminist Flora Tristan published *Promenades dans Londres*, an account of some visits to the capital between 1826 and 1839. In it she describes a visit to the western fringe of the Southwark area:

> There are so many prostitutes in London that one sees them everywhere at any time of day; all the streets are full of them, but at certain times they flock in from outlying districts in which most of them live, and mingle with the crowds in theatres and public places. It is rare for them to take men home; their landlords would object, and besides their lodgings are unfit. They take their 'captures' to the houses reserved for their trade . . .

Tom Hickman says in *The Sexual Century* (Carlton Books, 1999) that there were 80,000 whores in Edwardian London, although he does not say what the figure is based on. Gosling and Warner (1960) estimated that in 1958 there were 1,000 full-time streetwalkers in the West End, and about 3,000 in the whole of London. They believed that in addition there were between 6,000 and 10,000 women they called 'hidden prostitutes', that is women who did not solicit openly on the streets.

A report by a team under Professor Roger Matthews of Middlesex University (*Prostitution in London: An Audit*) found that street prostitution overall was declining, with only 1,100 'known' women involved in any one year and as few as 115 being on the streets on any one night. Whatever figures we accept for Georgian and Victorian prostitution there has obviously been a very great decline, even in fairly recent times. The Wolfenden Report which led to the STREET OFFENCES ACT OF 1959 pointed out that in 1953 there were 6,829 prosecutions of women working in the West End alone. Now there may be fewer than 200 women working in that area. Matthews concludes that the decline is 'partly due to pressure from the local community, police intervention and a growing awareness of the dangers of working on the streets'.

At the same time there has been an increase in 'off-street' prostitution, in saunas and massage parlours, clubs, hostess bars and private flats. At the top end of the trade escort agencies are flourishing. Matthews does not believe there is a link between the decline of street prostitution and the rise in its off-street conterpart – few street prostitutes make the transition to off-street work.

The Matthews study is the first major survey of prostitution in London since the Second World War. Although for various reasons the King's Cross area is the one most people will think of as a typical hot spot for vice, Matthews shows that Paddington has about eight times as many women on the streets – 400 compared to 50. 'This is probably not surprising since Paddington in fact comprises three distinct areas centred around Sussex Gardens, Cleveland Square and Porchester Gardens. Sussex Gardens is the most active of these areas and of the 16 women reported to be on the street on an average night the majority will be located in Sussex Gardens.'

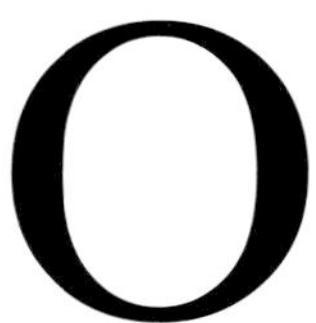

OATES, TITUS (1649–1705) Fraudulent clergyman and inventor of the notorious 'Popish Plot' against CHARLES II. Oates left Cambridge without a degree and condemned on all sides. One tutor called him 'a great dunce' and at another college 'his malignant spirit of railing and scandal was no less obnoxious'. He was appointed curate at Sandhurst but had to leave when parishioners complained that he stole their pigs. His father, an Anabaptist preacher at Hastings, gave him a job as curate. Oates falsely accused a local teacher of being a sodomite, and the teacher's father of high treason. Oates was fined £1,000 and jailed. He next served briefly in the Navy before being expelled for sodomy, then headed for London. Mixing with Catholics, he began to see the possibilities of his great plot. Feigning a conversion to Catholicism, he attended Jesuit seminaries on the continent to find out more about that religion. He returned to England and exploited anti-Catholic hysteria in 1677 to publicise his bogus plot to murder Charlies II, massacre Protestants, set fire to London and restore Catholicism. There was widespread panic and at least thirty-five innocent people were executed. He was granted a pension of £1,200 a year. Suspicions about Oates grew and two years later he was found guilty of perjury. He was sentenced to imprisonment for life and also to be whipped from Aldgate to Newgate, and then from Newgate to Tyburn. He was then to stand in the pillory on five days each year for the rest of his life. However, on his first day in the pillory he was almost killed, and thereafter he was excused the pillory. After the Revolution of 1688 he was freed and granted a pension.

OBSCENE PUBLICATIONS BILL In May 1857 the country got its first Bill dealing with pornography. The test of obscenity was later defined as whether the material was likely to 'deprave and corrupt'.

The Popish Plot perjurer Titus Oates in the pillory. He was sentenced to stand in the pillory on five days each year for the rest of his life. However, on his first day he was almost killed, and thereafter he was excused the pillory. After the Revolution of 1688 he was freed and granted a pension.

OLD BAILEY The Central Criminal Court stands at the junction of Newgate Street and Old Bailey in the City of London. NEWGATE PRISON, which stood on the site for centuries, was demolished in 1902 to make way for the court. Many of the major criminal trials of the last century took place there, including those of the KRAYS, the murderer DR CRIPPEN, and the traitor WILLIAM JOYCE.

OLDCASTLE, SIR JOHN (1378–1417) Leader of a Lollard revolt in 1414. Oldcastle seemed to have a dazzling future as a courtier and military man under his friend King Henry V. Successful military campaigns won him a 'European chivalric reputation'. His marriage to the great heiress Joan de la Pole brought the title of Lord Cobham and extensive territories. But he harboured proto-Protestant Lollards in his household and was in touch with the Hussites in Bohemia. When this became known in 1413 the clergy wanted to put him on trial, but Henry V offered him time to reconsider. Oldcastle, however, denounced the Pope and the clergy. He was condemned but Henry delayed his execution, still hoping that Oldcastle would change his mind. Instead Oldcastle escaped from the TOWER and, hiding out in London, planned a rising. Its main aim was the capture of the king. The plot was exposed, Oldcastle's few hundred followers were defeated and he went on the run. In 1417 he was taken near Welshpool and brought back to London to be executed. After his death Lollardry became a sect of the underclass, without appeal for the aristocracy.

OLD MINT, THE Notorious rookery in Southwark. It ran alongside the Borough High Street and had been exempt from City authority since Elizabethan times. Clearly an Act of 1623 and another in 1696 did not succeed in rooting out the criminals who mingled with the debtors who took refuge there, for another Act of 1722 declared that 'many evil-disposed and wicked Persons have . . . unlawfully assembled and associated themselves in and about a certain place in the Parish of St George in the

The Mint, Southwark, in 1825. In previous centuries it was a notorious criminal ghetto and refuge for debtors. When they were given amnesty in July 1723, the scene was 'like one of the Jewish tribes going out of Egypt'.

The Session House, the precursor of the Old Bailey, or Central Criminal Court. It was open to the air to stop court officials catching diseases from the prisoners. In April 1750 two prisoners with typhus infected everyone in the courtroom, and most died, including the judge and all the lawyers.

Woman witness at the Old Bailey in the eighteenth century. Trials were brief, often lasting only a few minutes. There were no defence lawyers – the judge was supposed to safeguard the interests of the defendant.

County of Surrey, commonly called or known by the name of Suffolk-Place, or the Mint, and have assured to themselves . . . pretended Privileges altogether scandalous and unwarrantable, and have committed great Frauds and Abuses upon many of his Majesty's good Subjects, and by Force and Violence protected themselves, and their wicked Accomplices, against Law and Justice'.

The new Act laid down that debtors owing less than £50 could not be arrested. HENRY MAYHEW and his colleague John Binney described what happened when the Act came into force:

> The exodus of the refugee-felons and debtors, in July, 1723 . . . is described as having been like one of the Jewish tribes going out of Egypt, for the train of 'Minters' is said to have included some thousands in its ranks, and the road towards Guildford (whither they were journeying to be cleared at the Quarter Sessions of their debts and penalties) to have been positively covered with the cavalcades of caravans, carts, horsemen, and foot-travellers.

In 1861 Hollingshead wrote that 'no speculator has been bold enough to grapple with the back streets – the human warrens – on the south side of the metropolis; to start from Bermondsey, on the borders of Deptford, and wriggle through the existing miles of dirt, vice and crime as far as the Lambeth Marshes'. He said scores of streets were 'filled with nothing but thieves, brown, unwholesome tramps' lodging houses and smoky receptacles for stolen goods'.

Things had not improved when Booth wrote about the area in 1891, finding nests of courts and alleys around St George's Church 'still harbouring an appalling amount of destitution not unmixed with crime' even though the Marshalsea Road had been cut through the Mint. He said the Mint still contained 'a very large amount of poverty and lawlessness, particularly in the many common lodging-houses'. Ten years later, visiting the area again, Booth 'brought away the same black picture, the same depression of soul'.

OLD ST PAUL'S The gothic pre-Great Fire cathedral was a haunt of thieves and conmen. They worked in packs, waylaying gawping country folk and tourists and going to great lengths to strip them of anything valuable. The playwright ROBERT GREENE, to whom we owe much of our knowledge of the Elizabethan underworld, wrote of them at work: 'There the nip [cutpurse] and the foist [pickpocket] as devoutly as if he were some zealous person, standeth soberly, with his eyes elevated to heaven, when his hand is either on the purse or in the pocket, surveying every corner of it for coin.'

The cutpurse might simply pretend to faint, then cut off the victim's purse as he leaned over to help, but some of the ploys were quite elaborate. Greene tells of a farmer who boasted that he had £40 in gold in his purse, and that no pickpocket or cutpurse was going to relieve him of it. A pickpocket who overheard him went away and gathered a team of criminals. One of them went to a debtor's prison and made a complaint against the farmer, and paid two sergeants to arrest him. The sergeants went to St Paul's and confronted the farmer, at which stage one of the criminal gang stepped forward and claimed the sergeants had no right to arrest a man within the precincts of the cathedral. A fight broke out and while pretending to rescue the farmer the criminals picked his purse.

OLIVER TWIST Hero of Dickens's novel (1837–8). An unhappy apprentice, he runs away and is taken in by FAGIN, Jewish leader of a gang of thieves. They include the murderous burglar Bill Sikes and the pickpocket 'The Artful Dodger'. Fagin was probably based on the famous Jewish fence IKEY SOLOMONS.

O'MAHONEY, MAURICE Violent criminal and SUPERGRASS. He admitted that in a long criminal career he got pleasure from maiming people with hammers or firearms. Arrested in 1974 he confessed to 102 offences, including armed robberies and burglaries. When he appeared at the Old Bailey in September 1974 the prosecution described him as the most guarded man in Britain. He was housed in what was called the 'grass house' at Chiswick police station, where he enjoyed regular visits from his girlfriend. He was also allowed to go on fishing trips and play golf. He was jailed for five years, and later helped the police successfully prosecute a large number of criminals. When he refused to give them any further help his armed guard was withdrawn. He told the *Guardian*: 'They've dropped me flat, the canary that fell from its perch. They told me to go out and get a decent job. The only trade I know is how to break into banks. I'm in a terrible state. I could go round the corner and cry.' O'Mahoney appeared at the Old Bailey in 1993 charged with a Post Office robbery, and said the police had asked him to do it so they could frame another man. He also claimed the police had been planning to kill him. He was acquitted.

ORDER OF SAINT FRANCIS Aristocratic exhibitionists and sensation-seekers who held orgiastic pseudo-religious rites at Medmenham Abbey on the Thames near West Wycombe. The guiding spirit was SIR FRANCIS DASHWOOD, rake, drunkard and a future Chancellor of the Exchequer.

ORDINARIES, THE Egregious prison chaplains at Newgate. They tried to persuade condemned prisoners to dictate their life stories, then sold them in pamphlet form on the day of the execution for up to 6*d*. If the prisoner refused the Ordinary would make up his biography. They were universally despised. John Allen, who was ordinary early in the eighteenth century, was also an undertaker. His successor, Paul Lorrain, had been Samuel Pepys's secretary. He was tireless in his efforts to get the condemned to confess and repent. The pirate Dalziel threatened to kick him downstairs, and another pirate, CAPTAIN KIDD, was drunk when he arrived at EXECUTION DOCK. Fortunately for Lorrain, the rope used to hang Kidd broke and the captain crashed to the ground. Lorrain claimed that before he was strung up again Kidd 'repented with all his heart, and died in Christian love and charity with all the world'.

OVEREND GURNEY & CO Bank whose collapse in 1866 caused a major financial panic and led to the prosecution of the directors. Overend, whose premises at the junction of Lombard Street and Birchin Lane were known as the 'Corner House', was among the most important financial institutions. The bank had unwisely diversified into shipbuilding, railway financing and trading in commodities, locking up capital. When it went public it was already secretly bankrupt. It collapsed on 10 May 1866 with debts of more than £5 million. The Bank of England, with which it had a difficult relationship, refused to help. In the ensuing crisis the Bank of England propped up the system by lending banks, discount houses and merchants the 'phenomenal' sum of £4 million in one day, and the situation was stabilised. Bank rate was increased to ten per cent, so high that a three-year industrial depression followed. There were other consequences: many finance and credit companies went bankrupt, 1,600 shareholders gave up their private carriages and the great railway contractors Peto and Betts went under with debts of £4 million. Corruption and mismanagement in other railway companies were exposed: shipbuilding in London, once an important industry, ended. Many thousands lost their jobs. In the trial which followed Gurney's failure the directors of the company were cleared (Kynaston, *The City of London*, Vol. 1).

OVET, JACK (?–1708) Highwayman who took the code of gallantry to extremes. A country squire he was robbing called him a coward because he was sheltering behind his pistols. Ovet dismounted and fought a sword duel with the squire, whom he eventually ran through. On another occasion he was smitten by a young woman on a stage coach he robbed. He wrote to her, promising to reform if she would marry him. She replied that she did not want to become a 'hempen widow'. Soon afterwards in 1708 he was caught and hanged. *See* HIGHWAYMEN

P

PAGE, DAMARIS (?–1669) Known to Pepys as 'the Great Bawd of the Seamen'. She operated in the Ratcliffe Highway area of Wapping, an ancient haunt of vice, and imported and exported whores, the former including Venetian women who were among the most expensive and expert in Europe. Her brothels at Ratcliffe were for poor seamen, but she also operated at the luxury end of the trade nearer the court. She was charged at Clerkenwell magistrates court with manslaughter over the death of a prostitute who died while having an abortion with an oyster fork. Page was sentenced to death but was reprieved after PLEADING HER BELLY. She spent some years in Newgate. After her death in 1669 her will showed that she had made a fortune from vice.

PAGE, WILLIAM (flourished 1755–8) One of the most successful of all highwaymen. A meticulous planner, ingenious and lucky, he committed more than 300 robberies with his partner Darwell. Page made maps of the areas where he intended to strike. He would dress in gentleman's finery, drive out in a phaeton and pair and having hidden the coach in a wood change into highwayman's attire. After the robbery he would return to the carriage and change back into his finery. Page's luck and audacity got him out of many scrapes. When stopped, as he often was when driving away after his crimes, he would warn those who questioned him that a highwayman was stalking the road. He sometimes even claimed that he too had been a victim of the highwayman. Inevitably he was finally arrested, and EARL FERRERS, who was among his victims, was one of the witnesses against him. Page put forward an ingenious defence. He found out that the year before Ferrers had been excommunicated for contempt of the Bishop of London's consistory court. Page claimed Ferrers could not give evidence against him because of his excommunication, and the court had to accept his defence. His respite was short. The following month he was arrested for highway robbery at Blackheath and hanged at Maidstone in March 1758. *See* HIGHWAYMEN

PALMER, JOHN Major time-share cheat and associate of London gangsters. In May 2001 John 'Goldfinger' Palmer, cleared fourteen years earlier of melting down gold from the BRINK'S-MAT raid at his West Country mansion before selling it back to the owners, bankers Johnson Matthey, was jailed for eight years. The Old Bailey heard how he cheated British tourists out of about £30 million in the world's biggest timeshare swindle. Police believe he used the cash from the bullion smelting to found a £300 million timeshare and money laundering empire. Palmer, 50, was said to be near to tears as he appealed to the judge for leniency. He is being sued for up to £80 million by people he cheated.

PARDONS In the eighteenth century judges who thought mercy appropriate would usually refer the case to the Home Office. GEORGE III scrutinised such cases himself (*see* DR WILLIAM DODD). Sometimes the pardon arrived after the prisoner had been hanged (*see* HALF-HANGED SMITH).

PAUL, BRENDA DEAN Actress and Bright Young Thing of the Twenties who became a drug addict. Robert Murphy (*Smash and Grab*) recalls that someone said of Paul that 'she wakes each morning with a song on her lips'. In the hedonistic London of BRILLIANT CHANG and other drug dealers and addicts she was introduced to cocaine and heroin. Her memoirs describe an attempt to cure her with hyoscine, which was supposed to put her to sleep for several days.

> For five hours I writhed without ceasing like a fish in a net, this way and that, sometimes arched back, so that my heels touched the back of my head. I fell on the floor. It took five nurses to hold me down and I remained painfully conscious the whole time in a complete terror of phantasmagoria. The kind of hallucinations and nightmare that no ordinary person could possibly imagine. Terrible faces, quite clear, seeming possessed with some supernatural force, floated before my eyes.

The effects on her health were so serious that her doctor decided she was better off taking morphine. She was still addicted in the 1950s.

PAYNE, CYNTHIA (1932–) The so-called 'Luncheon Voucher Madam'. She ran a brothel in Streatham, south-west London, which catered for pensioners and men with waning sexual powers, who got discounts. She was sent to prison in 1978 for 'keeping a disorderly house'.

Cynthia Payne leaving prison. Dubbed Madam Sin and the Luncheon Voucher Madam, she wanted to provide a public service but ended up in prison.

Her obsession with sex began early. She became a prostitute's maid and then a reluctant prostitute. Finally she found her *métier*, which was organising sex parties for other people. On 6 December 1978 she was giving a Christmas party at her brothel in Ambleside Avenue, Streatham, when it was raided by a large number of police. They found a queue of men on the stairs. In the Mirror Room a couple were close to climax. When ordered to stop what he was doing the man said: 'Not until I've come.' Other couples were copulating elsewhere. The men bought tokens which looked like luncheon vouchers for £25 on arrival. They gave them to the girls of their choice, and Cynthia later retrieved them and paid the girls their cut. For £25 the customers could eat and drink as much as they liked, watch a sex film and a live lesbian display, and have sex.

Sixteen months later, by which time she was a national celebrity referred to in the tabloid newspapers as 'Madam Sin', Cynthia Payne went on trial at Inner London Crown Court. She was sentenced to eighteen months' imprisonment for keeping a disorderly house. This was reduced on appeal to six months. She was also heavily fined. None of her clients was charged. *The Spectator*, pointing out that prostitution is not an offence, wrote: 'If prostitution be an offence punishable at law, then a law should be written and enacted to this effect; and, if offence it be, then the man and woman, clearly sharing the offence, should be held to be both of them culpable.'

Mrs Payne had no appetite for sex. She told the court: 'I know it makes some people happy but to me it's like having a cup of tea. One of my slaves said that sex with me would be like growing spuds in a Ming case.'

PEACE, CHARLES (1832–79) Burglar and murderer who became a Victorian bogeyman. In August 1876 he shot dead a police constable as he escaped after a burglary near Manchester. Two brothers, John and William Habron, were arrested for the murder and William, who had made threats against the policeman, was sentenced to death, later commuted to penal servitude because he was only 18. Peace went to the trial and later said he had greatly enjoyed it. He returned to his home in Sheffield, where he had a business as a picture framer and dealer in musical instruments. For some time he had been pursuing a neighbour's wife, Mrs Katherine Dyson. At first she encouraged him, was then embarrassed and moved to a new part of Sheffield with her husband Arthur. One night she went to the outside toilet and found Peace standing there with a revolver. She screamed and her husband chased Peace, who turned and shot him dead. Peace moved to Peckham in south London where he lived an outwardly respectable life, attending church and holding musical evenings at his home, at which he played the violin – rather well, apparently. At the same time he was carrying out a series of audacious burglaries. He would carry his housebreaking tools in his violin case and travel by his own pony and trap. In October 1878 two policemen cornered him in a back garden in Blackheath. He fired two shots, shouting warnings to the constables to keep away. One was hit in the arm but the other overpowered Peace. He confessed to the murder of the Manchester policeman, and William Habron was released. As he was being taken north to stand trial for the murder of Arthur Dyson he escaped from the train window, but hurt himself on landing and was soon recaptured. Peace was hanged in February 1879. 'Bloody poor bacon, this,' he grumbled about his last breakfast. On the scaffold he asked the hangman, WILLIAM MARWOOD, if he could have a drink. Marwood refused and pulled the lever activating the trap-door. Marwood said afterwards that he expected trouble from Peace, 'because he was such a desperate man. But bless you, my dear sir, he passed away like a summer's eve.' Peace became the anti-hero of many penny-dreadfuls, known as the devil man because of his simian features. Some women found him attractive.

PEARL, CORA (*c*. 1836–86) One of the most celebrated of all the *grandes horizontales*, as the courtesans of the later nineteenth century were known. Her real name was Emma Crouch, and her father wrote the popular Victorian song *Kathleen Mavourneen* before vanishing to America. Afterwards Cora, who was educated in France, stayed with her grandmother in London and was apprenticed to a milliner. Her *Memoirs* say she was first seduced by a diamond merchant she met on the way to church in Marylebone. She took to going to the notorious ARGYLL ROOMS in Great Windmill Street. The proprietor, Robert Bignall, took her to Paris, and she took the first of a series of her aristocratic lovers. They included William, Prince of Orange, several dukes, and Prince Achille Murat, who was only 17. Photographs reveal Cora to have been a rather ordinary looking little woman, but clearly she had that mysterious secret ingredient, sex appeal. She was described as having 'an almost superhuman knowledge of the art of love' and 'an inordinate talent for voluptuous eccentricities'. These attributes brought an appropriate income, and at one stage Cora had a stable of sixty horses. She created a scandal by riding astride in the Bois de Boulogne. She also introduced make-up to Paris in 1864, according to *Le Figaro*. She caused another sensation by appearing almost naked as Cupid in Offenbach's *Orpheus in the Underworld*.

Cora Pearl, the Englishwoman who became one of Paris's greatest grandes horizontales. *Despite her lack of beauty, it was agreed she had an incredible sexual allure and great experience.*

Her most important lover was Prince Napoleon, known as Plon-Plon. He was said to 'resemble a villain in a third-rate reportory company', but he kept her in splendid style in a great house. During the Franco-Prussian War Cora left Paris. She booked into the Grosvenor Hotel in London under an assumed name in 1870. She was recognised and the manager asked her to leave. 'That's how it is in England,' she remarked. Back in Paris Plon-Plon had lost his money and his influence, so she took up with the young son of a wealthy butcher. Her extravagance ruined him and, rejected, he tried to shoot himself in her house. Things went downhill for Cora from then on. She was forced to sell her house and its treasures, and then she wrote her *Memoirs*. She died of cancer in 1886 aged about 50 (Barker and Carr, *The Black Plaque Guide to London*).

PEEL, SIR ROBERT (1788–1850) Home Secretary who created the Metropolitan Police Force in 1829. Peel had long felt the need of such a force but had to fight the deeply entrenched prejudice against professional police. He also reformed penal legislation, reducing the number of offences carrying the death penalty. *See* POLICE

PERCEVAL, SPENCER (1762–1812) Prime Minister, assassinated in the lobby of the House of Commons in 1812. His killer, John Bellingham, had a long-standing grievance against the government which derived from his bankrupt shipping merchant business in Russia. He claimed compensation and during a long and unsuccessful campaign wrote to Perceval, who was then Chancellor of the

Exchequer. On the evening of 11 May 1812 he hid behind the folding doors of the lobby leading into the Commons chamber with a pair of pistols. When Perceval appeared he shot him in the chest. The Prime Minister staggered back dying, shot through the heart. Bellingham did not try to escape and simply attempted to vindicate himself. He was questioned by MPs who were also Middlesex magistrates. His motive, he said, was 'want of redress and denial of justice on the part of the government'. During his trial at the Old Bailey he made a long, rambling address to the jury. He was executed outside Newgate and his body sent to St Bartholomew's Hospital for dissection. Bellingham was almost certainly insane, but the law had not yet devised methods for dealing with such cases. Parliament voted a large sum of money for his widow and children.

PERREAU, DANIEL AND ROBERT Twin brothers executed for forgery. The brothers were London wine merchants. In 1775 they were charged with forging a money bond for £7,500 in the name of William Adair. Central to this affair, one of the most sensational criminal trials ever, was Daniel's mistress Margaret Rudd. An adventuress, she had been the mistress of JOHN WILKES and the DUKE OF CUMBERLAND. She gave evidence to the magistrate SIR JOHN FIELDING that she had forged a bond while Daniel Perreau held a knife to her throat. Fielding incorrectly admitted her as an 'evidence' or witness against the Perreaus: she had pleaded guilty to a forgery, but the brothers were accused of a *different* forgery. Probably because of this her evidence was not called, but her allegations against Daniel were well known and the brothers were sentenced to hang. They were almost certainly innocent.

It was widely believed that Rudd had framed the brothers, perhaps because she was tired of Daniel. A campaign to get them pardoned had widespread support. Rudd's former lover Wilkes thought it monstrous she should go unpunished. Newspapers came up with the story that Rudd was the mistress of William Adair, the supposed victim of the forgery. Seventy-eight bankers and merchants signed a petition pleading with GEORGE III to show mercy. He refused, and in January 1776 the brothers were executed at Tyburn before an unruly crowd of 30,000. Because of the crowd's hostility to the hangman three hundred constables surrounded the gallows.

Such was the public clamour something had to be done about Rudd. LORD CHIEF JUSTICE MANSFIELD overruled Sir John Fielding and Rudd stood trial for the forgery she had admitted. She was found not guilty, and after the trial she took up with Lord Lytton, who had used his influence behind the scenes during her trial. She wrote her memoirs in 1777 and they became a best-seller. Among her later lovers was JAMES BOSWELL.

PERRY, HENRY Soldier who murdered a family of four. Perry was staying with the Cornish family in Stukeley Road, Forest Gate, in April 1919. After a quarrel he stabbed and bludgeoned Mrs Cornish to death. He waited until her 5-year-old daughter Marie came home from school. He told the police: 'I hit her on the head with a hammer in the passage. She fell down and I struck her again, then picked her up and threw her in the cellar.' The Cornish's other daughter, 14-year-old Alice, then arrived and Perry killed her too. Finally Mr Cornish came in from work. He said to Perry: 'What game are you having? I am going to hand you over to the police.' Perry hit him on the head with an axe, and he staggered into the street saying 'that soldier . . .' He died two days later. Perry, who said he had been captured and tortured by the Turks during the war, claimed 'voices' had told him to murder the Cornishes. He was executed in July 1919.

PEWSEY, ISAAC Syphilitic crazed by the mercury treatment. Mary Hill told a court in 1698 that she heard her mistress, Sara Pewsey, cry out 'What, will you murder me?' and ran into the parlour of the house in Mile End Green, Stepney, to find Isaac 'twisting and squeezing his wife's hands over a cane chair'. Sara was heavily pregnant but Isaac kicked her all the way from the parlour into the kitchen. Apparently Isaac had violent outbursts when he was undergoing salivation – a stinking effusion from the mouth caused by the mercury. He would call Sara, who tried to look after him, 'bitch, whore . . . without any provocation or cause'. Once during his salivation he 'did . . . throw a basin of nasty spittle on her . . . which stunk so intolerably that the maid could hardly come near her to help her off with her clothes'.

PHILLIPS, TERESIA CONSTANTIA (1709–65) Beauty seduced by the future Earl of Chesterfield when she was only 12. The earl, author of the famous moralising *Letters* to his natural son Philip, offered her £200 to leave him out of her lively memoirs, *An Apologia for the Conduct of Mrs Teresia Constantia Phillips*. She countered with a demand for £500, he refused and she published. The *Apologia* contains details of her love affairs, many marriages and trial for bigamy. She may have been the Mrs Phillips who ran an important sex shop in

Half Moon Street. She settled in Kingston, Jamaica, where she was elected Mistress of the Revels at carnival time. *See* CONDOMS

PHYSICIANS V APOTHECARIES Medical practitioners constantly at odds. The physicians claimed that only they were competent to practise medicine, because of their long training – up to fourteen years at Oxford or Cambridge. The members of the Worshipful Society of the Art and Mystery of the Apothecaries of the City of London, on the other hand, served only a seven-year apprenticeship. At the beginning of the eighteenth century London had about 1,000 apothecaries and sixty to eighty physicians, nowhere near enough.

The antagonisms came to a head in 1701 when a butcher named John Seal sued an apothecary who had failed to cure him despite his expenditure of £50 on potions. He said he was 'forced to apply myself to the Dispensary at the College of Physicians, where I received my cure in about six weeks time, for under forty shillings charge in medicines'. The court found in his favour, but when the case went to the House of Lords they ruled that it was against the public interest to stop the apothecaries practising. There were too few physicians, and their treatment was too expensive for most people.

PICKERING, LAURENCE Called by the writer ROBERT GREENE the King of the Cutpurses in the Elizabethan underworld. Pickering seems to have been an underworld organiser. He held weekly meetings of thieves at his house in Kent Street, where intelligence about likely victims and the activities of the law enforcers was exchanged. He was the brother-in-law of the Tyburn hangman Bull.

PITTS, SHIRLEY Known as 'Queen of the Shoplifters' in the Fifties of the last century. By the age of 20 Pitts, who came from a noted south London crime family, was at the top of her profession. She and a large team she led plundered Harrods and other London stores. She also organised shoplifting trips to Berlin, Paris and Geneva. Pitts once escaped from prison while pregnant. When she died in 1992 the underworld laid on a suitable funeral: fifteen Daimlers, musicians playing 'I'm in Heaven' and a floral tribute in the shape of a Harrods shopping bag. *See* SHOPLIFTING

PLANTAGENET, MARGARET Victim of a shocking execution in 1541. Margaret, Countess of Salisbury and close friend of Mary Tudor, was 71 when she went to the block. She was the mother of Cardinal Pole, an outspoken opponent of KING HENRY VIII's break with Rome and divorce from Catherine of Aragon. She refused to lay her head on the block but instead ran about the platform shouting that she was no traitor. The executioner ran after her, hacking at her with the axe until she died.

PLEADING HER BELLY Women condemned to death were given a stay of execution if they could prove they were pregnant. It was held to be wrong to kill the child as well as the mother. As soon as they arrived in prison women would sleep with a man known as a 'child getter' and at the appropriate time present themselves to a committee of matrons. If they satisfied the matrons they were pregnant they were safe at least until the baby was born. Visitors to Newgate were shocked by the obvious soliciting of women desperate to be impregnated. Filch, in Gay's *The Beggar's Opera*, says: '. . . one would need to have the constitution of a horse to go through the business. Since the favourite child-getter [in Newgate] was disabled by a mishap I have picked up a little money by helping the ladies to a pregnancy against their being called down to sentence.'

PODOLA, GUNTHER (?–1959) The last person to be hanged for murdering a policeman. Podola, a German immigrant, was trapped in a call-box at South Kensington after making a blackmail call. He escaped and ran into a block of flats in Onslow Square, pursued by two detective sergeants. He was recaptured and guarded by one of the detectives, Raymond Purdy, while the other tried to find the housekeeper. Podola drew a pistol and shot Purdy dead. Three days later he was traced to a Kensington hotel. Police broke down the door of his room as he prepared to open fire. He was hanged in November 1959.

POLE-TYLNEY-LONG-WELLESLEY, WILLIAM (?–1857) Nephew of the Duke of Wellington who seems to have been without a single redeeming feature. He went to the Peninsular War on the duke's staff but was sent home, having shown interest only in horses, women and gambling. He married an heiress named Catherine Tylney-Long and soon got through her money, although he kept several of her names. He went to Italy, where he seduced the wife of a Guards officer on the slopes of Mount Vesuvius. He got her pregnant and his wife Catherine died of a heart attack. His treatment of her lost him custody of their three children. He set about trying to get his hands on the children's money. He threatened to kill their guardian, the Duke of Wellington, and accused him of having an affair with his friend, Mrs

Arbuthnot. His accused his widow's sisters, who were raising the children, of incest. He tried to kidnap his daughter, for which he was sent to the Fleet Prison. Released, he went with his younger son to Calais, where he stayed in a luxury hotel and employed a dozen servants. The managers allowed him to run up a bill of £29,000 in less than a year. After a period in prison in France he returned to London. By now he was Earl of Mornington, but he had to live on £10 a week allowed him by the Duke of Wellington. When he died in 1857 the *Morning Chronicle* said of him that he was 'redeemed by no single virtue, adorned by no single grace, his life gone out without even a single flicker of repentance'.

POLICE *see* following page

POOK, EDMUND Youth who almost certainly got away with murder. On the morning of 26 April 1871 a police constable discovered the body of Jane Clousen in Kidbrooke Lane, Eltham. Nearby was a hammer which had been used to beat her to death. Jane, a 17-year-old domestic servant, was pregnant. She had worked for a printer named Pook until twelve days before the murder, and had been dismissed for intimacy with Pook's son Edmund, who was 20. Edmund had been with Jane on the evening of the murder and had been seen running away from Kidbrooke Lane, covered in mud. There were bloodstains on his clothes, and he had bought the hammer used to kill the girl. On the evening she was murdered Jane had told her landlady that she was meeting Edmund. The evidence seemed conclusive, and Edmund's defence correspondingly feeble. He claimed he had spent the evening at Lewisham watching the house of a girlfriend. He attributed the bloodstains on his clothes to nosebleeds and a cut on his wrist. He denied getting Jane pregnant.

At his trial, however, the judge summed up in his favour, saying most of the evidence was circumstantial. Pook was acquitted, although almost no one except the judge and jury believed him innocent.

PORNOGRAPHY *see* pp. 196 and 197

PORN SQUAD The Soho pornography boom of the 1960s and 1970s brought extortionate demands for payoffs by the police. Some members of the Yard's Obscene Publications Squad – known as the Porn Squad and the Dirty Squad – and officers up to the rank of commander were involved. Pornographers including John Mason and JIMMY HUMPHREYS paid the officers anything from £2,000 to £14,000 to open new shops and a weekly £500 to be allowed to operate them. The wholesalers who imported the pornographic films and books paid £200 a week. They could afford it. One of them, Big Jeff Phillips, drove a Rolls-Royce and lived in a manor house in Berkshire.

The greed and indiscretion of the police were remarkable. Mason was given a CID tie to wear while he visited the storeroom in Holborn police station where confiscated pornography was stored. Some of it had been taken from his own shops – from time to time the Porn Squad had to raid the premises of their clients. Mason was allowed to buy back his own material from the police station.

BERNIE SILVER, the vice racketeer who had taken over the MESSINA vice empire, was among the most important figures in the early years of the porn revolution: but the most colourful was Jimmy Humphreys, a club-owner who with his wife Rusty would bring about the downfall of the Porn Squad.

Every bribe and gift and dirty weekend with Porn Squad members and girls from his clubs at his holiday home in Ibiza was secretly recorded by Humphreys in a series of diaries which he kept in safety-deposit boxes. Among the senior officers mentioned in the diaries were Commander Wally Virgo of the CID, Bill Moody, head of the Obscene Publications Squad, the greediest of all, and Commander Ken Drury, head of the Flying Squad.

In 1971 investigators from the *Sunday People* named Silver and Humphreys, among others, as pornographers. The *Sunday People* also claimed there was police corruption. There was a police investigation but it came to nothing. In February 1972 the paper said: 'Police officers in London, particularly some of those attached to Scotland Yard's Obscene Publications Department, are being systematically bribed by dealers in pornography.'

On page one of the paper was a photograph of Drury on holiday in Cyprus with Humphreys and his wife. Drury and his wife had been their guests during a two-week stay in Famagusta, and Humphreys had paid most of the costs, which came to more than £500. In March Drury was suspended from duty and on 1 May he resigned. He sold his story to the *News of the World* for £10,000. In it he claimed Humphreys was a police informer, a 'grass'. Humphreys, who still had his diaries, spilled the beans.

In February 1976 Drury, Virgo and Moody were arrested, with dozens of other officers. At their trial the judge estimated that Moody and Virgo had between them taken £100,000 from the pornographers, 'a scale which beggars description'. Virgo and Moody were each sentenced to twelve

Continued on p. 198

POLICE

When two families, seven people in all, were murdered in their homes on the Ratcliffe Highway in 1811 John William Ward, a future Foreign Secretary, said: 'I had rather half a dozen people's throats should be cut in Ratcliffe Highway every three or four years than be the subject of domiciliary visits, spies, and all the rest of Fouché's [the French police chief] contrivances.' This was typical of the attitude which kept London without a professional police force.

In the eighteenth century London was policed by about 3,000 unarmed men – Constables, Beadles and the parish Watch and Ward, overseen by Justices of the Peace and Magistrates. During the century the number of offences magistrates could deal with increased greatly, and this workload was a disincentive to take on the unpaid role. Some magistrates became notorious as 'trading justices' – men who would take payment in return for bail or other concessions. Payment could be in kind, particularly sex. Some magistrates were honest and hard-working. Among the first to bring order and honesty to the profession was the novelist and leading magistrate HENRY FIELDING. Fielding and his blind half-brother JOHN FIELDING took the first steps towards founding a police force by making the Bow Street court a police office, which sifted evidence and brought some order to the process of the law by weeding out malicious and trivial complaints. The Fieldings created a team of detectives, known as BOW STREET RUNNERS, paid one guinea a week and a share in the rewards from successful prosecutions.

Constables were unpaid and were elected annually from rotas of citizens. The job was unpopular and citizens would pay deputies to do it on their behalf. The constable, who answered to the magistrate, was a powerful officer at a local level. He policed prostitutes, gypsies, peddlers, and others regarded as

The decrepit men of the Marylebone Watch light their lanterns and prepare to go on patrol. Each man had a 'beat' to walk, but they preferred to stay in their sentry boxes. Tipsy Regency gents out on the town used to push the boxes over with the Watchmen, who were known as Charlies, inside.

semi-criminal. 'They could punish mothers for bearing bastards, whip vagabonds, force the unwilling to work, uphold apprentice statutes, confine begging to those licensed to beg, restrain lunatics and detain suspicious characters' (McLynn, *Crime and Punishment in Eighteenth-Century England*). They also had to detain and hold criminals. No wonder men were reluctant to take on the job. If they were lucky they got a 'Tyburn ticket', a certificate of exemption issued to those who had arrested an offender whose crime was serious enough to merit being sent to TYBURN.

The Watch, supervised by the Beadle, operated from the Watch House, and the officers, poorly paid, usually old and decrepit, issued forth in the evenings with their lanterns and cudgels to patrol the streets. Officers of the Watch had sentry boxes from which they were supposed to venture on the hour to patrol the streets. Because the responsibilities of the Watch ended at the parish boundaries criminals knew that they were unlikely to be caught: they could steal in one parish and lie low in another. The GORDON RIOTS of 1780, when Watchmen melted into the night as anti-Catholic mobs wrecked the newly-rebuilt Newgate Prison and burned and looted for days, were a further spur to the setting up of a regular police force.

While the FOOTPAD and the HIGHWAYMAN were the greatest threat to the public, the greatest incitements to crime in the capital were the shipping and the cargoes on the Thames. In 1798 the Thames Police Force was founded by PATRICK COLQUHOUN and John Harriott.

Between 1812 and 1827 five Parliamentary Select Committees rejected the idea of full-scale professional policing for the capital. The realisation that things could not go on this way came gradually, with a shift in both public and political opinion. Pitt made a modest start in 1792 with the Middlesex Justices' Act, which set up seven new police offices modelled on Bow Street. Each had paid magistrates and paid policemen. The Home Secretary, ROBERT PEEL, moved to get a new Select Committee in February 1828 and used the criminal committal figures, which showed that crime was indeed growing, to make his point.

In the end, the Metropolitan Police Bill had an easy passage through Parliament in 1829, and in May 1830, when the force was fully operational, the 'New Police' comprised 3,200 men. Peel was aware of the corruption of the Bow Street Runners, so he emphasised the preventive rather than the detective role of the new force. The police were to establish a visible presence on the streets and lower ranks were forbidden to mix with criminals and informers in public houses. Constables wore blue swallow-tailcoats and top hats, they were armed with truncheons and, on dangerous beats, cutlasses. A small detective force was formed in 1842. The City, which had strongly opposed the new force, retained its old inefficient watch system until 1839, when the City of London Police was formed.

Police searching for criminals scrutinise a queue of destitute men, women and children outside a dosshouse. The new police were hated by the underclass, who attacked and maimed them whenever they got a chance. In parts of London this attitude persists.

The new force faced bitter hostility, principally but not only among the poor. They were vilified, spat upon, stoned, blinded, mutilated, spiked on railings and generally molested. In 1831 an unarmed constable was stabbed to death at riots in Clerkenwell. A coroner's jury brought in a verdict of 'justifiable homicide'. An annual banquet was held to commemorate the event for many years afterwards.

Working-class fear and suspicion of the police has deep roots. The KRAY TWINS believed 'coppers is dirt' and the costers of the Victorian East End would have agreed. HENRY MAYHEW wrote: 'To serve out a policeman is the bravest act by which a costermonger can distinguish himself.' They would have a whip-round for those who attacked the police. A coster with a grudge against a particular policeman might track him for months waiting for an opportunity to strike.

At first low pay and drunkenness led to a huge turnover of staff. 'Within two years of 1829 nearly 2,000 men had been dismissed for drunkenness and over 1,000 had resigned, unwilling to endure the discipline, danger and unpopularity of police duty in return for less than £1 a week.' (Inwood)

The old Watch had been known as 'Charleys', and the Bow Street Runners as 'Robin Redbreasts' or 'Raw Lobsters' because of their red vests. Among their clients the new force were known first as 'peelers' and 'bobbies', obvious references to Sir Robert Peel. Then they were known as 'coppers' from cop for arrest, and 'crushers', perhaps from the size of their boots. More recently there have been 'bluebottles', 'rozzers', 'fuzz', 'filth' and of course Old Bill.

In 1877 some of the senior detectives at Scotland Yard were found guilty of corruption. The reputation of the police improved steadily throughout the twentieth century, and major gang trials made some senior detectives household names, the Krays' nemesis LEONARD 'NIPPER' READ in particular. Pay improved, as did the public perception, but there were setbacks. A series of trials showed that there was systemic corruption in the London force, especially among those officers who had contact with the porn and vice industries of Soho. Towards the end of the twentieth century tensions between the police and the black communities led to serious RIOTS. *See* PORNOGRAPHY

PORNOGRAPHY

Samuel Pepys bought *L'Eschole des filles* in 1688 and found it 'the most bawdy, lewd book that ever I saw'. He thought it rather worse than Pietro Aretino's *La puttane errante* and wrote in his diary that he was ashamed of reading it. Interestingly his copy came in plain binding. He resolved to burn it as soon as he had read it, for fear it might be discovered among his books. He did burn it, having read it first, and recorded that it was a 'rightly lewd work, but not yet amiss for a sober man to read over to inform himself in the villainy of the world'.

At the beginning of the eighteenth century London's main pornographer was EDMUND CURLL, who seems to have been the first Englishman to be convicted for publishing erotica when he was arraigned over *Venus in the Cloister, or The Nun in her Smock*, in 1727. At this time explicit guides to London prostitutes and what they had to offer were popular, the best-known being Jack Harris's *List of Covent-Garden Ladies*.

In 1830 there was a successful prosecution over the Marquis de Sade's *Juliette*, and publishers were repeatedly indicted over John Cleland's *Fanny Hill or Memoirs of a Woman of Pleasure*. The book had been banned on its publication in 1749 and was prosecuted again on its revival in 1963 under the Obscene Publications Act. Some of the nineteenth-century prosecutions were private actions brought by the Society for the Suppression of Vice, which was founded in 1802. The wit Sydney Smith called it 'a society for suppressing the vices of those whose incomes do not succeed £500 per annum'. Over the next fifty years the society brought 159 prosecutions, almost all of them successful. Street hawkers were prosecuted for selling indecent photographs. The important publisher Vizetelly was jailed for three years for publishing 'indecent literature', which in this case included Zola's *La Terre*, 'the obscenity of which is so revolting and brutal' that it was banned and destroyed. There were 'obscene' Christmas cards, theatrical and music hall posters and advertisements. A peddler was convicted of publishing an 'obscene' tooth-pick case: it had on its inside lid a picture of a copulating couple. In May 1857 the country got its first OBSCENE PUBLICATIONS BILL. The test of obscenity was defined by Lord Chief Justice Cockburn in 1868 as whether the material was likely to 'deprave and corrupt'. One of the centres of the trade was the tangle of streets later swept away by the building of Kingsway and the Aldwych. The most important concentration was in Holywell Street, and eleven years after the Obscene Publications Bill was passed the *Saturday Review* wrote of it: '. . . the dunghill is in full heat, seething and steaming with its old pestilence.' The Society for the Suppression of Vice had to admit that for all its zeal in prosecuting pornographers, they showed 'a tendency to revive'.

It was in the Holywell Street area that WILLIAM DUGDALE, Edward Dyer and other pornographers plied a lively trade, spied on by the agents of the society. Dugdale was an important pornographer: his premises in Holywell Street was raided several times and he was jailed.

Towards the end of the Victorian era the volume of pornography grew, with titles such as *Lady Bumtickler's Revels* and *Raped on the Railway: A True Story of a Lady Who Was First Ravished and then Flagellated on the Scotch Express*.

Soho had been a vice centre for centuries, and when Holywell Street and the surrounding area were demolished the pornographers found a new home there and in nearby Charing Cross Road. By the 1940s it was London's main centre for what was quaintly called 'erotica'. In the 1950s the police had a Home Office list of more than a thousand banned books. It included the works of the crime novelist Hank Janson and a novel by Maupassant, Defoe's *Moll Flanders* and James Hanley's *Boy*. Hundreds of magazines were also banned.

Much of the material sold in the 'dirty book' shops came from America. The more expensive items came from Paris. There was also an insipid domestically produced pornography. One of the most successful of these local pornographers in the 1950s was RON 'THE DUSTMAN' DAVEY. He began by selling photographs of women members of a nudist club he belonged to. Another figure to emerge in the fifties was Ronald Eric Mason, known as John. Mason, who made one of the biggest porn fortunes, would later claim that he started bribing police officers in 1953, and that in all he had paid off a total of 148 officers. These included Detective Chief Superintendent BILL MOODY, to whom he once gave £14,000 to get a friend off a criminal charge. The greed and indiscretion of the officers ended in trials and long prison sentences.

After the trials the Obscene Publications Squad was disbanded and their role was taken by a squad of uniformed officers. There was much for them to do. A new generation of young pornographers had moved in and business was booming. Videos and films were more explicit than ever, as were books and magazines. Sex shops blatantly advertised 'toys' and 'aids'.

One of the most successful of the new pornographers was David Sullivan, an economics graduate who quickly acquired a multi-million pound fortune and a property empire by publishing increasingly explicit magazines and films. He told the *News of the World*: 'I hotted the porn market up. I thought if the police were going to raid me for fairly soft porn, then I might as well make it hard.' In common with most of the new men, and in contrast with men like Silver, he courted the limelight, apparently thinking that any publicity was good for business. An example of this was his naming one of his magazines *Whitehouse* after Mrs Mary Whitehouse, a morals campaigner of the time.

Today many newsagents have shelves of soft-porn magazines on open display. No one could have imagined this situation arising when the state made its ill-advised attempt to suppress D.H. Lawrence's *LADY CHATTERLEY'S LOVER* in 1960. Roy Jenkins's new Obscene Publication Bill had become law the year before. It gave a defence of publication 'for the public good'.

One of the heroes of the struggle to stamp out pornography was Sir Archibald Bodkin (1864–1941). In 1923 when he was Director of Public Prosecutions he surprised delegates to a League of Nations conference with his strong objection to any attempt to define pornography. He argued that it was a matter of common sense. One of the authors whose works he described as 'disgusting filth' was Sigmund Freud. Freud's English publishers, Allen & Unwin, had to promise that his works would be kept in plain wrappers on top shelves among naturist magazine before Sir Archibald would allow publication (Donaldson, *Brewer's Rogues, Villains and Eccentrics*). *See* PORN SQUAD years in prison, although Virgo was freed after ten months. Drury got eight years. Of the seventy-four officers investigated, twelve resigned, twenty-eight retired, eight were dismissed and thirteen were jailed.

PRENDERGAST, SARAH Pioneering bawd of the late eighteenth century who was the first to see the possibilities of King's Place, then George Court, an insignificant alley off Pall Mall which later became an enclave of elite brothels. She was involved in an amusing sexual scandal. Among her clients was the Earl of Harrington, known as 'LORD FUMBLE' and described by *The Westminster Magazine* in 1773 as 'a person of the most exceptional immorality'. Mrs Prendergast kept only three girls as full-time whores in her seraglio, sending out for others when business was brisk. One night the earl rejected her three resident whores, so she sent to Mrs Butler's establishment at Westminster for 'a couple of fresh country tits'. The girls Mrs Butler sent over were Elizabeth Cummins, known as Country Bet, and a girl known as Black-Eyed Susan. The doddery old earl indulged in 'manual dalliance' for a couple of hours and afterwards declared that he was highly satisfied. The girls, however, were by no means satisfied with the three guineas he gave each of them. They had been led to expect much more.

When they got back to Westminster Mrs Butler demanded her cut of twenty five per cent. Susan paid up, but Country Bet, feeling that she had already been cheated, refused. Mother Butler took away her clothes, and Bet went to the police. No one could have foreseen the far-reaching consequences. Mrs Butler was convicted of stealing the clothes, and of keeping a brothel. Furthermore, she was convicted of 'causing Elizabeth to go in company with another woman of the lowest order to meet the Earl of Harrington at the house of Mrs Prendergast, who keeps a seraglio in King's Place'. Mrs Butler's husband, a sergeant in the Grenadier Guards, was convicted of helping his wife's brothel-keeping by transporting girls to the seraglios in King's Place, where they were dressed as country maids. 'The Earl attended Mrs Prendergast's seraglio on Sunday, Mondays, Wednesdays and Fridays, having two females at a time.'

The earl was furious. A scandal sheet had picked up the story, and he 'flew into a great Passion, stuttering and Swearing and Shouting' that he would not be able to show his face at court. The sensible Mrs Prendergast bought up all available copies of the paper and paid Betty £5 to drop the prosecution. She assured the earl that neither girl would work again in the King's Place brothels, a promise she had no intention or means of keeping.

To cheer everyone up she decided to hold a grand ball, at which 'the finest Women in all Europe would appear *in puris naturalibus*'. Lord Fumble contributed 50 guineas towards the costs. The ball was a great success. Aristocratic ladies flocked to join the professional beauties and danced nude for hours while an orchestra played facing the wall so as not to embarrass them. Afterwards there was a banquet. Mrs Prendergast made a profit of £1,000, but she soon lost one of her best customers, Lord Fumble dying a few weeks later in 1779. Nevertheless she retired wealthy (Burford, *Royal St James's*).

PRESS-GANGS Hired thugs who forcibly enlisted mariners and others to serve in the Royal Navy. Merchant ships which had just berthed might be stripped of their crews, from the master down, before they had time to go ashore or even collect their pay. The gangs were paid a bounty for every man they pressed, and although their victims were supposed to be able-bodied the press-gangs were not particular. They paid surgeons a shilling a head to pass the men as fit. In 1754 HMS *Bristol* was supplied with 68 pressed men. Only eighteen of them were fit for duty, and the rest had to be put ashore.The gangs broke into houses and dragged the occupants away. A Mr William Godfrey was dragged through the streets of London with only one slipper on and thrown into the stinking hold of a ship. A journeyman barber who was seized in 1770 managed to get a hearing before John Wilkes, who was sitting in the Guildhall as a magistrate. Wilkes freed him. A Mr Lewis was dragged from his house and clung to the railings outside. The gang beat his hands with their cudgels in order to make him let go. 'The Navy Board offered compensation, but Mr Lewis determined to go to law' (Picard, *Dr Johnson's London*). A gang who tried to press a bridegroom at his wedding were set upon by the guests, aided by the parson. If sailors got news of a press-gang they hid. In 1740 the Thames and the riverside haunts of sailors on leave were combed by the gangs. After they had gone 16,000 sailors came out of hiding (Hutchinson, *The Press-Gang Afloat and Ashore*). Lord Mansfield, who was Lord Chief Justice between 1756 and 1788, justified the press-gang on the basis that it was founded on 'immemorial custom', and was necessary to the defence of the realm. This attitude on the part of officialdom could frustrate attempts to bring violent press-gangs to justice. Seven of the men who seized Mr Godfrey, were arrested. The *Newgate Calendar* records their trial in 1755: 'Being brought to trial at the Guildhall of the City of London, Sturges and Dodsey, having surrendered themselves, and pleading for mercy, were acquitted; but the others were found guilty. While the Court was deliberating on the punishment to be inflicted on them some officers of Government interceded, and prayed that their country might not long be deprived of their services against the French, then at war with us; and in consequence thereof, and on their knees suing for mercy, backed by Mr Godfrey's generous forgiveness, they were sentenced to only ten days' imprisonment.' Pressing ended in 1833.

PRICE, CHARLES (?–1786) Ingenious swindler and forger who defrauded his victims of £100,000. In 1780 he forged the first of a series of Bank of England notes, getting his innocent servant to pass them. The servant was eventually caught and imprisoned but Price, who had by then forged notes with a face value of £1,400, got away. He also posed as a Methodist preacher to cheat people of large sums. At one stage he disguised himself with an eye-patch and used the name Brank. He cheated a man named Samuel Foote out of £500 by advertising for a partner in a brewery, and others through a phoney marriage agency. It was said he disguised himself to cheat his own father out of an expensive suit. He was arrested in 1786 and committed suicide in Tothill Fields prison.

PRINCESS ANNE (1950–) Royal involved in a kidnap attempt. On the evening of 20 March 1974 Princess Anne and her husband, Captain Mark Phillips, were being driven down the Mall towards Buckingham Palace. A car pulled across in front of them, forcing them to stop. The driver of the other car, Ian Ball, approached, firing a gun. A bullet hit the princess's car, and when her police bodyguard, Jim Beaton, moved towards the gunman he was shot in the chest. The gunman opened the door of the princess's car and grabbed the princess's arm. She shouted 'Get away! Get away!' Mark Phillips caught her by the other arm and pulled her back. The princess broke free of Ball's grip and slammed the car door. Jim Beaton put his hand over the muzzle of the gun, and Ball fired, hitting him in the hand and shoulder. Also shot were the chauffeur, a police officer and a journalist, Brian McConnell, who was passing and tried to help. More police arrived and Ball was arrested. He had planned to hold the princess for a £3 million ransom. He was sent to a psychiatric hospital.

PRISONS *see* following page

PROFUMO SCANDAL Affair that ruined the career of a senior Conservative politician, cost the life of an innocent man, showed the Establishment at its worst and thrust various denizens of the demi-monde into the limelight. In 1963, John Profumo, Minister for War, met CHRISTINE KEELER by the swimming pool at Cliveden, Lord Astor's country home. When he returned to London he phoned her and they began a brief affair.

Keeler was an unhappy woman with a lot of brief love affairs. She entertained Profumo at the London flat of a society osteopath, Stephen Ward. Another of her lovers was Captain Ivanov, the Russian Naval Attaché. The links between Keeler, the Russian Ivanov and Profumo became known to the security services, there were fears the minister could be blackmailed and eventually Sir Norman Brook, Secretary to the Cabinet, mentioned this to Profumo. The minister quickly broke off his affair with Keeler, and there the matter might have ended, had it not been for Christine Keeler's complicated love life. Two of her lovers, both West Indians, were involved in a fight and one, John Edgecombe, slashed the face of the other, Lucky Gordon. The following month Christine was visiting her friend MANDY RICE-DAVIES, mistress of the rack-renter PETER RACHMAN, who was living at Ward's flat in Wimpole Mews. Edgecombe turned up and when the girls refused to let him in opened fire on the door with a pistol. He was arrested and the Press began to take an interest in Keeler and Ward. When Keeler told them she had been sleeping with both Profumo and Ivanov a first-rate scandal broke.

In the Commons Profumo felt he had to deny the rumours that were now circulating. He said there had never been any impropriety between him and Christine Keeler, and threatened to sue anyone who repeated the allegations. Then the Home Secretary asked the Commissioner of Police to investigate the affair. Police put pressure on Ward, who wrote letters to senior politicians and the Press saying that 'my efforts to conceal the fact that Mr Profumo had not told the truth in Parliament made it look as if I myself had something to hide'. On 29 May 1963 the Lord Chancellor began an investigation and three days later Profumo confessed to his wife, the actress Valerie Hobson. Profumo issued a statement saying that he had lied to the House of Commons, and then resigned.

The hounding of Stephen Ward began. Dozens of potential witnesses were interviewed by the police, some of them several times. On 22 July 1963 Ward appeared at the Old Bailey. There were five charges, mainly of living on the earnings of prostitutes.

Continued on p. 203

PRISONS

The FLEET PRISON on the eastern bank of the Fleet River – now Farringdon Street – was the oldest of London's many jails, possibly dating from just after the Conquest. By the middle of the sixteenth century London had fourteen prisons. Virtually any offence, however trivial, could lead to prison: vagrancy, being away from your parish without good cause and with no visible means of support, debt, slander, suspicion of witchcraft and many others. Debt was also a common cause of imprisonment.

Prisons were regarded by those who ran them as machines for making money. They were woefully rewarded by the city authorities, and had to squeeze money out of the prisoners. At the end of the seventeenth century a Mr Geary offered the warden of the Wood Street Compter or Counter £1,500 a year for the contract to feed the prisoners. There were about 2,000 prisoners and he hoped to make a profit of more than 100 per cent. For those without money life in London's prisons was hell. The poet William Fennor wrote an account of his time in Wood Street after he had been sent there for assault in 1616. He described how a prisoner had to pay bribes – the word he used was 'GARNISH' – for even the slightest service or comfort. When he arrived he would be allowed to choose which part of the prison he would stay in. If he chose the best accommodation, the Master's Side, he passed through a series of doors, at each of which he had to pay a bribe, anything from a shilling to half a crown, to a turnkey for the privilege of having the door opened. When he reached the hall of the Master's Side he had to pay another two shillings or his cloak and hat and other items of clothing would be taken away. Finally he was ushered into his cell, 'a narrow, cobweb-festooned room with some straw and a pair of dirty sheets and a candle-end for illumination. And this was the best grade of accommodation which the Compter offered'. Fennor had to pay for his food and drink, and for his first meal also had to treat all the other prisoners on the Master's Side, as well as the keepers and even the vintner's boy who poured out the claret, to a meal. At the other end of the scale was The Hole, where those without funds were dumped to die of starvation, disease or cold. The playwright Thomas Dekker wrote: 'Art thou poor and in prison? Then art thou buried before thou art dead. Thou carriest thy winding sheet on thy back . . . Thou liest upon thy bier and treadest upon thy grave at every step. If there be any hell on earth, here thou especially shall be sure to find it. If there be degrees of torment in hell, here thou shall taste them.' Dekker was writing from experience, having spent time in one of London's prisons.

Men at hard labour in Coldbath Fields Prison. Two cringing prisoners, one touching his cap as a mark of respect for the warder, are directed to take their turn. Much of the labour had no product, and was designed to exhaust and humiliate.

In 1742, the year his father Robert's corrupt career as Britain's first Prime Minister came to an end, Horace Walpole described a truly horrifying incident involving some parish constables who locked up prostitutes in the prison known as St Martin's Roundhouse:

> A parcel of drunken constables took it into their heads to put the laws in execution against disorderly persons, and so took up every woman they met, till they had collected five or six-and-twenty, all of whom they thrust into St Martin's Roundhouse, where they kept them all night, with the doors and windows closed. The poor creatures, who could not stir or breathe, screamed as long as they had any

breath left, begging at least for water: one poor wretch said she was worth eighteen pence, and would gladly give it for a draught of water, but in vain! So well did they keep them there, that in the morning four were found stifled to death, two died soon after and a dozen more are in a shocking way. In short, it is horrid to think what the poor creatures suffered: several of them were beggars, who, from having no lodging, were necessarily found in the street, and others honest labouring women. One of the dead was a poor washerwoman, big with child, who was returning home late from washing.

London's prisons, particularly NEWGATE, were long known for sexual licence and riotous indiscipline as well as cruelty. In the seventeenth and eighteenth centuries prison sentences were short, and society meted out retribution by transportation, branding, whipping, the pillory or the gallows. Only a minority of offenders were imprisoned as a form of punishment. This began to change gradually around the end of the eighteenth century, and in the nineteenth century was replaced by a brutal regime of close confinement and deprivation. A Parliamentary report in 1836 suggested that the lax regime was turning first-time offenders into hardened criminals, and a wave of reforms followed. New prisons were built: Pentonville was started in 1840, Tothill Fields at Westminster in 1836, the Surrey House of Correction at Wandsworth in 1849, the same year as the City House of Correction at Holloway, and Brixton, for women, in 1853. Older prisons were modernised and improved. TRANSPORTATION was abolished altogether during the 1860s. Those of the capital's convicts who would formerly have been dumped in Australia or confined in the HULKS, dilapidated warships at Woolwich and Chatham, now faced longer sentences in tougher prisons. The new prisons aimed to inflict 'a just measure of pain'. The first step was to end fraternisation. Prisoners were masked with 'scotch caps' which covered the face, and it was an offence to 'reveal the features', punishable by solitary confinement on bread and water. Under the 'separate system' convicts were confined one to a cell, with their work brought in to them. The aim, as the Surveyor-General of Prisons, Sir Joshua Jebb, said, was to ensure that prisoners would be 'effectually prevented from holding communication with, or even being seen sufficiently to be recognised by, other prisoners'. The belief was that this isolation would cause the convict to reflect on his wickedness and to repent, and that it would also stop experienced criminals from corrupting the young. The capital's criminals were already recognised as the most hardened and expert in the country, and those the new system didn't break became even more fiercely committed to their code and their caste.

The system was abandoned in the 1860s. It didn't work, as the statistics for re-offenders showed. Crime rose by a fifth in the forty years or so it was in force, and the figures for re-offenders showed little improvement. The effects on mental and physical health were obvious: following the introduction of the system at Pentonville in 1842, mental breakdowns there were four times the level of other prisons.

There were other ways of breaking the spirit of recalcitrant convicts, of which solitary confinement was just the most severe. In solitary, men were kept in total darkness on a diet of bread and water. The ordinary prison diet was hardly adequate, and certainly not appetising. Detailed instructions were given to the prison cooks to make the food as unpalatable as possible.

The Irish revolutionary Michael Davitt, who became an MP, stunned the House and the nation with his description of the privations he experienced in prison. He had seen men eat candle ends, the marrow of putrid bones they were meant to grind up, even a used poultice found in a garbage heap by the prison cesspool.

Pointless work was another device for crushing the spirit. Shot drill was one example. Men would stand around three sides of a square, three yards apart, with a warder at the centre. At the end of each line was a pile of cannon balls. On command the first man would take a ball from the pile, walk to his neighbour and place the ball on the ground in front of him. The second man would pick it up and place it in front of the next man, and so on. When the whole pile had been transferred to the other end of the line the process was reversed. The task continued for an hour and a quarter every afternoon, and the men showed obvious signs of distress.

The TREADWHEEL, a series of steps on a giant wheel turned by prisoners endlessly climbing on it for up to six hours a day in compartments two feet wide, was simply a form of torture, which could

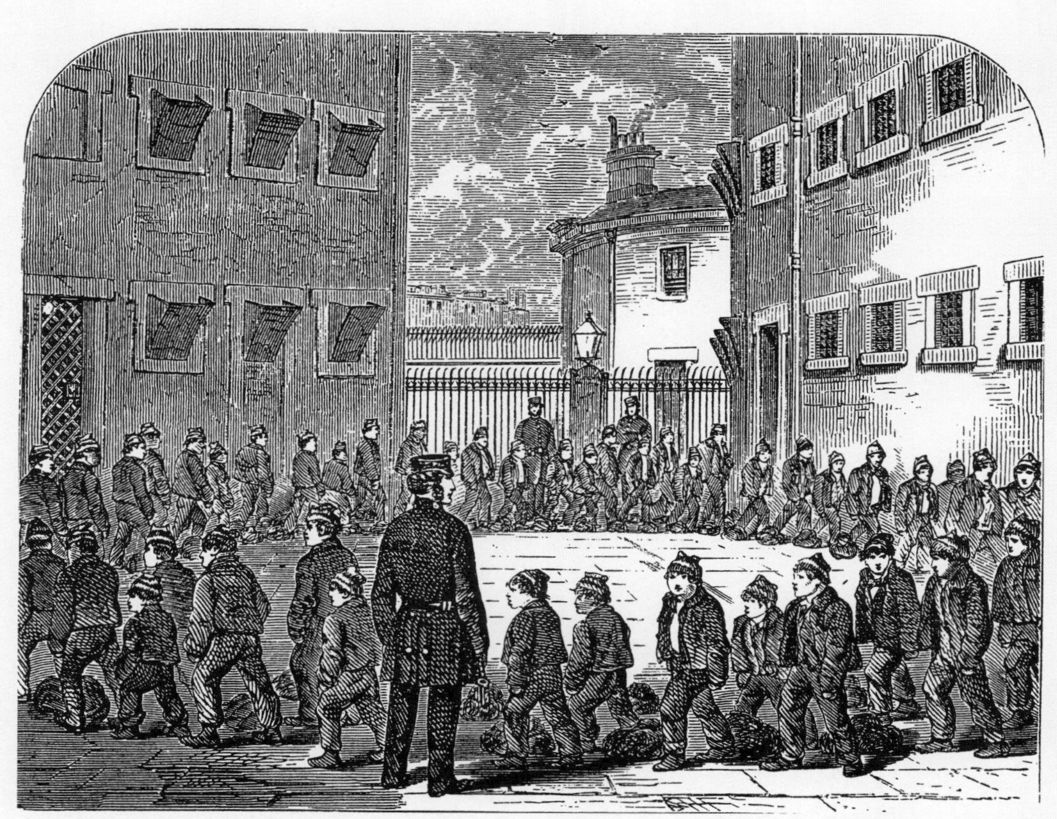

Children exercising at Tothill Fields Prison, Westminster. A child of 7 was held to be responsible for its actions in law: on one day in 1814 five children, one aged 8, were sentenced to death at the Old Bailey. There were many more in the throngs of homeless youngsters to take their places.

make men cry with pain and despair. It was justified on the basis that the hard labour the men had been sentenced to must be just that – hard. Another particularly pointless form of labour was the crank. Prisoners who were thought to be malingering by the medical officers would have this drum-like machine installed in their cells, and would be required to turn the crank handle ten thousand times a day. As the handle turned, sand was scooped from the bottom of the drum and tipped out again. The turns of the handle were recorded on a meter. It was reckoned that this lonely torture took the average prisoner eight hours and twenty minutes of continuous labour.

After transportation ended and the prison population grew hulks were introduced as temporary prisons in 1776, although they continued to be used well into the nineteenth century. The regime was harsh and vice and disease carried off many of those held on the ships. Others were shot trying to escape.

Reform came gradually. Advances in psychiatry led to an interest in the make-up of the criminal and the introduction of doctors and psychiatrists into prisons. A more liberal penal policy was possible after 1895 when the domineering Sir Edmund Du Cane, chairman of the Prison Commissioners for nearly 20 years, resigned. The ban on prisoners speaking to each other continued, at least informally, but many learned how to speak without moving their lips, like ventriloquists. Jim Whelan, an IRA gunman sentenced for a raid on a Liverpool Post Office in 1923, described hearing a working party returning to Maidstone jail: 'There was a strange susurration which I could not locate or identify. It was rather like the murmuring sound made by the wings of a thousand starlings when they are ganging up in the autumn. I was hearing the "silent system" of the English convict prisons for the first time.' This was the sound of prisoners speaking without moving their lips, what Whelan called 'the lip-still murmur'.

Discipline was still harsh in the inter-war years. Flogging was a common punishment. The prisoner would be strapped to a flogging triangle, his head held so that he could not turn and see who was inflicting the punishment. There were also punishment diets. The bread and water diet was still used, although it could be imposed for only fifteen days. The other punishment diet, bread, porridge and potatoes, could be imposed for as long as forty-two days. The burglar RUBY SPARKS was so hungry he ate the table in his Dartmoor cell:

> At Dartmoor I chewed away nearly all my wooden table in the punishment cell. Ate it, mouthful by mouthful, swallowing the chewed pulp of splinters to fill my empty stomach. The table wasn't anything particularly tasty. It was just a scrubbed wooden ledge, soggy from years of Dartmoor's eternal dampness. It's flavour was soap and firewood. But I'd eaten it. The lot!

He was given another fourteen days' punishment and put in a cell with a metal table.

The regular food was bad enough. Prisoner Wilfred Macartney recalled:

> The next thing the prison authorities do is to publish a false prospectus in the shape of a menu given to every convict; and how pleasant it is to read the various dinners! – 'treacle pudding' (it's like a dirty old rubber sponge); 'beef-steak pudding'; 'savoury bacon'; 'sea pie' ; 'beef stew'; 'pork soup' etc. The vile concoctions masquerading under these honest names would make a hungry pig vomit with disgust. 'Sea pie' is a mess in a filthy tin, defying analysis. The top is a livid scum, patterned with a pallid tracery of cooling grey grease, and just below this fearsome surface rests a lump of grey matter like an incised tumour, the dirty dices of pale pink, half-cooked carrots heightening the diseased anatomical resemblance. The stuff looks as if its real home were a white pail in an operating theatre.

Prisons today are badly overcrowded but not, it is hoped, as badly as one night in August 1984. A Report of Her Majesty's Chief Inspector of Prisons stated that on that night out of a prison population of 42,000 more than a quarter

> . . . were locked in a cell on their own and had to use chamber pots when they wished to urinate or defecate; over a third had to use chamber pots while sharing a cell (or occasionally in a dormitory) with one or more inmates; about a ninth were in accommodation with integral sanitation; about a quarter were in accommodation which allowed them access to communal toilets . . . when the time for slopping out comes the prisoners queue up with their pots for the few toilets on the landing. The stench of urine and excrement pervades the prison. So awful is the procedure that many prisoners become constipated – others prefer to use their pants, hurling them and their contents out of the window when morning comes.

During the trial Keeler and Rice-Davies, among others, admitted selling sex in Ward's flat and giving money to Ward. They also said that when he could afford it he gave them more money than they ever gave him. Nevertheless Ward was found guilty. By then he was beyond the reach of his persecutors, having taken a fatal drugs overdose.

PROGL, ZOE Burglar and jailbreaker. In July 1960 when Progl was serving her fourth term for housebreaking in Holloway Prison a rope was thrown over the wall and she climbed out to a waiting car. It was the first time a woman had escaped from the jail. She went on the run for five months with her boyfriend and daughter. When she was caught she had eighteen months added to her sentence. She sued the Metropolitan Police over a diamond ring which had been given to her by a former lover, TOMMY 'SCARFACE' SMITHSON. When she married for the second time in 1964 Progl, known as the 'Queen of the Underworld', told the *Sunday Mirror* that her husband knew 'about my days as a burglar, as a rich man's mistress and as a gangster's moll'.

PROSTITUTES' EARNINGS Comparison of prostitutes' rates over the centuries is difficult. The poet and playwright Thomas Nashe (1567–1601) says he visited an expensive whorehouse where the asking price was a steep half a crown, although the customers could try to negotiate a better rate. The going rate for what Pepys called a 'bout' was 6*d* in the country and up to 20*d* in the city. Christopher Hibbert writes in *The Road to Tyburn* that eighteenth-century street prostitutes, many of them little more than children, would hire out their bodies for 6*d*. BOSWELL wrote of 'the splendid Madam at fifty guineas a night down to the civil nymph with white thread stockings who tramps along the Strand and will resign her engaging person . . . for a pint of wine and a shilling'. The Victorian prostitute SWINDLING SAL got as much as £5 or as little as a few shillings. The diarist WALTER, who wrote *My Secret Life*, would pay widely different rates according to the state of his finances. When they were low he often paid 5*s*. When he could afford it he would pay a guinea, although he said ten shillings would get 'as nice a one as was needed' from among the streetwalkers. The sailor's tarts of the East End might have to accept shillings or even pence, or just a drink.

The gangster ARTHUR HARDING described in *East End Underworld* the prices the local girls charged around 1900:

> There were two kinds of girl. Those who went up West and mixed with the toffs. They would get as much as ten shillings a time or even £1 and they would ride home in hansom cabs . . . the girls who stayed at Spitalfields were very poor. That was what you called a 'fourpenny touch' or a 'knee trembler' – they wouldn't stay with you all night . . . Even if you stayed all night with girls like that it was only a couple of shillings.

After the First World War wages fell rapidly. In the 1930s when the average wage was about £3 5*s* street prostitutes in the better areas of the West End were charging 10*s* or £1, which was more than many men could afford. In the 1950s police who arrested the ponce of a Soho prostitute found a notebook kept by the woman's maid. In it were day-by-day records of the prostitute's earnings. These showed that in a six-hour period each night she would have about thirty customers. Her income over twenty days was nearly £1,000 – amounting to an enormous tax-free annual income of more than £18,000. The prostitute Edna Kallman told the Attilio MESSINA trial in 1959 that in eight years she earned about £40,000 working her beat in New Bond Street.

By the 1960s streetwalkers in Mayfair were charging between £5 and £10 for brief sex, in Soho the range was between £4 and £6 and the girls in South Kensington, Maida Vale and Bayswater were said to be charging from £3 to £5. Girls in Hyde Park charged £1 for sex standing up, and £2 for it lying down. The Hyde Park women also used taxis for sex, and charged between £2 and £3.

Call-girls at the top of the profession were said to charge up to £50 for the night, and girls further down the scale up to £30. Today the women at King's Cross charge around £30.

PROSTITUTION *see* opposite

PROTECTION Extortion of regular payments by threats or violence, practised by schoolchildren and gangsters. A certain stage in the development of gangsterism is characterised by widespread extortion of this kind. It is mostly a neighbourhood crime, and successful gangsters are usually those who have the imagination to see wider possibilities. ARTHUR HARDING remained a neighbourhood gangster, preying on spielers. Many of the Jewish gangsters of his time, the BESSARABIANS and ODESSIANS, and Harding's enemy DARKY THE COON, extorted money from prostitutes and stallholders.

'Chirrupers' operated a non-violent variant. They threatened music hall performers that unless they got a cut of their fee they would heckle. On the other hand, in return for a cut they would greet the performance with a storm of applause. The *East London Advertiser* reported in March 1888 a case that came before Lambeth Police Court. A large gang of chirrupers were in the habit of hanging around the music halls and accosting 'well-known artistes' as they approached the stage door. The magistrates 'rightly designated [the practice] as a very shameful one'.

PRYNNE, WILLIAM (1600–69) Puritan lawyer and pamphleteer. In 1632 he published *Histriomastix: The Players Scourge*, an attack on the theatre and on women actors. This was seen as an insult to Queen Henrietta Maria, who performed in masques. Prynne was condemned to the pillory, life imprisonment, had his ears cropped and his nose slit,

Continued on p. 213

PROSTITUTION

The first serious attempt to regulate prostitution was made in 1161, when Henry II set up London's first official red-light district. In granting the Bishop of Winchester rights to exploit the eighteen brothels on BANKSIDE in Southwark the king laid down regulations for the conduct of the sex industry. The rules have a strangely modern ring. Women in London today are allowed to sell sex but not to solicit, which makes it almost impossible for them to operate within the law. Henry's Act decreed that they were allowed to sit in their doorways, but not to solicit in any way. They were forbidden to get men's attention by calling or gesturing, or seizing them by the gown or harness. They could not swear, grimace or throw stones at passing men, 'on pain of three days and nights in jail plus a fine of eight and sixpence.'

The king's Act set out what rights the whores did have. The brothel-keepers were forbidden to detain prostitutes against their will. The women were not allowed to board in the brothels. They were not to be charged more than 14*d* per week for their rooms. This suggests that apart from the rent the women were allowed to keep the money they earned. Women were free to give up whoring if they wished. Married women and nuns were not to be accepted as prostitutes. The brothel owners were also forbidden to keep 'any woman that hath the perilous infirmity of burning'. Sexually transmitted diseases were already a problem, although they did not get their medical names until the sixteenth century.

In 1240 Cock Lane in Smithfield was also designated an official red-light district, acknowledging the fact that the area was already known for its brothels. In 1394 the Mayor and Corporation issued the *Regulations as to the Street Walkers by Night and Women of Bad Repute*. The first part ordered that

The harlot's descent continues in Plate 4 of Hogarth's series. She is pounding hemp, amid diseased and imbecile whores, one of whom is beginning to take away her fine clothes. The pitiless warder threatens her with a cane. Her bunter or servant leers on the right.

nobody should be so bold as to go about by night unless he had good reason and was a respectable person. The ordinance goes on to talk of broils and affrays and murders caused by those '. . . consorting with common harlots at taverns . . . and other places of ill-repute . . .' These women are to keep themselves in the assigned places, the stews on the south bank of the Thames and Cock Lane. If caught elsewhere their clothes would be forfeit, becoming the property of the City officers. In practice these officers were more likely to take the women's jewellery.

A woman named Margaret was accused of procuring a young girl named Isobel Lane and forcing her to sell sex to Lombards and others in the brothels of Bankside and elsewhere. Margaret was also accused of taking a girl named Joan Makelyn to a house in the parish of St Colemanstreet for sex with a Lombard who paid her 12*d*. This case tells us a lot about whoring, including what a whore charged a customer, although we don't know exactly what service was provided. It shows that whores found good customers among the foreign community, and that there was now little hope of confining the sex industry within a few ghettoes. In January 1440 there was a case involving 'immorality, common procurers and prostitutes' in Tower Ward. Katherine Frenssh, Sibil Eddon, Katherine Clerk and Alice Moysant all admitted many acts of immorality with Ralph Hislam, Simon Strengere and many others in the preceding month.

Economic changes under the Tudors deepened the reservoir of poverty which supplied the brothels with the constant source of new girls they needed. Enclosures, rising prices, changes in agriculture all forced people off the land, and the population grew after a long period of stagnation. Women were worst hit by the drift from the land.

Some women found work as servants in noble or bourgeois houses, but they were constantly preyed on by the men of the house. The feeling that it was better to sell sex than have to give it free to an employer led to many becoming prostitutes. Others simply had no choice. Bankside, with its inns and streets of brothels, beckoned. Brothels continued to multiply. A ballad of the time, 'The Merry Man's Resolution', laments:

The Haymarket, epicentre of the vice industry and haunt of hordes of streetwalkers, at midnight some time in the 1860s. Short skirts were an indication that the woman was a prostitute.

Farewell to the Bankside
Farewell to Blackman's Street
Where with my bouncing lasses
I oftentimes did meet . . .
And all the smirking wenches
That dwell in Redriff town . . .
Now farewell to St Giles
That standeth in the Fields
And farewell to Turnbal Street
For that no comfort yields.
In Whitecross Street and Golden Lane
Do strapping lasses dwell
And so there do in every street
Twixt that and Clerkenwell.
At Cowcross and at Smithfield
I have much pleasure found
Where wenches like to fairies
Did often trace the ground.

In 1546 HENRY VIII suppressed the brothels in Southwark, denouncing 'toleration of such dissolute and miserable persons as . . . have suffered to dwell beside London and elsewhere, in common open places called the stews, and there without punishment or correction to exercise their abominable and detestable sin.' Henry died the following year 'in agony of syphilitic periostitis in a stupor' at the age of 55. His successor, the sickly boy-king Edward VI, ordered the reopening of the Southwark brothels in 1550.

The court of James I, who came to the throne in 1603, has been described as 'extravagant and disorderly, with hard drinking and immorality winked at' (Davis, *The Early Stuarts*) and personal hygiene was not scrupulous. One English lady of the court complained that she was always lousy after visiting it, and the king was a dirty drunkard who seldom washed.

The case books of the Middlesex Sessions show that the loose morals of the court were echoed in society at large. In 1608 Emma Robinson was accused of being a 'Common Queane' and of sitting at her door until midnight 'to entertaine lewd persons that resort untoe her'. Ellen Allen was fined for enticing a Dutchman to lewdness. While he was kissing her, her maid stole his dagger. Elizabeth Basse 'keepeth a notorious bawdy house whereby murther was like to have been committed'.

The explosive growth of whoring was such that in 1622 even James I was moved to expostulate, issuing the ordinance *Touching on Disorderly Houses in Saffron Hille*:

> . . . of long time hath been and still is much pestered with divers immodest lascivious and shameless women generally reputed for notorious common whores, who are entertained into divers houses for base and filthy lucre sake accruing to the private benefit of the Landlords and Tenants of such houses . . . such women who do usually sit at the doors . . . do allure and shamefully call in . . . such as pass by to the great corruption.

Even reinforced by mass raids this does not seem to have worked. The following year another ordinance was issued, and the list of places raided gives some idea of the spread of prostitution: Cowcross, Cock Lane, Smithfield, St John Street

Whores and pickpockets combine to rob a man under the Piazza in Covent Garden. The area was the centre of the sex industry until late in the eighteenth century, when the centre of gravity of vice moved west to St James's.

THE "GHOST'S" HOUSE IN COCK LANE.

The 'ghost house' in Cock Lane. A Mr Parsons got his daughter to claim she had seen a ghost while in bed. It was exposed as a fraud and Parsons was put in the pillory, where the crowd had a whip-round to help pay his debts. In the fourteenth century the street was the only licensed walk for prostitutes.

in Clerkenwell, Norton Folgate (just outside Bishopsgate), Shoreditch, Wapping, Whitechapel, Petticoat Lane, Charterhouse, Bloomsbury and Ratcliffe. During just one day in August 1620 at Middlesex Quarter Sessions nineteen women were convicted of brothel-keeping. Sixteen of them were located in the Cowcross area.

Charles I, who came to the throne in 1625, brought in an Act which described how wayfarers in the old brothel areas of Cowcross, Turnmill Street, Charterhouse Lane, Saffron Hill, Bloomsbury, Petticoat Lane, Wapping, Ratcliff and other places were 'pestered with many immodest, lascivious and shameless women generally reputed for notorious common and professed whores'.

In 1641, on the eve of the Civil War, Parliament decreed that prostitution was no longer a crime, but only a public nuisance, to be treated as gross indecency if committed in public. If this was a first step towards liberalising the laws surrounding prostitution it was reversed by the events of the Civil War, which broke out the following year and ended with the victorious Puritans setting up the Commonwealth. Brothels had to go, and also theatres, gambling houses, race-courses, even maypoles. The death penalty was decreed for a second offence of adultery. Some brothels, such as Oxford Kate's in Bow Street, continued to trade, probably because their owners had influential customers. From 1652 whores found a new outlet: coffee houses became a meeting places for them and their clients. The Restoration brought an inevitable reaction. CHARLES II's court became 'one vast brothel'. The king, easygoing and cynical, had little patience for affairs of state, and spent much of his time with a string of mistresses.

Commercial theatres, which became popular in the middle of the sixteenth century, gave a new focus to the sex industry. Soon the theatres were thronged with whores looking for pick-ups. This situation continued into the twentieth century and for a long time 'actress' was synonymous with 'whore'. There was a gusto about eighteenth-century vice unmatched before or since.The pioneer criminologist and magistrate PATRICK COLQUHOUN reckoned that in 1800 there were 50,000 women living partly by prostitution. This is just an informed guess, and Colquhoun is tentative in his conclusions, but his estimate is close to that reached by others. In 1789 the German visitor J.W. von Archenholz (*A Picture of England*) said 'London is said to contain 50,000 prostitutes, without reckoning kept mistresses'.

The spectacle of swarms of young whores impudently soliciting in the fashionable streets and public entertainments of nineteenth-century London shocked visitors. One estimate put the number of prostitutes in London in the 1830s at 80,000, many of them little more than children. MAYHEW's collaborator Bracebridge Hemyng thought there were 80,000 around the mid-century, and he was in a better position to judge than most. To contemporaries the throngs of whores were a scandal that seemed to be getting worse, and there is no doubt that vice was one of Victorian London's biggest industries.

Whores paraded in the most fashionable parts of the city, particularly inside and outside the main theatres, calling out, plucking at the coatsleeves of passing men and making lewd gestures and suggestions. Covent Garden, the Haymarket, Regent Street, Cremorne Gardens, Fleet Street, the front of Somerset House and St James's were bazaars of sexual opportunity. There were women for every taste and every pocket. Child prostitutes pestered single men. At night hideous hags haunted the parks, their diseased bodies disguised by rags and darkness. During the day Hyde Park saw successful high-class whores flaunting their wealth by driving among fashionable upper-class promenaders in expensive carriages. Although Victorian moralists called it the road to ruin, prostitution brought relative affluence to many young women and riches to some. At the same time, a warning to the carefree young women promenading in the same streets were the ghastly diseased veterans of harlotry.

Soho in the Sixties. Soho remained the centre of the sex industry for many years after the Street Offences Act was passed in 1959.

The situation in the theatres was as bad as it had been in the eighteenth century. Fashionably dressed prostitutes roamed the bars and saloons, 'disturbing the performance, insulting the sober-minded and modest part of the audience, and exhibiting the most indecent appearance and gestures with perfect impunity, nay, apparently with encouragement from the profligate of the other sex' (*Address to the Guardian Society*, anonymous pamphlet, 1817). The women could be seen going from box to box, or flaunting themselves among the patrons in the saloons. Well-dressed whores with genteel manners – they could usually be distinguished from respectable women by their shorter skirts – mingled there with single men. These were superior prostitutes, whose appearance could stand scrutiny in the harsh light of the saloons, unlike their sisters in the streets outside.

As the century wore on the focus of the trade changed, moving west to follow the exodus of wealthy clients from the City, whose population was falling rapidly. Redevelopment had an inevitable effect. As the better-off residents moved out of Stepney and the run-down area was colonised by warehouses and offices prostitution dwindled, as it did in Lambeth. The Strand and Charing Cross were now the eastern end of the main prostitute belt, although the depopulation of the City would soon affect the Strand too.

Prostitutes who did not simply take their customers to a nearby alley for brief sex against a wall needed somewhere to entertain them. This was not a problem for the high-class courtesans, who would have houses of their own, perhaps as far away as Fulham or St John's Wood. All other prostitutes found their lives and their working practices dominated by this problem.

Girls who worked in brothels had a degree of security, as long as they did not succumb to disease or drink. Women on the game aged quickly and might lose their looks by their late twenties, so their careers were usually short. The women – occasionally men – who ran brothels were expert at keeping most of the clients' cash for themselves, so the prostitutes were unlikely to accumulate the kind of nest-egg that would attract a husband. For that a girl had to operate on her own, boldly advertising her charms by her presence in the theatres, night-houses, casinos, or even the most fashionable stores of the West End.

The rooms these successful whores took their clients to were often in lodging houses which were in effect brothels, in that all the rooms would be rented by prostitutes. These lodging-house brothels were found all over London, and varied enormously in the rents they charged the whores.

A round-up of whores by the authorities. One magistrate ordered the police to drive all the prostitutes they could find into the City at Temple Bar. As the City authorities resisted, this 'whimsical war' raged for two nights. The magistrate was sacked.

Another option, and one chosen by many prostitutes, was the ACCOMMODATION HOUSE. These establishments hired rooms for just a few minutes or for several hours. Food and drink might be available, according to the status of the house. There were many advantages for prostitutes in using accommodation houses. They could keep their working and home lives separate, vital if they wanted to keep up a facade of respectability, which many married prostitutes did.

In competition with the accommodation houses were cigar divans, chop houses, coffee rooms and particularly, shops. The latter included some exclusive West End establishments, and some of the elegant fronts in the Burlington Arcade were known among the cognoscenti to have rooms where a man and woman, entering the shop separately, might discreetly retire. Sometimes the girls behind the counter were available.

Street prostitution continued to be an embarrassment after the Second World War, particularly during 1953 when the Coronation drew many visitors to London. Dr Alfred Kinsey, the American sexologist and author of the famous Report, claimed he saw a thousand prostitutes at work in the West End one Saturday night in 1955. 'I have never seen so much nor such aggressive behaviour anywhere else,' he said.

Statistics suggested that there had been a big increase in the amount of prostitution. In 1958 there were 16,700 convictions, greatly above wartime figures and more than 50 per cent above the average for the years 1952–5.

> The curious investigator in the fifties could see evidence on the pavements, in Hyde Park, in doorways and alleys and under railway arches. From the edge of Notting Hill in the west, down Bayswater Road, through the Park to Piccadilly, and eastwards to Stepney, he could expect to be accosted at every few yards except across the City 'gap' from east of Charing Cross Road to

An old man knocking at the door of a brothel in Portland Street is distracted by the pretty street seller. Some commentators on vice refused to see the obvious – that prostitution was largely caused by poverty.

> Aldgate Pump. Similarly a walk north-south from Maida Vale, through Paddington to Victoria, or at a slightly different tangent from the mainline railway stations of Euston, St Pancras and Kings Cross, brought the same sights. The one-mile 'Prostitutes' Row' from Piccadilly to Waterloo Bridge had stretched over seven miles with only a one-mile break (Gosling and Warner, *The Shame of a City*).

There was certainly plenty of anecdotal evidence: citizens complained of having to clear contraceptives from their front gardens, and others that couples were copulating in Hyde Park in broad daylight. One of those scandalised was Billy Graham, the American evangelist. He commented on the antics he saw: 'It looked as though your parks had been turned into bedrooms, with people lying all over the place.'

The street girls operating on the eve of the Street Offences Act can be categorised by price. Those who charged the highest prices were the girls in Mayfair, who were naturally the most attractive. Next came the street walkers of Soho and Piccadilly. A further rung down the ladder were the girls in Hyde Park, Bayswater, Victoria and Maida Vale, and below them were the Euston-King's Cross women. As ever, the tarts of the East End were at the bottom of the earnings league table.

It is interesting that prostitution had returned to Stepney, a fact Gosling and Warner attribute to the arrival of many single coloured men. In 1952 the black journalist Roi Otley wrote of the area around Cable Street: 'Today, down by London dock in about a square mile of back streets there exists a dismal Negro slum. The neighbourhood, situated in the borough of Stepney, abounds with brothels and dope pads in tumbledown old buildings' (Otley, *No Green Pastures*).

The 1959 STREET OFFENCES ACT drove most of the prostitutes into the shadows. The estimated 5,000 women needed somewhere else to ply their trade. A few of the women may have joined the ranks of the 'call girls', the elite of prostitutes, but most of them would not have had the requisite looks or polish. Others put their cards in the windows of small shops, and later in phone boxes.

Another outlet was the escort agency. One called Eve International was said to have 200 girls on its books, charging from £14 a night upwards and bringing in £100,000 for the agency. When the man who ran it was charged his girls were said to be charging £40 for a 'quickie' and £100 for 'longer', and making £400 a week each for themselves.

Some girls used near-beer joints, which did not have a licence to sell alcohol, as places to pick up clients. They also began to advertise in phone booths all over London, which were soon wallpapered with explicit cards complete with photos. Vigilante groups would go round the booths ripping these up, and men employed by the girls would follow, pasting up replacements.

Technology had affected prostitution, particularly the phone and the automobile. The years after the Street Offences Act saw more girls cruising the streets in cars, and we have seen how some of the women advertised their attractions in phone boxes and shop windows. The film industry also contributed its innumerable 'starlets', who seldom or never acted in films but nevertheless made a good living as the companions or accessories of the rich and famous. In 1960 it was estimated that while her looks lasted such a girl could make between £300 and £500 in a weekend at some foreign resort or in London during 'the season'. Although in effect they were selling sex to a succession of men these women would not have considered themselves prostitutes.

The SOHO vice industry had burgeoned after the war as racketeers bought up the leases of premises housing small businesses as they expired and let and sublet them to prostitutes. Parts of the premises were turned into sex shops. In the 1980s new legislation enabled Westminster City Council to refuse licences to sex shops, and the police clamped down on what was left of the peep-show and porn clubs. Today even the miserable sex and porn shops seem to be on the retreat. However, the escort agencies are flourishing, as are the prostitutes, and there are still some strip clubs where customers are charged up to £10 for a bottle of alcohol-free lager. In others customers who paid a ten-pound entrance fee were expected to buy the 'hostesses' fake champagne at fifty pounds a bottle. *See* SOHO and was fined £5,000. He continued to pour out pamphlets, particularly against Archbishop Laud. In 1637 he was again tortured, losing the rest of his ears, and was branded on his cheeks with the letters S L for seditious libeller. This made him a popular martyr. Released in 1640 by the Long Parliament, he became a parliamentary prosecutor, taking malicious pleasure in proceeding against Laud. He turned against the Army and criticised the Independents and the execution of the king. He was imprisoned again and eventually became a Royalist, being rewarded with the post of Keeper of the Tower Records.

PSALMANAZAR, GEORGE (1679–?) Brilliant conman and linguist. Psalmanazar was born in France, and went to Rome when he was about 20, posing as a Japanese convert to Christianity. He then went to London, where the Bishop of London paid him to translate the catechism into Japanese. Psalmanazar did not speak Japanese but produced a fake which was convincing enough in a city where no one else spoke the language either. Another book proved to be his downfall. He said he was really a native of Formosa, and concocted the *Historical and Geographical Dictionary of Formosa*. This fooled many scholars, but the astronomer Edmund Halley unmasked Psalmanazar by asking him simple scientific questions about Formosa. Psalmanazar's reply to a question about the length of the twilight in Formosa convinced Halley he was an impostor, and soon everyone agreed. Psalmanazar was no longer courted, but saved himself from obscurity and poverty by another brilliant deception: he repented. Distinguished men, including the young Samuel Johnson, would gather to hear him hold forth at a public house in Old Street, and Johnson later described him as the best man he had ever known.

PUNISHMENT Prison sentences today are much longer than in the eighteenth and nineteenth centuries. In what could be seen as a kind of compensation, sadistic punishments have been abolished. These included hanging, drawing and quartering. The victim was cut down from the

Two wretches face the mob in the pillory at Charing Cross. This was the most dangerous of the secondary punishments. If the prisoner was hated, the mob might batter him to death with stones and refuse. Daniel Defoe, who had their sympathy, was pelted with flowers.

ANGLETERRE. — Le treadmill, punition infligée aux prisonniers dans la prison de Cold-Bath-Fields, à Londres.

Prisoners work the treadmill at Coldbath Fields Prison in Islington. This was a form of slow torture, and Coldbath was a notoriously severe jail. Prisoners weren't allowed to speak, and they could have one letter and one visit every three months. The aim was to break their spirits.

gallows while still alive, his bowels were torn from his body and burnt, he was then decapitated and his body divided into quarters. This terrible punishment was reserved for high treason. The heads of traitors were displayed on pikes at London Bridge and other important sites.

The bodies of common criminals were sometimes left hanging in chains near the scene of their crime, until they fell apart. Travellers on dangerous roads would see the bodies of highwaymen displayed thus on gibbets. Occasionally the condemned man would be suspended while still alive and left to starve to death.

The prospect of dissection after death was a form of mental torture, and was held to be a deterrent. An Act of 1752 allowed bodies of executed murderers to be handed over to surgeons for anatomical experiments and demonstrations. Until it was repealed in 1832 this law led to riots, with friends of condemned men fighting with law officers to prevent the bodies being taken away. The practice was repugnant to Christians who feared their dissected bodies would not rise again on Judgment Day. To the working class it was just another proof of the worthlessness of their lives in the eyes of the Establishment. They also felt there was always a faint hope that the hanged man could be revived, which occasionally happened. When JACK SHEPPARD was executed at Tyburn the driver of a hearse ordered by DANIEL DEFOE to take the body away so that attempts could be made to revive it was attacked by the crowd, who feared that the body was being taken away for dissection.

Although torture was specifically prohibited under common law some monarchs licensed it. The historian Lord Macaulay wrote: 'Those rulers who had occasionally resorted to it had, as far as was possible, used it in secret . . .' The Protestant martyr Anne Askew, who was burned at the stake in Smithfield in 1546, was first tortured on the rack 'till her bones and joints were almost plucked asunder'. Cuthbert Symson, a Protestant from Islington, was racked several times for refusing to name people

A prisoner works the crank at Surrey House of Correction. Prisoners who were thought to be malingering would have this machine installed in their cells, and would be required to turn the crank handle ten thousand times a day, a solitary torture. The pointlessness of the task was part of the torture.

who had attended a church service in English. He was burned at Smithfield in March 1558. GUY FAWKES was racked until he could no longer walk, and had to be helped to the scaffold.

Convicted felons who were hanged had their estate seized by the Crown. However, they could be found guilty only if they first agreed to plead. Some criminals who felt sure they would be found guilty refused to plead, so that their families could keep their property: the torture known as *peine forte et dure* was designed to change their minds. Increasingly heavy weights were placed on a prisoner's chest until he either relented or was crushed to death. SPIGGOT, leader of a gang of footpads rounded up by JONATHAN WILD in 1721, refused to plead, and was subjected to this judicial torture. After being pressed by iron weights of 400 lb Spiggott agreed to plead. He and his men went to the gallows. The author of *The New State of England* described the torture, which took place in 'some low dark room' . . .

> . . . all naked but his privy members; his back upon the bare ground, his arms and legs stretched with cords, fastened to the several quarters of the room, and as much irons and stones laid upon his body as he can well bear. The next day he is allowed but three morsels of barley bread, without drink; and the day after as much . . . water, and that without any bread. And this is to be his diet, till he die.

The eighteenth-century highwayman Nathaniel Hawes refused to plead when the judge at his trial said he could not go to his execution in the clothes he wearing when he was arrested. The judge ordered that he be subjected to *peine forte et dure*. Although Hawes had boasted '. . . as I have lived with the character of the boldest fellow in my profession I am resolved to die with it and leave my memory to be admired by all the gentlemen of the road of succeeding ages' he could bear the pressure of a weight of 250 lb for only a few minutes before giving in. He didn't get his clothes. The torture was abolished in 1772.

Courts were careful not to make defendants destitute by heavy fines, for fear they would become a burden on the ratepayers. Whipping was an alternative to fines in minor cases. The was commonly carried out in public, at the 'cart's arse' or tail. A cart would be driven through the streets with the offender tied at the back: he would be whipped until blood flowed.

The most dangerous form of secondary punishment was the pillory, especially for those whose crime had aroused high public indignation. The punishment usually lasted an hour, which was long enough for the prisoner to die under a hail of missiles. This was the fate of the crooked THIEF-TAKERS McDaniel, Berry, Egan and Salmon. MOTHER NEEDHAM was so badly battered that her life was despaired of, and she died not long afterwards. An informer named John Waller was put in the pillory at Seven Dials in 1731. He was pelted with stones and bottles, and after an hour a man dragged him down and tore off his clothes. The mob then trampled him to death. On the other hand DEFOE was pelted with flowers, and COBBETT emerged unscathed. A Wilkesite printer was treated to cheers and a whip-round which raised more than 200 guineas. The novelist Smollett, who detested Wilkes, wrote: 'If you are sentenced to the pillory your fortune is made . . .' When the Jacobite Shebbeare was pilloried in 1758 for a satire against King George I he was cheered and the crowd allowed a footman to keep the rain off him with an umbrella. One of the oddest cases of the public taking the side of the pilloried prisoner was that of Parsons, inventor of the 'Cock Lane Ghost'. To get revenge on a man who sued him for debt Parsons got his daughter to claim she had seen a ghost. This apparition accused Parsons' enemy of poisoning his sister-in-law, and said it could not rest until the man was hanged. Eventually it was shown to be a fraud and Parsons was put in the pillory. The crowd had a whip-round to help pay his debts.

Prison could be a form of torture for recalcitrant whores. The Swiss commentator on London low life César de Saussure describes a visit to the Bridewell or prison at Tothill Fields, Westminster:

> We entered a big court, on one side of which was a low building containing about thirty or forty robbers, pickpockets etc., male and female, occupied in beating out flax. Each of these unfortunate wretches was seated in front of a large block of wood, on which he beat the flax with a large and heavy wooden mallet. On one side of this room were the men, on the other the women, and between these two lines walked the inspector, or Captain Whip'em. This man had a surly, repulsive countenance; he held a long cane in his hand about the thickness of my little finger, and whenever one of these ladies was fatigued and ceased working he would rap them on the arms, and in no gentle fashion, I can assure you . . . In the women's part we saw a fine, tall handsome and well-dressed creature. Her linen was of the finest and so was her lace, and she wore a magnificent silk dress brocaded with flowers. The captain took great heed of her; he made her arms quite red with the little raps he gave her with his cane. The girl received these attentions most haughtily and with great indifference. It was a most curious contrast, this handsome girl or woman in rich clothes, looking like a queen and having a mallet in her hand with which she was forced to beat out hemp, and that in such a way that she was covered with large drops of perspiration, all this being accompanied with raps from the cane. I confess that the sight made me quite unhappy. [This scene is almost uncannily reminiscent of Plate 4 of Hogarth's *A Harlot's Progress*.] I could not help thinking that such a handsome, proud, queenly woman should at least be spared the blows. We were told that she had been sent here the day before because she had stolen a gold watch from her lover, and that it was not her first visit, because she always stole everything she could lay her hands on. At the opposite end of the room we remarked a girl from fifteen to sixteen years of age, extremely beautiful; she seemed a mere child, and was touching to look at.

This girl told de Saussure and his friend she had nothing to eat for three days except dry bread. The two men paid for her release, and exhorted her to lead a better life. She promised to do so, but some months later de Saussure saw her at the theatre, occupying one of the principal boxes, 'dressed like a duchess and more beautiful than ever'.

PUNKS Just one of the many terms for prostitutes which have dropped out of use. Others included bunters, smuts, trumpery, jilts, doxies, cracks, mawkes, brims, brimstones, brown besses, trulls, trugmoldies, molls, blowsabellas, buttock-and-files, wagtails, tails, twiggers, judies, buttered buns, squirrels, mackerels, cats, froes and punchable nuns. Fireships were diseased prostitutes. Bawds were known as Mother or Mother Midnight. At one stage they were called lenas and nappers.

QUEENSBERRY, DUKE OF (1724–1810) William Douglas was one of the most profligate characters of the eighteenth century, a patron of many of the best-known bawds and with a sex-drive which hardly flagged till his death. Known variously as 'Lord Piccadilly' or 'Old Q', he was immensely rich, and he had other passions besides sex: he gambled on a magnificent scale, he was a patron of the arts and the turf and he was a dandy. Old Q was a customer of the brothel-keeper SARAH DUBERY. His housekeeper, Maria Moreton, wrote in her memoirs that he 'employed that skilful Procuress Mrs Dubery to procure his *Sultanas* . . . candidates were paraded for inspection . . . she seldom served him with a dish that he could not make at least one meal upon. If he approved, he rang a bell and Mrs D . . . had to school the Novitiate in her duties . . .'. Old Q's appetite may occasionally have been greater than his

The Duke of Queensberry, too old and feeble to be anything more than a voyeur, watches the commerce of sex outside his mansion in Piccadilly. In his time he had been the lecher of the age.

capacity, however: one girl disclosed that 'the Piccadilly Sultan left me as good a maid as he found me . . . making a violent Fit of Coughing after an hour as an apology for his sudden retreat from the field of love'.

One of his mistresses was Kitty Fredericks, 'the very *Thais* of London'. She had originally been one of CHARLOTTE HAYES's girls, and was passed on to Catherine Matthews when that bawd took over the Hayes establishment at No. 5 King's Place. Mrs Matthews became one of several panders employed by Old Q, and he acquired Kitty for £100 a year, 'a genteel house' and a carriage. It was generally expected he would marry her. However, in 1779, when Old Q was in his middle-fifties, they quarrelled and parted. Kitty became one of the best-known and highest-paid courtesans of the epoch. Old Q never married.

When he was almost sixty the *Rambler Magazine* carried a caricature of the bawd Mrs Windsor bargaining with Old Q for the services of three young whores – one of them only 15. Old Q says: 'They are very young. Will you warrant them?' Mrs Windsor replies: 'Warrant, my Lord! I am astonished at you . . . They are chaste, virtuous girls . . . One has almost got her maidenhead!'

Old Q presided over tremendous orgies at his houses in Richmond and at 138 Piccadilly, and it was said that his sexual powers seemed to increase with advancing years. When he was in his eighties, a groom was permanently stationed at the door of the house. If a passing woman took the old man's fancy the groom was ordered to accost her and invite her in.

In his heyday 'Old Q' delighted in re-enacting the Judgment of Paris. The goddesses were played by prostitutes, and Paris by himself. His predilection for the drama was by no means confined to the home – he subsidised the Italian Opera in London for many years, and was indefatigable in his amours with singers and dancers.

In his later years it was the task of his doctor, previously physician to Louis XV, to keep him in a fit state to perform sexually. According to the *Gentleman's Magazine* a chemist, one Fuller, although receiving a legacy in the duke's will, claimed £10,000 for 9,340 visits made in the last seven years of the old man's life, and for over 1,000 nights in which he sat up with his patient! In the event he was awarded £7,500. 'Old Q' died at 85 years of age, worn out by a very full life. Thackeray wrote of him in old age in *The Four Georges*: 'This wrinkled, paralysed, toothless old Don Juan died the same corrupt, unrepentant fellow he had been in the most fiery days of his youth. In a house in Piccadilly there is a low window where old Queensberry is said to have sat in order to peer at passing women with voluptuous eyes.'

He was a lady's man to the end. 'The fact is that in December 1810, when at the point of death, his bed was literally covered with at least 70 billets doux and letters written by women of the most varied social positions, from duchesses to semi-prostitutes. Being unable to open and read the letters, he ordered them to be left unopened, and they lay there until his death.' After he died they were gathered up and burned (Jesse, *Literary and Historical Memorials of London*).

Three years before this there was a premature report of his death, and a wag wrote some verses which amused the duke:

And now this may be said of Q,
That long he ran all Folly thro',
For ever seeking something new:
He never cared for me, nor you,
But, to engagements strictly true,
At last he gave the Devil his due;
And died a boy – at eighty-two,
Poor Q of Piccadilly.

QUEENSBERRY, JOHN SHOLTO DOUGLAS, MARQUESS OF (1844–1900) Deranged peer who was OSCAR WILDE's nemesis. Queensberry was at odds with members of his family. In 1895 he faced a court for brawling in Piccadilly with his son and heir, whom he called 'this squirming skunk, Percy'. The Foreign Secretary, Lord Rosebery, arranged a peerage for Queensberry's second son, Lord Drumlanrig. Queensberry, who suspected Rosebery of being his son's lover, threatened the statesman with a dog whip. Apart from accusing Wilde of sodomy he is best known for giving his name to boxing's code of conduct.

QUINN, MARYANN Drug dealer who ran a drug club in the heart of London. In December 1998 armed police stormed a fortified drug den in the West End. The doors of the building, old EMI recording studios which had been turned into a club called Backbeat, were backed by steel shutters. Closed-circuit TV cameras watched at strategic points, and look-outs in the surrounding streets used mobile phones to keep in touch with those inside. Yardie gangsters, said to be armed with guns, machetes and electric cattle prods, stood guard. The club was run by Quinn, a woman with Jamaican roots. The Yardie guards were organised by her former lover Floyd Alexander, known in Yardie circles as Tank. The club was advertised in student magazines and inside it there were signs in four languages. Clients were said to have come from all over Europe. Upstairs, between 5.30 p.m. and 3 a.m., there would be between 300 and 400 clubbers dancing. In a special 'smoking' room up to 100 more would sit on the floor, passing joints. In the basement, drugs were being sold. Punters could pass £10 or £20 through a hole in the wall and in return be handed a packet of drugs. All they saw was a hand in a surgical glove which took the money and handed over the packet.

Police arrived outside the club concealed in two articulated lorries. Men of the Yard's SO 19 specialist firearms squad abseiled down from the roof and kicked their way into the building through the upper-floor windows. They threw stun grenades into rooms believed to be guarded by armed Yardies. With 120 armed policemen taking part, it was the biggest operation of its kind in British police history. More than 90,000 bags of drugs were seized, along with 21 kg of cannabis. Samurai swords, machetes and £125,000 in cash were also found. Quinn and Alexander were each jailed for five years for conspiracy to supply cannabis. Quinn, 39, had built up a property empire with cash from drug dealing.

RABBETT, MARMADUKE Nonconformist minister who packed his chapel in Clement's Lane off the Strand with bodies in shallow graves. In 1823 Rabbett built the Enon Chapel, and began an undertaking business. Over the next twenty years he crammed 12,000 bodies under the wooden floor. He later turned the chapel into a dancing salon, and enticed dancers with the prospect of 'Dancing on the Dead – admission three pence'.

RACHMAN, PETER (1919–62) Refugee who gave his name to a vicious new kind of exploitation. Rachman came to Britain from Poland at the end of the Second World War. He built up a property empire in the Notting Hill, Shepherd's Bush, Paddington and Earl's Court areas during the late 1950s and early 1960s, having spotted that the new Rent Act allowed landlords to charge new tenants much higher rents than existing tenants. All the landlord had to do was persuade or force the existing tenants to leave. 'Rachmanism' was the process of getting them out.

Savage dogs were used to assault tenants, intolerable neighbours were installed, all-night noisy parties were held and essential services cut off. When the sitting tenants were forced out the flats were let to prostitutes and West Indians at exorbitant rents. Some of the properties became brothels. He took rents totalling £10,000 a year from a single house in Hereford Road, Paddington, and he owned between 80 and 100 properties. He also began running call girls.

The KRAY TWINS found Rachman an easy target and forced him to pay protection money. He deflected their interest by telling them about Esmeralda's Barn in Wilton Place off Knightsbridge, a club they took over. Rachman enjoyed gambling with the gangster BILLY HILL. Other good-time companions were CHRISTINE KEELER and his mistress MANDY RICE-DAVIES, two of the girls in the PROFUMO SCANDAL. He died in 1962 at the age of 42. Rice-Davies said later in a TV interview: 'He was probably a racketeer but not during the two years I knew him. I adored him. I'm a one-guy girl. Only one at a time, that is. I got thousands from him and I've spent it all.'

RADCLIFFE, OWEN Club owner who saw off the KRAYS. Radcliffe was the proprietor of the successful Cromford Club in Manchester. In 1961 the Krays tried to take over, throwing the doorman down the stairs. The doorman was Jack London, former heavyweight champion of Britain. His son, Brian London, was also a successful heavyweight who lost a world title fight with Muhammad Ali. After their triumph the Krays were drinking in Manchester's Midland Hotel, where Radcliffe caught up with them. After seeing the meat cleaver he had under his Crombie coat the Krays caught a train back to London. Owen later opened MR SMITH'S CLUB at Catford in south London, which was a mistake.

RALEIGH, SIR WALTER (1552–1618) Courtier, navigator, writer and favourite of Queen Elizabeth I. The man who successfully introduced tobacco and potatoes into the Old World was sent to the TOWER in 1592 because of a secret affair with one of the queen's maids of honour. In 1603 he was again held there, this time for being involved in a plot against KING JAMES I. He was sentenced to death for high treason but reprieved on the eve of his execution. He continued to live comfortably in the Tower with his wife and son, and there wrote his *History of the World*, beginning with the Creation. He got only as far as 130 BC, despite spending from 1603 to 1616 as a prisoner. He was released to lead an expedition to South America to find gold. The venture was a disastrous failure, and Raleigh clashed with the Spanish just as James I was negotiating a Spanish marriage for his son Charles, the Prince of Wales. The death sentence imposed earlier was invoked and he was executed in Palace Yard, Westminster, in October 1618.

RAMPSMEN The Victorian equivalent of FOOTPADS. Their crime was known as 'propping' or 'swinging the stick'. Prostitutes would lure the victim into a dark alley and the rampsman would attack him and steal his money.

RAPE For a period during the reign of Edward I (1239–1307) rape was reduced from a felony to a 'mere trespass'. The results of this experiment were horrifying, and after ten years it became a crime again. By the eighteenth century rape was considered a crime against property, and what is more, a man's property. Naturally it was punished severely. However, Frank McLynn (*Crime and Punishment in Eighteenth-Century England*) quotes a survey which shows that between 1660 and 1800 in Surrey 60 per cent of those found guilty of rape were pardoned; in the same period all of those found guilty of sodomy were hanged.

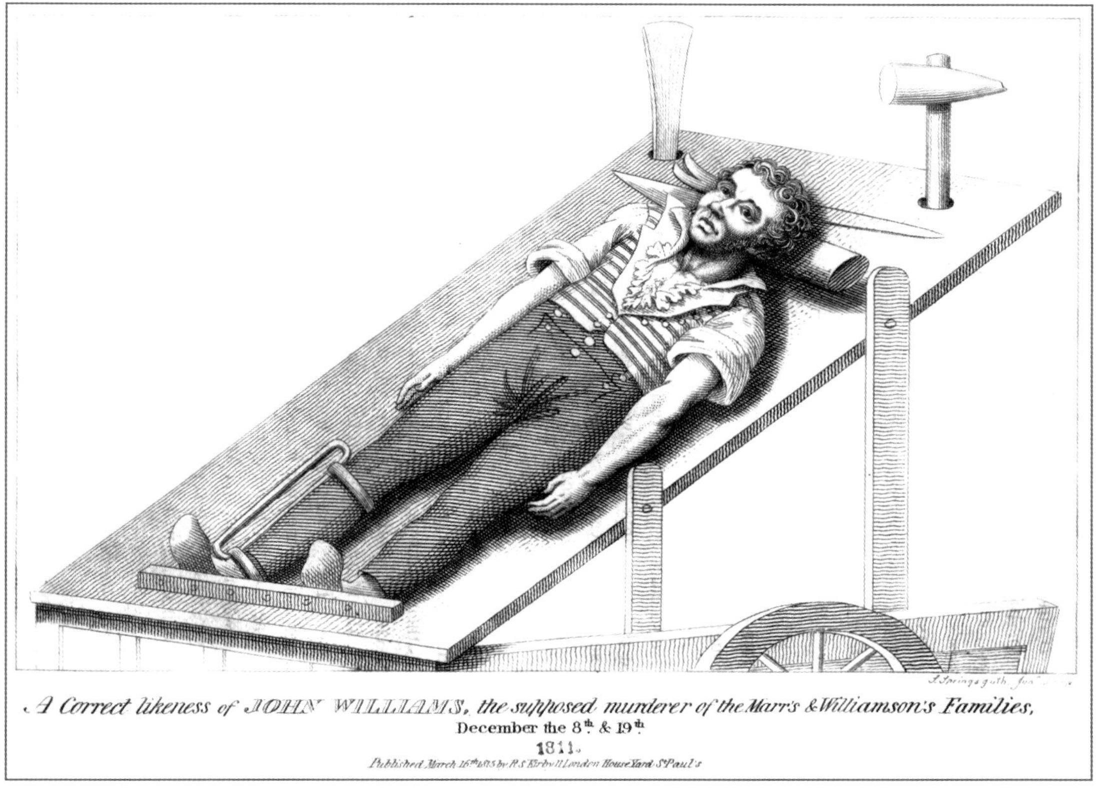

A Correct likeness of JOHN WILLIAMS, the supposed murderer of the Marr's & Williamson's Families,
December the 8th & 19th
1811.
Published March 16th 1815 by R.S. Kirby 11 London House Yard St Paul's

The body of John Williams, suspected of committing the seven Ratcliffe murders, as it was drawn through the streets on a cart. Williams committed suicide in prison. His body was buried at a crossroads near the present-day Cable Street, with a stake through its heart and covered in quicklime.

RATCLIFFE HIGHWAY MURDERS Seven people died in two related incidents in December 1811. At midnight on 7 December Timothy Marr, a draper, sent his maid out for oysters. He and his apprentice then closed the shop at 29 Ratcliffe Highway for the night. When the maid, Margaret Jewell, returned, the house was locked and in darkness. Eventually neighbours broke in and found Marr and his apprentice murdered, their throats cut and their skulls smashed. The murder weapons, a ripping chisel and a hammer, lay on the floor nearby. Upstairs Marr's wife and child were found, murdered in the same way. Nothing had been stolen.

Twelve days later a lodger at the nearby King's Arms tavern escaped nearly naked from a second floor window shouting, 'They are murdering the people in the house.' The publican, his wife and their maid were found with their throats cut and skulls crushed. A wave of panic spread across the city and there were many false arrests. Finally a young labourer named John Williams, who used the King's Arms and was in the neighbourhood on the night of the murders, was arrested. He hanged himself in his cell before he could face charges.

Williams's 'funeral' was highly symbolic. His body was placed on an inclined platform on a cart, with the maul and chisel by his head, and was taken in procession, stopping at the scene of the crimes and on through the East End, past crowds to a crossroads near the present-day Cable Street. The High Constable of Middlesex and hundreds of constables and parish officers accompanied it. The corpse was buried in quicklime with a stake through the heart. Suicides were traditionally buried at crossroads 'so as to confuse their restless souls' sense of direction' (Wilson and Pitman, *Encyclopedia of Murder*). The use of the stake was unusual. The murders, and the incompetent police reaction, gave impetus to calls for a professional police force. All the Watch men at Shadwell were sacked and new patrols of armed officers were formed. The evidence against Williams was merely circumstantial. Some commentators have doubted that he was involved in the murders at all, or even that he committed suicide, preferring to believe he was murdered in prison.

RAVEN, DANIEL Advertising agent who murdered his parents-in-law in 1949. Raven and his parents-in-law visited his wife at a Muswell Hill maternity home where she had given birth to their first child. Afterwards the wealthy couple, Mr and Mrs Leopold Goodman, returned to their home in Ashcombe Gardens, Edgware, not far from Raven's home. At 10 p.m. another relative called on them and, not getting an answer, climbed in through a window. He found their bodies in the blood-spattered dining room. Their heads had been crushed with a television aerial base. Robbery was clearly not the motive – there were piles of banknotes in various places in the house. Daniel Raven was called to the house and sat on the stairs crying and saying: 'Why did they tell me to go? Why didn't they let me stop?' He claimed he had taken the old couple home from the maternity home, and that they insisted on him returning home afterwards. Police quickly discovered that earlier in the day Raven had been wearing a dark suit, although he was now wearing a light one. An officer went to Raven's home where he found a partly burned dark suit in the boiler. The suit, and a pair of shoes, had traces of blood on them which matched the blood group of the Goodmans. Raven was charged with murder, and denied it, insisting that his father-in-law had made many enemies through illegal business deals. He was hanged. The motive for the crimes was not discovered.

READ, LEONARD Successful Scotland Yard detective, known as Nipper, who brought the KRAY TWINS to trial. He was conspicuously honest in a force saturated with corruption.

REFORMERS The spies and narks of the SOCIETY FOR THE REFORMATION OF MANNERS were not the only ones trying to make society more moral. Less rancorous reformers were dismayed by the failure of the authorities to make much impact on the growing numbers of prostitutes and brothels, and cast about for other solutions. Large numbers of prostitutes were sent to the penal colonies in Australia. Several authors suggested the setting up of state-run brothels. The Revd Martin Madan thought polygamy was the answer to what he saw as men's need for sexual variety. His suggestion got him sacked from his job of chaplain to the London Lock Hospital for venereal diseases. Other proposals were less radical and in some cases led to action. SIR JOHN FIELDING proposed a public institution to 'preserve the deserted Girls of the Poor of this Metropolis; and also to reform those Prostitutes whom Necessity has drove into the Streets, and who are willing to return to Virtue and obtain an honest livelihood by severe industry'.

Fielding proposed a public laundry where the women would labour for a pittance. They would also learn cooking, knitting and cleaning. In 1758 Dr William Todd took up some of these recommendations when he founded the Magdalen Hospital near Goodman Fields in London. The regime was harsh: the women worked from 6 a.m. to 10 p.m. in summer and 7 a.m. to 9 p.m. in winter making clothes or small saleable items. Any spare time was devoted to religious instruction. The aim was to fit the women for domestic service, a career which was already turning young women into prostitutes in large numbers. Although only 2,217 women opted to be 'saved' by the Magdalen Hospital during the first forty years of its life, more homes for fallen women, run on the same lines, followed. In 1885 there were said to be fifty-three Church of England penitentiaries for the reform of prostitutes. The Roman Catholic Church also set up such reformatories. The Evangelical Church of England was an important factor in the movement, with a more liberal approach. By 1908 the Evangelists' Reformatory and Refuge Union had 320 Magdalen Institutions. The Salvation Army opened the first English Salvation Army home in Whitechapel in 1884. The Church Army and the Jewish Ladies' Association also had homes, the latter setting up a home in Shepherds Bush. Individuals helped: the feminist and morals campaigner Josephine Butler would take ailing prostitutes to her own home, the wealthy philanthropist Angela Burdett-Coutts provided money for Charles Dickens to supervise Urania Cottage in Shepherds Bush, and Adeline, Duchess of Bedford ran an institution. Somehow Dickens found time from running a newspaper, writing major novels and stories and staging theatricals to visit prisons looking for likely candidates for Urania Cottage, and he wrote to Miss Burdett-Coutts: 'A most extraordinary and mysterious study it is, but interesting and touching in the extreme.' Another enthusiastic reformer was the Prime Minister, William Gladstone. When told by his private secretary in 1886 that the climate of opinion had changed and that he must cease his activities among prostitutes, Gladstone commented that 'there was among some people a baseness and lack of charity which enabled them to believe the worst. Because of this I will cease to visit clearing houses, brothels or places of assignation . . . and . . . promise never again to speak to women on the streets at night.' This should have been the end of a long series of encounters, during which he would sometimes accompany street walkers back to their rooms for long conversations. In July 1852, for example, he wrote in his diary in Italian of one such woman, Elizabeth Collins: 'Half a most lovely statue, beautiful beyond measure.' Even after his 1886 promise he did not completely desist.

REUBEN BROTHERS Murderers whose execution in 1909 brought an end to a wave of violent robberies in the East End. Two prostitutes took two drunken sailors back to their lodgings in Rupert Street, off Leman Street in Whitechapel. Waiting there were the womens' pimps, brothers Morris and Mark Reuben. Next morning one of the sailors, McEachern, was found semi-conscious in the street. His companion, Sproull, was lying dead nearby. The case was handled by FREDERICK WENSLEY of Scotland Yard. He found that after having sex with the women, the two sailors decided to return to their ship. The Reuben brothers, who had been listening outside the room, hoping to rob the sailors when they were asleep, attacked them. At their Old Bailey trial Morris said he did not know his brother had a knife, but to no avail. They were executed in May 1909. Wensley later wrote in his autobiography *Detective Days*: 'From that date robbery with violence grew unfashionable in East London and few unaccountable dead bodies were found in the streets.'

RICE-DAVIES, MANDY (1944–) Vivacious model, showgirl and club-owner, born in 1944, involved with her friend CHRISTINE KEELER in the PROFUMO AFFAIR. During the trial of Stephen Ward for living off the immoral earnings of the two women she gave the famous retort, 'Well, he would, wouldn't he?' when told that Lord Astor denied knowing her. She was the mistress of the property racketeer PETER RACHMAN. Unlike her friend Keeler she enjoyed celebrity.

RICHARDSON GANG, THE Gangsters and businessmen at the centre of the Torture Trial. This south London gang, led by the brothers Charlie and Eddie Richardson, were the main rivals of the KRAYS. The Richardsons had a wide-flung illegal business empire and were recognised as being better business brains than the Krays. MAD FRANKIE FRASER, who joined the Richardsons after working with BILLY HILL, said: 'Using racing terms, there would be no race, comparing the Richardsons with the Krays. The Richardsons were miles in front, brain power, everything.'

Charlie Richardson was born in Twickenham in 1934, the son of a former prizefighter. The family later moved to Camberwell in south London. Eddie Richardson was born in 1936. Charlie started out as a crooked scrap-metal dealer. He was called up for National Service, but like other underworld leaders the young man who was already forming his own gang was not prepared to take orders. After a court martial he was sent to the military prison at Shepton Mallet where he met the KRAYS. Other criminal alumni of Shepton Mallet included JOHNNY NASH and FRANK MITCHELL.

When he was freed Charlie Richardson set about expanding his business interests. He opened the first of his drinking clubs. Inevitably their kind of business involved a certain level of violence. He described how he and his men carried out a revenge attack on a local tough named Jack Rosa and members of his gang in the Reform Club at the Elephant and Castle in south London. After they had finished 'they lay unconscious at our feet in pools of blood and teeth'.

Charlie Richardson liked to think of himself as a businessman first, a criminal second. He wrote of 'heading the biggest firm on the manor . . . I was a businessman who had to protect his interests'. Those interests included LONG-FIRM FRAUDS. He added a new twist to this old swindle. A warehouse in Mitre Street, Aldgate, had been stocked with silk stockings. These were sold off, and the building was torched. The manufacturers of the stockings were told the stock was not insured. In fact the stock had been insured, so the Richardsons' profit was doubled. They made £250,000 from the swindle.

A group of clever fraudsters now gathered around the Richardsons. One was Brian Mottram, an old friend, who was also involved in the Mitre Street business. Another was Jack Duval, who was eventually to prove the Richardsons' undoing. Duval was a Russian-born Jew, a former Foreign Legionnaire who had served in the RAF during the war. He was a club owner and also an accomplished fraudster. Charlie Richardson would later call him 'a turd that floated down the Thames to my part of London'.

Duval ran a ticket fraud that swindled airlines out of £500,000, and he even managed to become owner of the Bank of Valletta. In March 1963 Duval's past began to catch up with him and he fled to Milan. At some stage he took some money from a firm in which he and the Richardsons had a joint interest. After he returned to Britain Charlie summoned him. Duval was given a beating and went into hiding. It was then that Charlie discovered that Duval had given him dud cheques. He went looking for the fraudster, and when he failed to find him decided to punish instead an associate of Duval's, Lucien Harris. Harris's testimony about his ordeal at the hands of Richardson's torturers was the main plank in the prosecution's case against the south London gang. He described how the infamous black box, which was to figure so prominently in the Richardson torture trials, was used on him. The box was a generator, a piece of old scrap. Harris said wires were attached to his toes and one of the Richardson gang turned the handle of the generator. Harris said the electric current flung him to the floor. He was then stripped and orange juice poured over him to make the shocks more effective. 'The leads were attached to my legs, my penis, the anus, the chest, the nostrils and the temples.' Another of the gang stabbed him in the foot.

Eddie Richardson, a less ambitious man than his brother, had teamed up with Frankie Fraser to install fruit machines in clubs. Through his old connection with ALBERT DIMES Fraser had contacts in Soho, then the most profitable area for fruit machines. Meanwhile the torture went on. One man who was given a gratuitous beating was involved in a swindle run by car park attendants at Heathrow Airport. After they had collected customers' parking charges the attendants would alter time clocks to show the customers had stayed for a shorter time. They were making £1,000 a week, and Charlie Richardson wanted half. Their leader had already agreed to pay up, but Charlie had him beaten just to show him who was boss.

A man named James Taggart who had been tortured by the gang went to see Gerald McArthur, the Chief Constable of Hertfordshire. Other victims of the gang now began to talk to the police. On the night of 7 March 1966 the Richardson gang were beaten and humiliated in the fight at MR SMITH'S CLUB in Catford, South London. Their clash with a local gang, the Hawards, left Kray associate Richard Hart dead and Eddie Richardson and Frankie Fraser badly wounded.

The Haward brothers, Billy and Flash Harry, had been acting as unofficial minders at the club in exchange for free drinks. When it seemed they were trying to turn the club into their headquarters the management asked Eddie Richardson if he would get rid of them. Seeing an opportunity to install his gaming machines there, Eddie agreed. On 7 March Eddie and Frankie Fraser were drinking in the club when the Hawards arrived. JIMMY MOODY, a friend of Eddie's, and more Richardson henchmen turned up later. The two groups drank together affably enough until about 3 a.m. when Eddie told the Hawards: 'Right, drink up. I'm running the club.'

A fight started between Richardson and one of the Haward gang, Peter Hennessey. Then Hart pulled out a pistol and opened fire, according to Frankie Fraser. Harry Rawlins was shot in the shoulder. The fight continued outside, where Fraser's thighbone was broken by a bullet, and Hart was shot dead. Another man was shot in the groin, and Billy Haward had serious head injuries. Eddie Richardson was shot in the thigh.

Fraser was later acquitted of Hart's murder but convicted of affray. He was sentenced to five years' prison. Billy Haward got eight years and a Haward ally, Henry Botton, five. The jury failed to agree on the cases of Eddie Richardson and Jimmy Moody. On retrial Eddie was jailed for five years, and Moody was found not guilty.

The police had continued gathering evidence on the torture allegations and early on the morning of 30 July 1966, the day of England's soccer World Cup Final against West Germany, a team of police led by Gerald McArthur arrested eleven of the Richardson gang, including Charlie Richardson. When their trial opened at the Old Bailey on 4 April 1967, prosecuting counsel Sebag Shaw told the jury: 'This case is not about dishonesty and fraud, it is about violence and threats of violence, not, let me say at once, casual acts of violence committed in sudden anger or alarm but vicious and brutal violence systematically inflicted deliberately and cold-bloodedly and with utter and callous ruthlessness.'

Charlie Richardson was jailed for twenty-five years – the longest punishment ever handed out for grievous bodily harm. Eddie got ten, as did Roy Hall and Frankie Fraser. The Richardsons were finished as a major force in London crime.

Eddie Richardson was released from prison in 1976. In October 1990 at Winchester Crown Court he was jailed again for twenty-five years for importing cocaine from South America. Botton was shot dead on his doorstep in Shooters Hill, south-east London, in July 1983.

RIDOUT, PORTER Child-killer whose trial established some important points of law. In October 1784 during the Jewish harvest festival some boys on their way home from a synagogue detonated fireworks near the home of Ridout, who kept a coffee-shop in

Duke's Place. Ridout called on them to stop, then went to an upstairs window and fired a blunderbuss at them. Two were killed, one died later and two others were seriously wounded. Lord Loughborough, who presided over the trial, said that shooting at a crowd constituted murderous intent, even if the perpetrator did not select a particular victim. If you aimed at one person, and by mistake killed another, it was still murder. However, having established that what had happened was clearly murder he told the jury that if they thought Ridout's mind had been disturbed at the time, they should acquit him of murder. The jury reached a verdict of manslaughter. It has been suggested that anti-Jewish prejudice played a part in that verdict (McLynn, *Crime and Punishment in Eighteenth-Century England*).

RIGG, FRANK An informer for the puritanical SOCIETY FOR THE REFORMATION OF MANNERS. He once 'peached' on the noted whore SALLY SALISBURY and was also one of the informers whose evidence led to the arrest of MOTHER CLAP, keeper of a homosexual brothel, and the subsequent hangings of homosexuals.

RILEY, WILLIAM Soldier hanged in 1750 for killing a spectator at a race. He was a trooper in the Foot Guards and an athlete who took part in walking contests. On the last day of a marathon walk, in which he was pressing for a record, Riley was impeded by a crowd. He lashed out and one of the spectators struck him back. Riley drew his sword and killed the man. Although it was clearly manslaughter the jury convicted him of murder. He was 19.

10 RILLINGTON PLACE The Notting Hill house where necrophiliac JOHN CHRISTIE murdered at least eight women in the years 1943–53. The street, a small cul-de-sac, was later demolished.

RINGING THE CHANGES Method of passing high-value dud coins. The crook would tender a real sovereign for some purchase, and it would be dropped on the counter to prove by the sound it made that it was genuine. Then he would take it back because he thought he had enough change to pay with. He would count out his change, which would not be enough, and hand back a sovereign – this time a fake one. It usually worked. *See* COINING, COUNTERFEITING AND FORGERY

RIOT ACT OF 1715 Drastic legislation introduced by a government shaken by Jacobitism. There was general public hostility to the regime, and the Act laid down that magistrates could order riotous assemblies of twelve or more to disperse within an hour. If they failed to do so they were guilty of a capital felony. Those who dispersed the rioters, including soldiers, were indemnified for any harm they caused. However, troops and the magistrates who ordered them to open fire could still be prosecuted if they overreacted. The constitutional lawyer Dicey wrote: 'The position of a soldier may be, both in theory and practice, a difficult one. He may, as it has been well said, be liable to be shot by a Court Martial if he disobeys an order, and to be hanged by a judge and jury if he obeys it.' Reluctance by magistrates to empower troops to open fire during the GORDON RIOTS was believed to have allowed them to get out of hand.

RIOTS *see* following page

RIVER POLICE The greatest criminal enterprise in London during much of the eighteenth century and part of the nineteenth century was the plunder of ships and quayside cargoes on the River Thames. The port was the richest in the world, with 620,000 tons of foreign shipping docking annually. Everything that Londoners needed was there: food, liquor, clothes, silks, tobacco, sugar, spices. It was a vast floating emporium, and a mighty force of thieves, both amateur and professional, assembled to exploit it.

A huge traffic jam built up as ships waited to be unloaded. They were still moored in mid-stream and their cargoes were taken off in open lighters which transferred the goods to the quays where supervision was lax. There were few secure warehouses and goods might lie about untended in the open for weeks on end. This led to pilfering on a vast scale. A third of the port's workforce were thieves or receivers, and the shipping companies were losing half of their cargoes.

The two most important groups of plunderers were the 'light horsemen', who worked by night, and the 'heavy horsemen', who worked by day. There were also mudlarks, scuffle-hunters and river pirates. The 'heavy horsemen' were the lumpers, what we would now call dockers, who loaded and unloaded ships. Dishonest lumpers dressed in specially adapted clothes; as PATRICK COLQUHOUN, the man who eventually brought some law and order to the river, wrote: 'Many of them were provided with an under-dress, denominated a "Jemmy", with pockets before and behind; also with long narrow bags or pouches which, when filled, were lashed to

Continued on p. 229

RIOTS

As clear an expression of the lawless spirit of London as the depredations of highwaymen and footpads was the readiness to riot. Often rioters were from the same pool of the desperately poor as criminals. Many were apprentices. Riots were sometimes whipped up by political factions, sometimes the expression of economic desperation and sometimes almost inexplicable. In London they were also sometimes the result of bigotry.

Jews were banned from the coronation of Richard the Lion-heart in 1189. When some were found they were attacked, and it was rumoured that the king had ordered a pogrom. There was a general attack on Jews, and their homes were looted. What seemed to be a general hatred of foreign merchants and craftsmen was responsible for the EVIL MAY DAY Riots in 1517. Troops were called in after a mob attacked the foreigners' homes and workshops. In June 1595 there were food riots, with apprentices seizing fish and butter, paying what they considered to be a fair price, not the going rate. The authorities responded by appointing marshals with the power to execute trouble-makers.

In 1668 thousands of Londoners attacked and destroyed brothels in what became known as the BAWDY HOUSE RIOTS. The riots lasted five days and caused a panic because of the rumoured participation of veterans of Cromwell's army. Four apprentices were found guilty of high treason and were hanged, drawn and quartered.

The Sacheverell riots of March 1710 were ostensibly an attack on Dissenters, although they were also a symptom of the strains between Tories and Whigs. A High Anglican Tory clergyman, Dr Henry Sacheverell, preached in St Paul's Cathedral attacking Dissenters and their friends in Church and State. He also implicitly attacked the 1688 Revolution, and he was tried for seditious libel in Westminster Hall in February and March 1710. There was popular support for Sacheverell, and on 1 March the riots began. There is evidence that they were directed by Tory gentlemen. The targets were very specific –

The great Chartist meeting on Kennington Common in 1848. More than 80,000 special constables were sworn in and Wellington called out the troops. The Chartists backed down and instead of marching delivered their petition to the House of Commons in cabs.

important Dissenter meeting houses, which were destroyed. Their furnishings were piled up in great bonfires. The rioters also planned to attack Whig targets, including the Bank of England.

In 1715 the RIOT ACT gave magistrates stronger powers, and it was soon in use. The silk weavers of Spitalfields, whose livelihoods were at the mercy of imports, seasonal demand, cheap labour and labour-saving machinery were quick to resort to collective violence. The new fashion for calico was a particular target, and they attacked women wearing it, tearing off their clothes and calling them 'calico madams'. When a group of silk weavers headed for Lewisham to destroy calico printing presses troops shot one dead. Eventually in 1720 an Act was passed banning the wearing of calico.

The economically troubled years of the 1760s saw a series of weavers' riots. In 1763 they smashed engine looms, and two years later when 8,000 of them marched on Parliament the Duke of Bedford's coach was wrecked. Once again the weavers won a temporary reprieve, all foreign silk imports being banned. Three years later the weavers, who had organised themselves into secret societies, attacked engine-looms and their operatives in an attempt to get higher wages. In one raid they damaged seventy-six looms. In September 1769 troops were stationed in Spitalfields, and two weavers were killed when soldiers raided the Dolphin Tavern, one of their strongholds. Two of the weavers' leaders were hanged at Bethnal Green in December.

The WILKES riots of 1768 led to bloodshed. Wilkes's attack on the government in his weekly journal the *North Briton* caused them to lose their heads and send him to the TOWER. Released, he was escorted home by a mob of many thousands, and for the first time the cry 'Wilkes and Liberty' was heard. When Wilkes was jailed again there was widespread unrest. A mob surrounded the King's Bench prison where he was being held. WILLIAM HICKEY was among those outside on 10 May. A justice, Mr Gillan, described by Hickey as 'a blockhead', ordered the reading of the Riot Act, and then ordered troops to open fire. At this point Hickey and a companion saw a soldier execute a man who had dropped to his knees to plead for his life. About nine other people were killed in what became known as the St George's Fields massacre. A soldier was charged but acquitted over the killing of the executed man, as was the magistrate. The very fact that a magistrate had been charged may account for the fact that when the GORDON RIOTS raged in 1780 it was some time before a magistrate could be found to read the Riot Act.

The Corn Laws riots of March 1815 marked the beginning of years of popular radicalism. Troops were used to restore order in 1815, but the postwar depression and high unemployment kept the working classes in a ferment. In December 1816 after a rally in Spa Fields in Clerkenwell a crowd which had seized weapons from gunshops threatened the Tower. They moved off before troops arrived.

Popular support for Queen Caroline, estranged wife of George IV, led to enormous demonstrations in 1820. They were some of the biggest the city had seen. When Caroline died in August 1821 the government, fearing fresh demonstrations, planned to get her body to Harwich by a route which bypassed the City. Huge crowds throwing stones at troops and Bow Street Runners harassed the procession as it made its way from Hammersmith to the New Road. The troops fired back, killing two men. Barricades at Tottenham Court Road forced the procession to turn south towards Fleet Street. It passed through the City, a triumph for the London mob.

The creation of PEEL's new police force in 1829 meant that rioters were confronted by a force without overwhelming firepower, although from time to time the police were stiffened with troops. For the great Chartist meeting on Kennington Common in 1848 more than 80,000 special constables were sworn in and Wellington called out the troops. Feargus O'Connor, the Chartist leader, backed down and instead of marching on Westminster delivered the great Petition to the House of Commons in cabs. There were other Chartist rallies in London in 1848, and increasing government repression, but when Chartist leaders joined Irish nationalists in planning an armed rising for August 1848 their cause was lost. They were betrayed, six were transported for life and another fifteen jailed.

The winter of 1886 was the coldest for thirty years and unemployment was high. On 8 February a vast mob of unemployed dockers and building workers, perhaps 20,000 strong, who had been attending a rally in Trafalgar Square went on the rampage through Mayfair and St James's, robbing the rich and plundering the shops of Piccadilly and Oxford Street. For two days there was panic as rumours spread that mobs were gathering all over London to sack the West End again. The following year, on Sunday

In 1789–90 a series of attacks on women by a man wielding a spike led to the arrest and imprisonment of Rhynwick Williams, who was dubbed The Monster. Colleagues said he was working at the times of the attacks and victims said The Monster was better educated.

13 November, police and soldiers reinforced by special constables dispersed a crowd of Socialist demonstrators, many of them unemployed workers, in Trafalgar Square. Two people died in what became known as the BLOODY SUNDAY RIOTS.

A mass meeting held at Cold Bath Fields in Clerkenwell in May 1833 by the National Union of the Working Classes led to a pitched battle with the police, who baton-charged the crowd. A constable, Robert Culley, was stabbed to death, and a coroner's jury later called it 'justifiable homicide'.

In the twentieth century the confrontations were bigger if not bloodier, with the police themselves sometimes becoming the focus of the protests. In August 1958 there were serious race riots in NOTTING HILL. In 1981 violent rioting, the worst in Britain in the twentieth century, broke out in BRIXTON, south London, an area with a large black population.

their legs and thighs, and concealed under wide trousers . . . By these means they were enabled to carry off sugars, coffee, cocoa, ginger, pimento, and every other article which could be obtained by pillage.' Ships that were easy targets were known by the cant phrase as 'game ships'. Some lumpers would work for nothing, so profitable was it to work on a 'game' ship.

The daytime thieves or 'heavy horsemen', who were large-scale pilferers, had their night-time counterparts, the more rapacious and organised 'light horsemen'. They were gangs of robbers who would steal whatever they could sell, but their main targets were the cargoes of sugar. It has been estimated that towards the end of the eighteenth century £70,000 worth of sugar was being stolen every year.

The greatest criminal enterprise in eighteenth-century London was the plunder of ships. An army of thieves preyed on the hundreds of vessels as they queued to be unloaded. Fences waited in taverns and safe houses to take the goods away. Sugar was the main target, but spices and drink were also stolen.

Sailors work on the rigging of a ship in London docks. This was one of the scenes that fascinated Dickens as he prowled London in search of scenes of 'prodigies of wickedness'.

Crime on this scale needed financing, and a network of riverside receivers or fences evolved to handle it. In particular they provided the bribe money paid to Customs officers to look the other way, to ship's officers and watchmen to be absent or asleep when the criminals came on board. The bribes to individual Customs officers could be as high as twenty or thirty guineas a night. Not all fences were professionals: publicans, pawnbrokers and second-hand dealers did good business on the docks.

The plunderers targeted West India merchantmen in particular. After they had boarded the ships in the dark they opened sugar casks and removed some of the contents before re-sealing them. The sugar was put into the 'black strip' – a bag large enough to contain one hundred pounds of sugar and dyed black so as to be invisible in the darkness. Meanwhile the watermen in the organisation would procure as many boats as possible. Lumpers would unstow the casks, coopers take out the heads, all would then fill and remove the bags, taking not just sugar, but coffee, rum, ginger etc. 'Mudlarks' would prowl in the mud under the ship to receive from the lumpers and others miscellaneous articles. At the riverside the receivers would be waiting to move the goods to safe premises. The work went on quietly and efficiently.

Other useful members of these gangs were rat-catchers, who were allowed on board ships at night to catch rats. Sometimes they moved the rats caught on one ship to another, thus getting paid for catching the same animals several times. All the while they would be carrying out reconnaissance missions for the gangs and sharing in the eventual plunder.

Patrick Colquhoun wrote of the light horsemen: 'Among the various classes of depredators on the West India trade in the Port of London, those denominated *Light Horsemen* seem to have been by far the most pernicious . . . The receivers who resided in the vicinity of the river on both sides were the chief leaders in this peculiar system of plunder; and it was carried on by the connivance of the mate and the revenue officers, in consequence of a preconcerted plan and agreement to pay them a certain sum of money for the liberty of opening and removing from such casks and packages as were accessible as much sugar, coffee and other articles as could be conveyed away in four or five hours during the dead of night . . . These infamous proceedings were carried on according to a regular system.'

Coopers were another problem. Many goods were shipped in barrels of various sizes. One of the cooper's tasks was to open the barrels so the goods could be quality tested. In some cases – sugar was one – he was allowed to draw off and keep three-quarter-pound samples, but he would also fill a bladder with pilfered liquor and take it ashore secretly in his tool bag. The barrels might be as much as 20 lb underweight because the cooper had caused excessive 'spillage'. This spillage was the sugar or other commodity left on the barrel when the cooper had taken the sample. It would be swept up and sold for the benefit of the warehouse workers. The coopers' perks were so valuable that when the West India merchants set up their own police force in 1798 the coopers demanded more money to cover their loss of earnings.

Against this highly organised and efficient system of plunder the authorities had as yet no answer. The Customs service had its hands full trying to control smuggling: they turned a blind eye to other crimes, as Colquhoun claimed. Sometimes they were well paid to do so. Ship owners did employ night watchmen. They found it wise to sleep through a robbery or even join in. When privately hired watchmen or vigilantes tried to intervene large fires were started in the close-packed warehouses by the Pool of London.

The West India Company, which suffered most from the plundering, approached Dr Colquhoun, a merchant and magistrate who had written a *Treatise on the Police of the Metropolis*. He set up a force of 200 armed men, called the Marine Police Institute, in 1798 and soon they were fighting bloody battles with the robbers. Colquhoun had notices entitled *Caution against Pillage and Plunder* nailed to the masts of ships which were about to be unloaded, and a marine police officer would read out the new regulations for unloading. As we have seen, the coopers demanded more money for their lost perks, and the lumpers sometimes left the ships immediately they realised there would be no more plunder. Colquhoun claimed that losses from the West India ships in the first year of the new regime were cut to *one-fiftieth* of the previous rate.

As the success of the new force became obvious other ships' owners and merchants sought to get its protection extended. Gradually the Thames River Police came into being, but not without resistance.

One night in October 1799 two coal heavers and a waterman's boy were arrested for stealing coal. They were taken to the Marine Police offices at Wapping New Stairs where a magistrate found them guilty and fined them forty shillings each.

A mob gathered outside and after the three were sentenced began hurling cobbles at the Marine Police office. They shouted that they would kill those inside. All the windows in the building had by now been shattered. One of the police officers fired a pistol from a window, and killed one of the rioters. The magistrates from the office went out to read the Riot Act but were driven back. A shot said to have been fired by the rioters killed a man helping the police, one Gabriel Franks. After order was restored one of the mob, James Eyres, was arrested and charged with murder. The authorities were by no means sure of their case. The indictment reads: '. . . not that any evidence can be offered to you that he discharged the pistol by which Franks was killed, but that he was an active man in the riot, encouraging and inciting it'. Eyres said the rioters were unarmed, and the shots came from inside the police office, but he was convicted and sentenced to death. In 1801 John Fisher, aged 23, was convicted of stealing 800 lb of sugar from the Dundee Wharf and hanged. It was 'the first case of a hanging for this crime recorded in the *Newgate Calendar*' (McLynn, *Crime and Punishment in Eighteenth-Century England*).

Lawlessness on the river had passed its peak by then, but the problems of protection for cargoes were not finally solved until the building of enclosed docks at the beginning of the nineteenth century. At first each dock company organised its own police force: they were united under the Port of London Authority in 1909.

RIX, SIR BRIAN Comic actor and mental health campaigner whose involvement in a traffic incident led to the 1960 Royal Commission on the Police. Rix was stopped for speeding while driving on Putney Heath in December 1958. While he argued with the police officer, a PC Eastmond, another driver stopped and became involved. He offered to be a witness to the fact that Rix had not been speeding. There was an argument and the second driver, a civil servant named Garrett, was pushed through a hedge. He was then arrested for assaulting a police officer, but when he was taken to a police station the officer in control refused to accept the charge. Mr Garrett sued PC Eastmond for assault. The Metropolitan Police denied liability but settled out of court, paying Mr Garrett £300. The Met also announced that they would not be taking disciplinary action against Eastmond. This led to a campaign by Labour MPs, and the setting-up of the Royal Commission. It led to the first steps towards the modern procedure for complaints against the police, and incidentally to massive pay rises for the seriously underpaid force. As one union leader put it: 'If you want to get a pay rise, push a civil servant over a hedge.'

ROBERTS, HARRY Post office raider and police killer. He and two other criminals, John Duddy and Jack Witney, were in a car stopped in Shepherd's Bush in 1966 by three police officers. The criminals were on their way to rob a rent collector. One of the officers noticed that the tax disc on their van was out of date. Roberts later told the *Evening Standard* what happened next:

> DC Wombwell was talking to Jack through the window of our van. He was shouting and trying to get the door open. Jack said: 'Let the slag have it, Harry.' I shot him point-blank with the Luger, one shot at the bottom of his eye. As Wombwell fell I turned towards DS Head on the other side of the van. He started running back towards their car. I aimed quickly and got him right in the middle of the back. He fell but he wasn't dead. I ran up and aimed at his head. I pulled the trigger. It misfired. I pulled the trigger again. It misfired again. He got up and staggered to the car but fell down in front of it. PC Fox tried to drive off but he jammed DS Head under the wheels. Then Duddy shot PC Fox in the head.

Roberts, a decorated former soldier, and his accomplices were jailed for life, with a recommendation that they serve not less than 30 years. Duddy died in prison and Witney was released in the 1990s. In 1993 Roberts, still in prison, told the *Guardian*: 'We were professional criminals. We don't react the same way as ordinary people. The police aren't like real people to us. They're strangers, they're the enemy.' For some time fans taunted police patrolling football grounds by chanting:

> Harry Roberts, he's our man,
> He shoots coppers, bang bang bang.

ROBINSON, BRIAN (1944–) Armed robber, known as the The Colonel. Robinson led the gang which stole £26 million in gold bullion from the Brink's-Mat warehouse at Heathrow in November 1983.

ROCHESTER, LORD (1647–80) John Wilmot, second Earl of Rochester, was wit, rake, poet of genius and debauched crony of King Charles II. He was described by the Count de Grammont:

> His manners were those of a lawless and wretched mountebank; his delight was to haunt the stews, to debauch women, to write filthy songs and lewd pamphlets; he spent his time in gossiping with the maids of honour, broils with men of letters, the receiving of insults, the giving of blows . . . For five years together he was said to be drunk . . . Once with the Duke of Buckingham he rented an inn on the Newmarket Road and turned innkeeper, supplying the husbands with drink and defiling their wives. . .'

Bishop Burnet wrote that Rochester was 'naturally modest till the court corrupted him'. He also paid tribute to his wit, which had 'a peculiar brightness to which none could ever arrive'. Burnet described some of the pranks Rochester got up to. Once the earl dressed a footman as a sentry and posted him outside the apartments of some high-born women involved in 'intrigues'. When the man had gathered enough evidence Rochester would repair to the country for a period in order to write up his 'libels' or satires against the women. He presented one of these to the king, hoping to amuse him. But Rochester was drunk, and by mistake he handed over a satire he had written about the king. As Burnet wrote: 'The king loved his company for the diversion it afforded, better than his person, and there was no love lost between them.' Rochester died aged 33 in 1680, apparently after seeking the consolations of religion on his deathbed from Bishop Burnet.

ROOKERIES *see* opposite

ROSE TAVERN Notorious hostelry in Russell Street, near the Drury Lane Theatre. The Rose, although not a brothel, was a meeting place in the eighteenth century for whores and their clients. It also served first-class food. At the turn of the eighteenth century the Rose was described as 'the Resort of the worst Characters in the Town, male and female, who make it the Headquarters of Midnight Orgies and drunken Broils where Murders and Assaults frequently occur'. Thomas Brown in *The Midnight Spy* called it 'that black school of SODOM' referring to men who paid 'posture molls' to flog them. These women were strip-tease artists who would also flog or be flogged. Plate 3 of Hogarth's *The Rake's Progress* shows a posture moll undressing for her act. Around her drunken whores are robbing their customers, becoming quarrelsome and getting ready for 'midnight orgies and drunken broils'. In the background a porter known as Leathercoat is bringing in a large pewter platter and a candle. These are the posture moll's props. She would strip naked and dance on the dish. Sometimes the posture molls played a version of the 'chuck game' made famous by the bawd and whore PRISS FOTHERINGHAM in the previous century. After stripping the posture woman would lie on her back, draw her knees up under her chin and clasp her hands under her thighs. Descriptions of this performance invite you to imagine what happened next as the drunken customers crowded round. At some stage the posture woman would snuff out a lighted candle in an obscene simulation of sex.

Posture molls were not prostitutes, and resented being asked for sex. 'They had a great aversion to whoring . . . their function was to flagellate or be flagellated to arouse sexual desire in the gentlemen.'

Most of London's famous whores, starting with SALLY SALISBURY, used the Rose. Pepys ate there with Doll Lane, and through its rooms over the generations passed the great Toasts of the Town, Betsy Carless, known as Careless, LUCY COOPER, Elizabeth Thomas and FANNY MURRAY, as well as princes and paupers, poets and playwrights, merchants and broken servants, conmen, mountebanks, rakes, lawyers and distinguished foreigners. Among its most famous customers were the actors and managers from the nearby theatre,

Continued on p. 237

ROOKERIES

The Devil's Acre slum in the shadow of Westminster Abbey by Gustave Doré. This was one of the rookeries, 'ancient citadels of vice and crime', that were seldom penetrated by police.

These teeming slums of Georgian and Victorian London were breeding grounds of criminals, referred to as rookeries and descibed as 'ancient citadels of vice and crime.' They extended east in a line very roughly from Westminster along the Strand and Fleet Street, then north and east in a great arc around the City, ending south of the Thames with the ancient and infamous Mint in Southwark.

Although Westminster was a wealthy district in the reign of Elizabeth I it had no industries. Already the poor were clustered around the Abbey, 'for the most part without trade or mystery . . . many of them wholly given to vice and idleness'. In Victorian times there was an area to the south and west of the Abbey inhabited by cracksmen, prostitute thieves and the males thieves who lived with them. There was an enclave known as Devil's Acre around Pye Street with a particularly bad reputation. After Victoria Street was driven through the worst part of Westminster John Hollingshead wrote of the

Dudley Street at Seven Dials, an area of strident vice, poverty and overcrowding from the seventeenth century on. Whores who lodged here plagued the nearby theatres. The area was also a nest of coiners.

overcrowding thus created, and described seventy streets and their courts either side of it. He singled out Orchard Street and Pye Street, the 'openly acknowledged high street of thieves and prostitutes'.

To the north of the Strand lies Covent Garden, long the centre of the capital's vice and entertainment industries. Further north was the hideous slum of ST GILES, the most feared of all the rookeries. It was easily accessible from Leicester Square, the Haymarket and Regent Street, the haunts of hordes of thieves and prostitutes. They could slip down dark alleys and courts and reach the asylum of St Giles in minutes. At the heart of the rookery was Rats' Castle, a 'large, dirty building' which stood on the foundations of an eleventh-century leper hospital. Dickens had visited it in the company of two police officers.

> Saint Giles's Church strikes half past ten. We stoop low, and creep down a precipitous flight of steps into a dark close cellar. There is a fire. There is a long deal table. There are benches. The cellar is full of company, chiefly very young men in various conditions of dirt and raggedness. Some are eating supper. There are no girls or women present. Welcome to Rats' Castle, gentlemen, and to this company of noted thieves!

Another rookery lay to the south of High Street St Giles – Seven Dials, where the gangster BILLY HILL was born in 1911 – and the streets around it, Drury Lane and its adjacent streets and alleys and Covent Garden nearby. For much of the eighteenth and nineteenth centuries these were known as places where thieves and prostitutes lodged.

Located between Fleet Street and the Thames, on the site of the former Whitefriars Monastery, was the rookery known as ALSATIA. After the monasteries were dissolved the inhabitants claimed they were exempt from the jurisdiction of the City. Their claim was upheld first by Queen Elizabeth, and then by James I in 1608, with the result that criminals flooded in. The privileges were withdrawn in 1623 but here, as in the other sanctuaries around the capital, it was many years before law and order was restored.

The rookery of Saffron Hill lay between Clerkenwell Green and Smithfield. Saffron Hill, which spawned the DARBY SABINI gang of Anglo-Italians in the twentieth century, was already notorious for its brothels in the reign of James I. Smithfield itself had many dangerous streets: they included Shoe Lane and Field Lane, and the courts and alleys around them. In the 1830s Dickens made the area the scene of the activities of the Jewish gang leader and fence Fagin.

In a flash house, young criminals gamble away the spoils of the day. The girls, little more than children, were mostly prostitutes. Henry Mayhew said of the street children 'their most remarkable characteristic . . . is their extraordinary licentiousness'.

Further east was Hoxton, where criminal families concentrated as demolitions and improvements destroyed some of the old rookeries. In 1902 the social reformer Charles Booth wrote: 'Hoxton is the leading criminal quarter of London, and indeed of all England.' In the early twentieth century the Hoxton Mob was one of the capital's more formidable gangs. The district also spawned the Nile Mob, a gang of pickpockets.

Further east again the districts of Whitechapel and Spitalfields were long known as criminal 'hot spots'. The eighteenth century burglar JACK SHEPPARD, hero of Gay's *The Beggar's Opera*, was born in Spitalfields. Nearby was the Nichol, the district called the Jago in Arthur Morrison's novel *A Child of the Jago*. ARTHUR HARDING, a noted gangster of the early twentieth century, was born there in 1886.

This area shared with others the advantage of being just outside the City, with easy access to its plunder. Before 1829 thieves could slip over the border away from the City and escape the attentions of its better-organised and more vigorous police. After the establishment of the Metropolitan Police in 1829 the process worked in reverse: thieves could slip into the City, where the police were not reformed until 1838–9, to escape the attentions of the new force. Young thieves would be taught from childhood the quickest escape routes from the City to the safety of the nearest rookery.

This borderland just beyond the City limits, an arc from Bishopsgate round to Aldgate and beyond, contained noted criminal areas. Perhaps the most famous street was Petticoat Lane, renowned for receiving and the sale of stolen goods. IKEY SOLOMONS, the 'Prince of Fences', had a house in Bell Lane.

Especially noted for criminal activity were Brick Lane, Church Lane and WENTWORTH STREET. Other notorious streets nearby were Essex Street, Church Street, Fashion Street, Flower and Dean Street, Thrawl Street, Lower Keate Street and George Yard.

In Wapping there was an area known as the Mint which was another Alsatia. In the mid-1720s law officers attempted to expel criminals who used it as a stronghold, but were driven off. One of them was ducked in a cesspit, and another frog-marched away with a turd in his mouth.

South of the River Thames, the OLD MINT in Southwark, alongside the Borough High Street, had been exempt from City authority since Elizabethan times. In 1861 Hollingshead wrote that 'no

Field Lane in Smithfield, about 1840. This was a dangerous criminal rookery. In the 1830s Dickens made the area the scene of the activities of the gang leader and fence Fagin.

speculator has been bold enough to grapple with the back streets – the human warrens – on the south side of the metropolis; to start from Bermondsey, on the borders of Deptford, and wriggle through the existing miles of dirt, vice and crime as far as the Lambeth Marshes'.

The Lisson Grove area of Marylebone was another criminal hot-spot. A policeman told W.A. Miles in the 1830s: 'Lisson Grove is the haunt of thieves . . . The worst and of all sorts . . . they spread themselves over London by day, in order to work (i.e. thieve). The neighbourhood is swarming with youth of both sexes, from eight to twenty years of age – all thieves. He thinks they fence the property in the Grove.'

There were many lesser criminal strongholds. The map of criminal haunts in the eighteenth century would show, besides the major sanctuaries, trouble spots in Holborn including Shoe and Fetter Lanes, and parts of Barbican and Bankside. The law-abiding would avoid Chick Lane in Clerkenwell, Thieving Lane near Westminster Abbey and Petty France in Westminster. 'The riverside area from St Catherine's to Limehouse was widely considered a "no-go" area.'

The rookeries of St Giles and Clerkenwell were partly obliterated in the 1840s and 1850s with the building of New Oxford Street, Queen Victoria Street and Farringdon Road. Victoria Street penetrated the Pye Street rookery in the shadow of Westminster Abbey in the 1850s, and Commercial Street was cut through Whitechapel and Spitalfields. The ruthless destruction gathered pace later in the century with Shaftesbury Avenue, Charing Cross Road, Queen Victoria Street, Clerkenwell Road and Holborn Viaduct being driven through working-class areas. Between 1830 and 1880 an estimated 100,000 people were evicted by the new roads. The Nichol went in the late nineteenth-century slum clearances. In the 1890s it was replaced by the Boundary Street Estate, the first of the London County Council developments.

In Holborn and the Strand about 6,000 tenants from thirty filthy courts and alleys between Bell Yard and Clement's Lane were evicted in the late 1860s to make way for the Law Courts, and thousands more were cleared out for the construction of Holborn Viaduct. Where did the poor who lived in these areas go? Superintendent G.W. Cornish of Scotland Yard believed the crimes associated with these areas were dispersed across London, but mostly the poor crowded into neighbouring areas such as Spitalfields, making conditions there even worse. Church Lane, one of the streets that survived the building of New Oxford Street through northern St Giles in 1844–7, was invaded by refugees from the demolished slums. The twenty-eight houses in Church Lane had a population of 655 in 1841: by 1847 it had risen to 1,095. These ousted Holy Landers were soon reinforced by a flood of Irish refugees fleeing famine in their homeland.

Slum clearance was inevitable, given the urgent need for new roads, railways and docks, but it was also seen as a cheap and easy method of getting rid of 'congregations of vice and misery'. It suited the authorities, and it suited the developers, who found slum land relatively cheap and slum dwellers easy to get rid of.

including David Garrick, Sheridan, Sarah Siddons and Peg Woffington. The *Covent Garden Eclogue*, published in 1735, catches something of the atmosphere:

> The Watch had cried 'Past One' with hollow strain
> And to their stands returned to sleep again.
> Grave Cits and bullies, rakes and squeamish Beaux
> Came reeling with their doxies from the Rose . . .

Leathercoat, a man of prodigious strength, would lie down in the street and allow a carriage to pass over his chest for the price of a drink.

ROUSE, ALFRED (1893–1931) Commercial traveller who murdered a hitchhiker so that he could fake his own death. Rouse was a philanderer reputed to have seduced more than eighty women. It was said that a brain operation carried out after he was wounded at Givenchy in 1915 increased his sexual appetites. He and his wife Lily had no children, but she looked after one of his many illegitimate offspring at their home in Finchley, north London. Rouse was a success in his work, earned a good income and was a popular member of clubs where he sang Victorian ballads. By 1930 however he was less prosperous and a woman in Wales was expecting his child. Rouse seems to have promised her a life of luxury. What followed was probably an attempt to start a new life with her.

On the night of 6 November 1930 two men walking home after a Bonfire Night dance to Hardingstone Village near Northampton saw a fire in a hedgerow. As they drew near a man climbed out of a ditch and said: 'It looks as if someone has had a bonfire.' They later identified him as Rouse. The two men found a blazing car, and called the police. Sprawled across the two front seats was the charred body of a man. It looked as though Rouse had died in a tragic accident. The car was traced to Rouse, then the man himself turned up, and questioned by police he said: 'I am glad it is over, I have had no sleep.' He said that he had picked up the hitchhiker near St Albans, and later stopped to relieve himself, asking his passenger to fill up the petrol tank. He claimed he walked fifty yards into a field, and turned to see the car was on fire. 'I saw the man was inside, and I tried to open the door, but could not, as the car was a mass of flames . . . I lost my head.' Rouse hinted that the passenger had started the fire by lighting a cigarette, but this would not explain how he came to be inside the car when the fire started. Rouse was charged with murder. He was tried at Northampton Assizes in 1931, and sentenced to death. After his execution the *Daily Sketch* published his confession, in which he described how he strangled the hitchhiker and then set fire to the car. Rouse's medical condition made the case controversial. His wife wrote afterwards to a friend: 'I cannot but grieve to think that it was only his head-wounds that made him a sex-maniac . . .'

RUSSELL, PATIENCE One of the great beauties of the second half of the seventeenth century: Marcellus Laroon left a portrait of her. She may have been the mistress of LORD ROCHESTER, who left her the large sum of £160. She probably worked in one of MRS CRESSWELL's brothels. She was named in *The Wandering Whore* as one of the great bawds of the kingdom.

Patience Russell, who probably worked in one of Mother Cresswell's brothels. Her mask and fan, symbols of the courtesan, give her away. Lord Rochester left her the large sum of £160.

RUSSO, VICTOR 'SCARFACE JOCK' Thug who saved the gangster JACK SPOT from prison. On 20 June 1956 Big Tommy Falco, who worked as a driver for ALBERT DIMES, was slashed outside the Astor Club near Berkeley Square and had forty-seven stitches in his arm. He claimed that Spot had attacked him. When Spot came to trial at the Old Bailey Russo was a witness for the defence. He said he was walking in Soho when BILLY HILL, Dimes and other mobsters drew up alongside him in a big Buick limousine. They asked him to allow himself to be slashed in the face by one of Hill's men, and say it had been done by Spot. The reasoning was that his face was so scarred already during his years in the Glasgow underworld it wouldn't make much difference. The payment was £500 before and another £500 after the court case.

Russo took the £500 and left for Glasgow, phoning Hill to say he wouldn't be back for the second instalment. The *Daily Mirror* columnist Cassandra called Russo 'a hacked-up rat' and 'a degenerate with treachery in his heart, compared with whom Judas was a thousandfold saint who had the decency to find a tree and a rope'. Yet Russo had shown considerable courage in speaking up for Jack Spot. The prosecution called Hill as a witness. The judge rebuked him for using underworld jargon. When Spot's counsel asked him if he called himself 'King of Soho' he denied it. Asked how he would style himself he replied: 'The Boss of the Underworld.'

The judge, Mr Justice Streatfield, called Russo's tale 'one of the strangest that can ever have been told even in the Number One court at the Old Bailey'. The jury took twenty minutes to find Spot not guilty, and although there were calls for Hill and his associates to be prosecuted for perjury, the matter was allowed to drop.

Hill's blatant claim to the title 'Boss of the Underworld' in the witness box at the Old Bailey raised official hackles. There were questions in the Commons, and newspapers speculated about exactly what a Boss of the Underworld did. The *Daily Herald* attempted to answer the question:

> Crime – even the shady rackets and 'concessions' that do not qualify for that title – does not pay to be disorganized. Gamblers want to run their dens without interference from ambitious 'gatecrashers'. So do the drinking club operators, the bookies and the smaller fry. Remember – they can't go running to the police for protection. Hence the Boss. He must be an organizer, must possess brains which in the respectable world of business would win him a high place. And he must be ruthless enough to dispense a rough justice throughout the underworld. He is the underworld's distorted symbol of the respectable morality it defies. Quiet crime is his motto.

RYLAND, WILLIAM (?–1783) Engraver to KING GEORGE III who was executed for forgery. Ryland was paid the considerable salary of £300 a year, but got into debt by gambling and keeping a mistress. He forged bills of exchange with a face value of £7,000 and used them as security for bank loans. When the forgery was detected he went into hiding with his wife at the Stepney house of a cobbler named Freeman. Mrs Ryland asked Freeman to mend one of her husband's shoes, and inside was the name Ryland. The cobbler turned Ryland in to get a reward, and when Bow Street Runners arrived to arrest him Ryland cut his throat. He survived to be executed at Tyburn in August 1783.

S

SABINI GANG, THE This combination of Anglo-Italians and Jews based in Clerkenwell dominated much of London's underworld in the inter-war years in a way that is unlikely to be achieved again. They began as racetrack thugs, preying on the bookies, and gradually took over the protection and gambling rackets in central London. They brought a new level of control and professionalism to gangland, and with it a greater degree of lawlessness. Their dominance did not go unchallenged, and there were shootings, stabbings and slashings in pubs, cafés and streets, particularly around their heartlands of Clerkenwell and Holborn. The racetracks of southern England were the scenes of pitched battles, often involving dozens of razor-wielding men. This warfare cost at least eight lives and countless broken bones and stitches. The degree to which society tolerated this level of violence, worse than anything the KRAYS caused, is surprising, although there were questions in Parliament and promises of a crackdown. Certainly the police did not target the gangs in the way they did the Krays and the RICHARDSONS in the sixties.

The gang's leader, Darby Sabini, was born in 1889 in Saffron Hill, in the area known as Little Italy. In the nineteenth century it vied with ST GILES in notoriety. An Italian colony developed there in the 1840s. Darby showed early promise as a boxer but preferred the easier life of a street tough before graduating to big-time gang crime. At the time, that meant gambling in one form or another. Gangsters offered protection to spielers, illegal gambling clubs. Street gambling was also illegal, so racecourse betting was big business. It has been estimated that illegal gambling had an annual turnover of between £350 million and £450 million a year, making it bigger than any other industry except the building trade. With his brothers Harryboy, Joseph, Fred and George, who were important members of his gang, Sabini worked the racetracks. As the East End gangster ARTHUR HARDING recalled, 'The racecourse business was a profitable one. When a gang went to a racecourse like Brighton they could clear £4,000 or £5,000 easy. At Epsom, on Derby Day, it could be £15,000 or £20,000.' Such easy pickings attracted rival gangsters, and widespread gang warfare raged throughout the 1920s and 1930s. The criminals were known as razor gangs, but in fact they used a wide range of weapons, including guns. Detective Chief Superintendent Edward Greeno of the Flying Squad said: 'Darby Sabini and his thugs used to stand sideways to let the bookmakers see the hammers in their pockets.' The bookmakers, or bookies, were forced to pay for the track-side pitches on which they set up their chalk boards showing the odds and runners. The Sabinis would drive bookies off the best pitches and then hire them out to other bookies, some of whom were allied to the gang. The gangs also charged the bookies for various 'services'. They had to pay for the chalk with which they wrote the odds on their boards, and even for sponging down the boards. The stools on which they stood also had to be hired from the gangs. Gangsters sold the sheets of runners, which cost a fraction of a penny to produce, to the bookies for half a crown (12½ p). Every so often there would be a collection for the wife or family of a gangster who had been jailed, and the bookies were expected to make a generous donation. If they didn't cooperate they might be beaten unconscious, but there were means other than crude violence to bring them into line. Gang members would surround their pitches so that the punters could not get through to place a bet. Or their boards would be wiped clean of the runners and odds before betting had finished. However some bookies were themselves powerful criminals, and several of them were members of the Sabini gang. Harding says the Sabinis would import recruits from Sicily, and Darby was said to have Mafia links.

The Sabinis fought a long war with a Birmingham gang called the Brummagem Boys, led by a bookmaker named BILLY KIMBER. But Sabini had connections with the police. 'Directly there was any fighting it was always the Birmingham mob who got pinched. They was always getting time, five-year sentences and that.' Darby Sabini was cornered at Greenford trotting track on 25 March 1921 and escaped a beating from the Brummagem Boys by shooting his way out of trouble. He was arrested but acquitted when he pleaded self-defence – it was not illegal then to carry a gun. That same year Kimber joined forces with a mob from Leeds to eliminate the Sabinis. An all-out attack was planned for the last day of the Derby meeting at Epsom. But in the confusion the Kimber gang ambushed the Leeds men by mistake, and a pitched battle followed. Twenty-three men were later convicted and the Home Secretary, Sir William Joynson-Hicks, vowed to wipe out the gangs. 'It may be difficult to get rid of these gangs all at once, but give me time,' he said.

There were periods of truce, and during one of them Kimber went to Darby Sabini's home at King's Cross to discuss an end to hostilities. He was later found in the street shot in the side. The powerful Jewish bookmaker ALF SOLOMON, a Sabini ally, gave himself up to the police. It was claimed Kimber had threatened Solomon with a revolver, and Solomon had taken it from him. Then, said Solomon, who was acquitted at a subsequent trial, the gun had gone off accidentally. It is more likely that Solomon had taken the pistol to the peace talks. Arthur Harding said that the Sabinis were too cunning for the Birmingham mob, who were 'all rough house, they weren't as clever as the Darby Sabini lot.'

Another gang the Sabinis clashed with early on were the TITANICS from Hoxton. There had been a fight in a West End gambling club and the Sabinis were driven out. Darby decided to take the battle to the Titanics' heartland. According to gangland legend, a convoy of cars drove eastwards towards Hoxton. In the cars were about twenty men with at least ten guns and a hamper of ammunition. The Titanics had been warned, and when the convoy drove into Nile Street on its way to the Albion they were armed and waiting behind upturned market stalls along a fifty-yard length of Nile Street. Other gunmen were placed in the Albion, which commanded a view west along Nile Street. The colourful gangland version of the tale has Darby's men taking cover behind fruit barrows on the other side of the street and opening a lively fire on the pub. Two of the Titanics were wounded. One reason the casualties were low in proportion to the firepower deployed by both sides was that no-one wanted a killing. The death penalty was still in force, and Darby had given strict instructions that no-one was to shoot to kill. The Sabinis also preyed on other criminals, demanding a cut of their loot. As the gangster Billy Hill, who felt that he and robbers like him were not being given the respect they deserved, was later to recall:

> Burglars and thieves had no chance. If they wandered up West they had to go mob-handed. And they had to be prepared to pay out if they were met by any of the Sabinis. If they went into a club it was drinks all round. The prices were usually especially doubled for their benefit . . . The Sabinis, who could rustle up twenty or thirty tearaways at a moment's notice anywhere up West, stood for no liberties, although they were always taking them.
>
> Night after night some thief or other was cut, or had his head bashed in. Merely because he was a thief, and not only a tearaway. Probably because he did not have enough loot on him to pay the Sabinis when they put the bite on him. That was the West End in the 1920s, when I was a kid.

The Sabinis had other rivals. Among them were the WHITE FAMILY from Islington, led by Big Alf White, who had been a lieutenant of the Sabinis. Lesser gangs were led by Hill, one day to become the self-styled Boss of Britain's Underworld, whose team started out as burglars and smash-and-grab raiders, and his later rival Jack Spot, a racecourse thug.

After years avoiding the limelight Darby was named in a Sunday paper as the king of the underworld, sued for libel and lost. He denied being the 'king of the Sabini gang' and also denied making 'twenty to thirty thousand pounds a year' – a fortune at the time. He was unable or unwilling to pay the £775 costs. Somehow he had managed to fritter away much of his huge income, according to Murphy (*Smash and Grab*).

He moved to Brighton, where he had a penthouse in the Grand Hotel. The gangster Colleoni in Graham Greene's novel *Brighton Rock* is based on him. His power was on the wane and when at the beginning of the Second World War the brothers were interned as enemy aliens, their West End empire was carved up between various rivals. Jack Spot was one of the claimants, as were the Whites.

Darby went to prison for receiving – having been framed by some of his old gang, according to one account – and while he was inside his son was killed in action with the Royal Air Force. Darby never recovered, and he died in 1950. After years of control over a large part of the London underworld he left almost no money. The Italians continued to be prominent in crime, but lacked a charismatic leader. Jews, as happened in America, had largely turned away from crime to the professions.

ST CLAIR, LINDI (1951–) Dominatrix who took on the Inland Revenue. When Britain became a member of the European Community the Inland Revenue was able for the first time to tax prostitutes. The tax authorities hired the accountants Deloitte Touche Ross to determine what allowances such sex workers could claim. It was decided these included wear and tear on the tools of their trade such as whips, bondage bars, irrigation pumps, surgical stirrups and rubber suits. St Clair was issued with a tax demand for £19,781 for the year 1974–5, on a turnover of £500,000. The magazine *Private Eye* claimed St Clair had produced a list of her clients, which included His Honour Judge Alan King-Hamilton QC. In 1973 he had sent the bawd JANIE JONES to prison for seven years, calling her the most evil woman he had ever sentenced.

In recent times Miss St Clair, who once claimed to have serviced 267 MPs, has been giving rural folk the benefits of her expertise. She operates from a farmhouse, and told the ITV programme *Girls Behaving Badly*: 'I specialise in men that want to dress up as women.' She described her clients as 'very nice men, clean, educated, kind, nice to talk to'. Obviously not politicians.

ST GILES Most notorious of the criminal ROOKERIES, teeming slums which were 'ancient citadels of vice and crime'. Also known as the 'Holy Land', perhaps because of the large numbers of Irish Catholic immigrants. It covered roughly the area enclosed by Great Russell Street, Long Acre, Drury Lane and Charing Cross Road. Eloquently described by DICKENS and HENRY MAYHEW. It was said to have had for Dickens 'a profound attraction of repulsion'.

As long ago as 1751 over a quarter of its 2,000 houses were gin shops, and it had eighty-two lodging houses which harboured prostitutes and receivers. Mayhew quotes a description by Inspector Hunt of the Metropolitan Police of St Giles in the 1840s, before parts of it were pulled down to make way for New Oxford Street. The streets were so narrow that in places a man had to turn sideways to get between the decayed and verminous buildings. On the corner of Church Street and Lawrence Street was an infamous brothel where the rooms were rented by prostitutes. As Inspector Hunt explained, robbery rather than sex was the business that went on there. The prostitutes would pick up drunken men in the streets round nearby Drury Lane or even as far west as Regent Street and take them back to the brothel. 'When they had plundered the poor dupe he was ejected without ceremony by the others who resided in the room; often without a coat or hat, sometimes without his trousers, and occasionally left on the staircase as naked as he was born.' When the brothel was pulled down it was found to be connected by a series of secret escape routes to other houses in the rookery. These escape routes were a feature of the houses in St Giles. They linked the houses in one street 'by roof, yard and cellar' to those in another, and made it almost impossible for the police to arrest a fugitive there. In some traps had been set for the police. One cellar held a large cesspool, so camouflaged that a pursuing officer might stumble in and disappear into the sewage. Some cellars had holes two feet square low down in their walls. These effectively stopped pursuit, for no police officer would risk crawling through the holes on his hands and knees in the dark. The area's impenetrability and the fact that it had a large Irish population made it seem even more alien. By 1851 it had 54,000 inhabitants, about one fifth of them Irish, living on average about twelve to a house.

SALA, GEORGE AUGUSTUS (1828–95) Journalist and writer of pornography. Sala, war correspondent with the *Daily Telegraph*, was known among the respectable classes for his account of London life *Twice Round the Clock* of 1858. In more louche circles he was known for books like *Miss Bellasis Birched for Thieving*, a tale of middle-class depravity set in a Brighton girls' finishing school. Readers with a taste for flagellation are treated to accounts of the girls being chastised while their spiritual adviser, the Revd Arthur Calvedon, watches through a spy-hole. Afterwards the school's proprietor, Miss Sinclair, assuages his lust. Sala also wrote *Prince Cherrytop and the Good Fairy Fuck*.

SALISBURY, SALLY (1690–1724) The most famous courtesan of early eighteenth-century London. Born Sarah Pridden in 1690, the daughter of a bricklayer, she grew up wretchedly poor in the slums of ST GILES, north of Covent Garden. She was the first working-class 'Toast of the Town'. By the age of 14 she had been seduced, poxed, cured, and, with the help of the famous bawd MOTHER WISEBOURNE, re-virginised. An early friend was the great actress ELIZABETH BARRY, who dropped Sally because of her rough manners and unpredictable temper. As a young teenager she had been the mistress of the notorious rake COLONEL CHARTERIS. When he abandoned her in Bath – perhaps again because of her violent temper – she went back to work for Wisebourne, proprietor of a high-class brothel in Covent Garden. Mother Wisebourne's clients included many aristocrats, and Sally was an asset. She was unabashed in high society, and counted some of the highest in the land among her conquests. They included Viscount Bolingbroke, Secretary of State, who paid 'the highest price for the greatest pleasure'. Others were the dukes of Richmond and St Albans, who was Nell Gwyn's son, the poet Matthew Prior and the Prince of Wales, later to become King George II. For a while she was part of the Duke of Buckingham's 'harem', and a ballad says she played the 'CHUCK GAME'. At a grand society ball the hostess commented on the splendour of Sally's jewels. The waspish whore replied:

Sally Salisbury stabs her lover. She died of jail fever, much lamented by aristocratic lovers and friends. Six gentlemen bore her coffin to the church. She was the first working-class Toast.

> 'They had need be finer than yours, my Lady,' said Sally. 'You have but one Lord to keep you, and to buy you jewels, but I have at least half a score, of which number, Madam, your Ladyship's husband is not the most inconsiderable.'
>
> 'Nay, my Lady' cried another guest. 'You had better let Mrs Salisbury alone, for she'll lay claim to all our husbands else, by and by.'
>
> 'Not much to yours, indeed, Madam,' replied Sally tartly. 'I tried him once and am resolved I'll never try him again; for I was forced to kick him out of bed, because his — is good for nothing at all.' (Walker, *Sally Salisbury*)

Lady Mary Wortley Montagu described in a letter the incident that led to Sally's death: 'The freshest news in Town is the fatal accident happened three Nights ago to a very pritty young Fellow, brother to Lord Finch, who was drinking with a dearly beloved *Drab* whom you may have heard of by the name of Sally Salisbury. In a jealous *Pique* she stabbed him to the Heart with a Knife. He fell down dead immediately but a surgeon being called and the Knife being drawn out of his Body, he opened his Eyes and his first Words were to ask her to be Friends with him, and he kissed her.'

Finch, who was the son of the Countess of Winchelsea, forgave Sally, but his family insisted on prosecuting her. At the trial Sally claimed she acted not from malice but from sudden passion, having discovered that Finch had given her sister a ticket to the opera. She suspected that he wanted to seduce her sister. Sally was found not guilty of attempted murder but guilty of assault and wounding. She was sentenced to a year in Newgate and fined £100. In spite of Finch's pleas she remained in Newgate, where she caught jail fever and wasted away. Here is how the Swiss commentator, César de Saussure, described her death in *A Foreign View of England*:

> You will suppose her lovers abandoned her in her distress. They did no such thing, but crowded into the prison, presenting her with every comfort and luxury possible. As soon as the wounded man – who, by the way, belongs to one of the best-known English families – was sufficiently recovered, he asked for her discharge, but Sally Salisbury died of brain fever, brought on by debauch, before she was able to leave the prison.

Sally was buried at St Andrew's Holborn in February 1724. Her coffin was followed by four coaches, and six gentlemen bore it to the church. She was about 32. Hogarth's print series *A Harlot's Progress* and JOHN CLELAND's *FANNY HILL* owe much to her life and legend. She failed to pay the fine.

SANDWICH, LORD (1718–92) Noted lecher and inventor of the snack which bears his name. A corrupt and inept First Lord of the Admiralty during the American War of Independence, he was a member of the MEDMENHAM ABBEY set of sexual sensation-seekers. Sandwich turned against another member of the set, JOHN WILKES, and on behalf of the government read extracts from the obscene poem the *Essay on Women*, then believed to have been written by Wilkes, in the House of Lords. The intention was to discredit Wilkes's political radicalism. Thereafter Sandwich was known as Jemmy Twitcher for his unspeakable treachery. This is a reference to the line in GAY's *The Beggar's Opera*, then playing in London, 'But that Jemmy Twitcher should peach I own surprises me.' There is a story that one reason for Sandwich's hatred of Wilkes was a joke the latter played on him when they were both members of the Medmenham fraternity. Wilkes acquired a baboon and dressed it up to look like the Devil. One night when the

Medmenham monks were holding a Black Mass, prancing about among the candles in the darkened abbey and calling on the Devil to appear among them, he released the beast from a cupboard where he had hidden it. It jumped on to Sandwich's shoulders and by the time it had been driven off Sandwich was almost insensible with fear. He never forgave Wilkes.

SAVAGE, THOMAS (*c.* 1651–68) Apprentice who was hanged twice for murder. Savage was an idle and drunken apprentice of 17 who murdered his master's servant and robbed his master's house at Ratcliff in 1668. He had been encouraged by his mistress, the 'vile common strumpet' Hannah Blay. He was sentenced to death and after making a short speech, was hanged at Ratcliff Cross. After a friend struck him several times to put him out of his agony he appeared to be dead. He was cut down, but began to breathe again, and was taken to a nearby house. The Sheriff's officers found him there, took him back to the gibbet and hanged him until he was dead.

SAVUNDRA, EMILE (1923–76) Car insurance fraudster. In 1963 he set up Fire, Auto and Marine Insurance and charged premiums which were only half those of his rivals. In 1966, when claims against policies exceeded £1.5 million he resigned and went to Switzerland. It was then discovered that his policies were useless, being written in a way that meant all claims could be refused. He had siphoned off £900,000 which he deposited in a Liechtenstein bank he controlled, and also paid himself £300,000. In 1967 he returned to Britain, was arrested and sent to prison for eight years. He had perfected a technique of simulating hearts attacks, and spent his sentence in hospital. He died of a heart attack in 1976.

SAWARD, JAMES, ALIAS JEM THE PENMAN (1805–?) Successful Queen's Bench defence counsel and criminal, known to his clients as 'Barrister Saward'. Secretly he was also a desperate gambler who had been a professional criminal for nearly forty years. Saward was the notorious forger Jem the Penman, who used his contacts in the underworld to acquire stolen cheques and then forged them for large sums. As he later revealed: 'I had made several thousand pounds a year by various sorts of crime.' He was the fence for the stolen gold in the first GREAT TRAIN ROBBERY. Saward was not named at the trial of the train robbers and was free to carry on both with his successful legal practice and his forgeries. When two of his henchmen were caught and sentenced to transportation for life, Saward went into hiding. He was arrested in a coffee-shop in Oxford Street after a tip-off. At the Central Criminal Court in 1857 he and another accomplice were transported for life.

Saward's *modus operandi* was almost foolproof. After forging a cheque he would pass it to his chief accomplice, a man named Anderson, who passed it to a man called Atwell. Heavily disguised in false beard and moustache, Atwell would hand the cheque to an errand boy and instruct him to cash it at a bank. If the forgery was detected and the boy was arrested, there was no link to Saward.

SAYER, MARY Unfaithful wife whose affairs led to murder. Mary married John Sayer in 1699, and soon began to run through his large fortune. She refused to have sex with her husband and had many lovers. He slept with prostitutes and caught a venereal disease. He sought treatment, and afterwards his surgeon told him he was cured. Mary agreed to have sex with him, and they found they both had the disease. Mary continued to have affairs, including one with a young clergyman. Sayer had bought a large house near Leicester Fields, and Mary's extravagance was in danger of bankrupting him. He sought the advice of an attorney, Richard Noble, who became the lover of both Mary and her mother. Noble and the two women conspired to cheat Sayer of his remaining fortune. Sayer was persuaded to settle most of his money on Mary. She also stole £2,000 from him and went to live with Noble, and Sayer was forced to seek refuge from his creditors in the FLEET PRISON. Sayer was unfortunately still in love with Mary, and he got a magistrate's warrant and went with a party of constables to the lodgings where his wife was living with Noble in the Mint in Southwark, a dangerous criminal ghetto. There was a fight and Noble ran Sayer through with his sword, killing him. Noble and the two women were tried. Noble was condemned and hanged, Mary and her mother were found not guilty.

SCHOOLS FOR THIEVES Fagin in *Oliver Twist* operates a typical school for young pickpockets. MOLL CUTPURSE ran one in the seventeenth century, and in 1585 William Fleetwood, Recorder of the City of London, reported that a man named Wotton was running such a school in his house near Billingsgate:

> There was a school set up to learn young boys to cut purses. There were hung up two devices, the one a pocket, the other was a purse. The

> pocket had in it certain counters and was hung about with hawks' bells, and over the top did hang a little sacring bell; and he that could take out a counter without any noise was allowd to be a Public Foister; and he that could take a piece of silver out of the purse without the noise of any of the bells, he was adjudged a Judicial Nipper.

The sharp increase in the number of juvenile criminals, starting in the Regency period and continuing well into the Victorian, seemed to suggest that the training of young criminals was widespread. In 1816, 514 prisoners under the age of 20 were committed to Newgate, of whom 284 were under 17 and fifty-one under 14. One was 9 years old. The figures from the prison HULKS were even more depressing. The Superintendent of the Hulks reported in 1828 that of the 300 boys in the *Euryalis* – they were all aged 16 or less and had been sentenced to transportation or had a sentence of death commuted to transportation – two were 8 years old, five were 9 years old and 171 were under the age of 14.

Henry Grey Bennet, M.P., chairman of the 1816 Select Committee on the Police, who reported the Newgate figures quoted above, said there were 'above 6,000 boys and girls living solely on the town by thieving, or as the companions and associates of thieves'. He pointed out that he had heard much higher figures quoted.

S.P. Day wrote in 1858 of 'several establishments throughout the metropolis . . . herein the novice is initiated into his future art, and practised daily in sleight-of-hand exercises . . .' In a sense a boy would be lucky to get into one of these schools, as there were far more young criminals than the market could absorb. The brighter and more skilful ones would be chosen, and if they became expert they would be valuable assets, so much so that their adult mentors would lavish money on them for food and drink and a woman.

SCOTLAND YARD The original headquarters of the Metropolitan Police Force was in Great Scotland Yard, part of the precincts of the old Whitehall Palace. In May 1884 Fenian terrorists detonated a bomb which blew in a wall of the building and wrecked a nearby public house. The offices were cramped and inadequate for the growing force, and in 1890 a new HQ, designed by Norman Shaw, opened on a site close to Westminster Bridge. The force quickly outgrew the new headquarters and nearby buildings were included in the complex. This too was eventually inadequate: in 1935 the Commissioner grumbled that his staff were 'crowded together like warehouse clerks in a Christmas rush'. The force moved to its present headquarters, on Broadway and Victoria Street, in 1967.

SCOTT, PETER (1930–) Successful burglar and playboy who stole Sophia Loren's jewels. Scott was an Irishman who claimed he felt a mission to relieve the rich of their surplus wealth. Like TATERS CHATHAM, he used insiders, servants who would tell him when their employers were at home and where they kept their valuables. Mayfair was where he found most of his victims, and after stealing mostly jewels and furs for a number of years he acquired a knowledge of antiques and paintings and began to take them too.

His most famous victim was the Italian film star Sophia Loren. She was making a film in England in May 1960 and staying at the Norwegian Barn in the Edgewarebury Country Club. Scott had read that she was to be paid in jewels. He kept watch and saw the actress putting empty wine bottles in a bin. He broke in and stole cash and jewels worth about £200,000 in what was then the biggest jewel theft ever.

Ms Loren later confronted Scott on television and told him she had put a curse on him. Scott, who remembered her as 'an attractive peasant girl', felt it may have worked because he lost all the money gambling. Having lived a glamorous life, mixing with the wealthy and with beautiful women, he ended up living alone in a council flat in Islington, north London. The man who estimated he stole valuables worth about £30 million spent twelve and a half years in prison and could not face the possibility of another sentence. 'I have no money but I have retained my arrogance. I am not reformed, I just have no more time to offer them, no more of my life to give them behind bars, so I have stopped. There was no road to Damascus, no burning bush, I simply didn't fancy being locked up again.'

SEDDONS, THE Couple accused of poisoning their lodger. Frederick Seddon, who worked for an insurance company, lived with his wife and children in Islington. In July 1910 they took in a lodger, wealthy Eliza Barrow. Miss Barrow, who was 49, was something of a miser, living on £1 a week but having £4,000 in stocks and other valuables. Somehow Seddon persuaded her to sign these over to him in return for an annuity of £3 a week. In September 1911 Miss Barrow began to suffer from vomiting and diarrhoea. She made a will appointing Seddon as executor. For two weeks Seddon's wife

The Seddons in the dock, a rare photograph of a trial in progress. Frederick Seddon ws found guilty of poisoning his lodger. A petition for mercy signed by 250,000 failed.

Margaret looked after Miss Barrow. A doctor who was called said Miss Barrow was suffering from epidemic diarrhoea. Her condition got worse and she died on 14 December 1911.

Seddon did not inform Miss Barrow's relatives of her death, but a cousin who called to see her was told she was dead and buried. When he asked about her fortune Seddon said she had transferred it to him in return for the annuity, which of course was no

Sir Edward Marshall Hall, the great defence barrister. He defended in several sensational murder cases, and won some surprising acquittals, including that of Marguerite Fahmy.

Frederick Seddon, who was hanged for poisoning his lodger. He made a poor impression in court and some felt that was the reason for the guilty verdict.

Miss Barrow. She was a wealthy miser.

longer being paid. The cousin called in the police and Miss Barrow's body was exhumed. She was found to have died of arsenic poisoning.

The Seddons went on trial for murder at the Old Bailey in March 1912. The prosecution claimed they had boiled up fly-papers to extract arsenic, and Mrs Seddon admitted buying the sticky papers to kill flies attracted to the sick-room. Mrs Seddon was acquitted, although the prosecution claimed it was she who had put the arsenic in Miss Barrow's food. Seddon, who was a cold and unsympathetic figure in the witness box, was convicted. He was executed on 18 April 1912 despite a petition for mercy signed by 250,000.

SELLON, CAPTAIN EDWARD (1818–66) Pornographer and railway-carriage seducer. Sellon went to India in the 1830s as an army cadet, returning ten years later as a subaltern without funds. He tried driving the mail coach between Cambridge and London but was put out of business by the growing popularity of trains. Other ventures failed and he began to write pornography for WILLIAM DUGDALE. He was a serial seducer, sometimes in railway carriages, but his own description makes his pornography sound restrained. 'A dream of pleasure without riot, of refined voluptuous enjoyment without alloy.' HENRY SPENCER ASHBEE, on the other hand, said it showed 'an ultra lasciviousness and cynicism worthy of the Marquis de Sade . . .'. In 1866, short of money, Sellon agreed to be the paid companion to a Mr Scarsdale on a tour of Egypt. As they prepared to set out he was waiting alone in a carriage for Scarsdale when he was joined by a young lady Scarsdale was taking along. Sellon hardly had time to find out that she was aged only 15 before they were happily copulating. As their train approached Vienna, Scarsdale fell asleep. Sellon told Dugdale in a letter that he pulled the girl onto his lap and made love to her again 'with her stern towards me'. While he was enjoying her Scarsdale woke up.

> I made a desperate effort to throw her on the opposite seat, but it was no go, he had seen us. A row ensued and we pitched into one another with hearty good will. He called me a rascal for tampering with his fiancee. I called him a scoundrel for seducing so young a girl! And we arrived at Vienna! 'Dammit!' said I as I got out of the train with my lip cut and nose bleeding, 'here's a cursed bit of business.'

Sellon was left adrift in Vienna with only £15. He met the girl again by accident, 'had a final poke and arranged to rendezvous in England'. He returned to London, took a room in a hotel in Piccadilly, wrote a farewell poem to a woman and shot himself.

SELMAN, JOHN Daring cutpurse who tried to rob KING JAMES I. On Christmas Day 1611 Selman was arrested in the chapel at Westminster Hall 'even at the King's elbow' as the monarch was about to take communion. He had earlier been seen picking another man's pocket in the hall. Selman was dressed as a gentleman, which seems to have infuriated the courtiers. He was stripped of his 'gallant apparel' and given suitably 'mean' clothes to appear before a jury and a panel of judges, among whom was the philosopher and statesman SIR FRANCIS BACON. He was found guilty and begged that his body should be given to his wife for Christian burial, and that 'the goods which he had (part of which was well-gotten, some otherwise) not be taken from her'. Bacon agreed to this, provided Selman named 'those of your faculty and fraternity, who are still . . . ready to enter into the presence Chamber of the king' to steal. Selman named a man who, he said, would identify 'many of that profession'. He was executed a few days later.

SEVEN DIALS Notorious criminal district just north of Covent Garden. The gangster BILLY HILL was born there in 1911. Today the area is filled with small boutiques, eateries and offices. In previous centuries it was a centre for coiners and prostitutes.

SHAKESPEARE'S HEAD TAVERN Covent Garden establishment where the WHORE'S CLUB met every Sunday evening. JACK HARRIS, author of the famous *List of Covent Garden Ladies*, is believed to have been head-waiter there at one time, although he had other businesses.

SHEPPARD, JACK (1702–24) Burglar noted for a series of daring escapes from London prisons, culminating in a breakout from NEWGATE the night before he was due to be executed. His defiance of the gangster and thief-taker JONATHAN WILD made him a working-class hero. Sheppard was born in White's Row, Spitalfields, in 1702. During his apprenticeship as a carpenter he showed great skill with locks. While he was living with his master, a man called Woods, he would be locked out at night if he was late, but he 'made a mere Jest of the Locks and Bolts and enter'd in and out at Pleasure'. After a series of thefts and prison breakouts Sheppard was trapped by Wild, on whose evidence he was sentenced to death. The irreverent young Cockney burglar had challenged Wild's control of the underworld by refusing to hand over his loot, and Wild was determined to destroy him. After Sheppard escaped again a team of Wild's men found him and an accomplice on Finchley Common. Sheppard was held in the strongest room in Newgate, the Stone Castle at the top of the prison. He was chained to the floor with iron staples, and special leg irons and handcuffs were made for him. He was under constant observation by the turnkeys. The stage was set for his greatest escape.

Working in total darkness, he first used a nail he had found on the floor to pick the locks of his handcuffs. Then he twisted asunder a small link in the chain binding his legs. Using the broken link as a tool he removed an iron bar from the chimney. With this he removed some of the chimney masonry, and climbed to the room above. There he found a large nail and with it broke through the wall, dislodged the door bolt and entered the chapel. There Jack broke off a spike from one of the railings, and with this he

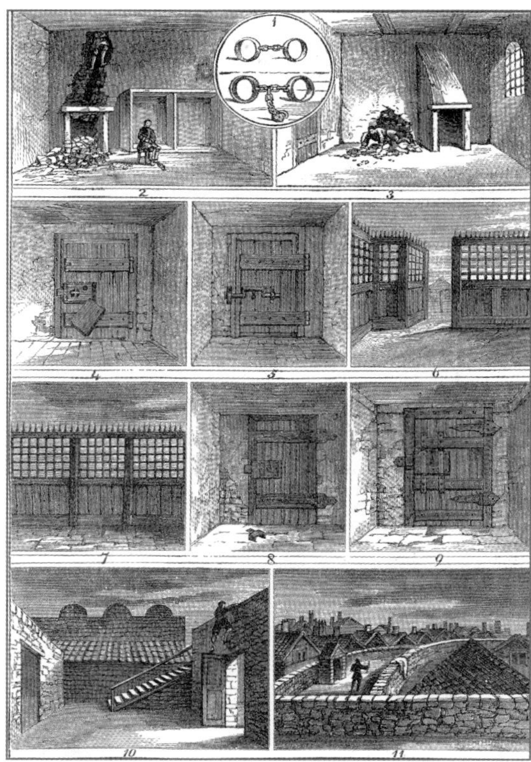

The burglar Jack Sheppard's extraordinary escapes. He refused to cooperate with the gangster Jonathan Wild, and was eventually executed. He became a popular hero, and Wild was demonised for his part in Sheppard's downfall.

wrenched off the bolt-box of the next door. This and the next two doors were all bolted on the other side, yet he broke through them. Now he came to the last door. Once through it he had access to the lower leads of the roof. 'The city lay below him. He knew that "the smallest Accident would still spoil the whole Workmanship",' so he did not risk leaping on to one of the adjoining houses, but retraced his steps through the doors, the chapel, all the way back into the Stone Castle where he retrieved his blanket. Once again on the roof, he drove the chapel spike into the wall, attached the blanket to it and gently lowered himself onto a neighbouring roof. He stole softly down two flights of stairs to freedom. DANIEL DEFOE interviewed the stunned turnkeys, who showed him Sheppard's chains and padlocks and the doors he had escaped through.

After going on the run Sheppard tore his clothes to make himself look like a beggar, and went round the taverns to hear what people were saying about him. With a sweetheart on his arm he set out by coach on a pub crawl. He even drove through Newgate itself. In his finery he paraded through the gin-shops and taverns of Clare Market. That evening he was recaptured. Sheppard was hanged at Tyburn on 16 November 1724.

SHERIDAN, RICHARD BRINSLEY (1751–1816) Playwright who survived a bloody duel. In 1772 he defended the reputation of his future wife against a Captain Matthews. The captain demanded a re-match and Sheridan, who was entitled to refuse, agreed. They fought first with pistols, then swords, then grappled on the ground. The captain stabbed the disarmed Sheridan five times and battered his face with the hilt of his sword so that it was 'nearly beaten to a jelly'.

SHOPLIFTING Probably as old as street trading. The term itself seems to date from the seventeenth century. The 1699 Shoplifting Act prescribed branding on the left cheek near the nose, rather than on the thumb. It was found that such branding condemned the victim to a life of crime, since nobody was going to give employment to somebody marked in this way. So after seven years the practice of branding on the thumb was resumed.

Shoplifting, regarded as a women's crime, seems to have been more commonly practised by men in the seventeenth century. There was usually a team of three, the 'lift', who dressed like a country gentleman, the 'marker' and the 'santer'. The lift would enter a shop and ask to see some bolts of cloth, one of the goods most easily disposed of. As he did not wear a cloak and so had nowhere to hide goods, the shopkeeper would be happy to leave him alone with several bolts of cloth while he went to fetch more. The marker would then enter the shop. While the shopkeeper was away finding yet more cloth, the santer would pass the open window and the marker would pass out bales of cloth to him. When the shopkeeper returned, his goods would be gone but the main suspects would protest their innocence and there would be nothing the shopkeeper could do.

In the eighteenth century London's shopkeepers were practically under siege from nimble-fingered thieves. The thieves' method was more or less the same, but by now they were usually women. Typically the shoplifters or 'hoists', who were often well-dressed, would ask to see rolls of cloth, then try to divert the attention of the assistant while an accomplice hid some of the material under her skirt. Losses were considerable, but the risks were great. Many women shoplifters were executed. Later they were transported in large numbers.

The voluminous clothes fashionable in the Victorian era were ideal for concealing many stolen goods. The full, heavily petticoated bell-shaped skirts reaching to the ankles could conceal a large pouch, extending all round the body. But such clothes made a quick getaway impossible. *See* MARY JONES and SHIRLEY PITTS

SIEGE OF SIDNEY STREET This famous event was the result of an earlier attempted robbery. A gang of anarchist burglars, led by a Latvian named George Gardstein, rented rooms in Exchange Buildings, which backed on to a jeweller's shop at 119 Houndsditch. On the evening of 16 December 1910 they attempted to smash their way through the wall into the shop, and neighbours called the police.

When officers entered the building the robbers opened fire. Two sergeants, Bentley and Bryant, were hit immediately. Bentley fell dead and Bryant, badly wounded, staggered from the house. A Sergeant Tucker was then shot dead and a constable shot in the thigh. Another constable, Choate, grappled with Gardstein. He was shot repeatedly and pulled Gardstein with him as he fell to the floor. In the confusion, Gardstein was shot in the back by one of his own gang. The gang fled, leaving three policemen dead and two badly wounded and dragging Gardstein with them. They took him to their base at 55 Grove Street off Commercial Road. There Gardstein was left with two women while the gang escaped. The horrified women watched as Gardstein died in agony, refusing to be taken to a hospital.

"THE BATTLE OF STEPNEY": The Anarchists' House on Fire

The climax of the Battle of Sidney Street in January 1911, with the anarchists' hideout ablaze. Churchill wanted to blast the building with artillery. He was criticised for calling in the troops.

On 22 December the City of London police offered a £500 reward for information, and an informer gave away two of the gang, Jacob Peters and Osip Federov. On 2 January 1911 another informer told police that members of the gang were hiding in a house in Sidney Street, Stepney. Armed police surrounded the house and the anarchists opened fire. Troops were brought in and the Home Secretary, Winston Churchill, arrived. He proposed that artillery should be used to blast open the front of the house. By the time it arrived the house was on fire in a kind of Wagnerian climax to the whole affair. The flames forced the men inside to retreat and one of them, Jacob Vogel, was shot. His accomplice, Fritz Svaars, died in the flames. During the assault on the house by police and troops a Sergeant Leeson was shot in the chest. He said to FREDERICK WENSLEY, the famous Scotland Yard commander: 'Mr Wensley, I am dying. They have shot me through the heart. Give my love to the children. Bury me at Putney.' He lived and wrote his memoirs. Some spectators were injured by gunfire, and one of the firemen died later. The government was criticised, particularly for calling in the troops. Only one person was convicted at subsequent trials, and that verdict was overturned. Peters was acquitted at the Old Bailey and was later to become deputy head of Lenin's infamous Cheka, the precursor of the KGB, and so was responsible for countless deaths before he too was liquidated in Stalin's purges of the 1930s.

SILVER, BERNIE Successor to the MESSINAS as overlord of vice in the West End. His alliance with the Maltese 'Big Frank' Mifsud was known as The Syndicate. They had run brothels and gaming clubs in the East End before making the takeover in Soho. Silver, a Jew from Stoke Newington in north London, served in the Parachute Regiment during the war. He was discharged on medical grounds in 1943. He later kept a brothel in Brick Lane and became one of the Messina's satellites. As the Messina empire crumbled other Maltese gangsters tried to move in but it was The Syndicate which came out on top. From a strip club they owned in Brewer Street Silver and Mifsud expanded until they owned most of Soho's strip clubs. With Silver providing the brains and Mifsud the muscle, the Syndicate was vastly profitable for two decades. When Silver was tried for running a vice racket there were reports that the Syndicate had £50 million in Swiss bank accounts.

As Silver grew wealthier he acquired expensive tastes – he was buying a £27,000 yacht when he was arrested on vice charges in 1973. By then the partnership with Mifsud was making £100,000 a week, according to the police. Mifsud, a former traffic policeman from Malta, was described as aggressive, generous, forever buying drinks, always loaded with money but dressed 'like a bum'.

Silver went on trial at the Old Bailey in September 1974. The Syndicate was accused of running what prosecutor Michael Corkery called 'a vicious empire . . . an unsavoury world of prostitutes, ponces and pimps'. After a trial that lasted sixty-three days, Silver was found guilty of living on immoral earnings and given six years in jail. He was also fined £30,000. Six Maltese men were also jailed. The judge, Lord Justice Geoffrey Lane, told them: 'The profits you reaped were enormous.' Silver and Mifsud were also charged with conspiring to murder the gangster TOMMY SMITHSON. They were cleared, but the Syndicate was now a spent force, and others moved in. Silver was also an important figure in the Soho PORNOGRAPHY trade.

SINGH, SIR HARI Wealthy victim of the BADGER GAME. Sir Hari, nephew and heir of the Maharajah of Jammu and Kashmir, was 27 when he was sent to England to learn something of English high society at the end of the First World War. He left his wife behind and was placed in the care of a former actor, 'Major' C.W.A. Arthur. One of the events Arthur sent the prince to was the Victory Ball held at the Albert Hall on the first anniversary of the Armistice of 1918. Arthur and his main accomplice, a crooked solicitor's clerk named William Cooper Hobbs, arranged for two attractive women to be in the box next to the prince's. They were Florence Maud Robinson, the wife of a businessman, and a Mrs Bevan. The occupants of the two boxes met and mixed, there were drinks at the Savoy later and the next day the prince and Mrs Robinson met again. Soon they were lovers. The prince's secretary began an affair with Mrs Bevan.

The four lovers went to Paris for Christmas. Mrs Robinson was in bed with the prince in their hotel when there was a knock at the door. The prince was led by Mrs Robinson to believe the caller was her husband, whereas he was another of those involved in the plot, a criminal named Montagu Noel Newton. The prince panicked, fearing that if there were a public scandal he might be disinherited. He turned to Arthur for advice. Arthur said Mr Robinson must be bought off for the extraordinary sum of £300,000. The prince gave him two cheques, each for £150,000.

The prince began musing on the affair and decided to consult solicitors. They advised him to stop the second cheque, which he did. The conspirators now fell out. Mr Robinson felt he had been cheated and sued. Newton told the court that the two Robinsons had been in on the plot from the beginning, and Robinson lost the case. Arthur and Hobbs were jailed.

SKITTLES (*c.* 1850–*c.* 1920) Otherwise Catherine Walters, courtesan. An equestrian portrait of her caused a great Victorian scandal. At the time high-class prostitutes known as 'the pretty horse breakers' used to parade on horseback in Rotten Row, to the scandal of respectable society. The portrait by the leading painter Sir Edwin Landseer, which was voted Picture of the Year in 1861, purported to be of a respectable woman but was clearly of Skittles. The newspapers were scandalised. Catherine was the mistress of Lord Hartington, heir to the Duke of Devonshire, described as the most eligible bachelor in London. She had been a prostitute in Liverpool, and when the duke learned of the affair she was bought off. Hartington went on to a distinguished

Women riding in Rotten Row. Courtesans flaunted their wealth and style by mixing with respectable women there. They were known as 'the pretty horse breakers' and were a great Victorian scandal.

political career, becoming leader of the Liberals in the 1870s. Skittles became one of the *grandes horizontales*, as the most famous courtesans were by then known. She found time to be the lover of the minor poet Wilfred Scawen Blunt, who made her the heroine of his *Love Sonnets of Proteus*. The Prince of Wales visited her parties and Gladstone dropped in for tea. Skittles was remembered for skating with 'memorable grace' at the new roller skating rinks in London and Tunbridge Wells. She was a tiny creature, loved like NELL GWYN for her gaiety, high spirits and warmth.

SLADE, HENRY (1840–1905) Conman and so-called 'slate-writing medium'. Slade cashed in on the Victorian weakness for spiritualism, the belief that the dead could be contacted. Before an audience he would contact his dead wife Alcinda and she would write the answers to his questions on a slate. It was a fairly harmless racket which gave some comfort to the bereaved, but a Professor Edwin Lankester, an evolutionary biologist who had studied with Charles Darwin, decided to expose him. He paid to attend a séance at Slade's London home and when Slade was receiving the answers to questions he snatched the slate away from him. Written on it was the answer to a question that hadn't yet been asked. Slade was prosecuted as a 'common rogue'. His séances had been society events, and the trial became another one. It divided the scientific world, with Darwin's colleague Alfred Russell Wallace appearing for Slade and Darwin providing funds to the prosecution. Slade was convicted and sentenced to three months in prison, but since he had been found guilty under a law against palmists and fortune-tellers, and he was neither, the verdict was overturned. Slade went to America where he died in an asylum in 1905.

SLEAZE As the seat of national government London has been the scene of much morally questionable conduct by politicians (*See* JONATHAN AITKEN, JOHN BELCHER, NEIL HAMILTON, LLOYD GEORGE, JOHN STONEHOUSE). In the 1980s there was a home-grown scandal, the selling by Westminster Council of 'homes for votes'. The council's Conservative leader, Dame Shirley Porter, devised a four-year plan to win the 1990 local elections. Council homes in key marginal wards would be sold to people likely to vote Conservative. People likely to vote Labour were dumped elsewhere, including in tower blocks contaminated with asbestos. A document circulated to her inner circle said: 'Imagine socialists running Buckingham Palace, militants lording it over Parliament and controlling Downing Street, left-wing extremists interfering in the daily running of business.'

The scandal was exposed by the BBC's *Panorama* in 1989, leading to a damning report by the district auditor and a surcharge of £27 million on Dame Shirley, daughter of Sir Jack Cohen, founder of the Tesco supermarket empire. She moved to Israel and her assets went with her. From there the diehard Thatcherite fought a bitter campaign to overturn the verdict of the district auditor and the surcharge. However, in May 2003 she apparently ran out of options when the European Court of Human Rights threw out her appeal.

SLOANES, THE Pillars on the community who were fiendishly cruel to a servant. In December 1850 George Sloane, attorney and director of the Church of England Assurance Association, with a house in Pump Court, Temple, and his wife were accused of cruelty by their servant Jane Wilbred. Widespread press coverage ensured that the case aroused considerable outrage and disquiet. Jane Wilbred told of constant beatings and worse. The following is from a newspaper report of the case:

> Mr Sloane often beat me; sometimes in the morning early and sometimes in the daytime. Mrs Sloane used to beat me because I wore my shift sleeves over my arms and shoulders in the morning [to keep warm]; and when I cried Mr Sloane used to beat me for crying. Mr Sloane called me round to the bedside one morning and beat me on the hands with a shoe. My mistress would not let me wear my shift on my shoulders and neck in the morning . . . she used to beat me on the back with a shoe. She would not let me wear anything on my neck, or any part of my body above the waist; so that, from the waist upwards, I was obliged to go about the house exposed, in the presence of Mr Sloane . . . (Sensation)

The girl's plight had come to light when she was admitted to a charity hospital covered with bruises and 'in a most frightful state of emaciation and debility'. There were 'marks of vermin' all over her body, and she weighed only fifty nine and a half pounds. She told the court:

> There was no watercloset of any kind in the chambers belonging to Mr Sloane. There was only one chamber utensil for the use of Mrs Sloane, Miss Devaux and myself, which was

> kept in a pan under the kitchen table. I was only allowed to use it once a day. I sometimes used it at night, and when she found it out in the morning she told me she would make me eat the contents. (Great sensation) I was generally locked in my bedroom all night, so that I could not use the chamber utensil. When she told me she would make me eat the contents she used to try and do so. (Prolonged hissing) She had made me eat it more than once, and when I struggled to prevent her, and it dropped on the floor, she picked it up and put it in my mouth. (Sensation) When I have not been able to get to the chamber utensil at all during the day I have dirtied the floor, but I could not help it. My mistress on one occasion got a piece of turnip and cut a hole in it and filled it with some of the dirt, and forced it down my throat by means of a large iron tablespoon. (Great sensation) Mr Sloane was not present when she at first attempted it, but he was when she succeeded in pushing it down my throat. He stood behind me, so as to keep me close in front of my mistress while she put it into my mouth. (Sensation) He beat me on that occasion with a shoe because I refused to do as my mistress wanted, and he beat me again after it . . .

After the hearing an angry mob was waiting when the Sloanes emerged from the court. They stoned them and chased them home. The Sloanes were found guilty and sentenced to two years' hard labour. 'It was generally believed that the depth and breadth of the news coverage of the trial had incited the public to retributory action, and, no doubt, had influenced the judge' (Boyle, *Black Swine in the Sewers of Hampstead*).

SMALLS, BERTIE (1935–) Bank robber and pioneer SUPERGRASS. He led a team who pulled off a series of raids in the late 1960s and early 1970s. By late 1972 he had been identified from a photograph by a witness as being one of the raiders on a National Westminster branch at Palmers Green in May of that year. After the £296,000 robbery at Ralli Brothers in Hatton Garden in March 1969 another witness identified him from a photograph. In December 1972 the Smalls' *au pair* took the police to the house near Northampton where the robber planned to spend Christmas. Smalls heard a noise at the door and, believing it was the cat, opened it. His wife Diane said: 'You let the rats in, not the cat.' Smalls offered to talk in return for a *written* guarantee that he would be given immunity from prosecution. The agreement, much criticised later, was drawn up with the Director of Public Prosecutions, Sir Norman Skelhorn. Smalls helped to jail twenty one men for a total of 308 years. Some got small reductions on appeal. In the Court of Appeal Lord Justice Lawton was scathing about the immunity deal. 'Above all else the spectacle of the Director recording in writing at the behest of a criminal like Smalls his undertaking to give immunity from further prosecution is one which we find distasteful. Nothing of a similar kind must happen again.' When he gave evidence at the Old Bailey one of his victims, Danny Allpress, sang 'We'll meet again, don't know where, don't know when . . .' but the expected underworld retribution never came. Some months after the trial his armed guard was withdrawn and the family lived under another name without molestation. Smalls said that if he went into a pub and saw a friend or relative of someone he had grassed he would simply leave.

SMITHFIELD Many people were executed at Smithfield, most of them by burning at the stake during the reign of the Catholic Queen Mary. A variation was BOILING ALIVE in an iron cauldron. Smithfield was also the site of Bartholomew Fair, first held in the twelfth century. The fair was finally suppressed in 1855 because of its raucous immorality. As long ago as 1691 *A Catalogue of Jilts, Cracks & Prostitutes, Nightwalkers, Whores, She-friends, Kind Women and other of the Linnen-lifting Tribe* listed twenty-one women who could be found in the cloisters of St Bartholomew's Church during the fair. *See* WHORES' GUIDES

SMITHSON, GEORGE Burglar also known as 'Gentleman George'. During the twenties the most successful burglar in Britain, mostly targeting country houses. That he spent fourteen years in jail was mostly due to his clumsy partner, George Ingram, whose value to Smithson was his ability to dispose of stolen goods, particularly works of art. Smithson, who was well-educated and came from a prosperous family, lived in a smart Kensington flat with his wife and children, who naturally had no idea what he did for a living. He avoided any contact with the underworld. In his autobiography, *Raffles in Real Life*, he described how he broke into a rectory and found a large retriever dog asleep in a chair:

> The drawers on the desk were locked. I forced each one of them open and ransacked them one at a time, carefully and systematically.

The dog still slept in the chair. In one of the drawers I found a safe key, and beside the desk stood the safe. With the same care and precision I opened the safe and rifled that too. The dog mildly snored in unison with my movements. After one final search and one last look round, I patted the dog on the head and commended it for its great faithfulness. It looked up at me in a sleepy canine way, as much as to say, 'Quite all right.' It then turned over and went to sleep again.

SMITHSON, TOMMY 'SCARFACE' (?–1956) Protection racketeer, murdered on the orders of Soho vice kings. Smithson preyed on Maltese spielers, illegal gambling clubs, taking a percentage of all bets. He was shot dead in a house in Carlton Vale in West London in June 1956 by a Maltese hitman, Phillip Ellul, who was arrested, convicted and sentenced to death, then reprieved forty-eight hours before the sentence was due to be carried out. Ellul served eleven years in jail. Police believed that Smithson was trying to muscle in on the West End vice rackets, and that he was shot on the order of The Syndicate's bosses SILVER and Mifsud. The pair were charged with conspiracy to murder. One witness, Victor Spampinato, did not turn up at the trial, and was traced to Malta. Police discovered that he had recently acquired a villa, drove a new car and was said to have a bankroll of £30,000. Ellul at first agreed to give evidence, but instead went to the United States and did not return. Underworld rumour said he had been paid £60,000 for his silence. Both Silver and Mifsud were cleared.

SMUGGLING One response to excessive taxation. The twentieth century saw a resurgence of the smuggling of alcohol and tobacco as domestic tax rates far exceeded those abroad, but levels are still nowhere near those of the eighteenth century. Out of a population of eight millions, as many as 20,000 people were full-time smugglers. Tea was for a time the mainstay of the trade: it has been reckoned that twenty one million pounds of tea were smuggled into Britain annually. Wine, brandy, gin, tobacco, coffee, silks and linen were also imported illegally. ROBERT WALPOLE, the country's first 'prime minister', used the Admiralty barge to smuggle in wine, lace and other goods. Lady Holdernesse, whose husband was Warden of the Cinque Ports and a former Secretary of State, used Walmer Castle to run a business selling smuggled French gowns and furniture. She had previously been caught in possession of 114 Parisian silk gowns.

London was the main focus of the rackets. Along the great roads leading into the city smugglers had caches. One was in the FLEET PRISON, but despite repeated attempts the excisemen could not find it. They were either driven off with stones or the warden and his turnkeys helped the inmates hide the contraband.

The smugglers operated in gangs of up to fifty men. They fought pitched battles with customs officers and troops, and for a time had the upper hand. Among the most violent were the HAWKHURST GANG in Kent. A parliamentary inquiry in 1745 was told that the gang could muster 500 men in an hour. In 1775 a large body of armed smugglers forced two witnesses who were to give evidence against one of their colleagues at Winchester Assizes to turn back to Southampton. There were battles between smugglers and the authorities at Orford and Southwold, and at Cranbourne Chase a party of dragoons who ambushed fifty smugglers were defeated, having to give up their arms and horses.

What had started as small-scale crime changed with the rocketing taxes after the Seven Years War (1756–63). When Edmund Burke took office in 1783 he called for a report on smuggling. The report, compiled by the Board of Trade, informed him that the illegal imports had trebled since 1780, and estimated that a staggering 21,132,000 pounds of tea were being smuggled in annually. The accountant of the East India Company believed that only one third of the tea consumed in Britain was legally imported.

The next government, headed by Pitt, struck a major blow against the smugglers by reducing the tax on tea from 119 per cent to 12 per cent. In 1784 4,962,000 pounds of tea passed through customs: the following year, the first year of reduced duties, the total was 16,307,000 pounds.

But the war against the smugglers was by no means over. Liquor smuggling had been big-time crime since the reign of William and Mary. The reason again was high taxation: the tax on French wines, rum and brandy in 1735 was £1 a gallon. Consumption of liquor was high: early in the century, 11.2 million gallons of spirits were being drunk every year in London. That is about seven gallons per adult.

The destitute drank gin: the better off drank wine and spirits. In 1774 at the Lord Mayor's dinner at the Mansion House the guests drank 626 dozen bottles of wine. Robert Walpole got his wine cheap when it was smuggled: nevertheless, his annual bills were prodigious. In 1733 his household consumed 1,200 bottles of White Lisbon alone. In 1733 Walpole spent the enormous sum of £1,118 12*s* 10*d* with the wine merchant James Bennett, and £48 2*s* with Schaart & Co. This was the income of a well-off minor aristocrat.

Cutting the duty on tea had been a striking success. In 1784 Pitt also struck at the alcohol smugglers. The duty on all French wines was slashed from £90 3*s* 10*d* a tun to £43 1*s*. Then he introduced the Hovering Act which enabled the excise to confiscate all ships under sixty tons carrying wine, tea or coffee within three miles of the English coast. Other restrictions on shipping tightened the screw on the smugglers. Shooting at naval or revenue officers was now punishable by hanging.

This left the very lucrative smuggling of tobacco. It has been estimated that about seven and a half million tons were smuggled in annually. The rewards were high. Tobacco could be bought on the Continent for three pence a pound. With added expenses of five and a half pence to cover the costs of importing it, smugglers were still able to make almost a shilling a pound when they sold it in England.

Pitt ignored advice to deal with the problem by slashing the duty on tobacco as he had done with tea and alcohol. Instead he proposed a system of warehouses for tobacco, and decreed that only London, Bristol, Liverpool, Glasgow and another seven ports could import it. These measures worked up to a point, but the war with France in the 1790s forced up duties and by 1806 the tax on tea had risen again to 96 per cent. The smugglers were back in business.

SOCIETY FOR THE REFORMATION OF MANNERS For more than two hundred years prostitution was the main target of groups of moral purists. Around 1700 the Society for the Reformation of Manners was making life difficult for all manner of transgressors. Essentially Puritans deeply affronted by what they saw as the lewdness and profligacy of society after the Restoration, their sour disapproval extended to swearing, drinking and Sabbath-breaking. Among many such complaints, the Middlesex Bench was told in 1671 that constables and headboroughs were taking bribes from the brothels in Whetstone Park at the northern side of Lincoln's Inn Fields. The Tower Hamlets Reformation Society issued this broadside:

> Here 'tis the Impudent Harlots by their Antick Dresses, Painted faces and Whorish Insinuations allure and tempt our Sons and Servants to Debauchery, and consequently to embezel and steal from us, to maintain their strumpets. Here 'tis that Bodies are Poxt and Pockets are picked of considerable sums, the revenge of which Injuries have frequently occasioned Quarrellings, Fightings, Bloodshed, Clamours of Murther (and that sometimes at midnight) pulling down of signs and parts of houses, breaking of windows, also other tumultuous Routs, Riots and Uproars . . . Here 'tis that many a Housekeeper is infected with a venomous Plague, which he communicates to his Honest and Innocent Wife . . . Here 'tis that Multitudes of Soldiers and Seamen get such bane that effeminates their spirits and soon rots their bodies. (Quoted in Bristow, *Vice and Vigilance: Purity Movements in Britain since 1700*)

The Reformation Societies had the backing of the royal couple, William and Mary. William had issued a *Proclamation for Preventing and Punishing Immorality and Profaneness* in 1698, in which he feared that 'the open and avowed practice of vice' might 'provoke God to withdraw his mercy and blessings from us, and instead thereof to inflict heavy and severe judgments'. With such high-level backing the societies spread across the country.

Thousands of secret informers, many of them small tradesmen such as James Jenkins and Bodenham Rewse from the Strand, were recruited to spy on prostitutes and others who infringed their rules. The informers were to take notice 'of all those, that for the time to come, shall impudently dare, in rebellion against the laws of God and man, to swear and curse, to profane the Lord's Day, or be guilty of the loathsome sin of drunkenness, also by searching out the lurking holes of bawds, whores, and other filthy miscreants, in order to their conviction and punishment according to law'.

Many of the victims of this crusade were the poor and miserable, the drunken labourer and the foul-mouthed working woman. As the author of *The Poor Man's Plea* pointed out, 'we don't find the rich drunkard carried before my Lord Mayor, nor a swearing lewd merchant punish'd . . . but if a poor man gets drunk, or swears an oath, he must to the stocks without remedy.'

The new morals police set about cleaning up the streets, to the great resentment of the general public. In 1699 the society reported that 500 disorderly houses had been suppressed:

> Some thousands of lewd persons have been imprisoned, fined and whipt; so that the Tower-End of the town, and many of our streets, have been purged of that pestilent

> generation of night walkers that used to infest them . . . forty or fifty of them have been sent in a week to Bridewell, where they have of late received such discipline, that a considerable number of them have chose rather to be transported to our plantations, to work there for an honest subsistence.

One society zealot, Samuel Cooke, arrested hundreds of prostitutes in the 1720s. Later the authorities were forced to admit that the warrants he was serving were illegal. By then many poor wretches had been tortured, including whipping and having their noses slit. One of these sadistic punishments, stripping the woman to the waist and whipping her, was sanctioned by a sixteenth-century statute which was not repealed until 1817. It stipulated that she 'should be stripped naked from the middle upward and whipped till the body should be bloody'. This was a charter for sadists.

There was widespread opposition to the methods of the odious Reformation Societies – particularly their use of informers – and hostile crowds sometimes intervened to stop prostitutes being arrested. In 1709 near Covent Garden a Reforming Society constable, John Dent, was killed by a group of soldiers as he tried to arrest a prostitute named Anne Dickens. The killers were later freed by a jury under the guidance of the Lord Chief Justice.

The societies were determined to drive whores out of public places and the playhouses. In 1730, for instance, a whore and her client were arrested for fornicating in a shop window and a group of women were 'taken at 12 or 1 o'clock, exposing their nakedness in the open street to all passengers and using most abominable filthy expressions'.

After reaching a peak around the beginning of the eighteenth century, when there were twenty in London, the societies went into decline. 'Their prosecutions for all offences, including prostitution and bawdy-house keeping, fell away from a high point of 7,251 in 1722 to 734 in 1730. The last set of annual figures published by the Societies, for the year to 1738, totalled just 545 prosecutions' (Henderson, *Disorderly Women in Eighteenth-Century London*). They had failed to make much impact on the growth of whoredom: given the prevalent poverty this was not surprising. Their agitation did however provoke a debate which was to become a dominant topic for the Victorians: how to make the working class more moral.

SOHO Area renowned for its bohemian and cosmopolitan ambience. Its association with the sex industry became more pronounced in the mid-nineteenth century, when theatres and music halls opened and large numbers of prostitutes took up residence. John Galsworthy caught the prevailing sense of its strangeness when he wrote in *The Forsyte Saga*: 'Soho is perhaps least suited to the Forsyte spirit . . . Untidy, full of Greeks, Ishmaelites, cats, Italians, tomatoes, restaurants, organs, coloured stuffs, queer names, people looking out of upper windows, it dwells remote from the British Body Politic.' Its reputation as a gastronomic centre began in the 1920s. Later it became the centre of the pornography trade. Its strip shows, clip joints and near-beer clubs drew outsiders, as did the prostitutes. Vice and pornography barons such as the MESSINAS and BERNIE SILVER flourished. Lobbying by the Soho Society led to legislation to control the sex industry by licensing. As a result the number of premises in use by the sex industry has fallen sharply, although there has been an influx of foreign prostitutes. *See* PROSTITUTION

SOLOMON, ALF Leader of the important Jewish faction in the DARBY SABINI gang. Solomon was a bookmaker, which in many cases at the time was tantamount to being a gangster. He shot and seriously wounded rival gangster BILLY KIMBER, but his plea of self-defence was accepted. He stabbed to death bookie Buck Emden in a fracas at a club near Warren Street. Emden had shoved a broken glass into the face of Solomon's companion Eddie Emmanuel. Solomon stabbed Emden in the head with a carving knife. The brilliant barrister SIR EDWARD MARSHALL HALL saved Solomon, partly by waving a jagged broken glass in the faces of the jury to suggest the terror Solomon had felt. The offence was reduced from murder to manslaughter, and Solomon got away with a three-year sentence. He was targeted by rival gangsters at the BATTLE OF LEWES in 1936, which led to mass jailings.

SOLOMONS, ISAAC 'IKEY' (?–1850) Receiver, the most important of the nineteenth century and probably the model for Fagin in *Oliver Twist*. The writer of programme notes for a performance of *Oliver Twist* at the Royal Surrey Theatre in 1838 cited Solomons to demonstrate the authenticity of Dickens's portrait of Fagin, and added: 'The City Officers, in pursuing that great receiver of stolen goods, Ikey Solomons, discovered cellars and trap doors, and all sorts of places of concealment, which they found full of stolen goods.' Property worth the enormous sum of £20,000 was said to have been seized when his house was raided.

Solomons paid the highest prices for stolen banknotes. He was arrested in 1827 and was found to have a fortune in cash, watches and jewellery on him. He escaped from the Black Maria on his way to Newgate – the police found out, too late, that it was driven by his father-in-law – and made his way to Australia where he joined his wife Ann, who had been transported with other members of his family. After a long legal battle he was sent back to England to face trial. He was found guilty, sentenced to fourteen years' transportation, and on 31 May 1831 left Newgate for the last time, bound for Van Diemen's Land. He and Ann were reunited but discovered that by now they loathed each other. When Ann was pardoned in 1840 they split up, and Ikey died ten years later. He left only £70.

SOUTH SEA BUBBLE Financial crisis arising from corrupt mismanagement of the South Sea Company. The South Sea Bill was introduced in the Commons in April 1720. It was proposed that the company should take over a large part of the National Debt in exchange for annual interest of 5 per cent and a monopoly of trade with the Pacific Islands and the West Indies. War with Spain meant there was no trade: nevertheless the stock was quoted at an inflated value. Large amounts of stock were given 'on credit' to MPs, ministers and members of the royal family. By the time the Bill became law in May the price had quadrupled. But the whole of the £2 million raised in subscriptions had been handed over as bribes to politicians and brokers. There were no trading profits to provide dividends and by August the value of the stock was slipping inexorably.

Some investors made large fortunes. The London bookseller Thomas Guy sold his huge holding in stages as the market rose: he made the immense fortune of £234,000, the largest of any speculator. He used part of it to build Guy's Hospital. Not so lucky was the scientist SIR ISAAC NEWTON, who sold £7,000 of stock in April and made a profit of 100 per cent. He went back into the stock and lost £20,000. 'I can calculate the motions of the heavenly bodies,' he is quoted as saying, 'but not the madness of people.' The politician ROBERT WALPOLE had been brought to the edge of ruin by inept speculation in the stock, yet he decided restoring public confidence and shielding the royal family and others was more important than punishing the guilty. One director of the company, Sir John Blount, had crossed Walpole by providing Parliament with evidence of the swindle. He forfeited most of his money. A clerk who absconded with £4,000 was hanged. Others paid fines and some were also expelled from the Commons. Walpole screened most of the the South Sea directors, the politicians and the Court from public scrutiny and punishment so successfully that he became known as 'Skreen-Master General'. Confidence in the market was eventually restored. Walpole became the first 'prime minister'.

SPAGHETTI HOUSE SIEGE On 28 September 1975 three gunmen, led by Nigerian Franklin Davies, forced their way into the Spaghetti House restaurant in Knightsbridge where the managers of the chain were meeting to hand over their weekly takings – a total of £13,000. Nine Italian staff were forced into the basement but another escaped and alerted police. During the six-day siege which followed the gang demanded a plane to fly them out of the country: Sir Robert Mark, head of the Metropolitan Police, refused. Police got a false message to Davies saying that one of his accomplices on the outside was being paid for giving information to newspapers. This helped to demoralise the gang and they surrendered without harming their hostages.

SPARKS, RUBY (1894–1972) Master burglar and smash-and-grab raider. With his partner and driver LILLIAN GOLDSTEIN, the 'Bob-Haired Bandit', he was the most famous of the 'motor bandits'. Sparks was born into a family of criminals in Tiger Yard, Bermondsey, in south-east London. His mother was a receiver, his father a bare-knuckle fighter who used to pickle his knuckles in brine. Ruby started his own criminal career by stealing registered letters from mail trains. His accomplices would pack him into a hamper and send it on the train. Once aboard Ruby would emerge from hiding and rifle the mailbags.

He got his nickname Ruby after a robbery at the home of an Indian maharajah. He found a box of red stones in a desk and after being told by a fence that they were fakes, gave them away to any friend who wanted one. Later he discovered that he had given away £40,000 worth of real rubies. His career of smash-and-grab raids and burglaries with Goldstein lasted about five years. In 1927 Sparks was jailed for three years for burgling a country house. Goldstein was acquitted. For Sparks a series of jail sentences followed. He was a leader in the 1932 Dartmoor Prison mutiny, and in 1940 he escaped from the prison after being sent there for five years in 1939. He hid out in the Bob-Haired Bandit's home in Wembley Park.

For a time Sparks teamed up with the gangster BILLY HILL, but Hill was caught during a raid in

Bond Street. After five months Sparks was recaptured and sent back to Dartmoor. When he was released he became an ice-cream salesman, then opened a newsagent's in the Chalk Farm area, and finally at the end of the war a club, the Penguin in Regent Street.

Sparks was a major underworld figure. When Billy Hill and JACK SPOT retired some gangsters approached him with a proposal that he should become the new Boss of the Underworld. Wisely he declined.

SPIGGOT, WILLIAM (?–1721) Leader of a gang of FOOTPADS and HIGHWAYMEN who was tortured at Newgate. Spiggot and two of his men, Thomas Phillips and Joseph Lindsey, a fallen clergyman, carried out more than a hundred robberies. For one crime they recruited a lunatic, one Borroughs, who had escaped from Bedlam. Together they robbed Charles Sybbald on Finchley Common. Borroughs boasted about their prowess and the gang were tracked down by JONATHAN WILD and tried at the Old Bailey. To save his own life Lindsey gave evidence for the prosecution. Spiggot and Phillips refused to plead, and they were returned to Newgate to be subjected to the torture known as *peine fort et dure* in which the victim was crushed with iron weights on his chest until he either died or agreed to plead. Phillips agreed to plead but Spiggot held out until the weight on his chest was increased to 400 pounds. He and Phillips were hanged at Tyburn in February 1721. Borroughs was sent back to Bedlam. *See* TORTURE

SPORTING UNDERWORLD, THE *see* following page

SPOT, JACK (1912–96) Jewish racecourse gangster and affable thug. Spot was born in 1912 in Whitechapel, the son of Polish immigrants. He started out as a petty crook and hustler, a protection racketeer and housebreaker. He was an unreliable bookmaker who would welch on the punters if he had a bad day. In spite of all this he achieved hero status for his part in defending the local Jewish community against OSWALD MOSLEY's Blackshirts before the Second World War. Spot later claimed he took on Mosley's top bodyguard, an all-in wrestler known as Roughneck, and knocked him unconscious with a chair leg filled with lead when the Blackshirts marched down Cable Street in 1936. This is unlikely, as the Cable Street confrontation was largely between the anti-fascists and the police, the Blackshirts having moved off elsewhere. In 1937 he was given six months' jail for attacking another Blackshirt. Spot probably did help protect the Jewish shopkeepers from the fascists but for a price: it was an old-fashioned protection racket. Early in the war there was a clamp-down on spielers and other gambling clubs, and Spot and his cohorts were rounded up and drafted into the army. He didn't like the discipline and got into a fight with an anti-semitic corporal. After that he made a nuisance of himself, and in 1943 the Marine regiment he was serving in discharged him on grounds of mental instability. He returned to a blitzed East End, and after a fight in a club in the Edgware Road where he seriously injured an anti-semitic gangster by striking him over the head with a teapot he fled to Leeds, the black-market capital of the north. He quickly achieved a commanding position in this thriving northern crime hub. Leeds became a kind of open city during the war years, attracting deserters, gamblers and racketeers, dominated by Poles. Spot's experience of the London underworld, which was intimidating for the local thugs, his strength and fearlessness and the fact that he didn't drink alcohol – like his future rival BILLY HILL – made him formidable. He and the Poles reached a power-sharing agreement: Spot would do what he knew best, looking after the bookies and gambling clubs, and the Poles would stick to their interests in taxis and petrol rationing. Spot brought order to the clubs and racecourses, dispensing rough justice. He recalled how his gang clashed with 'Fred, leader of a big mob in Newcastle . . . Newcastle Fred was not only a gangster but a racecourse operator as well. He thought he had the say-so on flogging out bookmakers' pitches, but he made a mistake when he tried to get nasty with me and a few of my pals at Pontefract races.' In the ensuing battle Newcastle Fred was left battered and bloodied in the mud. At the end of the war Spot returned to London and with the backing of powerful Jewish bookmakers opened an illegal spieler called the Botolph Club in Aldgate. By now he was a big, flamboyant, bombastic man usually smoking a large cigar. The club was a success, with Spot claiming he took £3,000 a week from the chemin de fer, faro and rummy. Gambling was flourishing in the immediate post-war period. Spivs and black-market racketeers were making small fortunes, and restrictions on travelling kept the rich at home. In an otherwise drab world gambling clubs offered glamour and excitement. Spot enjoyed his affluence. He also enjoyed talking to the newspapers:

Continued on p. 260

THE SPORTING UNDERWORLD

Gambling at Brooks's, the club in St James's Street. The upper classes were as affected by gambling mania as the poor classes were by gin mania. Estates would be won and lost on the turn of a card. The easy money generated by gambling attracted the underworld.

The easy money generated by gambling has always attracted the underworld. Almost as soon as there were professional bookmakers there were racecourse gangs to prey on them. Spielers or illegal card games were likely to be held up by gangsters such as ARTHUR HARDING. Prize-fighting, the bare-knuckle precursor of professional gloved boxing, attracted an unsavoury following. John Heenan, the American heavyweight champion, was doped before a fight in England in the 1860s and was so badly injured in the ensuing contest that he never really recovered. The match between Caunt and Bendigo in 1845 for the championship was so violent both inside and outside the ring that the referee was in fear of his life, and was induced to award the victory to Bendigo, although Caunt had clearly won. Prize-fighting was illegal anyway, so it was impossible for Caunt to seek justice through the courts. Bendigo later became a preacher with a mission among London's cabmen.

Prize-fighting had an interesting moral history. Some attributed the decline of duelling to the upper-class taste for the more manly way of settling disputes with fists. It was also rather absurdly believed to improve British prowess with the bayonet by strengthening soldiers' arms. It enjoyed a kind of glamour in the 1780s, largely because of 'Gentleman' John Jackson, with whom Byron used to spar, and his two predecessors as champion, Johnson and Mendoza. Two previous champions, Figg and Broughton, were much admired. Figg was one of those who visited JACK SHEPPARD in the condemned cell at Tyburn. Sheppard promised to stop on his way to execution at Tyburn to drink a glass of wine with Figg, a promise he kept. Broughton's patron, the Duke of Cumberland, bet Lord Chesterfield £10,000 to £400 that his man would beat a fighter named Slack. Broughton was blinded by a blow between the eyes and lost. The duke never forgave him, and thenceforth backed legislation to end prize-fighting. The bare-knuckle game gradually gave way to the gloved sport we know today, which at least had a code and a governing body. This code was partly the work of the mad peer LORD QUEENSBERRY.

Even more scandalous were the early years of the turf. The two worlds were united in many ways, perhaps uniquely in the person of JOHN GULLY, a prize-fighter freed from prison for a bout in 1808, later an MP and a horse-owner whose spectacular and dishonest coups made him rich. The tangled tale of the 1844 Derby, long after Gully's day, gives some idea of the scale of the skulduggery. The winner, Running Rein, was exposed as a 'ringer' – a successful horse entered under a false name. There was another ringer in the race but brevity demands we pass it over. A court case brought by a Mr Wood, ostensibly the owner of the so-called Running Rein, to silence rumours had the opposite effect and exposed the underworld background to the affair. Incidentally when the judge said he and the jury should inspect Running Rein the horse had vanished.

The real villain was a man named Goodman. He was the owner of Running Rein, real name Maccabeus, a successful horse which was too old to run in the Derby. It seemed he had run Maccabeus at Newmarket the previous year, where it did well. Only it was not Maccabeus that had run but another ringer. The real Maccabeus, *alias* Running Rein, was already in training for the Derby. When this emerged in court Wood withdrew the action, saying he had been made a fool. The judge summed up:

> Since the opening of this case a most atrocious fraud has been proved to have been practised; and I have seen with great regret, gentlemen associating themselves with persons much below them in station. If gentlemen would associate with gentlemen, and race with gentlemen, we should have no such practices. But if gentlemen will condescend to race with blackguards, they must expect to be cheated.

Gradually the sport was cleaned up and by the middle of the nineteenth century most races were probably fair. This growing respectability and professionalism was accompanied however by the rise of the professional bookmaker, and with him the racecourse gangsters, thugs who preyed on the bookies and fought each other in increasingly blatant displays of lawlessness. DARBY SABINI was the most successful of these gangsters in the twentieth century, but most prominent leaders of London organised crime until the 1950s had some role in racecourse crime. At a time when gambling was one of the biggest industries in the country there were rich pickings for all. JACK SPOT, ALBERT DIMES and FRANKIE FRASER were all associated with racetrack gangs.

Before the Puritan interlude brought a temporary halt the English were thought to be unusually addicted to gambling. As the underworld was addicted to cheating the odds were stacked against the honest gambler. There were at least fourteen different kinds of crooked dice. Some had faces of slightly varying lengths, others were filled with lead or mercury so that the thrower could predict the result. The skill lay in quickly being able to replace honest dice with the crooked ones at crucial moments, and then having the sleight of hand to switch back before the dice could be examined. Gilbert Walker said in *A Manifest Detection of Dice-Play* that there were workshops for making crooked dice in the King's Bench and Marshalsea prisons. However he recommended 'Bird of Holborn' as the 'finest workman, acquaint yourself with him'.

At the beginning of Elizabeth's reign gambling was illegal, but as the law did little to curb the craze licensed gambling dens were allowed. Official attempts to stamp out the use of crooked dice and cards – there was a fine of three shillings and fourpence for each offence – failed.

The Georgian era brought an explosion of gambling. John Wade, who wrote *Treatise on the Police and Crimes of the Metropolis* in 1829, thought it was largely an upper-class vice: 'The crimes and vices now most rife in London are gaming among the higher and more opulent classes – theft, swindling and fraud among the middle classes – drinking among the lower classes, chiefly labourers.' Bets were made on births and deaths: the betting book at White's club contains the following entry: *Ld Lincoln bets Ld Winchelsea One Hundred Guineas to Fifty Guineas that the 'Dutchess' Dowager of Marlborough does not survive the Dutchess Dowager of Cleveland*. Baron Alvanley, a wit who succeeded Beau Brummell as arbiter of taste, inherited an income of between £60,000 and £70,000 a year, and by dint of perseverance succeeded in squandering it. *January 11th, 1811 – Lord Alvanley bets Sir Joseph Copley twenty guineas that a certain person outlives another certain person*. Perhaps his friends laid wagers on the baron's longevity: he was known to extinguish his bedroom candle at night either by throwing it on the floor and aiming a pillow at it, or by thrusting it under his pillow while still alight.

Perhaps the most famous gambler of the age was the Whig politician Charles James Fox. By the time he was 24 his father, Lord Holland, was obliged to pay his debts of £140,000. Fox could go for long periods without sleep, so that he could gamble all night. HORACE WALPOLE describes one of these marathons:

> He had sat up playing Hazard at Almack's from Tuesday evening, 4th February, till five in the afternoon of Wednesday 5th. An hour before he had recovered £12,000 that he had lost, and by dinner, which was at five o'clock, he had ended losing £11,000. On Thursday he spoke [in the Commons], went to dinner at past eleven at night; from thence to White's, where he drank till seven in the morning; thence to Almack's, where he won £6,000; and between three and four in the afternoon he set out for Newmarket. His brother Stephen lost £11,000 two nights after, and Charles £10,000 more on the 13th; so that in three nights the two brothers, the eldest not twenty five, lost £32,000.

The Regency was the heroic age of gambling. There were many stories of estates and inheritances changing hands over the gaming tables. Georgiana, Duchess of Devonshire, lost several fortunes, and her gambling friends, including the Prince Regent himself, were constantly harried by their creditors. Many of them turned to the banker Thomas Coutts. He had a weakness for titles, and paid handsomely for it. When General Blücher, the Prussian who saved the day at Waterloo, visited the prince's residence, Carlton House, he was fleeced, if we are to believe the spiteful biographer Huish. He says the old soldier, who unfortunately mixed heavy drinking with gambling, lost £25,000 and left the country almost destitute. Worse, Huish accuses the Regent of cynically encouraging the fleecing. Certainly there were men in the Regent's circle who were capable of it.

In 2002 BBC TV's *Panorama* told a modern tale of horse doping by jockeys, of horses being pulled and of jockeys in league with gangsters. It left the feeling that backing horses was truly a mug's game. The Jockey Club, the venerable and aristocratic overlord of the sport, was complacent.

> I didn't have to buy nothing. Every Jewish business man in London made me clothes, gave me money, food, drink, everything. Because I was a legend. I was what they call a legend to the Jews. Anywhere they had anti-Semitic trouble – I was sent for: Manchester, Glasgow, anywhere. Some crook go into a Jewish shop, says gimme clothes and a few quid, the local rabbi says Go down London and find Jack Spot. Jack, he'll know what to do. So they did and I'd go up and chin a few bastards. The Robin Hood of the East End, a couple of taxi drivers told me once. 'You helped everyone,' they said.

Soon Spot was ready to claim the leadership of the underworld. Gang warfare at the time had a kind of comic opera quality, with more bloodthirsty threats and gestures than grievous bodily harm. However, people did get hurt. The WHITES were racecourse thugs who had seized much of the SABINI empire in Soho and the West End when the Italians were interned at the start of the war. Spot's showdown with them came in the Stork Club in Sackville Street off Piccadilly. Both sides later gave widely different accounts of what happened. Here's what Sidney Williams of the *Daily Herald* wrote after interviewing Harry White:

> His fear of Spot began in January 1947 in a club in Sackville Street, off Piccadilly. He was drinking with racehorse trainer Tim O'Sullivan and a third man. Spot walked in with ten thugs, went straight up to Harry and said: 'You're Yiddified' – meaning he was anti-Jewish. White denied it. He said: 'I have Jewish people among my best friends.' Spot wouldn't listen, and hit him with a bottle. As White collapsed in a pool of blood, the rest of Spot's men attacked O'Sullivan and the third man, who was employed by White. O'Sullivan was beaten unconscious and pushed into a fire in the corner of the club. The other man was slashed with razors and stabbed in the stomach.

Spot gave his version to the *Daily Sketch* eight years after the event:

> The biggest, toughest and most ruthless mob was the King's Cross gang, led by a bookmaker called Harry who had taken over the racecourse protection racket from the Sabini boys. Their word was law not only on the racecourses but in the clubs and pubs – even the fashionable nightclubs of the West End . . . We finally ran them down at a place in Sackville Street off Piccadilly. Harry had several of his toughest boys with him when I led my pals into the room. There wasn't any politeness this time. They knew what I'd come for and I sailed right in. At the first smack I took at them Harry scarpered. You couldn't see the seat of his trousers for dust.

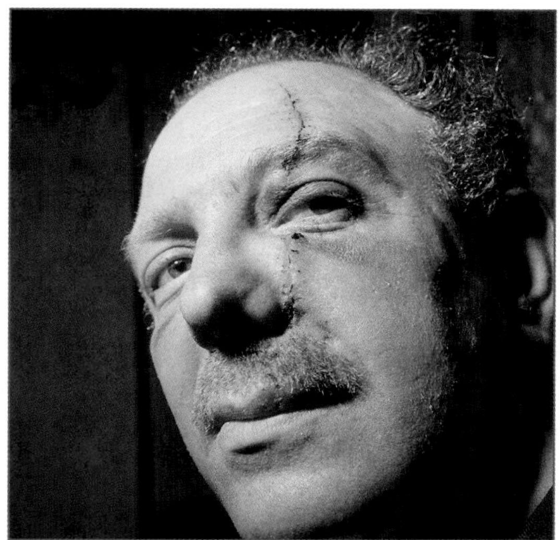

Jack Spot after the attack by the Hill gang. He said: 'I ain't afraid of anyone, but I want a quiet life now.'

For a time Spot's reputation for toughness kept him at the top of the more visible part of the underworld, in alliance with Hill and the Italians who were still the major power on the racecourses. Spot affected some of the style of successful American gangsters, dressing expensively, sitting in hotel lounges dispensing advice. As long as there was no serious challenge to his authority he was safe. But as crime reporter Michael Jacobson said, Spot was little more than a thug. 'He had no initiative of his own. He was never a gang leader. Hill was.'

Then it all fell apart. Hill later recalled: 'Jack was becoming insecure and a bit jealous of me. He was an older man, you see, and once he got this persecution complex he was impossible to work with any more.' Spot wrote: 'Billy Hill was a friend of mine. But he had his own way of working. His own personal ambitions and his own ideas and plans; ambitions and ideas can sometimes clash.'

Elsewhere he wrote: 'I made Billy Hill. He wrote to me when he was in jail, wanted me to help him. Then he got to be top over me. If it wasn't for me he would never have got there. I should've shot Billy Hill. I really should.'

While Hill was away on a trip to Australia Spot had come under renewed pressure. The take from the racecourses was falling away, and some of the Italian bookmakers, led by ALBERT DIMES, no longer recognised his rule. Spot was badly hurt by Hill's claim in his autobiography to be the boss of the underworld, and he hit back at the man who helped write it, DUNCAN WEBB. The journalist was lured to the Horseshoe pub in Tottenham Court Road, where Spot broke his arm with a knuckleduster. After Webb complained to the police Spot was tried and fined £50.

Gangster Jack Spot and his wife Rita. After he had been attacked by the Hill gang, she gave evidence to a court, although he refused to do so.

This clumsy act of revenge bore out what some had been saying: Spot was losing control. In *Jack Spot: Man of a Thousand Cuts* Hank Janson wrote: 'Jack Spot, who was the Boss of the Underworld, was now living a Jekyll and Hyde existence. He was a happy, contentedly married man in his home, and a scheming, planning master-mind at his club.' He had also grown soft and middle-aged. Spot announced that he was quitting the rackets and opting for a quiet life, running a small café. In May 1956 Hill heard that Spot was planning to attack him. Days later, as Spot and Rita were returning from inspecting a pub they planned to buy they were attacked on the steps of their Hyde Park Mansions flat by a large gang led by FRANKIE FRASER, who was wielding a shillelagh. Rita screamed, then clung to her husband. They were both knocked to the ground and the attackers, who were armed with razors and knives, set about cutting up Jack Spot. Later in hospital, after seventy-eight stitches and a blood transfusion, he agreed to name some of the attackers. A week later, his courage and fighting spirit restored, he changed his mind and told journalists: 'I'm the toughest man in the world. I am staying in London. Nobody will drive me out.'

Although he refused to name his attackers, Rita had no such scruples. She picked out Bobbie Warren, a member of the old White gang whose brother had once been beaten up by Spot, and Frankie Fraser at an identification parade. At the trial that followed Warren and Fraser both got seven years. Speaking later of the attack on the Spots, Fraser said: 'He must have been practising his scream because it was louder than his wife's. Hers was quite loud but his was even better. I just whacked him with the shillelagh a couple of times and someone else cut him and that was that.'

After the trial Spot said: 'I ain't afraid of anyone, but I want a quiet life now.' He fell on hard times. He was declared bankrupt and evicted from his flat. The Communist *Daily Worker*, of all papers, reported: 'Some of the more censorious neighbours of Mr and Mrs Comer – Jack Spot of Soho fame – have been appealing to their mutual landlord to tip the Comers the black spot by giving them notice to quit their luxury flat in Bayswater. It is just too painful, it seems, for a Queen of the Bridge Tables to have to meet a King of the Underworld in the lift.'

Rita sold her life story, and with the money she opened the Highball Club. Initially successful, it was wrecked by a gang and then burned down. It is not hard to see the hidden hand of Hill in all this. Spot got the message that his days as a kingpin in the underworld were over, and went to Ireland, where he was involved on the fringes of the racing world. He eventually returned to London and was to be seen from time to time at boxing matches. He and Rita parted, and he died, forgotten, in a nursing home in Eastbourne in 1996.

SPRING-HEELED JACK Entertaining Victorian bogeyman who breathed fire and could jump over high buildings. Jack made his first appearance in the autumn of 1837. Most of his victims were young women. He would leap out at them from behind walls, breathe fire into their faces and rip at their clothes with his claw-like hands. Then he would bound away with giant strides, his horrible laughter ringing in his victims' ears.

As reports of the attacks continued vigilante committees were formed to catch Jack. His ability to jump over high hedgerows made this impossible. His first London attack happened in the winter of 1838. Lucy Scales and her sister were walking home along a lonely street in Limehouse. As they passed Green Dragon Alley, a tall cloaked figure bounded out of the shadows, spitting blue flames. Lucy was blinded. Jack struck again shortly afterwards. Jane Alsop answered a violent knocking at her front door. A man standing in the shadows near the front gate said to her: 'I'm a police officer. For God's sake, bring me a light, we have caught Spring-Heeled Jack in the lane!' Jane gave him a candle and he held it to his face. It was Spring-Heeled Jack! He tore at her clothes and breathed great billows of fire. Jane screamed and her family rushed out. Jack got away again.

Jack had a long innings. He was sighted all over the country. In the 1870s he terrified army sentries by slapping their faces with a clammy hand before bounding on to the roofs of their sentry boxes. In 1904 he terrorised people in Liverpool, jumping from the streets on to their roofs. Author Peter Haining thinks the original Jack was the Marquis of Waterford, renowned for bad-taste jokes. He believes he wore spring-loaded footwear and had learned fire-eaters' tricks.

SPUNGING HOUSES Small prisons where debtors were held while their creditors sought satisfaction. They were a particular target of the mob during the GORDON RIOTS, who wrecked them and set their inmates free.

SQUIRES, DOROTHY (1915–98) Singer and enthusiastic litigant. When her husband, the actor Roger Moore, began an affair with an Italian starlet she was granted an order 'for the restoration of conjugal rights'. In 1982 she was forbidden to bring any further actions without the consent of the High Court. By then she had launched twenty-one actions in a five-year period, nine of which had been dismissed as 'vexatious' and none of which she won.

STANLEY, JOHN (?–1723) Seducer undone by sexual jealousy. Stanley was a war veteran, an expert swordsman and a bully. He would introduce himself to strangers in taverns and then pick a quarrel so that he did not have to pay for his food and drink. He lived with a Mrs Maycock, who was the mother of three of his children. Although he was promiscuous he insisted on her being faithful. When he found her talking to another man in a tavern a furious argument broke out between him and Mrs Maycock. On the way home he drew his sword and ran her through. He was executed.

STANLEY, SARAH Soldier and thief born in the 1760s. Stanley found a job as a clerk in the House of Commons after she began dressing as a man. She became a soldier in a cavalry regiment and was promoted to corporal. Two years later, when it was discovered she was a woman, she was honourably discharged with generous tributes from her superiors. She returned to London where, hard-up, she stole a cloak. She was convicted but unlike so many others she found mercy, being discharged from Newgate with a present of a small amount of money. The *Newgate Calendar* says she promised 'to seek an honest livelihood in the proper habit of her sex'.

STARCHFIELD, JOHN (?–1916) Hero who pursued a killer and was later charged with his own son's murder. In September 1912 Esther Towers was shot dead in the bar she managed at the Horseshoe Hotel in Tottenham Court Road. The murderer was a deranged 28-year-old tailor named Stephen Titus. He shot another barmaid in the shoulder and a customer in the cheek, wrist and hand. The customer died later. He also shot a man who had been at the hotel looking for a job. As he fled he was pursued by newspaper seller John Starchfield, who had seen him shooting the job-seeker. Starchfield tackled Titus, who shot him in the stomach. Titus was caught by another man as he reloaded the revolver. He was sent to BROADMOOR and Starchfield was given an award and a small pension for bravery.

In January 1914 Starchfield's seven-year-old son Willie was found dead on a train at Shoreditch. He had been strangled. His mother, who was estranged from John Starchfield, had sent the boy out on an errand and had no idea how he came to be on the train. John Starchfield was questioned and although he had an alibi an inquest jury accused him of murder on the basis of evidence from witnesses who said they saw him with the boy. When the case reached the Old Bailey it was stopped by the judge who said the evidence of identity was not satisfactory. Two years later John Starchfield died of the injuries he had received when tackling Titus.

STAUNTON, LOUIS (*c.* 1850–?) Auctioneer's clerk tried of the murder of his heiress wife. In 1875 Staunton, who was 24, married Harriet, who was ten years his senior, mentally feeble and unattractive. However, she was heir to a fortune of £3,000. At first they lived in Brixton. Harriet's mother, who was uneasy about the marriage, visited them. The following day she got letters from both Harriet and Louis telling her not to call again. In 1876 Harriet had a baby and Louis moved her to the Kent village of Cudham. He paid his brother Patrick to look after her. Louis moved to a nearby farmhouse, where he lived with Alice Rhodes, sister of his brother's wife. When Harriet's mother called at the farmhouse the door was slammed in her face.

In April Patrick and his wife Elizabeth took the baby to a hospital. It died of starvation within hours, and they claimed Harriet had neglected it. Days later the same couple took lodgings in Penge in south-east London for 'a sick lady'. At dusk they arrived with Harriet. She died there the following day. The three Stauntons and Alice Rhodes were charged with murder.

An inquest was told that Harriet had died of neglect and starvation. Her body was filthy and verminous. Medical experts at the trial disagreed about the cause of death. There was a suggestion by the defence that Harriet had died of tuberculosis. The judge was impatient with these conflicting medical opinions, and his summing-up leaned against the accused. In September 1877 they were found guilty and sentenced to death. Medical opinion was outraged: seven hundred doctors signed a petition protesting against the verdict, and all four accused were reprieved. Alice Rhodes was freed, the others were imprisoned.

STEAD, W.T. (1849–1912) Campaigning journalist and morals crusader who used a stunt to get the age of consent raised. Stead, editor of the *Pall Mall Gazette*, created a sensation with a series of articles titled 'The Maiden Tribute of Modern Babylon', in which he exposed the evils of juvenile prostitution. Stead was campaigning to have the age of consent raised from 13 to 16. Against him were ranged the brothel-keepers and their powerful political friends, particularly Cavendish Bentinck, the Member of

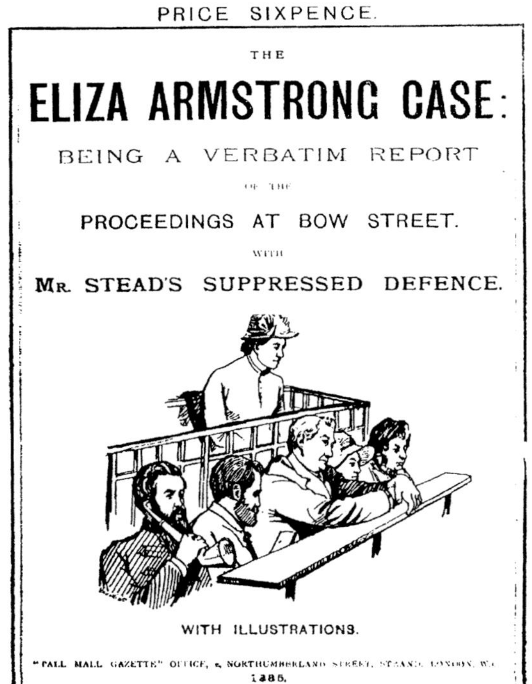
PRICE SIXPENCE.

THE

ELIZA ARMSTRONG CASE:

BEING A VERBATIM REPORT

OF THE

PROCEEDINGS AT BOW STREET.

WITH

MR. STEAD'S SUPPRESSED DEFENCE.

WITH ILLUSTRATIONS.

"PALL MALL GAZETTE" OFFICE, NORTHUMBERLAND STREET, STRAND, LONDON, W.C.
1885.

Rebecca Jarrett, the woman who helped W.T. Stead procure a child for his newspaper stunt, in the dock at Bow Street. She was jailed for six months. Her ordeal almost drove her back to drink.

Parliament for Whitehaven. Bentinck was a blustering upper-class politician of a familiar kind, with influential family connections in the House of Lords. He was suspected of acting on behalf of MARY JEFFRIES, the most important brothel-keeper in London in the last quarter of the nineteenth century.

Attempts to get a Criminal Law Amendment Bill raising the age of consent through Parliament had met with setbacks. Cynical aristocrats who regarded the daughters of the working class as fair game for themselves and their sons obstructed it. The Bill went to the Commons and was dropped. It was then reintroduced twice but in May 1885 was talked out in a hostile house by Bentinck. Stead announced that the next two issues of the *Pall Mall Gazette* would not be for 'all those who are squeamish, and all those who are prudish, and all those who prefer to live in a fool's paradise of imaginary innocence and purity'.

To back up his claims that there was a trade in young British virgins between London and Brussels Stead decided to show how the trade worked. The Salvation Army's Bradwell Booth and a reformed prostitute helped him buy 13-year-old Eliza Armstrong from her drunken mother for £5. On 3 June 1885 he took the child to a London brothel where her virginity was confirmed by a midwife. Finally he sent her to Paris in the company of a Swiss Salvationist.

When the articles, which told in lurid terms of young girls being drugged and raped in London brothels, appeared mobs rioted outside the offices of the *Pall Mall Gazette* to get their hands on the paper. Copies changed hands at twelve times the cover price, and the articles were syndicated in the US and published across Europe in book form from France to Russia. In fact, apart from the story of Eliza Armstrong the revelations were just a rehashing of well-known facts about child prostitution and the ravishing of young girls in brothels.

Official reaction was hostile. Cavendish Bentinck wanted to know whether Stead would be prosecuted for obscene libel, and the Home Secretary was said to be looking into it. However, he was told that Stead had gathered evidence against Mrs Jeffries' illustrious clients, and would call them as witnesses if he was prosecuted. Threatened with revelations about 'Princes and dukes, Ministers of the Crown and Members of Parliament', the Establishment held off.

However, Stead had given the Establishment the excuse they needed. He had committed a criminal offence in taking Eliza out of the possession of her parents while she was under the age of sixteen, and the examination in the brothel was indecent assault. He was charged in October 1885, together with Bramwell Booth and others who had helped. Stead, who had been elated at the prospect of prosecution, was sentenced to three months' imprisonment. The judge said that the Maiden Tribute articles had deluged the country with filth. Their publication 'had been – and I don't hesitate to say ever will be – a disgrace to journalism'. In prison Stead was given privileged treatment. For years afterwards he celebrated the anniversary of his imprisonment by wearing his old prison uniform. The woman who had helped him procure the child, Rebecca Jarrett, got six months and had a much more unpleasant time in prison. She had been a child prostitute, having been seduced at Cremorne Gardens at the age of 12 and then turned out of her home by her sailor brother. She was now a reformed alcoholic, and the aftermath of Stead's stunt almost drove her back to drink.

The publicity had the effect Stead and his allies desired. The Criminal Law Amendment Act was finally carried in the Commons by 179 votes to 71. It raised the age of consent to 16 and incidentally criminalised acts of indecency between men. It also outlawed brothels, throwing many prostitutes onto the streets. Perhaps the result of this shabby piece of sensationalism justified it, but it's hard to read Stead's excited prose without feeling the clichés echo to this day: 'Shuddering horror . . . maelstrom of vice.' There were chapter headings reading 'The Violation of Virgins' and 'Strapping Girls Down'. There were good judges who doubted Stead's sanity.

In 1912 Stead drowned on the *Titanic*. Moralists who had been pressing for a White Slave Act renewed their efforts as a tribute to his pioneer campaigns. The Act was eventually passed.

STEVENSON, SIR MELFORD (1902–87) Controversial High Court judge with a weakness for bad jokes. During the trial of the KRAY twins, at which he presided, Stevenson was overheard to say that Ronnie Kray had spoken the truth only twice: when he referred to prosecuting counsel as a 'fat slob', and when he said the judge (Stevenson) was biased. He stood against TOM DRIBERG as candidate for Malden, Essex in the 1945 general election. He announced that he wanted a clean fight and would not therefore mention Driberg's homosexuality. His judgment could be erratic: he told one defendant, 'I must confess that I cannot tell whether you are innocent or guilty. I am giving you three years. If you are guilty, you have got off lightly, if you are innocent let this be a lesson to you.'

STOCKWELL STRANGLER, THE Burglar who killed seven. Keith Erskine was sentenced to at least forty years for the series of murders which began in April 1986. His first victim was Nancy Emms, 48, who was strangled and sexually assaulted in her home in Wandsworth. His palm prints were found at the home of another victim, William Downes. Erskine, 24, who was said to have the mental ability of an 11-year-old, was sent to Broadmoor.

STONEHOUSE, JOHN (1925–88) British politician who faked his own suicide. In November 1974 Stonehouse, a former Labour government minister, sought to escape debts and personal problems by leaving his clothes on a beach in Miami and secretly fleeing to Australia. While there he was arrested by police who thought he was LORD LUCAN. He returned to Britain where his distraught wife sued for divorce and he and his mistress Sheila Buckley were charged with fraud and conspiracy. In Stonehouse's case the charges arose from a fraudulent secondary bank he had founded. The Board of Trade described it as 'a debt-ridden pack of cards, saturated with offences, irregularities and improprieties'. Just days before his trial began at the Old Bailey Stonehouse addressed the Commons on the 'evils of humbug, moral decadence and materialism afflicting England'. He was sentenced to seven years, and Sheila Buckley got a suspended two-year sentence. They later married. Stonehouse died in 1988.

STRAND RIOTS Violent reaction by sailors robbed of their wages in a brothel. Demobilised seamen returning from service in the War of the Austrian Succession were particular targets for brothel-keepers, who got them drunk and robbed them. When their end-of-service gratuity was stolen in 1749 some sailors wrecked a brothel in the Strand. Their numbers grew and they set out to attack other brothels. The magistrate HENRY FIELDING called out the military and the sailors dispersed, leaving Fielding looking foolish. A drunken servant, Bosavern Penlez, was found lying in an alley. He was executed although he probably had nothing to do with the riots.

STRATTON, ADAM Notorious medieval money-lender and forger. Stratton became chamberlain in charge of the royal treasury in 1276. He was also the holder of many benefices in the province of Canterbury. He ran his rackets from an office in Smale Lane in London. When he was arrested in 1289 he had the amazing sum of £12,666 in coin. This was equivalent to half the annual income of the crown. He was tried on charges reputedly ranging from homicide to sorcery. The king kept the money he had seized and Stratton was fined a further £333, yet he retained his twenty-three livings. Such was his financial expertise that although it was clear he had used his office to enrich himself it was 'almost impossible to prove even the most blatant crimes' (Hicks, *Who's Who in Late Medieval England*).

STREET OFFENCES ACT OF 1959 Measure which stopped prostitutes pestering men in the streets. The Conservative Home Secretary, Sir David Maxwell-Fyfe, decided in 1954 to order an inquiry into prostitution and homosexuality. John Wolfenden, an academic, who described his committee as 'we poor innocents', was given the task of examining the state of the law. Their 1957 report proposed heavier fines and even imprisonment to stop prostitutes making a nuisance of themselves. The committee also suggested that what homosexuals did in private was their own concern, as long as they were over 21. Two years

Boitard Inv. et Sculp.
The Sailor's Revenge or the Strand in an Uproar
a Tragi Comical Farce exhibited before a numerous Audience of ye Mobility & others July ye 1st & 2d
NB the Speeches adapted to the Characters
Publish'd according to Act of Parliament Aug. the 1749 by Rob. Sayer Map & Printseller facing Fetter Lane Fleet Street
Price Six-Pence

Sailors wrecked brothels in the Strand in 1749 after their end-of-service pay was stolen with the connivance of the brothel-keeper. A drunken servant was found asleep in a nearby alley and, although he probably had nothing to do with the riots, he was hanged.

later the proposals on prostitution became law. Eight years later the law on homosexuality was changed along the lines the Wolfenden committee had suggested.

STROUD, WILLIAM Conman whose career suggests the ineffectiveness of corporal punishment. Stroud had a long history of convictions, including one for defrauding tradesmen in 1752. To obtain goods without paying he dressed like a gentleman and had a footman. He was publicly whipped through the streets on six occasions.

SUICIDE Attempting this was a crime until 1961, when the Suicide Act was passed. BLACKSTONE had written: 'Self-murder, the pretended heroism, but real cowardice, of the Stoic philosophers, who destroyed themselves to avoid those ills which they had not the fortitude to endure.' He wrote of people 'rushing into [God's] immediate presence uncalled for'. How could society take revenge on someone who was dead? Their property was seized by the state and they were buried at crossroads with stakes through their hearts. The absurdity of financial penalties was compounded when, as was often the case, the act was the result of hopeless insolvency. The Church also had the right to refuse Christian burial to suicides. Because of these penalties coroners and their inquest juries usually brought in accident verdicts in all but the most blatant cases of suicide.

People dying slowly from the results of suicide attempts were sometimes hanged. The Methodist JOHN WESLEY was unsympathetic. He urged the government to check the 'suicide wave' by hanging the bodies of suicides in chains. A wag responded: 'The pious John Wesley has proposed a remedy for suicide, by gibbeting the unhappy victims of despondency. Would not a total extirpation of the gloomy and absurd tenets of Methodism be much more conducive to that purpose?'

Suicide was known as the 'English disease'. Beat Louis de Muralt commented: 'You must know the English die by their own hands with as much indifference as by another's. 'Tis common to hear people talk of men and women that make away with themselves, as they call it, and generally for reasons that appear to us but trifles: the men, perhaps, for the cruelty or inconstancy of their mistresses, and the women for the indifference of the men.' César de Saussure was perplexed by the suicide 'mania' but after a few months in London with its fogs and coal smoke he reported: 'Had I been an Englishman I should certainly have put myself out of my misery.'

Even in the twentieth century those who survived suicide attempts were sometimes prosecuted. *See* IRENE COFFEE

SUPERGRASSES Criminals who gave evidence against others in exchange for lenient sentences. The bank robber BERTIE SMALLS is generally accepted as the first supergrass. The doubling of jail terms for armed robbers in the 1970s was one reason for the fashion.

SWELL MOB, THE The elite of Victorian pickpockets. They dressed well or 'flash' and could steal as much as twenty or thirty pounds in a good afternoon. In *OLIVER TWIST* Fagin believed the Artful Dodger had the qualities to become such a 'great man', perhaps even to aspire to furnished rooms in Camden Town 'with a smart dolly to share them'. In 1839 the Committee on the Constabulary Force heard of the methods of the Swell Mob when they had chosen a victim:

> Two go before their man, the others close up behind; their victim is hemmed in, a push takes place, he is jostled and hustled about, the thieves cry out to those behind not to press so, the press is increased; the victim being surrounded, his pockets are presently turned inside out. No time is lost; if he does not readily raise his hands, but keeps them in his pockets, or at his side, to guard his property, his hat gets a tip behind, perhaps it is knocked over his eyes. To right his hat he raises his arms, nor does he get them down again till eased of everything in his possession. His fob and vest pockets are emptied by the thief standing beside him . . . the trouser pockets and coat-pockets are emptied by those behind.

SWINBURNE, ALGERNON CHARLES (1837–1909) Poet, flagellation addict and secret pornographer. Swinburne was thrashed at Eton, and emerged unable to have normal sexual relations. His friend Richard Monckton Milnes had a famous collection of erotica which impressed him. He referred in his correspondence to them as the 'most abominable bawdy books that ever were written . . . sodomy mixed with murder and hideous cruelty . . .'. Swinburne was a customer at 7 Circus Road, St John's Wood, where two matronly dames, rouged and golden-haired, flogged their guests for a price. He was an imaginative writer of pornography. His 'La Soeur de la Reine', about Queen Victoria's twin sister, a Haymarket prostitute, is splendidly subversive. The queen herself is overcome with passion when William Wordsworth gives a highly suggestive reading of his poem *The Excursion*, and they copulate. Her rampant sexual demands can afterwards be satisfied only by 'Sir Peel'. No pornographer had the nerve to publish 'La Soeur de la Reine' and it circulated in manuscript.

SWINDLERS Until well into the eighteenth century the law, so savage in other respects, did little to protect citizens from swindles. Embezzlement and fraudulent conversion flourished, and the law was likely, unless forgery could be proved, to take the view that a man was a fool to be taken in. 'In 1709 a man was charged with getting money from a debtor by pretending to be the creditor's agent. "Shall we," Lord Chief Justice Holt exclaimed to the Grand Jury, 'indict one man for making a fool of another?" False pretences was not made an offence until 1757 (Carswell, *The South Sea Bubble*).

Much swindling was petty. Sleight-of-hand games such as thimble-rigging and the three-card trick are probably ancient. Until fairly recently one sometimes saw the tricksters with their lurking accomplices in the Strand and Oxford Street. The success of these sleight-of hand swindles depends not just on the skill of the main operator, but also on the timing of accomplices and look-outs. At one moment they appear to be loungers strolling in a busy street. The next they have set up a tiny collapsible table covered with a cloth and are crowded round it apparently gambling for large sums. The thimble-rigger shuffles three tiny cups, under one of which he has placed a dried pea. The onlookers are invited to guess which cup the pea is under. Two of the gamblers choose the right cup and money changes hands. Gradually the onlookers are drawn in. They lose. (They cannot win because the thimble-rigger has an unusually long thumbnail, which he uses to pick up the pea and hide it.) Suddenly there is an alarm. Either a policeman has been spotted or it is time to move on before the crowd becomes angry. The table and the thimble-riggers vanish.

The three-card trick is a variant. Three cards, one a picture, the others plain, are laid face down on the table. The operator shuffles them and invites the onlookers to place bets on picking the picture card at odds of two to one. Again, an accomplice lays down a large bet and wins. After that the card sharp secretly substitutes a plain card for the picture, and players simply cannot win.

A Victorian swindle which was surprisingly successful was ring-dropping. The ring-dropper would suddenly stoop in a crowded street or at a fair and pick up a ring. He would ask a suitable passer-by if it could be gold. Another passer-by, in reality an accomplice, would opine that it was worth a good few shillings. With luck the ring-dropper would soon get several shillings for a brass ring worth a few pence a dozen. The conman, or magsman as they were known in the Victorian underworld, would simply let the greedy dupe snare himself. A variation on ring-dropping was the pawn-ticket LAY. A man would hesitate outside a pawn-broker's, clutching a watch or piece of jewellery. At last he would summon up his courage and go into the shop. Moments later he would reappear, holding a pawn ticket. This in a paroxysm of despair he would offer at face value to anyone who had followed his performance. He might even accept less than its face value. As soon as the dupe entered the pawnshop with the useless ticket the conman would take to his heels.

These are comparatively simple swindles. Some were more elaborate. John Binney, HENRY MAYHEW's collaborator, told of a trick worked by a couple of London sharps on a young master baker they met on a road near Croydon. One of them took the young man to a hotel for a drink, where he was introduced to a man who was prepared to lend large amounts of money at low interest to people who had been recommended. The baker was offered a loan of £100 if he could produce an equal sum to prove he was a good risk. The baker went home and returned with a £10 note. The lender indignantly refused. The baker went home again and returned with £100. The lender said he was prepared to go ahead with the loan in exchange for a stamped receipt. The baker went out to buy a stamp, leaving his £100 on a table covered with his handkerchief . . .

SWINDLING SAL Prostitute interviewed by HENRY MAYHEW's collaborator Bracebridge Hemyng. She was a powerfully built working-class woman of about 27. Hemyng interviewed her in a public house, and recorded her vigorous turn of phrase: 'She changed places, she never stuck to one long; she never had no things to be sold up, and as she was handy with her mauleys [fists], she got on pretty well. It took a considerable big man, she could tell me, to kick her out of a house, and then when he done it she always give him something for himself, by way of remembering her. Oh! they had a sweet recollection of her, some on 'em.'

This impression of truculence is strengthened by her reference to 'rows' she had been involved in. 'Been quodded [imprisoned] no end of times. She knew every beak as sat on the cheer as well as she knew Joe the Magsman, who, she *might* say, wor a very perticaler friend of her'n.'

Like many prostitutes, Sal had been a servant but hated the life. She chose to work in the sex trade instead:

> I was a servant gal away down in Birmingham. I got tired of workin' and slavin' to make a living, and getting a —— bad one at that; what o' five pun' a year and yer grub, I'd sooner starve, I would. After a bit I went to Coventry . . . and took up with soldiers as was quartered there. I soon got tired of them. Soldiers is good . . . to walk with and that, but they don't pay; cos why they ain't got no money; so I says to myself, I'll go to Lunnon and I did. I soon found my level there.

Her 'level' was that of a fairly successful street prostitute. She told Hemyng what she earned. The Joe she refers to is one of her lovers, a burglar:

> Well, I'll tell yer, one week with another, I makes nearer on four pounds not three – sometimes five. I 'ave done eight and ten. Now Joe, as you 'eered me speak on, he does it 'ansome, he does: I mean, you know, when he's in luck. He give me a fiver once after cracking a crib, and a nice spree me an' Lushing Loo 'ad over it. Sometimes I get three shillings, half a crown, five shillings, or ten occasionally, according to the sort of man.

She was called Swindling Sal because of her habit of 'chousing', or absconding without paying her rent. Sal told Hemyng that 'she never paid any rent, hadn't done so for years and never meant to'. The landlords were 'mostly Christ-killers, and chousing a Jew was no sin, leastways none as she cared about committing'.

Her friend 'Lushing Loo' had a more genteel appearance than Swindling Sal, and was neatly if cheaply dressed. At first she seemed too depressed to speak, until Hemyng gave her half a crown which she spent on brandy. After she had drunk it she became tipsy and began to answer his questions. 'My heart's broken . . . I wish I was dead; I wish I was laid in my coffin. It won't be long . . . I've just driven another nail in. Lushing Loo as they call me, will be no loss to society . . .'

Her story was similar to that of some other 'fallen women'. She had been seduced by a cousin when very young and this had been her 'ruin'. When Hemyng asked why she did not enter a refuge she replied: 'I don't want to live. I shall soon get DT [delirium tremens, a disease of alcoholics], and then I'll kill myself in a fit of madness.' When she had been plied with enough drink she sang a song:

> The first I met a cornet was
> In a regiment of dragoons,
> I gave him what he didn't like
> And stole his silver spoons.

SYPHILIS One result of the large numbers of prostitutes in London was rampant sexual disease. From about 1496 syphilis was treated with highly toxic mercury. 'A night with Venus, a lifetime with Mercury' was a popular adage. It was administered orally and also applied in ointments to rashes, scabs and ulcers. Mercury would also be injected into the nose and genitals. It was a drastic remedy whose side effects included loss of teeth, gum ulcerations, bone deterioration, nausea, diarrhoea and stinking salivation. All in all it was a distressing, doubtful and expensive treatment. But until the discovery of Salvarsan at the beginning of the twentieth century there was no other effective treatment.

In Leather Lane off Holborn a Madame Fourcade offered mercury baths, and they were used by wealthy and noble sufferers. This establishment may have been known to LORD ROCHESTER's friend Henry Saville, who wrote to him in July 1678 that he was undergoing a cure so drastic and painful that 'he would rather have turned Turk'. There was a Dr Fourcade, a specialist in venereal diseases, who was sent by the king 'post-haste to Newmarket to help out' in June 1675.

There were old wives' tales which recommended improbable cures. Sarsaparilla, opium, ammonia, sulphuric and nitric acids were thought efficacious. Some whores believed vigorous urinating was the answer. The seventeenth-century pamphlet *The Wand'ring Whore* describes 'Pissing . . . till I made it whurra and roar like the Tide at London Bridge to the endangering and breaking of my very Twatling-strings [sphincter] with straining backwards for I know no better way or remedy more safe than pissing presently to prevent the French Pox, Gonorrhoea, the perilous infirmity of Burning or getting with Child which is the approved Maxim amongst Venetian Courtesans.'

In 1547, the year that the syphilis sufferer HENRY VIII died, Dr Andrew Boord published his *Breviary of Health*, which recommended washing the genitals in 'white wine or ale or else with Sack and Water'. However, if the disease took hold he suggested recourse to an 'expert Chirurgeon'. Abstinence was even better. Dr Boord's prescription against 'Erection of the Yerde to synne' was: 'Leap into a great vessel of cold water or put Nettles in the Codpiece about the yerde and the stones.'

By the time of the Restoration venereal diseases were widespread and don't seem to have carried the stigma they acquired later. The poet and courtier Dorset wrote to a whore – possibly Moll Hinton – who had given him a dose: 'A little Advice and a great deal of Physick may in time restore you to that health I wish you had enjoyed on Sunday night instead of — your humble suffering servant.' The poet Dryden said CHARLES II caught a venereal disease from Lady Shrewsbury, and his mistress Louise de Kéroualle, Duchess of Portsmouth, accused the king of infecting her. Pepys wrote that Dr Alexander Frazier, physician-in-ordinary, 'was helping the ladies at court to slip their calves, and great men of their Clap.' John Aubrey recalled that the playwright Sir William Davenant 'got a terrible clap of a black [dark-haired] handsome wench that lay in Axe Yard, Westminster . . . which cost him his nose . . .' Davenant got little sympathy, Aubrey writing that 'with which unlucky mischance many wits were too cruelly bold . . .' JAMES BOSWELL tells in his diary for 1763 how he caught a venereal disease from an actress called Louisa, with whom he had a brief affair. 'Too, too plain was Signor Gonorrhoea.' He was treated by his friend, the surgeon Andrew Douglas, who cured him with the use of mercury. The treatment took about a month and Boswell was charged five guineas, which he thought rather high.

The Victorians were obsessed with prostitution and venereal diseases. An important and sympathetic Victorian commentator, Doctor William Acton, in *Prostitution Considered in its Moral, Social and Sanitary Aspects . . .*, wrote of 'rouged and whitewashed creatures, with painted lips and eyebrows, and false hair, accustomed to haunt

Langham Place, portions of the New Road, the Quadrant [in Regent Street] . . . the City Road, and the purlieus of the Lyceum' who were 'a mass of syphilis'.

Infection with syphilis and gonorrhoea was widespread, but guilt and secrecy made it difficult to gauge the true scale. The toll was great: in the 1830s, it was reckoned that 8,000 people died of venereal diseases each year, and in the capital's hospitals 2,700 children aged between eleven and sixteen were treated for syphilis annually. In 1856 three hospitals – Guy's, St Bartholomew's and King's College – treated 30,000 cases of VD between them. The children of infected parents were among the victims. In 1855, 269 babies under a year old died of syphilis in England and Wales. William Acton noted that syphilis was particularly deadly in children under a year old. Hereditary syphilis, which haunted the Victorian imagination, blighted generations. 'The innocent victims of syphilis are infinitely more numerous than the guilty; for it is a disease which follows vice down to the [third and fourth] generation . . .' (*Lancet*, 1846). Victorian medical statistics have to be used with caution, but venereal diseases were certainly widespread, and there may have been some truth in the belief among doctors that the country was suffering an epidemic.

The first specialist hospital for the treatment of venereal diseases, the Lock Hospital, was opened in Grosvenor Place in 1746 by William Bromfeild, surgeon to the Prince of Wales and to St George's Hospital. There was no revolutionary treatment, just a place where sufferers could find succour and soothing ointments and drugs. The need was immediately obvious – in 1758 442 patients were admitted, one hundred of them 'married women, many of whom were admitted almost naked, penniless and starving'. By 1836 the hospital had treated 44,973 patients and by 1808 claimed it had cured 20,222. Gaining admission was difficult: patients had to deposit the substantial sum of £1 11*s* 6*d* and once 'cured' could not apply for readmission, which meant that reinfected prostitutes had little choice but to go on whoring and spreading infection. Most victims of venereal disease were treated as outpatients, although whores could seldom find the privacy in their lodging houses for the recommended regime of personal hygiene which helped cure some venereal disease or keep it at bay. Hospitals allocated few beds to VD patients, and confined them in what were known as 'foul wards', as if to compound their shame. Inmate whores were subjected to a regime of severity and penitential work.

In 1864 the War Office and the Board of Admiralty, worried about the effects of syphilis on the efficiency of the armed forces, acted to stop the spread of the disease. The CONTAGIOUS DISEASES ACTS of 1864–9 authorised the detention and medical examination of suspected prostitutes near barracks and dockyards. If they were found to be diseased they could be detained for a cure. After protests from women's rights campaigners these Acts were repealed in 1886, although to judge by some of HENRY MAYHEW's collaborator Bracebridge Hemyng's observations the danger was great. A woman was pointed out to him as she solicited in the Knightsbridge Music Hall, 'who my informant told me he was positively assured had only yesterday had two buboes lanced . . . she was so well-known that she obtained the sobriquet of "the Hospital" as she was so frequently an inmate of one, and she had so often sent others to a similar involuntary confinement.'

'It was estimated that in a seven-year period in the middle years of the century one-fifth of the army quartered in Britain and one-seventh of the navy based on British ports was infected with syphilis or gonorrhoea. In London the estimate was that 50,000 patients were treated each year for VD' (Henriques, *Prostitution and Society*, Vol. 3). For comparison, in 1963 there were 1,099 cases of syphilis in England and Wales, and 31,547 cases of gonorrhoea.

T

TAYLOR, DAMILOLA Ten-year-old boy found bleeding to death in a block of flats in Peckham in November 2000. After a long police investigation four boys were charged with murder. The prosecution claimed Damilola died after being stabbed in the leg with a broken bottle. Police spent £10 million on the investigation but found only one witness, a girl of 14. The judge at the boys' trial refused to accept her evidence, saying she was an accomplished liar. Two of the accused boys were cleared on the direction of the judge and the other two, 16-year-old brothers, were found not guilty by a jury. They had a history of minor convictions and had also faced charges for assault, indecent assault and intimidation of witnesses. Police said they had been hampered by a hostile gang culture on the estate.

TEDDY BOYS Youngsters wearing 'Edwardian' clothes first appeared in the early 1950s in Southwark and Lambeth. This latest expression of Cockney chic – long velvet-collared jackets, bootlace ties, tapered trousers, suede shoes with thick crepe soles and the Brylcreemed DA or duck's arse hairstyle – was at first comical then, as the Teddy Boys became more aggressive, menacing. John Beckley, a 17-year-old apprentice, was stabbed to death on Clapham Common in 1954 by a gang of Teddy Boys wielding flick-knives. They were involved in riots in cinemas: one of them, in the Elephant and Castle Trocadero during a showing of the Bill Haley film *Rock Around the Clock* in 1956 was particularly destructive. In 1958 there were dance-hall brawls in which a young man and a police officer were stabbed to death. Teddy Boys had also been involved in instigating the NOTTING HILL race riots. *See* RIOTS and JOHN DAVIES

TEMPLES OF LOVE Three adjoining brothels in St James's Street in west London in the eighteenth century were described by their proprietor Miss Elizabeth Fawkland as temples. The first was the Temple of Aurora: it specialised in girls aged between 11 and 16. Here elderly customers were allowed to fondle the girls but not to have sex with them, at least in theory. These little virgins were said to be 'handpicked from those brought to the establishment by their parents'. From here the girls could graduate to the next-door Temple of Flora, which was a luxury brothel. Finally there was the Temple of Mysteries, which catered for those interested in flagellation and other sadomasochistic practices. These brothels were patronised by, among others, lords Cornwallis, Buckingham, Loudoun, Falkland, Bolingbroke and Hamilton, and the writers Sheridan and Smollett. Miss Fawkland put her girls through a training course before they took up their duties. The charges were exorbitant, and Miss Fawkland could afford to treat her girls well.

TERRISS, WILLIAM Actor-manager stabbed to death at the stage door of the Adelphi Theatre in December 1897. His killer was Richard Prince, a deranged Scottish actor. Prince believed that he rather than Terriss should have the lead role in the play *Secret Service* by William Gillette. He was sent to a mental asylum.

TERRORISM London has been afflicted by terror groups of various nationalities, but the spill-over of the Irish Troubles has been the main and most consistent source. The Fenian dynamitings of the nineteenth century, particularly the campaign of 1883–5, were a muted prelude to the bombings that accompanied the Ulster Troubles of the late twentieth century. In 1867 in an attempt to free two of their leaders who were being held at the House of Detention in Clerkenwell the Fenians detonated a wagon full of explosives against the prison wall. Nearby houses were demolished as was part of the prison wall, twelve people were killed and 120 injured. Michael Barrett, who was accused of lighting the fuse, became the last man to be hanged in public when he was executed outside Newgate Prison. In March 1883 the terrorists attacked the office of *The Times* and the Local Government Office in Whitehall. Over the next two years they struck at railway stations and prestige targets. Nelson's Column, SCOTLAND YARD, the TOWER, Westminster Hall and London Bridge were all bombed. More than sixty passengers were hurt when a bomb went off in a tunnel near Praed Street station. In response to the campaign the Special Irish Branch of the Metropolitan Police was established in 1885. It was later renamed the Special Branch. Its role of gathering intelligence about the Fenians was broadened to cover anarchists and left-wing revolutionaries. There was a new outbreak to accompany the successful campaign to set up an independent Irish state: in June 1922 Field Marshal Sir Henry Wilson was assassinated at his Belgravia home. In January 1939 the IRA launched a new campaign with time-bombs aimed at electricity generating and Post Office plants. Shopping centres were also targeted: six small bombs either exploded or were defused in the Piccadilly area in one night.

The campaigns of 1973–6 and 1978–82 which accompanied the Ulster troubles were an altogether more deadly affair. Fifty-six Londoners were killed, another 800 were injured, there were 252 bombings and explosive packages and immense damage. Some of the targets were the same: the Tower, Westminster Hall. Attacks on service personnel caused the greatest carnage, including bombings at a Woolwich pub, the Household Cavalry in Hyde Park, Chelsea Barracks and a regimental band in Regent's Park. The campaign continued throughout the 1990s with the IRA seeking what they termed 'spectaculars'. In April 1992 the BALTIC EXCHANGE was destroyed and a year later came the Bishopsgate bombing which led to the police throwing a 'ring of steel' around the City. This probably deterred the terrorists from striking there again, although it made life difficult for Londoners who worked in the City. The bombing of Canary Wharf was a catastrophic coda to the campaign. Later dissident republicans who disagreed with the IRA ceasefire returned to the city to attack, among other targets, the new MI6 headquarters.

In the nineteenth century London's reputation as an open city for political refugees attracted men who were regarded as terrorists in their own countries. The city became a centre for plotters hoping eventually to overthrow their own governments. In January 1858 two bombs were thrown at the coach of the French Emperor Napoleon III in Paris, and eight people were killed. The assassination attempt had been planned in London, and a French exile living in the city, Dr Simon Bernard, an explosives expert who lived by teaching languages, was arrested. At his trial at the Old Bailey he claimed the emperor was trying to stop London being used as an asylum by those opposed to his rule. He was acquitted. Towards the end of the century there was an influx of refugees fleeing police terror in Russia and eastern Europe. *See* SIEGE OF SIDNEY STREET

The presence in the city of many Arab refugees led to political murders. In December 1977 two Syrians died in a car bombing, and in the same year the London representative of the PLO was murdered. A former prime minister of Iraq was shot dead at the Intercontinental Hotel. There were assassination attempts on Jews. In the most spectacular event of all terrorists seized the Iranian Embassy in April 1980. They killed one of their hostages and were planning to kill more when the building was stormed by the SAS. Four of the terrorists died in the brief, shocking climax to the siege shown live on TV. The cathartic violence seemed to put an end to Middle Eastern sponsored terrorism on the streets of London, at least until March 1984 when PC YVONNE FLETCHER was shot dead by an official of the Libyan People's Bureau in St James's Square.

THEATRES Almost from the first there was a strong link between theatres and immorality. The word actress was synonymous with whore into the early twentieth century. Dryden commented bitterly in *Poor Pensive Punk* [prostitute]:

> The Playhouse Punks, who in a loose undress
> Each Night receive some Cullies' soft address;
> Reduc'd perhaps to the last poor half-crown
> A tawdry Gown and Petticoat put on
> Go to the House where they demurely sit
> Angling for Bubbles in the Noisy Pit . . .
> The Playhouse is their place of Traffic, where
> Nightly they sit to sell their rotten Ware.
> Tho' done in silence and Without a Cryer
> Yet he that bids the most is still the Buyer:
> For while he nibbles at her am'rous Trap
> She gets the Money: he gets the Clap . . .

It was during the seventeenth century that the connection between loose living and the theatre became particularly evident. Masked whores prowled the theatres in search of clients. Ladies of fashion also wore masks, and the ambiguity seems to have appealed to all. The theatres were divided by class and price into three sections, and the whores too: the pit, patronised by the most fashionable people, attracted the most expensive whores, the middle gallery attracted the middle class and their whores and the upper gallery, where the poorest playgoers went was infested by common whores. This section was notorious for brawls over women. In fact the theatres were constantly in an uproar.

The situation in the theatres, which have been likened to 'commodious brothels', was so bad that in 1704 Queen Anne issued an Order for their better regulation. 'We do hereby strictly command, that no person of what quality soever presume to go behind the scenes, or come upon the stage, either before or during the acting of any play, that no woman be allowed or presume to wear a vizard mask in either of the Theatres, and that no person come into either House without paying the price established for their respective places . . .'

Mixing with the whores, patrons and actors were the orange girls, who sold oranges, playbills and, sometimes, themselves. Some hoped to become actresses, and perhaps the mistresses of rich men, and some succeeded in both. None succeeded like NELL GWYN, who became the favourite mistress of CHARLES II. Nell was the most famous of the orange girls, but there were others of note. Among those named in a list of common whores published in 1660 were Orange Nan and at the Theatre Royal Orange Betty Mackarel, called 'the giantess Betty Mackarela'. Nobody took liberties with Betty, renowned for her strength, promiscuity and impudence. She could hold her own with the wits in the pit, 'hot at repartee with Orange Betty'.

In 1743 *The Tricks of the Town Laid Open* described a theatre bawd sitting in the pit at The Playhouse surrounded by her whores. 'In the pit she keeps her office by the concourse of whores and gallants perpetually crowding about her for advice and assistance . . . having a little more business among the Quality and the Gentry . . .' The prices of the girls were as low as 'a shilling and a glass of raspberry' and as high as five hundred guineas. *See* PIERCE EGAN

THIEF-TAKERS Bounty hunters who acted as a kind of police in the eighteenth century. The gangster JONATHAN WILD was the most successful of them. There was always a danger that ruthless criminals would frame innocent men just to claim the bounty, which was £40 for much of the century. In the 1750s a gang of thief-takers led by Stephen MacDaniel staged robberies in which the 'victim' was one of their gang. If a member of the public, seeing the robbery take place, intervened, he would be accused of the crime. In 1756 the gang arrested two men, Peter Kelly and John Ellis, accusing them of robbing a breeches-maker named James Salmon. Two witnesses, John Berry and James Egan, swore that Kelly and Ellis were the robbers. But the High Constable of Blackheath, Joseph Cox, was tipped off that it was a plot. Cox found a fence, a man called Blee, who acted as a receiver for the MacDaniel gang. Blee agreed to turn king's evidence in return for immunity. Cox arrested the four main conspirators and confidently expected their conviction.

Because of a legal technicality the men were found not guilty. A worse fate awaited them. They were tried for falsely obtaining rewards, and sentenced to the pillory. In their case it amounted to a death sentence. The mob were baying for the blood of these men who had sworn away innocent lives.

MacDaniel and Berry were first into the pillory. At the end of an hour they emerged bloody and battered from the missiles hurled by the mob. Egan and Salmon then followed, and the fury of the mob was if anything more intense. The barrage of stones and dead animals was so fierce the constables tried in vain to protect the two men. When they were finally released Egan was dead and Salmon was little better. He died soon afterwards in Newgate from his injuries, as did MacDaniel and Berry.

Nineteenth-century London threw up a similar racket in which innocent men were framed. Three Irishmen were looking for work in Cheapside. They met a man named Barry who offered them employment on condition they took an oath of secrecy. They swore, and Barry took them to a counterfeiters and put them to work. Shortly afterwards the BOW STREET RUNNERS raided the building and they were arrested. Although they were tried and condemned, they stayed silent because of the oath. When a priest told them that the oath was unlawful they told their story, and the Bow Street Runners were arrested. It emerged that for some time the Runners had been framing out-of-work men in order to claim the rewards. The Irishmen were cleared and a Lord Mayor's fund raised so much money they were able to go back to Ireland and buy a farm.

THOMPSON, EDITH (1894–1922) Woman convicted of inciting her lover to murder her husband in 1922. The husband, Percy Thompson, was a shipping clerk in the City of London, where Edith also worked as a book-keeper. On 3 October as the Thompsons walked towards their Ilford home after spending the evening at the Criterion Theatre in London, the lover, Frederick Bywaters, sprang from an alley and fatally stabbed Percy. Edith was heard to cry 'Don't, oh don't'. Bywaters insisted that Edith knew nothing of his plan to meet them that night. Nevertheless she too was charged with murder. Against her were the long love-letters she had written to Bywaters, some of which seemed to hint at ways of killing Percy. In one she said she had put ground-up pieces of light bulb in his porridge, 'big pieces too'. After a post-mortem the pathologist Bernard Spilsbury discounted this, and Edith was probably a bit of a fantasist. The judge's summing-up was unsympathetic, and the pair were found guilty. Against popular expectations the verdict on Mrs Thompson was upheld in the Court of Appeal. They were hanged at the same time in January 1923, Edith at Holloway and Frederick at Pentonville. Edith was so heavily sedated that she had to be carried to the scaffold. ELLIS, the hangman, who later committed suicide, described the execution as

Edith Thompson with her husband Percy, whom she was convicted of inciting her lover to kill. The trial in 1922 was sensational. When she was executed, she was so sedated she had to be carried to the scaffold.

Edith Thompson's lover Frederick Bywaters. He stabbed her husband Percy to death. She was heard crying 'Don't, oh don't' as he did it.

the most nerve-racking he had experienced. Mrs Thompson was 28, her lover eight years younger. F. Tennyson Jesse's novel *A Pin to see the Peep Show* is about the case.

THORNHILL, RICHARD Gentleman unusually tried for the murder of a man he killed in a duel. Thornhill dined with his friend Sir Cholmondeley Deering and others at the Toy at Hampton Court on 7 April 1711. A quarrel arose between the two men, Sir Cholmondeley struck Thornhill and then stamped on him and knocked out some of his teeth when he was on the ground. He later offered to apologise, but Thornhill said they must settle the matter in a duel. Two days later they went to Tothill Fields at Westminster 'and fired their pistols almost at the same moment'. Sir Cholmondeley fell dying, and Thornhill was arrested. At his trial witnesses testified that he was a peaceable man, while the dead man was 'of a remarkably quarrelsome temper'. Thornhill was found not guilty of murder but guilty of manslaughter, and was branded in the hand.

THORPE, JEREMY (1929–) Political leader acquitted of conspiracy to murder. Thorpe, a Liberal MP, was elected leader of the party in 1967 but resigned in 1976 following allegations that he had a homosexual relationship with a man named Norman Scott. In 1960 he met Scott, a neurotic and hysterical young man, and they stayed together at Oxted in Surrey, where Thorpe's mother had a house. Scott later claimed that they began a homosexual affair that night. He was given a flat near the House of Commons and Thorpe took him to restaurants and parties. Thorpe also wrote him a letter saying 'Bunnies *can* (and *will*) go to France'.

Scott claimed that after a three-year affair Thorpe tired of him and tried to brush him off. Scott was an embarrassment, particularly after Thorpe became Liberal leader. Scott was bitter, he was mentally ill, drinking too much and telling all and sundry that Thorpe had betrayed him. A court would later hear claims that Thorpe discussed with friends various methods of murdering Scott. For the role of hitman, friends were said to have chosen an inept schemer who turned out to be a hopeless assassin. Andrew Newton, an airline pilot, was hired for the enormous sum of £20,000 to kill Scott, it was claimed. In 1975 he drove with Scott to Exmoor and produced a Mauser pistol. Scott had brought his Great Dane Rinka with him, and Newton, who was afraid of dogs, shot it dead. The gun jammed when he tried to shoot Scott. It was pure farce. Newton drove off leaving the weeping Scott with his dead dog. Scott continued to tell anyone who would listen what had happened, and the Press at last began to take notice. In 1978 Thorpe and some associates were charged with conspiracy to murder. Thorpe, represented by the soon-to-be-renowned barrister GEORGE CARMAN, was acquitted. He had already lost his seat in the May 1979 election.

THURTELL, JOHN (?–1824) Murderer whose crime exposed something of the sporting underworld. In September 1832 Thurtell lost a large sum of money to William Weare in a game of billiards. Weare probably cheated, but the two men were part of a circle of gamblers and swindlers, and Thurtell would normally have been expected to accept his loss. Instead he decided to kill Weare. He and an accomplice, Joseph Hunt, bought a pair of pistols from a pawnbroker and then invited Weare to stay with them at a cottage near Elstree owned by the third member of the conspiracy, William Probert. As soon as they arrived at the cottage in Gills Hill Lane, Thurtell shot Weare in the face. Weare was only slightly wounded and leapt from the gig they had arrived in, shouting that he would repay Thurtell if he spared his life. Thurtell, a large, powerful man, ran after him and cut his throat with a knife. Some of Weare's blood splashed into Thurtell's mouth. He then drove the barrel of the pistol into Weare's head, penetrating the skull. After that he and his accomplices behaved with a mixture of almost suicidal carelessness and insouciance. Thurtell left the pistol and knife in the lane. Instead of looking for them, the trio went to the cottage and had supper with Probert's wife and his one-eyed sister-in-law. Thurtell gave Mrs Probert Weare's watch chain. At midnight the men put the body in a pond in Probert's garden. The next morning they searched for the weapons, but failed to find them. Two labourers who saw them searching later found the weapons and contacted a magistrate. By this time the body had been moved to another pond, some distance away. The BOW STREET RUNNERS were called in, and Hunt and Probert competed to be the first to turn king's evidence. Probert won, and Thurtell and Hunt were arrested.

It is a measure of the extent to which the public were fascinated by the case that a successful play depicting the crime was put on at the Surrey Theatre. Because of this the trial was delayed until January 1824. Thurtell made a long speech, ending with a plea to the jury not to upset his parents by having him executed. They rejected this and found him guilty, and at his execution two days later hawkers sold a ballad:

> They cut his throat from ear to ear
> His head they battered in
> His name was Mr William Weare
> He lived in Lyons Inn.

Hunt was transported to Botany Bay, and according to Wilson and Pitman (*Encyclopedia of Murder*) lived into old age.

THYNNE, THOMAS MP murdered on the orders of a jealous rival in 1682. Thynne, MP for Wiltshire and the owner of Longleat, married the wealthy heiress Lady Ogle, the 14-year-old only daughter of the Earl of Northumberland. A Swedish nobleman, Count Phillipp von Konigsmark, had also sought to marry Lady Ogle, and when Thynne declined his challenge to a duel Konigsmark decided to have him murdered. His men ambushed Thynne in his coach in Pall Mall in February 1682, one of them, a Pole named George Borosky, killing him with a blast from a blunderbuss. The assassins were arrested next day, and Konigsmark was found at Gravesend,

I. Nicholls delin.
I. Basire sculp.
The Murder of THOMAS THYNN Esq. in Pall-Mall

The ambush and murder of Thomas Thynne in Pall Mall in 1682. The murder was organised by Count Phillipp von Konigsmark, who was later murdered, probably on the orders of King George II, with whose wife, Sophia Dorothea, he was believed to have had an affair.

waiting to sail for Sweden. Konigsmark was acquitted, but the others were executed.

TICHBORNE CLAIMANT, THE Butcher's son who posed as the heir to a baronet. In 1871 Arthur Orton, who had been born in Wapping, launched a civil action claiming the Tichborne baronetcy and the family estates, which were worth £40,000 a year. He claimed he was Roger Charles Doughty Tichborne, who had been lost at sea. Lady Tichborne met him and was convinced that he was her son, but the rest of her family rejected him, with good reason. Tichborne had been slim, but Orton weighed more than twenty-one stones. He had none of Roger's tattoos, couldn't speak French, didn't know Lady Tichborne's maiden name, and was wanted in Australia for horse stealing. Nevertheless more than 100 people who had known Roger said Orton was the long-lost heir. After a 102-day hearing the Lord Chief Justice issued a warrant for his arrest for perjury. Orton's sensational trial lasted 188 days and led to him being jailed for fourteen years. He was released after ten and died in poverty.

TIPPING This practice, which reached insane levels, resulted in some of the oddest social strife in the eighteenth century. Tips or 'vails' were expected and demanded by servants. Not only house guests were expected to pay up at the end of a stay but even people who had simply been invited to dinner. Going visiting involved complicated considerations of expense for all but the rich. The demands were so great that they became 'a barrier to social intercourse . . . To dine with the nobility, with their considerable retinue, could be a ruinous business, costing at least a couple of pounds.' The philanthropist Jonas Hanway said servants in some houses charged a fixed tariff, 'so much to be paid by the guest for having taken breakfast, so much for having drunk tea, so much for having eaten dinner'. Servants in the great houses would expect a guinea. Those in an ordinary middle-class house got a shilling. A servant in the right kind of house could make £100 a year in tips.

Although resistance to tipping of all kinds had been growing for some time among the wealthy, the first concerted action was in Wiltshire in 1764, when the nobility, gentry and clergy agreed to end tipping. To enforce this new code there had to be sanctions against servants who resisted: a butler and two footmen were dismissed for behaving insolently to a visitor who didn't tip. At the Ranelagh pleasure gardens in May of the same year servants pelted their employers with stones and brickbats because they were forbidden to accept tips. Several men were wounded and four were arrested and held in NEWGATE PRISON. As resistance to tipping grew rural servants joined the drift to the cities.

TITANICS Gangsters from Hoxton. They were mostly pickpockets, hustlers and racecourse thugs. They clashed with ARTHUR HARDING's men and according to gangland legend fought a gun battle with the SABINIS at their stronghold, the Albion pub in Nile Street. Brian McDonald, who gives family trees for the major London crime organisations, suggests the Titanics were the forerunners of the KRAYS and the NASHES.

TOTTENHAM OUTRAGE Early in 1909 two Latvian revolutionaries held up a wages car outside a factory in Tottenham High Road. They were chased by a large crowd, and a policeman and a small boy were shot dead. Trapped, they shot themselves. During the chase they were said to have fired an improbable 400 bullets with their pistols, and wounded another twenty-seven people.

TOWER OF LONDON London's great fortress has been a place of imprisonment and torture, of daring escapes and despair. The first recorded prisoner was Ranulf Flambard, Bishop of Durham, who was held there for selling benefices in 1101. He got his guards drunk and escaped from a window down a rope. In 1278 some 600 Jews were imprisoned for clipping coins, and 267 of them were hanged. When the Treasury of Westminster Abbey was robbed in 1303 the suspects, many of them clergymen, were held in the Tower. The Keeper of the Royal Palace, Miles Podlicote, was hanged, although it was felt that the real culprits were never found. During the turbulent fourteenth and fifteenth centuries the Tower housed many hostages, including the kings of Scotland and France, and 300 burghers from Caen. In 1381 rebels led by WAT TYLER broke in and seized Archbishop Sudbury, Treasurer Hales, the man responsible for the poll tax, a notorious tax collector named John Legge and John of Gaunt's physician and dragged them to Tower Hill, where they were beheaded. Tower Hill later became the official site for beheadings, the first victim being Sir Simon de Burley, Richard II's tutor, in 1386. In 1414 the Lollard SIR JOHN OLDCASTLE, the model for Shakespeare's Falstaff, was held in the Tower awaiting execution for his religious views. He escaped and led the first Lollard revolt.

The rack was introduced to the Tower in 1446 by John Holland, Duke of Exeter, and afterwards known as 'the Duke of Exeter's daughter'. In 1471 Henry VI was murdered at his prayers in the Wakefield Tower.

The series of royal murders continued with the mysterious deaths of the boy princes Edward V and his brother the Duke of York. Their bodies were said to have been buried, but in CHARLES II's reign two skeletons were found under a staircase, and reburied in Westminster Abbey. In 1933 they were exhumed and it seemed that they were indeed the remains of the two young princes, reputedly murdered on the orders of Richard III.

HENRY VIII's reign saw the introduction of systematic ill-treatment of prisoners. Bishop John Fisher, who was sent to the Tower for refusing to take the Oath of Supremacy, complained to Thomas Cromwell that he was starving, and when he went to the scaffold in 1535 he was so weak he had to be carried. A fortnight later SIR THOMAS MORE, who had also refused the oath, went to his death. He asked an officer to help him mount the scaffold, saying: 'I pray you, Mr Lieutenant, to see me safe up, and for my coming down let me shift for myself.' The following year the most famous of all the Tower's royal victims, ANNE BOLEYN, was accused of adultery with her brother, Lord Rochford, a court musician and two courtiers. All were executed.

Four years later Thomas Cromwell, Henry VIII's once-powerful minister, was beheaded. The following year came the distressing execution of the COUNTESS OF SALISBURY, who refused to lay her head on the block but ran about shouting that she was no traitor. The executioner pursued her, hacking at her until she died. In 1542 Henry's fifth wife, Catherine Howard, was executed after being accused of infidelity.

The blood-letting went on. The Earl of Surrey was beheaded on Tower Hill in January 1547. His father, The Duke of Norfolk, was also condemned but on the day of his execution Henry VIII died and Norfolk remained in the Tower. The accession of the boy king Edward VI did not bring a stop to this tide of blue blood. Edward's uncle, the Duke of Somerset, was beheaded on Tower Hill in 1552 for plotting to overthrow the Duke of Northumberland, his successor as Lord Protector. The following year Edward VI was dying, and Northumberland, in a rash attempt to keep his family in power, arranged the marriage of his son Lord Guildford Dudley to the king's cousin, Lady Jane Grey. He persuaded the king to choose Lady Jane as his successor instead of his half-sister, the Catholic bigot Princess Mary. However, after the boy king died Londoners preferred Mary. Northumberland was sentenced to death and although he tried to save himself by becoming a Roman Catholic, he was executed on Tower Hill.

Mary's persecutions quickly claimed Archbishop Cranmer and the Bishop of London, Hugh Latimer. Both were imprisoned in the Tower and later burned for heresy at Oxford. Lady Jane Grey and her husband Guildford Dudley were tried and found guilty of treason. For the moment they were lodged separately in the Tower. But when Mary announced early the following year that she was to marry the Catholic Philip of Spain, a series of rebellions broke out. SIR THOMAS WYATT led the rebels in Kent. They caused panic in London before Wyatt was arrested and taken to the Tower. He was tortured and incriminated Princess Elizabeth, and she was arrested. The changed climate spelled doom for Lady Jane Grey and Guildford Dudley, and on 12 February 1554 they were executed. Dudley was beheaded on Tower Hill, and Lady Jane, who was awaiting her own execution, watched from a window as his headless body was brought back in a cart. She spoke briefly before her execution on Tower Green, claiming she had been the tool of others.

Princess Elizabeth was brought to the Tower on 18 March. She refused to become a Catholic convert, and on 19 May was released for lack of any evidence against her. Mary died in 1558 and Elizabeth came back to the Tower as queen. She touched the ground and said: 'Some have fallen from being princes of this land to be prisoners in this place. I am raised from being prisoner in this place to be the prince of the land.'

One of the most illustrious prisoners during her reign was EDMUND CAMPION, the Jesuit martyr. On 1 December 1581 he was executed at Tyburn, the executioner waiting until he was dead before drawing and quartering him. The long procession to the gallows continued. In 1586 John Ballard and Anthony Babbington planned a general uprising of Catholics, the murder of Elizabeth and her replacement by Mary Queen of Scots. They and their fellow conspirators were executed. In 1592 SIR WALTER RALEIGH was briefly held in the Tower for seducing one of the queen's ladies-in-waiting. He was sent there again for plotting against King James I. The queen's favourite, ROBERT DEVEREUX, second Earl of Essex, was brought there and later executed after his failed rebellion in 1601. The tensions between Parliament and CHARLES I brought a rich harvest of prisoners to the Tower. In 1629 nine Members of Parliament were locked up for harsh criticism of the royal favourite the second DUKE OF BUCKINGHAM. The health of one of them, Sir John Eliot, was broken and he died. In 1641 the king's principal adviser, Sir Thomas Wentworth, Earl of Strafford, and Archbishop Laud were impeached by Parliament and sent to the Tower. Strafford was found guilty of high treason and Charles, who had only recently promised him immunity, signed his death warrant. He feared an attack on his palace and family by the mob. On 12 May 1641 a vast crowd saw Strafford beheaded on Tower Hill. On his way to the scaffold Strafford saw Laud standing at a window, and was given his blessing. Laud followed him to the scaffold.

The great diarist Samuel Pepys was briefly held in the Tower in 1679, accused by the 'Popish Plot' perjurer TITUS OATES of giving naval secrets to the French. He later cleared his name. Religious strife claimed the life of CHARLES II's illegitimate Protestant son the Duke of Monmouth. After his hopeless rebellion against the Catholic James II he was beheaded on Tower Hill on 15 July 1685. The bungling executioner, JACK KETCH, took several strokes of the axe to dispatch the duke.

Jacobite attempts to restore the Stuarts to the throne in the eighteenth century brought a procession of prisoners to the Tower. In 1716 Lord Nithsdale escaped on the eve of his execution, disguised as his wife's maid. The last man to be beheaded in England, Simon Fraser, LORD LOVAT, was a Jacobite executed in 1747. As he surveyed the immense crowd which had come to watch one of the spectators' stands collapsed, killing several people. 'The more mischief the better sport,' he commented.

Famous eighteenth-century prisoners in the Tower included JOHN WILKES in 1762 and LORD GEORGE GORDON, instigator of the destructive riots, in 1780. During the First World War SIR ROGER CASEMENT was held there before his execution at Pentonville for planning the Irish Easter Rising with German help. Eleven spies were shot. During the Second World War Hitler's deputy Rudolf Hess, who had flown to Scotland on a peace mission, was held there for four days.

TOWNSEND Corrupt BOW STREET RUNNER who left a fortune of £20,000. The Regency diarist and commentator Captain Rees Howell Gronow described Townsend in action at the coronation of GEORGE IV at Westminster Abbey in July 1821:

> At this gorgeous solemnity it fell to my lot to be on guard on the platform along which the royal procession had to pass, in order to reach the Abbey. The crowd that had congregated in this locality exceeded anything I had ever before seen; struggling, fighting, shrieking and laughing were the order of the day among this motley assemblage. Little Townsend, the chief police officer of Bow Street, with his flaxen wig and broad-brimmed hat, was to be seen hurrying from one end of the platform to the other, assuming immense importance. On the approach of the cortege you heard this officious person, 'dressed with a little brief authority', hallooing with all his might, 'Gentlemen and ladies, take care of your pockets, for you are surrounded by thieves;' and hearty laughter responded to Mr Townsend's advice.
>
> When the procession was seen to approach, and the royal canopy came in sight, those below the platform were straining with all their might to get a peep at the Sovereign, and the confusion at this moment can be better imagined than described. The pick-pockets, of course, availed themselves of the confusion, and in the twinkling of an eye there were more watches and purses snatched from the pockets of his Majesty's loyal subjects than perhaps on any previous occasion.
>
> Amidst the crowd a respectable gentleman from the Principality [Wales] hallooed out in his provincial tongue, 'Mr Townsend, Mr Townsend, I have been robbed of my gold watch and purse, containing all my money. What am I to do? What am I to do to get home? I have come two hundred miles to see this sight, and instead of receiving satisfaction or hospitality, I am robbed by those cut-throats called "the swell mob."' This eloquent speech had a very different effect upon the mob than the poor Welshman had reason to expect: for all of a sudden the refrain of the song of 'Sweet Home' was shouted by a thousand voices; and the mob bawled out, 'Go back to your goats, my good fellow.' The indignities that were heaped upon this unfortunate gentleman during the royal procession, and his appearance after the King had passed, created pity in the minds of all honest persons who witnessed this disgusting scene: his hat was beaten over his eyes, and his coat, neckcloth &c were torn off his body. For there were no police in those days, and with the exception of a few constable and some soldiers, there was no force to prevent the metropolis from being burnt to the ground, if it had pleased the mob to have set it on fire.

TRAIN MURDER Britain's first train murderer was a German, Franz Müller. On 9 July 1864 he robbed and killed Thomas Briggs on a train between Bow and Hackney Wick, throwing the body out of the window. When he left the train he mistakenly took Briggs's hat, leaving his own with his name in it behind. He was hanged in front of Newgate Prison. *The Times* commented on the behaviour of the crowd who came to watch '. . . robbery and violence, loud laughing, oaths, fighting, obscene conduct and still more filthy language reigned round the gallows far and near'.

TRANSPORTATION The first convicts transported to the colonies were sent to the New World under an Act of 1597. They were welcomed as slave labour in north America, Jamaica and Barbados. By the end of CHARLES II's reign, however, the colonists in America had changed their minds. They regarded the convicts as a menace, and Benjamin Franklin asked how the English would feel if the Americans transported their rattlesnakes to England. For a while the trade lapsed. The 1718 Transportation Act gave it a new impetus. A London merchant named John Forward was paid £3 for every convict he transported to Virginia from London and the Home Counties. He got at least another £10 when he sold them to plantation owners at the other end. It was a flourishing business, with about 30,000 people being exported. When Virginia passed laws to end the trade Forward protested to the London government and they backed him. After the American colonies rebelled another dumping ground had to be found, and in May 1787 the first transports sailed for Australia. The ships carried 736 convicts, including Dorothy Handland, 82, convicted of perjury, and 9-year-old John Hudson, who had stolen some clothes. Handland committed suicide the following year. She was one of about 24,000 women sent to the antipodes. Another convict on the first transports was GEORGE BARRINGTON, a veteran of the Woolwich HULKS.

Many were whores who had been convicted of theft or coining, or one of the many other petty crimes which carried the death penalty. News of the horrors of the early voyages had filtered through, however, and some girls preferred a quick death to the lingering horrors of thirst, disease and depravity on the long voyage to New South Wales. In 1789 Sarah Cowden, 21, astonished the Old Bailey by preferring death to transportation. She insisted that she and another prisoner were innocent. 'I will die by the laws of my own country before ever I will go abroad for my life.' Three other women also refused transportation. The recorder tried to bully the women into accepting. Distinguished visitors to the court, who included the Prince of Wales's secret wife Maria Fitzherbert, went down to the cells to reason with Sarah and the others. When they still

Engraved for the Newgate Calendar.
Representation of the Transports going from Newgate to take water at Blackfriars

Chained prisoners sentenced to transportation are led to the river at Blackfriars at the start of their journey to Australia. Most elected to stay in the colony at the end of their sentences.

refused to accept their sentence the recorder ordered them to be put in solitary confinement and fed on bread and water. After more than a month the women gave in, Sarah being the last.

On board ship women convicts were expected to give sex freely to members of the crew, some of whom, including the senior officers, took women convicts as 'wives' for the duration of the voyage. However, most transported convicts were men. The voyage took from six to eight months, and although the prisoners were seldom allowed out of the holds most captains probably did their best to keep them alive. The government paid contractors £3 to ship the prisoners out, and the average prisoner might fetch an extra £13 when he was sold. Women surprisingly fetched less, £10 being the maximum.

The regime in the penal colonies was marked by sadism and depravity. On Norfolk Island, 1,000 miles off the coast of Australia, men got 100 lashes with the cat-o'-nine-tails for smiling or singing. The last transports arrived in Australia in 1868.

TREADMILLS AND TREADWHEELS A legal form of torture inflicted on prisoners sent to hard labour. As prisoners climbed on the steps of a great wheel it turned and they had to keep stepping up to avoid falling over backwards. Brixton was the first prison to install a treadmill, in 1824. After a riot in 1830 a treadwheel was installed at the notoriously severe COLDBATH FIELDS PRISON. Six hours on the treadmill would reduce a prisoner to tears of despair. The writer HENRY MAYHEW says the prisoners described working on the treadmill as 'grinding the wind', and adds: 'That is really the only denomination applicable to it.' Mayhew pointed out that prisoners would wound themselves severely in an attempt to avoid the treadwheel, and he suggested that it might put young offenders off manual labour for life. The fact that it was usually an entirely useless kind of labour added to its effectiveness in the eyes of those who opposed reform.

TRIAL BY BATTLE Ingenious device used by a murderer to escape justice. Abraham Thornton murdered Mary Ashford after a dance in 1817. Thornton, a bricklayer, claimed he had sex with Mary with her consent, and that they had then parted to go to their homes. However, there was blood on his clothes and footmarks found near the body matched his shoes. He stayed silent during his trial and was acquitted. Mary's younger brother William appealed against this verdict. When the appeal was heard at the Court of King's Bench in Westminster Hall in November 1817 Thornton demanded trial by 'wager of battle'. The judges ruled that such trials were still legal, and William Ashford refused to fight the stronger Thornton, who was discharged. Two years later trials by battle were abolished.

TRIAL OF THE DETECTIVES In 1877 some of the most senior detective officers at Scotland Yard were found to be corrupt. Two confidence tricksters, HARRY BENSON and William Kurr, had been operating a complex horserace betting swindle. They printed a bogus newspaper called *The Sport*, which carried reports of an English gambler who was so successful that bookmakers were refusing his bets. He would, the paper said, pay French residents to place his bets in their name. A wealthy Parisian, Madame de Goncourt, placed some bets for him and won. The swindlers sent her winnings, and soon she was prepared to invest £10,000 in the swindle. At this point the two conmen became greedy and demanded £30,000. Madame de Goncourt became suspicious and consulted a lawyer, who alerted the police.

For some time Benson and Kurr had been bribing senior detectives at Scotland Yard for information about police inquiries into horseracing scams. The officers who were put in charge of the de Goncourt investigation, Chief Inspector George Clarke and Inspector John Meiklejohn, were already on Benson's payroll, so inquiries stalled. Clarke advised Benson to leave the country, and he went to Amsterdam. Benson was arrested in Holland using the name Morton, but Clarke sent a telegram to the Dutch police saying they had got the wrong man, and that Morton should be freed. He said a letter would follow. When it failed to arrive the Dutch police sent Benson back to England in handcuffs. Benson, an ingenious and and successful crook who had at one stage been making £4,000 a week from crime, was sentenced to fifteen years' penal servitude for a series of outrageous frauds. Kurr got ten years. Benson decided that since he had not got the immunity from prosecution he had paid for the corrupt officers must pay the price.

At their trial Benson and Kurr appeared as the main witnesses for the Crown. It emerged that Benson had bribed police at Scotland Yard and in America, warders at various prisons including NEWGATE, Post Office inspectors, Superintendent Bailey of the City of London Police and others. He had paid the Scotland Yard officers for tip-offs when police were on his trail and about to arrest him.

Meiklejohn, Chief Inspector Nathaniel Druscovich, Chief Inspector George Palmer and a solicitor named Edward Froggatt were all sentenced to two years' hard labour. Clarke was acquitted. Confidence in the police, not yet strong, was shaken.

TRIALS The modern trial, with its careful sifting of evidence and the judge acting, ideally, as an impartial referee, took a long time to evolve. In the seventeenth and eighteenth centuries the savagery of the law was mitigated on many occasions by judge and jury ignoring the penalties laid down in the BLOODY CODE. Nevertheless, by modern standards criminal procedure left much to be desired. Prisoners could not give evidence on their own behalf – that was not allowed until the Criminal Evidence Act of 1898. Nor were they usually allowed counsel, except in cases of high treason. Although this rule was gradually relaxed, few could afford a barrister. As Ian Gilmour points out, as late as 1820 it was rare for a prisoner to be represented by counsel. The prisoner was not allowed to see depositions or a list of witnesses. These manifest unfairnesses were supposedly redressed by the judge acting as counsel for the prisoner. However, judges were frequently prejudiced. The wit Sydney Smith asked whether the judge ever gave 'the appearance of believing a prisoner to be innocent whom he thinks to be guilty . . .' After a Royal Commission in 1836 prisoners accused of felony were given the right to be represented by counsel.

Trials were breathtakingly brisk: in 1833 it was estimated that the average duration of a trial at the Old Bailey was eight and a half minutes. The jury's verdict was usually given equally quickly. They did not normally retire, but made their decision in the jury box.

Some of the quirks of the system worked to the prisoner's advantage. The terminology of the indictment had to be exact, down to the spelling of names, otherwise the case might be thrown out. The EARL OF CARDIGAN was tried at the Bar of the House of Lords in 1840 after wounding a man in a duel. There was no proof of his opponent's full name, so the earl was acquitted.

Death sentences passed in London and Middlesex were reviewed by the monarch, but the judge's recommendation was usually accepted.

TRUE, RONALD (1891–1951) Morphine addict sentenced to death for murdering a prostitute, but reprieved. True joined the Royal Flying Corps during the First World War but crashed on his first solo flight. His head injuries seemed to change his behaviour, making him moody and unpredictable. Invalided out of the RFC he went to America and became a flying instructor. After periods in hospital for drug addiction and mental problems he moved to London in 1922. He became involved in petty crime, stealing money and dishonestly obtaining goods, including a car. He became friendly with a prostitute named Gertrude Yates. True stayed with her in her flat in Fulham on the night of 5 March 1922. In the morning he strangled her and stole some money, but stayed in the flat until the maid came. She identified him, and in May 1922 he was sentenced to death at the Old Bailey after the jury rejected medical evidence of insanity. The Home Secretary ordered new medical examinations and he was found to be insane. True died in Broadmoor in 1951.

TURNBULL, JAMES Man who robbed the Mint. In 1798, when the Mint was still in the TOWER OF LONDON, Turnbull held his fellow employees at gunpoint and escaped with 2,804 newly coined guineas. He was caught after nine days and sentenced to death.

TURNER, ANNE (1575–1615) Court dressmaker, bawd and conspirator. Turner led a successful double life, devising costumes for the court revels of JAMES I and at the same time through her bawdy-houses and underworld contacts providing a range of sexual services to courtiers. She had brothels at Hammersmith and Paternoster Row which were used by men and women of the court as discreet places of assignation. An important contact of Turner's was Simon Forman, the celebrated magician and astrologer. She would keep him abreast of what was going on at court and he would provide her with love potions for her clients. His magic helped the great beauty Frances Howard, Countess of Somerset, win the love of the king's favourite, Robert Carr. Howard, who was unhappily married to Robert Devereux, the third Earl of Essex, confided in Turner. The bawd introduced Catherine to Forman, who gave her a magic figure of a man and woman copulating. The magic worked, and Carr and Howard became lovers, sometimes meeting at one of Turner's brothels. By 1611, when the infatuated King James I created Carr Viscount Rochester, Catherine decided to seek a divorce. She had sought the help of witches to make her husband impotent, and his impotence was one of the grounds put before a divorce commission appointed by James. The king successfully brought great pressure on the commission to grant the divorce, and in 1613 Frances married Carr, who was created Earl of Somerset. It was one of the great social occasions of the reign: Ben Jonson and Campion provided masques.

A loser in this affair was Carr's adviser Sir Francis Overbury. The pair had long been close friends and possibly lovers, and Sir Francis, a clever and wise counsellor, was a considerable help to Carr in his rise to power – apart from wealth and titles, the king made Carr Lord Treasurer. Overbury foresaw the loss of his influence over Carr. They quarrelled, and to get Overbury out of the way the king offered him a diplomatic post in Paris or Moscow. Overbury refused both in such an insolent manner that the Somersets were able to persuade the king to have him imprisoned in the TOWER. There they had him poisoned, with the help of Anne Turner. It is said that a young musician took a pie into the Tower and before handing it to Overbury slipped his finger under the crust to taste it. Afterwards his fingernail fell off. It is not recorded why he was not poisoned.

Without Overbury to guide him Carr was a less effective royal aide and besides became argumentative and domineering. The king found another favourite, George Villiers, later DUKE OF BUCKINGHAM. There were rumours about the death of Overbury, and Carr's enemies went to the king with circumstantial evidence which seemed to point to murder. A young man who had died recently had first confessed that he was the chemist's assistant who gave Overbury the fatal dose of poison. The king ordered the powerful jurist SIR EDWARD COKE, Chief Justice of the King's Bench, to carry out an inquiry. Carr was with the king when he was told that he had been summoned by Sir Edward. He refused to go, but the king told him: 'Nay, for if Coke summons *me*, I must go.'

Frances gave birth to a daughter in December 1615. It was taken away from her, and the following May she and Carr went on trial at Westminster Hall. She pleaded guilty and was condemned to death. When Carr was told he was to be tried he threatened to tell tales. At his trial two men stood behind him holding a cloak with which they were to silence him if he did attempt to disclose royal secrets. He was found guilty and condemned to death, but the king had promised him that no death sentence would be carried out. He and Frances were held in the TOWER, and after six years allowed to retire in disgrace to their country home, Grays. Their love had not survived their ordeal, and they never spoke to one another again. Frances died of cancer in 1632 at the age of 39, and Carr in 1645. He had been to see the king again, and James cried on his shoulder. Anne Turner had been found guilty of being an accomplice to murder and was executed in November 1615. The vindictive Sir Edward Coke ordered that she be hanged wearing one of the fashionable yellow ruffs she had introduced to the court.

TURPIN, DICK (1706–39) Butcher's apprentice who became a ruthless HIGHWAYMAN. His first venture into crime was cattle stealing, and when a warrant was issued for his arrest he joined a gang of deer stealers and smugglers in Epping Forest in Essex. Turpin was soon holding up stagecoaches, but he was adaptable, and had other criminal enterprises. He managed an inn, the Bull-Beggars' Hole at Clayhill in Essex, and used to rob his customers as they slept. He was associated with Gregory's Gang, a large band of housebreakers who used a clearing in Epping Forest as their base. Together they robbed graziers coming to market and the houses of London merchants. In one raid an old man had boiling water poured over him, and in another Turpin tortured an old woman by holding her over a fire.

In 1753 Turpin teamed up with the highwaymen Tom King, whom he had tried to rob. King is reported to have said: 'What, dog eat dog? Come come, brother Turpin, if you don't know me I know you, and shall be glad of your company.'

The two formed a successful partnership, so successful that they caught the attention of bounty hunters attracted by the reward of £100 offered for the duo dead or alive. When two bounty hunters tracked Turpin to a cave in Epping Forest he pretended to surrender, then shot one of them dead. The other fled. Turpin later killed King while shooting at a constable. This is the reality on which the legend of Dick Turpin, the highwayman with a burning sense of social justice, was built.

Turpin was so successful that he had to go north because things were getting too hot for him around London. He used the alias John Palmer and operated as a horse thief. When he shot a cockerel and had to give sureties for his good behaviour there were inquiries into his background. Turpin wrote to his brother in Essex for help in getting character references but did not pay sufficient postage. His brother refused to pay the postage and the letter was returned to the Essex postmaster's office, where the handwriting was recognised by Turpin's old schoolmaster.

Turpin's courage at his hanging in York was grist to the mill of the myth-makers. He showed no sign of fear except that his leg trembled, and he attempted to stop it by repeatedly stamping it on the scaffold.

TYBURN The main place of execution in London from 1571 until 1783. The earliest recorded execution at Tyburn (today's Hyde Park Corner) is that of William fitz Osbert in 1196. He had killed a guard of the Archbishop of Canterbury. He was the first in a great procession of victims great and petty:

it has been estimated that more than 50,000 people were hanged there. In 1534 Elizabeth Barton, the holy Maid of Kent, was executed for making a prophecy about the demise of KING HENRY VIII. Oliver Plunkett, the Roman Catholic Archbishop of Armagh, went to the gallows in 1681, a victim of the perjurer TITUS OATES. The bodies of the regicides Cromwell, Ireton and Bradshaw were dug from their graves in Westminster Abbey and hanged there. In May 1760 EARL FERRERS became the only peer to be hanged for murder. Celebrity criminals who died there included the HIGHWAYMAN CLAUDE DUVAL in 1670, the infamous Thief-Taker General JONATHAN WILD in 1725, the burglar and jail-breaker JACK SHEPPARD in 1724 and the clergyman and forger WILLIAM DODD in 1777.

The gallows at Tyburn was triangular in shape and eight people could be hanged from each of the three beams simultaneously. The Swiss commentator on London life César de Saussure (*A Foreign View of England*) described a multiple hanging at Tyburn:

> Some time after my arrival in London . . . I saw thirteen criminals all hanged at the same time . . . On the day of execution the condemned prisoners, wearing a sort of white linen shirt over their clothes and a cap on their heads, are tied two together and placed on carts with their backs to the horses' tails. These carts are guarded and surrounded by constables and other police officers on horseback, each armed with a sort of pike. In this way part of the town is crossed and Tyburn, which is a good half mile from the last suburb, is reached, and here stands the gibbet. One often sees criminals going to their death perfectly unconcerned, others so impenitent that they fill themselves full of liquor and mock at those who are repentant.
>
> When all the prisoners arrive at their destination they are made to mount on a very wide cart made expressly for the purpose, a cord is passed round their necks and the end fastened to the gibbet, which is not very high. The chaplain who accompanies the condemned men is also on the cart; he makes them pray and sing a few verses of the Psalms. The relatives are permitted to mount the cart and take farewell. When the time is up – that is to say about a quarter of an hour – the chaplain and the relations get off the cart, which slips from under the condemned men's feet, and in this way they all remain hanging together. You often see friends and relations tugging at the hanging men's feet so that they should die quicker and not suffer.
>
> The bodies and clothes of the dead belong to the executioner; relatives must, if they wish for them, buy them from him, and unclaimed bodies are sold to the surgeons to be dissected. You see most amusing scenes between people who do not like the bodies to be cut up and the messengers the surgeons have sent for the bodies; blows are given and returned before they can be got away, and sometimes in the turmoil the bodies are quickly removed and buried . . . These scenes are most diverting, the noise and confusion is unbelievable, and can be witnessed from a sort of amphitheatre erected for spectators near the gibbet.

The once free-flowing and navigable Fleet river gradually became a noisome sewer. Criminal communities grew up on its banks, with many notorious taverns. Eventually it was conduited and Farringdon Road built over it. Today it is still used as a sewer.

The progress to the gallows began in Newgate's Press Yard, where the prisoners' chains were struck off. The gates were opened and the procession of carts and horse riders set off through crowds lining the roads and rooftops. In front were the City marshal and the under-sheriff, flanked by peace officers armed with staves and javelins. The prisoners, unless they were rich and had their own carriages, sat on carts with the ORDINARY [chaplain] and the executioner. There were several halts on the journey. At the church of St Sepulchre's in Holborn the procession stopped while the bellman rang a handbell twelve times and addressed the crowd and the prisoners: 'All good people, pray heartily unto God for these poor sinners, who are now going to their death, for whom this great bell doth toll. You that are condemned to die, repent with lamentable tears; ask mercy of the lord for the salvation of your souls through the merits, death and passion of Jesus Christ, who now sits on the right hand of God, to make intercession for as many of you as penitently return unto Him. Lord have mercy upon you! Christ have mercy upon you!' The long slow way then wound through Snow Hill, across the Fleet Ditch, along High Holborn to the ROOKERY of ST GILES, an area that would feed the gallows year after year. Finally the procession made its way along what is now Oxford Street. The carts would stop up to half a dozen times so the prisoners could drink at inns. Sellers of gin also kept pace with the procession. By the time they reached Tyburn some of the prisoners were hopelessly drunk, and the hangman might be nearly as bad. One hangman was so far gone that, thinking he had three prisoners to hang instead of two he tried to put the noose around the neck of the Ordinary, and was with difficulty dissuaded from doing so.

At Tyburn the Ordinary would stand praying on the cart with the condemned man, who might address the crowd or read a confession. The theory of public executions was that the awful spectacle would deter others from following the same disastrous path, but the novelist and magistrate HENRY FIELDING pointed out that there were so many executions they had lost their power to shock, and were instead a form of entertainment. The mob was also moved to admiration for the condemned. 'The day appointed by the law for the thief's shame is the day of glory in his own opinion. His procession to Tyburn and his last moments there are all triumphant; attended with the compassion of the weak and tender-hearted, and with the applause, admiration and envy of all the bold and hardened.'

Another novelist, Samuel Richardson, was shaken by the spectacle; the clergyman was an object of ridicule, 'the psalm was sung amidst the curses and quarrelling of the most abandoned and profligate of mankind'; and 'unhappy wretches' preparation for death produced barbarous mirth not humane sympathy'.

The mob did not usually intervene to stop executions, although they would sometimes prevent a prisoner being rehanged if the rope broke. In 1717 the mob was responsible for three condemned men being reprieved. As they were being taken to Tyburn a writ was served on the hangman, William Marvell, and in the confusion he was knocked unconscious. The procession continued without him to Tyburn where a bricklayer offered to deputise for the absent hangman. He was beaten by the crowd and despite the offer of a large fee there were no further volunteers. The condemned men were eventually reprieved.

Fighting could break out between the hangman and friends of the condemned man over his clothes, which were a perquisite of the hangman. In 1447 five men sentenced to be hanged, drawn and quartered had already been hanged and cut down while still alive ready for the rest of the grisly ritual to be carried out when pardons arrived. The hangman refused to give them back their clothes and they had to walk home naked. Fights also broke out between the victims' friends and men sent by surgeons to take away the bodies for dissection.

After hangings ended at Tyburn the chief place of execution was outside Newgate prison, where the Central Criminal Court now stands.

TYLER, WAT (?–1381) Leader of the Peasants' Revolt, a popular uprising against a poll tax. On 12 June 1381 Tyler was recognised as the leader of the Kent and Essex men marching on London. King Richard II offered concessions which placated the Essex men, and they went home. Tyler was not satisfied and seized the TOWER, killing the chancellor, Archbishop Sudbury, the treasurer and others. An impulsive and violent man, Tyler pushed his luck too far, treating the king in a high-handed manner. At a Smithfield conference with the king there was a violent confrontation and he was wounded by the Lord Mayor of London, Sir William Walworth. He was taken to St Bartholomew's Hospital but Walworth had him dragged out and beheaded. His men dispersed, were pursued and punished. Tyler's rise from obscurity to arbiter of the future of the kingdom lasted a week. The chronicler Walsingham said he was 'beside himself in the insolent pride of success'.

TYRELL, SIR JAMES (?–1502) Royal agent reputed to have murdered the Princes in the Tower in 1483. He was greatly enriched by Richard III's usurpation, and was trusted with many difficult tasks by the king. SIR THOMAS MORE, who describes the murders in detail, attributes them to Tyrell, as does the historian Polydore Vergil, but both were writing long after the event. After Richard's death at Bosworth Tyrell prospered under his successor, Henry VII. In 1501 however he was implicated in a plot and executed the following year.

V

VANISHINGS, THE Series of disappearances of children which intrigued the Victorians. The children were all from East or West Ham. Colin Wilson in *The Mammoth Book of True Crime* says that because the mystery was never solved it is not clear how many youngsters disappeared. The vanishings began in 1881 with 11-year-old Eliza Carter, who went out one day wearing a blue dress with buttons down the front. A friend saw her some hours later and said she was too scared to go home. That was the last reported sighting of her. Her blue dress was later found at the East Ham football ground: the buttons were missing. In 1890 three girls from West Ham disappeared. One of them, 15-year-old Amelia Jeffs, was found murdered in West Ham Park. She had been strangled. Her two companions were the last to disappear, making a total, according to Wilson, of 'a dozen or more'. A woman had been seen talking to the girls shortly before they disappeared, and a coroner at the inquest on Amelia said 'women are susceptible to the lowest forms of mania as well as men'. A theory that might have struck a chord at the time would suggest the girls were kidnapped into WHITE SLAVERY, but to what extent this existed is controversial.

VASSALL, JOHN (1924–) Admiralty clerk who spied for the Russians. Vassall was serving at the British Embassy in Moscow in the 1950s when he was drugged and photographed taking part in a homosexual orgy by Russian intelligence officers. After he returned to London in 1956 he provided the Russians with navy secrets. He was unmasked after paying £46 in cash for a suit, and sentenced to eighteen years in prison, a sign of the paranoia of the times. Vassall later blamed the security forces who, he said, should have recognised that he was homosexual. Two journalists were sent to prison for refusing to disclose the source of information about the case.

VAUXHALL GARDENS The most popular of all London's pleasure gardens. It was of seventeenth-century origin. Pepys, who is frank about his own weaknesses, was shocked by the behaviour of the visitors. His diary entry for 27 July 1688 tells how he took his wife and servant Deb there to eat and walk in the gardens. He observed the 'coarse' behaviour of 'some young gallants from the town'. They took women into the leafy arbours and 'ravished' them. 'The audacity of vice in our time much enraged me.' Things had certainly not improved in the next century.

Light entertainment at Vauxhall Pleasure Gardens. Pepys complained about the behaviour of some visitors. 'They go into the arbours where is no man and ravish the women there.' The night would be rent by the cries of the raped or the sighs of the satisfied.

Vauxhall had many shady and secluded arbours which were ideal for prostitution. 'Those who purposely lost their way in the bushes did not bother to be discreet and made a tremendous uproar, no doubt added to by the screams of respectable women being raped' (Henriques, *Prostitution and Society*, Vol. 2). Yet the gardens were also popular with respectable Londoners of all classes and remained open until 1859. The entrance charge was 1*s* (5p).

VELTHEIM, KARL VON (1857–1932) Successful fraudster and blackmailer, real name Karl Kutze. Born in Brunswick, in 1886 he married an Australian and persuaded her to have an affair with a rich passenger she met on a boat to England.

Afterwards Von Veltheim obtained a large sum of money from the man by blackmail. Somehow he managed to get himself appointed American consul in the South American city of Santa Marta and stole the consular funds. In 1896 his wife identified a body found in the Thames as Von Veltheim's. In reality he was in South Africa where he tried to con the heirs of the millionaire Barney Barnato. He claimed he and Barnato had been business partners, and that Barnato owed him £50,000. When the heirs refused to pay up he became threatening, and confronted Barnato's nephew Woolf Joel in his office. Von Veltheim pulled out a revolver, as did Joel and his manager. The manager fired but missed. Von Veltheim then shot Joel dead. In court he pleaded self-defence: he was acquitted and deported.

After a series of amazing and lucrative adventures and many more 'wives', he again tried to blackmail the Barnato family. He was traced to Antwerp by Scotland Yard and arrested in 1907. He was tried in London, and given the very heavy sentence of twenty years' penal servitude. After the First World War he was released and returned to Germany, where he died in 1932.

VENNER, THOMAS Fanatic and rebel, executed in 1661. Venner was a London cooper and a member of the Fifth Monarchist sect who believed that with the coming of King Jesus the elect would rule over the ungodly. He was hostile to Oliver Cromwell. Jailed after an attempted uprising in 1657, he and about fifty supporters rose again in 1661 and were crushed by the Life Guards. Venner, who had been wounded nineteen times, was executed with twelve of his followers. Their heads were displayed on London Bridge.

VERE STREET COTERIE, THE In 1814 Robert Holloway published *The Phoenix of Sodom: or, the Vere Street Coterie* about a notorious male homosexual brothel at the White Swan in the street running north from Oxford Street. Holloway's book gives a description of the interior of the brothel:

> The fatal house in question was furnished in a style most appropriate to the purposes it was intended. Four beds were provided in one room: – another was fitted up for the ladies' dressing-room, with a toilette and every appendage of rouge, &c. &c.: a third room was called the Chapel, where marriages took place, sometimes between a female grenadier, six feet high, and a *petit maitre* not more than half the altitude of his beloved wife! These marriages were solemnised with all the mockery of bride maids and bride men; and the nuptials were frequently consummated by two, three or four couples, in the same room, and in the sight of each other! . . . Men of rank and respectable situations in life might be seen wallowing either in or on the beds with wretches of the lowest description . . . Sunday was the general, and grand day of rendezvous! and to render their excuse the more entangled and doubtful, some of the parties came from a great distance . . . to join the festivity and elegant amusements of grenadiers, footmen, waiters . . . and all the Catamite Brood . . .

In July 1810 officers from Bow Street, backed by a unit of troops, raided the premises and twenty-three people were arrested. Seven of them were sentenced to prison terms ranging from one to three years' imprisonment. They also had to endure a brief spell in the pillory. Here is a contemporary newspaper report of their ordeal, both in the pillory and travelling to and from it.

> About 12 o'clock the City Marshals arrived with more than a hundred constables mounted, armed with pistols, and a hundred on foot. This force was ordered to rendezvous in Old Bailey Yard where a caravan used occasionally for carrying prisoners from the jails of London to the hulks [prison ships] waited to receive the culprits . . . The miscreants were then brought out and placed in the caravan; Amos began a laugh, which induced his vile companions to reprove him, and they all sat upright apparently in a composed state, but having cast their eyes upwards, the sight of the spectators on the tops of the houses operated strongly on their fears, and they soon appeared to feel terror and dismay. At the instant the Church clock went half past twelve, the gates were thrown open. The mob at the same time attempted to force their way in but they were repulsed. A grand sortie of the police was then made. About 60 officers armed and mounted as before described went forward with the City Marshals. The caravan went next followed by about 40 officers and the Sheriffs. The first salute received by the offenders was a volley of mud and a serenade of hisses, shouting and execration, which compelled them to fall flat on their faces in the caravan.
>
> The mob, and particularly the women, had piled up balls of mud to afford the objects of

their indignation a warm reception . . . when the prisoners passed the old house which once belonged to the notorious Jonathan Wild they resembled beasts dipped in a stagnant pool. The shower of mud continued during their passage to the Haymarket. Before they reached half-way to the scene of their exposure they were not discernible as human beings . . .

At 1 o'clock four of them were exalted on the new pillory made purposely for their accommodation . . . Before any of them reached the place of punishment their faces were completely disfigured by blows and mud; and before they mounted their persons appeared one heap of filth.

Upwards of fifty women were permitted to stand in a ring who assailed them incessantly with mud, dead cats, rotten eggs, potatoes and buckets of grub, offal and dung which were brought by a number of butchers' men from St James's Market. These criminals were very roughly handled; but as there were four of them they did not suffer so much as a less number might. When the hour was expired they were again put in the cart and conveyed to Coldbath Fields Prison . . . When they were taken from the pillory the butchers' men and the women who had been so active were plentifully regaled with gin and beer procured from a subscription made on the spot. In a few minutes the remaining two, Cook . . . and Amos . . . were desired to mount. Cook held his hands to his head and complained of the blows he had already received; and Amos made much the same complaint and showed a large brickbat which had struck him in the face.

Cook said nothing but Amos . . . declared in the most solemn manner that he was innocent; but it was vouchsafed from all quarters that he had been convicted before and in one minute they appeared a complete heap of mud and their faces were much more battered than those of the former four. Cook received several hits in his face and had a lump raised upon his eyebrow as large as an egg. Amos's two eyes were completely closed up; and when they were untied Cook appeared almost insensible, and it was necessary to help them both down and into the cart when they were conveyed to Newgate by the same road they had come and in their passage they continued to receive the same salutations the spectators had given them on their way out. Cook continued to lie upon the seat of the cart but Amos lay down among the filth until their entrance into Newgate sheltered the wretches from the further indignation of the most enraged populace you ever saw. As they passed the end of Panton Street, Strand, on their return a coachman stood up in his box and gave Cook five or six cuts with his whip. (*Morning Herald*, 28 September 1810)

The ferocity of the crowd is difficult to explain. The women who took such a prominent part – as women were to do when OSCAR WILDE was tried later in the century – may have included many streetwalkers who resented the competition. Henriques (*Prostitution and Society*, Vol. 3) suggests that 'highly placed male homosexuals may possibly have fomented the feelings of the mob' to conceal their own complicity. *See* REVD JOHN CHURCH

VICTORIA, QUEEN (1819–1901) Survivor of seven attacks, most of them by lunatics. The first was on 10 June 1840 when the Queen and her husband, Prince Albert, were driving up Constitution Hill. The attacker, 18-year-old potboy Edward Oxford, raised a pair of pistols and fired. He missed and was overpowered. He was tried for high treason – still a capital offence – but reprieved because he was thought to be insane. He spent twenty-seven years in an asylum for the criminally insane, then was released and emigrated.

The next attempt took place on 29 May 1842 as the royal couple were driving down the Mall. A man fired at them and disappeared into the crowd. The following day the same man fired again as they drove down Constitution Hill. The gunman, John Francis, a cabinetmaker, was standing next to a plain-clothes policeman when he opened fire, and he was quickly arrested. He was sentenced to death but reprieved because of insanity and sent to prison. Just two days later a deformed youngster named John Bean fired a pistol at the Queen. It was loaded with paper and tobacco and could not have killed. Bean, who was 16, was sentenced to death but got a reprieve and a sentence of eighteen months' imprisonment. After this Parliament changed the law so that such crimes became misdemeanours.

The next attack was on 19 May 1849. William Hamilton, an Irishman, fired a non-lethal shot at the Queen as she drove on Constitution Hill. He was convicted under the new Act and got seven years' transportation. The next attacker, Robert Pate, got the same sentence. A retired army officer, he climbed on the the Queen's open carriage on 27 June 1850 and struck her on the head with his stick. The

Queen had bruises and a black eye. There was a long interval before the next attack. On 29 February 1872 17-year-old Arthur O'Connor climbed the railings of Buckingham Palace and ambushed Victoria as she was about to alight from her carriage. He was caught by the Queen's servant John Brown, and his pistol was found to be loaded with pieces of paper and leather. In many ways the O'Connor attack was more disturbing than the others, although he could not have caused great injury. He was the great-nephew of the Chartist agitator Feargus O'Connor, and in his pocket was a plea for the release of Fenian prisoners. O'Connor got a flogging and a year's hard labour. He went to Australia after his release but returned and on 5 May 1874 he was arrested outside Buckingham Palace. He was sent to a lunatic asylum. The last attack took place at Windsor station on 2 March 1882. A Scotsman, Roderick McLean, fired at the Queen and was attacked by two Eton schoolboys with umbrellas. McLean, a poet who was disappointed at the response to some poems he had sent to the Queen, had been released from a lunatic asylum some months before. He was locked up again. *See* LADY FLORA HASTINGS

VOISON, LOUIS Murderer whose conviction was a triumph for the detective FREDERICK WENSLEY. In November 1917 a roadsweeper found a sack with the torso and arms of a woman in Regent Square, Bloomsbury. In a parcel nearby were the legs. With the parcels was a piece of paper bearing the words 'Blodie Belgiam' and a sheet with a laundry mark which helped police to identify the victim. She was a Frenchwoman named Émilienne Gérard. In her flat in Munster Square police found an IOU for £50, signed by a butcher named Louis Voison. He was traced to his flat in Soho, and Wensley asked him to write the words 'Bloody Belgium'. Voison wrote 'Blodie Belgiam' five times. When his cellar was searched the head and hands of Mme Gérard were found in a cask. Voison was hanged. The 'Blodie Belgiam' note was intended to mislead police.

WAGES OF SIN This is a list of the charges the famous courtesan FANNY MURRAY had to pay when she worked in a brothel, before she became one of the Toasts of the Town in JACK HARRIS's *List of Covent Garden Ladies*. It is from the anonymous author of the *Memoirs of the Celebrated Miss Fanny Murray*, published in 1759. At the time Fanny was hardly earning enough to pay the greedy bawd's bill, a situation many brothel whores found themselves in:

Board and lodging (in a garret, on small beer and sprats)	£1 15*s*
Washing (two smocks, 2 handkerchiefs, two pairs stockings)	7*s*
Use of brocade gown (worth a crown [5*s*])	8*s*
Use of pair of stays (not worth a shilling)	3*s*
Use of pair silk shoes (not worth a shilling)	2*s* 6*d*
Use of smocks (old, coarse and patched)	7*s*
Use of ruffles (darned; worth only 2*s* 6*d* when new)	2*s*
Use of petticoats (all of the lowest rank)	4*s*
Seeing constables to prevent going to Bridewell (Peace officers' fees – in buckram)	10*s* 6*d*
Use of a hat (worthless)	2*s*
Use of ribands (unusable)	3*s* 6*d*
A few pins	6*d*
Use of a Capuchin cloak	8*s*
Use of gauze aprons (rag-fair quality)	5*s*
Use of gauze handkerchiefs (the same)	2*s* 6*d*
Use of silk stockings (yellow and pierced)	2*s* 6*d*
Use of stone buckles (most of stones out)	4*s* 6*d*
Carmine and tooth powder and brushes (brick-dust for the first two: brushes unseen	3*s*

The *Memoirs* go on to describe the kind of customers Fanny had to endure – it was obviously not a high-class establishment:

> The money thus supplied was mostly gained by apprentice boys who were seduced by the house to spend double the sum they gave to their doxy in bad punch, and worse negus. Perhaps their masters' tills were the only treasure for such debauchery, but good Mrs — the landlady never troubled herself with such reflections. If Tyburn carried off one set of her customers, which it frequently did, growing vice and the depravity of the times furnished her with another.

WAINEWRIGHT, THOMAS GRIFFITHS (1794–1847) Artist, art critic and poisoner. It is not clear how many people he killed, but he seems to have started in 1829 with an uncle, by whose death he inherited a house at Turnham Green. His mother-in-law, a Mrs Abercrombie, followed, and her daughter Helen. Taxed later over Helen's death he replied: 'Yes, it was a dreadful thing to do, but she had very thick ankles.' He had insured her life for £18,000 but the insurance company refused to pay. He was eventually transported for life for forgery, never having been convicted of murder. He died in Australia in 1847 aged 53, having become addicted to opium. Wainewright exhibited pictures at the Royal Academy, and was a noted art critic. His work was admired by William Blake. His acquaintances included Wordsworth, Charles Lamb, DE QUINCEY and Hazlitt.

WAINWRIGHT, HENRY (1832–75) Brush-maker driven to murder by the expense of keeping a mistress. Wainwright was a married man who owned a brush-maker's shop in the Whitechapel Road. He was intelligent and literate, giving popular lectures on Dickens and the poet Hood at Christ Church Institute. In 1871 he met Harriet Lane, an attractive 20-year-old milliner's apprentice. Soon she was his mistress, with a home and a generous allowance. They had two children. Wainwright's business got into difficulties and the cost of keeping two homes became too much. He cut Harriet's allowance, and she started drinking heavily and making unpleasant scenes at his shop. In September 1874 she apparently went abroad with a man named Frieake. A friend got a letter saying Frieake had promised to marry her if she broke off all contacts with her old acquaintances. Harriet's family were suspicious and hired a private detective, but he found no trace of her. Harriet's father begged Wainwright to say whether she was alive or dead. Wainwright told him he simply did not know.

Wainwright's money troubles continued, and in June 1875 he was declared bankrupt. His warehouse passed to a new owner. In September Wainwright dug up Harriet's body, which he had buried there after shooting her in the head and cutting her throat. Parts of the body were in two parcels as he prepared

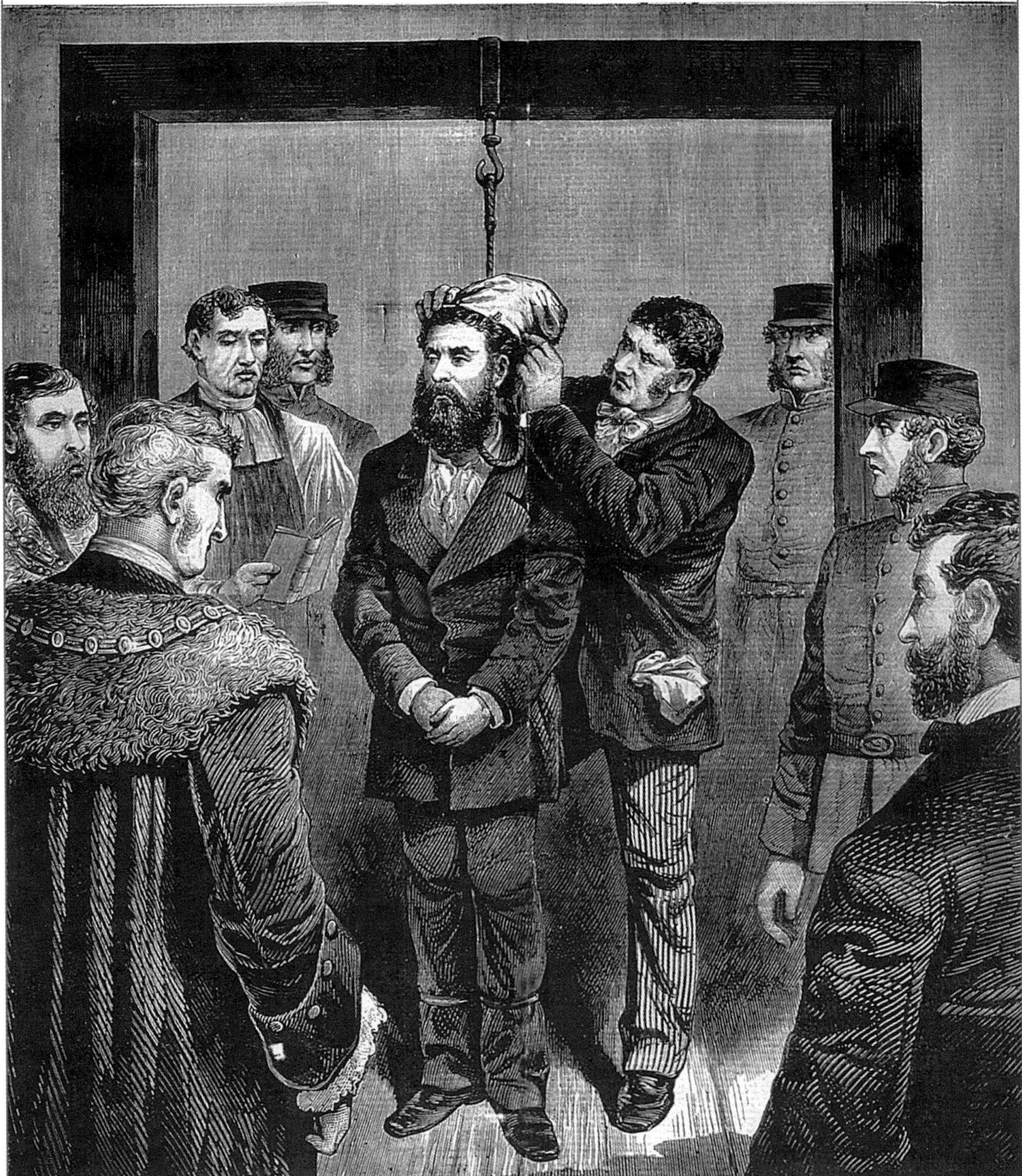

The execution of Henry Wainwright, a brushmaker who murdered his mistress. A large number of people had been invited to see the execution, and Wainwright said to them: 'Come to see a man die, have you, you curs!'

to bury it elsewhere. Wainwright asked a workman to look after the two foul-smelling parcels while he called a cab. The man looked in one of the parcels and saw a decomposing head and arm.

Wainwright and his brother Thomas, who had helped to cut up the body, were tried at the Old Bailey. Henry was condemned, and Thomas got seven years. A large number of people had been invited to see Henry die. When he saw them he exclaimed: 'Come to see a man die, have you, you curs!'

The judge who passed sentence on Wainwright, Lord Chief Justice Cockburn, was a known libertine with a weakness for women. Mark Herber says in *Criminal London* that when he was a barrister he had often climbed out of hotel windows to escape creditors or bailiffs, and had three children by the wife of a greengrocer.

WALL, GOVERNOR (?–1802) Sadist executed for murder nearly twenty years after his crime. Wall was governor of Goree, an island near the Gambia in Africa, in 1779. Some soldiers asked the garrison's paymaster why Wall had stopped their pay. Wall decided to make an example of one of them, Benjamin Armstrong. He sentenced him to 800 lashes, and stood by encouraging the floggers as they lashed him. He insisted on a thicker rope than usual being used. The following day Wall returned to England, and Armstrong later died of his injuries. News of the crime did not reach England until 1784, when a warrant was issued for Wall's arrest. He first escaped abroad, then returned to England in 1797, living discreetly near Bedford Square. The affair had been forgotten, and he could have lived out his life in peace, but he wrote a letter to the Secretary of State saying he had returned to answer the charge against him. He was arrested and given a trial, which was more than he allowed Armstrong. Wall claimed Armstrong had mutinied, but he had made no mention of mutiny when he returned from Goree. He was hanged outside Newgate in January 1802.

WALPOLE, HORACE (1717–97) Author who narrowly escaped being murdered by the highwayman JAMES MACLAINE. Here is how the great aesthete described being held up by Maclaine and his accomplice Plunkett in Hyde Park:

> As I was returning from Holland House by moonlight, about ten at night, I was attacked by two highwaymen in Hyde Park, and the pistol of one of them going off accidentally, grazed the skin under my eye, left some marks of shot on my face, and stunned me. The ball went through the top of the chariot, and if I had sat an inch nearer to the left side, must have gone through my head . . .

Walpole, 4th Earl of Orford, was the youngest son of the 'first Prime Minister' SIR ROBERT WALPOLE. He helped launch the taste for neo-Gothic with his pseudo-castle Strawberry Hill, and wrote the Gothic fantasy *The Castle of Otranto* (1764). He left acerbic but invaluable accounts of contemporary men and events. He visited Maclaine in prison, and felt it a pity he could not be pardoned.

WALPOLE, SIR ROBERT, EARL OF ORFORD (1676–1745) Statesman and first 'Prime Minister' of England, a description he angrily repudiated. His time in office was marked by bribery, nepotism, extravagance, adultery and a flagrant disregard of the rule of law. The wine he and his guests drank in huge quantities at Houghton, the great Palladian house he built in Norfolk, was often smuggled. He pulled down the local village and removed it from the park, rebuilding it elsewhere. He bought the office of Ranger of Richmond Park for his son and installed his own mistress, Maria Skerrett, in the hunting lodge there. Sir Robert's eldest son was given a post worth £7,000 a year and a peerage when he was 22; his second son one worth £3,000 a year plus other perks; his third son, Horace, was made Controller of the Pipe and Clerk of the Estreat when still at school and Usher of the Exchequer before he was 21. The rest of the family similarly prospered. Walpole opposed all parliamentary inquiries for fear that one day his own affairs would be scrutinised. He had made a huge fortune from office, and he needed it. He and his wife were recklessly extravagant. On resuming office in 1720 he said he was 'lean and needed to get some fat on his bones'. He succeeded in every sense: because of his great bulk George II called him '*le gros homme*'.

Despite his bluff front Walpole was hypersensitive to attacks by satirists and caricaturists. He tried to buy them off and if that failed, to arrest them. The most telling attack on him was JOHN GAY's *Beggar's Opera*, ostensibly the story of JACK SHEPPARD and JONATHAN WILD but really a thinly veiled satire on Walpole. The first performance was given at Lincoln's Inn Fields in 1728. The play ran for sixty-two nights, a record for the time, and the theatre owner, John Rich, packed the audiences in, even having nearly a hundred seated on the stage itself. It was said the play made Gay rich, and Rich gay.

The political innuendoes of the plot were not lost on the audience. Although the two central characters, Macheath and Peachum, are based on Sheppard and Wild, Gay had left room for other interpretations. It was possible to see Walpole as the highwayman Macheath, or as the gang leader Peachum, or even as Lockit, the Newgate jailer.

Walpole is said to have sat through a performance with his teeth gritted, and even called for an encore, an act of some political astuteness. Yet it rankled: he had the play's successor, *Polly*, banned, and Gay's patrons, the Duke and Duchess of Queensberry, banished from court. In the end, the attacks became too much for Walpole. FIELDING's attacks on him in his plays led to the government introducing a Licensing Act which effectively drove political satire off the stage.

A new word, Robinocracy, was coined by the opposition to characterise the Walpole administration. The Robinarch 'rules by Money, the root of all evils, and founds his iniquitous dominion in the corruption of the people'.

WALSINGHAM, SIR FRANCIS (1530–90) Statesman who developed a complex secret service for Queen Elizabeth I. He employed spies in foreign towns and courts, and spent his personal fortune on building up an extraordinarily efficient system of intelligence. He had fifty-three agents abroad and others throughout Britain – among them perhaps CHRISTOPHER MARLOWE. He exposed various Catholic plots against the queen, including the BABBINGTON plot. He was one of the commissioners who tried Mary Queen of Scots. *See* THE TOWER

WALTER Victorian lecher who left an account of encounters with hundreds of prostitutes. In one of them he entered a dangerous brothel and nearly came to grief. Many London whores worked with criminals to extort or steal, often with violence, from their clients. Walter must have been aware of the dangers, although he does not mention them. Perhaps the fact that he was not a heavy drinker – the women's victims were usually drunk – saved him. But one night in the Strand he met a young woman who took him to a house in a court near Drury Lane Theatre where an ugly scene followed. Walter begins as usual by describing the girl's charms:

> . . . there was an exceedingly well-dressed and very short-petticoated (they all wore them then) girl of about seventeen years of age; her legs especially pleased me, they were so plump and neat, and her feet so well shod. After my offer had been accepted we went to a house . . . She stripped and I plugged her, and recollect now my enjoyment of her.

When the time came to leave Walter paid her the ten shillings they had agreed, but she claimed he had promised her five pounds. 'Look at this room, look at my dress – do you expect me to let a man come here with me for ten shillings?' She called him a bugger, and opening the door called out: 'Mrs Smith, Mrs Smith, come up, here's a bilk, come up quickly.' An old woman, described by Walter as 'shortish, thick, hook-nosed, tawny-coloured, evil-looking', appeared and berated him.

> Was I a gent? She was sure I was, why not pay properly then? – a beautiful girl like that – just out – look at her shape and her face – she had written to a dozen gents who knew her house, and they had all come to see this beauty – all had given her five pounds, some ten pounds, and they were delighted with her – and much of the same talk. The girl began to whimper, saying she had never been so insulted in her life before.

The scam had obviously been well rehearsed. Walter said he had not got five pounds: the ugly old bawd demanded his watch, which she said she would pawn for the money. Walter, who had hidden his watch, countered that he had no watch either. The bawd shouted for a man called Bill and he replied from below in a loud voice 'Hallo'. Walter threw up the window and shouted 'Police! – police! – murder! – murder! – police! – police!' He saw a policeman under the window, but the officer ignored his cries and walked away: he had been bribed to turn a blind eye to the goings-on in the brothels on his beat. However, the two women were alarmed by the commotion and the ugly bawd said 'Go if you want, who is keeping you? This is a respectable house, this is.' But she demanded three pounds, then two. When they refused to open the door Walter seized a poker and smashed the window, then struck and broke a chair. They begged him to go, and he edged cautiously down the stairs, dropping the poker on the mat as he left. 'My blood was roused, I would have smashed woman or man who stood in my way, and eyeing the girl said, "Look at me well, if you meet me in the Strand again cut away at once, get out of my sight, or I'll give you in charge [have you arrested] for annoying me or robbing me, you bloody bitch, look out for yourself."'

A fortnight later he saw her again in the Strand, and followed her. He watched as she solicited various men. Not recognising him, she tried to pick him up, but, stepping into the lamplight so she could see him properly, he said: 'Look at me, you damned whore, you attempted to rob me the other night, go out of the Strand or I'll tell the next policeman you have picked my pocket.' The girl fled with her old bawd running after her, cursing. He saw her again some weeks later, chatting with a group of prostitutes. Walter approached them and said: '"That bitch attempted to rob me the other night . . .". "It's a lie", said she, but again turned round and ran up a side street as fast as she could. I don't recollect seeing her afterwards.'

Some years later a man died in a fight in the house where the whore had taken him. The owner was transported. 'I don't know if it was the same man who was called Bill, but suspect that it was, and that many a visitor had been bullied out of his money in that house' (Walter, *My Secret Life*). *See* YELLOW-HAIRED KITTY

WAR The two world wars forced the authorities to confront moral issues they would rather have left alone. The likelihood of high rates of infection from venereal disease during the First World War did not persuade the military to provide the soldiers going to France with condoms. Instead they got a leaflet signed by the Secretary of War Lord Kitchener, a bachelor:

> Your duty cannot be done unless your health is sound. So keep constantly on your guard against any excesses. In this new experience you may find temptations both in wine and women. You must entirely resist both temptations, and while treating all women with perfect courtesy, you should avoid any intimacy. Do your duty bravely. Fear God, honour the King.

There was a fear that by giving the men condoms or effective medical treatments the authorities would be seen to be condoning vice. General Childs of the War Office said there would be questions in the House of Commons 'which it would be impossible to answer'. After a royal commission on VD reported in 1916 the army decided to approve some form of treatment, but it was not clear what. To make the matter more confusing, the Army Council said it rejected any kind of preventive that might 'afford opportunities for unrestrained vice'.

The result of the confusion was that men went on getting VD, sometimes more than once. Some may have courted it, as a dose of VD meant a month out of the front line. There were more than a hundred thousand cases among troops in the UK during the first three years of the war, and a quarter of a million among British forces in France.

The war changed sexual relations in profound ways. Mass education of the troops, however tentative, on the dangers of venereal disease did much to break the old taboo on the subject. And the employment of women in factories and on other forms of war work led to a degree of sexual liberation.

Just as the moral panic of the First World War had led to the setting up of a 'MORALS POLICE', the Second World War produced Regulation 33B of the Defence of the Realm Act. This gave medical officers powers to request the examination of any woman suspected of being a source of venereal infection. There were few instances of this now forgotten regulation being applied. The first case was brought before magistrates at York on 5 March 1943. It involved a young married woman in the East Riding of Yorkshire who was suspected of having infected two people. She was requested to attend for examination, promised she would and then failed to do so. This occurred twice. She was subsequently arrested on a warrant, pleaded guilty and was sentenced to two months' imprisonment. Under the regulation, as under the old Contagious Diseases Acts of the nineteenth century, quite innocent women might be arrested by mistake and suffer public shame.

Conscription was a problem for prostitutes. In 1941 conscription was introduced for unmarried women aged 20 to 30. There were exceptions, but most prostitutes fell into the categories likely to be called up. They avoided it by writing 'prostitute' in the occupation section of the call-up paper. The authorities did not want young girls corrupted by mixing with hardened prostitutes, so women who described themselves so were not called up.

British troops were provided with condoms, but VD was still common. There were films, and advertisements in newspapers warning of the dangers, the impact of the latter spoilt when press magnates persuaded the Ministry of Health that they were too hard-hitting. The words 'on or near the sex organs' were excised from a paragraph explaining where a syphilitic ulcer would first appear.

WARD, NED (1667–1731) Author and tavern keeper, acute observer of the London scene around the beginning of the eighteenth century. His *The London Spy* (1698–1709) contains interesting sketches of London life and character. *See* BRIEF ENCOUNTERS and BRIDEWELL

WARREN, SIR CHARLES Police chief who didn't catch JACK THE RIPPER. In the 1880s the Press were demanding the appointment of an Army officer to bring order to the streets, and Warren, an officer, got the job. His use of troops to break up the BLOODY SUNDAY riots in Trafalgar Square in 1887 was criticised. Widespread criticism of police inefficiency during the hunt for the Ripper undermined his authority, and there was friction between him and his superiors in the Home Office. He resigned and returned to the Army. This coincided with the last of the Ripper murders, and led to suggestions that he had been dismissed for his failure to catch the killer.

WATNEY STREET GANG Brawlers who clashed with the KRAYS. The Watney Streeters were mostly dockers, not serious criminals, although GEORGE CORNELL, later shot dead by Ronnie Kray, had graduated from their ranks. They fought a bloody battle with the Krays at the appropriately named Hospital Tavern in 1959 and lost.

WATSON, REVD JOHN (1804–1884) Victorian scholar who murdered his wife. Some of Watson's translations of Greek and Latin classics were later reprinted in Everyman's Library, and he was a hard-working and popular headmaster of Stockwell Grammar School, a post he was appointed to in 1844. The job was poorly paid, and Watson's literary success brought him little money. He had become engaged twenty years earlier to Anne Armstrong, but had been too poor to marry her. His salary just about enabled them to marry, which they did in 1845 when Watson was 41. For a while the school prospered, but by 1870 it was failing. The struggle against poverty and overwork had worn Watson down. In September 1870 the governors of the school dismissed him without a pension. On 10 October 1871 he tried to commit suicide by taking poison. He left a note saying he had killed his wife. The servant girl found him and called a doctor. Mrs Watson was found dead in a bedroom with head wounds. Watson recovered, and was tried at the Old Bailey in January 1872. The jury recommended mercy, and he died in prison at the age of 80.

WATTS, MARTHE (1913–?) Prostitute and madam for the MESSINA BROTHERS. She wrote *The Men in My life*, an unsentimental account of life as a prostitute. She had worked in brothels in France, Spain, Italy and North Africa before coming to London, where she paid a drunken Englishman 30,000 francs to marry her. She became a street-walker, and at first found the long hours on her feet difficult. She was also astonished by the number of middle-class men who wanted her to tie them up and beat them. Her book provides much valuable information about organised crime and whoring in London just before, during and after the Second World War. Although she describes the viciousness of the brothers, she made large sums of money for them, picking up forty-nine clients on VE Day alone. She hoped to make it fifty, but could not find another man. She was the mistress of Gino Messina. *See* PROSTITUTION

The Messina madam and whore Martha Watts, with her lover, Eugenio Messina. She brought in a fortune for the family, which dominated London vice.

WEATHERBY'S Coffee house and haunt of low life. After the death of MOLL KING in 1747 Elizabeth Weatherby's Ben Jonson's Head coffee house in Russell Street, famous simply as Weatherby's, attracted her low-life clients. Some famous whores got their start there, including LUCY COOPER and the one-eyed Betsy Weems, or Wemyss. WILLIAM HICKEY, the memoirist, describes a visit to Weatherby's, 'an absolute hell upon earth', with some friends equally 'brimfull of wine'.

> At this time the whole room was in an uproar, men and women promiscuously mounted upon chairs, tables and benches, in order to see a sort of general conflict carried on upon the floor. Two she devils, for they scarce had a human appearance, were engaged in a scratching and boxing match, their faces entirely covered with blood, bosoms bare, and clothes nearly torn from their bodies . . . In another corner of the same room, an uncommonly athletic young man of about twenty-five seemed to be the object of universal attack. No less than three Amazonian tigresses were pummelling him with all their might, and it appeared to me that some of the males at times dealt him blows with their sticks . . .'

The *Nocturnal Revels* of 1779 says Weatherby's was a 'receptacle' for rakes, highwaymen, pickpockets, swindlers and prostitutes, 'from the charioted kept mistress down to the twopenny bunter [prostitute] who plies under the Piazza . . . [in Covent Garden]'. Weatherby's closed in the 1770s. A new owner had been refused a licence because of nightly affrays and riots, and when he was indicted for causing a nuisance he was pilloried and jailed.

WEBB, DUNCAN (1917–1958) Investigative reporter, largely responsible for the downfall of the MESSINA vice empire. He also ghosted the life story of his friend BILLY HILL, the so-called Boss of Britain's Underworld. The book is partisan, Webb regarding the notorious gangster, with reservations, as a 'genius and a kind and tolerant man'.

Webb's greatest journalistic triumph was the exposure of the Messina brothers, the Soho vice kings. After a long campaign in the *People*, during which he was threatened and attacked, on 3 September 1950 he named the 'four debased men with an empire of crime which is a disgrace to London'. He passed his dossier on to Scotland Yard and the Messinas had to flee the country. Because of his friendship with Hill he was beaten up by JACK SPOT, who broke his arm. Webb married Cynthia Hume, who had been a night club-hostess and former wife of DONALD HUME, a small-time crook who murdered the shady wartime businessman Stanley Setty. Webb died in September 1958 at the age of 41.

WEBSTER, KATE (1849–79) Murderer who boiled her victim and sold the fat. Webster, a servant who had made a career of robbing her mistresses and then moving on, was dismissed by Julia Thomas, a Richmond widow with whom she was living, in 1879. She killed Mrs Thomas with a chopper, then dismembered her body and boiled it in a copper saucepan. She scraped the fat off and sold it to neighbours as dripping. Parts of the body were found at Twickenham and Barnes. She tried to sell Mrs Thomas's furniture, saying the widow had gone away. This made the neighbours suspicious and the house was searched. The chopper and fragments of bone were found. Some of the fat was still in the copper. Kate Webster was hanged at Wandsworth Prison on 30 July 1879.

WEIL, DR LEVI Doctor, burglar and murderer. Weil came to London from Holland in the 1760s. At first he had little success because he was a Jew and a foreigner. Then a merchant called him to a house in Enfield to attend his sister, and paid him in cash. Weil was impressed by the merchant's obvious wealth. Later he went back to the house and stole £90. From then on, as he became more successful in his medical practice, he burgled the homes of wealthy patients. He recruited a gang of seven men, including a German Jew named Isaacs. Weil suspected Isaacs of cheating the rest of the gang, and sent him packing. In the autumn of 1771 the gang robbed a Mrs Hutchings in her home at Chelsea. A servant was shot dead, and a reward was offered for the arrest of the killers. Isaacs gave evidence in return for a pardon, and Weil, his brother Asher and two other Jews were hanged at Tyburn in December 1771. The *Newgate Calendar* says their crimes 'long roused the public indignation against the whole Jewish people'. Jews were attacked in the streets.

WENSLEY, FREDERICK Famous Scotland Yard commander. He witnessed the rise of the first modern gangsters in the East End, was present at the SIEGE OF SYDNEY STREET, and helped to jail ARTHUR HARDING. He arrested STEINIE MORRISON for the murder of Leon Beron. He wrote a disappointing autobiography, *Detective Days*, in 1931. *See* VOISON

WENTWORTH STREET Notorious criminal haunt near Spitalfields Market which had the distinction in 1836 of having six consecutive houses, Nos. 102–107, which were all brothels. HENRY MAYHEW said it ranked with ST GILES as the

Wentworth Street in Whitechapel by Doré. In 1836 six consecutive houses were all brothels. Mayhew said it ranked with St Giles as the worst London slum, 'both as regards filth and immorality'.

worst place in London, 'both as regards filth and immorality'.

WESLEY, JOHN (1703–91) Evangelist and founder of Methodism, who sought to bring salvation and comfort to the prisoners of Newgate and Marshalsea prisons. He recorded of his preaching in September 1738 'all Newgate sang with the cries of those whom the word of God cut to the heart'. He also rode on carts to Tyburn with the condemned. *See* SUICIDE

WHITE GANG Racecourse and protection racketeers from Islingon, led by Big Alf White. They were the leading racecourse gang after the SABINIS, with whom they had been allied, were interned at the beginning of the Second World War. They opposed the coalition of BILLY HILL and JACK SPOT in a struggle for control of the West End and lost. Hill, who called the Whites the Blacks in his book *Boss of the Underworld*, wrote:

> They took over the horserace-tracks and the dog-track concessions. They continued the blackmail of club-owners, cafe proprietors and publicans. They even ran some of the brasses [prostitutes] on the streets and got them to steer the mugs into their spielers and drinking clubs . . . No one could open a drinking club or spieler in the West End without the Blacks' permission. And their permission usually meant the payment of a dollar in the pound [25 per cent] out of takings.
>
> At that time I had my own manor [territory]. I was guv'nor of Camden Town, that part of London that is bordered by Regent's Park, Hampstead Road and King's Cross. The Blacks came out of Islington, which is next to King's Cross. So you can see they did not have much love for me.

WHITELEY, WILLIAM (1832–1907) Wealthy owner murdered in London's first department store. Whiteley was a notorious womaniser, finding willing partners among the young female staff of his store in Westbourne Grove, Bayswater. In 1882 when he was 50 he set up Louisa Turner in a house in Kilburn. He was also involved with Louisa's sister Emily, who lived with a man named Rayner. Later Emily had a son, who was called Horace Rayner. He was given to boasting that he was the son of a wealthy man and would inherit a fortune. On 24 January 1907 Horace tricked his way into Whiteley's and confronted the store owner. Whiteley refused to recognise him as his son. Rayner was overheard by staff saying 'Is that your final word? . . . Then you are a dead man.' He shot Whiteley in the head and then shot himself in the eye. He recovered and in a one-day trial in March 1907 was sentenced to death. Rayner revealed that Whiteley had three-in-a-bed sex with his mother and aunt. A wave of public sympathy and a petition signed by more than 200,000 people persuaded the Home Secretary to grant a reprieve. Rayner was released in 1919 and died two years later.

WHITE SLAVERY To what extent white slavery ever existed is unclear. The journalist W.T. STEAD campaigned against it and was sent to prison for his pains. There was a two-way commerce in prostitutes who were mostly willing migrants – English girls to brothels in France and Belgium, and Continentals to London. There was a widespread belief, however, fostered by the social purity campaigners and lurid novels and plays, that there was an organised and vicious international traffic in women. In these tales girls would be drugged and abducted, to wake up captive and terrified in a foreign brothel. The morals campaigner JOSEPHINE BUTLER wrote in the puritan paper *The Shield* on 1 May 1880: 'In certain of the infamous houses in Brussels there are immured little children, English girls of from ten to fourteen years of age, who have been stolen, kidnapped, betrayed, carried off from English country villages by every artifice, and sold to these human shambles. The presence of these children is unknown to the ordinary visitors; it is secretly known only to the wealthy men who are able to pay large sums of money for the sacrifice of these innocents.'

In 1880 Alfred Dyer, founder of the London Committee for the Exposure and Suppression of the Traffic in English Girls for the Purposes of Continental Prostitution, published a pamphlet claiming English girls were being abducted by the score, and forced to work in the licensed brothels of Brussels. A Parliamentary Committee was set up and discovered some migration of young women between Britain and the Continent. The British embassy in Brussels, which had helped about 200 women return home in the 1870s, knew about this. They also knew that 'the overwhelming majority of the young women who were recruited for the *maisons closes* of Brussels and Antwerp had already been prostitutes in Britain and had migrated voluntarily'.

Some light is thrown on the question of white slavery by the statement of a girl taken to Holland with a friend in 1876 by a man named Klyberg. The girl, whose name is given as Fanny, said that she was 18 and living with her mother in Chelsea when she met her friend Jennie one evening with a woman who called herself Mrs Dunner. Bizarrely, this Mrs Dunner asked if she could see Fanny's teeth. Then she asked her if she was 'all right', meaning did she have VD. Finally Mrs Dunner asked if she would like to go abroad, as an 'actress'. The association between the theatre and whoring was still strong, and Fanny must have known what Mrs Dunner was suggesting. After Fanny had fetched some clothes from home they all went to Klyberg's home in Soho, where the girls had supper with Klyberg and his wife. During the meal Klyberg asked if they had been told what they were going abroad for. When Fanny replied that they were to be actresses, Klyberg replied: 'Quite right.' His wife questioned the girls about their families, and discovered that they both had older sisters. The girls stayed the night, and next morning were taken to Somerset House, where they obtained copies of their sisters' birth certificates. That afternoon Klyberg told them he was taking them to Holland.

Next morning in Rotterdam Klyberg again asked if they knew why they were there. When Fanny repeated that they were to be actresses, Klyberg told them that they were to be prostitutes. Fanny angrily said she was going back to England, but instead was persuaded to go with Jennie to a brothel in the Hague. They were interviewed by the proprietress, and next morning Jennie was examined by a doctor, after which she was driven to a police station where she was registered.

Fanny was told the brothel did not want her, and Klyberg, after making unsuccessful sexual advances to her, began a tour of brothels, trying increasingly desperately to sell Fanny. He started at twelve pounds and progressively dropped the price. In the end, in spite of all his expense, Klyberg had to pay her return fare to London. White slavery, if it existed at all, was clearly neither a flourishing nor a highly profitable business.

WHITEWAY, ALFRED Brutal sex maniac who killed two young women. On a Sunday in May 1953 Barbara Songhurst, aged 18, and her 16-year-old friend Christine Reed set out to cycle along the Thames towpath near Richmond, Surrey. The following day Barbara's body was found in the river. She had been stabbed and raped. Several days later Christine's body was found in the river at Richmond. Her skull was fractured, and she had been stabbed and raped. At the end of June police arrested a labourer named Alfred Whiteway who had attacked a girl of 14 with a chopper and raped her. He had known Barbara Songhurst nine years before when she lived in the same road as his parents at Teddington. He told police he had not seen her since, but at Scotland Yard he confessed to the murders. 'It's all up. You know bloody well I done it. I'm mental . . .' However when cautioned he denied killing the women. At his trial the prosecution said he killed the girls because Barbara had recognised him. Whiteway's appeal against his death sentence was dismissed. The Lord Chief Justice, LORD GODDARD, said: 'This case is one of the most brutal and horrifying that has ever been before this court and any other court for years.'

WHORES' CLUB, THE This organisation, which met every Sunday night at the SHAKESPEARE'S HEAD TAVERN in Covent Garden in the eighteenth century, was a mutual-aid organisation with a membership of about one hundred women. It seems to have been the brainchild of JACK HARRIS. Certainly he was the main beneficiary. The aim was to help whores who were down on their luck or in prison. The rules included:

* Every girl must have been 'debauched' before she was 15.
* All members must be on Harris's *List*.
* No *modest* woman to be admitted.
* Each member to contribute half a crown, one shilling of which to go to support members who could not earn a living because they were being treated for venereal disease, or who could not get into the Lock Hospital for venereal diseases. Another sixpence to go to Harris for 'his great care and assiduity in the proper conducting of this worthy society'. The remaining shilling was to be spent on drink, 'gin not excluded'.
* No men to be allowed in except Harris, who could choose any girl he fancied for his bedfellow that night.
* Any member too drunk to walk to be sent home in a coach or sedan chair at the expense of the society, the fare to be paid back at the next meeting.
* Any member who broke glasses, bottles etc. or behaved in a 'riotous manner' to be expelled until she paid for the damage.
* Any member 'overcharged' with liquor who in 'clearing her stomach' soiled another's clothes must replace them.

There were lively Sunday nights at the Shakespeare's Head when these spirited young women, many of them still in their teens, let their hair down. Yet the *Memoirs of the Celebrated Miss Fanny Murray* tells us that this particular 'female naughty-pack' included women of noble birth.

WHORES' GUIDES The most famous guide to London's demi-monde was JACK HARRIS's *List of Covent Garden Ladies*, which first appeared in the 1740s. There were other guides for the sexually adventurous. In 1691 appeared among others *A Catalogue of Jilts, Cracks and Prostitutes, Nightwalkers, Whores, She-friends, Kind Women and others of the Linnen-lifting Tribe*. It was a list of twenty-one women who could be found in the cloisters of St Bartholomew's Church during Bartholomew Fair in Smithfield. Like Harris's guide it listed the women's physical attributes: 'Mary Holland, tall graceful and comely, shy of her favours but may be mollified at a cost of £20. Elizabeth Holland [her sister] indifferent to Money but a Supper and Two Guineas will tempt her.' Dorothy Roberts could be had for a bottle of wine, Posture Moll, a flagellant, wanted only half a crown, Mrs Whitby, who had obviously come down in the world, had previously charged more than five guineas but would now accept ten shillings from 'any ordinary fellow'. There are two black women in the list: 'Bridget Williams, a pretty little Negress ... not yet mistress of her profession so can be offered half-a-crown . . . and bullied out of her money again' and Mrs Sarah Heath, 'a Negress . . . her fee is higher . . . will make no concession about fee'.

GARFIELD's *The Wand'ring Whore* of 1660 listed the best-known women of the town, including the Queen of Morocco, Peg the Seaman's Wife, Long-Haired Mrs Spencer of Spitalfields, Mrs Osbridge's Scolding Daughter (how could this possibly be a turn-on?) and Mrs Osbridge herself, said to have practised within Bedlam. Other well-known whores were Jenny Middleton, Moll Hinton (who may have given the Earl of Dorset a venereal disease), Sue Willis and Doll Chamberlain. Garfield mentions the veteran whore Fair Rosamund Sugarcunt, and Burford says she operated around the Law Courts. London pullulated with brothels: in some areas tents were set up and the customers queued outside.

Towards the end of the eighteenth century another guide book was *The Ranger's Magazine*. 'This published, among a great deal that was scatological, a "Monthly list of the Covent Garden Cyprians; or the Man of Pleasure's *Vade Mecum*"' (Henriques, *Prostitution and Society*, Vol. 2).

In the 1850s *Hints to Men about Town* had echoes of Jack Harris, and was at the same time peculiarly Victorian in its preoccupations. There is a good deal about legs, which had not yet become unmentionable, and eyes. Jane Fowler had 'a full blue eye' and 'a beautiful leg' (presumably two of each). 'In the chamber, Jane has a peculiar method of disrobing, and possesses excellent tact in managing a charming repulse to the eager advance of a vigorous gallant for the purpose of enhancing the enjoyment, which she well understands how to take share of.' There is an echo of Harris in the description of Miss Merton, who had 'sister hills' that were 'prominent, firm and elastic'. Her charge for enjoying their use was a guinea.

The tradition was revived in 1960 with *The Ladies Directory*, which gave the phone numbers of prostitutes and the services they offered. Its publisher, Derek Shaw, was jailed for a year for conspiracy to corrupt public morals.

WILD, JONATHAN (*c.* 1683–1725) Criminal entrepreneur of genius who combined the roles of police chief and underworld overlord, the most powerful London has known. As the self-styled

A nineteenth-century depiction of Jonathan Wild's grim journey to execution at Tyburn. Wild had been at once London's chief policeman and its most powerful crime czar, a pitiless criminal mastermind who sent dozens of his own men to the gallows.

Thief-Taker General of Great Britain and Ireland he was a bounty hunter, courted by the authorities because there was no official police force to bring dangerous criminals to justice. On behalf of the government he consigned more than 120 men to the gallows, many of them his own gang members. He was also a fence and receiver, and the organiser of a vast network of thieves and highwaymen. He had a ship which would take 'hot' goods to the Continent for sale, and warehouses where they were stored and altered to make them unrecognisable. Any criminal who refused to cooperate by paying Wild off or fencing his goods with him was in danger of being framed.

Wild was born in Wolverhampton about 1683. He served an apprenticeship as a buckle-maker, moved to London and worked as a debt collector, then served four years as a prisoner for debt in the Wood Street Compter. He emerged in 1712 with an exceptional knowledge of the underworld and set about organising it with thoroughness and ruthlessness. Through his vast network of spies he would get word of a crime and where the criminals were hiding. Accompanied by members of his gang he would corner and arrest them. The prisoners would then be questioned separately, and each told that the others had confessed and implicated him. This way they would be persuaded to betray each other. Sometimes he offered reduced sentences as an inducement to inform. Thus he would add another recruit to his so-called 'Corporation of Thieves', a man who owed him his life.

Wild invented the double cross. He kept detailed notes about criminals and their crimes. When he had enough evidence to convict a man he would put an X against his name. And when he decided to betray him, he would add a second X – the double cross. His victims included destitute children whom he lured into a life of thieving, then betrayed for the £40 reward.

To establish total control of the underworld Wild destroyed all the other big gangs, including the largely Irish Carrick gang. The destruction of the Carricks alone brought him bounties of £900 – the annual income of a prosperous knight. The government was concerned about the level of mail robberies and Wild was consulted by the Privy Council. He recommended increasing the bounty, which was first raised temporarily to £100 a head and later to £140 – in effect a large pay increase for Wild. With his network of spies, convicts who had returned illegally from transportation, his bodyguards and his able lieutenants Quilt Arnold and Abraham Mendez, Wild gradually took control of the London underworld.

Wild greatly refined the dangerous business of receiving. He set himself up in Little Old Bailey in what he called the 'Office for the Recovery of Lost and Stolen Property'. He instructed his thieves to discover the identities and addresses of their victims, and offered to sell them back their own goods, saying he knew where the thieves had pawned or fenced them. In theory he never handled or even saw the goods.

One man who refused to be cowed by the great Thief-Taker General was the small-time burglar and popular hero JACK SHEPPARD. He was famous for a series of daring escapes from London prisons, culminating in a breakout from Newgate the night before he was due to be executed. Wild's men hunted him down and on Wild's evidence he was executed. Wild had made many enemies, including Sheppard's accomplice JOSEPH 'BLUESKIN' BLAKE. When Wild, who had arrested Blueskin, went to gloat over his last hours in the condemned cell Blueskin stabbed him, inflicting a dangerous wound. Wild had gone soft, aping the gentleman. DANIEL DEFOE, one of his first biographers, says

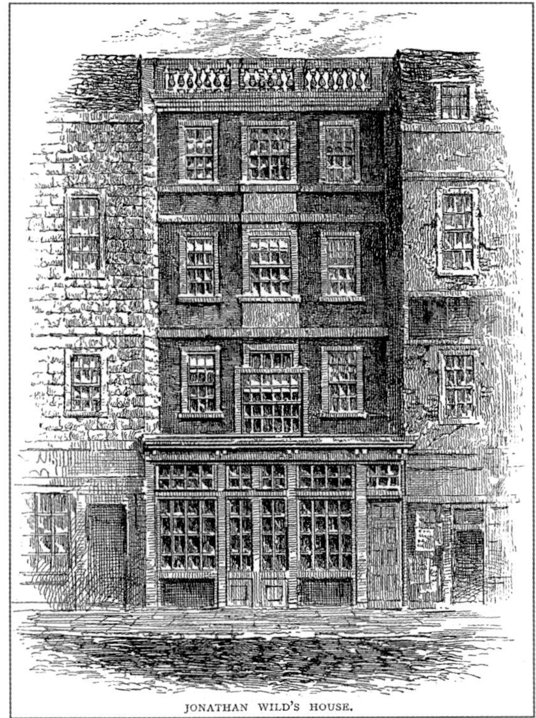

The house where the all-powerful criminal mastermind Jonathan Wild lived. He broke up the major London gangs and forced the survivors to cooperate with him. His feud with the popular jailbreaker Jack Sheppard was celebrated in Gay's The Beggar's Opera.

Wild 'made a considerable figure in the world, having a silver-mounted sword and a footman at his heels . . . and in company affected an air of grandeur'. In 1723 he had the effrontery to apply for the Freedom of the City of London, citing his 'great trouble and charge in apprehending and convicting divers felons'. His application was refused, a sure sign of the ambiguity of the official attitude to him. He was arrested soon after Sheppard's execution and hanged for a relatively minor crime, persuading two criminals to steal some cloth from a shop in Holborn. He had taken an overdose of laudanum in a failed suicide attempt the night before, and was so drugged that he did not suffer as the hangman 'turned him off' at the Tyburn gallows. Wild's personal courage was not in doubt. He arrested one highwayman by clamping his teeth on the man's chin and hanging on until he dropped his weapons and surrendered. He had the scars of 17 sword and pistol wounds on his body. His skull was mortised together with silver plates where it had been fractured.

Wild and Sheppard lived on in the popular imagination and particularly in the theatre: just two weeks after Jack's death *The Harlequin Sheppard*, a popular opera, opened at a Drury Lane theatre. It was the first of many dramatisations of story of the two men, of which JOHN GAY's *The Beggar's Opera* became the most popular opera of the eighteenth century. The two central characters, Macheath and Peachum, are based on Sheppard and Wild although the play is also a coded attack on the Prime Minister, Sir Robert Walpole, and his corrupt administration.

WILDE, OSCAR (1854–1900) Writer and convicted homosexual. He began an intimate relationship with Lord Alfred Douglas in 1891, when he was 36 and Douglas 21. Douglas's father, the MARQUIS OF QUEENSBERRY, a violent and spiteful man who was also mentally unstable, left a card for Wilde at his club accusing him of being a sodomite. Wilde had him arrested and charged with criminal libel. During the trial, where Wilde's wit and flippancy worked against him, his homosexual practices were revealed. Queensberry was found not guilty and Wilde was arrested and charged with gross indecency. There were revelations about a homosexual brothel in Little College Street, Westminster. The prosecutor spoke of 'these rooms, with their heavily draped windows, their candles burning on through the day, and their languorous atmosphere heavy with perfume'. At the end of two trials Wilde was sentenced to two years' hard labour. His prison experiences are reflected in *The Ballad of Reading Gaol*. After the trial W.T. STEAD, then editing the *Review of Reviews*, commented: 'Should everyone found guilty of Oscar Wilde's crime be in prison, there would be a very surprising emigration from Eton, Harrow, Rugby and Winchester to the jails . . .' In 1923 Lord Alfred Douglas, who had urged Wilde to bring the prosecution, was himself prosecuted for criminal libel against Winston Churchill. He was convicted and sentenced to six months. *See* TROOPER CHARLES WOOLDRIDGE

WILKES, JOHN (1727–97) Politician, journalist, lecher and champion of liberty. Wilkes was a prominent member of SIR FRANCIS DASHWOOD's Hell Fire Club at MEDMENHAM ABBEY yet he was a doughty champion of the rights of the individual against the state.

Wilkes became an MP in 1757. He founded the weekly paper *The North Briton* to oppose GEORGE

III's chief minister, Lord Bute. In the notorious issue No 45 he attacked the king's ministers, saying they had put lies into the King's Speech. For accusing the king of lying he was sent to the TOWER and the offending issue of the paper was burned by the public hangman. He was released, but the Establishment in the person of his fellow debauchee and Hell Fire Club member LORD SANDWICH, with whom he had quarrelled, accused him in the House of Lords of having published an obscene poem, *The Essay on Woman*. The spectacle of Sandwich, one of the most depraved men of the age, waxing sanctimonious outraged some of the peers. Sir Francis Dashwood was heard to comment that it was the first time he had heard Satan preaching against sin. Lord Sandwich told Wilkes: 'You will either die on the gallows or of the pox,' to which Wilkes replied: 'That depends upon whether I embrace your lordship's principles or your mistress.'

Hogarth's grotesque portrait of John Wilkes was an act of revenge. Wilkes had attacked him in his paper The North Briton. *Wilkes shrugged it off, calling it 'a* caricatura *of what nature had already caricatured'.*

Wilkes defending himself. In issue No. 45 of his paper The North Briton *he attacked the king's ministers, saying they had put lies into the King's Speech. For accusing the king of lying he was sent to the Tower and the offending issue of the paper was burned by the public hangman.*

Wilkes, who fled to Paris, was expelled from the House of Commons for libel. He returned in 1768 and was elected Member for Middlesex. He was eventually sentenced to 22 months in the King's Bench prison. By now he was a popular hero. He was re-elected to Parliament on several occasions and repeatedly expelled, until in 1774 he became Lord Mayor of London. In the same year he gained admission to Parliament.

Gradually Wilkes became almost a pillar of the Establishment, directing the Guards against the mob outside the Bank of England during the GORDON RIOTS and interesting himself in prison reform and religious tolerance. In 1771, when he was Sheriff of London, he ordered the Keeper of Newgate to stop 'the present illegal and inhumane practice' of keeping men in chains during their trials. He also intervened to save a man from the PRESS GANG. He told George III that he 'never was a Wilkite'. He died insolvent in 1797. Some historians have seen him as an opportunist, others believe he earned the epitaph he wrote for himself, 'A friend of Liberty'.

WILLIAMSON, JOHN Shoemaker executed in 1767 for starving and torturing his wife to death. Williamson was a widower who married a young woman of low intellect for her money, despite the objections of her guardian. He immediately began to beat her, keeping her handcuffed in a cupboard without food or water. A rope was drawn through the handcuffs and fixed to a nail above her head so that she had to stand on tip-toes. He was executed near his home in Moorfields.

WILSON, CHARLIE (?–1991) Train robber and murder victim. After serving his sentence for the GREAT TRAIN ROBBERY Wilson went to live near Marbella in Spain. On 23 April 1990 a young man arrived at the house on a mountain bike and told Patricia Wilson that he wanted to speak to her husband. Wilson took him out to the patio, where he had earlier been celebrating his wedding anniversary with some guests. Moments later there was the sound of an argument and two loud bangs. Patricia found Wilson dying by the pool, shot in the neck. His dog had been injured so badly it had to be put down. An inquest was held in London in November 1991 and Mrs Wilson told it: 'I heard the man say "I am a friend of Eamonn." I had a feeling there were two people there, although I couldn't say why. I heard two loud bangs, and at first I thought it was from the building site next door, but then I heard the dog screaming. Charlie was lying at the side of the pool face down. The man had gone and the gate was open. I saw blood coming from his mouth and Charlie did a sort of press-up and gestured in the direction the man had gone.' Police believed Wilson was involved in drug trafficking. Detective Superintendent Alec Edwards told the inquest: 'As far as the Spanish police and the British police are concerned, there is circumstantial evidence that this is a drug-related incident. We know of his meeting British criminals who are known drug dealers and who have been convicted of drug dealing and with one who has also been executed in a gangland killing.'

WILSON, HARRIETTE (1789–*c.* 1846) Celebrated courtesan who tried to blackmail the Duke of Wellington. Harriette was one of three courtesan sisters known as 'the Three Graces'. She cut a swathe through the aristocracy and when she fell on hard times wrote her memoirs, then sent copies of the manuscript to all her many high-born lovers with a note demanding '£200 by return of post, to be left out'. She had listed them in the index by rank: Dukes, Argyle, Beaufort, Leinster etc., Marquesses, Anglesey, Bath, Hertford, 'and so on down through Burke's Peerage to the modest Esquire' (Lesley Blanch, introduction to the Folio Society edition of her *Memoirs*). One of the few to resist this blatant blackmail was the Duke of Wellington, who is said to have scrawled 'Publish and be damned' on the manuscript before sending it back. This may account for the unflattering portrait of him in the *Memoirs*.

Harriette was born in Mayfair in 1786, one of fifteen children. It was said that of the nine who survived only three of the girls led respectable lives. Her sisters Amy, Fanny and Sophia were also whores. Sophia married Lord Berwick, and snubbed her sisters. Harriette got her revenge by taking the box directly above Sophia's at the Opera, and spitting down on her head. Here is an example of her lively style from the *Memoirs*:

> I was getting into debt, as well as my sister Amy, when it so came to pass, as I have since heard say, that the – immortal!!! No; that's common; a very outlandish distinction, fitter for a lady in a balloon. The terrific!!! that will do better. I have seen His Grace in his cotton nightcap. Well, then, the terrific Duke of Wellington!! the wonder of the world!!! . . . at three on the following day, Wellington made his appearance. He bowed first, then said – 'How do you do?' then thanked me for giving him permission to call on me; and then wanted to take hold of my hand.

Harriette Wilson, the Regency courtesan who blackmailed her lovers with her piquant Memoirs. *One of them, the Duke of Wellington, is said to have written 'Publish and be damned' in response.*

'Really,' said I, withdrawing my hand, 'for such a renowned hero you have very little to say for yourself.'

'Beautiful creature!' uttered Wellington . . . 'Beautiful eyes, yours . . .'

'Aye, man! they are greater conquerors than ever Wellington shall be . . .'

Wellington was now my constant visitor – a most unentertaining one, Heaven knows! and in the evening, when he wore his broad red ribbon, he looked very like a rat-catcher.

She admitted she had reason to be grateful to Wellington, saying 'he had relieved me from the duns, who else had given me vast uneasiness. God bless you, Wellington!' She may even have been reluctant to blackmail him, but been bullied into it by her lover, the shady and probably bogus Colonel William Rochfort. The book was a bestseller and should have made both Harriette and Rochfort rich. The publisher, Stockdale, had to erect barriers outside his shop in the Haymarket to hold back the crowds. Although the book is said to have earned them £10,000, Harriette and Stockdale paid a high price, he engulfed in lawsuits and she ostracised. In 1830 Harriette was charged with assaulting her French maid. 'There was a lot of noisy recriminations and the newspapers made much of Harriette's vanished looks, the Colonel's doubtful ancestry and their joint inability to raise bail' (Blanch, ibid). Others went further: she was attacked by a Mrs Campbell on Dover Pier, was knocked to the ground and had her hair ripped out.

Harriette died about sixteen years later in Paris. There was a story, probably untrue, that one of her lovers had once tried to lure her away to live in his house in the country, but Harriette, 'never one for ruralising', turned him down. Under the terms of his will the richly furnished house has stood shuttered and empty ever since.

WILSON, MARY Brothel-keeper whose establishments were designed for the gratification of women, those with lovers and those without. She had brothels in Old Bond Street, St Pancras and Hall Place, St John's Wood. In 1824 she published *The Voluptarian Cabinet*, describing her 'Eleusinian Institution'. This was divided into two sections, one for married women and their lovers, the other for women seeking sex. This is her sales pitch:

I have purchased very extensive premises, which are situated between two great thoroughfares and are entered from each by means of shops, devoted entirely to such trades as are exclusively resorted to by ladies. In the area between the two rows of houses, I have erected a most elegant temple, in the centre of which are large saloons, entirely surrounded by boudoirs most elegantly and commodiously fitted up. In these saloons, according to their classes, are to be seen the finest men of their species I can procure, occupied in whatever amusements are adapted to their taste, and all kept in a high state of excitement by good living and idleness . . .

Before making their choice the women viewed the men through a window. When they saw one they fancied they would ring for a chambermaid and point him out. Mary Wilson wrote that the woman client could 'enjoy him in the dark, or have a light, and keep on her mask. She can stay an hour or a night, and have one or two dozen men as she pleases, without being known to any of them . . .'

Two dozen men would have been extravagant in every sense. Brothels where women were the customers were rare, and they had to pay a premium. Mary Wilson's establishments were decorated with pornographic paintings after the Renaissance artist Giulio Romano. Patrons had to pay handsomely for all this: the subscription was a hundred guineas, and the fine wine and food had also to be paid for, as in a restaurant.

Mrs Wilson also specialised in flagellation. This interesting woman, who translated and published European erotic novels, wrote extensively about men's addiction to flagellation, and classified the different types drawn to this form of masochism:

> 1. Those who like to receive a fustigation, more or less severe from the hands of a fine woman, who is sufficiently robust to wield the rod with vigour and effect.
> 2. Those who desire to administer birch discipline on the white and plump buttocks of a female.
> 3. Those who neither wish to be passive recipients nor active administrators of birch discipline, but derive sufficient excitement as mere spectators of the sport.

Miss Wilson makes it clear that the taste for flagellation is not confined to the elderly debauchee or worn-out roué.

> Many persons not sufficiently acquainted with human nature, and the ways of the world, are apt to imagine that the *lech* for Flagellation must be confined either to the aged, or those who are exhausted through too great devotion to venery: but such is not the fact, for there are quite as many young men and men in the prime and vigour of life, who are influenced by this passion as there are amongst the aged and the debilitated.
>
> It is very true that there are innumerable old generals, admirals, colonels and captains, as well as bishops, judges, barristers, lords, commoners and physicians, who periodically go to be whipped, merely because it warms their blood, and keeps up a little agreeable excitement in their systems long after the power of enjoying the opposite sex has failed them; but it is equally true, that hundreds of young men through having been educated at institutions where the masters are fond of administering birch discipline, and recollecting certain sensations produced by it, have imbibed a passion for it, and have longed to receive the same chastisement from the hands of a fine woman . . .

Miss Wilson goes on to say that the expert flagellant or governess would have learned her skills from some older practitioner of the art. 'It is not merely keeping a rod, and being willing to flog, that would cause a woman to be visited by the worshippers of birch.' She mentions some of the teachers, including 'the late Mrs Jones, of Hertford Street and London Street, Fitzroy Square; such was the late MRS BERKELY, such is Betty Burgess of York Square, and such is Mrs Pryce, of Burton Crescent . . .' *See* FLAGELLATION

WINDHAM, WILLIAM (1838–64) Eccentric landowner who married a whore. In 1861 Windham bought Agnes Willoughby from her pimp, 'Bawdyhouse Bob' Roberts. Windham, who earned the nickname 'Mad' while at Eton, had inherited Felbrigg Hall in Norfolk, and he gave Roberts the timber on the estate in exchange for Agnes, although he allowed him to keep her until the wedding day. The following year three of his uncles, unhappy at this arrangement, tried to have him committed to an asylum as insane. They were Lord Bristol, Lord Alfred Hervey and General Windham. To prove Windham was insane at the time of his marriage the family gave evidence to the Commission in Lunacy of gluttony, masturbation, dirtiness, and Windham's enthusiasm for driving coaches and the engines of passenger trains without authority. They also complained that he dressed up as a policeman and patrolled the West End arresting prostitutes who took his fancy, and that he retained a broad Norfolk accent despite his years at Eton.

The flaw in the family's case was General Windham, who was apparently known himself for certain 'foul practices'. He had been accused of indecent exposure in Hyde Park and got off when his counsel put in a plea of insanity. Because of this he could not give evidence for fear of being cross-examined, and the jurors found his nephew to be sane. Mad Windham died four years later at the age of 26, leaving his bride and infant son in possession of his estate with an income of £5,000 a year. She enjoyed these in the company of Bawdyhouse Bob, who gave up his former occupation to be a country gentleman.

WISEBOURNE, ELIZABETH (1653–1720) Noted pious seventeenth-century bawd also known as Whyburn. Her brothel in Drury Lane was one of the most expensive in London. She was born in London in 1653 to a respectable family, and sent to Italy to acquire a veneer of good manners. While there she was seduced, and consequently took an interest in the Italian sex industry. She also acquired some knowledge of venereal diseases and 'cures', a subject in which she was later regarded as an expert. On her return to England she mixed in society high and low, was introduced to Court circles and got to know the most famous whores of the time, the most important of whom was SALLY SALISBURY. Mother Wisebourne – the keepers of brothels were usually called Mother – was the daughter of a clergyman and used to visit prisons, clutching her Bible, to buy the freedom of likely girls, and also looked for recruits among children whose parents rented them out to beggars for the day. Another source of recruits for her brothel was the children who were offered for sale outside the church of St Martin in the Fields. Those she chose would be 'drest with Paint and Patches . . . and let out at extravagant Prices . . . she was always calling them young milliners or Parsons' daughters'. She specialised in restoring their virginity after selling them to the highest bidder.

She taught them other tricks, such as touting for customers in church, as one of her girls recalled:

> We'd take all opportunities, as we came down stairs from the galleries, or as we past over the kennels [gutters] in the streets, to lift up our coats so high, that we might show our handsome legs and feet, with a good fine worsted or silk pair of stockings on; by which means the gallants would be sure either to dog us themselves, or else to send their footmen to see where we liv'd; and then they would afterwards come to us themselves; and by that means have we got many a good customer.

One of her customers, the Court physician Richard Mead, of whom Dr Johnson said 'he lived more in the broad sunshine of life than almost any other man', may have given her tips about treating venereal diseases.

WITCHCRAFT The sceptical British were far less given to prosecuting the old and afflicted as witches than some countries on the continent – in Como 1,000 people were burned at the stake in the single year 1524. There were 513 charges of witchcraft in the courts of the Home Counties between 1558, when Elizabeth I became queen, and 1736, when it ceased to be an offence in England. There were 200 convictions and 109 executions (Salgado, *The Elizabethan Underworld*, Sutton 1992).

WOOLDRIDGE, TROOPER CHARLES The condemned prisoner in Oscar Wilde's *Ballad of Reading Jail*, who 'looked so wistfully at the day'. Wooldridge married Laura Glendell, an assistant postmistress, at Kentish Town in north London in October 1894. He was a violent man who mistreated his wife and the marriage was soon in trouble. When his regiment was transferred back to Regent's Park Barracks from Windsor Laura stayed on in that town and continued working in the Post Office at Eton. Wooldridge, distraught at the separation, visited her at Windsor. There was a quarrel and he struck her. When she sent him a legal document asking him to undertake not to molest her in the future he again travelled to Windsor, having borrowed another man's razor and told a sentry that 'I have to go to Windsor tonight. I must go. I'm going to do some damage'.

There was another quarrel, he slashed his wife's face with the razor and when she rushed from the house followed and cut her throat in the street. He was hanged at Reading Gaol on 7 July 1896.

> The warders strutted up and down,
> And kept their herd of brutes,
> Their uniforms were spick and span
> And they wore their Sunday suits.
> But we knew the work they had been at
> By the quicklime on their boots.

WRONGFUL ARREST The arrest of two highly respectable professional men at the end of 1895 drew attention to police corruption and high-handedness. The first man, Ray Lankester, a professor of anatomy at Oxford University, was arrested for obstruction in October. He had witnessed and protested about the brutal arrest of a prostitute. He went to talk to a nearby prostitute about the arrest and a policeman told him to move along. When he refused he was arrested and held in a cell for two hours. When he was tried the magistrate was so partial to the police that Lankester's lawyer, Sir George Lewis, retired from the case, protesting: 'It seems to me, Sir, that you have absolutely made up your mind . . . instead of listening to any argument . . . you have interposed at every moment . . .' Lankester was found guilty of obstruction. He wrote in a letter to *The Times*:

> On my way from my club I stopped to ask some woman the explanation of an unusual scene of cruelty which I had witnessed. Before I had time to get an answer I was brusquely accosted by a policeman, and within three minutes . . . seized by both arms and taken to a police station . . . I ask whether it is tolerable that a man perfectly well known, talking to another person in the street . . . should be ordered to move on, and that on his remonstrating . . . he should be liable to be seized and treated as the vilest criminal?
>
> It is time that a departmental inquiry was held, in view of the allegations of violence and concerted perjury which have been repeatedly made against a portion of the police. These are not the only charges made, for it is a matter of common report that they levy blackmail on the women of the street, and receive bribes from persons whom they have arrested.

Early in November George Alexander, proprietor of the St James's Theatre, was arrested for indecent behaviour. He had gone to a friend's house near his own, and on his way back was accosted by a half-starved prostitute. Seeing, he said, that the woman was 'poor, miserable, starved and ill-clad', he gave her some money. A constable approached and accused him of 'having connection' with the prostitute. Among witnesses to his character at the court hearing was Arthur Wing Pinero, the playwright. Alexander was acquitted and two days later appeared on the stage of his St James's Theatre, where he was cheered by the audience.

An even more sensational case involved a Miss Cass. In July 1887 she was arrested for soliciting. The magistrate discharged her but wrote down her occupation as prostitute and warned her about her future conduct. Miss Cass, who was a respectable dressmaker and a member of the 'eminently respectable' Girls' Friendly Society, vehemently protested her innocence. The Press took up her case, there was a debate in the House of Commons, the Home Secretary resigned and there were enquiries into the conduct of the magistrate and the arresting constable, a PC Endacott. That officer had perjured himself by testifying that he had seen Miss Cass on the streets a number of times. He was charged with perjury but acquitted on the directions of the judge at his Old Bailey trial, and later reinstated as a constable. *See* GEORGE INCE

WYATT, SIR THOMAS (?1520–54) Soldier and rebel against Queen Mary Tudor. When Edward VI died Lady Jane Grey occupied the throne briefly but was sent to the TOWER when Mary Tudor was proclaimed queen on 19 July 1553. The following year Sir Thomas, son of the poet of the same name, and Lady Jane's father raised an army of 10,000 men in Kent and marched on London to overthrow Mary. They entered the city but failed to capture Ludgate, which had been barred to them. Wyatt surrendered and was executed for high treason. His head, exhibited on a gibbet near Piccadilly, was secretly removed by his friends for burial. About 400 of his followers were executed in various parts of London and at Maidstone and Rochester.

Queen Mary Tudor, the Catholic zealot who sent many Protestants to be burned at the stake. Most of these executions took place at Smithfield.

YARDIES Described by one police officer as 'disorganised organised crime', these Jamaican gangsters quickly established a reputation for violence when they arrived in Britain in the 1980s. Their turf wars over drug rackets have particularly affected areas such as Brixton in the south, Harlesden in the north-west and Dalston to the north of the City. They are also thought to supply contract killers to white gangs. A special squad of 160 detectives was set up to deal with black-on-black crime. *See* DRUGS

YELLOW-HAIRED KITTY Young prostitute the diarist WALTER had an affair with. Walter had a marvellous ear for the speech of the young street-walkers he picked up, and I have quoted Kitty at length because hers is the authentic voice of the Victorian street prostitute. She was 15 when Walter met her in the Strand. She was looking in a shop window with a younger girl. He offered them money, and heard Kitty saying to the younger girl, who was reluctant: 'You are a foole. You *are a foole*. Oh! you *foole*. Come he wants us. You *foole*.'

One day in bed with Kitty he asked her whether she was 'gay', which then meant a prostitute.

> 'I ain't gay,' said she astonished. 'Yes you are.' 'No I ain't.' 'You let men fuck you, don't you?' 'Yes, but I ain't gay.' 'What do you call gay?' 'Why the gals who come out regular of a night dressed up, and gets their living by it.' I was amused. 'Don't you?' 'No, mother keeps me.' 'What is your father?' 'Got none, he's dead three months back – mother works and keeps us. She is a charwoman and goes out on odd jobs . . .'
>
> 'Are you often in the Strand?' 'When I gets out I likes walking in it, and looking at the shops. I do if Mother's out for the day. 'Does she know you are out?' The girl had been lying on her back with her head full towards me, and giggling said in a confidential sort of way, 'Bless you, no – she'd beat me if she knew . . .'

Kitty has already decided, despite her protest that she is not 'gay', that she will be a whore: it is the only way she can get the clothes and the luxuries she craves. Those luxuries include food. She and Walter discussed what she did with the money she earned.

> 'I buy things to eat, I can't eat what Mother gives us, she is poor and works very hard, she'd give us more but she can't; so I buys food, and gives the others what Mother gives me, they don't know better – if Mother's there I eat some, sometimes we have only gruel and salt; if we 'ave a fire we toast the bread, but I can't eat it if I'm not dreadfully hungry.' 'What do you like?' 'Pies and sausage-rolls,' said the girl, smacking her lips and laughing, 'Oh! my eye, ain't they prime – oh!' 'That's what you went gay for?' 'I'm not gay,' said she sulkily. 'Well, what you let men fuck you for? Sausage-rolls?' 'Yes. Meat-pies and pastries too.'

Eventually the affair with Kitty tailed off. He returned from abroad to find her better-dressed and prosperous. She had become a man's mistress, but slept with Walter one last time.

YOUNG, GRAHAM (1948–90) Compulsive mass poisoner. He began trying out poisons on his Neasden family when he was 13. At Easter 1962 his stepmother died and his father, with whom Young had been having disagreements, became seriously ill. Tests showed the father was suffering from arsenic and antimony poisoning. Young had also experimented on his sister and a school friend. The boy was sent to Broadmoor. When he was released nine years later aged 23 after 'an extremely full recovery', he went to work at a photographic laboratory in Bovingdon, Herts. Soon his colleagues began to suffer mysterious illnesses which caused vomiting and diarrhoea. By the time he was arrested in November 1971 two of his workmates had died of thallium poisoning. Others had become seriously ill. He was jailed for life and died of a heart attack in Parkhurst prison in 1990.

Z

ZITO, JONATHAN Victim of a mental patient released into the community. On 17 December 1992 Zito was stabbed to death at Finsbury Park underground station by paranoid schizophrenic Christopher Clunis. Zito's widow Jayne afterwards founded the Zito Trust to help victims of community care.

BIBLIOGRAPHY

Ackroyd, Peter, *Dickens' London* (Headline, 1987)

— —, *London: A Biography* (Chatto & Windus, 2000)

Acton, William, *Prostitution Considered in its Moral, Social and Sanitary Aspects . . .* (1857)

Ainsworth, William Harrison, *Rookwood* (1843)

Anon., *The Life and Death of Mrs Mary Frith commonly called Moll Cutpurse* (1612)

Anon., *A Catalogue of Jilts, Cracks and Prostitutes. . .* (1691)

Anon., *A Genuine History of Sally Salisbury alias Mrs S. Prydden* (1723)

Anon., *An Authentic History of the Parentage, Birth, Education, Marriages, Issue and Practices of the Famous Jonathan Wild* (1725)

Anon., *The History of the Remarkable Lives and Actions of Jonathan Wild, Thief-Taker, Joseph Blake alias Blueskin, Footpad, and John Sheppard, Housebreaker* (1725)

Anon, *The Life and Character of Moll King* (1747)

Anon., *Memoirs of the Celebrated Miss Fanny Murray* (1759)

Anon., *The Nocturnal Revels – the History of King's Place and other Modern Nunneries, by a Monk of the Order of St Francis* (1779)

Anon., *Address to the Guardian Society*, pamphlet (1817)

Anon., 'Merry Man's Resolution', in the *Roxburghe Ballads* (1877)

Anon., *The Poor Whores' Complaint to the Apprentices of London* (n.d.)

Archenholz, J.W. von, *A Picture of England* (1789)

Archer, Thomas, *The Pauper, the Thief and the Convict* (1865)

Ashdown, Dulcie M., *Royal Murders: Hatred, Revenge and the Seizing of Power* (Sutton, 1998)

Bailey, Paul, *An English Madam: The Life and Work of Cynthia Payne* (Cape, 1982)

Barker, Felix, and Carr, Denise Silvester, *The Black Plaque Guide to London* (Constable, 1987)

Bartley, Paula, *Prostitution: Prevention and Reform in England, 1860–1914* (Routledge, 2000)

Baston, Lewis, *Sleaze: The State of Britain* (Channel 4 Books, 2000)

Baynham, Henry, *Before the Mast* (Hutchinson, 1971)

Beames, T., *The Rookeries of London, Past, Present and Prospective* (1850)

Bellamy, George Anne, *An Apology for the Life* (1785)

Berkley, Theresa, *Venus School Mistress* (1830)

Besant, Sir Walter, *All Sorts and Conditions of Men* (1882)

Beveridge, Peter, *Inside the CID* (Evan Brothers, 1957)

Bloch, Ivan, *Sexual Life in England Past and Present* (Arco, 1958)

Booth, Charles, *Life and Labour of the People in London*, 17 vols (1903)

Boswell, James, *London Journal 1763* (Edinburgh University Press, 1991)

Boyle, Thomas, *Black Swine in the Sewers of Hampstead* (Hodder & Stoughton, 1990)

Bristow, Edward J., *Vice and Vigilance: Purity Movements in Britain since 1700* (Gill & Macmillan, 1977)

Brome, Vincent, *Havelock Ellis, Philosopher of Sex* (Routledge, 1979)

Brown, Thomas, *The Midnight Spy* (1766)

Burford, E.J., *The Orrible Synne* (Calder and Boyars, 1973)

— —, *Wits, Wenchers and Wantons* (Robert Hale, 1986)

— —, *Royal St James's* (Robert Hale, 1988)

— —, *London: The Synfulle Citie* (Robert Hale, 1990)

— — and Wotton, Joy, *Private Vices, Public Virtues* (Robert Hale, 1995)

Burke's Peerage (published annually)
Butler, Josephine, *Personal Reminiscences of a Great Crusade* (Horace Marshall, 1896)
Campbell, Duncan, *The Underworld* (Penguin, 1996)
Carswell, John, *The South Sea Bubble* (Cresset Press, 1961)
Challenor, H., with Draper, A., *Tanky Challenor* (Leo Cooper, 1990)
Champly, Henri, *The Road to Shanghai* (1934)
Chesney, Kellow, *The Victorian Underworld* (Penguin, 1991)
Clarkson, Wensley, *Gangsters* (John Blake, 2001)
Cleland, John, *Fanny Hill, or the Memoirs of a Woman of Pleasure* (1748)
Colquhoun, Patrick, *Treatise on the Police of the Metropolis* (1796)
The Complete Newgate Calendar (Navarre Society, 1926)
Consistory of London Correction Book (1605)
Cox, Barry, Shirley, John, and Short, Martin, *The Fall of Scotland Yard* (Penguin, 1997)
Creighton, Louise, *The Social Disease and How to Fight It, A Rejoinder* (Longman Green, 1914)
Cunningham, Peter, *The Story of Nell Gwyn* (1903)
Davenport-Hines, Richard, *Sex, Death and Punishment: Attitudes to Sex and Sexuality in Britain since the Renaissance* (Collins, 1990)
Davis, Godfrey, *The Early Stuarts* (Clarendon Press, 1959)
Dawson, Nancy, *Authentic Memoirs of the Celebrated Miss Nancy Dawson* (1762)
Day, S.P., *Juvenile Crime, its Causes, Character and Cure* (1858)
Debrett's Peerage (published annually)
Defoe, Daniel, *The . . . Account of the Life . . . of the Late Jonathan Wild* (1725)
De Quincey, Thomas, *Confessions of an English Opium Eater* (1856)
Dickens, Charles, *Oliver Twist* (1837–9)
——, *Barnaby Rudge* (1841)
——, *Little Dorrit* (1855–7)
——, *Our Mutual Friend* (1864–5)
——, *The Mystery of Edwin Drood* (1870)
Dilnot, George (ed.), *The Bank of England Forgery* (Geoffrey Bles, 1929)
Donaldson, William, *Brewer's Rogues, Villains and Eccentrics* (Cassell, 2002)
Dormer, Joseph, *The Female Rake or a 'Modern Fine Lady'* (1763)
Dryden, John, *Satire on the Players* (1691)
Dunton, John, *The HE-Strumpet: A Satyre on Sodomites* (1707)
Egan, Pierce, *Life in London; or the Day and Night Scenes of Jerry Hawthorn and his elegant friend Corinthian Tom* (usually shortened to *Tom and Jerry*) (1820)
Ehrman, John, *Pitt the Younger* (Constable, 1969)
Ellis, Havelock, *Studies in the Psychology of Sex*, 7 vols (1900–28)
Evelyn, John, *Diary*, ed. William Bray (1951)
Fabian, Robert, *London after Dark* (Naldrett Press, 1954)
——, *Fabian of the Yard* (Cedar Books, 1956)
Fielding, Henry, *Life of Jonathan Wild the Great* (1743)
——, *Inquiry into the Causes of the Late Increase of Robbers* (1751)
Finch, B.E., and Green, Hugh, *Contraception through the Ages* (Owen, 1963)
Fitch, H.T., *Memoirs of a Royal Detective* (Hurst & Blackett, 1936)
Fordham, Peta, *The Robbers' Tale* (Hodder & Stoughton, 1965)
Foreman, Freddie, *Respect: Autobiography of Freddie Foreman, Managing Director of British Crime* (Century, 1996)
Fraser, Antonia, *The Weaker Vessel* (Mandarin Paperbacks, 1993)
Garfield, John, *The Wand'ring Whore* (1660–3)
——, *The Unparalleled Practices of Mrs Fotheringham* (1661)
Geijer, Erik, *Impressions of England 1809–10* (1932)
George, M. Dorothy, *London Life in the Eighteenth Century* (repr. Penguin, 1992)
Gibson, Ian, *The Erotomaniac: The Secret Life of Henry Spencer Ashbee* (Faber & Faber, 2001)
Gilmour, Ian, *Riot, Risings and Revolution* (Pimlico, 1992)

Goddard, Henry, *Memoirs of a Bow Street Runner* (Museum Press Limited, 1956)
Gosling, John, *Ghost Squad* (W.H. Allen, 1959)
—— and Warner, Douglas, *The Shame of a City* (W.H. Allen, 1960)
Greenwood, James, *The Seven Curses of London* (1869)
——, *In Strange Company: The Notebook of a Roving Correspondent* (1873)
Gwillim, John, *The London Bawd: With her Character and Life etc.* (1711)
Harris, Jack, *List of Covent Garden Ladies or the New Atlantis* (1764)
Hart, Edward T., *Britain's Godfather* (True Crime Library, 1997)
Hazzlewood, Charlotte, *True and Entertaining History of Charlotte Lorraine, Afterwards Mrs Hazzlewood* (1790)
——, *Secret History of the Green Room* (1795)
Head, Richard, and Kirkman, Francis, *The English Rogue* (1665)
Henderson, Tony, *Disorderly Women in Eighteenth-Century London* (Longman, 1999)
Henriques, Fernando, *Prostitution and Society*, 3 vols (MacGibbon & Kee, 1962–8)
Herber, Mark, *Criminal London* (Philimore, 2002)
Hibbert, Christopher, *The Roots of Evil* (1963)
——, *George IV, Prince of Wales* (Longman, 1972)
——, *The Road to Tyburn* (repr. Penguin, 2001)
Hickey, William, *Memoirs* (Hurst & Blackett, 1948)
Hickman, Katie, *Courtesans* (HarperCollins, 2003)
Hickman, Tom, *The Sexual Century* (Carlton Books, 1999)
Hicks, Michael, *Who's Who in Late Medieval England* (Shepheard-Walwyn, 1991)
Higgins, Bob, *In the Name of the Law* (Long, 1958)
Higgs, Mary, *Glimpse into the Abyss* (1906)
Hill, Billy, *Boss of Britain's Underworld* (Naldrett Press, 1995)
Hollingshead, J., *Ragged London in 1861* (1861)
Holloway, Robert, *The Phoenix of Sodom: or, the Vere Street Coterie* (1814)
Hudson, Derek, *Munby, Man of Two Worlds* (John Murray, 1972)
Hughes, David, *The Age of Austerity* (Penguin, 1964)
Hughes, Robert, *The Fatal Shore* (Folio Society, 1998)
Huish, Robert, *Memoirs of George IV* (1831)
Hutchinson, J.R., *The Press Gang Afloat and Ashore* (1915)
Inwood, Stephen, *A History of London* (Macmillan, 1998)
Janson, Hank, *Jack Spot: Man of a Thousand Cuts* (Alexander Moring, 1959)
Jesse, F. Tennyson, *A Pin to see the Peep Show* (Virago, 1979)
Jesse, J.H., *Literary and Historical Memorials of London* (1847)
Keeler, Christine, *Scandal* (Xanadu Publications, 1989)
Kray, Reg, and Kray, Ron, with Dinenage, Fred, *Our Story* (Pan Books, 1988)
Kynaston, David, *The City of London*, Vol. I (Chatto & Windus, 1994)
The Ladies Directory (Derek Shaw, 1960)
Lambrianou, Tony, *Inside the Firm* (Smith Gryphon, 1991)
Leeson, Ex-Detective Sergeant B., *Lost London* (Stanley Paul and Co, n.d.)
Leeson, Nick, *Rogue Trader* (Little Brown 1996)
Linebaugh, Peter, *The London Hanged* (Allen Lane, 1991)
Linnane, Fergus, *London's Underworld* (Robson Books, 2003)
——, *London, the Wicked City* (Robson Books, 2003)
Logan, William, *The Great Social Evil* (Hodder & Stoughton, 1871)
Low, Donald A., *The Regency Underworld* (Sutton, 1999)
Macartney, Wilfred, *Walls Have Mouths* (Gollancz, 1936)
Macaulay, Thomas, *History of England* (repr. Heron Books, 1968)
McCall, Andrew, *The Medieval Underworld* (1977)
McConnell, Brian, *Found Naked and Dead* (New English Library, 1975)
McDonald, Brian, *Elephant Boys* (Mainstream Publishing, 2000)
McLynn, Frank, *Crime and Punishment in Eighteenth-Century England* (Routledge, 1989)

McMullan, John L., *The Canting Crew* (Rutgers University, 1984)
Malcolm, J.P., *Anecdotes of the Manners and Customs of London during the Eighteenth Century* (1810)
Marks, Howard, *Mr Nice* (Minerva, 1997)
Masters, Brian, *The Mistresses of Charles II* (Blond and Briggs, 1979)
Matthews, R., *Prostitution in London: An Audit* (Middlesex University, 1997)
May, Erskine, *The Constitutional History of England* (Longmans Green, 1889)
May, Tiggey, Harocopos, Alex, and Turnbull, Paul J., *Selling Sex in the City*, South Bank University Faculty of Humanities and Social Study, June 2001
—— et al., *For Love or Money: Pimps and the Management of Sex Work* (Home Office, 2000)
Mayhew, Henry, and Binney, John, *The Criminal Prisons of London . . .* (1862)
——, Hemyng, Bracebridge, Binney, John, and Halliday, Andrew, *London Labour and the London Poor*, 4 vols (1861–2)
Memoirs of the Bedford Coffee-House (1751)
Meyrick, Kate, *Secrets of the 43* (John Long, 1933)
Misson, H., *Memoirs and Observations of his Travels over England* (1719)
Morgan, Kenneth O., *The Oxford History of Britain* (Oxford University Press, 2001)
Morrison, Arthur, *A Child of the Jago* (Penguin reprint, 1946)
Morton, James, *A Calendar of Killing* (Little Brown, 1997)
Moylan, Sir John, *Scotland Yard and the Metropolitan Police* (Putnam, 1929)
Murphy, Robert, *Smash and Grab: Gangsters in the London Underworld 1920–1960* (Faber & Faber, 1993)
Murray, Venetia, *High Society in the Regency Period* (Penguin, 1998)
Nead, Lynda, 'The Girl of the Period', *National Art Collections Fund Quarterly* (Autumn 2001)
Nokes, David, introduction to Henry Fielding's *Jonathan Wild the Great* (Penguin, 1982)
Orne, J., *The Streetwalker or Evening Rambles in Search of Lewd Women etc.* (1696)
Otley, Roi, *No Green Pastures* (John Murray, 1952)
Oxford History of the Prison, ed. Norval Morris and David J. Rothman (Oxford University Press, 1995)
Payne, Leslie, *The Brotherhood* (Michael Joseph, 1973)
Pearl, Cora, *The Memoirs of Cora Pearl: The Erotic Reminiscences of a Flamboyant Nineteenth-Century Courtesan* (Granada, 1983)
Pearsall, Ronald, *The Worm in the Bud* (Weidenfeld & Nicolson, 1969)
Pearson, John, *The Profession of Violence* (Panther, 1973)
Pepys, Samuel, *Diary, 1660–8*, ed. Robert Latham and William Matthews (HarperCollins, 1995)
Picard, Lisa, *Dr Johnson's London* (Weidenfeld & Nicolson, 2000)
Pike, L.O., *A History of Crime in England . . .* (1876)
Pitt, Moses, *Cry of the Oppressed* (1691)
Plumb, J.H., *Men and Places* (The Cresset Press, 1963)
Porter, Roy, *English Society in the Eighteenth Century* (Pelican, 1990)
——, *The Greatest Benefit to Mankind: A Medical History of Humanity from Antiquity to the Present* (Fontana Press, 1997)
——, *London: A Social History* (Hamish Hamilton, 1994)
Pringle, Patrick, *The Thief Takers* (Museum Press Ltd, 1958)
Prynne, William, *Histriomastix: The Players Scourge* (1632)
Read, Leonard, and Morton, James, *Nipper* (Macdonald, 1991)
Read, Piers Paul, *The Train Robbers* (W.H. Allen & Co., 1978)
Reynolds, Bruce, *Autobiography of a Thief* (Virgin Books, 2000)
Richardson, Charles, *My Manor* (Sidgwick & Jackson, 1991)
Richmond, Dr Guy, *Prison Doctor* (Nunaga, 1975)
Rees, Sian, *The Floating Brothel* (Headline, 2001)
Rendle, W., and Norman, P., *Inns of Old Southwark* (1888)
Roberts, Nickie, *Whores in History* (HarperCollins, 1992)
Rogers, Pat, *The Augustan Vision* (Weidenfeld & Nicolson, 1974)
Rose, Andrew, *Steinie, Murder on the Common* (Bodley Head, 1985)
Sala, George Augustus, *Twice Round the Clock* (1859)
Salgado, Gamini, *The Elizabethan Underworld* (1992)

Samuel, Raphael, *East End Underworld. Chapters in the Life of Arthur Harding* (Routledge & Kegan Paul, 1981)
Sanger, William, *A History of Prostitution* (New York, 1859)
Saussure, César de, *A Foreign View of England in the Reigns of George I and George II* (1902)
Shaw, D., *London in the Sixties* (1908)
Silverman, Jon, *Crack of Doom* (Headline, 1988)
Smithies, Edward, *Crime in Wartime* (George Allen, 1982)
Steevens, George Alexander, *Adventures of a Speculist* (1788)
Stow, John, *The Survey of London* (Everyman reprint, n.d.)
Tanner, Anodyne, *Life of the Late Celebrated Elizabeth Wisebourn, Vulgarly called Mother Whybourn* (1721)
Thomas, Donald, *The Victorian Underworld* (John Murray, 1998)
Thompson, Edward, *The Meretriciad, A Satire* (1765 and 1770)
Thornton, Bonnell, *Termagent – or Madame Roxana in Covent Garden* (1752)
Tietjen, A., *Soho* (Allan Wingate, 1956)
Tobias, J.J., *Crime and Industrial Society in the Nineteenth Century* (Pelican, 1972)
Tomkinson, Martin, *The Pornbrokers* (Virgin Books, 1982)
Tristan, Flora, *Promenades dans Londres* (1840)
Uglow, Jenny, *Hogarth: A Life and a World* (Faber and Faber, 1997)
Viccei, Valerio, *Knightsbridge, the Robbery of the Century* (Blake Hardbacks, 1992)
Wade, John, *Treatise on the Police and Crimes of the Metropolis* (1829)
Wakefield, E.G., *Facts Relating to the Punishment of Death in the Metropolis* (1832)
Walker, Captain C., *Authentic Memoirs of the Life, Intrigues and Adventures of the Celebrated Sally Salisbury* (1723)
Walkowitz, Judith R., *Prostitution and Victorian Society: Women, Class and the State* (Cambridge, 1980)
Waller, Maureen, *1700: Scenes from London Life* (Hodder & Stoughton, 2000)
Walpole, Horace, *The Castle of Otranto* (1764)
— —, *The Yale Edition of Horace Walpole's Correspondence* (Yale University Press, 1934–7)
Walter, *My Secret Life* (Panther reprint, 1972)
Ward, Ned, *The London Spy: The Vanities and Vices of the Town Exposed to View*, ed. Arthur L. Hayward (1927)
Watts, Marthe, *The Men in My Life* (Christopher Johnson, 1960)
Webb, Duncan, *Line-Up for Crime* (Frederick Muller, 1956)
Weinreb, Ben, and Hibbert, Christopher, *The London Encyclopaedia* (Papermac, 1993)
Wensley, Frederick, *Detective Days* (1931)
Whelan, Jim, *Jail Journey* (Secker & Warburg, 1940)
White, Jerry, *London in the Twentieth Century* (Viking, 2001)
Wilmot, John, *Earl of Rochester, A Panegyrick Upon Cumdums* (1674)
Wilson, A.N., *The Faber Book of London* (Faber & Faber, 1993)
Wilson, Colin, *The Mammoth Book of True Crime* (Robinson Publishing, 1990)
— — and Pitman, Patricia, *Encyclopedia of Murder* (Pan, 1984)
Wilson, Harriette, *Memoirs* (Folio Society edition; London, 1964)
Wilson, J.H., *All the King's Ladies* (Chicago, 1958)
Wilson, Mary, *Exhibition of Female Flagellants* (1777)